Collected Prefaces

Nicholas Hagger's Prefaces to 55 of his
Literary and Universalist works

T0386067

JOHN HUNT PUBLISHING

First published by O-Books, 2022
O-Books is an imprint of John Hunt Publishing Ltd., 3 East St., Alresford,
Hampshire SO24 9EE, UK
office@jhpbooks.com
www.johnhuntpublishing.com
www.o-books.com

For distributor details and how to order please visit the 'Ordering' section on our website.

Text copyright: Nicholas Hagger 2020

ISBN: 978 1 78904 273 3
978 1 78904 274 0 (ebook)
Library of Congress Control Number: 2019957211

Biblical quotations are taken from the Authorized Version of the Bible (the King James Bible), the rights in which are vested in the Crown, and are reproduced by permission of the Crown's Patentee, Cambridge University Press.

A CIP catalogue record for this book is available from the British Library.

Design: Stuart Davies

UK: Printed and bound by CPI Group (UK) Ltd, Croydon, CR0 4YY
Printed in North America by CPI GPS partners

We operate a distinctive and ethical publishing philosophy in all areas of our business, from our global network of authors to production and worldwide distribution.

Collected Prefaces

Nicholas Hagger's Prefaces to 55 of his
Literary and Universalist works

Nicholas Hagger

BOOKS

Winchester, UK
Washington, USA

Also by Nicholas Hagger

The Secret American Destiny
Peace for our Time
World State
World Constitution
King Charles the Wise
Visions of England
Fools' Paradise
Selected Letters
The Coronation of King Charles
A Baroque Vision
The Essentials of Universalism
The Promised Land
Fools' Gold

'Preface'. "An introduction to a book stating its subject, scope, etc."
(*Concise Oxford Dictionary*)

'Preface'. "The introduction to a literary work, usually explaining its subject, purpose, scope, and method, late Middle English."
(*Shorter Oxford English Dictionary*)

"The man of letters as such, is not concerned with the political or economic map of Europe; but he should be very much concerned with its cultural map.... The man of letters... should be able to take a longer view than either the politician or the local patriot.... The cultural health of Europe, including the cultural health of its component parts, is incompatible with extreme forms of both nationalism and internationalism.... The responsibility of the man of letters at the present time... should be vigilantly watching the conduct of politicians and economists, for the purpose of criticizing and warning, when the decisions and actions of the politicians and economists are likely to have cultural consequences. Of these consequences the man of letters should qualify himself to judge. Of the possible cultural consequences of their activities, politicians and economists are usually oblivious; the man of letters is better qualified to foresee them, and to perceive their seriousness."
(T.S. Eliot, *The Man of Letters and the Future of Europe*, 1944)

*

The front cover shows the titles of all Nicholas Hagger's works that contain Prefaces – 55 past works to date and the Preface for *Collected Prefaces*, making 56 Prefaces in all.

Acknowledgements

I am grateful to my PA Ingrid Kirk for her invaluable help during the assembling of these Prefaces.

CONTENTS

Sketch for a portrait of Nicholas Hagger by Stuart Davies

"The unexamined life is not worth living."
(Socrates, in Plato, *Apology*, 38a)

56*

Preface to Collected Prefaces
Renaissance Man and the One:
Literary and Universalist Thinking

Prefaces to 55 books as essays
In 1991 I revived the Preface. On 3 May 1991 I wrote to Tony Little, later Head Master of Eton, when I sent him copies of *Selected Poems: A Metaphysical's Way of Fire* and *The Fire and the Stones*: "You will see that I have revived the Preface, which has fallen into disuse since Wordsworth and Shelley." (*Selected Letters* p.115.) Wordsworth's 'Preface to the *Lyrical Ballads*', an essay for the second edition of 1801 and greatly expanded for the third edition of 1802, came to be seen as a manifesto for the Romantic movement. Shelley's essay 'A Defence of Poetry', written in 1821 and published posthumously in 1840, was a polemical essay rather than a Preface, but it was in the spirit and tradition of Wordsworth's essay-like Preface.

I have written Prefaces – sometimes called 'Prologues', 'Introductions' or 'Introductory Notes' – to all my 55 books, and this is my 56th Preface. Now I have reached the age of 80 it makes sense to collect them as essays that introduce each of my works. *Collected Prefaces* will eventually be joined by a companion volume, my *Collected Papers*.

The books the Prefaces introduce and often summarise are very varied. I was a man of letters from 1958 to 1991, and was first a poet and after 1966 also a writer of short stories. In my poetic quest I needed to do research within other disciplines, and from 1991 as well as works of literature (poems, short stories, autobiographies, epics, diaries, verse plays, masques and travelogues) I published works on history, mysticism, comparative religion, philosophy and the sciences, international politics and statecraft, and world culture.

I saw these seven disciplines as the seven bands of a rainbow, and they are symbolised in the rainbow on the cover of *My Double Life 2: A Rainbow over the Hills*. Later the seven disciplines are symbolised in one of the two seven-branched antlers of a stag (an inhabitant of my native Epping Forest). The other antler symbolises the seven branches of literature I have written within as a man of letters.

Chronological order and progression
I first considered grouping these Prefaces thematically under each of the seven disciplines (all historical works together, all philosophical

works together and so on); or under titles: for example, my epic poem on the Second World War *Overlord* appeared in four volumes at different times before coming out in a collected edition, and as each of the five volumes has a Preface it seemed logical to arrange all the *Overlord* Prefaces together.

However, I have decided to stick to the chronological order in which the books came out, so the Prefaces here appear chronologically. This way the progression of my thinking is not lost, and the development of my thinking as the Prefaces advance is thrown into relief. In *My Double Life 1: This Dark Wood* and *My Double Life 2: A Rainbow over the Hills* (two later autobiographical volumes) I seek "to catch the cumulative process of my thinking" (*My Double Life 1*, p.xxiv), and by arranging the Prefaces chronologically I am showing this cumulative process at work in this book.

All my Prefaces before Preface 34 originally appeared without subheadings. In the interests of conveying the progression of my thinking from one Preface to another more clearly I have inserted subheadings in these early Prefaces. Anyone who wants to compare the early Prefaces exactly as they were can simply ignore the subheadings before Preface 34. But I am confident that standardising subheadings throughout adds clarity to these Prefaces and assists the reader in following the progression of my thinking.

Development of my literary thinking: quest for the One and follies and vices
The progression in my thinking falls into two parts. First there is the development of my literary thinking. I started as a poet and my early work, such as 'The Silence', has a Modernist approach. Set in both the West and the East, it narrates a quest for the One. I reflect my journey along the Mystic Way, in which I experienced an awakening and eventually illumination (see Appendix 1, pp.437–447) and a unitive vision in which I instinctively saw the fundamental unity of the universe and adopted a progressively more unitive approach to life. Such a mystical approach inevitably expresses itself in Metaphysical poetry, naturally, but also in Romantic poetry for a while: looking back to Wordsworth's "unknown modes of being", Shelley's "The One remains, the many change and pass" and Keats' "Beauty is truth and truth beauty".

In the late 1970s I began what has become a lifelong correspondence with the literary critic Christopher Ricks, and in letters to him saw myself as first a Metaphysical poet (18 February 1979), then a Romantic poet (1 May 1982) and finally a Baroque poet blending Romantic and Classical attitudes (17 October 1982). [See Appendix 1, pp.461–468, which is taken from pp.868–873 of *Collected Poems*. These letters are also in *Selected Letters*.]

By the time the first literary Preface was written between 1982 and 1991 the development of my unitive approach was almost complete, and I was becoming more Classical. That Preface was about uniting the Romantic and Classical approaches to poetry in what I called "the new Baroque". Baroque art combined sense and spirit, and my quest for the One co-existed with my more Classical approach to European culture in my two epic poems *Overlord* and *Armageddon*, which both contain objective descriptions of harrowing incidents in the Second World War and the War on Terror; and in my 318 classical odes in *Classical Odes*, which set out the UK's cultural link to the European civilisation and anticipated the UK's desire to break away twenty or more years before the 2016 referendum. Both my *Collected Poems* and *Overlord* have Appendices which throw considerable light on my fundamental mystical experience and my Baroque approach in verse and on my approach to my first epic (including my visit to Ezra Pound to discuss it in 1970). I have included these as Appendix 1 and Appendix 2 – although they are long – as they are referred to in the Prefaces for these two works and as they illumine my approach to all my poetry and both my epics.

I progressed to demonstrating in *A New Philosophy of Literature* that the fundamental theme of world literature is an endless dialectic between a quest for the One and exposing social follies and vices, two opposing principles that have alternated for more than two thousand years. My attempt at unifying spirit and sense, individual communing with the One and social follies and vices, Romantic and Classical in my Baroque poetry was also an attempt to synthesise this fundamental theme of pursuing the One and exposing follies and vices.

I have now written more than 2,000 poems, 1,200 short stories, two long epic poems, five verse plays, three masques, three autobiographies, a book of diaries, two travelogues and a work on the fundamental theme of world literature, and I now see myself as having my poetic roots in the 17th-century Metaphysical poets and blending Romanticism and Classicism. I see all three of my early letters to Ricks (mentioned above) as containing valid approaches that have merit as literary Universalism reconciles opposites and blends the Metaphysical, Romantic and Classical into Baroque.

In my poetry I see myself as continuing the tradition of Wordsworth and Tennyson, and also the concerns of Eliot, Yeats and Pound (who I met at length in 1970). In my short stories I see my choice of titles with juxtaposed dissimilar images as being in the tradition of Dr Johnson's description of the wit of the 17th-century Metaphysical poets in his 'Life of Cowley' as "a combination of dissimilar images" in which "the most heterogeneous ideas are yoked by violence together". I see both my poetry and my short stories as being rooted in the 17th-century Metaphysical poets.

Development of my Universalist thinking
Secondly there is the development of my Universalism. The first Preface is titled 'Introduction to the New Universalism'. Universalism was the new philosophy I was developing before 1991. It attempted to focus on the whole of humankind's relationship to the whole universe, and saw, and still sees, all the seven disciplines as wholes within a greater whole, the One. Universalism sees the individual's engagement with the universe as an ongoing process; it is a process philosophy. The progression of my Universalism can be followed in every Preface, and can be seen to be a "cumulative process".

My literary Universalism, culminating in *A New Philosophy of Literature* as we have seen, combines my quest for the One (in the tradition of the Metaphysical and Romantic poets) with my exposure of social follies and vices (in the tradition of Classical poets such as Horace and the Augustan Neoclassical poets).

My historical Universalism culminating in *The Rise and Fall of Civilizations*, sees the rise and fall of 25 civilisations, all of which pass through 61 stages, the same pattern. I set out the pattern of history: The Law of History. (I had taught Gibbon, Spengler and Toynbee when I was a Professor at universities in Japan, and I had seen a fourth way of approaching civilisations, the details of which took me 25 years to work out in *The Fire and the Stones*.)

My philosophical Universalism, culminating in *The New Philosophy of Universalism*, sees humankind and all the sciences in relation to the universe, and announces a turning-away from philosophy as language and logic back to the view of the ancient Greeks that philosophy is about the place of human beings within the universe. For much of the 1990s I championed a Metaphysical Revolution against modern philosophy.

My mystical and religious Universalism, culminating in *The Light of Civilization*, sees all religions as having the same central experience and therefore essence: a vision of the mystic Light that was reflected in descriptions of Christ as the Light of the World and of the Buddha as the Enlightened One.

My political Universalism, culminating in *World State* and *World Constitution*, sees a democratic World State ahead with a new world structure to which we are heading, all too slowly in view of the distractions of populism and nationalism.

My cultural Universalism, culminating in *The Secret American*

Destiny, sets out the common basis of a world culture for such a World State.

By presenting the Prefaces in chronological order I am enabling readers to see that my Universalist themes remain consistent regardless of the discipline I am writing a Preface within, and that there is a powerful, interconnected, cross-disciplinary Universalist thrust that covers all aspects of the universe and every discipline throughout my Prefaces and works.

Cross-disciplinary approach to the One
In the course of my literary quest I developed Universalism and branched off into history, philosophy, international politics and statecraft and other disciplines to explore the ramifications of Universalism in these other disciplines. I see no conflict in this cross-disciplinary work just as Renaissance men such as Leonardo and Michelangelo worked in and were at home in different disciplines and saw no conflict in their cross-disciplinary work.

Because knowledge has increased since the Renaissance there are few truly Renaissance men today, and our time likes to pigeon-hole people in one slot within one discipline. I have refused to be pigeon-holed – it might have been more advantageous for my reception if I had stuck to one discipline – and so am cross-disciplinary in my literary and Universalist works. I am fortunate that my literary archive is held as a Special Collection in the Albert Sloman Library at the University of Essex, a university that is known for its support for cross-disciplinary thinking and works. In the cross-disciplinary sense – as well as in the sense of my Essex boyhood when I lived in Churchill's Essex constituency under the path of the V-1 and V-2 bombs – I have been, and always will be, an Essex boy.

But in all my works I have tried to hold a mirror up to Nature and to international society and reflect Truth, the truth about our world and the universe at every level and in every discipline. I hope that *Collected Prefaces* will give readers a better understanding of my approach and my works, and perhaps send some to individual books they are not familiar with; and that as they read they will be transported to Truth: the truth of the One.

3–4, 27, 30 August, 18, 28 October 2019

*This new Preface has been numbered 56 and is referred to as such in the Subject Index on pp.537–550.

William Wordsworth, who wrote 'Preface
to the Lyrical Ballads' (1801, longer version
1802), in contemplative, thoughtful, Preface-
writing mood, engraved from a painting by
R. Carruthers published in 1819.

THE PREFACES

1

The Fire and the Stones

A Grand Unified Theory of World History and Religion
The Vision of God in Twenty-Five Civilisations

Introduction to the New Universalism

Universalist history sees religions as central to the growth and decay of civilisations
We are at a turning-point when one age – the age of the Cold War and decolonising and nationalistic tensions – is ending and a new age is beginning. The European nations are discussing political union within a United States of Europe "or whatever name or form it may take" (a phrase from Churchill's 1946 Zurich speech). Many different nationalities are drawing together and increasingly feel part of a single, universal world-society, as is evidenced by the unanimous UN condemnation of Iraq's invasion of Kuwait. Universal history regards mankind as a single world-society and is to be contrasted with local national histories. Universalism is a way of looking that embraces all mankind, and is to be contrasted with nation-state nationalism.

However, the concept of Universalism must be defined in deeper terms than this. 'Universalism' suggests both 'universal' and 'universe'. According to *The Concise Oxford English Dictionary* 'universal' means "of or belonging to or done by all persons or things in the world or in the class concerned; applicable to all cases", while 'universe' means "all existing things; the whole creation; the cosmos; all mankind" or in logic "all the objects under consideration". At its best the philosophy of Universalism includes all these meanings. It embraces what is universal to all mankind in relation to the deeper mystery of the universe, i.e. the profoundest view of the human condition. It approaches what the purest souls have understood by God.

There have been attempts at Universalism in the past: religious Universalists have held that all mankind will eventually be saved, and Universalist historians have focused on the history of all mankind in relation to Providence. My Universalism offers a new perspective: it proposes a Grand Unified Theory which includes *all* religion and history. The new Universalism holds that *mankind's gnosis of a universal God perceived or known as the Fire or Light is central to all religions and civilisations, and controls and explains their growth and decay.*

The Fire or Light is central to all religions and the genesis of civilisations
It may seem paradoxical that a private experience of the Fire can profoundly affect a society and civilisation. In fact, inner religious experience has a private role within a particular religion, which is a social entity. Religion is a private matter between the individual contemplative mystic and the Fire or Light of God and can lead to unworldly disciplines such as the Desert Fathers practised in the Alexandrian desert. Religions, on the other hand, give social cohesion; they control societies and help civilisations to grow. Paradoxically, the contemplative mystic who renounces the world and pours his energy into religion also strengthens and renews a particular religion as a social force, and therefore strengthens and renews his civilisation.

It is therefore natural that we should start in one discipline (religion) and finish in another (history). The link is religions, the social entities which channel the contemplative mystics' Fire into historical civilisations. I seek to establish that the mystical experience of the Fire, which is universal in being available to all who seek it, founds and renews the religions; and I find in the spreading of the Fire through religions what Toynbee sought in vain in history, the motive force which explains the genesis of civilisations. This makes a new view of history possible, one that is based on the role of all the religions in history and on the performance of all civilisations.

Civilisations grow out of a vision of metaphysical Reality as the Fire and decay when they turn secular
Today knowledge of the Fire has been largely lost. We live in a secular time. Secularisation is at heart a sceptical movement away from the sacred, monastic-ecclesiastical vision. In our secularised, materialistic, money-seeking Western civilisation, the experience of metaphysical Reality – the vision of God – has been pushed to the margin when once (in the time of the Crusades, for example) it was at the centre. There is little official instruction from the Church on how to perceive, and therefore existentially confront, the Fire of God, which is still symbolised as a sun-burst in churches. In Prague's Old Town Square (a relic of Europe's 14th–15th-century high civilisation), for example, two churches have huge sun-bursts high on their outsides for all to see, yet Kafka, who lived in a house just off the square, evidently missed their significance, judging from the despair of his *Castle*. There is little understanding of the personal benefits that result from the experience of metaphysical Reality, even less of the benefits to the society in which the experience takes place. The contrast between a healthy metaphysical vision, a meaningful religious experience and a

4

dynamic, growing civilisation on the one hand, and a sceptical vision, meaningless religion and a decaying civilisation on the other hand, has never been fully explored although it is hinted at in the most important books of our century and in some of its greatest art (in the works of T.S. Eliot, for example).

The vision of the Fire is central to 25 rising and falling civilisations that go through 61 stages and leave "stones"
In this pioneering study I attempt to explore this contrast and show how illumination benefited the life and times of the contemplative mystic geniuses of the past; I focus on the personal and social benefits of the vision of "the Fire" during the last 5,000 years; and I draw together 5,000 years of experiences of the Fire for the first time. My Universalist assumption is that growing and decaying cultures (and therefore religions) can no longer be regarded in isolation from each other, and that growing and decaying civilisations must be regarded in relation to each other. This is true of primitive cultures and civilisations at the beginning of recorded history, and it is equally true of our own "global village" today. I attempt to demonstrate that all cultures and civilisations grow out of a metaphysical vision of God as Fire or Light, the "Fire" which inspired all their religious buildings and monumental ruins: their "stones".

In holding that the Fire of God is the Central Idea of civilisations, my historical theme goes beyond Gibbon, Spengler and Toynbee. It traces the impact of the Fire of God on the rise of civilisations and its absence during their fall. It follows 25 civilisations, some of which are still extant, and traces 61 stages in the life cycle of each, including our own Western civilisation (which is in fact an amalgam of two civilisations), as each civilisation grows through its response to the Fire and dies through its loss of the Fire. By comparing the stages of all the living civilisations with the succeeding stages of all dead civilisations we can make predictions about the coming Age.

Universalist cross-disciplinary approach
It will by now have become apparent that the new Universalism employs a cross-disciplinary approach to cultures and civilisations. In fact, I draw on religion, comparative religion, mysticism, metaphysics, philosophy, history, the philosophy of history, cultural and philosophical anthropology, cosmology, astronomy, physics, current affairs and the method of phenomenology, and the cross-disciplinary work can be categorised under several headings and is equally at home on the shelves labelled Comparative Religion, Mysticism,

Metaphysics, Philosophy, the Philosophy of History, and, perhaps more appropriately, Cultures and Civilisations. (I distinguish cultural and philosophical anthropology as follows. The discipline or listing of cultural systems as they pass through growth, peak and decay belongs to cultural anthropology. An understanding of the transformation of cultures in relation to the individual personalities of contemplative mystics belongs to philosophical anthropology, which in our case is reconciled with theology and cosmology.)

The personal basis for my Universalism
It would be natural for the reader to be curious about the personal basis for my Universalism. I developed it in the course of a 30-year-long search, an attempt to understand my time and the pattern underlying world events, a quest through inner experience, cultures and history that took me through sceptical Oxford to the Islamic Middle East, where I lived in General Kassem's Baghdad and visited Babylon and the ziggurats, Jerusalem and Qumran. (I first glimpsed my theme when studying the Metaphysical poets at Oxford. It was in a plane between Baghdad and Basra, high above Ur, that, as if by direct inspiration, I received, and scribbled down, the words "life cycle" and first pondered the rise and fall of civilisations in their light.) My quest took me to the Far East, where I absorbed the wisdom of the East while spending four years as a Professor in Japan, in the course of which I visited China (where in March 1966 I was the first to discover the Cultural Revolution). From Japan I visited the USSR, India and many Eastern cultural sites, such as Angkor Wat. In Japan I taught a year's course on Gibbon, Spengler and Toynbee, and glimpsed a way of solving the problem that had ultimately defeated them all, a fourth way. My experience of South-East-Asian Mahayana Buddhism, and in particular of Japanese Zen in Kitakamakura, was crucial in helping me to progress to a metaphysical outlook. In those Far-Eastern days I could have done with this book, for when I cast around in libraries and bookshops to support my researches into illumination I found bits and pieces in different books, but nothing drawn together. Quite simply this sort of book just did not exist.

My Universalist view of Christianity followed a deep experience of the Sahara Desert when I lived in Libya for two years (during which I was an eyewitness of the 1969 Gaddafi Revolution). At this time I visited Egypt and pondered on the Great Pyramid and the Valley of the Kings. Back in London in the autumn of 1971 I experienced the most intense two months of my life. [See Appendix 1, pp.437–447] The development is recorded in my poems, and the full story of my personal odyssey belongs elsewhere [*My Double Life 1: This Dark Wood*, see Preface 36] and reticence is proper here. Suffice it to say that I now knew what was missing from the Christian religion. I grasped from personal experience that there is a void in Western Christendom and I realised that I had been on a quest round the world to find among the typhoons and baking deserts of other cultures what should have been available in my own civilisation, what used to be available in it, but what secular Christendom now largely ignores.

Tradition of the Fire and civilisations' health
That was the starting-point for this present Universalist study, which has taken a further 15 years' pondering and musing to evolve, first in London and more recently among the oaks and silver birches of Essex's Epping Forest. During this time I was able to talk with a number of leading thinkers from many disciplines, and I became convinced that the void in the contemporary soul – I speak of my own sceptical generation as much as of the lost younger generation – can be attributed to an excessively Humanistic and diseased religion in which concern with social doctrine has replaced dynamic inner experience. Quite simply, pessimists about the human condition (such as Kafka and Beckett) have not had the inner experience of the Fire which in past ages they would have been encouraged to seek. I reached the conclusion that if the religion is too decayed to communicate its essence regarding the human condition then the only way forward is to restate the Tradition of the Fire in all cultures and civilisations, from a Universalist point of view, to remind the guardians of our decayed religion of what they are failing to do.

Rediscovering the Fire in mystical experience and a Metaphysical Revolution
Can there be a widespread acceptance of the rediscovery of the lost knowledge of the Fire? The search has always been open to all, and there are signs that despite the prevailing secularisation of our times Truth is now being revealed more widely than in recent years. The esoteric is becoming exoteric, and there are signs that what has hitherto been hidden among coteries is now being made more widely available to those of "the masses" who are prepared to seek. Those who seek *can* find, and there is evidence (largely gleaned from New Age conferences) that in our time the Fire is burning in the consciousness of ordinary people. This is a welcome development. If the growing North-American civilisation enters a worldwide phase, as this book argues it may, then the experience of the Fire will become increasingly available to all

mankind as it is always widespread during a civilisation's growth.

A movement to remysticise Christendom, and other religions, is the next stage in this widening of metaphysical consciousness, and it seems that our time will see a Metaphysical Revolution – a Metaphysical Restoration – in all disciplines and religions, which our world needs so badly. The existential vision of the Fire, the metaphysical Reality, in this book *existentialises* metaphysics and effects the beginning of this Revolution. The new Universalism points towards it and will come into its own when, as stage 44 of European civilisation and as a concomitant of stage 15 of the North-American civilisation, a new metaphysical movement eventually arrives. The deepening and widening of the European Community into an integrated conglomerate [the European Union] can be expected to be accompanied by a revival of the metaphysical vision.

An Age of Universalism, a new Baroque Age, is ahead
Baroque art combined the spiritual and the physical. A new Baroque Age, an Age of Universalism, is ahead. Through the universal Fire it will see man in relation to the entirety of the manifest universe, which operates at both physical and metaphysical levels, and then Humanism will seem very inadequate. The way forward for all our living civilisations, then, involves a fundamental shift in their perception – and therefore *our* perception – of the human condition, of the meaning of life and what it means to be a man. Our living civilisations will renew themselves by challenging the secular view of the human condition, as this book endeavours to make clear. To put it another way, our history of independence from foreign conquerors is linked to the health of our religion.

January 1991

2

Selected Poems: A Metaphysical's Way of Fire

Preface on the New Baroque Consciousness and the Redefinition of Poetry as Classical Baroque

This Preface first appeared in 1991 titled 'On the New Baroque Consciousness and the Redefinition of Poetry'.

In all there were six versions [see Appendix 1, pp.379–390, taken from Appendix 3 in *Collected Poems 1958–2005*, 'The Genesis and Shaping of the New Baroque Vision']. Versions 1, 2 and 3 were titled 'The New Romanticism: A New Consciousness'. Version 1 was written in September–October 1982. It was revised in August 1989 (version 2) and October 1989 (version 3) in Cornwall (within sight of the Black Head of Trenarren). Version 4 was at first titled 'The New Baroque: A New Consciousness', and this underwent minor revisions to appear in *Selected Poems: A Metaphysical's Way of Fire* in 1991 (version 5) when it was retitled 'On the New Baroque Consciousness and the Redefinition of Poetry'. The identical text with the same title appeared at the end of *Collected Poems 1958–1993: A White Radiance*, and it was updated in 2005 without changes to its poetic perspective but with a 2005 vantage point to appear in *Collected Poems 1958–2005* (version 6) under the present title 'Preface on the New Baroque Consciousness and the Redefinition of Poetry as Classical Baroque'.

The text below is therefore the 1991 text which spoke of a "selection" with a 2005 vantage point which speaks of a "collection" so it could appear in a Collected Poems fifteen years later, but with its poetic perspective unchanged. It was first written with a Collected Poems in view, and it makes sense to present the most updated text here rather than an outdated and superseded text.

This Preface presents the new Baroque consciousness as a blend of Classicism and Romanticism (pp.10–26), of classicism's social ego and Romanticism's infinite spirit or core. The new Baroque consciousness allows for a redefinition of poetic assumptions (pp.46–47).

The metaphysical Fire
My poems record a shift – a growth, a transformation – from the consciousness of the controlling social ego to the contemplative, unitive consciousness of a new centre in the inner core which includes the soul and spirit. (In Kabbalistic terms the shift is from *Yesod* to *Tepheret* or *Teferet*.) This shift of consciousness is significant because it

9

makes possible an approach to a metaphysical Reality and Being. For when the universe is perceived through the new centre it is perceived as being One through being permeated by a unifying metaphysical principle akin to Heraclitus' Fire, which unites the spiritual and physical outlooks.

This metaphysical Fire, and the consciousness that perceives it, have been known in every generation somewhere in each civilisation during the last 5,000 years. It breaks out at certain stages during the life cycle of a civilisation, and the vision of these poems should be related to the historical perspective of *The Fire and the Stones* and *The Light of Civilization*, in which I maintained that mankind's gnosis of a universal God perceived or known as the Fire or Light is central to all religions and civilisations, and controls and explains their growth, survival and decay. In *The Fire and the Stones* and *The Rise and Fall of Civilizations* I attempted to show that all civilisations pass through 61 stages.

The Age of Universalism
These poems are set against what in that work I designate as stages 42–45 of the European civilisation. *The Fire and the Stones* and *The Rise and Fall of Civilizations* hold that in stage 42 a civilisation decolonises (a stage the European civilisation has been in since 1910), that European civilisation is already passing into stage 43 (a conglomerate that deprives it of its national sovereignty, i.e. the enlarged European Union which by 2005 controlled more than 75 per cent of European legislation from Brussels), and that stages 44 and 45, which begin soon after the start of stage 43, are associated with this new unitive consciousness.

The Fire and the Stones and *The Rise and Fall of Civilizations* show that an Age of Universalism (in which the vision of metaphysical Supreme Being or God as Fire is widespread) is initiated in stage 15 of a growing civilisation – the North-American civilisation currently occupies stage 15 – and affects stage 44 of a declining civilisation (a syncretistic, Universalist stage about to be experienced by the European civilisation). In stage 45 civilisations experience a revival of cultural purity in which there is a yearning for the lost past of a civilisation. In both religion and art stage 45 draws on the artistic tradition of stage 28, and the coming revival of cultural purity soon after c.2005 can be expected to return to the pure vision of the European civilisation's own religion (a similar stage to the one the Arab civilisation has been in since 1956 under Nasser, Gaddafi, Khomeini and Saddam Hussein), and to glorify the Fire-based medieval vision which was expressed in the historical Baroque art which dominated stage 28 of the European civilisation and co-existed with Classicism.

Rediscovery of metaphysical Being
These poems are particularly concerned with the Universalist rediscovery of metaphysical Being in stage 44 of the European civilisation and with the coming revival of cultural purity in stage 45 of the European civilisation, and with the new Baroque/Classical consciousness that has already emerged in preparation for this stage. They draw on the historical Baroque Fire (stage 28) and the new Baroque's immediate antecedent, the Romantic Fire or Light (stage 33). Some regard the new consciousness I associate with Baroque as a development, or a new flowering in a different form, of the Romantic spirit, one in which Romanticism is crossed with Classicism to make a hybrid. To have a full grasp of the new Baroque/Classical consciousness and the outlook of stage 45, we therefore need to approach it through the traditions of European Renaissance Classicism, of the historical Baroque of the Counter-Reformation, of 18th-century Neoclassicism, and of the Romanticism which evolved from Neoclassicism and whose attitudes passed into Modernism.

*

Classicism and thought-based Metaphysicals
'Classicism', following the way of writing, painting and sculpting which the Greeks and Romans used, emerged from the Renaissance (during stage 24 of European civilisation). The Graeco-Roman order, clarity, balance, restraint, taste and sense of beauty were rediscovered during the Renaissance, which coincided with the Reformation, and historically European Classicism was at its height in 17th-century France, the Golden Age of Classicism or 'Neoclassicism' (if we seek to distinguish European Classicism from Greek and Roman Classicism). The French dramatists Corneille, Racine and Molière imitated the classical standards of the Greeks and Romans as set out in Aristotle, Horace, Quintilian and Longinus, standards rediscovered by the Renaissance. They trusted in the powers of the mind, and especially the reason of the social ego, and the scientific discoveries of the Age – for example, those of Newton – seemed to confirm that all things could be known.

In England, a parallel interest in reason led to the "thought-based" poetry of the Metaphysicals and of Milton, Dryden and Pope. T.S. Eliot sought to explain this Rationalism in his essay on Milton. Eliot argued that there was a "dissociation of sensibility" after the Civil War, as a result of which thought separated from feeling in English poetry, whereas earlier in the 17th-century thought and feeling were united in Donne as "felt thought". "To Donne," Eliot wrote, "a thought was an idea, invested with feeling." Neoclassical critics tend not to believe in this split which Eliot attributed to the Cromwellian Revolution, and though a similar separation can be observed immediately after any modern Revolution – I have witnessed it myself among Chinese and Libyans shortly after their Revolutions – the split Eliot noted can just as easily be explained by the growth of European Renaissance Classicism (or Neoclassicism) in 17th-century France.

17th-century Baroque
In fact, some of this "thought-based" poetry (notably the sensual-spiritual poetry of the Metaphysicals and of Milton) should be seen in terms of the vision of the 17th-century Baroque, the art produced c.1600–1750 by first the Catholic Counter-Reformation and then by the Protestants following the Renaissance and Reformation as they reasserted the pre-Reformation vision of the Fire and renewed the Fire or Light of European civilisation's central idea. Historically, the Baroque is the least understood of movements. Originally a term of abuse from the Portuguese *barroco,* meaning a large irregularly shaped pearl (see my dedication at the beginning of 'The Silence', 1965–6, which describes the poem as a "string of baroque pearls"), the Baroque sometimes has a pejorative connotation, of being overwrought and ornate, contorted and eccentric, full of strangeness, tension and irrationality, even grotesque. This connotation has been fostered by Neoclassical critics. If we get away from their pejorative disapproval, however, we can see that historically the baroque style was essentially full of movement and freedom, it was *dynamic.* Artificiality was stripped away (hence the masks and mirrors that appear in baroque art) and human beings were shown as everyday feeling people, whether they were saints from contemporary history like St Teresa or from the early Christian days, or the people of Bruegel or Velasquez or Rubens or Rembrandt. Baroque art emphasised metamorphosis, the protean quality of life, *transformation,* and as the Baroque began as a movement of religious architecture in the Catholic Church during the Counter-Reformation, the Fire or Light which unites Catholics and Protestants and therefore heals the divisions caused by the Reformation is never far away and can be found in the centre of baroque church domes (for example, the white centre of the dome of Wren's St Paul's). Baroque art aimed to involve the spectator's feelings in visions.

But perhaps the main feature of the historical Baroque was that it contained elements of the High Renaissance and of Mannerism. In other words, it was *a mixture of the world of the senses and the world of the spirit,* as in Bernini's *Ecstasy of St Teresa*. In fact, it sought to *remove the barriers between the world of the senses and the world of the spirit*, sometimes between the erotic and the spiritual, and to renew contact between art and Nature. If the baroque seems to be all movement across a sky with whirling clouds and children with wings, this is because the artist was trying to express his sense of *the Spirit – the infinite – within the finite world*.

The Baroque mixture of High Renaissance Classicism and Mannerism, of sense and spirit, can be seen in terms of Leonardo and Michelangelo. The High Renaissance (c.1490–1520) created works that were harmonious, well-balanced, clear and direct, in which order negated the artist's individuality, and out of this came Leonardo's universally perfect body and perfect work of art. The restless and powerful Michelangelo soon broke with the High Renaissance, and created the tense Mannerism of the Sistine Chapel. Both Leonardo's Classicism (which drew on the world of the senses) and Michelangelo's Mannerism (which derived from the world of the spirit) were present in Baroque, which was a Counter-Renaissance.

The Baroque was greatly present in the European poetry of the 17th century; in the thirty-three French, German, Dutch, Spanish and Italian poets Frank J. Warnke anthologised in *European Metaphysical Poetry* – poets such as Marino (Italian), D'Aubigné (French), Gryphius (German), Vondel and Huygens (Dutch), and San Juan de la Cruz (alias St John of the Cross, Spanish). Warnke, like Odette de Mourgues in *Metaphysical, Baroque and Précieux Poetry*, sees the literary baroque style as parallel to but distinct from the Metaphysical style, although many of the 17th-century European poets (like those just mentioned) are both baroque and Metaphysical: Baroque in being characterised by extravagance of language and a concern with appearance and reality, particularly in the religious impulse and the new science, and Metaphysical in being concerned with a protagonist who, with wit and wordplay, confronts the complexities of experience, and in the longing of the Soul to be liberated from the Body. The Dutch Luyken, like the English Vaughan, drew inspiration from the Hermetic books, the Kabbalah and the Alchemists, and wrote of the Inner Light. English Metaphysical poetry should therefore be seen within this European literary Baroque context.

18th-century Neoclassicism
The Baroque faded c.1750. It had co-existed with Classicism rather than replaced it, and first 18th-century Neoclassicism (an offshoot of stage 32 of European civilisation, the advent of scientific materialism) and then Romanticism (a creation of stage 33 of the European civilisation,

Collected Prefaces

the artistic reaction against scientific materialism) took its place. The revival – or survival – of Classicism in the 18th century is known as 'Neoclassicism' to distinguish it from 17th-century Classicism, which, as we have seen, is also confusingly called 'Neoclassicism' to distinguish it from Greek and Roman Classicism; and it is primarily in this 18th-century sense that I now use the term 'Neoclassical' to refer historically and aesthetically to the time when the 17th-century Materialism of the Age of Reason had given way to the 18th-century Materialism of the Augustan Age and the Enlightenment. It is important to distinguish Materialism with a capital 'M', the philosophy based on the supremacy of matter which holds that man is mere material, from materialism with a small 'm', the money-seeking attitude that can unconsciously result from a widespread acceptance of a Materialistic philosophy.

In England, the 18th-century Neoclassical poetry of Dryden and Pope was objective, impersonal and rational – written from the cortical or upper left brain. It was ordered, being concerned with harmony and proportion, and it was controlled by the reason of the social ego. "Reason alone countervails all the other faculties," Pope wrote in the 'Essay on Man', and in his 'Essay on Criticism' (1711) he asserted that the reason "methodises" Nature by obeying the Classical rules: "Those rules of old discovered, not devis'd/Are Nature still, but Nature Methodiz'd." Going back to Aristotle, the 18th-century Neoclassical tradition held that the main principle behind artistic creation was the imitation or representation of Nature. Thus, to Dr Johnson, poetry was "just representation of general nature". A glance at Pope's 'Rape of the Lock', 'To Burlington' and 'Epistle to Dr Arbuthnot', which span the years 1712–1735, reveals what the Neoclassical Nature showed. In these satires, Pope condemns the pride, vanity and self-interest of the beaux and belles, villa-builders and poets who made up the court society of his day, and he extols good humour and good sense: the common sense of the rational, social ego which was at the forefront of the Neoclassical view of human nature. Such a Neoclassical vision dwells on ordinariness and mocks anything that smacks of the heroic; hence the mock-heroic debunking of epic grandeur and supernatural "sylphs" in Dryden and Pope, for whom the heroic is simply not a Neoclassical subject.

Towards 1750, throughout Europe the Neoclassical tradition which had coexisted with the Baroque began to crumble. In Neoclassical art the imagination only had a decorative function, and the irrational side of the creative process was lost under what came to be a standardised, rigid, sterile, excessively rational formula. These weaknesses of stale formalism, lack of spontaneity and coldness led to a questioning of

Neoclassical standards during the Enlightenment (c.1750), for example by Voltaire, Diderot and Lessing. As a result, Neoclassicism fell into decline and its objective certainties disintegrated. Judgements consequently became subjective, hesitant, relative and ambivalent. Reason was still the god – through reason man could find knowledge and happiness – but genius was now admitted, even though it was beyond the reason and far from ordinary. England escaped much of this traumatic process as the Neoclassical rule had continuously been modified and as Shakespeare and the Elizabethans had anyway by-passed the Classical standards, so much so that *Hamlet* was considered "incorrect" by early 18th-century Neoclassical critics; and so 18th-century English writers had not been so constrained by the Neoclassical rules as had the writers in France. Similarly, Neoclassicism never took root in Germany.

The rise of Romanticism
Out of this Neoclassical decline grew the pre-Romantics (1740–1780), who revolted against the dull rules, the formal elegance and the orderliness of the Neoclassical conventions, and emphasised the natural instead of the rational, and feeling. Novels by Prévost (1731), Rousseau (1761) and Goethe (*Werther*, 1774) appeared on the Continent, but the English novelists led the way: Richardson (c.1740–1754), Goldsmith (1766) and Sterne (1768). The letter form made for a more subjective approach, and the Gothic novel became popular from the 1760s on. Inward contemplation made the heart conscious of its own melancholy, and Methodism in England and Pietism in Germany also emphasised the heart and the individual soul.

The Pre-Romantics had an organic view of Nature and the world, not a mechanistic one, and man and Nature became closer (for example in Gray and Cowper). The feeling was that civilisation and property-owning caused decadence and one should return to Nature, a Utopian ideal that was later found in the Pantisocratic project of Coleridge and Southey, and in Blake's Golden Age. The "natural" poetry of Ossian (by Macpherson, 1762) swept Europe, and the "natural man" was taken up by Goethe and Schiller in works of 1773 and 1781. The idea that a work of art was organic appeared in Young's *Conjectures on Original Composition* (1759), which was translated into German in 1760 and received wide attention, and this was taken up by the *Sturm und Drang* (Storm and Stress) movement of the early 1770s. Goethe and Schiller were the two most prominent writers, and they asserted that art was produced when the creative genius of the individual expressed personal experience freely and spontaneously. Lacking the slow modifications of English Neoclassicism, this German Romantic

15

movement was violent as it "caught on".

The Romantic Revolution itself broke in Germany first, through the early German Romantics of 1797. These were centred on Jena, and the leaders were the brothers Friedrich and August Schlegel – it was Friedrich Schlegel who first used the word 'Romantic' in a literary context – along with the poet Novalis, the natural philosopher Schelling, and other less well-known men. Hölderlin, Schiller's friend, was little known during his life but his poems were highly metaphysical. The "metaphysical" approach of these men was followed by a second phase, the High Romantics (1810–1820), some of whom came from Heidelberg. The main poet was Heine. These later Romantics were interested in the natural world rather than metaphysics, and they took their lyrics from folk songs.

Meanwhile, the English Romantic movement of 1798 took place. The English Romantics – first the lake poets Wordsworth and Coleridge, and later the cosmopolitans (1818–1822) Shelley, Keats and Byron (though we should not forget Crabbe, Clare, Scott, Campbell, Moore and Southey) – were comparatively very undoctrinaire. They did not seek a national literature like the Germans or oppose Neoclassicism like the French Romantics, and so there was no violent break with continuity. Rather, they thought of themselves as restoring a native tradition. (Hence the realistic, Neoclassical novels of Jane Austen could flourish during the Romantic period.) In fact, so undoctrinaire were the English Romantics that the word 'Romantic' does not appear in Wordsworth's *Preface to the Lyrical Ballads*, Coleridge's *Biographia Literaria* or Shelley's *Defence of Poetry*, all of which were anyway (like my own Prefaces) written after their poems rather than as manifestos. One consequence of this lack of doctrine was that both Realism and Idealism are found in English Romantic poetry. Wordsworth's poems about solitaries like Michael are very Realistic, whereas his sense of "unknown modes of being" suggests a metaphysical and Idealistic outlook, like Shelley's sense of the One. Whereas the Realistic view of the imagination perceived with full adequacy the sense-bound universe in which we live, the Idealistic view of the imagination emphasised the powers of the mind in perception and "imagined", or imaged, and located, a higher Reality beyond the reach of the senses.

French Romanticism was arrested by the Revolution, for from 1790 to 1820 it was dangerous to express new ideas or to question the Emperor Napoleon's restoration of Neoclassical literature for the glory of France. Romanticism was therefore at heart a German-English, or Anglo-Saxon, movement. It was not until 1820 that Lamartine introduced Romanticism into French literature, and not until 1830 that

Hugo brought it to the theatre. The French Romantics had very little appreciation of the creative imagination, and practised the opposite of Pascal's *"le moi est haïssable"* ("hateworthy") by stressing feeling. It was left to Baudelaire and the Symbolists of the mid-19th century (Mallarmé, Verlaine, Rimbaud) to recognise the imagination and preserve the metaphysical view of the universe, a cult of beauty, a mystical sense of a transcendental world beyond appearances, and the use of symbols to convey perceptions.

The Romantic Revolution of the brothers Schlegel (1797) and of Wordsworth and Coleridge (1798) was thus the result of a gradual evolution. Romanticism thus forms an essential continuity with the Augustan, Neoclassical tradition as W. Jackson Bate has pointed out (*From Classic to Romantic*), and this is especially true of the Realistic poems of Wordsworth, Keats and Byron. For all that, much of Romanticism was still a reversal of Neoclassical aesthetic theories (for example, a change from imitative reason to creative imagination), and a reversal of Neoclassical standards of beauty and ideals and modes of expression; and to that extent it was a revolution that directly opposed Neoclassicism, the social ego and the world of the senses.

Romantic Idealism and metaphysical Reality
And this brings us to the heart of Romanticism, the Idealist tradition. For as we have seen, with the imagination the best Romantics saw beneath the surface of the Neoclassical "inanimate, cold world" to the ideal, infinite, eternal behind it or within it. They did not describe the world with the "corporeal eye" ("bodily eye", Blake), but with the eye of the imagination. The best Romantics did not disregard the natural, physical world – Wordsworth and Keats loved the visible and temporal world more than most other poets and had an eye for its beauty, and the social ego was never abandoned altogether – but they were haunted by the presence of an invisible and eternal world, an ideal Being or Reality, behind or within the physical world. The prefix *meta* can mean 'behind', and they sought a *metaphysical* Reality in the sense that there was a Reality *behind* the physical world: the eternal behind the temporal, the significance behind the surface appearance – a dimension that had been missing during the Neoclassical time (although it had been present in the Baroque). The Idealistic Romantics expressed the inward and abstract by outward and concrete images, or, as August Schlegel put it, the transcendental could be made apparent "only symbolically, in images and signs" (*"nur symbolisch, in Bildern und Zeichen"*).

Neoclassicism had always been hostile to such Idealism. The

Neoclassical Dr Johnson had totally misunderstood the Idealist Berkeley when he simplistically said "I refute him thus" and kicked a stone to demonstrate that matter was not mental. His crude common-sense Materialistic position did not begin to see the subtleties of the Idealist position as they are contained, for example, in the manifestation of matter from the invisible through the four worlds of the Kabbalistic Tree of Life (a variation of which was proposed in the subatomic physics of David Bohm).

Meanwhile, at the Realistic level, Romantic individualism came out in confessional stories – Rousseau's *Confessions* (1781), Wordsworth's *Prelude* (1805), Byron's 'Childe Harold's Pilgrimage' and De Quincey's *Confessions of an English Opium-Eater* (both 1812) – and there were historical novels with a Romantic interest in the past (for example, by Scott). Now that the certainties of Neoclassical Rationalism were abandoned, the individual was forced to embark on a search, and so there was searching in aesthetics, metaphysics, religion, politics and the social sciences, and, of course, in how to write literature. This searching reinforced the Romantic's individualism, and it is notable that although the Romantic writers all have a 'family' similarity, they are fundamentally individuals.

We are now in a position to see that Romanticism was a revolt against tradition and authority, reason and classical science. It emphasised individualism – the individual consciousness – at the expense of the French Materialistic, Neoclassical tradition which treated Nature as a dead ornament. It opposed the authority of the contemporary political order, which was tyrannical by today's standards. It opposed the Rationalism of Descartes and the Enlightenment (which was in fact a Darkness). It opposed the empiricism of Locke and the mechanistic science of Newton.

Despite its slow evolution and relatively undoctrinaire intentions, Romanticism had the effect of reacting against Neoclassical "poetry of thought", and of restoring feeling to the European sensibility. Unlike the Neoclassical tradition, Romantic poetry is subjective, personal and irrational – written from the subcortical or lower right brain – and it is emotional in the sense that Wordsworth meant when he wrote: "Poetry is the spontaneous overflow of powerful feelings." It is daemonic – inspired by supernatural genius or impulse. If we leave aside the swoonings and extreme despairs, the Gothic sensationalism and the excessive adoration of Nature which the Neoclassical Jane Austen was caustically ironical about in *Emma* ("It led to nothing; nothing but a view"); then we find the Romantic feeling in the solitude of the heroes. Wordsworth's solitaries – his beggars and forsaken women – exemplify this feeling, as does the sentiment in his famous poem "I wandered lonely as a cloud". This feeling could go to extremes. All the Romantics sought to escape their solitude by flirting with the American and/or French Revolutions, which they saw as free-ers of oppressed individuals, and when they inevitably became disillusioned with the excesses of the guillotine, the isolation of their heroes was increased and heightened into an agony, as Mario Praz detailed in *Romantic Agony*. This agony was not always decadent; for example, Wordsworth's "We poets in our youth begin in gladness,/ But thereof comes in the end despondency and madness" ('Resolution and Independence', 1802). It could become decadent, as in Shelley's 'Alastor; or the Spirit of Solitude'.

The roots of political, libertarian Romanticism can be found in Rousseau, who developed his "back to Nature" philosophy as early as 1755. All men were equal in their primitive natural state, Rousseau argued. From this premise, he went on to hold (in T.E. Hulme's words) "that man was by nature good, that it was only bad laws and customs that suppressed him", or as Rousseau himself later put it, "Man is born free, and everywhere he is in chains" (*Du contrat social*, 1762). This outlook coloured the Romantic opposition to tyranny for years to come.

The attack on reason gathered force with the German *Sturm und Drang* (Storm and Stress) movement, which, as we have seen, included the young Goethe and Schiller. This sought to overthrow Rationalism – Descartes had placed the reason above imagination – and it exalted Nature and individualism, and Goethe's *The Sorrows of Young Werther* (1774) was the first really influential Romantic novel. Next came Kant, whose *Critique of Pure Reason* (1787) was enormously influential. Kant created a German Idealism which was followed by Schelling, who saw Nature as developing towards spirit (1795–1800).

The attack on science was on the 17th- and 18th-century Materialistic-Mechanistic belief, based on Newton and Locke, that Nature was material, and that there was a Cartesian duality between its material and mind. Romanticism now asserted that Nature was a living thing – organism, not material – and Schelling's philosophy of Nature, in which a plant was a tendency of soul, won the approval of Goethe, whose researches into biology and botany had already led him to see form in plants as being drawn out by an eternal, creative idea (1784–1790). Goethe would clearly have been very interested in Schelling's work.

*

Infinite "Spirit" in the Romantic Idealist poets: Wordsworth and Coleridge
The new Baroque consciousness is rooted in this Romantic Idealism;
in the Romantic spirit's consciousness of the infinite. We need to trace
this awareness of the infinite "Spirit" (or Being) in the main English
Romantic poets. The four threads enumerated above (revolt against
tradition, authority, reason and classical science) are never far away.

Wordsworth and Coleridge were very conscious that Nature is a
living thing or "Presence", that *Nature* is *Spirit* (or Being), that there
is an infinite world behind or within the finite one. 'Spirit' is a word
that lost its immediate accessibility during the 20th century, and it is
often dismissed as an imprecise use of language. The *Oxford English
Dictionary* defines it as "the supernatural power that controls our
destinies", while the *Shorter Oxford English Dictionary* gives a medieval
definition that is more specific: "the active essence or essential
power of the Deity conceived as a creative, animating, or inspiring
influence". It is this medieval "Spirit" that Wordsworth and Coleridge
rediscovered, and their rediscovery (akin to the metaphysical notion
that Being envelops sense-bound Existence) was independent of
German Idealism. Coleridge was steeped in the Cambridge Platonists,
and though he and Wordsworth visited Germany in 1798–1799 – it was
partly to pay for this trip that they published the *Lyrical Ballads* – and
though Coleridge studied German Idealism there, his sense of a Spirit
in Nature undoubtedly came from Platonism, which held that behind
the world was Soul, and further behind were the Forms in the Void
of what metaphysical thinkers would call Non-Being. Wordsworth
learned this vision from Coleridge, of whom he later wrote: "To thee,
unblended by these formal arts (i.e. the sciences),/The unity of all hath
been revealed."

Romantic poems are deeply rooted in the experience of the poets,
which is why they often seem mystical and existential, and the great
Romantic poem is undoubtedly Wordsworth's autobiographical
Prelude (1798–1805). Romantic poems are also frequently didactic in
intentions; it was certainly Wordsworth's intention to teach people
about the living "Presence" within Nature which challenged 18th-
century scientific Materialism, and his belief that poetry should
teach revolted against the Neoclassical opposition to didacticism.
Wordsworth knew, and taught, "the calm/That Nature breathes"
during the boyhood "seedtime" of his soul, and the experience of
"unknown modes of being", when he stole a shepherd's boat and
rowed out on Lake Ullswater and was pursued by a mountain, was an
experience of the Spirit or Platonic Soul within Nature which feeds the
passions of the soul:

Wisdom and Spirit of the universe!
Thou Soul that art the eternity of thought,
That givest to forms and images a breath
And everlasting motion, not in vain...
　　... didst thou intertwine for me
The passions that build up our human soul.
　　　　　　(Composed 1798–1799)

From "that still spirit shed from evening air" he learned "a quiet independence of the heart", and so sought Nature "for her own sake" so that "feeling... impaired power/That... /Doth like an agent of the one great Mind/Create". As a result:

　　　　　　An auxiliar light
Came from my mind, which on the setting sun
Bestowed new splendour....

This was the joy Coleridge was to miss in 'Dejection: An Ode', and it came from the mountains, lakes, cataracts, mists and winds that taught him to live with God and Nature. In 'Tintern Abbey' (1798) Wordsworth referred to the Spirit (or Being) in Nature (the "essential power of the Deity") as:

　　A motion and a spirit, that impels
All thinking things, all objects of all thought,
And rolls through all things.

Coleridge began as a Materialist, an associationist like Hartley, after whom he named his first son. However, his meeting with Wordsworth, whom he regarded as a genius, in 1795/6 led him to reflect on the mind, and his reading of the Cambridge Platonists (notably Cudworth) and of Berkeley, after whom he named his second son, and finally of Plato between 1795 and 1798 convinced him that the mind was far too *active* for the association of ideas to explain it. He turned against Hartley and made Wordsworth tone down the Hartleyan language of the 1802 *Preface*. He now asserted that the passive view of the mind of the empiricist Locke and the "cold world" of Newton were an error: "Newton was a mere materialist – *Mind* in his system is always passive – a lazy *looker-on* on an external World.... Any system built on the passiveness of the mind must be false as a system" (*Collected Letters* II, p.709). Only the imagination explained the active genius of Wordsworth's mind. Coleridge arrived at his theory of imagination "before I had even seen a book of German Metaphysics" (*Letters* II, pp.735–736), and it differed from the theories of Kant and Schelling. Schelling's philosophy, for example, was pantheistic – he identified Nature and mind – whereas (like Blake) Coleridge saw Nature as symbolising a transcendental Reality; and, believing in God, rejected Schelling as "a mere Pantheism" (letter of 24 November 1818).

Coleridge's theory of imagination is in *Biographia Literaria*, which began as a Preface and ended up as a mixture of autobiography and philosophy, the interweaving of his life and opinions. The theory distinguished fancy – an associative process as seen throughout the 18th century – from imagination, which was both an involuntary perception and a voluntary willing to unify the raw materials of experience and shape it, a psychological creative process which Coleridge called "secondary imagination". Coleridge held that through the imagination the mind perceives eternal Platonist Ideas in sense objects, and that since the reason receives the Ideas – and here it seems to me that Coleridge went astray for he should have used the word 'intellect' (see note to line 24 of *Fire-Void* [on p.306 of *Selected Poems: A Metaphysical's Way of Fire*]) – besides being under the will, the imagination is "the agent of the reason": "The poet brings the whole soul of man into activity.... He diffuses a tone and spirit that blends, and (as it were) *fuses*, each (faculty) into each, by that synthetic and magical power, to which I would exclusively appropriate the name of Imagination" (ch.14). By failing to distinguish intuitive "intellect" and analytical "reason" Coleridge is saying that the imagination is inferior to the reason, a strange reversal of the position taken up by later Romantics which Shelley did not hesitate to attack: "Reason is to imagination as the instrument to the agent," or: "Poetry has... no necessary connexion with the... will." Be that as it may, it was the imagination that grasped the Spirit within Nature. "An IDEA in the highest sense of the word," Coleridge writes in *Biographia* (ch.9), meaning the Platonist sense, "cannot be conveyed but by a symbol", and so Wordsworth's genius took objects of everyday perception, modified them with his imagination and transformed them into symbols of universal truth – though Coleridge readily acknowledged that in some of his poems which had a "matter-of-factness" (i.e. the Realistic poems) Wordsworth used fancy rather than the imagination. Thus, a poet showed the transcendent world by embodying his experience in symbols which reflected the essential organic unity, which the critic translated into thought, and Pope was at fault for writing down his thoughts without transforming them into symbols.

Coleridge, a would-be Unitarian minister until 1797, first expressed the Spirit (or Being) of Nature in terms of God. In 1795 he wondered, echoing Cudworth the Platonist:

> What if all of animated nature
> Be but organic harps diversely framed,
> That tremble into thought, as o'er them sweeps
> Plastic and vast, one intellectual breeze,
> At once the Soul of each, and God of All?
>
> ('The Eolian Harp')

In 1798, echoing Berkeley, he hoped that his baby

> shalt wander like breeze
> By lakes and sandy shores...
> ... so shalt thou see and hear
> The lovely shapes and sounds intelligible
> Of that eternal language, which thy God
> Utters, who from eternity doth teach
> Himself in all.
>
> ('Frost at Midnight')

He drank in "all adoration of the God in nature" from Britain ('Fears in Solitude', 1798) and this vision of Nature as being filled with God explains why the shooting of the albatross in 'The Rime of the Ancient Mariner' (1797–1798) caused disharmony in Nature, when a spirit followed the boat "nine fathoms deep" and parched the tongues of the crew in revenge; and it also explains how Geraldine could be possessed by the spirit of Christabel's mother in the Gothic 'Christabel' (1797–1800). In his 'Dejection' (1802), Coleridge made it clear that he could *feel* the beauty of Nature – a state then denied to him – if "the Passion and the Life, whose Fountains are within" would rise in his soul, for:

> Ah, from the Soul itself must issue forth
> A Light, a Glory, a fair luminous Cloud
> Enveloping the Earth!...
> This beautiful, and beauty-making Power!

This Power (Wordsworth's "auxiliar light") is Joy, "that wedding Nature to us gives in Dower". In other words, his soul must give out a cloud of luminous joy – the Divine Light – which gives meaning to the world of Nature, which in turn nourishes his soul. Failure to know the infinite in this way results in dejection.

23

Infinite Spirit: Blake and Shelley

The Romantic consciousness of the infinite continued with Blake, who really began it, for his Romantic *Songs of Innocence*, which were written under the influence of his Swedenborgian friends, came out in 1784, though without attracting any attention, and his *Songs of Experience*, which understood the devouring cruelty of the French Revolution in 'The Tyger', appeared in 1794. Blake went on to write about wars of liberation from authority in his longer works, but as early as 1793 he wrote of infinity in 'The Marriage of Heaven and Hell': "If the doors of perception were cleansed, everything would appear to man as it is, infinite." In 1788 in 'There is No Natural Religion' and in 'All Religions are One' he had challenged Locke's empiricism, his doctrine of the "corporeal eye", for Locke had chained the inner life of the mind: "Man cannot naturally Perceive but through his natural or bodily organs.... Man's perceptions are not bounded by organs of perception; he perceives more than sense (tho' ever so acute) can discover.... The desire of man being Infinite, the possession is Infinite and himself Infinite. He who sees the Infinite in all things, sees God." Similarly, he attacked Newton who had explained the outer world of Nature and the universe mathematically to further Hobbes' view of reality as matter in motion, and in a letter of 1802 he made his scathing reference to classical science as "Newton's sleep", and he wrote of Los, the imagination, as the spiritual sun (Los is *Sol* in reverse, the Fire or Light). Blake experienced the Fire or Light after visiting the Truchsessian Gallery in 1804 – he wrote that he had been in darkness for twenty years, which suggests he first saw it in 1784 – and he attributed many of his works (e.g. 'Milton') to his "celestial friends", from whom he took automatic dictation. (Compare Coleridge's spirits in 'The Ancient Mariner' and 'Christabel'.) By 1810 Blake took an extreme metaphysical, Platonist and Idealist position. In 'The Last Judgement' he wrote of the nature of the imagination and the "Eternal nature & permanence of its ever Existent Images": "the Oak dies as well as the Lettuce, but its Eternal Image and Individuality never dies" (cf. Plato's Forms and Goethe's view of plants). Again: "Mental Things are alone Real." Blake believed, like Wordsworth ('Intimations of Immortality'), that the soul existed before birth and was born with wisdom from the transcendent world of which Nature was a reflection, and that the imagination was the faculty that could see behind the appearance to the spiritual significance, the infinite. Blake's imagination was therefore less psychological and more transcendent than Coleridge's imagination.

The Romantic consciousness of "infinity" passed to Shelley rather than to Keats or Byron, although Shelley's Idealism is mixed with the

Neoplatonism of Thomas Taylor the Platonist. In two poems Shelley wrote in Switzerland in 1816, 'Hymn to Intellectual Beauty' and 'Mont Blanc', Shelley refers to the Spirit in Nature as "the awful shadow of some unseen Power" which "floats though unseen among us", and as "the everlasting universe of things" which "flows through the mind". And of course he hailed the west wind (in 1819) and the skylark (in 1820) as "spirit" – the one embodying the Spirit in Nature, the creative principle behind the universe, and the other its material reflection in the creative gladness of the poet. It is hard to believe that Shelley was sent down from Oxford for professing atheism, and that he is today sometimes regarded as "a Red", when he could write in 'Adonais', his elegy on Keats (1821):

> The One remains, the many change and pass;
> Heaven's light forever shines, earth's shadows fly;
> Life, like a dome of many-coloured glass,
> Stains the white radiance of Eternity.

It was his *spirit* that had the imagination to grasp this and feed his heart, and it is a measure of our age's Materialism that a poem like "When the lamp is shattered/The light in the dust lies dead" (1822) is not understood today – and is regarded as *afflatus* by Neoclassical critics – because readers have difficulty in distinguishing the lamp/spirit from the light/echoes in the heart, and therefore in giving meaning to:

> The heart's echoes render
> No song when the spirit is mute.

In fact, Shelley is saying that his spirit is his creative source because it reflects the creative Spirit in Nature.

Keats, of course, wrote about the joys and beauties of Nature, but he was haunted by the transience of life ("I was one whose name was writ in water") rather than by its infinity, and he did not write about the Spirit in Nature. He longed for a permanent beauty that was also truth, which his imagination could seize, and he found it in the perennial song of the nightingale and in a 2,500-year-old Grecian urn, and there are traces of a Platonic Ideal Beauty in "Beauty is Truth, Truth Beauty" (which came from his reading of Thomas Taylor the Platonist at Bailey's) and in the letters ("the mighty abstract idea I have of Beauty"); but by and large he was a Romantic of the visible world, not of unseen power. He rejected reason, preferring to be "in uncertainties, mysteries, doubts without any irritable reaching after fact and reason" (letter of 22 December 1817), but this "negative capability" – or capability of making his rational, social ego negative – merely led him to feel the beauty of the visible world more deeply, to enter into the being of a sparrow picking on the gravel (letter to Bailey postmarked 22 November 1817), and to accept the mystery of its beauty without seeking a rational explanation; and he never located the "power of Deity" or the creative principle of the universe, as Shelley did. To put it in the words of contemporary brain physiology, he made his left brain negative so that his right brain could feel into the visible forms of Nature. Although he wrote of revolt (in 'Hyperion') and emphasised feelings and individuals in his poems, and imagined he flew ('Ode to a Nightingale') and received and channelled images from the unconscious ('Ode on Indolence'), and was on the verge of receiving "knowledge enormous" – of Beauty – that "makes a God of me" ('Hyperion'), and although he had advanced to Moneta's inward contemplation ('Fall of Hyperion'), he lacked the vision of spirit or Being which Wordsworth, Coleridge and Shelley had, and lived far more in the world of the senses. The same is true of Byron, who was really a Romantic version of Pope. Byron did not proclaim the creative imagination, a fact which demonstrates his closeness to 18th-century poets, and his subject was the social ego – albeit treated with Romantic attitudes – and not the soul or spirit, which he implicitly lampooned by lampooning poets who write of the soul and spirit. In a sense, Byron was a classical Augustan who continued the outlooks of Dryden and Pope and struck a Romantic stance in a Romantic time.

Romantic consciousness after 1830
Romanticism after 1830 is a mere ghost of its former self and its Idealism was soon replaced by Realism. Although we have contrasted Romanticism with 18th-century Neoclassicism, Romanticism ("transformation through the imagination") is more naturally opposed to empirical, Materialistic Realism ("observation of the '*res*'", as in Zola) – this in spite of the fact that, as we have seen in Wordsworth and Keats, Idealist Romanticism could be combined with Realism, which soon collapsed without the imagination, making way for a Neo-Romanticism in Germany through the young Rilke.

As we have seen, the Romantic consciousness was taken up by German poets such as Heine, and by French symbolist poets like Baudelaire, Mallarmé and Laforgue, and of course by composers like Beethoven, Brahms and Tchaikovsky, and by painters like Constable and Turner. In English poetry though there are traces of it in Tennyson's mysticism and Arnold's 'Scholar Gipsy', Romanticism eventually paled into William Morris, Pater and Ruskin. During the Victorian Age, the settled spiritual values of the Romantic Age weakened in the face of Darwin's theory of evolution and in the face of positivism, and faith became doubt. In Victorian poetry we can see the beginning of that neglect of spiritual values which was to lead to Europe's decline in the 20th century; the bridge between the Romantic spirit before 1830 and the scepticism of T.S. Eliot's 'Waste Land'.

The view of Nature as a living thing passed into the Vitalism of Nietzsche, Bergson and Shaw, and was taken up by two men who lived in Grantchester, just outside Cambridge, in the first decade of the 20th century: Rupert Brooke and Whitehead. Brooke saw Nature as a living thing in his 'Grantchester', which is sometimes dismissed as being too sentimental, and he wrote of becoming "a pulse in the eternal mind" in 'The Soldier', and of his "mysticism" in a letter to Ben Keeling. Whitehead, one of the few 20th-century philosophers to believe that "the purpose of philosophy is to rationalise mysticism", opposed the Materialistic view of Nature held by traditional classical science with a philosophy of organism. Significantly, in his tremendously important *Science and the Modern World* (1925), Whitehead picked out Wordsworth and Shelley as reacting against the Materialism of 18th-century science: "Berkeley, Wordsworth, Shelley are representative of the intuitive refusal seriously to accept the abstract materialism of science."

Romanticism made a come-back in disguise in the early 20th century with the three great Modernists, Eliot, Pound and Yeats. As Kermode has argued in *Romantic Image*, this triumvirate did not understand themselves as Romantics, going for the image rather than the experience as they did, but they share the Romantics' preoccupation with the image, organic form and their view of the artist as a solitary; and therefore they have the Romantic consciousness. They saw themselves rather as Classicists, and the confusions of T.E. Hulme (ably pointed out in pp.32–35 of Hough's *Image and Experience*) have contributed to their misinterpretation of themselves. Hulme's 'Romanticism and Classicism' correctly points to the infinite as the goal the Romantics sought, but wrongly contrasts it with the religious attitude, by which he means the religion of the social ego ("man as a fixed and limited animal"). (The Romantic spirit's contact with the infinite Fire or Light is arguably a more truly religious attitude than the subordination of the Classical, rational social ego to a theoretically, rationally proposed God, Blake's Nobodaddy; and the major objection to Hulme is that he fails to distinguish the religion of the social ego – church religion – from the religion of the core, the mysticism of the Romantic spirit.) In fact, the truly Classical religious attitude is not the subordination of the social ego to "Nobodaddy" in church, but the Classical soul's contact with and awareness of the One and the profound sense of order and meaning that brings.

The Romantic spirit of Blake, Coleridge, Shelley and Yeats, and their emphasis on imaginative truth, was continued in the 1930s and later under the shadow of Modernism by Edwin Muir, Vernon Watkins and David Gascoyne, and by Saint-John Perse. All these have written of the imaginative tradition, by which they meant Jung's Collective Unconscious, Yeats' *Anima Mundi*, Blake's world of Imagination and Plato's world of Ideas, and therefore "that Plato's is the truest poetry" (Muir). For all of them the poet was a seer and eternal life could be contacted and known. In David Gascoyne's case, the sorrow on his return led to acute depression and a spell in which he relived Hölderlin's madness.

Neoclassical critics
Most of the English poetry since the Second World War has been Neoclassical and anti-Romantic. The now unimportant but still powerful Movement of 1956, for example, harks back to the 18th-century Augustan Age, to Rationalism and to Neoclassical, mechanistic form. It is a poetry of rational statement, like Dr Johnson's poetry which was written in the 18th century, and it is hostile to anything that smacks of Romanticism. It makes sincere feeling or realistic description the test of merit. It emphasises ordinariness as in Larkin, and opposes epic grandeur as in Amis's "Nobody wants any more poems on the grander themes for a few years". This attitude is now widely prevalent among the universities and modern publishers, those two powerful conditioners of modern taste, and few voices – Kathleen Raine is one in *Defending Ancient Springs* – have spoken out against it on the grounds that it lacks a metaphysical dimension and perspective, an awareness of "eternal life". Such an archaic return to the 18th century on the part of English poets suggests that the European civilisation has temporarily lost its creativity during its time of decolonisation and has retired to imitate past forms.

As soon as Neoclassical critics look at Romanticism in its wider, historical context, they argue that Romanticism was a disaster for the European tradition; that it was a sickness (Goethe) that led to a decline in spiritual effort, to self-expression and abstract art, to decadence and a sense of nothingness as artists tried to find the infinite, eternal world and ended in disillusioning failure. To this, the new Baroque artist who is rooted in Romantic Idealism has to reply that, on the contrary, the old imitative Neoclassicism is dead, along with its mechanical view of the universe, and that though much 20th-century art is appallingly decadent and spiritually barren, it was Romanticism that highlighted the spirit. Moreover, the disillusioned pessimism is no longer appropriate, for a new mysticism and an awakening of the spirit have put an end to the Age of Anxiety in which Modernism flourished – which was in fact an Age of Blindness and Sloth when there was an inability to see (with the imagination) beneath the surface to the core that knows the Divine Fire or Light, and which, accepting defeat too readily, never really made the effort to reconstruct a *new* vision, a fusion of the best of the Romantic and Classical ways of looking, such as is the new Baroque vision.

*

Neo-Baroque vision
Today, this new Baroque vision, which is partly a new – disguised – Romanticism, is abroad. It flowered in the so-called New Age consciousness movement, where such figures as Sir George Trevelyan and the more precise Neoplatonist Kathleen Raine briefly fulfilled the function for a modern young Shelley that Thomas Taylor the Platonist fulfilled for the early Romantics. If we leave to one side the astrology, the psychic research, the Steinerian doctrine – the more extreme manifestations of the New Age's spiritual and metaphysical vision – we can see that the new Holism restored the vision of the whole, the One, and of man as an incarnating spirit, which was declared a heresy at the Fourth Council of Constantinople in 869; and that its consciousness took an Idealistic view of the universe, seeing matter as infinite "Spirit". Nature is once again Spirit or Being, only now it has manifested from the Divine Fire or Light.

Metaphysical Fire or Light and the new science
We have seen that Romantic Idealism presented the world of the senses in order to reveal an invisible force that is beyond the senses. Once again man is infinite, for at his core his consciousness is filled with the invisible power of the mystic Fire or Light which flows through all Nature and the heart of man; which, through spiritual effort, he can see with his inner eye (see my volume *The Gates of Hell*); and which can "flash upon that inward eye/Which is the bliss of solitude" (Wordsworth).

This holistic view of man and Nature is supported by the new science, which has overthrown classical science and 18th-century

Materialism. It is supported by the new cosmology, and in particular by the new subatomic physics, which has challenged the Mechanistic, Newtonian view of the universe, and by the new biology, which has challenged Darwin's directionless evolution and restored Goethe's view of plants. It is supported by the new neurophysiology which, contrary to Locke's view, more and more sees mind as controlling the brain and causing chemical changes in its cells, rather than being dependent on the brain. The new vision's view of the mind is an anti-Materialist one: our incarnating spirits grow minds that link with the Universal Mind which flows all about the brain like the cosmic background radiation which is a perpetual echo from the Big Bang. According to some anti-Materialist scientists, consciousness flows into a person through certain centres (*chakras*) which act like gates and admit it into the nervous system, whence it flows up to the limbic centre in the brain, the child-like area linked with the soul and spirit (the core) where images and symbols are received and creative ideas flow. Wordsworth insisted that "the child is father of the man" because he knew that a child's spirit was closer to its divine origins than an adult rational, social ego, and both Wordsworth and Milton composed in the mind before writing anything down because they had an anti-Materialist view of the mind and sought to contact the Universal Spirit or Muse.

The new science, then, assumes that the universe is a whole, and Descartes' split between the mind of the social ego and matter is now criticised as, at our core, our minds merge into the whole universe of Spirit or Being. Thus our separation from the universe is an illusion based on the faulty perception of the rational, social ego. ("If the doors of perception were cleansed," Blake wrote, meaning 'if the grime of the social ego can give way to the core', "every thing would appear to man as it is, infinite.") We are each a wave in one sea of energy or Being, and what we do affects the whole, just as the whole affects us. Both mind and matter manifest from the One and are conscious in varying degrees, according to physicists like David Bohm, and photons within "matter" (which is in fact energy) have a kind of consciousness in so far as they are "aware" of each other and order themselves. In *Supernature* Lyall Watson sees Nature (mind and matter) as being governed by a supernatural, or supra-natural, power; an unseen, invisible force of Being – the Fire or Light – that is more fundamental than the world of the senses and which is very close to the Romantics' conception of the Spirit in Nature.

It is possible that this metaphysical Fire is associated with, i.e. manifests in, the cosmic background radiation which is a still-surviving product of the Big Bang which created the universe 13.7 billion years ago. Discovered in 1964/5 at Holmdel in New Jersey, America, this radiation is received as a persistent hiss. It is dispersed throughout the known universe as a diffuse glow at constant microwave tendencies, and the American NASA satellite Cobe (Cosmic Background Explorer) was launched in November 1989 to investigate this. This perpetual hissing echo of the fiery birth of the universe may be regarded as the physical and temporal manifestation of a metaphysical and eternal principle: the Fire or Light, whose silence preceded the universe and will succeed it, and which can be experienced as the vision of God as Fire or Light, a vision which has inspired the genesis of 25 civilisations. This radiation is the equivalent of the ether for which 19th-century scientists searched unsuccessfully. This hugely important idea reconciles time and eternity, physics and metaphysics, and offers the theory of everything which the physicists are seeking, for the cosmic background radiation which cooled into matter and organisms can be expected to organise gravity, electro-magnetism, strong and weak forces into one unifying law. (A theory of everything is impossible without cosmic rays because two of the three families of elementary particles, all of which existed naturally a fraction of a second after the Big Bang, can now only exist naturally on earth in cosmic rays as the universe has cooled since the Big Bang.)

What is the Baroque Fire or Light, this mysterious Divine Fire or Light that is so baffling when it first arrives, and which, after years of observation, is found to be full of symbols from the eternal world? It was better known to the ancient sages of Egypt, India and China than it is to us today, and as I showed in *The Fire and the Stones* and more recently in *The Light of Civilization* it is to be found in every religion. In Christian terminology it is the Holy Spirit which fills Creation and flows into the spirit as "the inner Light" of divine guidance and Providence. The workings of this "Spirit" are best seen outside the West, and in Hindu and Yoga terminology, where it has been known for thousands of years, it is *prana*, the cosmic vital essence which is experienced in *Kundalini* Yoga. This *prana*, or immaterial life energy that has been in existence since a fraction of a second after the Big Bang of creation, is everywhere: in every atom of the earth, in the sun and the moon and in the stars. Hence the tradition that there are planetary influences, or "flowings-in". *Prana* is an immaterial substance that pervades the universe in which it becomes material, a unified principle that contradicts the Cartesian division of experience into material and mental. It is the vital energy which acts on matter as force ("*Sakti*") and on mind as life ("*Prana Sakti*"). It is the architect that shapes organic structures out of elements and compounds. It is, in a sense, the agent of the divine imagination which shapes everything we know: trees, flowers, sunshine, seas, everything. So far it has not been tested empirically, and its radiation is too subtle to show up in a laboratory without reference to cosmic background radiation, but Gerard Manley Hopkins (for one) was on its track when he wrote of "instress" and of the world being "charged with the grandeur of God".

Some hold that this immaterial Fire or Light or *prana* flows into the body's subtle centres or *"chakras"*, perhaps within the manifested cosmic background radiation, and that, in the case of most people, it is extracted from the surrounding organic mass by nerves. Now a very fine, delicate, volatile, biochemical essence, they claim it is conducted up the spine to the brain where it resides, constantly leaving it to circulate the body as a motor impulse and sensation, and guiding choices providentially. Most people are unaware of this process. However, some Yogis have discovered voluntary control over it, and can channel it and use it voluntarily in healing when it rises as four or more "shivers" up the spine and leaves the laid-on hand as a surge. Such Yogis can see it as deathless in *"samadhi"*, the enlightenment that occurs in the course of my volume, *The Gates of Hell*. (The central experience of my life – both my active life and my poetic life – has undoubtedly been my experience of this Fire or Light which so fascinated Wordsworth, Coleridge, Blake and Shelley. [See Appendix 1, pp.437–447]) On death it departs; hence the Tibetan Clear Light of the Void which dying people are supposed by Tibetans to see as the *prana* gathers itself to leave and the immortal spirit is released, provided the spirit's immortality has been assured through an experience of illumination. *This Fire or Light – this immaterial* prana *which becomes material*, this vital energy which fills matter and mind like the cosmic background radiation and acts as the medium of the divinity – is the Romantic infinity.

Neo-Baroque synthesis of Romantic infinity (Fire or Light) and Classical harmony
In the new Baroque vision, the Romantic infinity (the Fire or Light, now a part of the poetic tradition as a result of the work of Wordsworth and Coleridge) is synthesised with Classical harmony, just as the historical Baroque vision combined harmony and dynamic movement. The stillness of the contemplative gaze amid the dynamic world of the new subatomic physics and of the immaterial *prana*/Holy Spirit is a Baroque paradox. It is because the New Age consciousness movement combines a celebration of the world of the senses with a great striving, even

yearning, for the infinite spirit that it should properly be regarded as a Baroque movement, and the same processes are at work in artists (such as the Catholic Margaret Riley of Shoreham) whose landscapes and bodies show the influence of a peaceful, divine order. And this is the main feature of the new Baroque: the Classical sense that there is order behind the physical world is synthesised with the Romantic infinite and movement. This "mix" is to be found in T.S. Eliot's *Four Quartets*, which anticipates the new Baroque vision in lines like "at the still point of the turning wheel". In synthesising Romanticism and Classicism, the new Baroque synthesises Modernism and Neoclassicism and makes for a continuity between their scepticism and the Baroque Reality.

It may be objected that art and literature are different, and that aesthetic categories applied to art ("the Baroque") should not be applied to literature. I would disagree. Both art and literature are products of minds – and souls and spirits – that are affected by, or reacting against, their Age. The Age dominates both art and literature, and there is, for those who have the eyes to see and the ears to hear, a fundamental parallel between the Baroque St Paul's Cathedral (started 1675) and Milton's *Paradise Lost*, a Baroque epic published eight years earlier in which the spirit is within the world. The same is true of the Baroque music of Bach or Handel, and the literature of the Metaphysicals, who were of the Baroque period and whose work is steeped in the Church of England Light: Marvell's 'Garden' for example, in which spirit and world are intertwined.

Neo-Baroque literary style combines Classical social ego and Romantic spirit
The Baroque literary style includes both Classicism and Romanticism. Let us contrast the way a Neoclassical writer works with the way a Romantic writer works, paying attention to the role of the social ego. A Classical writer concentrates on the social being, as we have seen. In 18th-century Neoclassicism, too, the writer hides his ego behind the ego of Man, but it is the social ego – the social ego of Man – that he is interested in. For the Classical hero is always a social being, he is never a mystic or solitary or social parasite like the Romantic hero (and contemporary anti-hero). The Neoclassical writer never delves far below the social surface of life, and as a generalising moralist he seeks to present not the unique individual but the social type: the greedy man, the liar etc. (Compare Ben Jonson's types.) The Neoclassical writer sees social types, and consequently praises empirical observation, tending not to believe in genius. In typifying or rationally classifying Nature, he "imitates Nature". A Neoclassicist's work thus reveals very little of

the writer, and he creates a social world to be shared by all.

On the other hand, the Romantic writer reveals his ego – often in a confessional context, as we have seen – and he is often a mystic or solitary who creates a world that is different from anyone else's: unique and individual. The Romantic Idealist relates his revealed *spirit* – for he is ultimately more soul and spirit than ego – to the invisible world behind the world of the senses.

The Baroque writer combines Classicism and Romanticism by reflecting both the social ego of the Classical writer and the mystic infinite spirit of the Romantic writer. It is most important to stress this: the Baroque writer includes much more of the social ego than does a Romantic writer. (Compare the social ego of Adam or Eve in Milton's Baroque *Paradise Lost* with the dream self that received the images from "the other mind" in Coleridge's Romantic 'Kubla Khan', for example.) The Baroque writer relates his revealed social ego and its feelings to the core that lies behind it and its deeper feelings, and to the metaphysical truth of the Fire or Light which is the same for all men. See the "Reflection" and "Shadow" in my early Baroque work, 'The Silence'. Hitherto, Classical writers have not included the sub-social, unconscious depths, but the Baroque writer is aware that the core is a *type*, as well as being unique and individual – compare the collective unconscious of Jung – and that the universality of the core in relation to the universal Fire or Light could have classical undertones in the right hands.

This invisible power, the Fire of Light, is perceived by the core of man's being, not his social ego, and so the new Baroque blends with mysticism, transcendental or Metaphysical Existentialism and Idealism and *reveals that core, the soul and spirit of Romantics, in conjunction with the social ego of Neoclassicism. It is the purpose of the new Baroque poetry to show the relationship between the social ego and the core, to reveal* through all the confusion of human emotions and feelings and thoughts and sensations the *core that can perceive the Fire or Light.* And just as Wordsworth had a didactic aim, to teach that Nature was a living thing, so the new Baroque has a partially didactic aim: to teach the presence of the core that glimpses the metaphysical, that mystically perceives the Fire or Light, and to offer its consciousness which differs so greatly from the consciousness of the controlling social ego – while at the same time creating a work of harmony and beauty that catches the harmony and beauty of the universe of Fire or Light and of the world of the social ego, and that may seem at times close to Classicism. However, whereas Romanticism was to some extent egotistical, in as much as Wordsworth had to be self-absorbed in *The Prelude* in order to dig out from his own experience his sense of the "Spirit of the universe" – hence John Jones' Neoclassical view of him in the title of his book *The Egotistical Sublime* (Keats' words) – the new Baroque seeks to *loosen the hold of the social ego* and free the core of the human being, his soul and spirit, and it is thus relatively *un*egotistical; although it is concerned with the individual and inwardness as it traces a dying away from lower consciousness to higher consciousness and awareness of Being which gives meaning to life. The new Baroque *revolts against the tyranny of the social ego*, Blake's rational, Materialistic "spectre" which oppresses the immortal self:

Each man is in his Spectre's power,
Untill the arrival of that hour
When his Humanity awake
And cast his Spectre into the lake.
                    ('Jerusalem')

Of course the new Baroque writer never completely escapes his social ego or spectre or "Reflection", for everyone without exception always has an outer social side. It is all a matter of control. All men and women spend a large amount of time living through their social ego: at parties, when talking in the High Road, through their job. Property developers and politicians spend large parts of their time in their social ego. A personality becomes disharmonious and unbalanced when a person is imprisoned in the social ego, and cannot locate the inner core. A shift from the controlling social ego to this inner core (the thread of these poems) liberates a person. Kabbalists offer an exercise to illustrate this. They arrange ten chairs in the hopscotch-like pattern of the *sefirot*, and ask you to sit in each chair in turn. Only chair 2 represents the social ego, and if you are centred in the equivalent of chair 5, which controls all the chairs (*Tepheret* or Beauty), then from your true centre you perceive things as they are and are in contact with the spiritual and divine as well as the physical and psychological worlds. You can then sit in the centre of the social ego which is equivalent to chair 2 at will to do your negotiating or social transactions, but you can leave it and return to your true centre which is equivalent to chair 5 at will, aware that you are not controlled by the centre which is equivalent to chair 2, not chained to it or imprisoned in it.

The new Baroque recognises that the social ego is not to be, and cannot be, finally rejected or obliterated, and so in a sense the new Baroque writer is in permanent revolt against it. He can, however, *escape its power*, loosen its spectre-like grip, so that though it still features in art, giving all the benefits of the Neoclassical range of subject matter and orderliness, it appears in conjunction with the deeper core, as do the social egos of the characters in D.H. Lawrence's *The Rainbow* in which the social and unconscious characteristics are distinct and almost separate. The point needs underlining. In view of the underlying continuity of the Augustan tradition into Romanticism, it may seem that in liberating the spirit of Romantic Idealism from the social ego of Augustan Neoclassicism and Romantic Realism, which depends on the world of the senses, the new Baroque must pay a price in human terms. On the contrary. The new Baroque is not exclusively about the invisible Fire or Light. It seeks to relate the social ego to the core, to deepen the Neoclassical definition of what a human being is, and consequently the new Baroque is as interested in everyday life as was the historical Baroque. Thus, like light, the new Baroque shows a protean self that can be both a particle and a wave, both social ego and core (Blake's two "contrary states"), both the spectre's social hardness *and*, at the core, a wave in the Oneness that the mystic consciousness can know, whose powerful Light flows through the self during the inner, contemplative vision. The new Baroque has its source in the spiritual, intuitive right brain – and more specifically in the subcortical, emotional limbic area of the brain where the Fire or Light is known during the theta brain rhythms of the creative trance – rather than in the analytical, cortical, Materialistic left brain, but it is still very human. Holistic poetry covers the whole brain (mind/psyche/soul); it is poetry in which both the social ego and the core are involved, and while it originates in the core it is interpreted by the social ego.

Baroque Imagination
The new Baroque Imagination – like the Romantic Imagination – originates in the core, not the interpreting social ego. It continues to find the infinite as Spirit or Being. For Coleridge, as we have seen, it was the *unifying* power, the faculty by which we reach towards and perceive and *know* the indivisible One behind creation. Coleridge called it the "esemplastic" power that "shapes into one", and he derived the word 'esemplastic' from the Greek '*eis hen plattein*', "to shape into one". Hence his reference in 'Dejection' to "My *shaping* spirit of Imagination". For all the Romantics, including Coleridge, the Imagination from the synthesising area of the right brain perceives a symbolic truth which the cortical reason of the left brain cannot know (even if it is superior to the Imagination, as it was for Coleridge), and it serves the eternal part of our nature whereas associative Fancy serves the temporal part of our nature, the social ego. Neoclassical critics who do not acknowledge an eternal part of ourselves and only acknowledge

the social ego, tend not to find the distinction between Imagination and Fancy helpful, but Wordsworth was very clear on this: "Fancy is given to quicken and beguile the temporal part of our nature, Imagination to incite and to support the eternal." Both Fancy (associative metaphor) and Imagination (eternal symbols) are found in new Baroque poems as they reflect both the temporal and eternal parts of man's nature.

Let us be quite clear about this. There are three distinct views of the imagination:

1. The temporal view: the 17th-century Neoclassical and 18th-century Augustan Neoclassical view which regards the imagination as the decorative verbal playfulness, associative elaboration and metaphorical grace of Fancy with which the reason embroiders poems, comparing dissimilar phenomena from the temporal social world; and as a faculty of the temporal rational social ego (e.g. the Neoclassical Larkin's "Why should I let the toad *work*/squat on my life?" in which "toad" is decorative and "squat" purely associative, a view that is related to the novelist's temporal imagination, i.e. imagining oneself into different characters' shoes).

2. The eternal view: the realistic Romantic view which regards the imagination as the power (associated with the Fire or Light) that synthesises raw experience into concrete images, apprehends order and organic form, and fuses feeling, vision and thought into a unified whole which suggests "the Translucence of the Eternal in and through the Temporal" (Coleridge on the symbol) so that the laws of the lower world are seen to correspond to the realities of a higher order; and the Idealistic Neo-Romantic view, which regards the creative imagination as receiving from on high in the trancelike "other mind" images and symbols from the eternal world. (Both these views are at work in the river-caverns-sea symbols in the Xanadu of Coleridge's 'Kubla Khan' "where Alph, the sacred river ran/Through caverns measureless to man/Down to a sunless sea".)

3. The contemplative mixture of the temporal and eternal views: the new Baroque view, in which the temporal rational social ego reflects upon the reception and synthesising of images and symbols which correspond to or reflect the eternal world or metaphysical Reality, recollecting in tranquillity and quietness and contemplating the emotion, feeling, vision and thoughts that arise when in a social setting the eternal Fire presents itself from on high, relating the temporal self (social ego) to the eternal One, i.e. a small part to the unified whole.

Today, the new Baroque has redefined the Romantic Imagination as the faculty with which we grasp *the whole* (i.e. unity of Being) during contemplation (when "emotion is recollected in tranquillity"), and poetry is the expression of the "whole behind everything" or the Fire behind a particular social setting, in which it is present, and therefore of the meaning of life, the perspective of meaning which is given by an awareness of the whole. In Blake's words (c.1803), the whole, or infinity, is everywhere:

To see a world in a Grain of Sand
And a Heaven in a Wild Flower,
Hold Infinity in the palm of your hand
And Eternity in an hour....
('Auguries of Innocence')

This meaningful vision from the synthesising area of the brain where the Light flows in is like a spring of inspiration that flows behind the eyes, and it is buried when the earth-like distractions of the social world of work are flung upon it. The Romantic Imagination could "see into the life of things" (Wordsworth). The new Baroque Imagination sees *into* each form and relates it to the one Fire or Light behind all, employing a metaphysical vision that is known to all mystics. The new Baroque Imagination thus approaches a cosmos filled with one "Spirit" or being, and lifts consciousness to levels which are cosmic and transcendent, so that it can attain the objective, unitive consciousness of the one Fire or Light.

Into this cosmic consciousness – this metaphysical vision and contemplative imagination which unite with the Idea-filled Void of Non-Being or non-manifestation – flow symbols which represent Reality. Or to put it the other way round, metaphysical Reality (the Fire or Light) manifests from eternity into temporal, psychological and physical forms which are symbols. These symbols are received in the soul (the mind's eye) or by the physical eye. They can be seen as transparencies of Reality or as being identified with Reality, which they veil and then reveal so that a reader can get to know, approach and have the unitive vision of the metaphysical Fire or Light. According to the Kabbalah Reality has layers and the symbol embodies the layers of the four Kabbalistic worlds, the physical, psychological, spiritual and divine worlds. René Guénon wrote of a law of correspondence which operates throughout the cosmos, in which "all things are locked together and correspond in such a way as to contribute to the universal and total harmony" and a consequence of which "is the plurality of meanings contained in the symbol" as "anything and everything can in fact be regarded as representing not only the metaphysical principles, but also realities of orders higher than its own". To a contemplative poet, symbols are signs which point to Reality, suggesting that the parts of our universe (its physical manifestations) are identified with a greater whole, and they pale to relative insignificance beside the central unitive vision of the Fire, which offers a theory of everything and governs the whole. In the Rationalistic 18th century there was a de-symbolisation, but the Romantic movement revived symbolism and the new Baroque vision welcomes the symbols that come into the core of consciousness from the beyond for they represent, contain and are identified with a layered Reality of Fire whose presence is not far behind.

Politically, the new Baroque (unlike Romanticism) is not dedicated to totalitarian revolutions, which are exclusively social and materialistic. The new Baroque aspires to a better, cleansed world on holistic principles in which man's spirit can prosper, and man can live in true harmony with Nature – the world of the senses – like the early Taoists. The ideal is some sort of world government, in which man relates to the *whole world*, but as that will take time to achieve, the more immediate ideal is of a supranational European State that has a wise attitude, for example, towards organic food and insecticides. More than ever, the Romantic "back to Nature" attitude is expressing itself in a return to the countryside, where people can grow fresh food and have healthy bodies, like the Essenes of the two centuries before Christ. Educationally, the new Baroque seeks to open the imaginations of the young to the eternity that is all round them, and within Nature.

The new Baroque's rejection of totalitarian political revolution – the Russian, Chinese and Libyan revolutions in my poems – emphasises again the solitude of the Romantic at the level of the social ego, and provides a new emphasis on inwardness, and therefore on heightened consciousness, which can lead to a holistic view of mankind. Just as Wordsworth's disillusion with the French Revolution led to *The Prelude*, so the new Baroque artist's rejection of materialistic Marxism which is based on the social ego alone, can afford similar opportunities and possibilities. Because his life-style is opposed to much of the materialism of the West – he may seek to live close to Nature, eat natural food, be largely vegetarian, non-smoking and teetotal, and have values that differ from the materialistic round of work-and-pleasure of the city, where Nature is forgotten – it may be thought that he seeks to overthrow European civilisation, but this is not so. He is aware of the importance of preserving European civilisation, which transmits the tradition of the European Fire or Light, and of the danger of that even greater materialism, Communism, which until the fall of the Berlin Wall could still be expected to succeed a destroyed European civilisation.

As to reason and science, despite the inroads made on them by Jung and Einstein, the heirs of Descartes, Locke and Newton are still abroad, and Rationalism, Empiricism and scientific Materialism have regrouped after the early Romantic attacks on them, and have combined with a regrouping of Neoclassicism in England (all the Movement poets and critics, for example) and with practitioners of Scepticism and atheistic, egocentric Humanism (as opposed to the early Christo-centric or theocentric Humanism), particularly in the universities. The result is a world-view that is totally inimical to the new Baroque writer – and to the Fire or Light. The new Baroque must challenge these obstructions to a true world-view, the heirs of Darwin, the evolutionists, the empirical linguistic analysts (the Ayers and Ryles) and the heirs of the positivists who have threatened to bankrupt the Western spiritual tradition. It must put forward the anti-Materialist alternative which is not based on the Neoclassical social ego, so that it is still available for the younger generation. It must proclaim the message that the reason of the ego serves the core, which includes the unifying Imagination. The reason is in the service of the irrational, or supra-rational, supra-empirical Divine Fire or Light, one glimpse of which burns away Scepticism; the reason does not dominate the core, as Descartes held. The new Baroque Fire or Light differs in emphasis from Coleridge's Platonism. Instead of Platonist Ideas flowing into the higher reason and thence to the Imagination as symbols, and the phenomena of the natural world in turn being regarded as symbols of the Ideas (Coleridge); the inspirational Fire or Light – *prana* – flows into the core – the spirit, which includes the intuitive intellect (the Kabbalistic *Binah-Hokhmah*) and which is nearest to the Fire or Light being furthest from the world, and then the soul (the Kabbalistic *Neshamah*), which is nearer to the world (being moved by poetry and music), both of which awaken when the reason of the social ego slumbers. And its eternal symbols proceed thence to the Imagination (the Kabbalistic receiving *Tepheret*, where the physical, psychological and spiritual worlds meet). The phenomena of the natural world are also "symbols", forms that have manifested from the eternal world of the Fire or Light and the Void of Non-Being. The intellect is only involved when it has received Ideas or other communications from the Fire or Light, and it may be baffled at the symbols which the Imagination has received directly from the Light. The new Baroque writer, then, works for change within our materialistic Christendom along these lines, seeking to make its consciousness blossom from the Materialistic dead wood.

*

Classical and Baroque artistic styles
The new flowering in Europe should be seen as a new stage in the life cycle of the European artistic style. This new stage coincides with the Universalist rediscovery of metaphysical Being and the Fire in stage 44, and the revival of cultural and metaphysical purity in stage 45 of the 61 stages in the life cycle of European civilisation.

Although the history of art and literature (like the history of a civilisation) is a continuous process through different Ages, there are undoubtedly stages within the life cycle of a civilisation's artistic style that spans all Ages (and, indeed sub-stages within the life cycle of the artistic style of each Age). Whereas Neoclassical critics have concentrated on the social environment which produced the style, the material, moral and intellectual climate of each Age, Romantic critics have had a vitalist approach, and have seen an Age's style as organically going through stages of growth, like a plant. (See the development of the Gothic style, for example.) In other words, the determining factors in a work of art were not in circumstances outside the work, but in the artistic activity itself.

Returning to the life cycle of the artistic style of a civilisation, it was the vitalist Swiss Professor Heinrich Wölfflin, in works published in 1888 and 1898 (*Renaissance und Barock* and *Die klassische Kunst*), who first defined the two main stages of a style in terms of the psychological concepts of "classical" and "baroque", two mutually hostile attitudes to life which he removed from their historical context (historical Classicism and the historical Baroque). In this last sentence and in what follows the historical Classicism and Baroque have a capital 'C' and 'B', whereas the universal styles removed from their historical context have a small 'c' and 'b'. In Bazin's words (*A Concise History of Art*, pp.524–525), the European Renaissance style's classicism, according to Wölfflin, "which attempts to strike a balance between form as it is conceived by the intellect on the one hand and the direct observation of nature on the other, expresses itself in centred compositions and through a strict arrangement of component parts, each of which retains its distinct unity; classical forms are ponderable and static, and obey the laws of gravity, while movements are governed by rhythms and may be reduced to a harmonious cadence." European Baroque, on the other hand, "expresses uneasiness and a longing for freedom, and shows itself in open compositions, fragments of the world rather than a world in themselves, which overflow the limits of the frame. Baroque forms are very imponderable, weightless, they soar into space, which they cut across with movements that set the eye moving in every direction, far beyond what they actually show. The unity of baroque compositions is not of an intellectual" (he means "rational") "order, but it is organic, living, comprehensive, resulting in a close dependence of the forms one upon the other." Thus, "Classicism means cohesion, it reduces nature to the human scale. It is a state of being, while baroque is a state of becoming, a dispersion, so enamoured of nature that it absorbs man into the cosmic rhythm. Baroque tries to depict human passion, grief and pain, love and death, all the ages of man; whereas classicism is only interested in the mature man at the height of his powers, when all his faculties are controlled by reason. The favourite medium of baroque is painting or music, while classicism expresses itself most fully in architecture and sculpture. In extreme baroque, architecture tends to abandon abstract principles, becoming as it were plant-like, closely wedded to the organic forms of nature."

A new Baroque Age and Counter-Renaissance
The view that in every civilisation there are differing stages in the life cycle of its artistic style was first suggested by Déonna in Geneva in 1913, and developed by Faure (1927) and Focillon (1934). On this view, the complete evolutionary life cycle of a style passes through the following stages. There is first a primitive, archaic, pre-classical, experimental stage or Age, in which there is no clear distinction between the soul and the world. The artist projects mental data into his work, and has little awareness of the external world and does not use his powers of observation. There follows a classical stage or Age in which the reason and soul are in balance, with reason informing the soul of its observation and the soul being aware of the harmony in the external world. There is then an academic or post-classical stage or Age in which artists have an undue respect for the forms of the previous generation and out of exhaustion obey conventional rules (Neoclassicism). Nothing new is invented, and the result is an anaemia that results in artificiality and drives artists to revolt and create the extremes of the ensuing pre-baroque Mannerist stage or Age. In this they create a world of their own as a substitute for the everyday world around them, and the body is distorted and lengthened. The end of mannerism – its cure – is *in the baroque stage or Age* in which "the spirit is again in contact with the world, the imagination drinks deeply

of its forms, and at the very source, with an eagerness born of long deprivation. The cosmos itself seems to be throbbing in the soul, filling it with inspiring emotion" (Bazin, p.528).

If the life cycle of an artistic style is seen as lasting centuries, its stages as lasting 100–200 years or more and its sub-stages as lasting for several decades, then in the style of all civilisations we can recognise similar classical/baroque stages in equivalent Ages. In the European style which emerged from the decay of ancient classical forms we can recognise broad sweeps or Ages; a primitive, pre-classical stage or Age in the Medieval Age; a classical stage or Age in the High Renaissance and after; an academic or post-classical stage or Age in Neoclassicism; and a Mannerist or pre-baroque stage or Age in Romanticism and its aftermath, when, and I quote Bazin again: "with his mind obsessed and arrested by conventional memorised forms, his soul impoverished by the sudden lowering of vitality that cuts it off from the outside world, the artist can only create a world of his own, a substitute for the real one around him. This anaemia results in artificiality and drives artists to extremes, for instance such deformities as the exaggerated lengthening of the body or frantic gestures, feverish attitudes and caricatured expression" (p.527). We have seen that "the world of the artist's own" passed from Romanticism – compare the world of Blake's own in his long poems – to Modernism and abstract art. In this case, the dynamic "baroque" stage or Age, the psychological term as used by Wölfflin, corresponds to the new Baroque Age into which European art is now beginning to pass – in which Classicism is combined with Mannerism just as in the historical Baroque the High Renaissance was combined with Mannerism as we have seen. In this Baroque Age we are now entering, soul and spirit, with heightened consciousness, contact the invisible source of the cosmos with the baroque Imagination, and depict (to recall Bazin's words) all human passion, grief and pain, love, death and the ages of man, uneasiness and a longing for freedom, the whole human life cycle in fact. For the new Baroque Age *redefines man*.

On the evidence of the consciousness movement, we are now proceeding into a period that is really a Counter-Renaissance. The Italian Renaissance's rediscovery of the classical past in Rome and Greece, along with its rediscovery of the human body, is paralleled by the Romantic rediscovery of the Middle Ages and of Gothic architecture, both of which were ended by the Renaissance. Hence such Romantic poems with medieval settings as Coleridge's 'Christabel' and Keats' 'Isabella' and 'The Eve of St Agnes', and the medieval subjects of the Romantic novels of Walpole and Scott. In our day a new and parallel Renaissance has a new concern with the past. There is a revival of interest in the ancient wisdom and ancient religions, and in particular in the old Neolithic shamanism, the journey of the shaman, which gave birth to them. There is also a rediscovery of the soul and spirit, which were well known in the past, and of the Fire or Light which was widely known in the Middle Ages. *We are living at the beginning of a kind of Counter-Renaissance that is restoring the soul and spirit to Renaissance Humanism.*

It is enormously difficult to pigeon-hole periods and styles, but if we look more closely at the life cycle of the artistic style of the European civilisation, which *shows* man's relation to the civilisation's central idea of the metaphysical Fire, and therefore to his soul and to Nature, in different Ages, we can identify some of the historical sub-stages within the broad classical/baroque stages or Ages within the one main style in our European civilisation. As we have just seen, there was a long pre-classical, primitive, archaic stage (the Medieval Age) as the civilisation grew round its spiritual élan of Christianity, in which there was no clear distinction between the soul of the artist and the world. (Hence the use of the halo in all social settings.) This became Mannerist in 14th-century French Madonnas. Out of this sub-stage grew a classical stage (the Renaissance, c.1425–1590) in which the mind's observation dominated the soul, a trend anticipated in Chaucer in the 1380s, a Christo-centric Humanism that culminated in the High Renaissance of Leonardo and Michelangelo (1490–1520). Then followed the first post-classical or Neoclassical or academic stage ("the academy" of the late 15th century and early 16th century) when artists belonged to "schools" of past masters, and decorum was taken from rules based on the great masters, with the result that artists did not have to invent. After this there was a first pre-baroque or Mannerist stage in which artists revolted against the academic rules (16th century, for example the ecstatic trance of El Greco who lived during the time of St John of the Cross). Finally, there was a first dynamic, baroque stage in which the barriers were removed between the world of the senses and the world of the spirit, and in which there was a mixture of classicism and Mannerism (sense and spirit) as artists used the body to express the spirit (the historical Baroque, c.1600–1750). This baroque stage was in turn succeeded by its academic and Mannerist stage (Rococo), which was based on the wave-like lines of Nature.

After a civilisation breaks down, its central idea of metaphysical Fire goes into decline and its religion ceases to inspire new artists, who gradually turn to secular subjects. In due course the civilisation ceases to be artistically creative, and artists continue past modes of thought, notably the struggle between reason and the irrational spirit.

It seems that the last three stages of the cycle repeat themselves. In the European civilisation which broke down c.1453–1550, a new, second post-classical or academic stage continued with Rationalistic Neoclassicism and the Augustan Age (17th and 18th centuries), which resisted the Baroque and led eventually to the Realism of the Victorian social novelists. Secondly, there was a new, second pre-baroque, Mannerist trance, ecstasy and extreme emotion in the Romantic movement (late 18th and early 19th centuries), which freed artists from Neoclassical shackles. If we bring literature into our look at art, this turned academic (Matthew Arnold, Pater, Ruskin), while Romantic expressionism – when intense emotions are poured out in a monologue – really marked a pre-baroque stage in which sense and spirit are merged (in Romantic Idealism). Hence, though Blake is often regarded as a Mannerist "shackled" by a Neoclassical form, he was full of pre-baroque elements; while Rodin's feverish, tormented art was also Mannerist, although in *The Burghers of Calais* (a copy of which stands outside the British Houses of Parliament in London) he anticipated the new Baroque. In the 20th century, as we have seen, Romantic expressionism and Mannerism developed into fragmented and abstract Modernism (for example, abstract art), and into the symbolist Neo-Romanticism of poets like Katherine Raine. Meanwhile, there has been a Neoclassical revival since World War 2, at least in England. Out of the conflict between these two repeated stages, a new, second baroque stage, a mixture of Classicism and Mannerism, of sense and spirit, is set to emerge. This new – repeated – mode of thought will redefine spirit or metaphysical Being in relation to sense and will save European civilisation – which cannot survive without the Fire of the spirit as *The Fire and the Stones*, *The Light of Civilization* and *The Rise and Fall of Civilizations* attempt to demonstrate – for a while.

We can now place this new Baroque Age/Counter-Renaissance in a more sharply focused historical context. It was perhaps anticipated by metaphysical or religious (as opposed to atheistic) Existentialism, and it significantly preserves the central feature of the Medieval stage of the Western style, the Fire or Light. It emphasises the baroque "transformation" of consciousness – what I at the outset of this Preface called "a shift, a growth, a transformation" in consciousness – and by transforming consciousness to an awareness of the Fire or Light it can hand on the medieval Fire or Light to European civilisation. As the new Baroque Age has emerged from the collapse of classical Humanism due to the new science and the rediscovery of the ancient wisdom surrounding the Fire or Light, it fits in with the dynamic view of the world held by the new subatomic science and with the workings of irrational *prana*, and can be expected to last as long as stages 44 and 45 of European civilisation last, i.e. as long as the coming United States of Europe lasts before European civilisation enters its long process of disintegration. Now – and here I introduce a note of optimism and hope – it is possible that the new Baroque Age will be the crowning glory of Western literature, and perhaps of the whole of Western civilisation (i.e. the European and the North-American civilisations). For just as medievalism gave way to Humanism from about 1450 (when the halo disappeared from paintings), and the glory of the High Renaissance was only forty years in coming; so our Humanism is giving way to a new anti-Materialistic, spiritual or metaphysical Baroque Age whose High Counter-Renaissance may be only forty years in coming and as great as the 16th-century High Renaissance. The foundation of this Counter-Renaissance is the Fire or Light which, through the writings of St Augustine, Pope Gregory the Great and St Bernard, was central to the growth of European Christendom; for without the Fire or Light there could be no coming new age. Such a baroque new age within the European style – new age in values and in an aesthetic and artistic sense rather than an astrological sense – can be expected to have its own classical sub-stage (in Wölfflin's sense of 'classical'), and it will emphasise the unity of the universe. (Compare Toynbee's prediction that the idea of unity will dominate Europe's disintegration.) Thus our anti-Humanist stage within a European Christendom that has known the Humanist Renaissance is charged with the task of restoring the soul and spirit to Renaissance Humanism by restoring the Fire or Light, and *this redefinition of man can produce the greatest art and literature Western civilisation (i.e. the European/North American civilisations) has known.*

This is a huge subject, involving as it does considerations of the rise and fall of civilisations and the relation of the life cycle of a civilisation's artistic style to the salvation of its civilisation, which I have dealt with in *The Fire and the Stones*, *The Light of Civilization* and *The Rise and Fall of Civilizations*. But it does fit in with T.E. Hulme's broad scheme (Middle Ages – Humanism – and a coming Religious, i.e. Metaphysical, Age) and with the concept of a New Age that has nothing to do with astrology and everything to do with a rebirth of the spirit and an awareness of Being. The conclusion is clear. We are on the verge of a new Baroque Age, or, as I wrote in 1965 (though I do not think it found its way into the text of the poem until 1970) in a passage which came straight from the beyond and which for some years I did not fully understand:

I heard a cry from the old Professor's darkened room,
'The Age of Analysis is dead!'
Books lined with dust, a buzzing fly....
                              While, naked on the petalled lawn,
A new Baroque age is born.
                              (1348–1352 of 'The Silence',
                              which the dedication describes as
                              "a string of baroque pearls".)

*

The role of poets in the new Universalist Baroque Age
What is the role of poets in this Counter-Renaissance and in this new
Age? We have seen that this new Baroque Age casts a respectful look
back to Romantic Idealism, and indeed to the Metaphysicals of the
original Baroque Age, and we have said that writers and artists living
in a declining civilisation cannot help echoing earlier stages in that
civilisation, in so far as stage 45 echoes stage 28. Nevertheless, there
is no question of going back, archaistically, to the old Baroque. Rather
the new Baroque Age *looks forward,* for it is creating something new out
of everyday life and a new climate for the coming age, to which writers
and artists will in due course react, as did Milton, Handel and Bach in
the past. It is appropriate that the Christian mysticism of stage 45 will
feature strongly in the new Baroque Age along with the Universalist
New-Age consciousness of stage 44, as the original Baroque began as a
Catholic movement and traditionally the Church has been the guardian
of the soul and spirit in Christendom.

In the past, the great poets have been the best interpreters of their
Age. ("No man," Coleridge observed in chapter XV of *Biographia
Literaria,* "was ever a great poet without being at the same time a
profound philosopher.") Just as the poets of the Victorian Age saw a
time of settled Christian faith turn to doubt, so today in our Space Age –
compare the whirling clouds and the blue skies of the original Baroque
– we are seeing the traditional view of the universe being overturned,
with consequences for our view of the world and ourselves.

A very important aspect of the coming Age of Universalism is
what is universal to mankind in relation to the deep mystery of the
universe. It is fundamental to the coming Universalist, Baroque Age
that it is not enough to define man in purely social terms, in terms
of the social egos of his society. Man also has to be defined in terms
of the stars and metaphysical Being that gives oneness to the vast
interstellar spaces. It is a salutary and sobering experience to stand on

the end of a completely deserted Cornish harbour on a moonless night, a unifying laburnum tree sweeping branches of stars round your head, each bright and gleaming like a yellow laburnum flower, and to reflect on the vast distances involved and the millions of light-years that separate you from the stars 180,000 light-years from the Magellanic Clouds, the two satellite galaxies of our galaxy the Milky Way which is 100,000 light-years in diameter, and nearly 15,000 million light-years from the remoter quasars, high-energy sources which may be centres of galaxies which were created about the same time as our Big Bang. Orion, Cassiopeia, the Plough – you identify familiar friends. You stand there on one of two hundred thousand million stars in our galaxy, and out there across the quiet sea there are another two hundred thousand million galaxies equally large, and so far as we know there is only life on our planet. 'The Silence', written at a time when the universe was thought to contain only half this number of stars and galaxies, contains a similar experience in Japan:

> The sea sighed like a lover,
> Explored the face of the shore with webbed fingers,
> Blind in the dark phase. And in a glittering sweep
> Some of a hundred thousand million suns
> In one of a hundred thousand million galaxies
> Whirled on in a fiery band, shot out rays
> To traverse the silence for a hundred thousand years
> And beam on the man who crouched by a whelk-shell.
> On a Japanese beach, my terrestrial illusions shattered,
> I fell headlong into a deep, dark silence....
>   (896–905)

This metaphysical dimension is missing from the social view of Neoclassical art. Metaphysics, the philosophical study of Reality, traditionally includes ontology, the study of Being; epistemology, or what can be known with certainty about Being, which overlaps with psychology; and philosophical cosmology, which relates the findings of astronomical cosmology to ontological Being. It sees the One (or Fire or Light) as enfolding the Void or Non-Being, which pre-existed the Big Bang and which is unmanifest; which in turn enfolds or envelops Being which is manifestation; which in turn envelops Existence, the world of the senses and of the rational social ego, the world of physics and astronomical space probes. The metaphysical dimension is never far from astronomy, and *Voyager 2*'s journey round the planets has brought it back to us. Man in relation to the entirety of the universe, not just in relation to his immediate society, and the meaning of life – these are themes of Universalist, new Baroque art. It is an art of Metaphysical Existentialism for its subject is direct, existential experiences of ontological being, the Reality behind the cosmos and the unity behind all existence.

"What good are metaphysics or an understanding of our Space Age to the common man?" I am sometimes asked. And when I begin to explain I am told, "You're speaking Greek, the common man doesn't understand about ontology, and it's no good to him. There are many views of what life is about, and they are all equally right to those who hold the views. The idea that there is something beyond the social world of the senses is a theory, an opinion. It is useless to the common man and only as true as the contrary opinion that there is nothing beyond it. All opinions are relative and equally true."

In fact, many "common" craftsmen and artists – particularly stonemasons – are instinctive metaphysicians, and it is extremely patronising to the common man to suppose that he is only aware of the social world of the senses, of his pay packet and beer and girlfriend, of the physical and material, and that he is not aware of a higher or divine layer of Reality. To those who have read deeply about the last 5,000 years and have unearthed the Tradition (which I have described in full in *The Fire and the Stones* and *The Light of Civilization*), there is ample proof that there is something more than sense-bound Nature, and to suggest otherwise is like denying the existence or benefits of all libraries because the common man apparently never visits them. Spiritual improvement or purification of consciousness as an end in itself in this life and as a possible preparation for the next world, and understanding the structure of the universe as an approach to the human condition whose context it is, are both better goals than "being ignorant and proud of it". The Tradition is quite clear that all opinions are *not* relative, that the "fourfold vision" is more absolute than (to quote Blake) "single vision and Newton's sleep", and if you are not prepared to visit the libraries or look in encyclopaedias and dictionaries and delve, you will never have an informed as opposed to an uninformed opinion or learn the terminology in which truth is expressed, and it will always "seem Greek" to you, just as classical Greek does to those who have never made it their business to master the Greek script. (In the same way, the terminology of the "commonest" electrician will seem Greek to the greatest Professor Emeritus at Oxford or Cambridge unless the Professor takes himself to a library and masters the terminology of electricity.) The common man can place his social (working and family) life within the context of the meaning and purpose his life has if he will open his mind to the metaphysics which used to be so widespread and which have again gained ascendancy. This Preface, and the poems it introduces, are addressed to the common man despite their admittedly complex ideas, in the hope that his life will take on an added quality and existential authenticity and consciousness as he faces the question of what the environment of the universe is in relation to his life's goal and destiny. By facing metaphysical questions, the common man's life can become satisfyingly religious or blessed with a philosophical certainty, depending on how and at what level he responds to the answers a metaphysical vision gives him.

Traditionally the poet has always interpreted his Age. Now such a poet would interpret the new Space Age, and see that the conflict of the Counter-Renaissance is between Materialism and the spiritual or metaphysical "something more", the awareness of ultimate Being that gives meaning to life. Matthew Arnold believed that religion would be supplanted by poetry, that the poet would take over the function of priest (as Eliot in a way did) "to interpret human life afresh and to supply a new spiritual basis to it". (Taken literally, the belief that religion will be supplanted by poetry is absurd, but taken somewhat metaphorically in the sense that poetry would take on a spiritual role as it did in the hands of Eliot, or a metaphysical role, this belief can be seen to have been prophetic.) It is to be hoped that our poets can rise to the task of interpreting this fundamental conflict in our Age and break out of sense-bound, social poetry into a metaphysical vision.

If our poets can rise to the metaphysical vision of the coming Age, there will be a redefinition of poetry and of poetic assumptions that differs from both the Neoclassical and Neo-Romantic definitions of *their* assumptions.

Consider the Neoclassical and Neo-Romantic assumptions as regards subject matter and language, for example. Neoclassical poets and social rationalists regard poetry as a rational statement from the social ego in social situations, and the language of their poems is a plain one of statement and uses fancy, decorative simile or metaphor and association. Its merit is to be found in its presentation of sincere feeling or realistic description. The drawback of such poetry is that it ignores the soul and the universe. On the other hand, the Neo-Romantic or imaginative or imagist-symbolist poets regard poetry as the language of the soul speaking to the spirit of the reader, and the language of their poems is dream-like and incantatory, from the "other mind", and presents its theme in a succession of images and symbols which are received or channelled from another world. Its merit is to be found in its presentation of the eternal world behind the phenomenal world of appearances. The drawback of such poetry is that it ignores the social world, which is a very important facet of existential living, and it regards the current everyday language in which the soul attempts to express itself as being polluted and corrupted by television and the press. Life is about more than the soul as the soul has to live and act within the context of the social world, and to reject the social world completely is to be the artistic equivalent of a monk or nun and write in etiolated language.

Plato and the Neo-Romantic "other mind"
Let us turn aside and examine the Neo-Romantic position more closely by considering the attitude of Plato, whom the Neo-Romantics admire. Plato does not present poetry as a rejection of the social world, although he does see poetry as an irrational pursuit. Let us comb the pages of Plato's *Collected Dialogues* and list the main statements of his doctrine of poetic inspiration. According to Plato the poet is divinely inspired and receives "sublime messages without knowing in the least what they mean" (*Apology*, 22c). The poems are "divine and from the gods, and... the poets are nothing but interpreters of the gods, each one possessed by the divinity to whom he is in bondage" (*Ion*, 534). "If any man comes to the gates of poetry without the madness of the Muses, persuaded that skill alone will make him a good poet, then shall he and his works of sanity with him be brought to nought by the poetry of madness, and behold, their place is nowhere to be found" (*Phaedrus*, 245a). Socrates points out with some humour that "there are two kinds of madness, one resulting from human ailments, the other from a divine disturbance of our conventions of conduct.... And in the divine kind we distinguish four types, ascribing them to four gods: the inspiration of the prophet to Apollo, that of the mystic to Dionysus, that of the poet to the Muses, and a fourth type which we declared to be the highest, the madness of the lover to Aphrodite and Eros" (*Phaedrus*, 265a, b). "Poets..., singing as they do under the divine *afflatus*, are among the inspired and so, by the help of their Graces and Muses, often enough hit upon true historical fact" (*Laws*, 3.682a). "When a poet takes his seat on the Muse's tripod, his judgement takes leave of him. He is like a fountain which gives free course to the rush of its waters, and since representation is of the essence of his art, must often contradict his own utterances in his presentation of contrasted characters, without knowing whether the truth is on the side of this speaker or that" (*Laws*, 4.719c).

Nowhere in these passages is Plato saying that the poet hears the words of his poem in the course of his divine inspiration or that the poet must not write about the social world. Rather he talks of the poets being "possessed" by the divine, i.e. the Fire or Light; of "interpreting" the divine; of becoming "mad" (in the sense of out of their reason through inspiration) because they are too close to the divine. The inspiration is "*afflatus*" ("the communication of supernatural knowledge" or "divine creative impulse") or a "fountain"; it quickens the flesh and tingles up the spine, causing (in Coleridge's words) "flashing eyes" – the images in 'Kubla Khan' were divinely inspired. Inspired poetry is in a language of the soul but Plato does not say it has to be exclusively about the world of the beyond. The inspiration can flow into and be very much about the social world, as were the dramatic epics of Homer and the poetic dramas of Aeschylus, Sophocles and Euripides, who presented "contrasted characters". Plato says there must be contact with the divine – the madness of the Muses – and if a poet is not inspired from the divine then his works will not last. In Hindu terms the poet must be a *rsi* ("inspired one" in whose heart the universal and internal Light shines) to be a true poet.

Our view that inspiration flows into and informs the social world amounts to a guided rather than an abandoned view of poetic inspiration. The baroque poet, inspired from the beyond and contemplating the social world, unites his being into a new whole that unifies time and eternity, and his poem is an artefact of this unification. The poet retains the control over himself and the social world of a meditator who channels the divine; he does not abandon himself into an extreme Bacchic frenzy or babble incomprehensible words that defy meaning. In the politics of inspiration the baroque poet is an Orphic, not a Dionysian; a moderate, not an extremist. To adapt Wordsworth, he offers inspiration recollected in tranquillity.

Let us return to the conflict between Neoclassical and Neo-Romantic poetry. The 1,200-year-old tradition of European poetry, like the poetry of all cultures and civilisations over the last 5,000 years, includes both the Neoclassical and Neo-Romantic traditions of language at different times. Each side defines poetry in terms of its own outlook and denies the definition of the other side. In our time the early Eliot redefined symbolist poetry in terms of his symbolist outlook in his essays, while Yvor Winters wrote *In Defense of Reason* to reaffirm the rationalist view and to deny the symbolist view.

Neo-Baroque poetry blends Classical social and Romantic spiritual outlooks
A middle way is to combine the two, and this is what the new Baroque poetry will do and in my work has done. In the social-spiritual poetry of the new Baroque which combines the Classical and Romantic

visions, the language of the poets will combine statement and image as the social ego writes *about* the Fire, starting in social settings and employing both decorative fancy and imaginative images. In other words, the social world of the Neoclassicists is informed by the soul's reality of the Neo-Romantics: as the soul with a goal (Shadow) looks at Nature it includes the social ego (Reflection). In Kabbalistic terms the consciousness in *sefira* 5, *Tepheret* (Beauty), can look at Nature and include *sefira* 2 (*Yesod*), the social ego. Such a poetry concentrates on the consciousness that receives the images – social setting included – rather than on the images themselves. It is the same phenomenological approach to consciousness which I outlined in *The Fire and the Stones* and *The Light of Civilization*. It records the experience in everyday consciousness of inspiration from an unseen metaphysical Reality beyond it. This can be a conflagration from the beyond – a catching fire with inspiration, being seized or "rapt" – or an advance from a specific social setting which can turn into a raid on the eternal world and a Promethean "stealing", or more accurately borrowing, of the divine Fire. Whether the Fire approaches him or he approaches the Fire, the poet is a seer of a Paradisal world which nourishes his sojourn – indeed exile – in the social world. Such a poetry looks back to the Wordsworth of *The Prelude* who wrote *about* "the unseen power" in a language of statement that appealed to common men (the language of "a man speaking to men") but which included images which had flashed upon the "inward eye". For example, the mixture of image and statement which in one and the same passage could show the image of an animate mountain – "a huge peak, black and huge,/As if with voluntary power instinct/Upreared its head" – and at the same time make a profound ontological-metaphysical statement: "for many days, my brain/Worked with a dim and undetermined sense/Of unknown modes of being." The late Eliot of the *Four Quartets* was working towards such a poetry. As philosophical as he was inspired, he touched on the Fire at the end of 'Little Gidding': "And the fire and the rose are one." In our time such an approach makes a new kind of poetic language possible.

To put it another way, the social rationalists define poetry as the unpictorial rational statement about a human experience which suggests an empirical, social truth. The imaginative imagist-symbolists define poetry as images or symbols which are channelled from an imaginative Reality. The social-spiritual Baroque poets will redefine poetry as a statement by the reflecting soul of a metaphysical Reality which is received along with images and symbols; which is sometimes in the form of images and symbols; and which flows into and is combined with the consciousness of the social ego. This glimpse of Reality may come to the soul unexpectedly, or it may arise out of a visit to a particular place in a specific social setting – as if Larkin's 'Church Going' had resulted in a vision of the divine Fire instead of the social observation of "some brass and stuff/Up at the holy end". Instances of both can be found in my work: for example, there is an unexpected glimpse in 'The Silence' (line 1202), "And golden gods with Egyptian heads were drawn past my closed eyelids", while a visit to a particular place results in a glimpse in my volume *The Gates of Hell* in which "visions wobbled up like bubbles". The images are there. It is how they are presented that is crucial. They are described, deliberately written *about*, rather than strung together in an incomprehensible way in the interests of a purely imaginative logic.

Baroque redefinition of poetry and humankind

Such a redefinition of the subject matter and language of poetry in our Europe will at one and the same time revivify and detrivialise Neoclassical poetry and revitalise and de-etiolise Neo-Romantic poetry. It makes possible a new reflective poetry that speaks to ordinary people by relating individuals, social settings, and scenes of Nature to the deeper meaning of the universe, to the stars and the metaphysical Reality that is behind all things and flows through all things.

Poets looking back on the 1,200-year-old European tradition can connect themselves to the poetry of many different branches of the tradition: Pre-classical Medieval poetry, High Renaissance Classical poetry, Neoclassical poetry, and Romantic and Modernist poetry. There is a poetry for each of these branches of the tradition, and each has its own assumptions as to whether it is statement or image, whether it has architectural or organic form and as to whether the poet-artist has a social role or is isolated. Each poetic tradition is rooted in a different area of the creative brain (whether it be cortical thought, feeling, vision or the centre which receives unconscious images from the beyond), and each claims it alone guards the right way and that other ways are wrong. (We have seen that 20th-century Neoclassicals despise Neo-Romantics, and *vice versa*.) The consciousness of the new pro-metaphysical Baroque Age allows for a redefinition of poetic assumptions in a number of areas that amounts to a Metaphysical Revolution, and its points of difference from the other traditions can be summarised as follows:

1. Subject matter: the vision of Reality/God as Fire or Light, human passion and grief, pain, loss, death and freedom, the correspondence

between the temporal, natural world and the infinite, eternal world of the Void/Being;

2. Form: architectural and organic (like a climbing rose by an orderly country house);

3. Language: both statement and image/symbol (which embodies a psychological or physical form that is a manifestation of a divine Reality and spiritual Void);

4. Centre: both Neoclassical social ego and Romantic soul and spirit (all of which are connected in the *sefirotic* centre which the Kabbalists call *Tepheret*, or Beauty);

5. Imagination: both temporal comparison and eternal correspondence to present the whole/unitive metaphysical Fire;

6. Metaphysical outlook: both awareness of physical reality and an ontological, epistemological and cosmological approach to the eternal metaphysical Supreme Being and Reality (the Fire) which is behind both the Void of Non-Being (or non-manifestation) and unitive Being (or manifestation);

7. Perspective of man: both man as a member of his society and man as a member of the universe which has a metaphysical order behind it;

8. Philosophical outlook: scepticism presented within the context of metaphysical Being and Reality, and unitive anti-Materialism;

9. Psychological outlook: the reason presented within the context of the irrational;

10. Cosmological scientific outlook: scientific Materialism presented within the context of the unitive new science (subatomic physics and anti-Darwinian biology) and metaphysical cosmology;

11. View of the universe: the multiplicity of phenomena presented within the context of the Oneness of the universe when seen with the unitive vision of Being;

12. Historical outlook: themes of contemporary social history (including rejection of totalitarian and particularly pro-Communist political revolution), presented within the context of support for a unifying, holistic, altruistic, benevolent rather than self-interestedly malevolent world government/supranational state that genuinely seeks to benefit rather than exploit all humankind.

(To this can be added:

13. Purpose of the teaching of English Literature: to take pupils from a response to, and judgement of, temporal imagination, i.e. imagining themselves temporally into the shoes of others and associatively, to an awareness of eternal imagination, i.e. of metaphysical Being/Reality. Minor poets operate in an exclusively temporal mode, major poets operate in both temporal and eternal modes, i.e. a metaphysical mode.)

Besides being points of difference from other traditions, some of the above threads of the new metaphysical Baroque poetry of the coming Metaphysical Revolution can reconcile and synthesise other traditions, for while Baroque poetry differs from both Classical and Romantic poetry in its assumptions regarding subject matter, form and language etc., it also reconciles Classical and Romantic poetry at each of the above points as we have seen.

If poets can rise to the challenge of the Age, then once again poetry will drip with experience as the soul drinks deep from the natural world and finds the eternal Being within Nature. Once again poets will contemplate and point the way for the young. The followers of the new Baroque are contemplative, illuminated souls who live very much in the world of the senses. They are a generation of Contemplatives. Baroque artists of the world, who have one foot in the social world of the senses and one foot in the metaphysical world of contemplative spirit/Being and Void/Non-Being and who have much in common with Classical serenity and sense of order, unite and contemplate the Supreme Being or Fire or Light. You have nothing to lose but your sceptical, Neoclassical sense-bound chains.

*

Classical and Romantic features in my Baroque poetry
This selection [1991, collection 2005] spans thirty-three [1991, forty-seven 2005] years of my poetic life, and traces the growth of my Baroque consciousness and increasingly Classical outlook, and the marrying of sense and spirit, social and unconscious, everyday thoughts and symbols during my development as a Metaphysical Existentialist and later Universalist who sees the unity of Being behind Existence. Collections present whole works, selections present excerpts. I am pleased to present whole works as organic form demands to be read as a whole. Some of these works can now be seen to have been written before their time, in view of their contemplative, Baroque content.

This Baroque selection [1991, collection 2005] reveals an interest in the interpretation of contemporary history, notably in stages 42 to 45 of the European civilisation. As to stage 42, the decolonising of European civilisation and the shedding of Empire are caught in 'Blind Churchill and the Night', in 'Old Man in a Circle', and in the anti-Western attitudes of the Libyan Revolution. Stage 43, the winning of the Cold War, the expansion of Europe and the global domination of America are also foretold in 'Old Man in a Circle' and in 'Archangel', with its closing vision of benevolent world government; while the resurgence of Japan is present in Part Three of 'The Silence'. The coming tussle between stage 44 of the European civilisation (Universalism and syncretism) and stage 45 (a revival of the purity of Christian religion)* is anticipated in the 16 poems of *The Fire-Flower* and is more deeply explored in *Beauty and Angelhood*.

This Baroque selection [1991, collection 2005] reveals the Romantic elements I have identified: in the early works an autobiographical element, emphasis on the solitude of the artist, an obsession with the image and a challenge to the social ego and the reason (e.g. in 'The Silence', which is a latter-day abridged version of *The Prelude* as well as the journey of a latter-day shaman in an early Mannerist-Baroque style, a 20th-century idiom of abbreviated narrative which is essentially Baroque as it is all movement and the images flow into each other); fascination with, and rejection of, totalitarian revolution (e.g. 'Archangel'); extreme passion, grief, pain and love as the ego is dismantled, and illumination (*The Gates of Hell*); and then a growing sense of the whole as the ego's hold is loosened (in 'The Night-Sea Crossing' and 'The Labyrinth'), an increasingly spiritual and unitive vision (e.g. 'The Four Seasons'), an absorption of the new science which is in revolt against classical science, and the sense that eternity is within Nature (the 16 poems of *The Fire-Flower*). The poems reveal a concern with organic form until the later works; a Romantic feature. As the starting-point of each longer poem is a feeling or state of mind within a particular level of consciousness, the form grows organically like a plant by an emotional logic, through an emotional linking of juxtaposed images, either with abbreviated narrative ('The Silence'), or more musically – the favourite medium of baroque being painting or music – as in 'The Night-Sea Crossing' or the narrativeless 'The Four Seasons', both of which follow an anti-rational sonata form.

Being Baroque, a mixture of Romanticism and Classicism, this collection also reveals some Classical elements. Thus these poems are written from the social ego – the mature man and his reason who opens to, and receives, images from beyond – rather than exclusively from the dream-like "other mind" of totally irrational verse, and there is a strong grasp of the world of the senses in which the infinite operates. There is verbal play, and especially towards the end, as the Baroque method matures, there is a harmonious, well-balanced, orderly, intricate approach that is very Classical, and a sense of stillness. The poems are progressively undisturbed by anguished agony ("the Romantic agony" of Praz). In other words, there is often a Classical – orderly – way of proceeding about Romantic material, or a presentation of the infinite in a context of the finite, of the eternal within the temporal, which is one of the ways by which we recognise metaphysical Baroque. The poems become progressively impersonal as the control of the ego, the enemy or "Reflection" of 'The Silence', is progressively obliterated and lower consciousness dies into higher consciousness, lower emotion into higher feeling. The form becomes more orderly as order and harmony predominate towards the end of this selection [1991, collection 2005]. Organic form gives way to carefully sculptured stanzas. The same movement can be observed in the metres, which initially depart from traditional disciplines into freedom and irregularity as the social ego is challenged and its control dismantled. The iambic line gives way to anapaests and they pass into Stress Metre to combine discipline and natural speech rhythms, strict form and free verse, "in correspondence with some transition in the nature of the imagery or passion" (Coleridge on the 4-stress line of 'Christabel'). Eventually this too becomes more orderly as the power of the social ego is subjugated for mystical ends, and metrical strictness returns as a Classical stillness is reached within the dynamic flow of the universe. The classical poets of the ancient world regarded rules and metre as providing harmony. One cannot say that the poems become more Classical as the mystical subject matter and sense of the One is the very antithesis of Neoclassicism's concern with the social ego; but later poems present the social world and human scale within the context of the One with a sense of the meaningful order and harmony in the universe; and one can say they are Classical with the One, Classical Baroque rather than Romantic Baroque. (The Baroque has its own sub-stages, and in Classical Baroque a harmonious and well-balanced, orderly form and world overrules the personal individuality of the artist.)

The language combines Classical statement and Romantic image. It is conversational in social situations and seeks to be direct when catching the freshness of the world of Nature, and ruminative – or even sublime and elevated – when the poetic consciousness ponders on and contemplates the Spirit or Being within Nature. (In the same way, Wordsworth and Coleridge in their *Lyrical Ballads* sought at one and the same time to catch the language of common speech, and to approach the supernatural Spirit with a Miltonic, "sublime" diction.) The amount of directness or ruminativeness depends on the degree of contemplation the poetic consciousness is doing as it approaches Reality, the truth which the Imagination can grasp but which the reason cannot. It should be pointed out that the relationship between consciousness and Reality is two-way. Sometimes consciousness penetrates into Reality and grasps the Oneness of the universe, while sometimes Reality penetrates into the Imagination, which receives it quietly in contemplation with a "wise passiveness" (Wordsworth) and channels its images and symbols. These come from the divine ocean of Light and are, as Blake pointed out, eternal. Contemplative writing is a bit like reflective prose, which combines the freshness of description with the toughness of a more abstract, reflective thought – only in the case of contemplation, the thought is imaginative (in the Romantic-Baroque sense of the word).

My Classical Baroque consciousness
The Baroque consciousness combines the rational ego and the spiritual core. Its *attitude* to metaphysical Reality, the vision of God as Fire or Light, differs from that of the Neoclassical reason in that it is ultimately one of acceptance. This is especially true of the artistic Romantic-Baroque consciousness, whose attitude is well summed up in Keats' "being in uncertainties, mysteries, doubts, without any irritable reaching after fact and reason", for "with a great Poet the sense of Beauty overcomes every other consideration, or rather obliterates all considerations" (letter of 22 December 1817). In other words, a sense of beauty obliterates all *rational* considerations, and so Keats could write to Shelley, "My imagination is a monastery and I am its monk" (letter of 16 August 1820). Thus, Baroque poets can accept the mystery and beauty of the Fire or Light in their core, without the social ego's having to *explain* it in rational and scientific language – after all, what is essentially divine cannot be explained by the human ego – although hints from the new science can help a poet achieve a true perception of the Fire or Light and its relation to Nature (see the 16 poems of *The Fire-Flower*).

According to Horace, "A poet should instruct or please or both," and how much instruction or pleasing depends on how puritanical the poet is. Classical poetry emphasises the pleasing, whereas Romantic poetry instructs regarding the vision. Baroque poetry marks the opening of the social ego to the core, and the outpouring of the soul's delight when, in the course of contemplating the natural world, the spirit unfolds to Reality and perceives the infinite and eternal world of the Fire or Light which is immanent in creation, and whose symbols control the Imagination. The composition of Baroque poetry, as opposed to the process of its inspiration, is thus a receiving by the social ego of an outpouring from the deeper core as, in harmony with the social ego and at one with the universe, the deeper core channels the still deeper eternal world within appearances, and knows that all Nature is filled with the Fire or Light. Baroque poetry both instructs and pleases.

I have already said that these poems have a partially didactic intention. They seek to teach Being or the Fire or Light and the perception and consciousness of the mystic (to "instruct") as well as to create works of harmony and beauty (to "please"). Wordsworth wrote that "every great and original writer, in proportion as he is great or original, must create the taste by which he is to be relished; he must teach the art by which he must be seen" (letter to Lady Beaumont). I offer this Preface as an instruction in the redefinition of man and his consciousness which have made possible a redefinition of poetry and a new Baroque Counter-Renaissance (a Universalist stage 44 of the European civilisation), the beginnings of which are now already taking place in our midst and which can be relished once they are understood. Classical Baroque offers a poetry of synthesis.

September–October 1982; revised August, October 1989 and October 2005

*The revival of stage 45 emphasises the culture of an earlier phase of the civilisation. In the UK's case this has been reflected in Brexit, a revival of the independence the UK enjoyed during the reign of Queen Victoria and the rise of the British Empire.

Preface on the Metaphysical Revolution

This Preface first appeared in *Selected Poems: A Metaphysical's Way of Fire* in 1991 and like 'Preface on the New Baroque Consciousness and the Redefinition of Poetry as Classical Baroque' it was updated to appear in *Collected Poems 1958–1993: A White Radiance* and *Collected Poems 1958–2005* to present a 2005 vantage point.

This Preface was first written in May–June (especially 22 June) 1980 as the Preface to *The Fire-Flower*, a volume containing 16 poems, and appeared as such in *Collected Poems 1958–2005*. All these poems are to be found in this Selection [*Selected Poems: A Metaphysical's Way of Fire*] but are grouped in a different sequence. The numbers in brackets on pp.61–62 refer to the numbered poems in *The Fire-Flower*: (1) 'A Metaphysical in Marvell's Garden'; (2) 'A Crocus in the Churchyard'; (3) 'Fire-Void'; (4) 'Sea-Fire'; (5) 'A Mystic Fire-Potter's Red Sun-Halo'; (6) 'An Aesthete's "Golden" Artefacts'; (7) 'Pear-Ripening House'; (8) 'Clouded-Ground Pond'; (9) 'The Bride of Time' [later version, 'Two Variations on One Theme', 1. 'Time and Eternity (Second Version)', 2. 'The Bride of Time']; (10) 'A Stonemason's Flower-Bowl'; (11) 'An Obscure Symbolist's Rock-Tree'; (12) 'The Tree of Imagination'; (13) 'Firethorn'; (14) 'A Temple-Dancer's Temple-Sleep'; (15) 'A Metaphysical's Light-Mandala'; and (16) 'The Fire-Flower'. This Preface was subsequently revised in August and October 1989.

This Preface presents a new Existential Metaphysics linking cosmology and subatomic physics, transpersonal psychology and epistemology and ontological mysticism; all of which approach Reality as the metaphysical Fire or Light which can be seen. The Preface shows four layers of Reality [pp.66–67] which manifest downwards from the Infinite to Non-Being or Void, to Being, to Existence, and incorporate the layered meaning of the symbol.

The three main branches of metaphysics

Metaphysics is the philosophical study of the real nature of things, of the meaning, structure and principles of what is. Traditionally it was ranked the highest of the university studies, and its three branches are ontology, the study of Being, of the basic characteristics of Reality; epistemology, or what can be known with certainty about Being or Reality, which overlaps with psychology; and philosophical cosmology, which follows astronomy's cosmology in studying the origin and physical structure of the many galaxies of the universe (which in the 20th century became galaxy-centred, not earth- or sun-centred), but relates it to ultimate principles, i.e. Being or what is Real. Metaphysics was originally theoretical and speculative, as in the philosophers from Plato to Leibniz and Kant, but in the 20th century metaphysics became practical, existential and empirical in the phenomenological existentialism of Husserl and Heidegger and in the cosmological observations of American space probes.

The 16 poems of The Fire-Flower *and Reality*

Metaphysical poems are penetrations into Reality. Being a linked sequence, these 16 metaphysical poems (of *The Fire-Flower*) aim to present a consistent vision. The thought progresses through complementary pairs and reconciles all sixteen poems into the harmony of the whole scheme, so they can all be read in terms of each other as well as by themselves and in pairs. In view of the revolutionary novelty and complexity of their subject matter, it may help if I briefly outline the progression.

The metaphysical Fire or Light, the Supreme Being which permeates all creation and which can be known by turning within from the five senses, is presented obliquely at first. Contact is made with it and with "timeless" Eternity (1). Eternity is then explored in relation to death (2). This Eternity contains a Void, the fiery Idea that brings in all forms and transforms souls (3). It also contains the spiritual Sun which, though found within, is paradoxically at the heart of the universe (4). This Sun is the inner Light of the halo of the Christian mystic tradition (5), in contrast to the roaring fire of the unmystic aesthete who does not know the Light (6). The Sun aids spiritual growth from ego to soul, and according to tradition enables the soul's genes to reincarnate (7). It enables the soul to unite with the *Tao* (as manifested Being) (8). Eternity (the *Tao* as unmanifested Void) is in panting love with the forms of time (9), and it takes the initiative in entering the imagination of stonemasons who fix it in changeless images (10). The symbolist artist draws back the veil and shows the unity of the physical world in terms of the spiritual world (11). Symbols come from the spiritual world (12). They have a religious force when they embody the Idea or Fire of God (13). Far memories – images from past lives – are symbols, being divine reminders of past spiritual glories (14). The central Sun in the soul is one with the eddying power of the universe, whose tides flow into mystics, healers and poets (15). This eddying power is the swirling "implicate" *Tao* (as Void) or Idea which forms matter, the Fullness which creates (16). The progression, then, is from metaphysical intimations of Eternity to a deeper grasp of the Void, which is also Idea, *Logos*, and *Tao*, and thence to its spiritual power, which symbols communicate, and finally the eddying, swirling power of creation, the Fullness, Sun or Inner Light which forms matter and all created things.

A new model of Reality
These poems offer a new model of Reality. All poems, novels, plays, cinema and television films, and critical works, all paintings and scientific hypotheses – indeed, all art and language itself – are, in effect, constructions of different models of Reality in varying degrees of simplicity or complexity. They say "Reality is like this", and as reality can be material, physical, social, intellectual, psychological, educational, financial, criminal or what you will, as well as philosophical and religious, all at the same time, Reality may very well be "like this" in part, to some extent, on one occasion, at one level or layer. Since Reality is layered, the simplified or complex models that appeal to a reader, listener or viewer are those which correspond to the layers of Reality he or she is groping towards at that particular time, the level or layer he or she is nearly at. Thus, what seems to be a good model to a 20-year-old student may not seem a good model when he or she has reached a mature 40. Some models claim that only one layer of Reality is absolute, and if it is demonstrated that the "absolute" Reality is limited and incomplete, then the model collapses as an absolute statement, in which case it is incorporated into a newer, better, truer, more real model. This happened to Newton's model of the universe, which has been incorporated into Einstein's model.

These poems demonstrate that the physical, social sense-bound reality of much modern poetry is limited and incomplete, and in providing a layered metaphysical context within which the social layer operates, they incorporate the social layer into a truer, *more real* metaphysical model. As they draw on the very latest, often bewildering ideas of post-war physics and psychology in constructing a new metaphysical model, it is important to make clear the central premise that underlies them, an understanding of which will aid interpretation of the whole. This premise is the relationship between post-Newtonian and post-Einsteinian subatomic physics and cosmology, the collective unconscious of transpersonal psychology and epistemology, and the spiritual Eternity of ontological mysticism, which together make up an entirely new metaphysical outlook that is best conveyed by poetry, and by a poet who observes some impersonality, or transpersonality.

The expanding universe and matter
According to post-Einsteinian cosmology, the universe is expanding outwards with galaxies moving away from each other. (Einstein himself was wrong to accept the then prevailing idea that the universe is static.) According to post-Einsteinian subatomic physics, the universe of "matter" is in fact a sea of dynamic, organic energy whose inter-relating subatomic particles are also waves, and are even to some extent "conscious", since all photons in the sea "know" what other photons are doing exactly when they are doing it. In quantum theory, this sea comes from the quantum vacuum, the underlying reality of all that is. All basic physical properties – mass/energy, charge, spin – are conserved in this sea of potential, and under the laws of physics this vacuum or Void will continue to exist even if the universe one day collapses down a black hole. The American physicist David Finkelstein has linked a Theory of Everything with this quantum vacuum: "A general theory of the vacuum is thus a theory of everything."

According to Bohm's theory (1980), the whole sea of matter is explicate (manifest in forms, particles) and implicate (Void-like, eternal unformed whole) at the same time. Space-time, the fourth dimension, is curved and finite, and physicists now postulate an infinite "Superspace" which is timeless, eternal and transpersonal, an implicate Reality which manifests into form, from which different universes or "many worlds" (a concept made possible by the discovery of black holes) "explicate" into being, a concept that appears to confirm Einstein's words: "Anyone who studies physics long enough is inevitably led to metaphysics." The non-local theory, a consequence of the enormously important Bell's theorem (1964), states that events do not take place in localised space but affect the whole sea of "matter" that includes our universe, and according to the superluminal information transfer theory (1975), events are linked by a velocity faster than that of light, a phenomenon which affects theories of perception and makes telepathy and psychic phenomena – and communication with other universes (if they exist) through black holes – theoretically possible, and brings physics to the verge of metaphysics. Events, then, have to be understood in relation to the whole, and one wave is affected by, and affects, the whole ocean and cannot be considered to have a "local" identity only; it is part of the ocean and is the ocean, has "implicate" identity. As matter is a whole sea of "conscious" organic energy, the old distinction between mind and matter has collapsed, along with the old distinction between the observer ('I') and what he observes, for the part is inseparable from the indivisible whole, and to see from a fixed point distorts Reality.

In the transpersonal psychology and epistemology of later Jung, who derived his idea of the psyche from his meetings with Einstein in Zurich, there is a sea of collective unconsciousness, the Alchemists' *unus mundus*, outside time, an eternal, transpersonal world of "dead spirits" which pours archetypal images into the Self (the core), whence they are communicated to the ego just as waves become particles. This concept closely resembles "Superspace". In what Jung called "synchronicity", a symbolic image in the *unus mundus* or timeless psychic inner world (a dream, waking vision, communication from a "dead spirit", or hunch) coincides with an event in the outer world, as when a mother suddenly has an intuition that her child has had an accident. Such psychic and physical events coincide simultaneously in time without being connected causally – indeed, images from the *unus mundus* can break into time and manifest as synchronistic events – and psyche and matter are thus linked. (Jung's collaborator, Marie-Louise von Franz, strengthened this link in *Number and Time*, which develops Jung's view that numbers regulate the unitary realm of psyche and matter.) Jung's findings confirm both Bohm's theory, in which implicate "energy" can manifest into form as explicate "matter", and the non-local and superluminal transfer theories. Again, the old dualism of mind and matter has collapsed, and the psyche has no local identity only (the ego), but is a part of – and is – the whole ocean, which can be mystically known.

Reality as Fire or Light
Ontological mysticism sees Reality as an ocean of Fire or Light or Idea outside the cosmos, that manifests into form. Though interest in

mysticism has never been greater than today – witness the many New Age sects – there is a 5,000-year-old mystic tradition which has always maintained this process of manifestation, a tradition I have dealt with at great length elsewhere (in *The Fire and the Stones*, *The Light of Civilization* and *The Rise and Fall of Civilizations*). One of the models in this tradition is the Kabbalistic one, in which manifestation takes place through four worlds (the divine, spiritual, psychological and physical worlds) down an inverted Tree of Life, through ten *sefirot*, relevant details of which appear in the Notes [of *Selected Poems: A Metaphysical's Way of Fire*, and of the two subsequent volumes of *Collected Poems*]. All periods in the tradition agree that the soul or Self can return to the Fire or Light of its origin if it takes the Mystic Way and journeys away from the centre of the ego, the social 'I' or vantage point which misses the Being or Idea or Fire or Light within all forms. The soul turns within from the five senses, and, by-passing outer space and therefore space-time in inner vision, contacts the timeless, and therefore eternal, spiritual Reality which is a dynamic present of Fire or Light and images. This sea of Fire or Light closely resembles "Superspace" and the *unus mundus*. The soul rises to cosmic and transcendent levels of consciousness in which the observer knows he is not just a part of the Eternal totality or implicate Void he observes, he *is* the totality, and is inseparable from the whole. The distinction between mind and matter collapses, and in ontological mysticism, as well as in cosmological physics and epistemological transpersonal psychology, the perspective of the ego or social 'I' gives an unreliable, distorted picture of Reality, alienating and separating the observer from the whole sea of Fire or Light and spiritual being. The 'I' must be obliterated if a truly objective picture of Reality is to emerge.

The link between cosmological subatomic physics, epistemological psychology and ontological mysticism may be found in modern cosmology, which is based in astronomy and reflected in metaphysical philosophy: notably in the cosmic background radiation (CBR), a still-existing perpetual hiss from the Big Bang, the non-localised explosion which created a fireball everywhere and which cooled into the universe 18 billion to 15 billion years ago. This radiation was discovered in America in 1964/5 by Penzias and Wilson, and has been found to be evenly dispersed throughout the known universe as a diffuse glow at constant microwave tendencies (with a temperature of 2.7° Kelvin). The NASA satellite Cobe (Cosmic Background Explorer) was launched in November 1989 to investigate this radiation.

The discovery of CBR, for which Penzias and Wilson were awarded the 1978 Nobel Prize for Physics, has been enormously important as, together with the existence of quasars, it is now held to confirm the Big Bang theory and to discredit the Steady State view of creation. As a result, cosmologists are now probing the vacuum that existed shortly before the Big Bang, the Void of nothingness or Bohm's "implicate order" out of which "something" came, which existed before the Big Bang and which will exist after the universe. Although there are arguments (e.g. by the sceptical Hume) against the necessity of placing the divine immediately before the Big Bang, I have already linked this Void with the metaphysical Fire in *The Fire and the Stones* and *The Universe and the Light*. The CBR, which dates back to 300,000–500,000 years after the time of creation, may be a manifestation of the implicate, mystical, metaphysical Being or Reality or Quantum Vacuum or Void of the Fire or Light which influences the psyche and which can be experienced as the vision of God as Fire or Light, a vision which has given rise to all history's civilisations. Our bodies are composed of material that came out of the Big Bang and which had cooled when the universe had ceased to be radiation-dominated and had become matter-dominated (after hydrogen ceased being ionised and the radiation decoupled from the gas) about one million years after the Big Bang, and our bodies can therefore be expected to have an affinity with, and receive and absorb, the radiation from which matter condensed. (Penzias himself has said that we receive and absorb the CBR as a slight warmth.) As our bodies are composed of material that emanated or manifested from the vacuum or Void (which has been called a superdense blob) that preceded the Big Bang, our souls can be expected to have an affinity with, and receive and absorb, the metaphysical Fire which, the new metaphysics argue, manifested into CBR, the spirit-like radiation from which bodies congealed.

Four layers of Reality
There are therefore four levels of Reality which link cosmological physics, epistemological psychology and ontological mysticism, and which mirror the four worlds of the Kabbalah; and from a metaphysical point of view the scheme of things looks as follows, with alternative descriptions for each layer, the highest layer being no. 1 and the lowest no. 4:

Four layers of Reality	Religious interpretation	Four Kabbalistic worlds	Metaphysical discipline
Eternity:			
1. Infinite/Supreme Being/Reality/Fire or Light/the One/absolute Good (and Ontic realm above intellect)	God	divine	ontology/ mysticism
2. Non-manifestation/ Non-Being/Quantum vacuum (before Big Bang)/Void/implicate order of Reality/ Nonduality (*advaita*)/ Idea/Archetypes/ Forms/*Logos*/*Tao*/ Superspace/Sea of Fire or Light/ Alchemist's *unus mundus*/metaphysical Zero/Divine Mind/ Intellectual principle (or Nous)/Totality of Possibilities of Being/ Holy Spirit/ Heaven	Holy Spirit known by spirit	spiritual	intellectual Idealism/ transpersonal psychology/ transformation to new centre
Time:			
3. Manifestation after Big Bang/Being/Totality of Possibilities of Existence/invisible cosmic background radiation/Ocean of Being/Unity of Being known by soul	Oneness of creation known by individual soul illumined by Fire/Light through spirit	psychological	epistemology/ psychology
4. Existence/matter/ organism/world of senses	world known by social ego/ body	physical	cosmology/ physics

Being has been variously regarded as belonging to divine, spiritual, psychological and physical layers of Reality by the varied approaches of Idealism, Materialism and Existentialism. Despite attempts by Materialists and Realists to connect Being with matter of the observable world, and by Logical Positivists to define Being as non-existence, in metaphysics Being is regarded as manifestation (layer 3 above) and also as the Supreme Being (layer 1) which includes the Void or non-manifestation/Non-Being (layer 2). More specifically, Being (layer 3) envelops universal Existence, which is the sum total of manifestation of all Being's possibilities. (The oneness of the pebbles and rocks in the stone garden at the Zen Ryoanji temple in Kyoto, Japan, images this relationship between Being and Existence.) Unity contains multiplicity, and there are many degrees of Existence (layer 4), all of which are multiple manifestations of Being (layer 3) (e.g. trees, flowers, birds, animals, humans etc.). The anti-metaphysical Existentialists were wrong to see Existence as particular and individual without being enveloped by universal Being (for example, Sartre's Roquentin in *La Nausée* who lacked the vision of Being that relates the particular and individual chestnut tree to the universal whole of Being and therefore felt disgust at the gratuitousness of the cosmic order); and it was the Materialistic error of the 20th century to regard Reality as being confined to layer 4.

Being is the sum total of everything manifested, and Non-Being (layer 2) contains everything unmanifested, including the possibilities of Being which have not yet manifested. In other words, as Guénon points out in *The Multiple States of Being*, Non-Being (layer 2), or the non-manifested (i.e. the Void, *"la vide"* or the metaphysical Zero, layer 3), "envelops Being" "or the principle of manifestation, so silence contains within itself the principle of the word". Universal Possibility or the Infinite (layer 1) therefore contains both Being (layer 3) and Non-Being (layer 2), or as the famous Eastern thinker and Japanese poet Junzaburo Nishiwaki scribbled out for me in 1965 in a *saké* bar with sawdust on the floor next to Keio University's Mita campus, "+A (to be) + −A (small zero) = 0 (great nothing)", an equation my poem 'The Silence' carries as a pentameter: "(+A) + (−A) = Nothing". In other words, Being + Non-Being (metaphysical Zero) = Infinity (layer 1), which encompasses both time and unmanifested eternity.

The idea that the metaphysical Fire or Light which preceded the Void and Big Bang (or unmanifested Non-Being and manifested Being) manifests in cosmic background radiation unites physics and metaphysics and enfolds time within eternity, and it offers a theory of everything which includes all four layers of Reality. A theory of everything cannot exist unless it includes cosmic rays and CBR as while all the three families of elementary particles existed naturally a fraction of a second after the Big Bang, now that the universe has cooled two of the three families are only found in cosmic rays and in this cosmic background radiation.

New metaphysics, what is behind physics
Ontological mysticism has derived renewed strength from the scientific corroboration of cosmological physics and epistemological psychology, and it is the renewed drawing together of the three disciplines in our time that has led to the Metaphysical Revolution in which ontological Being can be epistemologically known through illumination (as St Augustine maintained) and related to the cosmological first cause (the Big Bang of astronomy). The mystic's sea of Fire or Light is the traditional metaphysical Being which metaphysical ontologists have always claimed was behind creation and therefore Existence. Metaphysical philosophy is a philosophy of Being and Knowing, and in the new metaphysics, Supreme Being (Fire or Light) can be known during contemplation as an existential, mystical *experience*. It is not a theoretical concept to be argued, speculated about and reasoned in the manner which has given the word 'metaphysical' its popular derogatory connotation of "abstract and subtle talk", "mere theory". (It was in this pejorative sense that Drummond, Dryden and Johnson dismissed as "metaphysical" the 17th-century poets who drew on the new learning and science, and who knew the Fire or Light.) Traditionally, 'metaphysics' has wrongly been thought to mean "*beyond* physics", the "science of things transcending what is physical or natural" – in fact, "*ta meta ta phusika*" were the works of Aristotle which were placed "*meta*" or *after* his *Physics* by his early students – but as physicists move towards a traditionally metaphysical model of the universe in which an infinite, implicate quantum vacuum or Void or "Superspace" outside space-time manifests into explicate form as Being and Existence, and as Einstein's prophecy that physicists are "inevitably led to metaphysics" is fulfilled in more books like Fritjof Capra's *The Tao of Physics*, then the *workings* of the timeless, eternal, transpersonal and extra-cosmic Fire or Light which can be seen in contemplation become increasingly accessible to physics; and metaphysics will increasingly cease to be the traditional, popular "what is *beyond* physics" and will increasingly become almost a new branch of physics, "what is *behind* or *hidden within* (or implicate within) physics, which is now being revealed". Physics will try and "catch" the metaphysical manifesting into the physical, the Void into Being and Existence, the "supernatural" into the natural, and the manifesting process will be seen to be to some extent a physical and natural one, though the implicate Void through which Being or Fire or Light becomes form is outside space-time.

The new metaphysics, then, includes a physics-based study of the first principles of ontological, epistemological and cosmological Being, substance or essence (the manifesting Fire or Light) which is *behind* time, space, cause and identity, as well as a description of existential, contemplative experiences of the great *"behind"* or *"hidden within"*, and this important perspective of an ontological, epistemological and cosmological Reality *behind* the physical world is contained in the very word 'metaphysical'. For interestingly, the prefix *'meta'* occasionally has the sense of *"behind"* rather than "after", as in "metaphrenon" ("the part of the back that is behind the diaphragm"). 'Metaphysics' can therefore mean *"behind* the physical" or *"behind physics"*, and the new metaphysical perspective and approach to Reality marks a break with the speculative past precisely because this *behindness* can be directly known. In other words, the Supreme Being or Reality – God – *behind* the physical world can be known directly as an experience of the Fire/ Light, which is simultaneously (1) an ontological truth, in the sense of a non-contradictory fundamental principle, (2) an epistemological truth that can be directly known through mystical experience, (3) a cosmological truth which offers a first cause in the physical world as it preceded the Big Bang, (4) a teleological truth which links design in nature to the purpose or end of the universe, and (5) a moral truth which is the "Good", the supreme object of knowledge. All these five traditionally theoretical approaches to Being or Reality or God can now be directly *experienced* through Existential Metaphysics in which Metaphysical freedom involves participating in the unity of Being, escaping the chains of multiplicity and Existence for the oneness of Being through the experience of the Fire. The new metaphysical perspective is in fact a Metaphysical Existentialism, for it is concerned with direct existential experiences of Being, with existential glimpses of the unifying Reality that is *behind* the phenomenal cosmos and Existence. It is of course this break with the past that makes it necessary to speak not of a Metaphysical Restoration, but of a Metaphysical Revolution.

Metaphysical revolutions might seem to be the province of philosophers who inquire and penetrate into the nature of Reality. With the very honourable exception of some of the Continental Existentialists and Whitehead, whose organic Reality (or process metaphysics) took the side of poets against Newtonian scientists, the philosophy of recent years has been in such a state that philosophers now have little chance of penetrating into anything very important, let alone Reality. Moreover, the post-Relativity philosopher is a part of – and is – the Reality he seeks to describe, and the old technique of an on-looker observing and cogitating is no longer as appropriate to an inquiry and penetration into an existential Reality as is direct experience of it through image- or symbol-channelling.

Metaphysical poets' symbols of Reality

Metaphysical revolutions are more properly the province of traditionalist poets. Symbols point to, and indeed embody, Reality. Metaphysical poets open to Reality, the highest level of Being (layer 1), and their symbols present Reality as a manifestation in a psychological or physical form. The symbol (Greek *symbolon* meaning contract, token, insignia, means of identification) therefore represents Reality; it is certainly a transparency of, or reference to, Reality, the supreme vision of the Fire, the sacred or holy Being which has manifested in time and space, and may be identified with it, i.e. the psychological or physical manifestation may be identified with the spiritual power symbolised in it. The symbol mediates between Reality and conventional physical forms. As religion and metaphysics involve man's relationship to the sacred or holy (i.e. Reality), the symbol always represents a religious or metaphysical idea. The four worlds of the Kabbalah, the physical, psychological, spiritual and divine worlds, are all present in the layered meanings of the symbol for those who have eyes to see. The symbol shows a part (the psychological or physical form) representing a whole (Reality) with which it is identified. In epistemological terms, the symbol helps a reader to *know* Reality (layer 1) by veiling and then revealing its Fire or Light either instantaneously or gradually, by giving the reader access to the sacred or holy Reality. (In this the symbol is helped by myth, sacred stories that define the human condition and man's relation to the sacred or holy.) In ontological terms, the symbol points the reader in the right direction and enables him to *experience* the existence of Being (Reality) as a fusion of his own being with the divine Fire or Light (layer 1). The symbol can startle a reader into an experience of the Fire or Light, the delicate *yugen* (flower) which is regarded as a moment of perfection in the Japanese culture. The reader must therefore learn to interpret the symbol as a pointer to Reality (layer 1), and this places on the poet the onus of instructing the reader in the metaphysical Reality embodied in his symbolism.

The layered meanings within the symbol which reflect the four worlds of the Kabbalah are illuminated by the metaphysician René Guénon's view of the law of correspondence which operates throughout the cosmos:

> By virtue of this law, each thing, proceeding as it does from a metaphysical principle from which it derives all its reality, translates or expresses that principle in its own fashion and in accordance with its own order of existence, so that from one order to another all things are linked together and correspond in such a way as to contribute

to the universal and total harmony, which, in the multiplicity of manifestation, can be likened to a manifestation of the principal unity itself. For this reason the laws of a lower domain can always be taken to symbolise realities of a higher order.... A consequence of this law of correspondence is the plurality of meanings contained in the symbol. Anything and everything can in fact be regarded as representing not only the metaphysical principles, but also realities of all orders higher than its own.

Elsewhere he says:

Rites and symbols fundamentally are only two aspects of a single reality, and this is none other than the correspondence that binds together all the degrees of universal existence in such a way that by its means our human state can enter into communication with the higher states of being.

Reality, the Fire or Light that comes into form through an eternal "Superspace" or *unus mundus* or sea of Light, is best penetrated existentially by channelling symbols and images. Symbols and images originate in the divine ocean of Light – according to Jung they manifest into form by "synchronicity" – and they contain all Reality in a layered form. (As can be gleaned from the poems and the Notes, an "image" is an external pictorial form, whereas a "symbol" is an image which is perceived to have a layer higher than layer 4, i.e. a spiritual layer, and so the words are interchangeable depending on which association is required.) Symbols and images therefore apply at both spiritual and physical/material levels at the same time. The poet's soul was always traditionally a channel for images of this metaphysical Reality, and in past times, simply to be a channel for it (some would say be inspired by it) was the most important thing that could happen to a man, and certainly to a poet. Image- and symbol-channelling is the proper – I would go so far as to say the true – subject for poetry, and is the basis of true poetic aesthetic, although the social, rational poetry of the worldly 'I' of recent years has helped us to forget this. The image has always traditionally played a part in healing – modern researchers are rediscovering that visualising, or intentional imaging, can heal disorders in the body – and poems that channel images and symbols of Reality are not bourgeois entertainments, but *transmissions of healing* to the receiving civilisation. Such poems raise consciousness to higher worlds and enable Imagination to see into the form and to perceive within it the Idea or Fire or Light of Reality, and today they heal (as if with healing flower potencies) the anxiety which was caused by distorted appreciation of Reality during the now happily defunct Age of Anxiety, whose legacy of dis-ease is still with us. The poet is therefore a priest-healer who merely passes on the images and symbols he has received, much as a medium passes on communications from a higher source, and like a "de-egoed" healer, he is a pipe through which the waters of spiritual image can flow without being blocked by the stone of an ego. The poet must therefore ensure that his personality does not intrude between the divine source he is channelling and the reader whose attitudes are being transformed, transmuted and "healed".

As he is a link between the physical, material, temporal world of the reader, and the spiritual, Eternal source, the contemplative, metaphysical poet-healer stands half-way between the two. He blends realism with a sense of Eternity; the everyday with the mystical; social meetings with a spiritual dimension; the disorderly with a teleological sense of the meaning of life. Though his poems are finally poems of the soul that have won free from worldly attachments, they all begin in the world as poems of the heart. They begin in precise moments (like the 17th-century Metaphysical poems), but develop into ruminative contemplation. The poet-healer ruminates half-way between the social and the unconscious, at the place where the withdrawn contemplative mystic gazes upon Reality, receives images and symbols of Reality and interprets them with his receiving mind. In existential phenomenology, the phenomena of consciousness are studied by examining what is in *the receiving mind*, by investigating what is in the perceiving, interpreting consciousness and bracketing out, or forgetting, the source from which it came. The poet-healer is a receiving, perceiving, interpreting consciousness, and, being closer to society than trance-like imaginatives whose poems are a string of automatically received unconscious images which are not interpreted for the rational, social mind, he can urge the reader to take part in the transforming, healing power of the image and symbol. He can become a contemplating voice over the reader's shoulder, issuing the imperatives and precise instructions of a spiritual director.

Language for the metaphysical vision
A poet who channels the metaphysical vision has an obvious problem in the language and vocabulary he uses. With the decline of the old speculative metaphysics, the traditional metaphysical words and concepts have lost much of their freshness. A word Donne used to excess in *The Exstasie*, "soul", does not have the precise, widely experienced meaning in our sceptical Age that it once had in the

Elizabethan Kabbalistic Age. Other, similar words which have tended to become ciphers or slogan-words, and therefore "dead language", are: "mind", "spirit", "heart", "Idea", "Eternity", "God", "order" and "Nature", while recent additions from psychology like "ego", "centre", "self", or from Eastern religion like "Void" or "Fullness", have blurred the metaphysical terminology. Words like "universe", "world" and "Time" have been given new, confusing meanings by physics, and words like "meaning", "pattern", "images" and "symbols" have been blurred by the rational, social, sceptical philosophy and criticism of our time.

So what does a poet who is half-way between social and spiritual worlds do? Avoid all such words altogether and build up his metaphysical vision through symbols without any super-structural terminology at all? Or boldly seize the dilemma by its horns and attempt to renew metaphysical language by a reasonably sparing use of such words – without most of the traditional capital letters which tend to sloganise – in precise and, where possible, fresh contexts? The social ego and critical judgement advocate the second. All these words once had precise metaphysical meanings, and as a Metaphysical Revolution is bound to reinstate and rehabilitate some wrongly discredited traditional concepts in stating its new vision I believe it is part of the metaphysical poet's task and function in his criticism to restore some precision to traditional words that have lost their meaning, and to redefine and revivify, through use, the metaphysical "metalanguage" which enables a society to absorb its metaphysical experiences. To this end it will be helpful if his poems are accompanied by Notes that take the form of a Metaphysical Commentary [as is at the end of *Selected Poems: A Metaphysical's Way of Fire*]. However, criticism is not the exclusive language of poetry, and although he must employ a certain amount of metaphysical terminology, as the cosmos is One the metaphysical poet should present the metaphysical in terms of the physical, between which there is a correspondence through Reality's layers. In other words, the metaphysical poet of the core should also use symbols. The metaphysical poet will therefore use a mixture of metaphysical terms to which he gives precision, and symbols, thus reflecting both the social and the spiritual approaches to his material.

The self and four layers of Reality
It will be extremely helpful to form a clear idea of the metaphysical terminology for the structure of the self. We need a clear chart of the structure of the self, and it will help our restatement of the metaphysical vision if we list again the four layers of Reality in descending order,

using the Kabbalistic headings we have already given, and relate these to the different parts of the self involved, first in the Greek tradition and then in our Western metaphysical tradition. Our structure of the self will then look as follows:

Four layers of Reality/ Four Kabbalistic worlds	Greek concepts of part of the self involved	Western part of the self involved	Level of Reality received by part of the self
1. divine		Crown centre or *chakra*, divine spark of potential Angelhood	Fire or Light of One Being
2. spiritual	*pneuma* (spirit which receives breath and *gnosis*)	spirit (the 'I' which has lived before, which receives *gnosis*)/intellect of the intellectual vision/spiritual soul/*Ruah* in the Kabbalah)	Spiritual power from Void/ Fullness
3. psychological	*psyche* (soul which animates)	higher mind including intellect (which has concept of self)/mind's animating soul (*Neshamah* in the Kabbalah)/heart centre or *chakra* (which sees global one-ness)	Being
4. physical	*soma* (body)	body/brain function & reason/social ego of judging mind/ lower sensation/ bodily soul (*Nefesh* in the Kabbalah)	Existence

It will be seen that there is some overlapping, and that spirit, intellect and soul make contact with the psychological as well as with the spiritual and divine worlds. The spirit is distinguished from the intellectual in that it is enduring and eternal whereas the intellectual centres are temporal. The soul is a receptacle for the Fire or Light; it is a link between the mind and the vision, and so it is often portrayed as a butterfly or a bird which can fly between worlds and bring back the divine vision.

Metaphysical poets' ordering technique

The Reality a metaphysical poet channels is reflected in the technical side of his poetry, for form and style always serve the subject matter. The unity between the channelling egoless observing psyche and "matter", which is known in meditation when the body, emptied of mind, is perceived as a rock, and rock in turn is perceived as becoming dynamic like mind, is expressed in rock-like stanzas that lack an ego. The Reality – the Fire or Light – is an orderly principle which it is the purpose of evolution to express, and so the form in which the images come to rest will express a sense of order in strict stanzas, metres and rhymes, to distinguish it from the unstanzaic, unmetred, unrhymed, *random* or "entropied" poetry of so many poetry readings, which is to ordered poetry what electronic music is to Bach, or splodges on a canvas are to Rembrandt. In the poems that follow, the contrast – initially discord – between the transient physical world and Eternal spiritual vision is caught by the rhyming couplet, and the growing harmony between them, a growing sense that one is a manifestation of the other, emerges as alternate rhyming, in which the earlier "pairing" of the contrast is not so pronounced. Similarly, the development from unipart to multipart sectioning obviously reflects a growing sense that multiplicity and complexity are manifestations of a unity, a sense which the growing harmony makes possible. The layering of Reality's divine, spiritual, psychological and physical levels is caught in a symbolic, layered language in which words carry deliberately ambiguous associations which apply at different levels simultaneously. The total effect of the obliteration of the ego is to throw attention onto the "thing made", and create an objective art.

Metaphysical poets' whole view

When specialised knowledge in several disciplines draws together, someone has to be able to take a "whole" view and experience and recreate the whole knowledge, or Reality is lost among the various compartments of learning. Today, the poet-mystic is the person who can best embody and express the whole, not the philosopher or the physicist or the psychologist, who approach part of the whole, a greater part than the social-rational sceptic, no doubt, and one that is nearer to the Fire or Light, but nevertheless a part. (I am reminded of Whitehead's words, "The purpose of philosophy is to rationalise mysticism.") A phenomenological poetry of the Mystic Way which continues the Einsteinian-Jungian tradition and channels images and symbols is a better metaphysical path than the path of philosophy. It is one that can restore the stature of poetry, which, in turning away from the grand themes, has been trivialised and impoverished in recent years. The urgent task is to renew poetry's traditional contact with its metaphysical source.

May–June 1980; revised August, October 1989, 12 October 2005

Both these Prefaces appeared in *Selected Poems: A Metaphysical's Way of Fire* in 1991, and omit references to all Nicholas Hagger's works written after 1989. They were included in *Collected Poems 1958–1993: A White Radiance* and *Collected Poems 1958–2005* as offering useful background on the Baroque and metaphysical perspective of many of the poems.

3

The Universe and the Light

A New View of the Universe and Reality and of
Science and Philosophy
Essays on the Philosophy of Universalism and the
Metaphysical Revolution

Introduction

Three essays on the Fire or Light, Universalism and metaphysical science
These three essays were written independently and where they overlap
they complement one another. The first one is a fuller version of
'Illumination and Metaphysics: A Grand Unified Theory of the Mystic
Light in History, Nature and Cosmology', the opening lecture I gave
to 450 scientists at the 1992 Scientific and Medical Network's Mystics
and Scientists conference at Winchester. The second one was written to
introduce Universalism as the metaphysical antithesis of reductionism
and to explain the thinking behind my centre at Epping (the Foundation
of the Light), which is opening many people to the Light. The third one
was written as a paper for a Symposium on Reductionism's Primacy
in the Natural Sciences, which was held at Jesus College, Cambridge,
in early September 1992. The paper was circulated among fifteen
speakers who included ten Professors of Physics, Biology, Physiology,
Neurology, Astronomy and Philosophy in Britain and the USA.

Taken together the three essays provide an introduction to my
thinking. The first covers the theoretical framework, how the Fire or
Light unifies all disciplines and triggers a Metaphysical Revolution
in each. The second covers the practical side, explaining how
Universalism is creating a global network of inter-religious groups
which are bringing down the Light. The third deals with the movement
against reductionism in philosophy and science, and sees metaphysical
Universalism as an extension of physicalist holism and as creating
a new metaphysical science which has launched the Metaphysical
Revolution.

A Mystic Revival, a Metaphysical Revolution and Universalism
The penultimate paragraph of *The Fire and the Stones* says:

A new 'Fire of the World Movement' would devise a new Universalist terminology and would have three aims, which would correspond to the three levels on which we said at the outset the Tradition of the Fire can be read: to bring individuals to an existential confrontation with the Fire; to bring to pass a Metaphysical revival within all societies, cultures and civilisations, particularly within the European and North-American civilisations, so that university syllabuses contain metaphysical as well as secular texts; and to show that the Fire is the common ground for all civilisations, whose central idea it is, that the Fire provides the common ground for the coming worldwide culture, and that it is an impetus for world peace. It is time to establish a Foundation – a Foundation of the Light – which will further these aims and safeguard the Metaphysical Revolution.

The Foundation of the Light was created in May 1992 and it thus has three planks to its platform: at the personal, practical level it encourages people to see the divine Light, which is the way of mysticism and involves a Mystic Revival; at the theoretical level it promotes a Metaphysical Revolution in all disciplines, which involves the academies or universities; and at the universal level it promotes Universalism, the essence of all religions, a philosophy that has replaced Existentialism and involves the arts and all religions.

This book follows this pattern. The first essay covers the mystic Light and the Metaphysical Revolution. The second essay covers Universalism and amplifies the themes in the first essay. The third essay focuses on the Metaphysical Revolution in philosophy and science, and amplifies themes in the previous two essays. The Universalist history theory, touched upon in the first essay, is presented in embryo in Appendix 1 [of *The Universe and the Light*], and it may be useful to grasp it as a whole there before plunging into the detail of *The Fire and the Stones*. Appendix 2 and Appendix 3 [of *The Universe and the Light*] flesh out the metaphysical view of the origin and creation of the universe, and of evolution and brain-function.

The rise of Universalism

All the main themes of the new movement in mysticism and metaphysics, known as Universalism, are here. The history theory shows that the rise of Universalism is linked to the rise of the North-American civilisation (as its heresy) and to the decline of the European civilisation (as an expression of the coming conglomerate's cosmopolitanism): to stage 17 of the American civilisation and stage 44 of the European civilisation. Universalism is ahead for both the North-American and European civilisations. In this respect I am a historicist in believing that historical events reveal the motive forces of culture as photons reveal waves of light; in asserting that historical events are governed by the laws of the freely-chosen stages I have outlined in *The Fire and the Stones*; and in affirming that movements in the soul and cultural phenomena express themselves at certain times, in certain stages, and are therefore determined by history, i.e. by the laws that underlie and bring in these freely-chosen stages.

September 1992

4

Collected Poems 1958–1993: A White Radiance

Introductory Note by the Poet

This Introductory Note first appeared in 1994 and was updated to include the most recent poems in 2005, when it appeared in *Collected Poems 1958–2005*.

Turning-point and mature work
These 1,272 poems represent all my finished works to date. They are grouped in 27 volumes, the titles of which head each section. The poems are in broadly chronological order to reflect my growth, with three qualifications: sometimes dating is approximate; sometimes there is overlapping as two poems were worked on simultaneously; and sometimes a poem has been added to an earlier group for thematic reasons. The *juvenilia* are thus at the beginning; the Light is first properly opened to in 'The Silence' and *The Gates of Hell*, which are the turning-point; the gain is consolidated in *The Fire-Flower*, and the fully mature work, such as *A Rainbow in the Spray* and *Question Mark over the West*, is therefore towards the end.

Like any artist, I have grown through different periods and styles, some of which I would not practise now. I have left these as they are as this is a historical presentation of works from different times of my life when I was growing into the person I am now. Where a poem has been revised I have sometimes given both versions; when I have not, the revision has always been within the idiom of the style that applied at the time the poem was first drafted.

Influence of Roman poets and growing metaphysical perspective
For a full account of the life from which the poems arose, see first my long autobiography *A Mystic Way*, which includes many references to particular poems and quotations from all my *Diaries*; and secondly *Awakening to the Light*, Volume 1 of my *Diaries* which covers 1958–1967. These two works account for many of the influences on my work, for example my thoughts about the Roman poets who influenced my poems during the 1970s, and my growing metaphysical perspective and declaration of the Metaphysical Revolution, which has already entered philosophy and the sciences and which now enters poetry with this collection. In this respect, the second version of 'A Metaphysical in Marvell's Garden' is clearly an important poem.

Neo-Baroque poems combine Neoclassical and Neo-Romantic approaches
In art, the metaphysical manifests as the Baroque, as it did in the 17th century. My Baroque and metaphysical perspectives are outlined in the two Prefaces [see pp.9–60 and 60–77 of *Collected Prefaces*] and in the Notes. It will be helpful for the reader to know at the outset that Baroque poetry combines the Neoclassical (social situations and attitudes in rational statement) with the Neo-Romantic (emphasis on inner feeling and mystical contact with Reality in image). Neo-Baroque poetry blends statement and image, and unites both strands of 20th-century poetry: the active and contemplative lives, and sense and spirit. It will help the reader to know that just as Bernini shows St Teresa swooning in a sexually suggestive pose, so the new Baroque sometimes presents the Light of Reality and inspiration in contemporary sensual imagery.

Universalist poetry: One Reality behind the universe
As a sometime Existentialist and now Universalist poet, I have sought to reflect the Reality behind the universe in poetry. The Baroque Revolution – the manifestation or emanation of the Metaphysical Revolution in poetry which results in a Poetry Revolution – presents hints and *glimpses* and chinks of this One Reality in everyday situations. Universalist poems blend experience and tradition; they relate the poet's inner experience to the 5,000-year-old Universalist tradition which I have stated in full in Part 1 of *The Fire and the Stones* and in *The Universe and the Light*, and references to which can be found in the Notes [pp.592–701 of *Collected Poems 1958–1993: A White Radiance*]. Universalist poems offer perceptions and eternal truths about the universe (and the energy of the Light) in imagery that draws on or is associated with the tradition of the last 5,000 years.

1 February 1994

5

A Mystic Way

A Spiritual Autobiography

Note

Cumulative process of events, the Light and my thinking
The construction of this Autobiography presents a succession of events in accordance with the view of time and memory stated on p.159 and pp.776–777 [of *A Mystic Way*], that the present is endlessly added cumulatively to the past so that new layers are endlessly added to previous layers. The theme of the Light and the Mystic Way is thus presented within a philosophical context of a creative process, Being within Becoming.

Later on I have regarded my *Diaries* entries as events, and similarly each new entry modifies or qualifies the layering of the past. *Diaries* entries written at the time retain the freshness and accuracy of an event on the day it happened, and to some extent avoid imposing a present construct on past experience. Using my *Diaries* entries as a source catches the cumulative process of my thinking as each thought emerges from my life, and the cumulative effect of the Light on me as I progress up the Mystic Way to the summit where all paths meet.

6

Awakening to the Light

Diaries: Volume 1, 1958–1967

Introduction

Finding myself as a poet
These *Diaries* were not written for publication. They fulfil the same function for my poetry as Coleridge's *Biographia Literaria*, Yeats's *Autobiographies*, Kafka's *Diaries*, and Gascoyne's *Journal* did in relation to their work. They help the reader to understand the poems. In Volume 1 the reader can see a poet's discipline taking shape as I learn to take charge of my experiences and motivate myself, as I find myself as a poet. The reader will observe a poet behind the scenes, groping through false starts towards the work he should be doing, producing 'The Silence', 'Archangel' and 'Old Man in a Circle', transforming himself spiritually and in the process throwing up the concepts of the chapter headings.

A Mystic Way
These *Diaries* also state a Mystic Way: my own journey from mechanism to metaphysics. They follow the events I have narrated in *A Mystic Way*, but contain the different perspective and detail of entries written on a specific day. The daily entries show a young man on the Mystic Way in many different situations and kinds of experience, in many postures and poses, and contain snapshots of a mind taken over the years from every conceivable angle. These *Diaries* are distinguished from all other works by their daily search and their successful journey from unhappiness and craving for purpose to a mystical position. They show a journey from confusion to certainty, from despair to hope, from darkness to Light, from Hell to Paradise. While Volume 1 ends before the Paradise is attained, the movement is clearly present.

Process philosophy
These *Diaries* attempt a philosophical self-definition. They amount to a work of process philosophy. The philosopher is in process, in a flux of Becoming from day to day, and is groping towards Being, which in several entries he glimpses, although his full apprehension of Being will fall within Volume 2. As he proceeds through time his ideas and

perceptions change. Each observation and reflection must therefore be related to his present position and stance within a changing process, and many of the more sceptical observations in Volume 1 will be contradicted by the more metaphysical observations of Volume 3.

My literary and historical predictions and gropings towards Universalism
Rereading these early *Diaries* now, I am struck by how from the very beginning I seemed to have an inner knowledge of what I had to do and of where I would go, and some of the earliest entries anticipate developments that took place years later both in myself and in the current affairs of the Age. For example, I see that I predicted the post-Modernist movement on 20 January 1965 before I started 'The Silence', which is arguably the first post-Modernist poem as well as the first Neo-Baroque poem; and there are several predictions of a coming European Union (such as the entry for 19 January 1967), which anticipate the European Union we are now citizens of. It can now be seen that in the 1960s I was at least 25 years ahead of my time, and my gropings towards a new Baroque Age (a mixture of Classicism and Romanticism), a new post-Existentialist philosophy of Universalism and a post-Communist world order must be seen in that perspective. Here can be found the germs of the work that became *The Fire and the Stones*, and the concern for my fellow human beings throughout Asia which resulted in my support for a benevolent world government that puts an end to famines and wars.

My literary and Universalist works
The entries are selections from writings that have survived. Certain key points in my life, which I have described in *A Mystic Way*, passed without any reference or comment in my *Diaries*. Confronted with this almost arbitrary body of work, I have adhered to strict principles. I have put in anything that aids an understanding of my literary, philosophical or historical work. I have included anything which shows my development from a sceptical Oxford position to the metaphysical outlook of my Metaphysical Revolution and Universalism. I have omitted anything of a personal family nature, and anything which can hurt any living person.

My inner development amid events
These *Diaries* record an inner development against a background of events. At first they show a young man who is disenchanted with his life and who is seeking something beyond him which he associates with eternity. At Oxford in 1958 and in the holidays I had already awakened

to this "something beyond" and was at odds with society and changed from Law to English in 1959. In 1961 I married and began my search among other cultures, religions and civilisations, beginning in Iraq. No Diaries for this period have survived. In 1962, back in England, I attempted writing, living with my in-laws in Dulwich. I spent all our money and we elected to go to Japan; I took short-term jobs, as a gardener in Dulwich Park and a library assistant, while I waited. My father died and everything seemed to have gone wrong. I had only £5 in the world, but found I was a Professor in Tokyo at three universities: Tokyo University of Education, Keio and Tokyo University. My boss, the Representative of the British Council, was the philosopher E.W.F. Tomlin. I taught the Vice-Governor of the Bank of Japan one day a week and was eventually made tutor to the younger brother of the present Emperor. I was exploring the theme of eternity in a novel, which was not going well.

My literary development
In late 1964 and in 1965 I underwent a development, purging myself and turning to poetry, writing 'The Silence' and remaking myself as a writer. I had my first glimmer of illumination. This development coincided with the arrival of the novelist and writer of short stories, Frank Tuohy, in Japan, but otherwise I was on my own, and without any objective yardstick by which to measure or interpret what was happening to me. My research among different civilisations and cultures took me to China and Russia in 1966, and I deepened my vision and produced poems such as 'Archangel', which predicted the collapse of Communism, and 'Old Man in a Circle', which anticipated the European Union. I did not know that when I returned to Essex at the end of 1967 I would lose my way and that there would be a swing back into inner darkness. It would be several years before the development begun in Japan could be seen to be the beginning of an illuminative way and a lifetime of inner growth.

14 April 1994

7

A Spade Fresh with Mud

Introductory Note

Ordinary people and revelations of Being
These 220 mini-stories were written between 1966 and 1972, over twenty-five years before the miniatures of Margaret Atwood's *Good Bones* (1992) or John Fuller's *The Worm and the Star* (1993). Many of my stories grope towards the unified view of the universe that can be found in my philosophy and poems. Many hint at Reality through humdrum living. They show ordinary, unaware people saying or doing everyday, often inadequate things against an implied backdrop of Being, which peeps through into and invades their veiled consciousness when they least expect it, and which can be glimpsed when their souls are awake. Some are epiphanies: revelations of Being within the process of Becoming in moments of heightened awareness.

Images of horror in fresh language and associative order
With the exception of some of Hemingway's short pieces, these mini-stories are much shorter than most. They present an image and create a mood or even a spasm (a sudden convulsive response). They are prose-poems that use concreteness and realism (fidelity to observation of facts and feelings) in a fresh, rhythmical prose language to present the pain and horror and wonder in the world of the Fifties, the Swinging Sixties and Seventies. Each story can be read in isolation, but at another level each Part can be thought of as a meditation in Rawley's mind in which some stories – in Part One, the Japanese ones – set off associations in Rawley's memory. The stories follow an associative rather than a chronological order. Each Part is itself a kind of image-poem, with each image being linked emotionally to the one before and the one after in an emotionally-linked sequence of images; the theme being symbolised in the title.

A painter of human life in words
I am a painter in words, and each of these stories is a painting. I show, for example, a baronial house, a learned man and some girls, just as a painter in the Tate shows a dead girl, a staring doctor and tormented parents. My technique and his are the same, and this is my Tate Gallery exhibition. Believing that philosophy should be rooted in concrete

experience, I paint samples of human life from which to deduce an unspoken hypothesis about human possibilities, and I hang them round my gallery. You pass from picture to picture, and just as you do not necessarily see every painting at the Tate in one visit, but wander and select, so here too you may select. Though I hope you will revisit and go on revisiting until you know my gallery from start to finish. And I hope some of the images which show the ordinary, everyday life of Becoming surprise or even startle your soul into awareness of the extraordinary freshness of Being.

1 January 1995

8

Overlord
Books 1–2

The Triumph of Light

Preface to Books 1–2

How to recognise epic and an epic poem
Epic is recognised by: its subject matter; theme; heroic tone; narrative length; complexity; unity of action; the scope of its setting; the scale of its action; the moral stature of its heroes; its supernatural elements; its conventions; its accessible language; its exact metre; and its distinctive cosmology.

An epic poem's subject matter includes familiar and traditional material drawn from history and widely known in popular culture, which reflects the civilisation that threw it up. Its theme has a historical, national, religious or legendary significance. It narrates continuously the heroic achievements of a distinguished historical, national or legendary hero or heroes at greater length than the heroic lay, and describes an important national enterprise in more realistic terms than fantastic medieval Arthurian (Grail) romance; it gives an overwhelming impression of nobility as heroes take part in an enterprise that is larger and more important than themselves. Its long narrative is characterised by its sheer size and weight; it includes several strands, and has largeness of concept. It treats one great complex action in heroic proportions and in an elevated style and tone. It has unity of action, which begins in the middle (*"in medias res"*, to use Horace's phrase). The scope of its geographical setting is extensive, perhaps cosmic; its sweep is panoramic, and it uses heroic battle and extended journeying. The scale of the action is gigantic; it deals with good and evil on a huge scale. Consequently, its hero and main characters have great moral stature. It involves supernatural or religious beings in the action, and includes prophecy and the underworld. It has its own conventions; for example, it lists ships and genealogies, and the exploits that surround individual weapons. Its language is universally accessible, and includes ornamental similes and recurrent epithets. It uses exact metre (hexameters or the pentameters of blank verse). It has its own cosmology, and explains the ordering of the universe.

Overlord's epic theme: the liberation of Europe from tyranny

Homer's *Iliad*, which is about the Greeks' war against Troy, and Virgil's *Aeneid*, which is about the foundation of Rome, established the epic genre and defined these epic elements or components, and Milton's *Paradise Lost* conformed to them; while Dante's *Divine Comedy* and Ezra Pound's *Cantos* echo the lofty epic tone. My poem *Overlord*, the first two books of which I now offer, is about the liberation of Europe from tyranny and also reflects the characteristics of epic.

The subject matter of *Overlord* includes familiar and traditional historical material drawn from the Second World War, which has shaped the world of the last fifty years and reflects Western civilisation in a time of conflict, division and crisis. The Second World War is often referred to as an epic struggle, and is known to all people through living memory, books and films, regardless of age, wealth, position or social class; it has passed into popular culture. My theme, the liberation of Europe from Nazi tyranny, is of historical, national and legendary significance, and is still regarded as being of national importance in both the US and Europe. Eisenhower is a distinguished hero involved in a great complex action which has unity – the invasion of German-occupied France and the advance to Berlin – and he is involved in a noble enterprise of complexity and scope. *Overlord* begins with D-Day in June 1944 and narrates the American and British – and later, Russian – drive against Hitler, which ended with the fall of Berlin and led to the explosion of the atomic bomb. Book 2 narrates Stauffenberg's plot to kill Hitler.

Overlord's narrative length

A word about *Overlord*'s narrative length. The massiveness of the theme of the Anglo-American triumph over Hitler following his conquest of and overlordship over Europe, and his onslaught on the Jews and Christendom, requires *Overlord* to be of greater narrative length than past epics. Whereas Homer's twenty-four books tend to be around five hundred lines each and Virgil's and Milton's twelve books around a thousand, give or take a hundred or two, *Overlord*'s first two epic books are respectively over 2,900 and 2,200 lines long; the events before and after D-Day, the bomb plot and their supernatural context simply cannot be done in less.

The scale of Hitler's killing and evil

The scale of the action in *Overlord* derives from Hitler, who dwarfs all his predecessors in sheer awfulness and evil. To Marlowe, writing in the 1590s, the worst and cruellest military tyrant was the 14th-century

Timur Lenk, or Tamburlaine the Great. To Dostoevsky in *Crime and Punishment* and Tolstoy in *War and Peace* Napoleon was the most wicked man who could be imagined, a military tyrant who flouted all moral laws. On precise analysis, the Napoleonic Wars of 1800–1815 killed no more than half a million French people (one sixtieth of the French population at the time), and if we agree that Napoleon killed more of his enemies, then he was responsible for the death of between a million and a million-and-a-half human beings in all, 0.43 per cent of mankind, which then totalled 1 billion (i.e. 1,000 million). The total dead in the First World War amounted to no more than eight-and-a-half million, and according to the best studies Stalin is thought to have been responsible for killing 20 million. Census records recently discovered in the Kremlin show that Hitler's Operation Barbarossa resulted in 49 million Soviet dead alone (see *Barbarossa: The Axis and the Allies*, edited by John Erickson and David Dilks, pp.256–258), which puts up the conservative estimate of the total number of dead in World War Two from just under 36 million (including 18 million Russians) to 67 million, nearly 3.4 per cent of the total population of the world in 1939, which was 2 billion (or 2,000 million); and the higher estimate of 60 million dead to a staggering 90 million, or over 4.5 per cent of all mankind, nearly one in twenty human beings. Never in human history has one tyrant stood accused of being responsible for killing 67 million of his fellow humans, let alone 90 million. On a statistical count of the numbers of deaths and taking just the conservative figures into consideration, Hitler was almost forty-five times as bad as Napoleon, and nearly eight times as destructive as the entire First World War. He was responsible for killing more than three times as many people as the tyrants Stalin or Mao (although it has recently been claimed that Mao killed 70 million in all), and this is the context for the genocide he presided over, the liquidation of over 5.9 million out of the 8.86 million European Jews, one third of the world's Jewish population.

Stauffenberg's moral stature
The heroes who resist tyranny have moral stature, and the larger the tyrant the greater their stature. In opposing the killer of at least 67 million, and possibly 90 million, people, the pragmatic Eisenhower and the idealistic Stauffenberg therefore take on an awesome moral and human stature. The moral choices take place in situations of everyday ordinariness, even banality, and the evidence for Eisenhower's strange affair with his driver is detailed in Kay Summersby Morgan's *Past Forgetting: My Love Affair with Dwight D. Eisenhower*. Full accounts of the long influence of the poet Stefan George, whose poem *Antichrist* is

about Hitler, on Stauffenberg's life can be found in Joachim Kramarz's *Stauffenberg* and Michael Baigent and Richard Leigh's *Secret Germany: Claus von Stauffenberg and the Mystical Crusade Against Hitler.*

Supernatural elements in Overlord
In *Overlord* supernatural elements blend with history. Scenes of realistic everyday life take place within the context of the supernatural as the forces of Light and Darkness, personified by the Cosmic or universal Christ and Cosmic Satan in Heaven and Hell, attempt to influence the action on earth. (Yeats said we make art out of the quarrel with ourselves and rhetoric out of the quarrel with others, and my quarrel with myself is inextricably connected with this conflict, or quarrel, between Light and Darkness, and its Christian and Luciferian manifestations on earth, where genocidal dark forces such as the Illuminati and Nazis claim to follow the mystic Light.) Hitler's – and the Nazis' – interest in the occult and the influence of the poet Dietrich Eckart on Hitler are dealt with in a number of books, notably in Nicholas Goodrick-Clarke's *The Occult Roots of Nazism*, Nigel Pennick's *Hitler's Secret Sciences* and Dusty Sklar's *The Nazis and the Occult.* Hermann Rauschning, Governor of Danzig, hinted in *Hitler Speaks* (1939) that Hitler was possessed by the Devil, the Beast, and the circumstantial evidence for his Satanism is cited in such books as H.G. Baynes's *Germany Possessed* (1941), Pauwels and Bergier's *The Morning of the Magicians*, Trevor Ravenscroft's *The Spear of Destiny* and Francis King's *Satan and Swastika: The Occult and the Nazi Party.*

Christ's new Universalist era and world rule brought in by Eisenhower
Overlord connects Hitler's dark mania for destruction to the contemporary legend of the millennium and the Second Coming, and identifies the Battle of Normandy as the Battle of Armageddon which, under Satan's leadership, succeeds a thousand years of Christ's rule through the Holy Roman Empire during the time of nations, and precedes a thousand years of supranational universal religion. In *Overlord* the Cosmic or universal Christ is endeavouring to set up a new Universalist era which will express itself in a world government. Through Hitler, Satan is trying to set up his alternative millennial thousand-year *Reich*. Like Michelangelo's vision on the Sistine Chapel ceiling, *Overlord* addresses and explores good and evil on a huge scale, and their origins in and connections with Heaven and Hell.

Eisenhower is the instrument for bringing in the universal Christ's world rule. Eisenhower will eventually be shown the new age, and will realise that although he is working for the defeat of Hitler in the short term, he is endeavouring to bring in a globalist world government. My Universalist work of history, *The Fire and the Stones* (since revised in two parts, the second of which is *The Rise and Fall of Civilizations*), shows that such a world rule occurs in stage 15 of the 61 stages a civilisation goes through, that the North-American civilisation is currently in this stage and that such a stage is always associated with epic. As well as marking the British contribution to victory, *Overlord* is a celebration of the rise of globalism within the American worldwide civilisation, and its hero Eisenhower is the figurehead in establishing the foundations for this US world rule, first on the battlefield in 1944–1945 and then as President of the US from 1953 to 1961. *Overlord* is essentially an American epic.

Epic conventions
Overlord adheres to the epic conventions. For example, a catalogue of Angels and demons echoes Homer's catalogue of ships, and the spear of Longinus is introduced within the context of a list of historical events with which it has been associated. The language of *Overlord* is accessible and includes ornamental similes.

Iambic pentameters
Overlord uses strict metre. I eschew the Stress Metre that can be found in places in my *Collected Poems*, and use a blank verse that can be both elevated and descriptive. It has strictly five feet to a line, although an occasional effect requires an extra half-foot. My verse consists of iambic pentameters with occasional trochees and spondees, but no anapaests or dactyls, which I have employed in my two verse plays about the last year of the Second World War, *The Warlords*, Parts One and Two. Whereas spoken dramatic verse benefits from the loosening effects of anapaests and dactyls, epic poetry must be metrically tighter, variations being achieved in other ways than mixed metres. The one poetic licence permits some words to be scanned in either of two ways. Thus "Heaven", "seven", "driven", "General", "cruel" and "power", for example, can be scanned as one syllable or as two; "Admiral", "areas", "Eisenhower", "genius", "Aetius", "history", "Aryan", "Emperor", "Catholic" and "several" can be scanned as two syllables or as three; and "military" and "spiritual" can be scanned as three syllables or as four. In all these cases, when the lower number is used the stresses of contemporary spoken English are allowed to override a strict syllabic count. On very rare occasions an elision is allowed, as in "the angelic".

Genesis of Overlord *and discussion with Ezra Pound*

Overlord has its own cosmology, and passages such as lines 182–315 in book 1 give an account of the creation and ordering of the universe. As readers of *A Mystic Way* will know, I have had the idea for this epic since 1969 and I discussed it with Ezra Pound in Rapallo in 1970. [See Appendix 2, pp.498–501.] I have put it off for over twenty-five years, until my vision had developed sufficiently to cope with the idea. The trouble was, existing philosophy could not encompass the cosmology of the Fire or Light, and so on the way I have had to found a new school in philosophy, Universalism. Now I can at last tackle this work, the starting-point of which is a unified vision of the universe, and understanding of the rise and fall of civilisations and of the laws of history, a sound grasp of perspective that includes the supernatural, and a knowledge of the laws by which the universe is run: the laws of the Light. My writings on mysticism, history, science, philosophy and metaphysical cosmology have been the perfect preparation for this daunting work, which revives the epic in our time and of which the following pages represent but the first sixth.

13 February 1995

9

The Warlords, Parts One and Two

From D-Day to Berlin
A Verse Drama

Preface to the 1995 edition

This 1995 Preface was updated in 2006 without any significant changes to appear in *Collected Verse Plays* [2007, see Preface 24], which included *The Warlords*, Parts One and Two, and an abridged single play in its Appendix [as explained on p.172]. This is referred to in the last line of this Preface.

The last year of the war
The Warlords puts the last year of the war on stage. Its two Parts are therefore necessarily long and rival the length of Goethe's *Faust*, Parts One and Two.

At one level *The Warlords* has been written as a celebration of the 50th anniversary of VE Day (8 May 1995) and, besides creating imaginatively realised, living, solid characters who move in and out of known events, I have wanted to leave the audience with a clear, historically accurate – and verifiable – picture of the main issues. The Second World War dominated my childhood; I lived in the path of the air raids and the flying bombs. The men in the assault craft were heroes for my generation, and my awe of their bravery in leaping into water under fire on D-Day with men dying all round them has, if anything, increased over the years. There is still great interest in what happened. After fifty years an event passes into history and people who were once living take on the force of historical characters and appear to represent historical forces. I met both Churchill and Montgomery, and it is with reverence that I now present them in terms of the drives and forces which shaped our lives.

Revival of verse drama
I have found the medium of verse liberating; I have been acutely aware that the sweep of my settings would be impossible in the medium of realistic prose drama. This revival of contemporary verse drama is essentially practical; it gets the job done better than prose could by escaping the constraints of realistic settings and by reviving

monologues, soliloquies, asides. As Marlowe and Shakespeare found, and as Goethe also discovered in *Faust*, Parts One and Two, verse drama can range over battlefields and heaths and get inside the soul of characters.

The verse in The Warlords

The verse in *The Warlords* varies the strictness of iambic pentameters (⏑ –) by including trochees (– ⏑), anapaests (⏑ ⏑ –) and dactyls (– ⏑ ⏑) where feeling requires a loosening, and even tribrachs (⏑ ⏑ ⏑), bacchiuses (⏑ – –), cretics (– ⏑ –) and sometimes amphibrachs which reverse cretics (⏑ – ⏑). On rare occasions there may be 4-syllable feet such as paeons (– ⏑ ⏑ ⏑ or ⏑ ⏑ ⏑ –) or Aeolic choriambs (– ⏑ ⏑ –).

A verse dramatist writing today follows in the footsteps of Marlowe, who developed blank verse (which Surrey had imported from Italy and which Sackville and Norton first used dramatically in *Gorboduc* in 1561), and Shakespeare, and their historical plays *Tamburlaine the Great* and *Henry the Fourth* (both in two parts); Webster, whose *The White Devil* draws on the history of Renaissance Italy, and Dryden's *All for Love*; and more recently Eliot's *Murder in the Cathedral* and Fry's *The Lady's Not for Burning*.

Sources and documentary evidence for Hitler, Montgomery, Stalin and Eisenhower

Every historical dramatist has a source. Marlowe used an English version by P.F. of the German *Historia von D. Johann Fausten* of 1587; Shakespeare North's Plutarch and Holinshed's *Chronicles*; Webster a German newsletter written from the Fugger banking house in Augsburg; and Dryden Plutarch's *Life of Antony* as well as Appian's *Civil Wars* and Dio's *Roman History*. I have assembled a library on the Second World War of a couple of hundred books. The British accounts of the last year of the war (such as Nigel Hamilton's) support Montgomery, the American accounts (such as Stephen Ambrose's) Eisenhower. I have tried to be even-handed, and to show both sides. I have gone to some pains (notably visiting Normandy, Berlin, Warsaw, Auschwitz and Munich, and many other such places on the Continent) to achieve historical accuracy and veracity. I went with the view, recently confirmed by the eyewitness Traudl Junge (whose book *Until the Final Hour* came out in 2002 shortly before she died), that Hitler dictated his will to her before his wedding to Eva Braun rather than after (as some books assert). Generally speaking, the dialogue reflects established events, while the soliloquies provide imaginative interpretation based on documentation.

My interpretation of the characters has been based on documentary evidence. To focus on some of this, a number of books on the occult influences on Nazism show that Hitler must be seen in relation to the Thule Society and the occult practices of Dietrich Eckart, which included forays into black magic; and that there was at least a suppressed Satanism in the Nazi drive against Jehovah, the Jewish god. Several books show that after the bomb plot Hitler declined into a shuffling, trembling human wreck who was but a shadow of his former dictatorial self. His fascination with the spear of Longinus has been documented in Trevor Ravenscroft's *The Spear of Destiny* and there are several books on the Nazis and the occult, the most sober and academic of which is Nicholas Goodrick-Clarke's *The Occult Roots of Nazism*, the most interesting Nigel Pennick's *Hitler's Secret Sciences*. The first was Pauwels and Bergier's *The Morning of the Magicians*, and the most comprehensive is Francis King's *Satan and Swastika: The Occult and the Nazi Party*. All these books look back to Hermann Rauschning's *Hitler Speaks* (1939) in which the Nazi Governor of Danzig describes his conversations with Hitler between 1932 and 1934, and H.G. Baynes's *Germany Possessed* (1941). Lawyers wanting convictions and executions at the Nuremberg trials suppressed some of the occult material as it might have given the defendants cause to plead diminished responsibility.

That Hitler was shown the *Protocols of the Elders of Zion*, which he mentioned as a Jewish work in *Mein Kampf*, by Rosenberg, to whom Eckart introduced him around 1920, is documented in many books, for example Lucy S. Dawidowicz's *The War Against the Jews, 1933–1945*. The Final Solution to kill the Jews was decided on at the Wannsee Conference of January 1942, chaired by Heydrich, but it had its roots in the early 1920s and is heralded in *Mein Kampf*. (For the eschatological connotations in the word "Final", which led Malraux to speak of "*le retour de Satan*", see Dawidowicz, p.18.) How Hitler saw the Jews can be found in a number of books, including the chapter "Jehovah as Satan" in Dusty Sklar's *The Nazis and the Occult*. The Allies' knowledge of events in Auschwitz from May 1941, and certainly in March and June 1944, is documented in Martin Gilbert's *Auschwitz and the Allies*.

Montgomery was at heart a very religious man. His father was a clergyman, he always went to church when he could, he wrote of "the Lord mighty in battle" and, according to his deputy chef (who travelled with him from Broomfield House to Luneburg Heath and with whom I have had a long discussion), he always went to bed at 9pm to pray in his caravan. It was generally known in 'A' Mess that Montgomery could not be disturbed on any account after 9pm because he was in prayer, obtaining God's Providential guidance for the huge decisions he faced. For some years he lived simply in a caravan close to Nature, both on North-African sand and European grass, and he did not smoke or drink, and thus represented the puritanical tradition.

That the Jewish Paulina Molotov, the Soviet Foreign Minister's wife, became Stalin's mistress after his wife died is suggested in Larisa Vasilyeva's *Kremlin Wives*. Files in the KGB archives show that Niels Bohr gave Stalin nuclear secrets via Beria's agents Vasilevsky and Terletsky, as reported in *The Sunday Times* of 26 June 1994.

Eisenhower's relationship with the Irish driver Kay Summersby is documented in her book (written under her later name, Kay Summersby Morgan), *Past Forgetting: My Love Affair with Dwight D. Eisenhower*. It is not known if she told the whole truth; but if she did then Eisenhower was sexually impotent during the whole war. I have chosen not to believe this entirely.

Universalist reconciliation of good and evil
The conflict between the Christian Montgomery, the occultist Hitler and the Materialist Stalin goes deeper than social disquiet and raises metaphysical considerations of good and evil. After fifty years the time has come to present Hitler's racism in its true context, de-demonising Hitler but not hiding his involvement with the occult, without which the Holocaust cannot be understood. (Indeed, failure to address Hitler's occult beliefs about Jehovah is the main reason why the Holocaust has so far not been understood.) Philosophers who study the universe seek to reconcile the opposites of war and peace within the total scheme, as did Tolstoy, and Montgomery's belief in a Providential power for good that orders events in a fallen world offers such a reconciliation.

Issues that dominated the next 50 years
The Warlords honours the men who delivered us from evil and enslavement by a totalitarian dictatorship and shaped the world we know. The last year of the war threw up so many issues that have dominated the last fifty years: the Russian domination of Eastern Europe; the atomic bomb; the rise of American world power; the decline of British world power, which can be dated back to the demotion of Montgomery on 1 September 1944; the dream of a united Europe; the Final Solution of the Jewish problem which saw five million Jews killed; and the need for a world government. Against a background of conflicting ideologies, philosophies and historical forces, *The Warlords* explores the warlords' leadership, and, I hope, presents an eternal image of the relationship between power and good.

The Warlords can be produced as two separate plays or as one play with excisions (see Appendix [in *Collected Verse Plays*]). Asterisked blocks [within *The Warlords*] are candidates for excision.

13 February 1995; revised 2 February 2006

10

A Smell of Leaves and Summer

Introductory Note

Knowledge of spiritual Reality
These 162 mini-stories were written between 1973 and 1981. They appear in thematic rather than chronological order. Whereas the stories in the first volume, *A Spade Fresh with Mud*, examined the horror of the Materialist position and revealed Being as the way to meaning, the stories in this volume focus on knowledge of spiritual Reality through illumination and enlightenment. The experience itself I presented in *A Mystic Way*, pp.195–200 (and also in *Collected Poems*, pp.854–859 [see pp.437–447 of *Collected Prefaces*]), and these stories explore the peace the vision brings – the "peace that passeth understanding" – and a growing awareness of spiritual love through the Light, and of people who know spiritual love. Death is present in the opening stories of both Parts, but knowledge of the Light brings relief from the bleakness and finality of death and enables consciousness to move beyond Materialism.

Heterogeneous images yoked together
As with the stories in the first volume, these stories are visual prose poems or paintings. Even when the subject matter is spiritual and inward, they go for the vivid, fresh, observed detail as would a painting, and often combine dissimilar ideas. Dr Johnson defined the wit of the Metaphysical poets as when "the most heterogeneous ideas are yoked by violence together". When a Metaphysical sensibility replaces ideas with perceptions and observations, and presents "heterogeneous *images* yoked by violence together", then the ensuing *frisson* is akin to wit but distinct from it as the medium is not rational but observational, not ideas but things seen; heterogeneous impressions being associated or yoked together. Behind all multiplicity is a unity, and some phenomena of multiplicity correspond to each other within the unity in a way that surprises and delights.

Revealing Truth
In his *Ars Poetica* (c.19–18BC or c.12–8BC) Horace wrote: "A poet should instruct or please or both." In a letter to Pope (1725) Swift wrote: "The chief end in all I propose to myself in all my labours is to vex the

world rather than divert it." My aim is not to vex mankind, though the bleak Materialistic consciousness – whether proletarian, bourgeois or aristocratic – *needs* to be vexed into a change. It is not primarily to divert or please, to delight or entertain, though I hope these prose-poems or paintings are diverting, pleasing, delightful and entertaining. My aim is to reveal the Truth: which means showing that behind all Becoming and all surface beauty there is Being, Reality, eternity; knowledge of which makes a difference to living as it cleanses, purifies and enhances consciousness and its appetite for life. To the extent that I reveal Truth I instruct. I show healthy, optimistic images of man and the universe despite an ever-present awareness of horror, suffering and death. I show images which present a vitality and zest for life that transcend bleakness and despair.

1 March 1995

11

Overlord
Books 3–6

The Triumph of Light

Preface to Books 3–6

Eisenhower's conflict with Hitler
Books 3–6 of *Overlord* carry the story of Eisenhower's conflict with Hitler forward through Falaise, Arnhem, Auschwitz and the Ardennes. I visited each of these places and areas, and all the places in the invocations, in 1994 or 1995, and as my interpretation of events is distinctive, it is important that I should draw attention to some of the corroborating sources, particularly those I have not mentioned in my 'Preface to *Overlord, books 1 to 2*'.

Sources for the occult roots of Nazism
My sources for the occult roots of Nazism (books 3 and 5) include some books that are now hard to find. The suggestion that Hitler sold his soul to the Devil in a Faustian pact in 1942 further to Eckart's Satanic Annunciation can be found in a number of books, for example Nigel Pennick's *Hitler's Secret Sciences: His Quest for the Hidden Knowledge of the Ancients*, p.175. Pennick also sees the SS's genocide as a State act of black magic. Nazi links to the *Fehme* can be found in Paul Winkler's *The Thousand-Year Conspiracy: Secret Germany Behind the Mask*. Details of Hitler's Rosicrucianism (and Stalin's) and information on Rosicrucianism's Satanic aspects (for example, that the rose round the cross represents the serpent, Lucifer) can be found in Volume 1 of John Daniel's *Scarlet and the Beast: A History of the War between English and French Freemasonry*, which chronicles the eight-hundred-year-old war between the Priory of Sion and its English Rosicrucian and Illuminati descendants associated with the Grand Lodge on the one hand, and (its creation) the French Knights Templar and their descendants associated with the Grand Orient on the other hand. Daniel's book sees Hitler as a product of the Priory of Sion and English Freemasonry, which financed him to destroy French Freemasonry. Hitler was originally a member of his teacher Lanz's Rosicrucian Order of the New Temple, and his interest in Templar-related Catharism can be corroborated in Jean-Michel Angebert's *The Occult and the Third Reich: The Mystical*

Origins of Nazism and the Search for the Holy Grail.

Hitler's interest in the Grail and Himmler's search for the Grail in Montségur on his behalf (which is referred to in an epic digression in book 5) can be found in Col. Buechner's *Emerald Cup: The Quest of SS Lt Otto Rahn of the Third Reich*. Himmler's fascination with the Holy Lance and details of the rituals of the Knights of the Holy Lance at Wewelsburg can be found in Col. Buechner and Capt. Bernhart's *Adolf Hitler and the Secrets of the Holy Lance*. Details of Himmler's SS Headquarters at Schloss Wewelsburg can be found in the German *Wewelsburg: Kult-und Terrorstätte der SS*.

Sources for Allies

I have drawn on many sources for the passages involving Eisenhower, Montgomery and SHAEF (books 3–6). While I have been at pains to ground all their conversations in the correct historical time and place, I have used poetic licence in setting Christ's approach to Eisenhower on Mont-St-Michel (book 3). Shortly after this imaginary episode Eisenhower *did* have a room overlooking Mont-St-Michel, although I have again used poetic licence in giving him alternative visions of the future there (book 4). By contrast, Patton's prayer (book 6) is almost exactly as recorded. Some of the more minute details of the Arnhem operation (book 4) can be found in Urquhart's *Arnhem*, and some vivid details of the battle round Bastogne (book 6) can be found in Guy Franz Arend's *The Battle for Bastogne*.

Sources for the Jews' revolt in Auschwitz

The bare facts of Dorebus's 7 October revolt of the Jews in Auschwitz (book 5) are in Danuta Czech's *Auschwitz Chronicle 1939–45*, pp.724–729 and p.775 (the final hangings), and in Martin Gilbert's *The Holocaust: The Jewish Tragedy*. An eyewitness view, which is not reliable as regards dates and times, is in Dr Miklós Nyiszli's *Auschwitz: A Doctor's Eyewitness Account*. I have also drawn on Höss, Broad and Kremer's *KL Auschwitz Seen by the SS* (State Museum in Oswiecim), Swiebocka, Webber and Wibach's *Auschwitz: A History in Photographs* and Swiebocki (*sic*) and Bujak's *Auschwitz: Voices from the Ground*. There is a picture of Roza Robota in Michael Berenbaum's *The World Must Know: The History of the Holocaust as Told in the United States Holocaust Memorial Museum*. Evidence for Himmler's ending of the Holocaust soon after the 7 October revolt can be found in Martin Gilbert's *Auschwitz and the Allies*, ch.33 and Heinz Höhne's *The Order of the Death's Head: The Story of Hitler's SS*, ch.18.

Blank verse
My strict blank verse allows for certain two-syllable words to be scanned as one syllable where contemporary pronunciation usage permits ("fuel", "seventh", "iron", "given", "power"), and for certain three-syllable words to be scanned as two syllables ("conference", "personal", "senior", "Frederick", "serious", "travelling", "Hungary", "dangerous", "victory", "prisoners"); and for some five-syllable words to be scanned as four syllables ("crematoria"). Elision is allowed ("the offensive", "the Americans").

Universalist reconciling of worst evil and highest good
As with all epic, despite the grounding of the story in historical fact the poem is essentially a work of imagination. My imagination has taken known characters and recreated and presented them in a form that seeks to make sense of the worst horror of our time and locate its origins in the Satanic outlook and influence of certain occult secret societies within the neo-Illuminatist ambience of Rosicrucianism, to which both Hitler and Himmler belonged. I am now half-way through my epic, and have yet to resolve the long quarrel with myself that contrasts and seeks to reconcile a nightmare vision of the worst evil and a dream-like vision of the highest order and good, and explains how if all is One there can be a force of evil that can be reconciled with the underlying unity. I am on my way to resolving it, and am confident that the horror of the Holocaust will be justified and transcended in the final Paradisal vision of the poem.

5 January 1996

12

Overlord
Books 7–9

The Triumph of Light

Preface to Books 7–9

Stalin allowed to advance on Berlin
Books 7–9 of *Overlord* take Eisenhower's conflict with Hitler through the Yalta conference, the crossing of the Rhine and Stalin's advance on Berlin after Eisenhower's controversial cable to him which allowed the Russians to take the city. I visited Yalta in October 1995 and went to all three palaces, and I visited the other places and the sites of the invocations at various times between 1994 and 1996.

Epic rooted in history
Ever since Homer epic has been rooted in history. The historical reality of the Trojan War has been confirmed by Schliemann's discoveries at Troy and by discoveries in the Peloponnese. Menelaos's palace on Mount Therapne above Sparta can be visited by really intrepid explorers, and the list of ships in book 2 of *The Iliad*, long thought to be legendary, has been confirmed as being largely historical following recent discoveries of clay tablets at Nestor's palace at Pylos. The geography of Homer's Ithaca is very precise, and *The Odyssey* can only have been written by someone who knew the island intimately. Similarly, some material in *Overlord* that may seem legendary (even incredible) has historical reality.

Sources for involvement of Illuminati élites: Rothschilds, and Rockefellers' CFR
As I am offering an unfamiliar view of twentieth-century history I must indicate some of my sources. Evidence for Illuminati involvement in the Second World War can be traced back to the letter of 15 August 1871 written by the Satanist Albert Pike, Head of the US Scottish Rite and of the US Illuminati, to Mazzini, Italian revolutionary and Head of the world Illuminati after Adam Weishaupt. Pike wrote, "We shall unleash the Nihilists and the atheists, and we shall provoke a formidable social cataclysm." Pike's letter set out a plan for three world wars, which would: use communist atheists to topple the Tsar; give the Illuminati

a base in Moscow from which they would capture part of Europe; and restore Israel, from which they would make war on the Arabs and after both sides had destroyed each other bring in a New World Order or world government under Lucifer. This letter was first referred to in the 1920s in A.J. Gwynne, *The Cause of World Unrest*, and is alleged to have been on display in the British Museum Library from 1906 until a few years ago. Details of the letter can be found in two books by Des Griffin, *Descent into Slavery?*, pp.38–39 and *Fourth Reich of the Rich*, pp.64–71; and in William T. Still, *New World Order: The Ancient Plan of Secret Societies*, pp.127–128.

Illuminati involvement in 20th-century history would fill a whole library. Dozens of books on the subject, many only available in the US, can be bought by mail order or from specialist bookshops, and it is necessary to read them all to obtain a full picture as each supplies something the others do not. Broad accounts can be found in Gary Allen and Larry Abraham, *None Dare Call It Conspiracy*; John Daniel, *Scarlet and the Beast*, volume 1; and David Allen Rivera, *Final Warning: A History of the New World Order*. How the Illuminati *élite* have pulled the strings on all world events is revealed in Dr John Coleman's *Conspirators' Hierarchy: The Story of the Committee of 300* and in Antony Sutton's books on the Order.

It is extremely hard to influence world events. No human endeavour can be all-powerful: no matter how much organisation there is behind the scenes, things can go wrong in any local undertaking, let alone at world level. The outcome of a UN resolution can never be guaranteed. Nevertheless, in such books there is clear evidence that world leaders have been influenced to further the hidden agenda of a coming world government. One of the main influencing organisations has been the Council on Foreign Relations or CFR (first formed in 1921 and funded by the Rockefeller Foundation from 1927), the American headquarters of the Illuminati which has always supplied the backbone of US administrations including the President. (For example, it supplied a hundred members of President Nixon's administration.)

The Rothschild-Rockefeller background to the decisions reached at Yalta, which affected the world for fifty years, can be found in such books, as can [Mayer Amschel] Rothschild's link with the Satanist Weishaupt in the 18th century. Details of the Rothschilds' involvement in the Order of the Golden Dawn, which was linked to the Scottish Rite through first Pike and then Aleister Crowley and which was behind Hitler's Thule, can be found in Rivera, page 6, and in Daniel, volume 1. Evidence of Rockefellers' control of Roosevelt from the 1920s to the 1940s, and of Rockefellers' oil deal with Stalin in 1926, which became the basis of the Rockefeller-Soviet axis, can be found in two books by Emanuel Josephson, *The Truth about Rockefeller, Public Enemy No. 1* (e.g. chapters 3, 6 and 11) and *The Strange Death of Franklin D. Roosevelt* (chapter 22), which also covers Rockefellers' capture of Saudi-Arabian oil from the British (pp.71 and 91) and Stalin's waiter's attempt to poison Roosevelt and Churchill at Tehran with curare (chapter 23). Details of Roosevelt's affair with Lucy can be found in Peter Collier with David Horowitz, *The Roosevelts: An American Saga*. Hints of Baruch's hold over Churchill can be found in John Toland, *The Last 100 Days*, pp.357–358, 418–419. (Links between the Illuminati and world leaders continue. The link between the Illuminati and the Malthusian advocates of population control who in our time produced *The Global 2000 Report to the President*, i.e. Jimmy Carter, in 1980 can be found in Daniel, pp.285–288.)

The existence of a secret Illuminati Council of Elders which ran the ex-Soviet Union is confirmed in John Cotter, *A Study in Syncretism*, page 105, which reports that dictator Khrushchev proposed Bulganin as Prime Minister "on the instruction of the Central Committee of the CPSU and the Council of Elders" (speech made on 8 February 1955). John D. Rockefeller's presence on the Council of Elders can be connected to a later Rockefeller's visit to the Kremlin which led to the dismissal of Khrushchev (Allen, pp.105–107).

I am indebted to Svetlana Stalin, Stalin's daughter who spent the war years living in the Kremlin, for some of the local colour and background material on Stalin, particularly that covering the suicide of his wife. In conversation with me she stated that there was something "demoniac" about Stalin. For Stalin's link with Gurdjieff and his own Rosicrucianism, see John Daniel, *Scarlet and the Beast*, volume 1.

Legendary-historical Illuminati, like Arthurian legend
I have used poetic licence in transporting Eisenhower from Rheims to Hell in book 8, but there is no poetic licence in the account (substantiated by Des Griffin and others) of the CFR and Illuminati's control of the Allied war effort and of the CFR and Illuminati's, and therefore the Allies', deliberate avoidance of Berlin so that Stalin could dominate Eastern Europe and take mankind towards a world government. The voluminous literature on the Illuminati, the secrecy surrounding their rituals and the symbolism of the Lance of Longinus give them a mystery and near-legendary status in our time that corresponds to Arthurian legend in Tennyson's *Idylls of the King* and the symbolism of the Holy Grail. The legend of the hidden hand behind the Western governments of the 20th century is as rooted in history as the legend

of Arthur, the Roman-British king who succumbed to the Saxons, and is more contemporary and topically urgent than the remote story of Arthur; and at the artistic and imaginative level my use of this material is akin to Tennyson's use of Arthurian legend.

A good work of art reveals Truth

But the important thing is that, regardless of whether it draws on history, legend or everyday life, poetry points readers to the Truth, like an eagle soaring towards the sun. My view of a work of art differs from that of the logical positivists. Wittgenstein held that a work of art is a proposition in feelings and perceptions, to which the reader answers Yes or No. I hold that a good work of art is an image or symbol which represents and reveals Truth; a narrative, description or reflection in feelings and perceptions which the audience recognises with a Yes or fails to recognise with a No. Taken as a whole, a work of art is an epiphany of Truth which offers new insight into the interconnectedness between the metaphysical, cultural, social and personal levels of life within a civilisation. And the entirety of *Overlord* is therefore an image of Truth which the reader either recognises or does not recognise: an image made up of realistic images and statements, of observations, feelings and perceptions drawn from history, legend or everyday life, which confronts readers with Truth. And to the extent that readers recognise Truth in this poem, they mirror and thus confirm their soul's progress to Truth.

22 November 1996

13

Overlord
Books 10–12

The Triumph of Light

Preface to Books 10–12

The end of the war
Books 10–12 trace the end of Eisenhower's victorious war through the fall of Berlin, the German surrender and the dropping of the atomic bomb. I visited all the places, including the places of the invocations. I visited the bunker site in Berlin in July 1994, and the site where Montgomery accepted the German surrender and Eisenhower's Rheims schoolroom in April 1995. I visited Hiroshima when I gave a lecture there in 1964.

Sources and evidence for events
For details of the death of Hitler I have by and large followed Hugh Trevor-Roper's *The Last Days of Hitler* but I have also taken account of the apparent discovery of Hitler's skull, which shows a bullet hole, in Russia in 1992. The evidence for its being Hitler's is reviewed in Ada Petrova and Peter Watson, *The Death of Hitler: The Final Words from Russia's Secret Archives*. Details of how the Lance of Longinus and Hitler's ashes were transported to Antarctica in 1945 and returned in 1979 can be found in Col. Howard Buechner and Capt. Wilhelm Bernhart, *Hitler's Ashes* (which also refers to Hitler's son by Eva Braun, Horst).

Those who compare *Overlord* with my two-part verse play *The Warlords* will see that I have changed the times and sometimes the order of events. The trouble is, historians often disagree; and whereas several have Hitler dictating his last Will and Testament before marrying Eva, for example, as many again have the marriage first, on different authority. I have reviewed the conclusions I came to while writing *The Warlords* with an open mind, and sometimes I have felt it necessary to move on from them in the light of fuller evidence. It should also be remembered that epic poetry, which is not bound by the constraints of writing for the stage, affords a more panoramic perspective than drama.

Detailed evidence for Shakespeare as the 17th Earl of Oxford (invocation to book 11) can be found in Verily Anderson, *The De Veres of Castle Hedingham*, and Charlton Ogburn, *The Mystery of William Shakespeare*. I am indebted to discussions and correspondence with two of the 17th Earl's descendants, who are cousins and who at the time of writing have not met: Lord Burford and the Hon. Tom Lindsay, the owner of Castle Hedingham. Details of wartime atrocities by the Ustashe in Croatia can be found in Avro Manhattan, *The Vatican's Holocaust* and Vladimir Dedijer, *The Yugoslav Auschwitz and the Vatican*.

Illuminati pressure on the Scottish Rite Freemason Truman to drop the atomic bomb can be gleaned from reading the many accounts of the Illuminati in conjunction with Alonzo Hamby, *Man of the People: A Life of Harry S. Truman*, pp.327–335. Niels Bohr's involvement in Russia's atom bomb was exposed in *The Sunday Times* of 26 June 1994. The identification of Mlad as Theodore Hall was reported in *The Daily Telegraph* of 3 October 1996. The idea that Britain fought the Second World War to stop Hitler developing an atomic bomb once nuclear fission was discovered by Otto Hahn in Berlin in 1938 is a relatively novel one, but there is considerable evidence that this was the case. Thomas Powers, *Heisenberg's War: The Secret History of the German Bomb* (chapter 7, pp.67–72) recounts how British scientists feared a German uranium bomb in the first nine months of 1939. That Heisenberg deliberately delayed the German discovery of the atomic bomb is suggested in *Heisenberg's War* and in the Farm Hall tapes. That the USSR stole the German V-2 rocket design and was given some US nuclear secrets and stole the rest can be found in Des Griffin, *Descent into Slavery?* and in David Holloway, *Stalin and the Bomb*. Evidence that Eisenhower dropped Kay Summersby is in Kay Summersby Morgan, *Past Forgetting: My Love Affair with Dwight D. Eisenhower*.

A world government
I have used poetic licence in book 12 in transporting Eisenhower to Heaven, where the Holocaust is seen within the context of Paradise. Eisenhower is an eyewitness of the inauguration of the Aquarian New Age as the Cosmic Christ's Millennium. Whether we like it or not, we are progressing towards a world government. According to the American weekly newspaper *The Spotlight* of 3 April 1995 the Rockefeller-inspired world government, which was originally scheduled to begin in the year 2000, is now running two years late and is due to start in 2002. By that date two tiers of government have to be in place above the national tier in each country: a regional tier (in Europe's case, a European Parliament and single European currency) and a world tier (a world Parliament and single world currency). The main question

for our time is, what kind of New World Order is ahead? What is the nature of the coming world government (if it comes)?

Universalist conditions of Heaven in an era of world peace
I hope that there will be an era of world peace ahead that resembles Augustus's Roman Peace – the yearning for this is very strong at present, although nationalists still criticise "liberal internationalists" quite violently – but this depends on the right kind of world government being formed early in the new millennium: one that tries to bring the Universalist conditions of Heaven down to earth by redistributing food and the world's resources, not one that replicates the Illuminatist conditions of Hell with Malthusian population reduction (as seen in Cambodia and Rwanda) on a huge scale.

Light triumphing over Darkness, harmony over conflict
I have shown the democratic vision of the Light triumphing over the totalitarian nightmare of Darkness, and I have trusted my vision that our leaders will put our highest hopes into practice rather than our worst fears: that the Czar of the coming world government, our Overlord, will be a goody and not a baddy, a follower of Christ and not a follower of Satan. For a full view of the significance of the workings of the Light in philosophy and history, see my revival of metaphysics, *The Universe and the Light*, and my fuller cultural history, *The Fire and the Stones*. For a detailed account of the experience of the Light, see my autobiography *A Mystic Way*, pp.195–200. [See Appendix 1, pp.437–447] For a clear contrast between this mystic, Illuminative vision and the false Light of Satan and the Illuminati, see Texe Marrs, *Dark Majesty: The Secret Brotherhood and the Magic of a Thousand Points of Light*.

I have seen Hitler, Stalin and Roosevelt as being manipulated by American-European internationalist forces that seek world domination. My Aeneas, Eisenhower, who is in charge of the war, has to work within these forces as he tries to create a more decent world, and the struggle between good and evil, Light and Darkness, in both war and peace straddles Europe and America: I have set *Overlord* in practically every European country and in the US, and out of the temporary triumph of Darkness in Auschwitz comes a Paradisal, millennial vision of Light in America. I maintain that I have a European-American sensibility, and I have sought to relate the most important European-American event of the 20th century, behind which lurks the entire Christian-Luciferian cultural and intellectual conflict of the 20th century, to the divine order behind and within the universe. My concern with conflict and harmony has preoccupied the likes of Michelangelo and Tolstoy before me.

Reconciliation of genocidal Hell and visions of Paradise, and of Romantic and Classical styles
In this work, the first poetic epic in the English language since 1666, I have described the fall of a modern Troy before contemporary engines of war, and I have shown how the Holocaust happened in terms of occult belief-systems. I have expressed the tension in my being between the West's worst nightmare and its highest hope, between a genocidal Hell and an angelic Paradise. I have tried to express the unitive vision in relation to contemporary world history, seeing the Light as the measure of human affairs. My Eisenhower is the Western figure who most determined the conditions, pace and outcome of the Second World War, the establishment of peace and the spreading of the democratic American way of life throughout the world, and choosing him as the heir to Aeneas (or Octavian, on whom Aeneas was based) and following his progress through illumination to a vision of Paradise and a benevolent New World Order, has enabled me to combine realism with the visionary and mystic traditions and to achieve that blend of Romantic and Classical styles (the dynamic and harmonious) which I call New Baroque – with what success others must judge.

23 November 1996

14

The Tragedy of Prince Tudor

A Nightmare

Preface to the 1999 Edition of *The Tragedy of Prince Tudor*

Revival of unnaturalistic verse drama
I have long held the view that there should be a revival of verse drama
to create a new unnaturalistic contemporary theatre. Naturalism is
limiting with its realistic settings, and conveys a social view of people
in naturalistic, mundane language. The unnaturalistic verse drama of
Sophocles or Shakespeare is liberating in its settings and heightened
language: a dramatist can set a scene literally anywhere (on the Falaise
battlefield or Luneburg Heath, as I discovered in my last two-part
verse drama about General Montgomery, *The Warlords*) and can use
imaginative language with verbal pictures, evocative comparisons
and Marlovian rodomontade. Soliloquies carry the audience behind
the social surface deep within the soul of the characters, who reveal
a universal dimension as we become party to their inner thoughts.
Unnaturalistic verse drama on a contemporary historical theme is
Universalist as characters can be connected through their inner life to
the central force of the universe, as Sophocles' Oedipus is to Fate and
Shakespeare's sovereign Henry V, who championed the autonomy of
the soul, is to God.

A new unnaturalistic verse drama looks back to the plays of
Sophocles, Shakespeare and Marlowe, and to the plays of Ben Jonson,
Webster and Middleton, which flourished before c.1640. The Civil War
closed the theatres and when they opened Restoration comedy was
in vogue. The only unnaturalistic verse plays in the Shakespearian
tradition since c.1640 are Dryden's *All for Love* (1677) and Eliot's *Murder
in the Cathedral* (1935). I exclude the plays of Shelley, Byron, Yeats
and Auden, which are more poetic than dramatic; and the plays of
Christopher Fry, who has recently acknowledged that he did not write
true verse. (The realistic plays Eliot wrote after *Murder in the Cathedral*
must also be disqualified.) A contemporary verse drama embodying
the Elizabethan tradition of eschewing realistic sets can be as topical
today as was the drama of Shakespeare and his contemporaries, who
were "modern" in their day.

National sovereignty and world government
The idea for *Prince Tudor* came to me during the spring of 1998, when a number of events – in Britain, Europe, the US and the Middle East – impinged themselves on my consciousness simultaneously and I saw that they were all interconnected and could not be understood in isolation (a Universalist view of contemporary history). Events involving Britain in particular raised the question of the relationship between national sovereignty and the coming world government, a preoccupation in *The Warlords*. Shakespeare wrote some of his greatest plays as acts of political will – to warn Elizabeth I against the manoeuvrings, machinations and plots of the Cecils, who consequently made life difficult for him (if we accept one reading *of Hamlet*). At one level *Prince Tudor* is a warning against the impending break-up of the United Kingdom by hostile international forces. By showing the Prince as a man who grasps the danger and refuses to collaborate with the modernisers who seek to bring about the break-up on behalf of the world government, the play elevates the Prince into a national hero and presents his reaction to the national predicament in heroic terms. The Prince's own predicament and dilemma echo Hamlet's, and like Hamlet he feigns madness – to preserve British sovereignty.

Three sovereignties under attack, and the splitting-up of the UK
Sovereignty exists on different levels. There is the sovereignty of a nation (in the sense that a nation's independence guarantees power over its own destiny without interference from other nations); there is the sovereignty of the monarch (in the sense that the monarch has supreme power within the nation without interference from subjects within the realm), which is traditionally derived from God by the divine right of kings; and there is the sovereignty of the soul (in the sense that the soul has autonomy and self-governing independence without interference from the State or any of its bodies). All three sovereignties are under attack today. The United Kingdom may not be a nation-state much longer, but may be split into four states within the European Union, one of which (England) may be fragmented into nine Euro-regions. The United Kingdom may therefore become twelve mini-states.* The Crown may lose its constitutional power to dismiss a government. And when its existence is not denied, the soul is disregarded by shallow governments which erode people's individual choice and the private control they exercise over their lives. Not since the Civil War has there been a more urgent time in our history to focus on the threefold, interconnected concept of sovereignty.

Benevolent and malevolent world government
In our time the advantages and disadvantages of world government need to be aired. A benevolent world government can abolish war, starvation and much disease. A malevolent world government using Stalin's or Hitler's concentration-camp methods would be a nightmare. The Western and Pacific countries are seeking to establish a world government, but at present it is divided. We hear little about it as it operates in the shadows through its proxies, the Presidents and Prime Ministers who, it is said, owe their appointments to their willingness to go along with its transnational aims. Never since Augustus's world rule has there been a more urgent time in Western history to focus on the quality and attitudes of the world government that is being mooted.

Topical allusions and universal theme
Some of English Literature's best works have contained allusions to contemporary events. Shakespeare's *Hamlet*, for example, contains no fewer than 81 topical allusions out of the 593 allusions in 25 Shakespeare plays listed by Admiral Holland in *Shakespeare, Oxford and Elizabethan Times*. When specific names are referred to in plays they date quickly, as in John Osborne's *Look Back in Anger*. When the allusions are incorporated into the imaginative framework of a play, they do not date in the same way. The 81 topical allusions have not dated *Hamlet* but have served to give a universal theme added resonance.

An artist is a maker of an artefact, a work of beauty, regardless of whether he makes a picture, sculpture, symphony, poem, short story or play. As an artist I am a weaver of dreams, and *Prince Tudor* is intended to stand outside our mercantile time as does an intricately woven silk tapestry of a unicorn – or like Eliot's Chinese jar or Keats' Grecian urn. I have woven a pattern, and we follow a Prince concerned about the impending dwindling of the Kingdom he expected he would one day rule, and we see how the paradigm of the inexorably divided American-European world government works, and how Presidents and Prime Ministers have apparently acted as its pawns. His wife is a victim of its machinations, and there are references to events in the US and Iraq. But any topical allusions are as incidental to the imaginative universal theme as are the 81 topical allusions in *Hamlet*.

16 July 1998

*A plan to split the UK into twelve mini-states was leaked to NH from within the Suffolk County Council, and he questioned the former British Prime Minister, Sir John Major, about it. See p.175 for details.

15

The One and the Many

Universalism and the Vision of Unity

Preface

The Presocratic source of Western philosophy
At the beginning of the 20th century a second scientific revolution was set in motion with Einstein's Relativity theory and the discovery of quantum mechanics. This new physics influenced the philosophy of the day, and found its way into the work of Bergson (the philosopher of Vitalism), Whitehead, Husserl, T.E. Hulme and others. In the metaphysical tradition of Plato, Leibniz and Kant, they attempted to create models of Reality by which every element of our experience could be interpreted. After 1910 this process was curtailed by the ascendancy of the Vienna Circle whose logical positivism and linguistic analysis insisted that metaphysical principles must be verified. I have endeavoured to retrieve the Vitalist tradition and return to the source of Western philosophy, to its Presocratic origins: Heracleitus's Fire and (Vitalist) flux, and Parmenides' One.

The vision of the One
The vision of the One has inspired all the deepest philosophers, poets and mystics in all cultures. According to this vision the universe is fundamentally One not only in terms of spatial area – it is a Whole, the aggregate of its parts, just as a forest is the aggregate of all the individual trees within it – but also in terms of its originating principle. According to the vision, the universe originated in and emerged from one seed, Dante's "infinitesimal point", the "singularity" of modern cosmologists. Whereas the holistic view of the Whole's spatial "area" is often as Materialistic as the opposite, reductionist view of its parts, the view of an "origin" beyond physics is only metaphysical. All the multiplicity, the manifold phenomena within Nature and the cosmos, the many, originated in and emerged from the One which is beyond physics and whose manifest ingredient and texture it shares.

The One principle as the Fire or Light, and a Metaphysical Revolution
According to the vision, this One principle is the Fire or Light, the metaphysical principle which permeates the universe it produced

and which can be known within as Inner Light in the experience of illumination. This One principle has inspired the stone temples of past tradition, much of which is buried under the Materialistic brambles and undergrowth of recent times. It is best approached through present experience, for which there is no substitute. The focus for philosophers, poets and mystics must therefore be on the metaphysical universe in which they operate, and which needs to be described. Such a description requires a Metaphysical Revolution in philosophy to scythe away 85 years of humanism, scepticism and Materialism that have obscured an approach to the One just as jungle and low cloud obscure the peak of a high mountain and the sun. The purpose of the Metaphysical Revolution is to clear the jungle so that what is – both above and below – can be truly seen. Part One of this book begins on this process.

Universalism, a new metaphysical philosophy
A new metaphysical philosophy is needed, and to this end I have been developing Universalism throughout the 1990s. My philosophy of Universalism sees and describes the universe as a Whole which has originated in the One metaphysical principle of the Fire or Light. Universalism starts with the premise of Oneness and explores the consequences of Oneness in all disciplines – most notably in physics, history, philosophy and literature. Each attempt to define Universalism is like an expedition into the jungle round Angkor Wat in Cambodia, and each attempt brings back more information about the stones between the tree-roots, some damaged by iconoclastic occupiers, rationalistic, Materialistic Khmers Rouges. A new metaphysical philosophy has to be hewn out of the jungle of humanism, scepticism and Materialism before a cleared view can be presented to the world, a coherent, self-consistent and symmetrical philosophy like the main temple at Angkor Wat standing in a clearing open to the sun. Part Two of this book represents further probes and further clearing of the ground in preparation for a full revelation of the new philosophy. [See Preface 29, *The New Philosophy of Universalism*.]

Vision of the One, Fire or Light as the metaphysical sap of civilisations and cultures
A metaphysical approach has a huge effect on civilisation and culture. Cultures deprived of metaphysical sap are like gardens of brittle, etiolated trees and flowers. Our culture is one-dimensional – Materialistic – and following the deaths of Eliot, Jung and Toynbee has almost entirely lost contact with its metaphysical roots, its origin.

The waste land has extended. My mission is to redeem the waste land, and the vision of the metaphysical Fire or Light can do this by bringing about a Revolution in philosophy and culture and starting a new mystical direction in poetry and literature. At a time when a world government is looming and all cultures are drawing together into one globalist civilisation, it is important that a coming common culture should be "origin"-based (based on the metaphysical One Fire or Light, which is common to all cultures) rather than spatial-"area"-based (based on a shallow one-dimensional, materialistic multiculturalism that has no rootedness and merely weakens each regional culture's traditional energy). In short, the coming common culture should be Fire-based rather than money-based. Part Three of this work makes a start on redeeming the waste land of our culture by clearing it like a dynamic gardener tackling the back-breaking task of creating order and symmetry where Nature, out of control, has left a jungle.

The One metaphysical universe and the multiplicity of materialistic culture
The aim of this book is to leave the reader with an understanding of the metaphysical universe in which he or she lives; of the need for physics, philosophy, history and literature to describe it accurately; and of the importance of transforming our arid, humanistic, sceptical, Materialistic culture in which souls too readily wither and atrophy. In short, I call for a Revolution in all disciplines to hew a track through the jungle of multiplicity towards the life-saving One.

August 1998

16

Wheeling Bats and a Harvest Moon

Introductory Note

Belief, harmony and acceptance
These 209 mini-stories were written between 1982 and 1991, and represent volume 3 of my *Collected Short Stories*. The stories in the first volume, *A Spade Fresh with Mud*, examined the horror of the Materialist position and searched for meaning. The theme of the stories in the second volume, *A Smell of Leaves and Summer*, was knowledge of spiritual Reality. These stories focus on belief, harmony and acceptance. My work – in poetry, verse drama, diaries and autobiography as well as short stories – redeems the Waste Land, and by revealing people in their beliefs, their sense of harmony and their tranquillity I hope to indicate the positive values by which it is possible to live.

Paintings of moments: people like bats, the Light like a harvest moon
These stories are paintings of moments, like Metaphysical poems. Like a painting by Holbein they squeeze a situation for its significant detail and symbolism. People move back and forth in their everyday lives like bats, but never far away is the Light which hangs above them like a harvest moon. Our lives are lived against everyday social situations, but now and again our Being is revealed and we relate to the enduring One.

Images that reveal universal truth
Each story is a kind of meditation, a reflection on an aspect of life and its teeming vitality. The art is in the economy, the balance between the fresh, concrete everyday world and the eternal, and in the logic of the images which culminates in perception or revelation. My method is akin to Holbein's method in *The Ambassadors* (1533) in which two French ambassadors, one ecclesiastical and one secular, stand in their contemporary dress and milieu, which is highly significant – they are on Westminster Abbey's hidden high altar pavement, the mystical heart of the English Church – on the very day Henry VIII broke away from the Church of Rome. All the literal and symbolic details of the painting combine to give a sense of unease at the impending division of Christendom. Chaucer uses a similar method in his *General Prologue*, in which a Prioress wears a bracelet with a secular message (*Amor*

vincit omnia) and a pleated wimple to attract men when she should be wearing a habit that symbolises separation from the world and the life of prayer. Just as the artistic eye of a Holbein or a Chaucer reveals both the particular and the universal truth of a situation, so these mini-stories use vivid images to suggest truths that reverberate beyond and transcend the disquieting or serene events being described.

1 September 1998

17

The Warm Glow of the Monastery Courtyard

Introductory Note

Homecoming and Reality

These 181 mini-stories comprise volume 4 of my *Collected Short Stories*. They were written between 1991 and 1998 and they bring my tally of mini-stories to 750. The stories in the first volume, *A Spade Fresh with Mud*, state the horror of the Materialist outlook and seek meaning. The stories in the second volume, *A Smell of Leaves and Summer*, emphasise spiritual Reality. The stories in the third volume, *Wheeling Bats and a Harvest Moon*, examine people in terms of their beliefs and focus on harmony and acceptance. These stories carry forward the positive vision by emphasising homecoming and Reality.

In all my stories, what happens in the moment – and I catch moments like a painter – is somehow related to the Being that lurks behind Existence, which peeps through into human consciousness in moments of great awareness. We live our everyday, social lives largely in forgetfulness of the universe which is their context – forgetfulness of Being – until awareness of death reminds us of Reality. In my vision, life and death are in stark contrast, but both are part of a greater unity which reconciles all opposites and contradictions.

Revelations of the One Light, Truth

Very few stories (or novels, plays and poems) these days present human beings in relation to the One Light. My stories show a universe in which a Seeker finds himself as an exile in the everyday social world of existence, from which he feels alienated. At first his feeling that he does not belong causes him acute distress. Eventually, through perceptions and revelations that light up his soul, he glimpses Truth and begins the journey back to Reality. He overcomes his misery and his return feels like a homecoming. This is to some extent a Gnostic view of existence; it is certainly a mystic view that Universalists recognise.·

A beneficent universe and the Universalist vision

These stories paint a universe that seems indifferent to human beings but which, when perceived truly, is in fact beneficent. And so, despite their closeness at times to despair, these are optimistic stories. In the

Universalist vision optimism and tranquillity ultimately triumph over nihilism and despair.

1 November 1998

18

The Syndicate

The Story of the Coming World Government

Prologue

The Queen of England is alleged to have told her butler Paul Burrell a few months after Princess Diana's death in a car crash, "Be careful. There are powers at work in this country about which we have no knowledge." Mis-reporting? Or is she wrong? Or could it be true? The theme of this book is that it is.

Currents determine events and patterns
The history and current affairs we are taught in schools, read in the newspapers and books, tends to focus on public figures – kings, prime ministers, nations. It highlights the events that are most visible. But there are currents that determine these events, and figures hidden from the public eye that move them. It can be hard to discern these figures, and the sequence of events can be hard to unravel.

It's hard enough to unravel the events in front of our noses. Did Iraq for instance have weapons of mass destruction or not? You might think that with all the modern technology at the disposal of Western governments, down to satellites that can spot cigarette packets, there could be little room for doubt. If our governments can get it so wrong, what chance do we have? Who can we trust? What can we believe? It's easy to lose our bearings and believe any conspiracy theory. The opposite is equally true; it's easy to believe what the government says, and everything is open and above-board. I believe the answer is to look at the broader picture, to look at patterns over decades rather than single events.

Sudden appearance of terror
Many of the conclusions here are tentative. They may sound impossible. But then many things do without the benefit of hindsight. Who would have guessed in 1930 that the following decade would see the attempt to create a New World Order involving the extermination of most of Europe's Jews and the overall deaths of 70 million? Who would have guessed in 2000 that the following year would see the politics of the West dominated by a war against terror, with troops now in

Afghanistan and Iraq? Who is really behind this terror? How has it suddenly appeared, with such vigour and success, seemingly from nowhere?

Pattern behind recent events: drive to a world government
There is a pattern behind recent events which I attempt to uncover. The overall explanation is that these events are not random, not driven by individual acts of evil. They are the result of a gradual, inexorable drive on the behalf of certain parties to a world government. The dreams of past empires are not dead, but very much alive. The drive to world government is not a past fad, limited only by the lack of knowledge of how big the world is and the ability to get around it all, but present today. It is not the fantasy of alien cultures, of fundamentalists of different hues, but has been slipped into our own democracies by people and organisations we've never really understood were there in our midst.

These dreams have driven the creation of the United States as well as the European Empires. They are behind the push to a united Europe, and many of the recent events in the Middle East. They will be realised, if we let it happen, in a United States of the World, a world government. With modern communications, in a small planet, this is inevitable. The question is whether this world government is going to work for the good of everyone, coming from a universalist, global democratic perspective, or whether it's going to be run in the interests of the few. This is the key question we face over the coming decades.

Evidence for the Syndicate
In covering so much ground in one book I realise I often make assumptions and judgements that may seem questionable, particularly in the case of recent events. As in any court of law, some of the evidence for the Syndicate and its actions will be less than satisfactory – circumstantial, hearsay and inadmissible. But a judgement has to be made. Otherwise the twenty-first century could prove even more violent than the twentieth. Wisdom with hindsight is easy, but too late for many. I leave it to you to decide.

19

The Secret History of the West

The Influence of Secret Organisations on Western History from the Renaissance to the 20th Century

Preface

The influence of secret organisations through revolutions from 1453
This is the first major study of the influence of secret organisations on Western history – through its main revolutions. It explains the revolutions in terms of secret societies, situations and influences that have hitherto been unexpressed, hidden, "secret". It relates revolutions to the activities of factions within Freemasonry and of families such as the Rothschilds, and therefore narrates "a secret history of the West." In drawing together much new material this study is ground-breaking. It prepares the way for the book's companion volume, *The Syndicate: The Story of the Coming World Government* (published in October 2004), which carries the story forward from 1900 to our own day.

Four-part revolutionary dynamic: from occult Utopian vision to massacres
In the course of charting the activities of the secret organisations, the book offers a chronological narrative of all the revolutions from the Renaissance (which began in 1453) to the Russian Revolution. It covers the exploits of all the legendary revolutionaries such as Robespierre and Lenin. It shows how Utopian visions of ideal societies end in massacres and guillotinings, and is therefore something of a cautionary tale. I present each revolution in terms of a completely new and original four-part revolutionary dynamic. An idealist has an occult vision, which others state in intellectual terms. This becomes corrupted by a political regime, and results in physical suppression (such as Stalin's purge). The Summary at the end of each chapter includes tables summarising this dynamic as it applies to each revolution.

Revolutions within a tide of world revolution
The book sees all the secretly-inspired revolutions as waves within a tide of world revolution that has reached high-water mark in the world government which is being established in our own time. It will therefore help you understand the roots of the New World Order Revolution, which I have dealt with separately in *The Syndicate*.

The cultural map of Europe and the hidden hand
A Western man of letters focuses on the cultural map of Europe and the way events such as revolutions have affected the health of European culture. For me there has been a personal fascination in considering this material, for poets from Sidney to Yeats, playwrights from Marlowe to Shaw and writers from Ficino to Dostoevsky have written works coloured by secret organisations. In particular, in my capacity as an epic poet (of *Overlord*, which draws on secret history) I have been very interested in the way Milton based Satan on Cromwell, whom he knew, and wrote admiringly of revolution, as did Blake and Wordsworth. Many writers have performed the will of secret organisations as devotedly as revolutionary activists, and it has been a joy to fix their attitudes within the secret history of the West so that their true worth can be assessed and our grasp of the crisis facing European culture can be advanced. While such poets, playwrights and writers can be understood in terms of their dealings with secret organisations, the healthiest European culture is to be found in those poets, playwrights and writers who have stood apart from, and resisted, the Freemasonic hidden hand.

March 2005

20

The Light of Civilization

How the Vision of God has inspired all the Great Civilizations

Preface

Religion: the soul opening to God as Light
Religion is about more than hymns and prayers, the outer forms and rituals you will find in any church, temple or mosque. It is fundamentally about the inner experience of the soul unfolding to God, which the outer forms and rituals are designed to encourage. And how is God characterised? There is a large body of opinion, accumulated over the centuries, that God is Light and is experienced as Light, in inner illumination. Different religions interpret the experience in different ways, but there is much evidence that all who open to God as Light are having essentially the same experience. In fact, for many centuries religion has been based on the experience of the Light, although today the Light is not as well-known as it was in the past.

Religions are central to civilisations
Religions are very important to history. At school we were taught a history of monarchs and generals, and today many people associate religions with wars: Catholics and Protestants in Northern Ireland, bin Laden's Islam and Judaism/Christendom. In fact, history is about more than *élites* and wars. In certain times civilisation flourishes and is expressed in the arts: great painting, sculpture, literature and music. Much of the great art – civilisation – has been inspired by a particular religion. A moment's thought about the world's main geographical areas suggests Western art's indebtedness to Christianity and Eastern art's indebtedness to the Buddha and other deities. Religion is the basis for civilisation, and is itself based on the experience of the Light. The Light is therefore extremely important to civilisation. Is it also important to the history of geographical regions? Can the illumined – the mystics of the great religions – be as important to the sweep of history as kings and wars?

God as Light dominates religions
That is the theme of this book – that the (today) little-known experience

of the Light, which was once universally known, is fundamental to religion and may be crucial to the history of the world's regions. Recorded history began c.3500–3000BC. As we recount the tradition of the Light from earliest times and advance towards the present, we find certain local traditions of the Light dominate religions and through them play a part in history.

A Grand Unified Theory of World History and Religion
This book should be read in conjunction with its companion volume, *The Rise and Fall of Civilizations*, which is based on the premiss established at the end of this book. The two books together offer a Grand Unified Theory of World History and Religion.

Universal history: Universalism and nation-state nationalism
Looking at all the world's history as one field is called universal history. Universal history regards mankind as a single world-society and is to be contrasted with local national histories. Universalism is a way of looking that embraces all mankind, and is to be contrasted with nation-state nationalism. Universalism incorporates 'universal' ("belonging to or done by all persons") and 'universe' ("all existing things, the whole creation and the Creator; all mankind"). Religious Universalists have held that all mankind will eventually be saved, and Universalist historians focus on the history of all mankind in relation to the universe and God ("the whole creation and the Creator"). The new Universalism holds that mankind's experience of a universal God perceived or known as the Light is central to all religions and historical traditions, and to civilisation and civilisations.

The personal basis for my Universalism
The personal basis for my Universalism can be found in my 45-year-long quest to understand our time, the Age and the pattern underlying world events. This quest through inner experience, cultures and history took me through sceptical Oxford to the Islamic Middle East, where I lived in Baghdad and visited Babylon and the ziggurats, Jerusalem and Qumran. It was in a plane between Baghdad and Basra, high above Ur, that I received and scribbled down the words "life cycle" and first pondered the rise and fall (life cycle) of civilisations. My quest took me to the Far East, where I absorbed the wisdom of the East while spending four years as a Professor in Japan. There I taught a year's course on Gibbon, Spengler and Toynbee to the postgraduate students, and first glimpsed a fourth way of approaching Western history, which finds its basis in this work. From Japan I visited China (where in March 1966 I

was the first to discover the Cultural Revolution) and later the USSR, India and many Eastern cultural sites, such as Angkor Wat. I absorbed South-East Asian Mahayana Buddhism, having already experienced Japanese Zen in Kitakamakura.

My quest then took me to Libya for two years (during which I was an eyewitness of the 1969 Gaddafi Revolution). From there I visited Egypt and pondered on the Great Pyramid and the Valley of the Kings. Back in London in the autumn of 1971 I experienced the most intense two months of my life. [See Appendix 1, pp.437–447.] The development is recorded in my poems, and the full story of my personal odyssey belongs elsewhere and reticence is proper here. Suffice it to say that I now knew what was missing from the Christian religion. I grasped from personal experience that there is a void in Western Christendom and I realised that I had been on a quest round the world to find among the typhoons and baking deserts of other cultures what should have been available in my own civilisation, what used to be available in it – but what secular Christendom now largely ignores. I could have done with this book at that time, for when I cast around in libraries and bookshops to support my researches into illumination I found bits and pieces in different books, but nothing drawn together. Quite simply this sort of book just did not exist.

Theme: religions and civilisations are based on the experience of God as Light

The main theme of this book, then, is that religion is based on the experience of the Light, which is interpreted differently in different religions. And that civilisation and civilisations are based on religion. Civilisation and civilisations decline when the Light is dimmed. The implication therefore is that Western civilisation needs a recovery of the Light via its religion if it is to survive and flourish.

August 2005

21

Classical Odes
1994–2005

Poems on England, Europe and Global Theme, and of Everyday Life in the One

Preface on Classical Odes

Odes on European culture and the essence of Western civilisation
Eliot, Yeats and Pound described a crisis in European culture and the decline (as they saw it) of Western civilisation (which is an amalgam of the European and North-American civilisations). More recent poets such as Hughes have spectacularly failed to address their concerns, which I believe I have found a new way of carrying forward. I spent a long and memorable evening with Ezra Pound at Rapallo in 1970. An unfinished canto lay on his table. These odes represent the first major attempt to define the European culture and essence of Western civilisation in verse since Pound's *Cantos*.

My odes show the British Establishment in decline and on the verge of dissolving into a United States of Europe
My odes show the British Establishment as a waste land in deep decline and decay. But in spite of its disintegration it is dissolving into new forms: a United States of Europe and, in the wider scene, a world government. The feeling in these odes is in part elegiac: the feeling of Tennyson's "The old order changeth, yielding place to new" (*The Idylls of the King*, 'The Passing of Arthur', line 407). An old system, an old way of life, is collapsing, and those who have grown up within it regard the future with a mixture of hope and apprehension. These poems look both backwards and forwards, and reveal the present as a time of transition. Mostly written over ten years, they capture this transition which is experienced in many civilisations.

The vision of the four books of odes
The four Books reveal a changing, shifting perspective from England-centred, Europe-centred, globalist vision to intimations of the One. (These differing perspectives are dealt with historically in my work *The Syndicate* and its companion volume *The Secret History of the West*.)

A transitional Age and a new European and globalist identity
As an approach to our transitional Age, the scheme is innovatory. A cross between Herodotus and Pausanias, both of whom visited classical sites, and Virgil and Horace, who wrote of everyday life in the countryside, these classical odes attempt to catch the mood of our time: the general dismay at the end of the Great Britain of Churchill and Montgomery; and the hesitant fumblings for a new European and globalist identity.

The endnotes are integral
The endnotes are integral to the scheme. They make the poems accessible, conveying snippets of history that bring instant understanding to particular lines. They bring out historical precision and exactness of language and meaning. I often use words that require a knowledge of specific dictionary meanings. Some of my words carry multiple shades of meaning at the same time; they demand a precise knowledge of dictionary usage. They capture aspects of Western culture as succinctly as do some of the lines. These imaginative and, I hope, sometimes witty notes are full of gleams and insights into the mood of Western civilisation at the end of the 20th and in the early 21st centuries.

Cross-disciplinary reflective odes
I see the reflective poem as a cross-disciplinary *genre* which can accommodate within a few dozen lines perceptions from very different disciplines, such as archaeology, classical studies, history, art, literature, astronomy, physics, philosophy, biology, industry, politics and the professions of everyday life (law, accountancy, etc.). Within this volume, somewhere, perceptions relating to all disciplines can be found.

The stanza form of my odes
The reflective ode has developed over 2,500 years. I have arrived at a basic stanza, mostly consisting of 8 lines, sometimes of 10, that combines rhymed pentameters and blank verse. On occasion (where order predominates over a combination of order and disorder) each entire stanza is rhymed. I have stamped the ode with my own idiosyncratic shape, form and line.

Western civilisation's cultural heritage
My sweep through the cultural sites of England, Europe and the world of the Great Powers presents Western civilisation's cultural heritage. It opens the treasure chest of the West's cultural tradition and relates

classical sites and specific places to the eternal, timeless vision of the One, which imbues them with meaning.

*

Classical odes presenting the layered complexity of the Age
I believe with Wordsworth that a poet should "create [i.e. give some instruction in] the taste by which he is to be relished" (letter to Lady Beaumont). (The Japanese poet Junzaburo Nishiwaki, regarded by many as Japan's Eliot, told me in 1963, "You must teach the taste by which you wish to be relished.") Now I have arrived at a classical phase in my poetic output, I should make clear the sense in which I am "classical" in presenting the layered complexity of our Age. [See the Preface of each Book for the layer it contains.]

Classical odes in restrained, formally harmonious style
We should start with a dictionary definition of 'classical'.

> 'Classical', "of ancient Greek or Latin literature or art; having the form used by the ancient standard authors; based on the study of ancient Greek and Latin; following traditional principles and intended to be of permanent rather than ephemeral value; following the restrained style of classical antiquity; in or relating to a long established style".
>
> (*The Concise Oxford Dictionary*)

In other words, classical work (as in the Augustan poets Dryden, Pope and Johnson) follows a restrained style and aims to be of permanent value, like the work of the Greek and Latin authors. When it refers to a style classicism is spelt with a lower-case 'c'.

Here is an attempt to define 'Classicism' as an aesthetic movement and historical manifestation – when it refers to a historical movement Classicism is spelt with a capital 'C':

> There is no clear-cut definition of the term *Classicism*. Encyclopaedias use phrases such as *an aesthetic tendency characterised by a sense of proportion, by a balanced and stable composition, by a search for formal harmony and by understatement; imitation of ancient writers; aversion to the exceptional; well-nigh exclusive interest in psychological and moral analysis; control of sensitivity and imagination; submission to rules governing specific kinds of writing,* and so on. *Classicism* has been equated with Beauty, with Reason, with Health, with Tradition.... Classical means first and foremost ordered and controlled.... *Classicism: a way of writing or*

painting marked by serene beauty, taste, restraint, order and clarity....
The student of Classicism... must perforce cast his eyes back to antiquity,
for it is there, in Greece and Rome, that the sixteenth, seventeenth and
eighteenth centuries, to a greater or lesser degree, found their sources
of inspiration.

(Dominique Secretan, *Classicism*)

In other words, Classical works (like the architecture of some of the
palaces reflected in these poems, and Eliot's *Four Quartets*) have
proportion, balance, formal harmony, control, order, serenity, clarity
and submit to rules. We are getting warmer.

Graeco-Roman order, clarity, balance, restraint and sense of beauty
The Graeco-Roman order, clarity, balance, restraint and sense of beauty
were rediscovered during the Renaissance, which coincided with the
Reformation. The golden age of Classicism (or of Neoclassicism if
we are distinguishing European Classicism from Greek and Roman
Classicism) was in 17th-century France. There the dramatists Corneille,
Racine and Molière imitated the classical standards of the Greeks
and Romans as set out by Aristotle, Horace, Quintilian and Longinus
(which the Renaissance rediscovered).

The classical tradition in Western literature
In *The Classical Tradition*, Gilbert Highet gives a full account of the
Greek and Roman influences on Western literature. His massive study
details the classical influences on Old English poetry, e.g. Cædmon,
Cynewulf; Middle English poetry, including *The Romance of the Rose*;
Dante (Virgil); Petrarch, Boccaccio and Chaucer (Ovid, Virgil, Boethius,
Statius, Claudian, Cicero, Seneca, Juvenal); Renaissance epic including
The Faerie Queene and *Paradise Lost*; Renaissance Pastoral including
Sidney's *Arcadia*; Rabelais and Montaigne; Shakespeare (Ovid, Seneca,
Plutarch and Plautus, but also Virgil, Caesar, Livy, Lucan, Pliny and
Juvenal); the Renaissance lyric poetry, including Milton, Jonson,
Cowley, Marvell, Pope, Collins (Pindar, Horace); Swift's Battle of the
Books; Baroque tragedy, satire and prose, Baroque tragedy including
Corneille, Racine, Milton, Dryden, Johnson; Baroque satire and prose,
including Gibbon; the time of revolution, including Goethe and
Byron; the Parnassians, including Tennyson, Arnold and Browning;
the Symbolist poets and Joyce (through *Ulysses*); Pound's *Cantos*
(Virgil); and many 20th-century reinterpretations of myths, including
Camus (*The Myth of Sisyphus*). His conclusion is that there has been
a continuous stream of classical influence on Western literature. All

the poets and authors just mentioned were influenced by the classical tradition. In all can be found the characteristics I have identified: proportion, balance, control, clarity and the rest.

My Baroque poetry a blend of Classicism and Romanticism, developing into Classicism
In the past, I have seen Classicism as a movement of felt thought and the social ego, and Romanticism as a movement (as in Wordsworth and Shelley) of the soul, spirit and the One. And I have called for a poetry that is a mixture of sense and spirit, of Classicism and Romanticism. I saw this mixture of sense and spirit as "Baroque". Baroque art reveals a tension between passion and control; as Highet puts it, "beauty compressed but almost breaking the bounds of control". I should point out that the development that has taken me back towards Classicism has brought with it a profound sense of the One, which is behind all these poems.

My classical approach: felt thought in precise language and clarity
There are a number of stanzas in these classical odes that state my classical outlook and method. Here is one extract:

Why do I do this, spend my time each day
Drafting a poem, polishing it twice?
I sharpen my thought, hunt for precise words,
Make a statement in language that's concise,
Associate a place with a giant,
See poems as cross-disciplined, in rhyme,
Mix disciplines, felt thoughts, in a fresh whole,
Imaged perceptions that can withstand time....

I have a need to keen clarity, search
For new ways to relate to and present
The One in words, as some need prayers in church.
(From: 'In Cornwall: A New Renaissance')

In other words, a classical approach involves felt thought in sharp and precise, concise language. And clarity.
Here is another extract:

I write to achieve clarity of thought
About complexity, simplified view,
And to express classical clarity,

Reflect on experience digested, true,
Mind grappling with complex issues, precise,
Ending on top with exactness yet dense;
Catch the situation's total content,
Sense first, careful exact verse serving sense.

(From: 'After the Pisan Arno')

In other words, classical poetry has clarity of thought and expression, puts sense first and is on top of complex subject matter.

The ode is a form for classical reflection
I should now say something about the ode. In what sense can the ode be said to be a classical form? Consider the following:

(Odes by Marvell, Wordsworth and Keats) are reflective, philosophical, descriptive...; "generally dignified or exalted in subject, feeling and style".... Edmund Gosse takes as an ode "any strain of enthusiastic and exalted lyrical verse, directed to a fixed purpose, and dealing progressively with one dignified theme"; William Sharp suggests "that any poem finely wrought, and full of high thinking, which is of the nature of an apostrophe, or of sustained intellectual meditation on a single theme of general purport, should be classed as an ode"; Robert Shafer, who quotes both of these in his *English Ode to 1660*, requires "that a true ode be a lyrical poem, serious in tone and stately in its structure; that it be cast in the form of an address; that it be rapid in style, treating its subject with 'brevity and variety'; and that its unity be emotional in character"; and George N. Shuster, after quoting further attempts in his *English Ode from Milton to Keats*, declares that the "element of address is of no especial significance, being merely a reflection of the classical influence", and for the purposes of his treatise takes an ode to be "a lyric poem derived, either directly or indirectly, from Pindaric models"....

Many English odes belong to a tradition stemming from the work of the Classical Greek poet, Pindar, and many others belong to a tradition stemming from that of the Classical Latin poet, Horace. The two traditions can mingle, Horace himself having become something of a Pindarist. From the Romantic period onwards, we lose sight of each for long stretches; but before that period, if they are often inseparable they are rarely indistinguishable....

Horace... was a keen observer, and in his poetry he raised worldly common sense to the level of wisdom.... Political themes remain subordinate to personal themes in the earlier books of the *Odes*.... Gilbert Highet in *The Classical Tradition* distinguishes clearly between

144

the Pindaric and Horatian traditions in Western literature.... "Pindar represents the ideals of aristocracy, careless courage and the generous heart. Horace is a *bourgeois*, prizing thrift, care, caution, the virtue of self-control.... Pindar loves the choir, the festival, and the many-footed dance. Horace is a solo singer, sitting in a pleasant room or quiet garden with his lyre.... Brief, orderly, tranquil, meditative, [Horace's poems] are less intense and rhapsodical but deeper and more memorable than those of Pindar. Cool but moving, sensitive but controlled, elusive but profound, they contain more phrases of unforgettable eloquence and wisdom than any other group of lyrics in European literature."

(John D. Jump, *The Ode*, ch.1, 'Classical Models')

In other words, an ode can be reflective, philosophical, descriptive, enthusiastic, dignified, full of high thinking and a sustained intellectual meditation. The Horatian (as opposed to the Pindaric) ode is bourgeois, and its virtues are self-control and profundity. These qualities make the ode an ideal form for a classical reflection.

Visits to places, 318 odes addressed to posterity
My classical odes draw on some of the above ideas. Each visit to a specific place occurs within a social situation, and fuses place and idea in an objective mode, in which such classical ideas naturally reside. Echoes of them can be found in many of my 318 odes. In reflecting the Age in England, Europe and the world I endeavour to employ a controlled clarity and precision which are classical. All the "classical odes" are addressed to posterity.

Four books of odes like the four dimensions of Relativity theory
There are four books of classical odes. Relativity theory is an approach to the measurement and study of the three dimensions of space and one dimension of time. The first three books are spatial and examine classical culture from the perspective of England, Europe and a globalist view of the world. All these books cover the same time span. They operate within historical time. The fourth book overtly covers the same time span but focuses on everyday local life in relation to the One. As the One is timeless, the fourth book focuses on a different dimension: the Reality behind the universe.

To explain this in greater detail, Relativity theory includes the postulate that results depend on the relation of the observer to the objects measured. The relation between observer and England, observer and Europe, and observer and the world gives a different perspective in each case. The fourth book shifts the focus from time to eternity, to the One, Being, the Light, and reveals the Western universe through local everyday life, for example in a specific part of Essex. The poems in the fourth book are Universalist because they present the unity of the universe which can be apprehended in all times and places, in all three dimensions of space-time and the one dimension that connects the universe to "beyond-time", the One Being that is a classical constant. See the Preface on p.633 [of *Classical Odes*, see pp.152–153 of *Collected Prefaces*] for the poetic aesthetic behind the approach to the One.

A quartet of odes about Western everyday life
According to the *Concise Oxford Dictionary*, a 'quartet' is "a composition for four voices or instruments; any group of four". *Classical Odes* is a quartet about Western everyday life in the sense that Horace's *Odes* (also in four books) is a quartet about Roman everyday life two thousand years ago. I have been as open to Graeco-Roman life as the early rediscoverers of Ficino's Florence who gave the Renaissance its impetus.

A new classical Renaissance and rebirth of knowledge
It is possible that we are living at the beginning of a new classical Renaissance ("rebirth") as new classical masterpieces are about to be made available. Four hundred thousand previously unseen scraps of papyri filling 800 boxes were salvaged from a rubbish dump in the Graeco-Egyptian town Oxyrhynchus ("city of the sharp-nosed fish") in central Egypt at the end of the 19th century. In all of them the ink has faded, the scraps are decayed, worm-eaten and blackened, and they have been illegible. However, in April 2005 a team from Oxford University has found that placing them under infra-red light, using techniques developed from satellite imaging, can enable them to be read. The prospect ahead is that by 2015 we will be familiar with hundreds of new ancient Greek comedies, tragedies and epic poems, and new Roman works: new works by Archilochus (the 7th-century-BC Greek poet whom Horace imitated), Hesiod, Aeschylus, Sophocles, Euripides, Lucian (a lost novel), Ovid and a series of Christian gospels. Fragments retrieved and translated include a 30-line paragraph of text from Archilochus' *Elegies* and part of an epic poem about the events leading up to the Trojan War, and a fragment from a lost play by Sophocles, *Epigonoi* ("The Progeny"), about the siege of Thebes. The language of the scraps is mainly Greek, but some are in Latin, Hebrew, Coptic, Syriac, Aramaic, Arabic, Nubian and Persian.

The collection of Greek and Roman writings is the biggest hoard of classical manuscripts in the world. It is so vast that it could increase the number of Greek and Roman works in existence by 20 per cent and rewrite classical history. The Oxyrhynchus papyri alongside the recently discovered library of papyri at Herculaneum (see 'On the Rediscovered Library at Herculaneum' within these odes) gives a situation comparable to that in 1453, when Constantinople fell and hitherto unseen classical Greek and Roman texts arrived in the West from its libraries. We are in a new 1453 – a new rebirth of knowledge about the classical world, a new or second Renaissance. The hi-tech development that has made these rediscoveries possible will have a profound impact on English Literature in the 21st century.

Inspiration: Classical Odes *glimpsed whole along with* Overlord *by the Arno*

These classical odes are a *prolegomena* to this coming literary movement. For all their connection with literary antecedents, the inspiration for this work came as a blinding flash that was swiftly followed by a surge of realisation of what work lay ahead. Those few moments revealed not one but two vast works. In one thrilling vision I glimpsed my epic poem *Overlord* (which I had discussed with Ezra Pound in 1970) and *Classical Odes* as finished works while sitting by the Arno (where Dante too found inspiration) in Pisa in May 1993 (see the two poems 'By the Arno, Pisa' and 'After the Pisan Arno'), and it has taken me ten years – twelve if time spent in preparing the odes for publication is included – to complete the two works that were revealed to me in a matter of seconds. I was aware in those first few minutes that the range and scope of these two works have been missing from English literature since Ezra Pound's *Cantos* and that a new movement should start with this perception: to let the tradition and example of the ancient Greeks and Romans back into English verse, grounding it in place rather than by recreating myths, and in so doing to restore to poetry the dimension of Western civilisation that Pound and Eliot had in the early 1920s, and to let the culture of Europe back into English Literature as our participation in the new Europe requires.

Massiveness: like a range of mountains

Finally, I am aware that there is a massiveness – some would say gigantism – about this work, and, indeed, all my works. As in the case of all my works, bulk may prove daunting. I make no apologies for this. It is my hope that this work will take its place in the reader's consciousness like a peak in a range of mountains which is always there, towering in the distance, and which can be repeatedly tackled, sometimes by walks into the foothills and sometimes by climbing to the top. A climb will be like walking up Ben Nevis on foot rather than scaling the Eiger face with ropes and crampons. This work is not to be read through once and discarded; it is not intended that every poem and note should be grasped and understood at one sitting. Rather, it is meant to be permanently on the landscape of the reader's consciousness, observed and related to from a distance and returned to from time to time, different features being discovered during different visits like grassy slopes, beetling crags and foaming waterfalls. After all, the culture of Europe, from its classical origins, through the Renaissance to today, is too vast to be assimilated at one sitting.

The English soul split by Europe: letting the culture of Europe back into English literature
In my vision by the Arno I was clear that letting the culture of Europe back into English Literature should in no way deny the Tudor origins of the English tradition. The English soul has been split by Europe as much as it was split by the Civil War – and that perception is the starting-point of *Classical Odes*.

The Principle Behind the Order of these Odes

The poems appear in the order in which places were visited and poems were conceived rather than in the order in which poems were finally written with the exception of: the first two poems of Book 1, Part I, the last poem in Part II and the last two poems in Part IV (all moved for thematic reasons so that all parts begin and end with poems about Otley Hall and/or England); the first and last poems of Book 2, Part I, the last poem in Part II, the last poem in Part III and the last two poems in Part IV (all moved for thematic reasons so that all parts begin and end with poems about ruin, loss of empire, death and immortality); the first and last poems in Book 3, Part I (both moved for thematic reasons so that all parts begin and end with poems about world administration and the changes it will bring); and the first and last poems of Book 4, Part I, the first and last poems of Part II and the first poem of Part III (all moved for thematic reasons so that all parts begin and end with poems about the Western universe and the One).

The full chronological order in which all the poems in all four Books were written appears at the end [of *Classical Odes*].

April 2005

Prefaces to individual Books within Classical Odes

Preface to Book One
A Tudor Knot
Poems on England

Odes on the roots of Englishness and Anglo-Americanism, and the tangle in the English sensibility over Europe
A Tudor Knot goes back into England's past and explores the historical roots of Englishness and of the Anglo-American ideal and the decay of the present English Establishment, at a time when the English sensibility is in a tangle over Europe. The ideal solution may be to undo the knot: to retain a Eurosceptical position while remaining within the European Union in a clear way that satisfies everybody. So hard is it now to untie the knot that the only practical solutions are to cut it like the Gordian knot, to leave the European Union and reject Europe; or to embrace integration in a European Union, with the euro replacing the pound. As Book Two, *In Europe's Ruins*, makes clear, it would be undesirable to cut British ties with Europe because of Europe's great cultural heritage.

During my tenure of Otley Hall the Tudor knot of the knot-garden was a symbol for the One. This positive view of the knot can change our way of looking, help us to accept the tangle we are in over Europe and move forward from it to a new destiny. The artist is a leader of his nation's consciousness in every age, and it is the duty of a responsible poet today to find words that articulate this tangle in our sensibility.

Universalist odes: Classical treatment of the anguish caused by schism in the soul
My classical approach seeks an ordered, controlled, serene view of a time when there is as much of a split or schism in the English soul as there was during the Civil War. The anguish caused by this schism is experienced Romantically. The blend of a Romantic agony and a Classical treatment is Universalist, and these odes are fundamentally Universalist despite their classical style.

Opposites reconciled into harmony
A Tudor Knot and In Europe's Ruins complement each other as two opposites that, put together, are reconciled and make a harmony (rather as Blake's *Songs of Innocence* and *Songs of Experience* do).

Preface to Book Two
In Europe's Ruins
Poems on Europe: A Grand Tour

Europe's cultural heritage
In my epic *Overlord* I drew on the culture of Europe. *Overlord* is set in every European country, and in apostrophes at the beginning of each book I invoke the main European cultural figures of the past: Milton, Goethe and Dostoevsky, for example. *In Europe's Ruins* continues this process of defining Europe's culture. The poems delve into places that are associated with Europe's cultural heritage – many of them classical sites – and bring out the universal idea that they keep alive and which is relevant to European civilisation today.

Universalist odes blending realistic Classical style and sumptuous Romantic ruins
These poems treat classical locations Romantically – in the tradition of Wordsworth (in 'Tintern Abbey'), Keats, Shelley and Byron – but with a classical style that pursues order, control, restraint, clarity and balance rather than a Romantic retelling of Graeco-Roman myths (the deeds of Hyperion and Prometheus). Universalism blends Classicism and Romanticism, and focuses on what is universal, what applies to all mankind. These are Universalist poems despite their classical style.

As a mental traveller, I use the imagination to reconstruct the historical places I have visited, just as Wordsworth did when reconstructing Tintern Abbey and Shelley the Baths of Caracalla. The wealth of cultural riches to be found in Europe makes possible a new poetry of Romantic sumptuousness tempered by Classical realism, that is far removed from the drab side of our time. There has been a tradition of English poets reflecting on classical ruins in Italy: Milton, Keats, Shelley, Byron and Browning. Book Two is an addition to, and widening of, that tradition.

Poetry, history and imagination
As Book Two is a combination of poetry and history, the notes are integral to the reader's response and contain material that will illuminate the poems. Combining history and imagination brings history alive.

Metaphysical vision behind "stones"
Many of the places in these poems are the "stones" left behind by a civilisation during its growth. In *The Light of Civilization* and *The*

Rise and Fall of Civilizations I show that a civilisation grows through the energy of a metaphysical vision and creates pyramids, temples, cathedrals and mosques which have vitality, which become tourist sites, "stones", as the civilisation declines and turns secular and the energy that once surged peters out. The stones are now moribund like empty snail shells on a lawn. They are very often linked with giants; for example, the ruins of Samos will always be linked to the work of the giant Pythagoras.

Books One and Two reconciled into harmony
In Europe's Ruins reveals Europe's great cultural legacy whereas Book One, *A Tudor Knot*, dwells on Englishness and the English tradition. The two Books therefore complement each other as two opposites that, put together, are reconciled and make a harmony (rather as Blake's *Songs of Innocence* and *Songs of Experience* do).

Preface to Book Three
A Global Sway
Poems on a Global Theme

Poems on American globalism and the global vision of internationalists
A Global Sway looks beyond Europe and is principally concerned with poems about the Great Powers: America, Russia and China. It includes areas outside Europe such as Iceland, North Africa and the Middle East – notably Libya and Iraq. I have worked in both countries. There is a contrast between the troubled present and the past.

Threads running through Book Three of these odes are: America's globalism, and how it affects our perception of the world; and world administration along with the destructive effect of American globalism on peace, population and the environment.

The odes' fourfold vision and the One
A Global Sway moves on from England-centred and Europe-centred perception to the global vision of contemporary internationalists. This is a third tier in the fourfold vision of these odes. As well as having national and European identities, Europeans have a globalist identity as citizens of the world.

There are strong hints that the three geographical regions of the first three Books will pass into a metaphysical vision of the One in the fourth Book.

Preface to Book Four
The Western Universe
Poems of Everyday Life in the One

Everyday local life and the One
The Western Universe takes the odes away from the geographical regions of the first three Books – and from England-centred, Europe-centred and globalist vision – to everyday local life; they confront the One, eternity, which, in truth, has never been far away in the first three Books.

Unity is perceived through the imagination, which shapes into One
The perception of unity is the prerogative of a certain kind of poet and philosopher. Unity is perceived through the imagination, not by analytical thought (which makes distinctions and finds differences). Coleridge wrote of the "esemplastic power" of the imagination: in Greek, 'esemplastic' means "shaping into one". This shaping power brings together the world's many different phenomena and combines them, shapes them, into One, sensing that there is one principle behind all conflicts and contradictions. The imagination's shaping leads to a special form of intuitive perceiving, in which the universe is seen to be One.

The Classical poet reshapes the apparently chaotic universe into an ordered One
Through his poetic imagination, the classical poet can reshape the apparently chaotic universe that surrounds him into a structure of order and meaning by writing a poem; a model (as it were) of how things really are. The act of reshaping the universe in a poem brings heightened awareness, and in this mode of being the poet is then in a state of readiness and open to a perception of the One, which he receives back from the universe. A poet approaches the One by his classical reshaping in the poetic act and is rewarded with a glimpse – a reassurance – that the universe is in fact an ordered One with a purpose and meaning, and not chaotic and meaningless. His glimpse brings about a metamorphosis, a transformation, a turning from the everyday to a sense of a permanent and enduring Reality.

The One renews the health of a declining civilisation
The perception of the One is vital to the health of our civilisation. From the One, Light pours into Being and thence into Existence, creating the forms and phenomena of Nature and enlightening the soul of the

aware poet and alert philosopher. The vision of the One brings hope to the waste land of declining Western civilisation and offers the prospect of renewal.

The vision of the One perceives the universe as a well-ordered whole
Through the vision of the One the physical universe is perceived to be a cosmos, a well-ordered whole. This vision is approached from within the social situations of everyday life in a tiny part of the West's great territories: the Essex countryside where I grew up, the Epping Forest landscape that inspired me and nourished me; and the Cornish seaside. The soul's direct perception of the One in local and personal settings transcends the England-centred, Europe-centred and globalist regional outlooks. The resulting fourfold vision reveals the order and meaning in the multifarious universe.

The odes: three regions/dimensions of space and one of time
Just as Relativity theory studies the three dimensions of space and one dimension of time, so these odes study three spatial regions and a dimension of timelessness; and timelessness is as important to understanding the regions as time is to understanding space. In each region/dimension the observer is part of what is observed, and each region/dimension affects the perception and perspective of the observer.

22

Overlord

The Triumph of Light
An Epic Poem Based on the Events of 1944–45

Preface to One-Volume Edition of Overlord

Genesis of Overlord
It is now ten years since the first volume of *Overlord* appeared. The work was conceived in 1968, finally decided on in May 1993 and begun in June 1994. It was written piecemeal, like a serialised Dickens' novel, and came out in four consecutive volumes between 1995 and 1997. I am delighted that it can now appear in one volume and be seen as a whole, as readers have requested. The text is unchanged but I have made one or two corrections, added some large capital letters to make the rests or breaks more coherent, and have italicised foreign words.

Overlord's *roots in my childhood*
I am now clear that this work had its roots in my childhood when I lived in Churchill's constituency in the path of the V-1 and V-2 bombs. I can recall setting off with my father to walk to the Post Office after dark in March 1944 when I was four, and by the garden gate a white flash lit up the house as a string of six bombs landed in Loughton cricket field nearby, blowing out all our windows. I can see my father turn round and hurry back to the house without saying a word. At the old Oaklands School by the cricket field I was put in a Morrison shelter in the garden during daytime air raids, and I can remember lying in bed night after night from June 1944, listening for doodle-bugs and filled with dread. I can recall seeing Churchill speak at Loughton war memorial, standing next to Mrs. Churchill, during the General Election campaign of 1945, just before he left for Potsdam. I was chosen to meet Montgomery at Chigwell School in October 1953. He sat on a bench by the chapel and I asked him questions about the war, and later he spoke to us in New Hall and said, sawing the air with his right hand, "I went through the Germans at El Alamein like a knife going through butter." (See pp.844 and 784 [of *Overlord*] for references to these encounters.) Such memories, combined with my infant apprehension at being bombed, left me determined to make sense of what had happened and to find out what had brought war to my childhood skies.

Evidence for Hitler's prior knowledge of Holocaust
At this remove, the first thing to stress is that all the war scenes and discussions of Generals were accurately researched, as the individual Prefaces that follow make clear. For Heydrich's role in devising the Holocaust, and Hitler's prior knowledge of it, see Christopher Browning, *The Origins of the Final Solution: The Evolution of Nazi Jewish Policy 1939–1942*. Evidence is a problem as the files of Himmler and Heydrich were destroyed, but Browning suggests that Hitler approved the killing of the European Jews as early as, or even before, May 1941, long before the Wannsee Conference of 12 January 1942; and he reinforced his approval in August–September 1942.

A Universalist work, conflicting New World Orders
The vision of human souls and the Light is Universalist in as much as it draws on the religious experience of all cultures and all humankind, including New Age thinking. *Overlord* is nothing if not a Universalist work. Those who want to research further into this aspect of the work may like to consult my prose study, *The Light of Civilization*. The visions of conflicting New World Orders which are shown to Eisenhower are historical, contemporary and actual rather than fanciful, and the background for these, and for the references to Rockefellers, Rothschilds and the Illuminati, can be found in my prose studies, *The Syndicate*; *The Secret History of the West*; and *The Rise and Fall of Civilizations*.

I now distinguish "the Syndicate" (the network of families dynastically attempting to introduce a world government) from "the Illuminati" (the historical Order founded by Weishaupt in 1776 and its vision of world rule, with which all the families are connected), and would now write "the Syndicate" for "the Illuminati" in many places, but have not disturbed what I originally wrote.

Sources for Hitler's pact with Satan
The "occult" theme was also accurately researched. See the Prefaces for books 1–2 and 3–6 [numbers 8 and 11] on pp.94–95 and 107–108 for my sources for Hitler's pact with Satan. When I wrote *Overlord* I was not aware of Bob Rosio's *Hitler and the New Age*, which focused at some length on Hitler's initiation into Luciferianism. Quoting Dietrich Eckart's "Follow Hitler! I have initiated him into the secret doctrine, opened his centres to vision and given him the means to communicate with the powers", Rosio writes: "He established communication with Lucifer, from whom he openly coveted possession... entering into the service of Satan through a Luciferic initiation." He writes of Satan's thirst for sacrificial death:

Robert Cecil said, "The Blood of Christ was replaced by the blood of the German war dead." Their true value to Hitler was as a sacrifice to the bloodthirsty god he served. "From the Mayas to the Nazis, the shedding of blood to attract the attention of indifferent powers was the magic significance of human sacrifice."... This mentality caused Hitler to say, "Our losses never seem to be high enough."... Hitler's war in Russia illustrated his total confidence in the occult powers which owned him and his willingness to sacrifice human lives. Hitler believed that his covenant with the occult powers enabled him to control the weather. He felt that the Russian winter would melt away before him as his forces invaded Russia.... When the German offensive was halted within sight of Moscow, Hitler saw it only as a test, requiring more human sacrifice. He saw Stalingrad, however, as the true test, recognising Stalingrad as the sacred city of the ancient Aryans. He felt that no amount of human suffering or death was too high a price to pay for its conquest, that if he were faithful to Satan at Stalingrad, he would be given final victory.... The Holocaust was Hitler's fiery offering of human sacrifice to Satan, just as in the days of the heathen Amorite god, Moloch.

'Holocaust', coming from a 3rd-century Greek word 'holokaustos', means "the whole burnt", suggesting the burnt sacrificial offering of the Jews dedicated to Satan. According to Rosio, the Holocaust was a dress rehearsal for the Final Solution under the rule of the Antichrist, who is invoked as Lucifer by the New Age movement. Rosio's findings confirm my view of Hitler's pact with Satan.

Hitler's will
In the mid-1990s books were divided as to whether Hitler dictated his will before or after his wedding. In my verse play *The Warlords* (1995) I had the will *before* the wedding. In book 10 of *Overlord*, after further research and guided by narrative (as opposed to dramatic) considerations, I have the will *after* the wedding. In 2002, shortly before she died, Traudl Junge, to whom Hitler dictated his will, described in *Until the Final Hour* how the will preceded the wedding. I have stuck with what I wrote and the artistic dictates of fluent narrative. In book 11 I invoked Shakespeare as the 17th Earl of Oxford, a theme that fascinated me at the time of writing. I do not now believe that Shakespeare's works were written by the 17th Earl of Oxford – I believe they were written by William Shakespeare – but, again, I have left the text untouched.

Overlord *an American epic*
Returning to *Overlord* ten years after the first volume appeared,
I am struck by the extent to which it is an American epic. Its hero,
Eisenhower, pursues Hitler and witnesses the advent of America as
a superpower. *Overlord* is the first poetic epic to deal with America's
coming of age as a superpower – Stephen Vincent Benét's *John Brown's
Body* was about the Civil War, and sections of it are in prose. In *The
Rise and Fall of Civilizations* – and also my earlier study, *The Fire and the
Stones* – can be found the idea that epic follows closely on stage 15 of
a civilisation's 61 stages – which makes the US (currently in stage 15,
the same as the expansionist stage Rome entered which culminated in
the worldwide Roman Empire) ripe for epic now. Between 1995 and
1997 *Overlord* crept out in England in parts. It can now be seen as an
American epic, which I discussed with the American expatriate Ezra
Pound in Rapallo in 1970 [see Appendix 2, pp.498–501]. Ezra Pound
wrote: "For forty years I have schooled myself... to write an epic which
begins 'In the Dark Forest', crosses the purgatory of human error, and
ends in the light" – in the "moment of metamorphosis" which occurs
when the everyday world ("quotidien", i.e. quotidian) approximates
to the "divine or permanent world" (letter to his father, 11 April
1927). *Overlord* follows a similar path and though equally Universalist
manages to retain an American perspective.

Liberty from tyranny, Citizens of the World
The theme of liberty from tyranny has found echoes in Bush Jr's second-
term inauguration address. The visions of conflicting New World
Orders, which Eisenhower is shown, are prophetic of a development
towards world government that is happening in our own time (see
The Syndicate). Ezra Pound stated that "an epic is a poem including
history" (*ABC of Reading*). Besides being a narrative of a heroic episode
taken from history, epic defines what a human being is, and the
metaphysical motifs involving Heaven and Hell, and Christ and Satan,
and accounts of the origin and workings of the universe enabled me
to redefine a human being in terms of a metaphysical self (soul and
spirit), as a Citizen of the World. This is a perspective that would have
been familiar to Dante and in our own time to T.S. Eliot.

26 July 2005

23

Collected Poems
1958–2005

Preface to Collected Poems

The 'Introductory Note by the Poet' on pp.83–84 also appeared in this 2005 volume with the first sentence amended to: "This collection of 1,478 poems brings together the 30 volumes of my poetic output (excluding my *Classical Odes* and epic), the titles of which head each section."

These poems represent a new presentation of my *Collected Poems 1958–1993*, with many new poems and Notes added. This volume accompanies new one-volume editions of *Overlord* (my epic poem, written 1994–1996) and *Classical Odes* (1994–2005). These three volumes include all my poetic works to 2005, excluding my four verse plays that are to appear in a forthcoming volume, and this volume thus includes everything to date that is not epic or classical ode.

Themes and poetic development
Reading through these poems in 2005, I am struck by a number of perceptions. First, by how the themes of my later and more mature work can all be found in my early poems, such as 'Ode to a Prospect from a Window Frame' (1961, written when I was still an undergraduate, the prospect being across Port Meadow, Oxford), which anticipates my concerns with Truth, Light and the universe, and whose last line ("Behind each shadow reigns a glorious sun") anticipates my mature view of Reality. Secondly, by how prominent is the development from autobiographical *résumé* and reflection on the Cold War (Communism and the state of Europe) in the 1960s, through anguished suffering – the troubled Dark Night which first loomed through sudden deprivation and unstructured chaos and which led to an unhealthy focus on self which is distasteful to me now but which I have left intact as it is an essential part of the process of purgation; to illumination and a new consciousness that is serene, outward-looking, unitary and universalist, at one with the universe and the lot of mankind, which as in the 1960s has post-2001 concerns over the War against Terror (the American invasions of Afghanistan and Iraq), concerns I have dealt with fully in prose in *The Syndicate*.

Mystic Way: Dark Night and unitary consciousness
This development was a consequence of a pivotal freeing of self
from body, a turning away from youthful sense-attachments to the
spiritual life of maturity, of Light and Truth. This turning is a feature
of the traditional Mystic Way along which the soul journeys from an
awakening to detachment from sense-involvement; through suffering
and purgation; to illumination; then into a Dark Night which separates
the self from dependence on sensual desires; into unitary consciousness,
seeing all as manifestations of the One, seeing the world as One – not
as a fiefdom to be conquered and looted for a few bent on cornering
its natural resources and oil, but as a place where all mankind can live
in brotherhood.

It is a characteristic of the journey along the Mystic Way that
those lost in its "Dark Wood" and experiencing its Dark Night are
unaware of the explanation for what is happening to them and what
lies ahead; this is only grasped later when, from the serene calm of
unitary consciousness, the self can look back and understand the
detaching that suffering brought as a gift. Experiences that at the time
seemed chaotic, inexplicable, accidental and even cruel, are then seen
to be Providential, perhaps even intended in order to bring about
a development that is necessary to the self's journey and destiny.
The self can then see that the Dark Wood and Dark Night had to be
gone through to remake the self into a permanently serene, unitive
consciousness. So it was in the case of my Dark (Epping) Forest, and
those who follow my journey while in their own Dark Wood may be
encouraged to grasp that the Way does end in serenity. It is no accident
that this turning coincided with my remarriage, following which my
work increasingly reveals a selfless approach to, and vision of, the
universe. I acknowledge the infrastructure of support it provided in
making possible such a large output.

Technical innovations
I am also struck by the extent of my technical innovations in the
1960s and 1970s – compressed narrative in a sequence of images
('The Silence'), stress metre ('The Gates of Hell', 'The Pilgrim in the
Garden') and sonata, fugal and symphonic form ('The Four Seasons',
'Lighthouse', 'The Weed-Garden'); carried forward in the 1980s and
1990s into a quartet and a quintet ('Beauty and Angelhood', 'American
Liberty Quintet') – before I settled back into more traditional stanzaic
forms and metres. I am struck by how active – indeed, prolific – a poet
I was in the 1970s and 1980s. My reduced output in shorter lyrics in
the 1990s reflects the time I spent during that decade in producing

Overlord and many of the odes in *Classical Odes* (both out in separate volumes) and publishing historical and philosophical works on themes that surfaced in my pre-1990 poetry. Undoubtedly time spent on these necessary activities was at the expense of lyric poetry.

Romantic and Classical outlooks reconciled in new Baroque consciousness
Looking back, I contrast the Romantic outlook of my early works with the Classical outlook of my later works. 'The Silence' begins in the consciousness of the Romantic ego, and locates the One Light. Following the illumination chronicled in 'The Gates of Hell', some poems mix sense and spirit, and this mixture is Baroque. [See 'Preface on the New Baroque Consciousness and the Redefinition of Poetry as Classical Baroque' in Preface 2, p.9.] I am aware that in the course of these poems I begin writing from a different centre, a more unified consciousness, than when I began. This unifies the social ego, the soul and the One, and my later verse is restrained, ordered and emphasises clarity – all features of Classical writing – while still perceiving the universe in terms of the One.

Constancy of poetic aesthetic
I am struck by the constancy of my underlying poetic aesthetic. Throughout my work, from the very beginning I have used the poem as a means to order experience and to reflect the order in the universe. This underlying outlook does not change, although I progress from trying to justify suffering by relating it to the Whole; to reflecting human life (the dying men of 'The Night-Sea Crossing' and 'The Labyrinth') and Nature ('The Four Seasons' and 'The Weed-Garden'); to the One; and then to relating direct individual experience of the Light to the One ('The Fire-Flower', 'Beauty and Angelhood'). By the end, I am relating the torments in America, Afghanistan and Iraq to the One. Though billed as "political poems", these last poems are not so much political works as works expressing humanitarian concerns and relating them to the One.

A poet reshapes the universe and receives a vision of the One
As I state in the Preface to book 4 of *Classical Odes*, I believe that a poet puts himself in readiness to approach and receive the One by restructuring, reshaping, the universe in poems which are models of the One – simplified orderly versions of chaotic complexity, models that bring out the order in the cosmos – and that in this state of readiness he then receives a reassuring glimpse of the One. The best poems are models of the One, and at its best, the poem, with its cross-disciplinary

possibilities (incorporating perceptions from many disciplines such as history, philosophy, archaeology, physics, geology, astronomy etc., all within the space of a few lines), is the best way of approaching the One and of receiving the vision of the One which confirms that the universe is an ordered Whole, with meaning and purpose, and not a chaotic mess.

A developing view of the universe and the Age
I am struck by my progress from blind gropings near the beginning to mature articulation of the order within human life, Nature, the physical and metaphysical universe; the profound connection of all these; and the extent to which, in the course of revealing this connection, I have been able to catch the flavour of the Age. I am struck by my range. I of course wrote each poem individually, but I believe that when these poems are taken as a whole, they reveal a developing consciousness that reflects a developing view of the universe and Age of which it is an inextricable part. For in post-relativity thinking the observer is an inextricable part of the universe he observes.

A self in process of development
These poems, in short, reveal a process: a self in process of development, conveying a view of human life, Nature and the universe which is also in process of development; behind which the One, Being, is a fixity. It is this fixity that makes the later poems Classical; for the social ego and soul are held within a Reality that is changeless. It strikes me, however, that Heracleitus and the Presocratic Greek philosophers would be deeply sympathetic towards my view that both self and the universe is a process of flux, behind which – within which – is the Light, which Heracleitus called Fire. See the last line of 'The Laughing Philosopher': "For all is flux, but underneath – the Fire!"

All my poems are included except for Overlord and Classical Odes
These poems span 47 years, and as one would expect the self-in-process that is writing at the beginning is quite different from the self-in-process that is writing near the end. Yet that "other person" writing near the beginning is still unmistakably and identifiably "me". Consequently I have included all my poems, regardless of whether "I" am shown in a flattering or unflattering light. They were written out of conflicts, tensions and questionings that were overpowering at the time, even though some now may seem unworthy and even shaming thirty or more years later. It is important to grasp the entire sweep of the whole process; this is a collection, not a selection, of my works

not covered by *Overlord* and *Classical Odes*. Therefore the only changes I have made to previously published works involve corrections of minor typographical errors. Relevant technical Notes now appear at the beginning of each volume, and interpretative notes at the end of each of the 30 volumes.

Truth

Yeats wrote: "Man can embody truth but cannot know it." These pages represent my embodiment of Truth.

December 2005

24

Collected Verse Plays

Preface to Collected Verse Plays

Revival of unnaturalistic verse drama on the shaping of national power and the abuse of power

These four verse plays, written between 1994 and 2000 and presented together in one volume for thematic comparison, develop my preoccupation with the forces that shape national power and with the abuse of power. They represent my revival of verse drama in our time – single-handed in the sense that I operated in isolation – following the efforts of Eliot, Auden and Fry between the 1930s and 1950s. They were written as a kind of sideline while I was deeply engaged in producing books in other disciplines and very busy.

Looking back now, I am struck by the scale of what I was trying to do in my unnaturalistic settings. To put the last year of the Second World War on stage in two Parts with 219 speaking parts (and four choruses of four, i.e. 235 characters in all)* – even the abridged version has a cast of 94 – and then to put the entire English Civil War and Puritan Revolution with a cast of 38, and 31 or more minor parts – what did I think I was doing? I was clearly not writing with budgets in mind. (The ideal budget for actors' wages is a cast of two.) Like Goethe in *Faust*, Parts 1 and 2, I was trying to catch a historical trend that required an epic sweep: the shift from Britain to the United States as ruler of the world stage and the marginalising of Britain that took place in 1944/5, the consequences of which have shaped our own time; and the degeneration of the libertarian Cromwellian vision into regicide (which is called tyrannicide) in 1648/1649, echoes of which can be found in the Blair government's reform of the Lords in the UK in our own day, and will be found in future British governments forced to implement the world-government agenda.

These plays develop my preoccupation with the forces that shape national power, and represent different treatments of the abuse of power. Whereas Montgomery in the two Parts of *The Warlords* sees his nation lose power to a world government-in-waiting that wants Stalin to reach Berlin first, and Prince Tudor observes with dismay the break-up of the kingdom whose crown he is waiting to inherit, my latest two historical plays take the exploration of the abuse of power into new areas. Augustus, who rules the Roman world, banishes Ovid to silence his criticisms – a fate that can befall any artist who stands up to supreme power. Cromwell, on the other hand, rises to supreme power as Protector – in effect, Augustan dictator – of England, Scotland and Ireland with the help of international interests keen to replace Charles I. With Augustus and Cromwell, the focus shifts from the victims of supreme power to the perpetrator. The four victims in the four verse plays – Montgomery, Prince Tudor, Ovid and Charles I – are all defeated by a world government which is hidden in the case of Montgomery, Prince Tudor and Charles I and naked in the case of Ovid.

Plays on the theme of world government
In fact, these four plays explore one theme: world government, the imminent prospect of which I have investigated very fully in *The Syndicate* (published in 2004). In *The Warlords* (written in 1994/5) Montgomery is blocked by Eisenhower's Rockefellerite world-government superiors from taking Berlin as they want Stalin to found an East-European empire there. In *Prince Tudor* (written in 1998) the two factions of the world government are set to abolish the British monarchy and the Prince is confronted with having no kingdom to rule – a predicament that will become a reality if the new European constitution is ratified by four-fifths of the EU's member nation-states for this would replace all member nation-states by a superstate under which they would all be substates. In *Ovid Banished* (written in 1998/1999) Augustus, the leader of the world government of the day, banishes Ovid, the poet, for knowing too much about a plot against his rule and (arguably) for questioning his policy towards the barbarians. Ovid, the (partly inadvertently) dissident artist, has to live among non-Latin-speaking barbarians for the rest of his life. In *The Rise of Oliver Cromwell* (written in 2000), the world-government Rosicrucians and Jews of Amsterdam fund Cromwell's army in return for a pledge to kill Charles I – so that the Jews can return to England from which they had been banned since their expulsion in 1290. (See my book *The Secret History of the West*, ch.2 for full details and for the letters between Mulheim Synagogue and Cromwell.) Again, there is an attack on the integrity of the nation-state, which has been mirrored by Cromwellian New Labour today. One way or another, world-government thinking defeats an English General, an English Prince, a Roman poet and an English King.

Plots and counter-plots
All four plays deal with plots or conspiracies, and counter-plots: in *The Warlords* the world-government Syndicate's 1944–1945 plot to allow

Stalin to take Berlin and advance towards world government via the Yalta negotiations, and the resistance of Montgomery and Churchill; in *Prince Tudor* a world-government Syndicate plot to replace the British monarchy and sovereignty with a European republic and split England into smaller states within a United States of Europe, and a counter-plot to defend the monarchy by eliminating a threat; in *Ovid Banished* an imperial world-government plot to reintroduce morality in Rome and a counter-plot to replace the Claudian imperial line with the Julian line; and in *The Rise of Oliver Cromwell* an internationalist, potential world-government plot between Cromwell and Dutch Rosicrucians to overthrow the king, and Charles I's resistance and counter-plot to escape.

Research into secretive, shadowy world government, the most important issue of our time

All four plays are based on meticulous research and are factually accurate. They therefore dovetail with *The Syndicate* and its companion volume *The Secret History of the West* and flesh out a picture of a secretive, shadowy world government that intrigues against the West, swallows its sovereign independence, censors artists and breaks down national barriers. Within the tentacles of world government individuals such as Montgomery, Prince Tudor, Ovid and Charles I put up heroic resistance but barely understand the forces that crush and defeat them.

This issue is the most important issue of our time, yet my fellow-writers have totally ignored it. Indeed, most are unaware of it. A friend (Kingsley Shorter) wrote to me in 1966 of our time at Oxford, "I see now that you were perhaps fighting for your life when most of us didn't even know there was a war on." History has repeated itself – the same could be said of today.

My verse

As to the technical side, I began *The Warlords* before writing my epic *Overlord*. *Overlord* is in strict iambic pentameters. *The Warlords* allows anapaests and dactyls, even paeans (4-syllable feet), and the verse is consequently loose. The act of writing *The Warlords* tautened my verse so that it was more classical by the time I came to *Overlord*. The last three plays reflect this tautening. In all the four verse plays I have sought to use verse, including dramatic monologue and rodomontade, to catch characters making existential decisions and choices in unnaturalistic settings, appealing to the imagination, evoking the scenery in words as the settings are not realistic.

Historical unnaturalistic verse plays as analogies for contemporary political themes, their words create scenic effects
Two of these plays are contemporary – *Prince Tudor* and *The Warlords*, which is set in my lifetime but is further back in time – and two are clearly historical. In a sense, all four plays are historical verse plays. The *genre* of the historical verse play presents historical subject matter to draw an analogy, and make a point, about a contemporary political theme. This *genre* was perfected by Shakespeare, who commented on contemporary events through such historical plays as *Henry IV*, Parts 1 and 2, *Richard II*, *Julius Caesar*, and *Hamlet*. Shakespeare has to be the model for a contemporary revival of the verse play. In all his plays Shakespeare was able to achieve his range and depth by foregoing realistic scenery and appealing to the imagination to supply scenic details by suggesting them through his words. Shakespeare invited the audience to imagine the scenery and surrounding nature, such as the house-martins round the eaves (Banquo's "temple-haunting martlets"); and Lear's heath. Through his use of language he stimulated the imagination into "seeing" the scenery. In this Shakespeare followed the unnaturalistic method of Sophocles whose Greek plays depended on his words for their scenic effects.

The end of unnaturalistic verse drama, and its revival
The unnaturalistic Sophoclean-Shakespearean verse play was abolished in 1642 as a result of the Civil War, which closed the theatres. Cromwell finally banned dramatic performances in 1655. Drama returned with the Restoration, but with the exception of Dryden's *All for Love* (1672), which is about Antony and Cleopatra, prose took over. After that there were dramatic poems (rather than poetic dramas) by Byron, Shelley and Yeats, but the unnaturalistic drama that employs pictorial language in place of scenery was not revived until Eliot's *Murder in the Cathedral* in 1935, which has some elements in common with this *genre*. The true revival of the verse play had to wait 350 years until the 1990s (in my own work, beginning with *The Warlords*, first published in 1996) launched a new movement in verse drama.

My work with four casts of Globe plays
This movement has coincided with the work at London's Globe Theatre, with which I have been privileged to have a link. From early 1998 I urged Mark Rylance, then Artistic Director at the Globe and (then) my co-trustee of the Shakespeare Authorship Trust's library at Otley Hall, at that time my Tudor house in Suffolk, to put on contemporary verse plays. Shakespeare and his contemporaries wrote plays about

contemporary or nearly contemporary events, I said at some length; some plays at the Globe should now similarly include works with a contemporary analogy or angle. My suggestion was not taken up but I was asked to have the entire casts of the Globe productions of *As You Like It* (1998), *Julius Caesar* (1999), and *The Tempest* and *Hamlet* (2000) to stay at Otley Hall for up to three days each. During these four visits I must have encountered more than 120 actors and speakers of verse, including the Masters of Verse and directors who have had experience of putting verse on stage. These visits led to an exchange of views on the revival of verse drama.

I found these visits of immense benefit. I took part in their rehearsals: I was Antony's standard-bearer in the final battle of *Julius Caesar* on nearby ploughed fields, a Doctor of Philosophy at the University of Wittenberg instructing Hamlet and Horatio on the Lutheran philosophy of the 1580s, and the priest who married Gertrude and Claudius before the beginning of *Hamlet*, presiding over a candlelit "altar" in the summerhouse after dark wearing an Elizabethan frock coat with the entire Globe cast as congregation before me. The *Hamlet* actors rehearsed the players' scene in the enclosed space of Otley Hall's Linenfold Room to see if it could be performed in such a small space – the effect on the court, of whom I was one, was extremely intimate – and there have been times when I have felt like Hamlet coaching the players. We were all aware of the ghosts of the players of the 1590s watching our activities with approval. Elizabethan plays may have been performed in the "plahouse" wing at Otley Hall, which was dated by dendrochronology I commissioned to 1588 and appears to be an early version of a Fortune-style square-yard theatre with a north-south alignment (which guaranteed afternoon sun on the west side on open-air theatre days). Plays seem to have been performed indoors in the Banqueting Hall, then my bedroom, or outdoors in the Elizabethan courtyard (now under the rose-garden). The actors' "tiring-room" (attiring-room) below the Banqueting Hall, where the actors prepared themselves behind the open-air stage, was my study. The "rehearsal theatre" that the Tudor rooms and grounds of Otley Hall became during these visits was as inspiring to me as Lady Gregory's Abbey Theatre and Coole Park evidently were to Yeats.

The iambic pentameter as the basic unit of verse drama
I recall good discussions with Giles Block and Tim Carroll, Masters of Verse of *Julius Caesar* and *The Tempest* respectively, when, sitting in the Literary Room at Otley Hall, we focused on what the verse is doing in verse dramas and how to treat the verse in Shakespeare's plays. We

agreed that Shakespeare tried to hear – and catch – the human voice. The iambic pentameter is the basic unit of verse drama. To this day people tend to speak in iambic pentameters in everyday life. Although Shakespeare varies the iambic pentameter, adding half a foot with a feminine ending, for example, and including irregularities that enable him to catch the struggle of thinking while it is happening to create a natural effect in which the structures, philosophy and imagery heighten the language, the discipline of the iambic pentameter is always there in the blank verse. It is a mistake to free it too often, to break a pentameter in half with a central pause or to stress an unstressed word so that a line sounds like a 4-stress line. Nevertheless, the pentameter must be varied so that it does not become monotonous. The aim of the Master of Verse or director is to allow the characters to communicate naturally through it while preserving the beauty and on occasion rhetoric of the language.

The iambic pentameter as a medium for sincerity
Essentially the iambic pentameter is a medium for sincerity. People fully express their feelings in verse and conceal them in prose. Verse is perfectly suited to an age in which characters tell us the truth about themselves, whereas prose is more suited to characters who lie to us about themselves and each other, as did the characters of the mannered Restoration sexual comedies. Giles Block was fond of quoting the 18th-century Goldsmith's *The Citizen of the World; or, Letters from a Chinese Philosopher, Residing in London, to his Friends in the East* (1762): "We speak to conceal rather than reveal our feelings." In other words, the mind of prose censors the heart. In my four verse plays I have revived the soliloquy, in which characters tell the truth and reveal their feelings. In my verse plays I want to get behind the social façade to the inner thoughts. I am therefore a devotee of the iambic pentameter, which conveys sincerity.

Verse
I am using verse to revive the timeless, unnaturalistic bare-stage setting of Sophocles and Shakespeare and to paint the scenery in words that suggest the context of the situation as well as react to it. Speech should combine the naturalness of the iambic pentameter with heightened language and imagery that can accommodate switches into soliloquy. Speech has various modes. It is partly transactional – it is designed to achieve a particular goal such as to sell someone something or wheedle something out of someone or persuade someone of the rightness of a particular idea or course of action – but it is also partly responsive: it

responds to people and their situation. A manipulative character will use speech transactionally part of the time and may let us know in soliloquy what his real feelings are; a sincere speaker, on the other hand, may express emotion through verse. Speech can also be partly (on occasion) descriptive as it dwells on verbal scenery through an image.

Verse can therefore be more mannered than the grunts and inarticulate "ums" and "ers" of hesitant contemporary speech, and yet still be natural, as the Elizabethans (notably Marlowe) discovered. In the best verse drama, the rhetoric of verse carries the meaning along through image and gracefully poised pentameter while seeming natural to the audience.

Rapid unfolding of events in Universalist drama
The structure of *The Rise of Oliver Cromwell* needs some comment, for it is more fluid and more panoramic than *Ovid Banished*. The scenes are shorter and flow into each other more rapidly, as if influenced by cinematic techniques. The reason for this is the dynamic view of action held by Universalism. Universalism sees a perpetual present, a process, and a rapid unfolding of events, and the many scenes within each act are a consequence of this Universalist vision. As I have written elsewhere, the Universalist view of a work of art is idiosyncratic (i.e. peculiar to itself), like the Romantic or Classical view of a work of art.

Universalist plays and structure
All four plays are in fact Universalist plays. They deal with the universal theme of the manipulation of power and the shortcomings of world government, which at its best is a desirable utopian end if approached with the right state of mind – or heart. Augustus and Cromwell both lack this right state of mind – hence the shortcomings of their governments. As I have written elsewhere, Universalism combines the Romantic and the Classical – social, rational debate with a dynamic sense of growth – and a Universalist structure is ideal for showing Ovid and Charles I enmeshed in a process that is both ever-changing and yet constantly limiting.

Historical and contemporary verse plays without natural scenery
The historical play is more difficult to write and more demanding on the dramatic poet than is a verse translation, in which the characters and plot are given to the translator who can as a result concentrate totally on his use of language without worrying about characterisation, plot or structure. (In his translations of Sophocles, Euripides and

Seneca, Ted Hughes was able to take the characters, plot and structure as already given. Ted Hughes, also a translator of excerpts of Ovid's *Metamorphoses*, wrote me a number of letters and cards, and had he lived he would have been extremely interested in *Ovid Banished*, which I told him I was writing.) The historical play lends itself to foregoing natural scenery more than the contemporary play, as T.S. Eliot discovered. The verse of *The Confidential Clerk* and *The Elder Statesman* sits awkwardly beside the realistic settings in which they were produced: the 1950s drawing-rooms with curtains. It was a mistake for him to move away from the Sophoclean-Shakespearean bare stage of *Murder in the Cathedral*.

Two other verse dramatists in the present movement that has revived verse drama have written historical plays: Peter Oswald, dramatist of *Augustine's Oak*, and Tony Harrison, whose play on Cromwell approves of Cromwell and his changes, and is written from the other side of the fence. So far as I am aware, *Prince Tudor* is the only contemporary-set (as opposed to historical or translated) unnaturalistic verse play. *Ovid Banished* and *The Rise of Oliver Cromwell* offer a new historical verse drama for our time. The challenge now is to write unnaturalistic contemporary plays in verse, as did Shakespeare's contemporaries.

For years I have mused over verse plays on Alexander the Great, Suez, J.F. Kennedy and the 1984 British miners' strike. Perhaps one day I will get round to these. If any theatre company is receptive and would like to commission one of them, please get in touch. It will be helping to keep the revival of verse drama going in our time.

17 January, 2 February, 20 March, 6 April 2006

*A recount in 2019 shows 201 speaking parts and 6 choruses times 6 people = 36, making 237 speaking parts.

Prefaces to individual verse plays in Collected Verse Plays

Collected Verse Plays (2007) included *The Warlords*, Parts One and Two, and an abridged single play in the Appendix [of *Collected Verse Plays*]; *The Tragedy of Prince Tudor*, 2007 version; *Ovid Banished*, 1999; and *The Rise of Oliver Cromwell*, 2000. Besides the 'Preface to *Collected Verse Plays*' there were individual prefaces for these plays. The Preface to *The Warlords* is the same as the 1999 version in Preface 9. The last three follow.

Preface to the 2007 Edition of The Tragedy of Prince Tudor

Changing 1999 obfuscating names
This play was written in 1998, when I first learned that Britain was being split into 12 regions, each of which would have tax-raising powers, within what can only be described as a coming United States of Europe. About this time an official in a certain County Council [it can now be said, Suffolk County Council] leaked to me a secret document issued when John Major was British Prime Minister, which proved this.* When the play first came out in 1999 it was too close to the painful events surrounding Princess Diana's death in 1997 to give characters their original names. And so I used other names to obfuscate. As a result the play had the appearance of being a *roman-* (or drama-) *à-clef* ("a novel in which real persons or events appear with invented names"), and the serious message of the play was obscured.

Now we are at some distance from the events leading up to 1997, and I have since published *The Syndicate* about the plan for a world government (which includes regionalisation), and its companion volume *The Secret History of the West*, both of which focus on the Rockefellers and Rothschilds and supply numerous sources. I feel it is now time to restore these two original names, and to remove most of the obfuscating names so that the message can come through more clearly, and to include the original subtitle, *A Prince without a Kingdom*. The obfuscating names can be found in the 1999 edition of the play.

Proposed European Constitution and the abolition of England
The abolition of England is now a very real possibility. The new European constitution [*The Treaty Establishing a Constitution for Europe*, also known as the European Constitution] has to be ratified by the end of October 2006. If 20 out of the 25 members of the European Union vote for ratification (i.e. four-fifths), then the European Council of heads of government are empowered by the constitution document itself to recommend the adoption of the constitution, which would impose a superstate on all member nations, including the UK, and turn them into states. (The actual wording in the document is: "If, two years after the signature of the Treaty establishing a Constitution for Europe, four-fifths of the Member States have ratified it and one or more Member States have encountered difficulties in proceeding with ratification, the matter will be referred to the European Council", 'Declarations', 30.) The UK would fragment into 12 Euro-regions: Scotland, Wales, Northern Ireland, London and eight English regions. This process, which I confirmed through the leak of the County-Council document,

has progressed. *The Syndicate* gives full details, and more recently Lindsay Jenkins' *Disappearing Britain* lays out further evidence. This play is now very much a creature of its times.

Composite and imaginary characters
The leaders of the two Syndicate factions are composite characters and are not based on particular individuals; rather they embody a particular emphasis of commercial pattern – an emphasis within the ethos and outlook on life of the Syndicate rather than the influence of specific individuals. Both represent the commercial drives of conglomerates of companies or corporations with a shared common interest in the Syndicate, and I make no imputation against the specific behaviour of any individual, family, company or corporation.

The courtiers remain imaginary and have composite, multiple inspiration. Sir William Hawkes has no connection with (the then) Sir Robert Fellowes or Sir Robin Janvrin (who did not become Private Secretary to the Queen until 1999, *after* the events in the play). Lord Green is not based on Sir Stephen Lamport, Mark Bolland or Sir Michael Peat (all of whom have done stints as Private Secretary at St James's Palace), and any resemblance is coincidental; I was not thinking of any particular courtier. The politician Wormwood is not based on Peter Mandelson, dubbed in the popular press "the Prince of Darkness"; it must be borne in mind that in recent times although he has attended the Bilderberg Group Mandelson has been a close adviser to the Rothschilds rather than a Rockefellers' hatchet man. Mrs. R was probably based on a newspaper account of a highly publicised visit Princess Diana and Dodi al-Fayed made to clairvoyant Rita Rogers at her Central-England home in Chesterfield a few weeks before their deaths; my obfuscation allowed me to exercise some dramatic licence with the timing and content of the consultation, as it did with the manner of Rabin's killing. The Fool – the Goon jokingly appointed Fool – may have echoes of Spike Milligan, but again he is a composite character who is much more akin to Shakespeare's Tudor Fools than our modern Goons. (It is significant that on 3 July 1998 I had lunch with John Southworth, author of *Fools and Jesters at the English Court* and an expert on Shakespeare's Fools, whom we discussed for most of that afternoon.)

It goes without saying that the Prince is also a composite character. No Prince of our realm has gatecrashed a Bilderberg Group conference and denounced the world government. Nor has one been murdered and replaced by a double.

The Minister of World Culture in 2100
Finally, I should point out that it is the Minister of World Culture, in 2100, not me, who accepts his scholars' view that the Prince was murdered and replaced by a double to perpetuate the Windsor line. It must not be ruled out that the Minister of World Culture in 2100 has slipped the idea of the murder and the double into the text for spin and propaganda purposes – to discredit the ex-regime that preceded his world-government superstate. To put it more strongly, his claim that the Prince was assassinated for seditiously opposing the world government and replaced by a pretender who had no title to the throne is outrageous black propaganda on the part of the world government, and is patently absurd and in no way credible. His claim reveals much about the Utopia of 2100 towards which we are creeping.

16 January, 2 February 2006

*NH encountered Sir John Major at a dinner on 9 October 2014, and raised the linking of UK regions to Continental regions. Major said he thought the linking was due to twinning, not the EU's attempt to put in place a latent structure for a United States of Europe. (See 'Twinning and a Rodeo' in *The First Dazzling Chill of Winter*.)

Preface to Ovid Banished

Freedom of speech under a world government
This play is about freedom of speech particularly in relation to a world government. It is clear that Ovid, the artist, has offended Augustus, and (as the epigraph from Milton's *Areopagitica* indicates) not because of his sexually-frank *Ars Amatoria*, which mocked the fashionable *genre* of didactic poetry. For a reason never disclosed be was banished to the Pontus, where he died. He refused to say what his offence was.

How Ovid offended Augustus
In *Tristia*, "Sad Poems" (also "Sorrows"), II, 207ff, he addresses Augustus:

> Though two crimes, a poem and a blunder (*carmen et error*), have brought me ruin, of my fault in the one (i.e. the blunder) I must keep silent, for my worth is not such that I may reopen your wounds, O Caesar: it is more than enough that you should have been pained once. The other remains: the charge that by an obscene poem I have taught foul adultery.

Elsewhere he makes it clear that his "offence" (*offensus*) wounded Augustus. It was something he saw:

> Why did I see anything? Why did I make my eyes guilty? Why was I so thoughtless as to harbour the knowledge of a fault? Unwitting was Actaeon when he beheld Diana unclothed....
>
> (II, 103–105)

What he saw happened by chance:

> It is not a brief tale or safe to say what chance made my eyes witness a baleful evil. My mind shrinks in dread from that time.... Nothing then will I say except that I have sinned, but by that sin sought no reward; folly is the proper name for my crime, if you wish to give the true title to the deed.
>
> (III, vi, 27ff)

He took his secret to the grave.

Ovid's "mistake": discovering a plot to restore the Julian succession
Ovid Banished narrates a set of events which have baffled historians. It draws on new historical research. The "mistake" (Latin *error*) for which Ovid is banished has been a subject of speculation in many articles and books over the years. What had Ovid done that deserved banishment for the rest of his life by Augustus personally, with no pardon contemplated by any of the imperial family, not even Augustus's son Tiberius when he succeeded his stepfather? It cannot have been a sexual peccadillo alone, for perpetual banishment would have been too extreme a punishment for its time for such a misdemeanour.

I have researched the background to the banishment and follow Peter Green in *Classical Bearings*, who believes that Ovid stumbled across a Julian conspiracy. The Julian line was descended from Julius Caesar and included the line through Augustus's first wife Scribonia, by whom Augustus had a daughter Julia, who in turn had a daughter (his granddaughter) also called Julia. The Claudian line was through Augustus's second wife Livia, who had had a son Tiberius by her first husband: Tiberius Claudius Nero, who gave his name to the Claudian line. Her son Tiberius was Augustus's stepson. The Julian line was plotting to succeed Augustus. The strong Livia was determined that her son Tiberius would be the next Emperor, and she achieved this outcome. It seems that Ovid stumbled across Julian plotters and that his crime was not to inform Augustus. He knew too much for his own good, and had to be removed from Rome.

Analysts now agree that Ovid inadvertently discovered and was suspected of being involved in a plot to restore the Julian imperial line (the two Julias) in place of the Claudian line (Tiberius). Such a plot would have struck at the very basis of the *imperium*, Augustus's "new" world order.

Ovid opposed Augustus's imperium

I have been faithful to the history of the time. There is considerable evidence that Ovid opposed Augustus's *imperium*, Rome's world empire or new world order which pacified barbarian tribes by military massacres. Ovid was a dissident in relation to Augustus's world government, and this must have been a factor in his banishment. The two men shown being executed after the two conspiracies – Iullus after the first, Paulus after the second – were actually executed. Paulus's crime, *laesa maiestas*, high treason (i.e. plotting against the State), may well have been Ovid's crime. News of Silanus's escape from execution can be found in Tacitus, *The Annals of Imperial Rome*, 3.24. There is some evidence to suggest that Livia finally poisoned Augustus, and I have gone with this interpretation.

Ovid's banishment in Tomis

The details of Ovid's voyage to the Black Sea and his exile I have taken from his *Tristia* and his *Epistulae Ex Ponto* ("Black Sea Letters"), both of which include letters to his wife. Both are full of autobiographical detail. A literal translation can be found in the Loeb *Tristia Ex Ponti* and a verse translation in Penguin's Ovid, *The Poems of Exile*.

My view of the reason for Ovid's banishment is historically-based and is not a mere fancy. Ovid is thus a universal victim of the excesses of world government. I have used more poetic licence in interpreting Ovid's transformation in Tomis on the Black Sea, where his complaining, self-absorbed, self-pitying letters (*Tristia* and *Epistulae Ex Ponto*) give way in the end to dignified acceptance and silence. There is nevertheless considerable historical evidence for seeing Ovid as transforming himself into a mystic in his relative solitude away from the cultural desert of Rome.

The artist living in a time of world government – like Virgil, Horace and Ovid, who lived when Rome ruled the known world through Augustus – has a duty to tell the truth. He is at risk, and if he is banished for the remainder of his life, he only has his pride and his personal growth with which to occupy and console himself. My Ovid ends as a mystic who comes to see the shallowness of Rome. The barrenness of Tomis, so bleak when contrasted with Rome's opulence at the beginning of his exile, finally appears desirable as it lies outside the materialism of metropolitan Rome.

Plight of a dissident
I have always been fascinated and appalled at the knowledge Ovid came by, a knowledge it would have been safer for him not to have had. The plight of the dissident who knows more than is good for him is a universal one. It was Solzhenitsyn's plight in the Communist USSR. The spurned artist can embody true values to which the all-powerful but shallow world government of his day cannot aspire.

A Universalist play
A Universalist play, besides relating its story to a global theme and perspective and to the Light, seeks echoes in all civilisations and times. Shakespeare drew on the Roman time, and I have found focusing on Rome at its most powerful liberating. The Universalism of the play should not blind the reader to the fact that *Ovid Banished* is fundamentally a play about our own time, in which State censorship, though more subtle than in Augustus's Rome, is still a hazardous weapon of government.

Revival of unnaturalistic verse drama, and freedom of speech
This play continues the revival of verse drama I began with *The Warlords* and *Prince Tudor*, and later developed with *The Rise of Oliver Cromwell*. It is written in tight blank verse, with fewer characters than appear in my other historical verse plays, which are of epic scale and scope. But first and foremost it is a play that sides with freedom of speech against the self-interested immorality (or amorality) of the most powerful government there had ever been.

27 October 2000; revised 17 January, 2 February 2006

Preface to The Rise of Oliver Cromwell

Genesis of staging the English Civil War
This play puts the entire English Civil War on stage and therefore has an epic scope.

I knew very young that I would one day write a play on Cromwell. In 1961, while still at Oxford, I wrote to Jim Campbell, the history tutor at Worcester College, telling him I wanted to write a play on the Spanish Inquisition, to be called *The Holy Brotherhood*, and asking him for a reading list. He replied helpfully. Slowly the Holy Brotherhood turned in my mind into a play about Cromwell. I did not then know it would be a verse play. I wrote a poem on Cromwell while sitting on a boat travelling between Russia and Japan in 1966. It was a 'Moral Letter after Horace' entitled 'An Epistle to an Admirer of Oliver Cromwell', and was a preliminary covering of the ground. It raised questions that puzzled me, and it has taken forty years to discover the answers. I do not think that I had remembered that youthful title *Holy Brotherhood* when I began this play. (I also knew in 1961 that I would own a writing base in a Cornish harbour, and I am writing this overlooking the sea in the harbour I then visualised and later found, or was led to.)

Cromwell's Rosicrucian revolution: Jews in Amsterdam
Cromwell is fascinating because he overthrew the monarchy and achieved a revolution in England. I have always been interested in revolutions. I lived under the first Iraqi Revolution, and visited (and wrote poems about) the Russian and Chinese Revolutions. I was caught in the Libyan Revolution of 1969; I had driven to work and had to drive back through it with soldiers firing at every street corner. I researched Cromwell again in 1998, and interrupted this play to write a book on revolutions, *The Secret History of the West*. The reader can trace Cromwell's Rosicrucianism more fully in chapter 2 in that work, and in particular how two little-known letters involving the Mulheim Synagogue make it clear that Cromwell was offered funding for his New Model Army by Rosicrucian Jews in Amsterdam in return for killing Charles I and resettling the Jews in England. Cromwell, in fact, has to be understood in relation to Samuel Hartlib's Invisible College. The title *The Holy Brotherhood* could not be more appropriate. I have preferred *The Rise of Oliver Cromwell* as it focuses on the forces behind his rise rather than on the secret brotherhood of Rosicrucians that surrounded him.

Charles I beheaded on the instruction of international forces
Charles's final speech from the scaffold, relevant parts of which appear in *The Secret History of the West*, shows that he was aware he was being beheaded by international forces; he actually mentioned Alexander the Great and "conquests by forces of world imperialism", showing that he saw himself as the victim of internationalism. I have added Rosicrucian Freemasonry to his drift in the interests of clarity, but the spirit of what he says is unaffected. I have reviewed the evidence for Charles's executioner, and after reflecting on all the accounts have adopted the view that Cromwell, aided by Ireton, personally beheaded

Charles: hence his non-appearance anywhere during the execution, and the executioner's disguise.

Dutch Jews funded New Model Army so Jews could return to England
The Rise of Oliver Cromwell narrates a set of events which have baffled historians. It shows Cromwell's rise to power as being abetted by Dutch Jews. The full deal was that in return for additional funding of the New Model Army, Cromwell would kill Charles I and become King himself and (after a decent lapse of time) then allow the Jews to return to England, from which they had been expelled in 1290. At the same time Cromwell would return the monarchy from the Templars (who controlled the Stuarts) to the Rosicrucian Grand Master of the Priory of Sion, to whom the Dutch Jews were linked. In *The Secret History of the West* can be found details of the letter dated 16 June 1647 from Oliver Cromwell to the Mulheim Synagogue, and their reply on 12 July 1647 ordering Cromwell to allow Charles I to escape as "his recapture will make trial and execution possible". During the summer and autumn of 1653 Cromwell several times proposed an Anglo-Dutch union, and Menasseh Ben Israel's visit to Cromwell in 1655 to negotiate the return of the Jews to England is well documented. I have followed this less-well-known view of the Civil War, which focuses on Cromwell's links with Rosicrucian Freemasonry. Such an approach gives rise to an entirely new view of the Civil War and of the 17th century, in which Charles I is the victim of an internationalist conspiracy.

The Venetian Ambassador, who is a source for many events of the time, says (see *Venetian State Papers* 1655–6 collected by Edward, Earl of Clarendon, ed. by Scrope and Monkhouse, 1767–86, p.160) – and Antonia Fraser in *Cromwell, Our Chief of Men* includes the story – in December 1655, after Menasseh's visit to London, that Cromwell had met Menasseh in his youth while travelling in Flanders. The evidence for this is not conclusive. However, I have adopted this view as it explains how the 1647 letters came to be written, and why Cromwell opposed the Council of State in championing the readmission of Jews into England.

Cromwell's 12 administrative regions in England and contemporary parallel
There are contemporary echoes in what Cromwell set out to do. Cromwell has become a topical figure as a result of the constitutional changes in England since 1997. Cromwell abolished the monarchy and then the House of Lords, and attempted to change the English constitution fundamentally by splitting England into 12 administrative regions run by Major-Generals. Britain's "New Labour" government

under the neo-Cromwellian Blair has abolished the voting rights of hereditary peers, thus fundamentally changing the composition of the House of Lords, which is now filled with his "yes-men" who rubber-stamp his Commons policies, and thus undermining and threatening the hereditary monarchy. He has split and devolved the United Kingdom into 12 administrative regions or Euro-regions: Scotland, Northern Ireland, Wales, London and 8 English regions that are to have tax-raising powers and to form separate entities in the coming United States of Europe. All modern Cromwells achieve power through foreign help, and there is a parallel between the Dutch-funded Cromwell and the Dutch origin of the Bilderberg Group, which backed the Blair government; indeed, the two are linked historically through their Rosicrucianism.

Cromwell's revolutionary alliance with Freemasons
My Cromwell is in league with the Freemasons of the day, shadowy forces outside England who sought to make changes for their own benefit. Today the British Prime Minister operates within a context of similar pressure from the shadowy world government. At one level, my study of Cromwell is about the betrayal of England. But of course it is not as simple as that. All revolutions begin with a noble spiritual Utopian vision which somehow goes wrong and degenerates into political and physical dictatorship and military rule. My Cromwell is the archetypal revolutionary, facets of whom can be found later in Washington, Napoleon and Stalin. In trying to preserve the revolutionary vision while compromising his principles due to the requirements of his own corrupting revolutionary government, my Cromwell is a universal revolutionary.

Historical derivation of Puritanism from Rosicrucianism
There is a historical basis for every situation and discussion in this play. There is evidence for every scene, and nothing has been invented. The evidence may be little known and the story may shock, but that is a different matter. I have endeavoured to be historically truthful. My derivation of Puritanism from Rosicrucianism is considered. (For a full account see chapter 2 of *The Secret History of the West*.) This is a view of the English Revolution which is faithful to the facts but conveys a new interpretation. T.S. Eliot remarked that the Civil War is still with us, and putting it on stage as a whole is worthwhile, despite its epic proportions (and cost implications). The English Revolution is an important part of our national heritage and it holds lessons that we need to learn today. I have no doubt that one day this play will be staged.

Revival of unnaturalistic verse drama, and blank verse
This play could not have been written in prose. Scale and scope of this order can only be tackled in the kind of verse play I revealed in *The Warlords* and *Prince Tudor*: the historical, Sophoclean-Shakespearean sceneryless, unnaturalistic play which uses words to evoke settings, a poetic drama not known since 1640 (or possibly Dryden's *All for Love*, 1677). Shakespeare characterised this drama in his Prologue to *King Henry the Fifth*:

> Can this cockpit hold
> The vasty fields of France? Or may we cram
> Within this wooden O the very casques
> That did affright the air at Agincourt?
> O, pardon! since a crooked figure may
> Attest in little place a million;
> And let us, ciphers to this great accompt,
> On your imaginary forces work.
> Suppose within the girdle of these walls
> Are now confin'd two mighty monarchies,
> Whose high upreared and abutting fronts
> The perilous narrow ocean parts asunder.
> Piece out our imperfections with your thoughts:
> Into a thousand parts divide one man,
> And make imaginary *puissance*;
> Think, when we talk of horses, that you see them
> Printing their proud hoofs i' th' receiving earth;
> For 'tis your thoughts that now must deck our kings.

So it is with the battlefields and armies in conflict in Cromwell's time in this play. Whereas *The Warlords* contained a number of metres, I have stuck to blank verse in this play just as I have in *Ovid Banished*.

Universalist approach to modernising revolutions
I regard myself as the only man of letters, and therefore dramatist, operating today to have a full appreciation of the nature of the world government we are moving towards, which I have written about extensively elsewhere. I have also written about Universalism elsewhere. Besides being sensitive to the impact of the world government on national life and heroes like Cromwell who live by the Light, I have again adopted Universalism's own fluid method of narrative, which involves a structure of many dynamic scenes, some of which can be quite short, and an eye for the universality of the

central figure. Montgomery, Prince Tudor and Ovid are all in a sense, Everyman. They could just as easily be Arjuna unsure whether it is right to kill his enemies in a coming battle in the *Bhagavad Gita*; Henry V regarding his State as a garden; and Solzhenitsyn being deported by the KGB-ruled USSR. Cromwell is also many of the revolutionaries who have conducted revolutions in different parts of the world (for example Gaddafi in Libya), but he is first and foremost an attitude found in British life today, which shows no respect for our history and tradition and believes that change is a good thing for its own sake. Cromwell is the archetypal moderniser.

27 October 2000; revised 17 January, 2 February 2006

25

Collected Stories
1966–2006

Introductory Note to Collected Short Stories

1,001 mini-stories: novelty of the form
These mini-stories or verbal paintings are in five volumes. The first
four have already appeared. The stories in them essentially remain as
they first came out, though I have corrected some typographical errors,
punctuation and italicising. The stories in the fifth volume are all new.

As I look back on a thousand and one mini-stories written over forty
years, I am struck by the novelty of the form I alighted on one day (15
July) in 1966 when I wrote 'Limey' and resolved to write a hundred
such stories that would focus on intense experiences that shaped
people's lives. I am also struck by the sureness with which I settled
on the idea of verbal painting that day, and by the tenacity – some
would say stubbornness, obstinacy – with which I have carried the idea
through to complete a thousand and one stories over so many years.

Verbal paintings
The verbal painting can sometimes actually be a *series* of paintings
within one story – sometimes a triptych (a relief on three hinged
panels), sometimes more like the paintings about Becket's life in
the Miracle stained-glass windows in Canterbury Cathedral which
tell a story through pictures for illiterate people. Though seemingly
innovatory, story-telling through pictures is probably the oldest form
of all. Each story throws up an image which is signalled – headlined –
in the title. An imagistic poetic technique applied to prose abbreviates
and heightens, so these verbal paintings are also a form of prose-poem,
using action to say things through images.

Meditations on scenes and images
Each volume is a meditation on scenes and images which are
thematically linked to the next scene and image. So, in a few stories'
time we may encounter a story that takes place at an earlier time than
one we have just read. Though each story has a thematic place in a
meditation, each story can be pondered – reflected on, meditated
on – before passing on to the next story. The form is therefore ideal
for a short time-and-attention span. A train or air journey, lying on

a hospital bed, bedtime reading, school comprehensions within the confines of one lesson – all are windows in our busy lives and benefit from a literary form that offers brevity and limited space. It is possible to absorb a few stories a day and put the book aside just as it is possible to visit a gallery and focus on just a few pictures.

Revelation on Being and character
I am struck by how these mini-stories reveal character. They are all epiphanies – moments of manifestation and revelation, sometimes of Being, mostly of character. They catch the essence of people's lives, either as people reveal themselves or as they are revealed by events, caught as on canvas. There is cross-referencing, some characters appear in other stories, and there are further revelations, as if a painter used the same face or figure in more than one painting, but each time in a different posture or light.

Range of people presented
I am struck by the range of the people presented: expatriates, educational people (university professors and lecturers, schoolteachers, academic and backward pupils), literary figures, people from political and military life, professional people (solicitors, accountants, doctors), people from alternative medicine, people living off the sea, workmen who service utilities, people in families, people at leisure (dinner parties, suburban entertaining, clubs and pubs, carnivals), people from within the established religions and the New Age alternative scene, people at rites of passage (christenings, weddings, funerals), non-believing people. All have dreams and aspirations, all reminisce and know loneliness. Many are haunted by extreme situations they have experienced (wartime events such as the dropping of the atomic bomb). Such memories intrude into everyday consciousness, thrown up under pressure from within, and reflect the Age. People at work, people relaxing, people from a cross-section of high life and low life, from the Queen to the dustman – all have souls. All reveal themselves by their words or deeds, and the revelation is often expressed in terms of an image. I am glad to note that humour is never far away.

Correspondence within the One
In the one universe, everything corresponds to everything else as the many are all aspects of the One. Phenomena can therefore be seen in terms of – or as similar to – other phenomena. Behind the imagistic technique is a perception that the universe is a unity, and that to know this intuitively gives meaning, purpose and order to a life. To be cut

off from this perception brings feelings of meaninglessness, futility, fragmentation and disorder, even chaos. Those living in harmony with the One, the *Tao*, relate easily and correctly to others. Those who are unaware of this harmony have assertive egos, act in self-interested ways and spoil things for other people.

Death lurks behind social situations
I am struck by how from the very first story in this collection Death lurks behind the social situations. It is an abnegation of the aspirations of those who do not know the harmony of the universe, but part of the orderly process for those who do. All orders of society are overtaken by Death without warning.

Universal values
Between them these thousand and one mini-stories – a number which echoes *A Thousand and One Nights* (the *Arabian Nights Entertainments*) – reveal what makes life worth living. Flawed people deceive themselves and others and behave in treacherous and less-than-satisfactory ways, but the meditating consciousness above them is aware of the eternal and universal values of goodness, openness, honesty, sincerity, love, compassion, kindness, patience, courage, tolerance and peace. The wisest have a sense of purpose that is linked to the One, the Light, and the universal harmony.

A Bildungsroman *on Rawley*
A *Bildungsroman* is a novel dealing with one person's early life and development. These mini-stories amount to a *Bildungsroman* about the life and development, and long education, of Philip Rawley as he progresses from late youth to early old age in a thousand and one different situations, witnesses a Dance of Death involving the whole of society and triumphantly transcends nihilism and despair.

3 August 2006

The Introductory Notes for the individual volumes of *Collected Stories* are under *A Spade Fresh with Mud* [Preface 7], *A Smell of Leaves and Summer* [Preface 10], *Wheeling Bats and a Harvest Moon* [Preface 16] and *The Warm Glow of the Monastery Courtyard* [Preface 17]. Below is the Introductory Note for *In the Brilliant Autumn Sunshine*, volume 5, which first appeared in *Collected Stories* [Preface 25]. See the Preface to *The First Dazzling Chill of Winter* [Preface 42] for volume 6.

Introductory Note to
In the Brilliant Autumn Sunshine
(Volume 5 of Collected Stories)

Stories on retirement and readiness
These 231 mini-stories or verbal paintings were written between 1999 and 2006 and form volume 5 of my *Collected Short Stories*, which follow Philip Rawley from his late twenties to his late sixties, from late youth to early old age. Stories in the previous volumes state the horror of the Materialist outlook and show Rawley's developing spiritual awareness and sense of meaning in terms of the One that pervades Nature and the universe. The stories in volume 5 focus on retirement and wise "readiness", preparing the soul for what death may bring while retaining all faculties and powers.

A hermit surrounded by Nature
"Retirement" suggests both the act of retiring and the condition of having retired, but it also suggests seclusion from the world, a turning-away into solitude, a retreat into contemplative reflection from the bustle of everyday action. Rawley has always removed himself from the hurly-burly to reflect on the vivid situations he recalls, but now he is able to be more apart from the daily rushing-about that impedes the growth of souls, and is living more like a hermit surrounded by Nature. The hermits of the early Christian period lived in simple stone huts in solitary but stunningly beautiful places. Rawley, being a child of his century, lives in considerably greater comfort but he has time to ponder and prepare himself for what is to come while still observing the lurches of the Age (as when a pre-emptive West attempts to rearrange the Middle East to suit its – and internationalists' – security and wealth).

The ubiquitousness of Death
In all these last stories he is preoccupied with finding meaning despite the ubiquitousness of Death. The paintings in this gallery show a Seeker engaged in the perennial task of finding his way back to the One; not in reclusive, monastic isolation but while continuing to move freely about in a social framework that is apparently orderly. His questing existence is never long separated from the encompassing rhythms of Nature and the universe.

3 August 2006

26

The Secret Founding of America

The Real Story of Freemasons, Puritans and the Battle for the New World

Introduction
Skeleton of a Planting Father

The US the world's most advanced civilisation
The United States of America boasts the most advanced civilisation the world has ever known. Its technology is awesome. It has reached the moon, sent spacecraft to the far reaches of our solar system and produced images of our galaxy. Its satellites transmit instant pictures from across the world on our television screens. Its computers send instant messages round the globe via the internet. Its precision-bombing has raised war to a new level, enabling surgical strikes to be made while limiting damage. Its skyscrapers, aircraft, cars, housing and potential for wealth are unrivalled, and it has opened its doors to the tired, the poor, the homeless "huddled masses yearning to breathe free" and admitted refugees from all corners of the world. It stands for liberty and democracy and is a beacon of freedom to the rest of the world, which is apprehensive, fearing US domination and world hegemony.

The time of the first settlers
All this technological inventiveness and administrative genius has developed very rapidly in a country that only 400 years ago was an empty landscape occupied only by Native Americans, a place of great scenic beauty but also a terrifying wilderness. Into this vast, seemingly sparsely-populated tract came Europeans – from England, Spain and France – at a time when navigators were exploring the limits of the Earth. The prevailing view was still that the Earth was the centre of the universe and the planets travelled round it in spherical orbits. New heresies were asserting that the Earth revolved around the sun and that its movement caused the stars to appear to move. But it was only a theory that the world was round and that a ship sailing west might reach the Indies of the East. Rumour had it that beyond the mariners' horizon there was a huge waterfall that ships would plunge over and be lost forever more.

In this bewildering time European voyagers set sail in small-masted ships that leaked like old tubs to unknown destinations, knowing they would be absent for a year or two and unsure whether they would ever return home. What drove them? Some, like Vasco da Gama, were in quest of knowledge. Some, gentlemen adventurers, were seeking their fortune and hoping to bring back cargos of gold and diamonds, or at least precious wood that they could sell for commercial gain. Some hoped to own land, an impossibility for the poor under the medieval feudal system. Some were fleeing religious persecution and yearned for the freedom to worship in the way they wanted without being penalised by the State.

When they reached America after their heroic voyages, they planted settlements, and a backwoods life of great primitiveness, of hand-hewn wooden huts, shacks and fences, grew up along the eastern coast. As more colonists arrived, the lands that were settled grew more extensive. For more than 150 years there were English colonies in the north. Eventually these threw off their colonial yoke, became independent and wrote themselves a constitution, which enabled the United States to grow into the superpower it is today.

The founding, planting and Freemasonry
This book is about the founding of the United States from the planting of the first settlements to the constitutional founding of 1787. It shows that while religion was behind the first plantings, circumstantial evidence indicates that Freemasonry was also present and that a secret Deistic Freemasonry, subscribing to a non-Christian concept of God and hiding behind a religious façade, inspired the constitutional arrangements that prepared the way for today's superpower. Indeed, the first United States was a Masonic State. As we shall see, Freemasonry remained strong during the Civil War and is still a very powerful force behind the apparently Christian United States today. We shall see that today Freemasonry has an agenda for a new world order, a federal-continental United States of the World in which nation-states are subsumed as states within regional blocs.

All was not as it seems in the early planting of America. The story that schoolchildren learn is that Separatists came over on the *Mayflower* in 1620 and settled at New Plymouth. But they were not the first. Before this there is a real story involving Jamestown, which was settled in 1607. That is what America has chosen to base its 400th anniversary on in 2007. But, as we shall discover, even that is not the true start of America....

My interest in the founding: my study of civilisations and Bartholomew Gosnold at Otley Hall
I first became interested in the founding of America when I did research for my study of the origin, growth, rise and fall of 25 civilisations, which became *The Fire and the Stones* (Element Books, 1991). My view has recently been updated and is appearing in two volumes, *The Light of Civilization* (O Books, 2006) and *The Rise and Fall of Civilizations* (forthcoming). In these works I have identified North-American civilisation as separate from European civilisation, though the two together form Western civilisation. I have found that it is the most recent civilisation and has now arguably reached the same stage that the Roman civilisation reached while Rome was still a republic. I became further interested in the founding of America when I acquired Otley Hall in Suffolk, eastern England, in 1997. Otley Hall is a Tudor moated house where the Jamestown settlement of 1607 is thought to have been planned. There Bartholomew Gosnold is thought to have interviewed and recruited the crews and passengers for his two voyages, first in 1602, when he named Cape Cod and Martha's Vineyard, and then in 1606–7, when he was "prime mover" in the founding of the Jamestown settlement. We shall see that Gosnold inspired this second voyage. He organised it and his wife's cousin funded it. John Smith, who later awarded himself much of the credit, was very much an underling who took no part during the first six months of the voyage.

My visit to Jamestown and meeting with Kelso
I conducted research into Bartholomew Gosnold for a year and wrote an illustrated guidebook to Otley Hall – indeed, I also wrote a film script about Gosnold's life – and by October 1998, when I visited Jamestown, I was steeped in Gosnold. I gave a lecture on him to the English-Speaking Union in Richmond, Virginia, and showed slides. (One Virginian correspondent[1] described it as "the Hagger gospel of Gosnold".) There were some 200 in the audience. When I told them, "You've got the wrong man. You've erected a statue to John Smith, but there should be a statue to Bartholomew Gosnold, who did more to establish Jamestown than John Smith," some were shocked and several shook their heads. But many were extremely interested in the alternative pedigree I was proposing for Virginia – one which, as we shall see, stems from the politics of the Elizabethan and early Jacobean court rather than the disreputable, semi-piratical Smith. Indeed, I was told by several prominent Virginians, "We would rather see ourselves descended from Gosnold than from Smith."

In the audience was the deputy of the chief archaeologist at

Jamestown, Dr William Kelso. He had discovered the Jamestown Fort in 1994, thereby proving it was not a myth, in the same way that Heinrich Schliemann proved Troy was not a myth. Between April and December 1994 APVA Jamestown Rediscovery archaeologists recovered 30,000 artefacts of the early 1600s, at least half of which dated back to the earliest years of the Jamestown settlement. Dr Kelso has since uncovered some 350,000 artefacts that had lain buried within the Jamestown Fort.

I had met Bill Kelso during a visit to Jamestown before my lecture. The morning after my lecture he rang me up and said he wanted to see me. I went to Jamestown and met him again, a white-haired man of great bearing and dignity whom I now think of as America's Schliemann. We sat on a wooden seat by the river James, which lapped near our feet, the statue of John Smith towering above us, behind and to our right.

Bill said to me, "I've been trying to figure out how three English ships arrived here in front of us in 1607 and led the way for others to come, which all brought with them the stuff we've been finding under the ground here. Who was behind it? Who organised it?"

I said without hesitation, "Bartholomew Gosnold," and talked Bill through the main points I had made in my lecture. I explained that Gosnold had died in the fort in August 1607 and had been buried there. I said to Bill, "Please dig for him."

Digging for Gosnold's skeleton at the centre of the Jamestown fort
He said, "The ground's severely impacted, it's like concrete, and sub-ground radar won't work here. We have a triangle 140 yards by 140 yards by 140 yards. It's like looking for a needle in a haystack. It'll take decades to find him."

I replied without hesitation, "He'll be in the centre of the fort. There were cannons in each of the three corners, and all the ordnance was shot off during his funeral, so all three cannons were fired. Out of courtesy to the dead leader they'd have laid him in the centre of the cannons, not in one of the corners where he could only hear one. The fort was a palisaded stockade, as you know, and there were hostile Indians outside with bows and arrows. They wouldn't have stood outside the palisade with their eyes closed in prayer during the interment. They'd have buried him in conditions of relative safety, where they would not have been at risk of being shot."

Bill was interested. "I'm going to work with that theory," he said. "The trouble is, I don't know where all the corners of the fort are. One, I know, is under the river James out there somewhere. If I can find the other two I might be able to calculate the centre."

Bill visited me at Otley Hall three or four times during the next few years and I took him round some of the villages adjoining Otley, including to Letheringham and Wetheringsett, so he could see where Gosnold's crew and passengers had come from. Forty of the 108 passengers had lived in the nearby villages. One Sunday he rang saying that he was in Lavenham with the Virginian crime novelist Patricia Cornwell and others, could he come straight along? I gave them all lunch and we talked the whole afternoon. He came again when the First Lady of Virginia, Roxane Gilmore, came to Ipswich.

Jamestown and Ipswich to be sister cities, visit of First Lady of Virginia to Ipswich and Otley Hall
This was a highly publicised visit. At a civic reception held in Ipswich's Christ Church Mansion, the First Lady of Virginia formally requested that in view of the Gosnold connection as outlined in my lecture Jamestown and Ipswich should become "sister cities". Governor Gilmore of Virginia had earlier sent a representative and delegation to meet the Mayor, Leader and Chief Executive of Ipswich Borough Council to discuss the requested visit. I had been present at the meeting before hosting a lunch for the Americans, and had been dismayed that in their formal statements the Leader of the Council and Mayor had been unenthusiastic about the request. The Leader had said that the Council might be accused of "junketing on the rates". I had made a speech about the importance of the connection, but the Americans had been rebuffed. Roxane's formal approach now was therefore deliberately low-key, but set the request on record – her speech was filmed, as were the Mayor's speech and mine – and at the time of writing, five years later, it is being taken up again by the Council. So the thunder of my lecture is still reverberating today.

On the morning of Roxane's visit I gave a long television interview in Otley Hall to the American History Channel. She later told me it had been "broadcast to schools all over the US and the world".

Bill came once more and we toured every local house associated with Gosnold. We also spoke regularly over the phone. Each time I would ask him, "Have you found him yet?" and Bill would say, "No, but...." One year he told me he had found one corner of the fort and the next year he said he had found a second corner.

Finding Gosnold's skeleton
Then, in January 2003, when I asked, "Have you found him yet?", he said, "Yes, I think so." He told me he had found a remarkably well-

preserved skeleton of a man in his thirties with a staff that indicated he was the leader of the colony. There was also a decorative captain's staff on the lid of the coffin (coffins at that time were reserved for people of higher status). "I'm sure we've got Bartholomew," he said. "He was only 50 feet away from where we were sitting that day."

Bill held a press conference in Virginia to announce the find and I had to sit by my phone in England that day and give interviews to various US newspapers. There was considerable interest in the skeleton in the USA and it was displayed in the Smithsonian for a while.

Verification by DNA

Verification then became the problem. Bill wanted to locate a relative or descendant in the female line so that he could do a DNA test. He trawled the historical records and came up with Bartholomew Gosnold's sister, Elizabeth Gosnold Tilney, who died in 1646 and was buried inside All Saints' church, Shelley, Suffolk, and his niece Katherine Blackerby who, it is believed, was buried at St Peter and St Mary church, Stowmarket, Suffolk, where a tombstone bears the name of her husband. He applied for permission to dig up the floor of Shelley church. Edward Martin, an archaeologist who had at my request dug up the Otley Hall rose-garden lawn to find the old Tudor courtyard, lent the application weight and, for the first time ever, the Church of England agreed to an exhumation for purely historical reasons.

I attended the beginning of the exhumation on 13 June 2005. The church was in a deeply rural area and cars were parked in an adjoining field. Some 20 press, radio and television employees were milling before the altar, together with about eight people like myself who were either experts or associated with the project. Bill was of course present, looking very spruce. *National Geographic* magazine had exclusive rights to the project, having funded it in return for the rights to make a film and, under the deal, as soon as a workman began hammer-and-chiselling the tiles of the ancient floor, we were all ushered out.

The verdict was leaked in October 2005 and confirmed when the television programme was shown in the UK at the end of March 2006: there was no DNA match. It was, however, claimed that the woman dug up was not Gosnold's sister. She was supposed to have died at around 70, whereas the woman exhumed is thought to have died in 1690, plus or minus 50 years, in her fifties. Edward Martin maintained that the right skeleton was exhumed.

The ancient tiled floor had been broken up and the identification of Gosnold was no further forward. At his request I sent Bill my slides of Bartholomew Gosnold's relatives Robert Gosnold III and V. During

Otley Hall open days I had been approached by getting on for 30 people who claimed to be descendants of the Gosnolds. I used to stand claimants between the portraits of these two relatives and do my "nose test". The Gosnold nose was distinctively hooked. I would appoint a panel of visitors to adjudicate as to whether the claimant was a true Gosnold or not in terms of how hooked the particular nose appeared to be in relation to the portraits. I suggested that Bill should compare facial measurements in the slides and his skeleton.

At the time of writing Bill is focusing in greater detail on the skeleton. He is doing a DNA test on one of its teeth in the belief that it will give a more accurate reading than the previous test, which was based on an area of bone. Minerals from drinking water are deposited in teeth as they form during infancy and leave a chemical signature that can be co-related to ground water. Tests on the tooth sample may therefore prove that the skeleton is of a man who did not grow up in Suffolk, as Gosnold did. The bone-sample test has confirmed that the Jamestown skeleton was an immigrant to America who had had a diet rich in wheat, as opposed to an American corn diet.

That is where we are at the time of writing. Bill is convinced that he has Bartholomew Gosnold, but it will take a bit more time to establish this. There is still another skeleton, that of Bartholomew Gosnold's niece, to try – if it can be located.

Research more impartial after selling Otley Hall
I no longer own Otley Hall. Some 40,000 people passed through during the seven years I owned it, most of whom our staff and six guides coped with, but eventually I found that running it was too time-consuming and I sold it to concentrate on my literary activities.

But the experience of the skeleton had whetted my appetite for getting to the bottom of the founding of America. I renewed my research while preparing other books. And having shed Otley Hall, I found I was researching much more impartially. Bartholomew Gosnold was just one of those involved in the founding of settlements and I was keen to be objective about him, to place him in the pattern of settlement without distorting or exaggerating his achievement. I began looking further....

Note:
1. Kenneth Haas, an ex-professor to whom I am indebted for a day's intense discussion on the Southern mind as we toured Civil War sites, a focus he will recognise in chapter 8.

27

The Last Tourist in Iran

From Persepolis to Nuclear Natanz

(In this book, the Preface was incorporated into Chapter 1, which is
reproduced here.)

Behind the Negative Image

The Persian invasions of Greece
Persia. The country had loomed large in my imagination ever since, as
a schoolboy studying Greek literature, I had read of the mighty invader
that threatened to crush Greece. Herodotus referred to the Persians
as "the barbarians". Their awesome power gathered in 492BC under
Darius I, King of kings, who was incensed at the burning of Sardis
by Athenians, and was miraculously repulsed by Greek heroism at
Marathon. They came again in 480BC in a revenge attack under Xerxes
I, Darius's successor, crossing the Hellespont on a bridge of boats with
180,000 men. They were held up at Thermopylae but burned Athens.
Then, with Xerxes watching on high from a throne of rock, they were
defeated at Salamis. After further battles during the next two years
including the battle of Plataea of 479BC the civilised Greeks were saved
from an implacable foe, Ionian cities became independent and the
Athenian Empire was born. That led to Rome, to Christendom, Western
culture and the world we know today. In my boyhood, the Persians
were the enemy. Reviled, they stood for barbarism and everything bad.

The carvings in Persepolis
Now I was standing in Persepolis, "city of the Persians", among the
superlative Achaemenian carvings there. I had the massive 33-acre
site all to myself. I had been looking at meticulously realistic carvings
on the Apadana platform, and I had a startling – indeed, stunning
– revelation that sent a shiver up my spine, a thrilling moment that
seemed to turn my boyhood – indeed, the West's – understanding of
ancient history on its head. All the carvings had been executed around,
or soon after, 515BC. This was *before* the Persian expeditions to Greece,
before Greek philosophy rose in Persian-ruled Ionia, long before Greek
art flourished and reached its highest achievement in Pheidias's
carvings on the Athenian Parthenon.

The "One" reached Greece from Persia, the true source of Western civilisation
The Persians believed that Ahura Mazda – who may have been shown as the winged soul (*Faravahar* or *Fravahar*) displayed on early Persian monuments although this may merely be the Achaemenian crest – was the supreme, if not sole, god and that the universe was "One" within him. The vision of an ordered and whole universe, inspired by a single spirit, which was at the source of Greek – and then Western – philosophy, had arisen from this developing Persian monotheism. It had travelled from Persia to Ionia, been taken to Elea in Southern Italy by Xenophanes of Colophon, who passed it on to Parmenides, the grandfather of Western philosophy. But it was originally *Persian*. Therefore in c.515BC the idol-worshipping Greeks, not the nearly monotheistic Persians, were the true barbarians; and Persia, which had been behind Greece, not Greece, was the true source of our Western civilisation.

Terrorist-supporting Iran and nuclear weapons
And now we, the beneficiaries of early Persian culture, were as mighty in our time under the leadership of Bush II as Persia had been in the time of Darius I and Xerxes I. We had this troublesome, backward country of Iran to deal with, full of people who dressed oddly, behaved strangely, and seemed to go their own way irrespective of our strategic interests. Obligingly, we had destroyed their enemies on either side, removing the threats from Iraq and Afghanistan. By some miscalculation we had let it become, by default, the main force in the region. Even worse, the Iranian President Ahmadinejad had threatened to wipe Israel off the map and was defiantly developing nuclear energy, a policy felt by many to be a cover for a nuclear bomb, as if he was the spiritual descendant of Xerxes rather than ourselves. So we in turn were proposing to crush terrorist-supporting Iran and with it, no doubt, some of the early Persian culture that had inspired our civilisation's Greek precursor, just as the "barbarian" Persians had tried to crush early, pre-imperial Greece. Who were the barbarians now?

*

My interest in the Middle East's early religions, and Iran
"Please don't say you're an author on this form," the travel agent said. "It'll take forever to obtain a visa. Just put down retired teacher." And so that was how I went in (Tehran – "Teheran" with

an "e" is an incorrect, French spelling – having authorised my visa in a fortnight and the Iranian Embassy in London having issued it a week later).

Why Iran? I had long had an interest in the Middle East. I had spent eight months lecturing in English Literature at the University of Baghdad back in 1961–1962 and had visited the cradle of civilisation in Mesopotamia: the ancient site of Paradise where the Tigris joined the Euphrates, out of which had grown the Sumerian, Akkadian, Babylonian and Assyrian empires in lands around nearby Babylon. In Iraq I had encountered young men who spoke enthusiastically about Iran, and I had been offered a job there in 1968 but had gone to Libya instead to be closer to ancient Egypt.

Iran was as much a cradle of civilisation as Iraq. Although, influenced from Mesopotamia, the Elamites were progressing between c.3000 and c.2500BC. The Iranian civilisation was the result of two migrations: of Indo-European Aryans through Mesopotamian Akkad c.2250BC and of Indo-Iranian Aryans from the east c.1500BC. It was unified by Cyrus the Great and his Achaemenian dynasty. It then expanded with the Sasanians before being conquered by Arab Muslims by AD 640. It eventually passed into the Arab civilisation when the Safavids completed their subjugation of Iran and made Shiite Islam Iran's official religion in 1511.

For me, a student of the rise and fall of civilisations, going to Iran would be an opportunity to study a civilisation that had passed through all the stages in a civilisation's life cycle, and which boasted a great tradition. In 1971 the last Shah had proudly honoured 2,500 years of kingship, which began with Cyrus the Great. He had planted 2,500 trees at Persepolis to symbolise the antiquity and continuity of Iranian kingship, and had famously and grandly proclaimed before the tomb of Cyrus, the first Iranian king, at Pasargadae: "O Cyrus, sleep calm and peaceful for I am here."

I had always been fascinated by early religions as well as civilisations, and had been particularly interested in Zoroaster, founder of the earliest religion based on revealed scripture, the *Avesta*, which probably originated c.600 BC (although there are claims that it was much earlier). He proclaimed Ahura Mazda as the god of the early Persians. Ahura Mazda was transmitted to the Jews held in exile in Persian-ruled Babylon. In the seven generations or so that they lived in Persia they assimilated many of the Persian beliefs – the idea of a holy, just God who all men should worship, with evil embodied separately in Satan, rather than the local tribal god of the Hebrews; the immortality of the soul, along with life after death, resurrection, heaven and hell, and the judgement of the dead; and the final prophet, the world saviour, the Holy Spirit (the Persian Spenta Mainyu), down to the details of the seven archangels, the seven-branched candlestick (*menorah*) and the Sabbath, the full moon day. When Cyrus liberated Babylonia in 539BC and permitted the Jews to return home the following year, the Jews took back with them the concept of Ahura Mazda as supreme god. Zoroastrianism had influenced Jewish monotheism and is therefore perhaps the most influential religion of all time. I knew that Ahura Mazda is still worshipped in Iran, particularly in remoter areas.

I was interested in Iran's ethnic diversity. In 1935 Reza Shah, the father of the last Shah, called on the world to refer to his country not as Persia but as Iran ("land of the Aryans"), a name first used by Ardashir I, founder of the Sasanian dynasty, to reflect all ethnic groups, Persian and non-Persian, which now include the Kurds, the Turkmen, the Baluchis and the Lurs. The Sasanian "Iranshahr" (or "Eranshahr") meant "Empire of the Aryans".

The Iranian Revolution and Persia's cultural heritage
I also appreciated Iran's modern significance in international politics. The story had been a turbulent one. The rise of Ayatollah Khomeini ("*Ayatollah*" means "sign of God") and his replacement of the last Shah in a Cromwell-style (but civil-warless), puritanical revolution in 1979 marked the highest point of the Islamic movement and inspired bin Laden to attempt to replace the House of Saud. 9/11 struck at the House of Saud's main ally. More recently President Ahmadinejad's determination to make Iran nuclear in defiance of US wishes and a UN Security Council resolution (1737) has made military action against Iran by the new Coalition a very real possibility. Indeed, given the uncompromising stance of both sides at the time it seemed unavoidable. Iranian intransigence was now a byword, and could have profound implications for the supply of the world's oil.

I wanted to see Iran's cultural heritage before the country became impenetrable and before its monuments were destroyed. Not much, alas, has been left of Iraq's cultural treasures after five years of relentless war and civil war. I was fortunate enough to see Iraq's early Islamic caliphate buildings in conditions of relative peace and security under the military dictatorship of Abdul Karim Kassem, and this might be my last chance to absorb early Iranian culture in similarly peaceful conditions.

Research for my second poetic epic
So what is the aim of this book? My immediate personal reason was that

I was planning a long poem on the Middle East [*Armageddon* (Preface 31)], and, as in the case of my poetic epic *Overlord*, which I researched on the Second World War's battlefields, I wanted to do some on-the-spot research and absorb some local colour for this new work before Iran became a no-go area. More broadly, I thought my traveller's notes might help a wider audience appreciate the sheer wealth of Iran's cultural and spiritual heritage. Iran was richly diverse, and in its tourist sites and ruins Achaemenian, Sasanian, Islamic, Safavid and modern motifs were woven together into a fine pattern, like the pattern on an exquisite Persian carpet. Its awe-inspiring mix of culture, history, politics and spirituality could not fail to impress the most casual observer and nourish all personal quests for universality, the philosophy of embracing the "whole" whilst retaining our individual distinctiveness which I see as the only way forward for our troubled world. It was lamentable that some of its beauty might be about to be lost in war. Maybe in tracing its history and culture I could see how we came to this impasse, and how it might be negotiated.

Iran's capture of American hostages and support for militias
No country had been the recipient of a more negative image than Iran. President Ahmadinejad had been identified by one of the hostages as one of the student leaders who held 66 American diplomats and citizens hostage in their own Embassy in Tehran for 444 days in 1979–1981. An AP picture of this particular student leader can be found in Mark Bowden's *Guests of the Ayatollah*, and he certainly looks like a younger version of Ahmadinejad. It was suggested that a "fanatic" who allegedly climbed the gates to the US Embassy and paraded the blindfolded Jerry Miele on 11 November 1979 was now on the verge of acquiring, allegedly with Pakistani and perhaps North Korean help, a nuclear weapon that can be used against the United States.

To the US, if true this was a preposterous state of affairs and was a possible factor in the US's decision to urge the UN to introduce targeted sanctions against Iran under resolution 1737, which banned the export of nuclear technology to Iran, and to call on a reluctant Europe to implement an economic squeeze against Iran to foment internal dissent. Iran had been given 60 days to comply with a list of demands, and had so far ignored them. Tehran had just turned down applications for visas from 38 UN nuclear inspectors. The situation looked potentially more dangerous than the situation in Iraq, which had 1,200 UN inspectors looking unsuccessfully for nuclear weapons in 2003, and the US and Britain still went to war.

Furthermore, there had been allegations that the Supreme Leader has been host to al-Qaeda and has funded Hamas in Palestine, Shiites in Iraq and Nasrallah in the Lebanon, all of whom were anti-US. It is hard to know how much of this is true, but there does seem more evidence of substantial involvement with these groups than was produced for similar involvement by Saddam Hussein. There had been claims in the press that Iran had been responsible for the insurgency in Iraq, through the 31,690 Iranian agents (named by an opposition group, the National Council of Resistance) allegedly working in Iraq, paid in Iranian *rials* and supplying Shia militias with money, bomb-making equipment and expertise. To the US this was unacceptable, and according to press reports, Bush had authorised American troops to kill these agents. Put all this together and it is easy to see why word was out that Iran was a pariah state and was not a safe place to visit, and why a country that should be in the top ten destinations in terms of its attractions has not been in the top one hundred over the last couple of years.

Areas not safe for Westerners
Tour operators confirmed this image. "I'd like to go to Susa," I told the travel agent, "which was the Elamite capital and also one of Cyrus's and Darius's capitals in the south-west; to the tomb of Daniel, the *Old Testament* prophet; and to the two ziggurats, Chogha Zanbil and Haft Tappeh, nearby."

The answer came back from the ground handlers that the area was not safe for Westerners. "It's just across the Shatt al-Arab from Basra. It's a strongly Arab area, there are al-Qaeda present. The tour company can't guarantee your safety in the south-west. They don't allow any tourists to go to the Ahwaz area; they may be kidnapped on the sites."

And Bam in the south-east, where there was a terrible earthquake on 27 December 2003?

"There are still many homeless camping round the ruins. Visitors are discouraged from going there. It's also not safe. Visitors can be attacked."

The UK's Foreign-and-Commonwealth-Office website reflected this concern. Iran was listed as a second-category country, meaning a country "the FCO advises against all travel to parts of". "There is a threat from terrorism in Iran. Attacks could be indiscriminate and against civilian targets." The FCO website continued, "We strongly advise against all travel to the border areas with Afghanistan, Pakistan and Iraq. Westerners have been the target of kidnaps by armed gangs in south-east Iran.... We cannot rule out the possibility of further kidnaps." (The Lonely-Planet website said that one should only go overland to Iran if one has a death-wish.)

Israeli threat to Natanz
The week before I went Bush Jr announced that 21,500 more US troops would be sent to Iraq. A front-page *Sunday Times* article about Israel also appeared, claiming that Israeli planes were rehearsing sorties to Iran by flying to Gibraltar and back, the distances being comparable. Israeli pilots were being trained to bomb the nuclear sites near Isfahan and Arak with conventional bunker-busters and the nuclear site near Natanz with nuclear-tipped tactical nuclear weapons one-fifteenth of the size of the Hiroshima bomb. If this happened, Natanz would soon be as well-known as Hiroshima.

My itinerary, no other tourists
With all these considerations in mind I chose my itinerary by looking at books and maps and aiming to be compact. The main principle was to see as much as possible, operate out of a car and keep moving, and to sleep in a different place each night so that if any ill-disposed "terrorists" heard of my presence I would be gone before they could locate me. I was clear that it was too risky on several counts to take my wife, who had been my travelling companion to so many places that feature in my literary works. This was a journey I should undertake alone. I designed a tailor-made itinerary in conjunction with a tour company who liaised with their "ground handlers" in Iran. The itinerary was agreed before I left the UK. I consulted my doctor's surgery and was deemed to be covered for typhoid. I was given tetanus, diphtheria and polio in one arm and hepatitis A in the other. I made sure I had good travel and medical insurance.

The tourist season in Iran is from March to December. Few tourists go in January and February because of possible snow and hazardous ice. I had originally planned to go in December but my visit was delayed until mid-January as it became clear that my visa would not be through in time. The compensation for this was that the "nuclear crisis" had caused the hardy souls who might otherwise have braved the anticipated winter weather in January to cancel, and I seemed to be the only tourist in Iran. I pretty much had Iran to myself. I was the last tourist in Iran before the bombing was expected to begin.

28

The Rise and Fall of Civilizations

Why Civilizations Rise and Fall and what Happens when they End

Prologue

Religions based on the experience of the Light
In the precursor and companion volume to this work, *The Light of Civilization*, I saw that religion is about more than hymns and prayers. It is an inner experience of the soul opening to God, who is experienced as Light. Different religions interpret the experience in different ways, but all who open to God as Light are having the same experience.

I focused on 25 Light traditions from different parts of the world, spanning the last five thousand years, and established that the experience of God as Light is the basis of religion and all religions.

I saw that during the five thousand years of recorded history there were many periods of high civilisation which have left behind stone monuments and exquisite art, and I identified the principle that has stirred different peoples from nomadic, pastoral culture to the heights of civilisation that we still admire today.

25 civilisations based on religions and their Light, 14 still living
I maintained that civilisation is based on religion and that religion is based on an experience of the mysterious Light which is interpreted differently in different religions. I identified 25 different civilisations that have reached high civilisation through their religions. To recap, the civilisations are, in broadly chronological or geographical order:

1. Indo-European Kurgan (perhaps builders of megaliths in Old Europe)
2. Mesopotamian (Sumerian-Akkadian and later Babylonian)
3. Egyptian
4. Aegean-Greek (including Minoan and Mycenaean)
5. Roman
6. Anatolian (including Hittite)
7. Syrian
8. Israelite (Judaistic)
9. Celtic (including Irish-Celtic and Druid)

10. Iranian
11. European together with 12 forming Western civilisation ⎫
12. North-American (now centred in Europe and USA)   ⎭
13. Byzantine-Russian (Christian Orthodox)
14. Germanic-Scandinavian
15. Andean (including Peruvian)
16. Meso-American (including Mexican and North-American Mississippian)
17. Arab (Islamic)
18. African
19. Indian (Hindu)
20. South-East-Asian (mainly Mahayana and later Theravada Buddhist)
21. Japanese
22. Oceanian (including Polynesian and Australian)
23. Chinese
24. Tibetan
25. Central-Asian (including Mongolian) from c.500BC

Of these 25 civilisations the first ten and no. 14 are dead, and the other fourteen are still living. Between them, these 25 civilisations were based on, and reached high civilisation through, 21 different religions/ distinctive gods, which I saw as:

	Civilisation	Distinctive god
1.	Indo-European Kurgan and Megalithic in Old Europe	Dyaeus Pitar/Magna Mater (Sky Father/Earth Mother)
2.	Mesopotamian	Anu/Ogma/Utu Shamash/Tammuz/Marduk Shuqamuna/Ashur
3.	Egyptian	Ra/Amon/Aton Horus/Osiris/Apis
4.	Aegean-Greek (Minoan/ Mycenaean)	Zeus/Apollo Anat/Athene (or Athena)
5.	Roman	Jupiter/Apollo Gnostic God as Light
6.	Anatolian Hittite Phrygian	Mistress of Animals/ Storm and Weather god Tarhun or Teshub/Sharruma/Arinna Cybele/Attis

7.	Syrian	
	Canaanite	El/Dagon/Baal/Mot/Resheph/
		Molech (or Moloch)
		Koshar/Astarte/Anath (or Anat)
	Phoenician	Baal/Astarte/Adonis
	Philistine	Dagon/Ashtoreth/Baal
	Aramaean	Hadad/Rammon/Atargatis
8.	Israelite (Judaistic)	El Shaddai/Yahweh
9.	Celtic	Du-w ("Yoo-we", cf. "Yahweh")/Lug/
		Beli (cf. Baal)/Taran/Yesu
10.	Iranian	Mithras/Zurvan (of Medes)/Ahura Mazda/Mani
	Elamite	Inshushinak/Kiririshna (cf. Indian Krishna)/Nahhunte/Huban
11.	European (Christian)	God as Light
	*North-American	God as Light
	*Byzantine-Russian	God as Light
	(offshoots from Christian)	
12.	Germanic-Scandinavian	Wodan/Odin
13.	Andean	Smiling god ("El Lanzon" "the Great Image")
		Sun-gods: Inti/Quetzlcoatl/Kukulan
14.	Meso-American	Kinich Ahau (or Itzamna)/Huitzilopochtli
15.	Arab (Islamic)	Allah
16.	African	Mwari/Nzambi/Cghene/Ngai/ Leza/Ndjambi Marunga/ Raluvhimba/Olodumare
17.	Indian	Agni/Brahman/Atman
		Siva/Sakti
		Vishnu/Rama/Krishna
		Om Kar
	South-East-Asian	The Buddha
	(Mahayana Buddhist)	The Buddha
18.	Japanese Shinto	Kami/Amaterasu
		The Buddha
19.	Oceanian (Polynesian and Melanesian) (offshoot from Indian/Andean)	The Buddha?
		Andean Smiling god/Inti?
		Io (Maoris)

20.	Chinese	*Shang Ti/T'ien Ti*/The *Tao*
21.	*Tibetan *Central-Asian (including Mongolian)	The Buddha The Buddha

Four civilisations (see asterisks) have related religions.

How 25 civilisations rise and fall through their religions and the Light
I now carry the argument forward by showing in detail how civilisations rise and fall through their religions and Light. We will consider the genesis, growth, arrest of growth, breakdown, renewal, decline, decay and demise of the 25 civilisations in terms of the Light which inspired their religions. When their Light is strong, they rise; when their Light dims and fades, they turn secular and begin to fall. As with all patterns, the devil is in the detail; the evidence has to be presented before it can be said that the patterns work, the proof of the pudding is in the eating. Much of the detail can be found in the respective Light traditions and subtradition presented in *The Light of Civilization*. I now give, in summary form, historical detail for the progress of civilisations, which should be read in conjunction with *The Light of Civilization*. I give the evidence for my thesis. I show that the Light – the experience of what has been called the divine Light – inspired the religions within 25 civilisations and propelled their growth. In the eleven dead civilisations, when the Light was dimmed the civilisation declined. The same may now be true of the fourteen living civilisations, including Western civilisation.

Western civilisation, an amalgam of the European and North-American civilisations
In *The Light of Civilization*, we saw that Western civilisation is an amalgam of two civilisations: the European civilisation, which goes back to the Germanic tribes who sacked the Roman Empire; and the North-American civilisation, which, despite its discovery by Columbus in 1492 really began with the founding of the Jamestown settlement, the first English-speaking settlement to survive, in 1607 (the date on which the US has based its observance of its 400th anniversary). [Also see Preface 26.] One of my conclusions in this book is that the European civilisation is old and may need a recovery of the Light if it is to survive and flourish. The North-American civilisation, however, is relatively new and young, and contains within it the Light that it needs to survive – and, indeed, expand.

61 similar stages of 25 rising and falling civilisations
We will see that each civilisation goes through the same 61 stages. By overlaying the living civilisations on the dead ones we can anticipate the coming stages of living civilisations, including our own. This will enable us to make some predictions. We shall see that the dead civilisations pass into other living civilisations with different gods and continue their flow; thus, the Egyptian and Mesopotamian peoples woke one day to find that their civilisations had come to an end and that they had passed into the Arab civilisation, that their religions and gods had been replaced by Islam and Allah. We can thus grasp that the flow of history is endless in the sense that it is without end until human history ends. By looking at the past of living civilisations and considering what happened to the dead ones as we chart the rise and fall of 25 different civilisations, we shall be treading in the footsteps of Gibbon, Spengler and Toynbee, whose works I taught in Japan where I first glimpsed this fourth way of approaching Western and world history more than forty years ago.

My Universalist way: a Grand Unified Theory of World History and
Religion revealing the pattern and Law of History
My fourth way is a Universalist way. For Universalist history focuses on the history of all mankind as a whole in relation to the universe, and not on regional parts. It seeks to reveal the pattern of history. By offering the endless rise and fall of 25 civilisations based on religions I am able to offer a Grand Unified Theory of World History and Religion, which to my knowledge has never been attempted before and which is surely timely now that globalism is on the verge of creating a world government that will view us primarily as world citizens.

August 2007

29

The New Philosophy of Universalism

The Infinite and the Law of Order
Prolegomena to a Vast, Comprehensive Philosophy of the Universe and a New Discipline

Prologue

Greek philosophy and the Reality behind the universe
This book calls for a revolution in Western philosophy. The Presocratic Greeks, Plato and Aristotle focused on the Reality behind the universe. I hold that Western philosophy should return to its origin in them. This book seeks to overthrow the Establishment orthodoxy of Western philosophy which has been entrenched in logic and language for nearly a hundred years, ever since Einstein bewildered philosophers with his two relativity theories of 1905 and 1915. It calls for the universe to be let back into philosophy. Explaining the universe and Nature should once again be the business of philosophy.

It is sometimes said of our knowledge of the universe, "It's all theories. We don't know how the universe began. The Big Bang is a theory. All that physicists and mathematicians say about the universe is just theories. Nothing is known." This is too pessimistic. I have tried to sift what can be safely known, and in this book I have built up a picture of what we can know about the universe. I have been careful to distinguish fact from theory. What is missing today is a university course that does this. And yet in the Middle Ages such a course was central to university life.

Medieval schools of philosophy: metaphysical and scientific traditions
One of my favourite quadrangles, which I always look in on when I visit Oxford, is the Schools Quadrangle at the Bodleian Library. It was built between 1613 and 1619 as an extension to Thomas Bodley's 1602 Library, and the ground and first floors were used as lecture rooms for the university students of the seven liberal arts. These *"scolae"* or "schools" are named in Latin lettering over the stone Quadrangle doorways: Logic, Grammar and Rhetoric (the *trivium*); and Arithmetic, Geometry, Music and Astronomy (*the quadrivium*). As the Renaissance had flourished by 1613, "modern subjects" are over other doorways: Hebrew, Greek, History, Medicine and Jurisprudence. Beside them is

the oldest and most important subject: Divinity. As the Quadrangle looked back to the medieval time of Duke Humfrey's 1443 Library, which Bodley restored from 1602, also present in Latin lettering are the three branches of philosophy found in all medieval universities to which the seven liberal arts were introductory: the very important subjects of Moral and Natural Philosophy and Metaphysics, which were the centre of the curriculum of all medieval universities.

Two thousand years previously, philosophy was at the centre of the Greek curriculum in the Academy Plato founded, where Aristotle was a pupil. For nearly two hundred years before then, Greek philosophers had looked at the universe – sky, sea and land – and had attempted an explanation. I was fortunate enough to be introduced to these first Western philosophers at school, where I also spent long hours reading Socrates' arguments in the original Greek of some of Plato's dialogues. Plato continued this metaphysical tradition of attempting to explain the universe, and since then, despite changes soon after the Renaissance, some philosophers have offered quite theoretical explanations involving an invisible Reality. Other philosophers have seen the world of Nature as the real world and have offered more scientific explanations. Aristotle continued this scientific tradition of natural philosophy, and since then many philosophers have been scrupulously evidential and wary of excessive theorising. Some philosophers have been more interested in human conduct, or moral philosophy.

The definition of philosophy has therefore varied in accordance with the interests of particular philosophers, who have defined philosophy to reflect their interests. The *Shorter Oxford English Dictionary* defines philosophy as "the love, study, or pursuit of wisdom, or of knowledge of things and their causes, whether theoretical or practical". It adds, "That more advanced study to which, in the mediaeval universities, the seven liberal arts were introductory; it included the three branches of natural, moral and metaphysical philosophy, commonly called the three philosophies." These are all defined separately in the *Shorter Oxford English Dictionary*. 'Moral philosophy' was "the knowledge or study of the principles of human action or conduct; ethics", "the part of philosophy that treats of the virtues and vices, the criteria of right and wrong, the formation of virtuous character". 'Natural philosophy' was "the knowledge or study of natural objects and phenomena; now usually called 'science'". 'Metaphysical philosophy' was "that department of knowledge or study which deals with ultimate Reality, or with the most general causes and principles of things". 'Metaphysics' is more specifically defined as "that branch of speculation which deals with the first principles of things, including such concepts as being, substance, essence, time, space, cause, identity etc.; theoretical philosophy as the ultimate science of Being and Knowing".[1]

In the later Middle Ages the philosophical disciplines of logic (including disputations), ethics (the Aristotelian version of moral philosophy), natural philosophy and metaphysics were central to the curriculum as they were studied as a preparation for the higher calling of theology (or divinity).[2] Little attention was paid to epistemology (how we know) as scepticism was not an issue due to the dominance of theology (or divinity) and the importance of direct intellectual vision with the aid of divine illumination. Likewise, little attention was given to psychology as soul and body were thought of as being dualistically distinct.

17th-century rise of science crowds out philosophy
The two main traditions of philosophy – the metaphysical and the scientific – developed until in the late 17th century the rise of science began to crowd philosophy out. Newton, whose physics revolutionised science in the 1660s, saw himself as a 'natural philosopher', but in the 18th century 'natural philosophy' had been renamed "science". Scientists ("natural philosophers") occupied the philosophers' traditional ground including the ground once occupied by metaphysics, and in the 20th century theoretical physicists theorised about the universe as metaphysicians had done – often no more evidentially: there is only circumstantial evidence to support their black holes, dark matter and dark energy, which have not been observed. (However, if they do not in fact exist there will have to be new hypotheses to explain the fact that only 4 per cent of the universe's matter is visible, according to mathematical calculations; which means that 96 per cent of matter is missing without any explanation.)

During the last 350 years of increasing Materialism and reductionism, and of scientists fragmenting the universe into smaller and smaller bits, philosophy has vacated its metaphysical and scientific ground to science. Philosophy has been left with Phenomenology (and its focus on consciousness) on the Continent – Existentialism is now dead – and linguistic philosophy in the Anglo-Saxon world; and moral philosophy. These are all separate and in some degree of conflict with each other. They are all removed from the universe and Nature, which first inspired philosophy. There is no prospect within the existing movements and structures that, if left to their own devices, philosophy can be reunited, and a return of the universe into philosophy offers the only prospect of such a reunification. The existing groupings only explore parts of Reality, which for 2,600 years has included both the finite universe that emerged from the Big Bang and the infinite from which it came.

Universalism: new philosophical reunification of metaphysical and scientific traditions
It is time for philosophy to return to its original purpose of looking at the whole of Reality (the finite *and* the infinite) and of seeing man in relation to an orderly universe. The name I give to this way forward and renewed focus on the universe is "Universalism". The term has been used variously in the past to describe the salvation of the whole of humankind (universal salvation), or the recognition that all religions have equal validity (religious universalism or universal religion) or that the whole of humankind should have equal political rights, an increasingly aired view as thinking becomes more global (political universalism or universal suffrage). Thus the *Shorter Oxford English Dictionary* defines a Universalist as "one who believes or maintains the doctrine that redemption or election is extended to the whole of mankind". In this book I use the term 'Universalism' to describe the new philosophical worldview and movement that seeks to take philosophy back to its origins and which like Romanticism or Classicism may one day have a life outside philosophy as well as within it. My Universalism can eventually put philosophy back at the centre of the university curriculum which it occupied until the rise of science. For the study of the philosophy of the universe incorporates the findings of all the sciences.

My term 'Universalism' incorporates 'universe', 'universal' and 'universality'. It is a philosophy focusing on (1) the universe, (2) universal science, (3) a universal principle of order ("universal" in the sense that its effects are found in every aspect of Nature and its organisms) and (4) humankind as a whole and its place in the universe. It also refers to (5) the universal being, the deeper self below the rational, social ego, which is open to (6) universal cosmic energies which stimulate the growth of plants and organisms and convey the principle of order. The universe is the earth, galaxies and intergalactic space regarded as a whole: all that is, all existing things. It has become the fiefdom of Materialist scientists who focus on its matter and energy, using mathematical methods. 'Nature' is the system within the universe in which we are integrated.

'Order', in the first of its 20 meanings in the *Concise Oxford Dictionary* (one present in Middle English during the Middle Ages), is "the condition in which every part or unit is in its right place, tidiness", which covers the behaviour of insects, fish, birds, reptiles, mammals and humans within Nature's system. It is also "a state of peaceful harmony under a constitutional authority" (as in "order has been restored"), suggesting organisation, and "the nature of the world society" (as in "the order of things"). Thus 'order' suggests an organised, basically tidy world scheme or system in which everything knows its defined or right place (until randomness intrudes). Such a system is described in systematic philosophy, which proposes a Grand Unified Theory of Everything.

The theme of this book, then, is that philosophy should now return to its traditional task of understanding and explaining the universe and the world of Nature, and that it should reunify the existing conflicting groupings and movements. In a sense, this book is an introduction or *Prolegomena* to a vast philosophy of the universe – to a new discipline, for it redefines the scope of philosophy and subsumes many existing scientific disciplines from a new angle. I hope that, seeing the new direction that I offer, young philosophers will come forward and use their skills to articulate Universalist philosophy and turn it into as detailed and wide-ranging a movement as Phenomenology and Linguistic Analysis are.

Metaphysical and scientific philosophical traditions: two wings of reunifying Universalism

This book explains why Universalism is needed in philosophy; what it derives from the evidence of science; what the new metaphysical philosophy is; and its applications. In Part One we look at the history of Western philosophy since the Greek Thales, c.585BC. We shall see that for 2,600 years there have been two main emphases in philosophy, stemming from the Presocratic Greeks, Plato and Aristotle. These passed into the Christian era, and since the Renaissance fragmented. These two tendencies have changed their names since the Renaissance, but in essence they have remained the same though they have declined in importance: one metaphysical and focusing on Reality, the other scientific and focusing on Nature. Part Two deals with the scientific view of the universe. I give an up-to-date view of all the main scientific disciplines, and have tried to be scrupulously objective and factual, as if I were trying to explain it to the satisfaction of Aristotle, the founder of the scientific tradition, and of Sir Francis Bacon, the first Empiricist. To synthesise all scientific disciplines and distil a whole view was possible in the time of the Renaissance but is very difficult today as knowledge has become specialised and fragmented. Only the philosopher contemplating the philosophy of science is in a position to draw the specialised subjects together and attempt a synthesis, and if he makes mistakes of detail, that is surely a price worth paying for achieving a whole view.

This scientific view of the universe is one wing of Universalism. Part Three deals with the metaphysical view of the universe. It assimilates the hidden Reality of the metaphysical view over 2,600 years. This metaphysical view of the universe is the other wing of Universalism. Universalism now reunifies the two emphases in philosophy by incorporating Plato's tradition of hidden Reality emerging from the infinite and Aristotle's tradition of a scientific approach to the universe. We shall see that the first focuses on the unchanging and infinite, the second on finite, changing Nature. Part Four gives some modern applications of Universalism and integrates moral philosophy's focus on human conduct.

I use a dialectical method which was anticipated by Eastern thinking. This was first explained to me in 1965 by the Japanese poet Junzaburo Nishiwaki, who has been called Japan's T.S. Eliot. (He was a contemporary of Eliot's.) As we drank *saké* (rice-wine) in a bar with sawdust on the floor round the corner from Keio University, he wrote out on a reply card which is now framed on my study wall: "+A + −A = 0, Great Nothing". The 0 is zero; the Great Nothing is the One. In this thinking, two opposites are reconciled into harmony within the One. The opposites can be Being and non-Being, Being and Becoming, life and death, the world of time and the world of eternity, the finite and infinite, the metaphysical and the scientific. Universalism as a reconciler as well as a revolution employs this dialectic to unite the two traditions, and within the context of this unity to unite Continental Phenomenology's ontology and Anglo-Saxon Analytical philosophy's focus on language.

In attempting a reunification of the two traditions after 2,600 years, I am by definition attempting to reunite largely untestable metaphysics and testable science − which were united at the origin of Western philosophy.

Philosophical categories
Categories are very important. The metaphysical emphasis is often theoretical and speculative (as can be seen from Idealism), and has Rationalistic and Intuitional forms. Its reasoning is often untestable. As I have already observed, theoretical physics is in a similar position, with little proof outside mathematics for its various theories, such as superstring theory. Mathematics is not evidential. The scientific emphasis is empirical and testable. Theoretical, speculative reasoning

and empirical handling of data must be kept separate. The philosophical category can handle opposites of different categories (+A + −A) so long as it is clear what the categories are. There are other categories – for example, categories of interpretation, faith, myth and culture – and philosophy must be wary of these.

Just as the philosopher uses a philosophical category to consider theoretical reasoning and scientific evidence, so the universal principle of order is a philosophical category. It may, however, also be a scientific hypothesis based on evidence of its cells' operating effects within Nature. There is no anomaly in its being a philosophical category *and* a scientific proposal at the same time. Indeed, it may one day be proved to be a scientific law – perhaps sooner than we realise in view of CERN's search for a hitherto undetected field of bosons from September 2008 – just as for 2,500 years the atom was both a philosophical category and an unproved scientific proposal until it was proved to have operational existence. Similarly, infinity and timelessness are philosophical categories which may similarly be scientifically evident.

Need for evidence and endnotes
Works of philosophy tend not to have endnotes so that their general ideas may appear more enduring. Today ideas by themselves are insufficient to describe the universe. Gone are the days when philosophers can make sweeping generalisations about the universe without a discerning reader rightly wishing to know, "Where's your evidence?" The process of thought, though an indispensable tool, is by itself incapable of approaching the truth about the universe, which demands the allegiance of other disciplines besides thought. The philosopher of the universe must be up-to-date on all the recent advances in thinking and scientific discoveries such as those that might be made at CERN. Today the philosopher of the universe must be evidential and transparent about his sources. No book of modern philosophy about the universe can be taken seriously if it does not offer sources.

The philosopher as sage
The main theme of this book, then, is that philosophy needs to be reconnected to Nature and the universe, and that the evidence of a principle of order in cells will enable philosophy to be reunited and reassume a more central position in Western life. The philosopher can come to be regarded as a man who has explored all the cross-disciplinary scientific knowledge of the Whole, the One, and has an

up-to-date view of the structure, substance, cause, first principles and reality of the scientific universe. The philosopher can cease to be thought of as an abstruse, irrelevant figure lost in minutiae of language, and can be regarded once again, as he traditionally was: as a sage. The dictionary definition of a sage is "a profoundly wise man", a fitting description for a "lover of wisdom".

Notes:
1. Some useful introductions to metaphysics are: Brian Carr, *Metaphysics*; D.W. Hamlyn, *Metaphysics*; George N. Schlesinger, *Metaphysics*; and Alan R. White, *Methods of Metaphysics*.
2. See the *Routledge Encyclopaedia of Philosophy*, https://www.rep.routledge.com/.

30

The Libyan Revolution

Its Origins and Legacy
A Memoir and Assessment

Preface

New information on the 1969 Libyan Revolution
I was an eyewitness of the military *coup* which began the Libyan Revolution in 1969 when I was working in Tripoli. I have seen no other eyewitness accounts in print of what it was like. More than that, I was party (in more than one sense) to events before the *coup* which enabled me to observe how the Revolution was allowed to succeed. During this time I got to know the Libyan who would emerge as Gaddafi's most controversial Prime Minister.

In October 1978 I found myself drinking in an Oxford buttery with the historian (Lord) Asa Briggs, then a chubby, tousled-haired, bespectacled, twinkling-eyed Oxford Provost of great charm. He questioned me in some detail about Libya. I told him the story in full, and he said, "You must write a book about your experiences. You have told me something I have often wondered about and did not know, you must write it down. You have just explained how the West came to accept the Gaddafi Revolution. I have not seen this written anywhere else. You must write the full story. It is of historical importance."

Here, thirty-one years later, is part of the story, the public one. The more private one will have to wait for another occasion. [See *My Double Life 1: This Dark Wood*, Preface 36.]

My accurate prediction Gaddafi would be in power for 40 years
When I left Libya I was asked to write an article for *The Sunday Telegraph*. In my first draft I compared Gaddafi to the youthful Alexander the Great and predicted that he would be in power in 40 years' time. The paper did not want to be hearing that – they wanted me to be saying that he might not survive his first year in power – and they did not want me to be indulging in far-sighted predictions, but to be reporting on what I could see a month or two ahead. So they edited my prediction out. (I had similar treatment when I submitted the world scoop on the Chinese Cultural Revolution to Fleet Street's China experts, to be told by all of them, "I do not believe that such a purge is about to happen.")

Now, once again, I can wryly say to the editor who knew better, "I told you so."

This unique view of Libya is timed to coincide with the 40th anniversary of Gaddafi's despotic seizure of power.

31

Armageddon

The Triumph of Universal Order
An Epic Poem on the War on Terror and of Holy-War Crusaders

Preface

Epic in a growing civilisation
An epic poem is "a long poem narrating the adventures or deeds of one or more heroic or legendary figures", "an imaginative work embodying a nation's conception of its past history" (*Concise Oxford Dictionary*). Ezra Pound wrote that "an epic is a poem including history" (*ABC of Reading*).

Epic, a narrative of a heroic episode taken from history, is thrown up by heroic deeds during a civilisation's time of growth. This is true of the *Rig Veda, Gilgamesh,* the *Iliad,* the *Aeneid,* the *Chanson de Roland* and *Beowulf* in the growing Indian, Mesopotamian, Greek, Roman, European and Germanic-Scandinavian civilisations. When there is no growing civilisation there is no epic.

The Greek epic of the primitive and oral tradition of Homer, who wrote about the capture of Troy, is less sophisticated and psychological than the Roman literary epic of the tradition of Virgil, Homer's imitator, who wrote about the founding of Rome. The literary epic was designed to be read rather than recited, and whereas Homer admired the deeds of rugged individuals whose code of honour often acted against society, Virgil made Aeneas the embodiment of Rome's civic virtue. He had a deeper awareness of society and how heroic deeds achieved national destiny.

The rediscovery of Virgil during the Renaissance led to Torquato Tasso's epic of Christian knights, *Gerusalemme liberata* (*Jerusalem Delivered*), 1575. Two lesser-known epic works had appeared in 1572: Camões' *Os Lusiadas* (1572) narrated Vasco da Gama's discovery of the route to India, and Pierre de Ronsard's *Franciade* (1572) connected the founding of France with the Trojan hero Francus. Milton's *Paradise Lost* (1667) was the last distinguished epic. Joel Barlow's *The Columbiad* (1807) narrated how Columbus had a vision of America's destiny. He anticipated the coming American epic. The Romantic poets valued spontaneity, particularity, self-expression and classical mythology as in Keats' *Hyperion*, and the Victorian Tennyson wrote a 12-book romance on the fortunes of King Arthur in a pre-industrial world. No one attempted poetic epic in the 19th or 20th centuries, though Ezra Pound's *Cantos* touched on epic narrative with Modernist brevity, and John Heath-Stubbs approached the epic tone in *Artorius*, which subordinates narrative to focus on the nine Muses.

My two epics within the growing North-American civilisation
In our time the only youthful, growing civilisation is the North-American civilisation, which is on the verge of reaching its epic stage. We reflect our Age, and now is a time of epic works on historical themes like Homer's *Iliad* and Virgil's *Aeneid* – on historical themes that include the United States, until recently the sole superpower, and modern Crusader war. Heroic American deeds during the Second World War and the War on Terror await poetic treatment. The epic is due for a revival within the North-American civilisation.

I, an Englishman living in the time of American global domination, am not unlike a Greek living in the time of the Roman Empire and writing in Latin. Very often an outsider can see more clearly than an insider, and by writing about America from within England I believe I have grasped the pattern of contemporary American global events more objectively than many Americans. Just as my historical work *The Secret Founding of America* [see Preface 26] has revelations about early (and later) American history that have startled many American readers, so my epic works, which I discussed with the American poet Ezra Pound in 1970 [see Appendix 2, pp.498–501], can be seen as North-American epics about heroic deeds within a global perspective.

I wrote in the Preface to Books 1–2 of my first poetic epic, *Overlord*:

Epic is recognised by: its subject matter; theme; heroic tone; narrative length; complexity; unity of action; the scope of its setting; the scale of its action; the moral stature of its heroes; its supernatural elements; its conventions; its accessible language; its exact metre; and its distinctive cosmology.

An epic poem's subject matter includes familiar and traditional material drawn from history and widely known in popular culture, which reflects the civilisation that threw it up. Its theme has a historical, national, religious or legendary significance. It narrates continuously the heroic achievements of a distinguished historical, national or legendary hero or heroes at greater length than the heroic lay, and describes an important national enterprise in more realistic terms than fantastic medieval Arthurian (Grail) romance; it gives an overwhelming impression of nobility as heroes take part in an enterprise that is larger and more important than themselves. Its long narrative is characterised by its sheer size and weight; it includes several strands, and has largeness of concept. It treats one great complex action in heroic proportions and in an elevated style and tone. It has unity of action, which begins in the middle (*"in medias res"*, to use Horace's phrase). The scope of its geographical setting is extensive, perhaps cosmic; its sweep is panoramic, and it uses heroic battle and extended journeying. The scale of the action is gigantic; it deals with good and evil on a huge scale. Consequently, its hero and main characters have great moral stature. It involves supernatural or religious beings in the action, and includes prophecy and the underworld. It has its own conventions; for example, it lists ships and genealogies, and the exploits that surround individual weapons. Its language is universally accessible, and includes ornamental similes and recurrent epithets. It uses exact metre (hexameters or the pentameters of blank verse). It has its own cosmology, and explains the ordering of the universe.

Universalist epic has a global perspective associated with the North-American civilisation, the world's globalist superpower. It presents a universal theme that is integral to the world's common culture and currency. My *Overlord* was about the Second World War, an Anglo-American war of liberation, which is a common global currency: everyone alive regardless of nationality knows about Eisenhower and Hitler to some degree. *Armageddon* is about the War on Terror, Anglo-American pre-emptive war, which is on the tongues of all living people and is, again, a common global currency.

Universalist epic is cross-disciplinary and factually accurate
Universalist epic draws on the approaches of traditional Greek, Roman, Italian and English epics (the epics of Homer, Virgil, Dante and Milton) and Old Norse sagas, but it differs from traditional epic in two key respects. First it draws on the up-to-date knowledge of a number of different disciplines, including cosmology and astrophysics, mysticism and comparative religion, and modern warfare and weaponry, but principally history and philosophy. In combining history, philosophy and literature (a three-legged stool) I am treading in the footsteps of, and am a successor to, Albert Camus, whose history included *The Rebel*, whose philosophy included *The Myth of Sisyphus* and whose literature included *The Plague*. (My history is of the rise and fall of civilisations, revolutions and the New World Order, my philosophy is of the universe and Universalism rather than Existentialism, and the

medium of my literature is poetry rather than fiction, but Camus is still a forerunner.) However, I am welding such a cross-disciplinary approach, and insights into the fundamental order and unity of the universe, into epic.

Secondly, we live in a time of 24-hour global news, which has turned the world into a global village and brought pressing historical change and religious conflict into our rooms. Interpreting a modern international story that is in the public domain to present a universal theme requires reference to precise events, facts and dates. If an event or fact is imprecise or in the wrong order, the epic poet's interpretation of the modern historical story will be inaccurate and just plain wrong. Dwelling on precise facts and dates to reveal universal aspects of war and the modern international tale may bewilder readers who are accustomed to the most general poetic treatment of events and have not encountered Universalist thinking in which the general co-exists within the particular and the universal within the specific. However, in innovative Universalist epic, the universal arises from specific events which are given a precise time and place. All poetry makes the personal and particular universal. Universalist poetry also makes the personal and particular universal, but pays greater attention to the particular.

Sources

A panoramic narrative epic poem on the War on Terror immediately faces one obvious difficulty. As the events have all happened relatively recently, sources are sometimes scanty and it is difficult to establish what happened, let alone how everything was connected and fits into an international story and pattern. In my previous epic, *Overlord*, I at least had the distance of 50 years which allowed events to settle into a broadly agreed story and pattern. In the case of the War on Terror the settling process is still happening. Nevertheless, I believe I have been able to establish what happened from many sources, and to connect everything so there is a clear, historically-accurate story and pattern. And the pattern will come through more clearly in a poetic work than in a more diffuse prose work detailing all its sources.

Some of the material relating to the War on Terror will be unfamiliar to many readers. As in the Preface to *Overlord* I should indicate some of my sources. Below are some – not all – of the books I have drawn on in different places. Dates in brackets indicate the extent of the War on Terror they cover.

For the account of bin Laden's purchases of nuclear-suitcase bombs, of his claim in November 2001 to have nuclear weapons and of his plan to organise ten simultaneous nuclear explosions in ten American cities (and at the very least seven cities, as mentioned on p.vi), see Yossef Bodansky, *Bin Laden: The Man Who Declared War on America* (2004) and three books by a former consultant to the FBI on organised crime and international terrorism, Paul Williams: *Osama's Revenge* (2004), *The Al Qaeda Connection* (2005) and *The Dunces of Doomsday* (2006). The suitcase bombs have been featured in the Western press, for example the front page of *The Times* of 26 October 2001 and *The Daily Mail* of 8 November 2001. For bin Laden's many attempts to purchase nuclear materials, see the Historical Addenda, pp.582–585 [of *Armageddon*]. *Osama's Revenge* includes three of bin Laden's long letters: 'Declaration of War', 'Jihad Against Jews and Crusaders' and 'A Letter to America'. Many more of his letters and essays can be found in *Messages to the World*, ed. Bruce Lawrence. Also see Brad K. Berner, *Quotations from Osama Bin Laden*. There is material about these writings in Peter L. Bergen, *The Osama bin Laden I Know* and *Holy War*. *Hunting Bin Laden* by Rob Schultheis suggests that bin Laden is near Zhob in Pakistan. Lawrence Wright's *The Looming Tower* has background on al-Qaeda.

Bin Laden has obliquely accepted overall responsibility for 9/11 in a number of opaque references to the event. (See p.x [in *Armageddon*].) Khalid Sheikh Mohammed has admitted to his captors that he had operational responsibility for 9/11.

I have followed Richard Miniter, *Shadow War: The Untold Story of How America Is Winning the War on Terror* (2004), and the evidence of his interviews with Iranian ex-intelligence officers, in seeing bin Laden as relocating after Tora Bora in Iran, which is positioned between, and is therefore central to, both Afghanistan and Iraq. This line is followed in Ilan Berman, *Tehran Rising* (2005) and in *The Dunces of Doomsday*. Much can be gleaned regarding Iran's role in the War on Terror from Ali M. Ansari, *Confronting Iran*; Alireza Jafarzadeh, *The Iran Threat*; and Vali Nasar, *The Shia Revival*. Also, a particular conversation in my book, *The Last Tourist in Iran* (2008) [pp.198–199].

There is an account of Bush's transformations in Stanley A. Renshon, *In His Father's Shadow*, and the impact of Bush senior on the son is well-handled in Jacob Weisberg, *The Bush Tragedy*. My Bush is genuinely trying to prevent nuclear proliferation, having come to grasp the seriousness of al-Qaeda's acquiring nuclear weapons. For Bush's outlook on freedom, see Natan Sharansky, *The Case for Democracy*, which Bush drew on. Also see Bruce Cumings, Ervand Abrahamian and Moshe Ma'oz, *Inventing the Axis of Evil*.

For confirmation that Kissinger of the Syndicate met Cheney monthly and Bush every two months, see Bob Woodward, *State of Denial*. For the Syndicate's work, see my book *The Syndicate*. Also see David Ray Griffin, *The New Pearl Harbor*. Antonia Juhasz, *The Bush Agenda* covers the role of multinationals under Bush. *Vice*, by Lou Dubose and Jake Bernstein, is revealing on Cheney's role. For the neo-cons, see Stefan Halper and Jonathan Clarke, *America Alone*; and Murray Friedman, *The Neoconservative Revolution*. Also, Andrew Cockburn, *Rumsfeld*.

For the insurgency I have drawn on Loretta Napoleoni, *Insurgent Iraq* (2005), but have gone with Jean-Charles Brisard, *Zarqawi: The New Face of Al-Qaeda* (2005), who provides more evidence that Zarqawi was an al-Qaeda operative from an early stage and bin Laden's endorsed heir. For the surge I have drawn on Thomas E. Ricks, *The Gamble* (2009). Israel's wars against Hezbollah in the Lebanon and Hamas in Gaza happened too recently to be covered in accurately-researched books, and I have relied on newspaper reports, internet material and my own notes based on television film.

Books on the background to the War on Terror include: *Understanding the War on Terror*, ed James F. Hoge and Gideon Rose; Paul Berman, *Terrorism and Liberalism*; Richard Falk, *The Great Terror War*; John L. Esposito, *Unholy War*; Nafeez Mosaddeq Ahmed, *Behind the War on Terror*; Walid Phares, *Future Jihad* and Ron Suskind, *The One Percent Doctrine*. Some books claim that America is winning the War on Terror, such as Richard Miniter, *Shadow War*. For the context of the War on Terror, see Charles Allen, *God's Terrorists*, which is on the Wahhabi cult and the roots of *jihad*; Philip Bobbit, *Terror and Consent*; Lt. General Thomas McInerney and Maj. General Paul Vallely, *Endgame*, which is a military assessment; and Anonymous, *Imperial Hubris*. [Anonymous was later revealed to be Michael Scheuer, a CIA veteran who ran the CIA's Counterterrorism Center's Bin Laden Issue Station from 1996 to 1999.]

Books hostile to Bush's Iraq adventure include Bob Woodward, *State of Denial*; Thomas E. Ricks, *Fiasco*; and Jonathan Steele, *Defeat*. Con Coughlin, *Saddam* contains an account of Saddam's life. For Saddam's links with al-Qaeda see Stephen F. Hayes, *The Connection* (2004), which details some telling contacts. Also see Paul William Roberts, *The Demonic Comedy*; and John Lee Anderson, *The Fall of Baghdad*. For the American Occupation of Iraq, see Michael R. Gordon and General Bernard E. Trainor, *Cobra II*; Patrick Cockburn, *The Occupation* and *Muqtada Al-Sadr and the Fall of Iraq*; Jeremy Scahill, *Blackwater*; Rajiv Chandrasekaran, *Imperial Life in the Emerald City*; and Joseph Stiglitz and Linda Bilmes, *The Three Trillion Dollar War*.

There are a number of books on specific issues covered in *Armageddon*. For the Vatican's finances after 1928, see Paul Williams, *The Vatican Exposed*. For Bush's links with Saudi Arabia, see Craig Unger, *House of Bush, House of Saud*. For books on oil, see David Strahan, *The Last Oil Shock*; and Michael Clare, *Blood and Oil*. For the Temple, see Simon Goldhill, *The Temple of Jerusalem*. There is no book about the missing American gold, and I have drawn on press cuttings, internet material and my own emails from well-placed sources.

There are more general works on the Middle East. The Western perspective can be gleaned from Robert Kagan, *Paradise and Power*; *Dangerous Nation*; and *The Return of History and the End of Dreams*. Also Cullen Murphy, *The New Rome*. The Islamic background can be found in Hugh Kennedy, *The Court of the Caliphs*; Efraim Karsh, *Islamic Imperialism*; and David Pryce-Jones, *The Closed Circle*.

There are many differing perspectives in these works, and the overall perspective in *Armageddon* is mine and only mine. Armed with some of these books the reader can, if so inclined, broadly check my interpretation of events and track my journey through my sources. However, I have drawn on many other works and on my files of newspaper cuttings that have helped me with specific events.

Blank verse, iambic pentameters
On the technical side, a poem is traditionally defined as "a metrical composition, usually concerned with feeling or imaginative description, an elevated composition in verse" (*Concise Oxford Dictionary*). I have remained loyal to metrical composition, and my chosen medium for telling my international story is again blank verse, which is rooted in the English tradition from Surrey and Marlowe to Tennyson. This is pretty strict verse in iambic pentameters with very occasional variations for emphasis. As in Latin verse, elision is allowed, as when 'the' or 'to' is followed by a vowel. Some words, such as 'seven', 'given' and 'Heaven', can be treated as having either one or two syllables depending on how the line is read, which will be governed by stress and emphasis. When a character is speaking I have sometimes followed the pronunciation of the speaker's ethnic group. Thus an American Southerner may say 'following' as two rather than three syllables, and on occasion 'Afghanistan' may be three rather than four syllables and 'organisation' may be four rather than five syllables if that is how the words would be spoken in their context. Blank verse in iambic pentameters is the medium that best allows verse to accommodate a tale involving international events.

Quarrels with myself
All poetry is a kind of quarrel with oneself rather than a quarrel with the world, when it becomes political propaganda. The quarrel

in *Armageddon* concerns some of the following issues. Is there a clash between Christian and Muslim civilisations? Is the West nobly intentioned or governed by commercial motives and greed for oil? Is bin Laden's hostility to the West valid in terms of the Muslim perspective? Are Islamic terrorist and al-Qaeda methods sanctioned by the *Koran*? To what extent is the War on Terror a noble thing on both sides? How much of it is idealism and sacrifice, and how much self-interest – on both sides? Is the suffering it has caused justified? In my quarrel with myself I have tried to understand all sides and have reconciled my internal conflicts – but in no way glorify terrorism or take part in quarrelling with the world.

Myths

The poet who deals with the modern clash of religions, cultures and civilisations soon discovers that his historical subject is intertwined with myth ("traditional narrative usually involving supernatural or imaginary persons", *Concise Oxford Dictionary*): the myths of Armageddon, the Great Tribulation and the Second Comings of Christ and of the Mahdi or Hidden *Imam* which have influenced the historical decisions of key modern leaders: Bush, bin Laden and Ahmadinejad.

These myths express "the unconscious metaphysic" of our time. E.M.W. Tillyard in *The English Epic and its Background* quotes Lascelles Abercrombie as seeing the epic poet as "accepting, and with his genius transfiguring, the general circumstance of his time... symbolising, in some appropriate form, whatever sense of the significance of life he feels acting as the accepted unconscious metaphysic of the time" (*The Epic*).

Many books relate recent events in the Middle East to the myth of the end days, the tribulation, the Antichrist and Armageddon from a Western point of view. These include J. Dwight Pentecost, *Things to Come* and with Charles R. Swindoll and John E. Walvoord and others, *The Road to Armageddon*; Walid Shoebat with Joel Richardson, *God's War on Terror*; Grant R. Jeffrey, *The Next World War* and *The New Temple and the Second Coming*; John P. McTernan, *As America Has Done to Israel*; Richard Booker, *Radical Islam's War against Israel, Christianity and the West*; and Robert Livingston, *Christianity and Islam: The Final Clash*. Many focus on Jerusalem and Iran: John Hagee, *Jerusalem Countdown*; Mark Hitchcock, *Iran: The Coming Crisis* and *The Apocalypse of Ahmadinejad*; Michael D. Evans with Jerome R. Corsi, *Showdown with Nuclear Iran*; and Ron Rhodes, *Northern Storm Rising*.

Joel Richardson, *Antichrist: Islam's Awaited Messiah* focuses on the Mahdi or Hidden *Imam*. Also see Al-Fadl ibn Shadhan, *The Return of the Mahdi*. Compare Ed Hinson, *Antichrist Rising* and Joye Jeffries Pugh, *Antichrist: The Cloned Image of Jesus Christ*. Hal Lindsey, *The 1980s: Countdown to Armageddon* provides background. Tom Kovach, *Tribulation 2008* has insights but his time scheme differs from that in the poem (2002–2009). Many books offer a Christian perspective on the last days, including Robert Lightner, *Last Days Handbook*; *The Meaning of the Millennium*, ed. by Robert G. Clouse; J. Oswald Sanders, *Certainties of Christ's Second Coming*; and W.J. Grier, *The Momentous Event*.

Books on the end of the world on 21 December 2012 include Adrian Gilbert, *The End of Time: The Mayan Prophecies Revisited*; Geoff Stray, *Beyond 2012: Catastrophe or Ecstasy – A Complete Guide to End-of-Time Predictions*; Patrick Geryl and Gino Ratinckx, *The Orion Prophecy*; and Lawrence E. Joseph, *Apocalypse 2012*.

Epic Heaven, and Hell as a place of Self-Improvement
All epics have a mythical upper world where events interact with and parallel events in the world below. I have continued the Light-based Heaven and Light-deprived Hell of *Overlord*, but those comparing and contrasting the upper worlds in the two epics will notice differences and an advance in my thinking about how the two worlds interact and how the dead relate to the living. Hell is now primarily a place of Self-Improvement which prepares for Heaven. Particular attention should be paid to what happens to the newly-dead who have been involved in acts of violence. The philosophical background for this advance may be found in my work of philosophy, *The New Philosophy of Universalism* (2009). To some extent, but only to some extent, my Christ and Satan can be seen as personifications of the order and disorder principles set out in that work.

My aims
In *Armageddon* I have attempted to unite poetry, history and myth in my own Sistine-Chapel ceiling. I have painted the War on Terror and the suffering it has caused, and have related it to "the ways of God", which I have attempted to justify to men. I have tried to balance the moral certainties and confusions of the two warring sides, and have focused on the US's need to prevent al-Qaeda from implementing their plan to set off nuclear-suitcase bombs simultaneously in ten US cities (see pp.x and xix [of *Armageddon*] for sources) and to re-establish the Caliphate in Baghdad (see maps on pp.xi and 624–625 [of *Armageddon*]). These real aspirations and goals of al-Qaeda's may come as a surprise to readers of Western newspapers and viewers of Western media, who will not have encountered them in such stark terms. Napoleon said

ironically and bitterly from his island exile, "History is a myth that men agree to believe." The version of contemporary history conveyed by Western media is a myth that Westerners agree to believe. In being truthful about the issues of our time I am concerned not to demoralise readers. On the contrary, I seek to convey a vision of hope.

My Bush

My Bush is a very misunderstood man who was genuinely trying to protect the West from what he believed to be a real threat that has not been fully reported and which was exaggerated and exploited by the Syndicate, of whom he was to a considerable degree something of a prisoner. (See my book *The Syndicate* for a historical, evidential account.) The Western duty to avoid dwelling on news items that may "unnecessarily" alarm the public has left the Western world bewildered at, and therefore critical of, the scale of military action in Central Asia and the Middle East. Bush is therefore a tragic figure with well-intentioned, noble ideals who through his own single-mindedness in pre-emption ended up widely reviled. In contrast, Eisenhower in *Overlord* also had noble ideals and, despite indecisiveness that infuriated Montgomery, through his genial bravery and defiance ended up widely admired.

32

The World Government

A Blueprint for a Universal World State

Prologue
World Government and Peace

Plato's ideal state
Plato wrote his *Politeia* (*Republic*) c.380BC, following his visit to Italy and Sicily when he was about forty in 388BC. In it he set out his ideal state and government for Dionysus I of Syracuse, who promised to implement his political ideas. Plato argued that a society is best ruled by a single individual. Later in his *Laws*, which he wrote towards the end of his life, he proposed replacing a single ruler with a set of laws, an executive, a group of oligarchs and all citizens.

Ever since Plato philosophy has been interested in proposals for the ideal state, and the thinking of Kant in *Perpetual Peace: A Philosophical Sketch* (1795) is particularly relevant. However, it is only relatively recently that a philosopher could realistically contemplate an ideal World State, for it is only relatively recently that 20th-century air travel, instant communications via the Internet and globalisation have made world government a realistic possibility.

Modern calls for a world government
These days world government is often mentioned, and has been on the lips of some of the most famous people of our time as the following passages demonstrate:

> Unless we establish some form of world government, it will not be possible for us to avert a World War III in the future.
> (Winston Churchill, Prime Minister of Great Britain, 1945)

> The emergency committee of atomic scientists, having explored for two years all means other than world government for making responsible the control of atomic energy [meaning nuclear weapons, really, and by implication, all weapons of mass destruction], has become convinced that no other method than world government can be expected to prove

effective, and that the attainment of world government is therefore the most urgent problem now facing mankind.

(1948 UN Resolution)

There is no salvation for civilisation, or even the human race, other than the creation of a world government.

(Albert Einstein, 1945)

The world no longer has a choice between force and law; if civilisation is to survive, it must choose the rule of law.

(President Dwight D. Eisenhower)

There is an increasing awareness of the need for some form of global government.

(Mikhail Gorbachev)

The international community should support a system of laws to regularise international relations and maintain the peace in the same manner that law governs national order.

(Pope John Paul II)

Yet despite such views at the highest level and despite a world federalist movement in the aftermath of the First and Second World Wars, there has surprisingly been no accessible study of the concept of world government. In fact, so far as I am aware this is the first book to be entitled *The World Government*.

World government is the concept of a political body that would make, interpret and enforce international law within a system that would allow it to have legally-binding authority over sovereign nation-states. Under a world government, all humankind would be united under one common political authority.

My political Universalism
The actual starting-point of this book is a section on political Universalism in my challenge to modern philosophy, *The New Philosophy of Universalism*. Besides restoring the universe to philosophy after a hundred years of focusing on logic and language, Universalism returns to the view of the universe of the Presocratic Greeks, Plato, Aristotle and Kant. It identifies a universal principle of order and focuses on universality. It sees the universe as latently contained within an infinitesimal point that preceded the Big Bang. It sees all humankind as having emerged from an interconnected unity, from one

cell and later one species. Universalism therefore treats all humankind as a whole in all disciplines.

In the course of covering the applications of Universalism, which include political Universalism, I wrote:

> Political Universalism sees the whole world as being ordered as one political entity, an interconnected unity, a whole. In short, under a world government it would be a reflection of the unity of the cosmos (or ordered universe). As all humans are world citizens they have human rights, which include a human right to live under a world government that has abolished war, famine and disease. The world order's world government must be democratic so every member of humankind has a democratic vote. Political Universalism affirms a world government... that is not totalitarian but allows each human being the maximum freedom and attacks poverty.... Political Universalism minimises the conflicts that divide people and eliminates divisions by negotiation.... Political Universalism is Utopian in wanting to improve the lot of humankind and bringing universal freedom, democracy and relief from poverty, war, famine and disease.[1]

This book examines the concept of world government in more depth than space permitted in my challenge to philosophy.

Political philosophy is philosophical reflection on how best to arrange our political institutions and social practices, our economic system and family life. Political philosophers – such as Plato, Aristotle, Augustine, Aquinas, Hobbes, Locke, Hume, Hegel and J.S. Mill – establish principles that justify a particular form of state, and this involves analysing and interpreting the concepts of freedom, justice, authority and democracy with a view to portraying an ideal state. Social and political thinkers who have contributed to political philosophy include Cicero, Marsilius of Padua, Machiavelli, Grotius, Rousseau, Bentham, Fichte and Marx.

I have always been interested in universal states. I have a classical background – I had to translate several books of Plato's *Republic* at school – and in Ancient History I studied the Athenian Empire and its hold over the Aegean, and the Roman Empire and its hold over the known world, and was encouraged to draw parallels between them and the British Empire, which had been battered by two world wars. I had to translate a report of a Second-World-War battle into Latin. Montgomery had to be spelt "Montegomerius".

My view of the rise and fall of civilisations and the Law of History
In Japan, where I was a Professor, I taught a course on Gibbon, Spengler

and Toynbee to eight doctorate students. I steeped myself in Toynbee's view of civilisations' universal states and his conviction (expressed in Book 12 [of *A Study of History*]) that all civilisations would eventually pass into a worldwide civilisation. My poem 'Archangel' (1966) ends with a glimpse of a future world government under a "World-Lord". (See pp.167–168 [of *The World Government*].) However, although seeing nation-states as being within civilisations like Toynbee, I had criticisms of Toynbee's choice of civilisations and his uniform dating. Toynbee admitted at the end of his work that he had been unable to find the motive force of civilisations. I was convinced that I had the answer: civilisations rise after someone has had a vision of a metaphysical Reality, round which followers gather and a new religion is formed that develops into a civilisation. This insight enabled me to propose the Law of History.

I had seen a fourth way of accounting for the rise and fall of civilisations that differed from Gibbon's, Spengler's and Toynbee's. It enabled me to identify 61 stages through which 25 civilisations have passed or will pass. After 25 years of research I implemented the details of this view in *The Fire and the Stones*, a work of philosophy of history. This has recently been updated in two parts, the second of which is titled *The Rise and Fall of Civilizations*.

Self-interested élites *and world government*
In the course of my research I came up against a group of contemporary oligarchs who were trying to effect a world government by secrecy and deception. (See ch.6 [within *The World Government*].) In the late 1980s I dismissed them as I was convinced history was, is and always will be the endless interplay of stages within civilisations. The attempt of these *élites* to create a world government would, if successful, bring this interplay to an end as they wished to subsume all civilisations. I felt, and still feel, that any world government will be a tier above the rise and fall of civilisations, which will continue their rise-and-fall patterns. Nevertheless, in a chart in *The Fire and the Stones*, which also appeared in *The Light of Civilizations* and which I reproduce in this book (see pp.178–179 [of *The World Government*]), I followed Toynbee in showing all civilisations as passing into one worldwide civilisation for a while. It could be said that the worldwide civilisation would occupy a tier above the lower tier of rising and falling civilisations, which would continue beneath this higher tier.

I kept track of this group and found that by 2003 its *élites* were actually doing rather well. They seemed self-interested rather than philanthropic, and I distanced myself from what they were trying to achieve in *The Syndicate* (2004). It was not the institution of a World State that I was distancing myself from, but the would-be incumbents, as I made clear at the end of that work.[2]

In 1992 I had heard Francis Fukuyama, who was representative of their way of thinking, speak in London. In *The End of History* he claimed that in a Hegelian sense history as an evolutionary process has a direction and will reach an end when it achieves a form of society that satisfies humankind's deepest longings. For Hegel this meant a liberal state, for Marx a communist society. Fukuyama suggested that history reached its "end" with the end of the Cold War as there would now be permanent liberal democracy. He seemed to be saying that the world was about to pass very soon into a permanent World State. In support of this view, it is worth noting that while there were no liberal democracies with universal suffrage in the world in 1900, in 2009 119 out of the 193 nation-states (including Taiwan) were deemed to have an electoral liberal democracy.[3] (See pp.230–231 [of *The World Government*].)

In 2009 a more precise survey found that 89 nation-states were deemed to be free, 62 were deemed to be partly free and 42 not free.[4] (See pp.231–235 and 235–242 [of *The World Government*].) 119 were deemed "electoral democracies" when only 89 were deemed free. Thus the 119 figure includes 30 partly free.

Ideal World State and world government
I hope that a World State – of the right kind, with the most appropriate incumbents, form and structure – is ahead for the world, but it has not happened yet and, though (as I shall explain in ch.8 [of *The World Government*]) it could happen quite rapidly, there is no immediate prospect of its happening. In the meantime, civilisations continue in their rise-and-fall pattern, which will continue beneath a World State if one comes into being. The rise and fall of civilisations has been endless, for when a civilisation ends it passes into another civilisation. As a way of distancing myself from Fukuyama's belief that a universal state would replace civilisations, my most recent book on civilisations [*The Rise and Fall of Civilizations* (Preface 28)] was originally entitled *The Endless Rise and Fall of Civilizations*, the word "endless" making it clear that the rise-and-fall pattern of civilisations will never end so long as there are historical events.

My encounter with Fukuyama made me think carefully as to whether world government can be superimposed on civilisations forever. I have concluded that it cannot, as world government is itself the expression of a stage within a civilisation, and no stage can last for more than a limited period of time. I have concluded that I have lived during the development of a stage within the system of civilisations which will express itself for a while as a World State that will be above the continuing events of civilisations. Civilisations flow under a worldwide civilisation and continue beneath it, as river currents continue under a majestic cloud.

The theme of this book is that eventually, through the evolutionary process of government and the state, there will be an ideal world government. I describe as a philosophical concept, but also as a practical and feasible course of action, what its model, structure and feel would be, and the process by which it would come into being. The book describes the human dream and longing for a world government; the reality that is already unfolding in our time; and the form it will ideally take. Just as Plato in an effort of statecraft wrote his *Republic*, for which a better translation might have been *Constitution*, so this work in an equivalent effort of statecraft offers a World State. It can be read at both philosophical and practical levels. In a similar vein, Jean Monnet devised the EU in conjunction with the Council on Foreign Relations in the early 1920s, and lived to see it brought to birth via various intermediary stages in the 1957 Treaty of Rome and in the European Parliament, which opened in the year he died, 1979. (The European Parliamentary elections were held in July 1979, a few months after Monnet died in March.)

There are many practical difficulties to be overcome before there can be a world government, and bringing it into being will be even more of a process than was the EU. It may take until the 22nd century to realise and implement the idea fully to achieve a minimum standard of living for all humankind. This work is nevertheless timely in our age of globalisation, and even though some parts of my thesis may not be fulfilled for another hundred years, Universalism requires that the concept of world government should receive a fuller treatment than the two pages in my work of philosophy.

World government to prevent wars
Having written two epic poems on contemporary war I can see very clearly that contemporary wars are linked to the interests of nation-states or empires, to a clash of interests which cannot be resolved by current international law as the legal framework does not exist. World government would create this legal framework and prevent wars. Most epic poets who have lived through wars yearn for peace. As we shall see, the epic poet Virgil was aware of a new order of world rule in the 'Fourth Eclogue' and in the *Aeneid*; the epic poet Dante was extremely

interested in world government; and the epic poet Milton who wrote *Paradise Lost* had been Latin Secretary to Cromwell who saw himself as founding a universal republic. Milton proposed an ideal republic in *The Ready and Easy Way to Establish a Free Commonwealth* (1660).[5] James Harrington wrote that the duty of a free Commonwealth was "the intent that the whole world may be governed with righteousness".[6] I ask myself if there is a special link between epic poetry and the conviction that there should be a World State that prevents war.

My innovatory vision of World State in 1966 poem 'Archangel'
All my works are innovatory in some way. My innovatory philosophical and historical works have been thrown up by the need to address philosophical and historical issues I encountered in my innovatory literary, often poetic, work. It was my literary, poetic work that gave me my first glimpse of a World State: see pp.167–168 [of *The World Government*] for the end of my 1966 poem 'Archangel' and the glimpse that came to me in Moscow. Many of my philosophical and historical probings work out what has gone wrong in the past and in the present, and suggest a way forward, as does this present work.

This is a work that begins in philosophy and ends with an innovative proposal for a World State with a fair amount of precision as to how to realise it – and a safeguard for such a state against the wiles of self-interested *élites*. As such it is a contribution both to political philosophy and to the philosophy of history, and may in the fullness of time, when attitudes have changed, be used as a blueprint to benefit the lot of humankind which has been living through a long time of trial and tribulation.

Notes:
1. Nicholas Hagger, *The New Philosophy of Universalism*, pp.355–357.
2. Hagger, *The Syndicate*, pp.283–284 and 291–293.
3. Survey conducted by Freedom House, an organisation opposed to tyranny that supports the expansion of freedom in the world, between 1972 and 2005. In this survey, updated to 2009, "free" nations up to a certain ranking were considered to be liberal democracies. See http://www.freedomhouse.org/.
4. Freedom House Survey of 2009.
5. John Milton, *The Ready and Easy Way to Establish a Free Commonwealth*, ed. by Evert Mordecai Clark.
6. Sir Charles Firth, *Oliver Cromwell and the Rule of Puritans in England*, p.382.

33

The Secret American Dream

The Real Story of Liberty's Empire and the Rise of a World State
How the Whole World is to Share in the American Dream

Prologue
Liberty's Dream

The Statue of Liberty
Liberty has come to represent much of what America stands for. Her statue was unveiled in the US in 1886 as a gift from the people of revolutionary France to the people of revolutionary America. "Miss Liberty" or "Lady Liberty" is a representation of Libertas, ancient Rome's goddess of freedom from slavery, oppression, and tyranny.

She wears a Roman *stola* (a long outer garment) and a Roman facial expression. Her head is modelled on the Graeco-Roman sun-god Helios, a version of the sun-god Apollo as shown on a marble tablet in the archaeological Museum of Corinth, Greece. She has the seven-spiked rays of Sol's radiate solar crown. These seven spikes represent the seven seas and seven continents.[1] She is moving forward. Her right foot is raised and her left foot tramples broken shackles.[2] Her torch represents enlightenment, and the keystone she holds represents knowledge and shows the date of the United States' Declaration of Independence in Roman numerals: July IV, MDCCLXXVI.

The Colossus of Rhodes, erected between 292 and 280BCE and one of the Seven Wonders of the World, also represented the sun-god Helios.[3] It is shown in a 16th-century engraving by Maerten van Heemskerck holding a torch[4] to guide ships into harbour in the dark. The torch in this engraving was based on what is believed to be the genuine dedication text for the Colossus of Rhodes: "To you, O Sun, the people of Dorian Rhodes set up this bronze statue reaching to Olympus, when they had pacified the waves of war and crowned their city with the spoils taken from the enemy. Not only over the seas but also on land did they kindle the lovely torch of freedom and independence."[5]

Like the Colossus of Rhodes (if this dedication is genuine), Liberty functioned as a lighthouse, and from 1886 to 1902 it shone an electric light that could be seen on board ship for 24 miles (39km). One and a half times the height of the Colossus of Rhodes – 151 feet (46m) from base to torch as against 107 feet (33m) – Liberty was the first image that immigrants saw as they steamed into New York to begin their new lives. To them, Liberty was a guarantee of personal liberty from oppression, of a prospect of freedom. Emma Lazarus wrote these haunting lines in her sonnet, 'The New Colossus', which was written during fund-raising for the pedestal of the Statue of Liberty in 1883:

> Not like the brazen giant of Greek fame,
> With conquering limbs astride from land to land;
> Here at our sea-washed, sunset gates shall stand
> A mighty woman with a torch, whose flame
> Is the imprisoned lightning, and her name
> Mother of Exiles. From her beacon-hand
> Glows world-wide welcome; her mild eyes command
> The air-bridged harbour that twin cities frame.
> "Keep, ancient lands, your storied pomp!" cries she
> With silent lips. "Give me your tired, your poor,
> Your huddled masses yearning to breathe free,
> The wretched refuse of your teeming shore.
> Send these, the homeless, tempest-tossed to me,
> I lift my lamp beside the golden door!"

The first two lines refer to the Colossus of Rhodes. The bronze plaque in the pedestal omits the comma after "Keep" in line 9.[6]

The American Dream
The 'American Dream' is one of prosperity for all within the American democracy. For many it has been the prospect of an escape from misery and persecution in Europe and of a new life in which they would be able to stand on their own feet. The phrase was first expressed in 1931 by James Truslow Adams, who in his book *The Epic of America* wrote: "The American Dream is that dream of a land in which life should be better and richer and fuller for every man, with opportunity for each according to ability or achievement.... It is not a dream of motor cars and high wages merely, but a dream of social order in which each man and each woman shall be able to attain to the fullest stature of which they are innately capable, and be recognised by others for what they are, regardless of the fortuitous circumstances of birth or position."[7]

It has been the dream of countless immigrants who came to the United States in the 19th and 20th centuries seeking a prosperous life. It looked back to the 1776 Declaration of Independence, which proclaimed all men's "inalienable rights" including "Life, Liberty and the pursuit of Happiness". For many, seeing the Statue of Liberty as their ship approached American shores represented a fresh start in a free society where all had the opportunity to succeed, regardless of their past. For arriving immigrants, Liberty with her torch embodied the American Dream.

The American model of empire

The American Dream emerged during bouts of expansion which culminated in the rise of the United States to superpowerdom and a global role. Not since the Roman Empire has one nation-state dominated the world to such an extent. There is a feeling abroad that America controls an empire, defined by the *Concise Oxford Dictionary* as "an extensive group of states or countries under a single supreme authority, especially an emperor".

The Greek model of empire which the Athenians put into practice was that of a city-state holding colonies in subjugation. The Roman model of empire was more ecumenical. It spread the benefits of Roman citizenship without enslaving the inhabitants of colonies. The American model of empire was the Roman one rather than the Greek one, under a presidency akin to the Roman Caesars' imperial rule. It is no accident that Liberty is based on a Roman lady, Libertas, rather than a Greek one.

America's anti-empire: an extensive group of states

Yet empire is what the Founding Fathers stood against. They proclaimed liberty in the Declaration of Independence. This meant liberty from religious persecution, the principle that drove the Separatists to board the *Mayflower* in 1620, and liberty from the colonialism of the British Empire. From the outset, the United States sided with revolutionary countries that opposed colonialism. One of these was France, which fraternally gave the United States the Statue of Liberty. Having crowned Napoleon Emperor in 1804 and having been under a Second Empire from 1852 until 1870, France was now a Third Republic and against all emperors, who were regarded as arbitrary despots. (It should be pointed out that the French Third Republic went on to establish colonial rule in Tunisia in 1881 and Indo-China in 1884–1887.)

Today the United States sides with the oppressed and downtrodden, the victims of tyrannical empires. Ideologically, the United States commands an anti-empire: a network of nation-states that have broken free from their colonial masters. And so Donald Rumsfeld, US Secretary of Defense, when questioned by an *Al-Jazeera* correspondent, stated on 25 February 2003: "We're not a colonial power. We've never been a colonial power. We don't take our force and go around the world and try to take other people's real estate or other people's resources, their oil. That's just not what the United States does. We never have and we never will. That's not how democracies behave. That's how an empire-building Soviet Union behaved but that's not how the United States behaves."[8] He also asserted on 29 April 2003: "We don't seek empires, we're not imperialistic, we never have been, I can't imagine why you'd even ask the question."[9]

President George W. Bush agreed: "We're not an imperial power, as nations such as Japan and Germany can attest. We are a liberating power, as nations in Europe and Asia can attest, as well."[10] Nevertheless, the fact remains that Liberty runs what can only be described as a loose, Roman-style empire: "an extensive group of states".

America's seven expansions and paths
Whether or not America has a formal empire, it has undergone a number of expansions during its growth. Each one is a strand, and they appear to be intertwined like seven strands of spaghetti tangled in a small bowl. Each strand is actually a path, and now America has reached a crossroads. President Obama has tried to bring change in place of the policies of the Bush era. Yet there is a profound sense in the world that no one is sure where America is going, what the future will bring.

What should America's direction be now? This book is about the course America will take – has begun to take – in the immediate future. It is about what America will do next and how it can benefit all the world's citizens. To understand the new direction America is taking we need to consider the past direction, or differing directions, it has already taken, the route which has brought us to this point. We need to review America's past dealings with the outside world. We will then see that its next direction is emerging both as a reaction against, and as a continuity with, what has already happened.

The first three parts of this book identify seven bouts or strands of expansion that are behind the rise of the United States to superpowerdom. Each has its own individual characteristic, and each is of a different kind. Part One tells when Liberty's empire apparently began: in the late 1890s when the US founded a colonial empire with what was widely understood to be Christian zeal and an embracing of what Kipling called the "White Man's burden". It carries us forward to America's subsequent isolationism and interventionism and on to America's Cold-War hegemony. Part Two tells when Liberty's empire really began: further back in time with the federal unification that was encouraged by Freemasonry, and the ensuing westward expansion that built the United States. Part Three brings the story up to date by focusing on America's world empire and supremacy, which have been covertly backed by commercial *élites*.

Each of the seven bouts of expansion represented an attempted direction. The seven expansions are like the seven radiate spikes of Liberty's crown. These seven directions can all in theory be continued by the Obama Administration. Examining each in turn will make it clear why a new direction is needed now, one that leads on from these past efforts.

America's eighth path
It is as though America has reached a 'double crossroads' shaped like an eight-pointed star. There is such a place in Denmark, in the Gribskov Forest not far from Copenhagen, where eight radial paths meet at Stjernen. ('Stjerne' is "star" in Danish, and associations include "many-pointed star" and "eight-pointed asterisk".) The paths were made for huntsmen from 1680 to 1690 by King Christian V, who had spent time at the court of Louis XIV, the "Sun-King", at Versailles.

The Danish philosopher Søren Kierkegaard wrote of the intersection in *Stages on Life's Way* (1845):

> There is in Gribskov a place called the Eight Roads' Nook; only he finds it who seeks it worthily, for no map gives it. The name itself also seems to hold a contradiction, for how can the collision of eight roads make a nook?... It really has eight roads, but is still very lonesome; off-place, hidden.... Eight roads and no traveller!

The intersection inspired the choice in *Either/Or: A Fragment of Life*, which came out two years earlier. I tried to find the spot in 1987, but discovered that the intersection amid high beeches can only be reached on foot and is not marked on most maps.

America's future direction
If one imagines that seven of the radial forest paths symbolise the seven directions America has tried, the question is: where does the eighth way lead? This is addressed in Part Four of this book, where it becomes clear that distancing ourselves from the directions of the past helps us to identify America's future direction.

I was impelled to chart America's future course by my research when owner of Otley Hall in Suffolk, England, where the 1607 Jamestown Settlement is thought to have been planned. In May 2001 I was visited by the First Lady of Virginia, Roxane Gilmore, who had led some 20 Americans to Ipswich to request that Jamestown and Ipswich become sister-cities. That evening I was invited to meet her husband, the Governor of Virginia, at the US Embassy in London. I gave him a copy of my study of 25 civilisations, *The Fire and the Stones*, to present to George W. Bush. In my dedication to President Bush at the front of the book I wrote that the 21st century belonged to America. I knew exactly what I meant. I did not mean that it belonged to American supremacy and the pre-emptive strikes that succeeded 9/11, which stunned the world just over three months later.

A few years later my book *The Secret Founding of America*, this book's predecessor, narrated the planting and founding of America to coincide with the 400th anniversary of the Jamestown Settlement in 2007. It followed the interplay between early Christianity and Freemasonry in the growth of the North-American civilisation, which culminated in attempts by self-interested *élites* to found a federal New World Order in our time and absorb civilisations and nation-states, including the United States itself. I subsequently wrote my second poetic epic, *Armageddon*, about the War on Terror and the New World Order's commercial gain from US military activities. I followed this up with *The World Government*, a philosophical approach in the tradition of Kant's *Perpetual Peace*. It advanced a political Universalism that would counterbalance and control the *élites* pressing for a New World Order. I became convinced that America has a hitherto-undisclosed agenda, which will soon be revealed and to which my present title alludes.

It is completely understandable that in his first year of office Obama did not fully disclose his program. Any president elected on a ticket of 'change' would have done the same. For a new president to carry a program through requires the winning of substantial support, precise timing, and political savvy. Obama's way forward has been necessarily enmeshed in the dictates of political strategy. A program cannot be fully blazoned across the US press until mid-term has been reached, by which time the necessary support can be presumed to have been built.

The word 'secret' in my title in no way impugns Obama or suggests underhand deviousness on his part. The *Concise Oxford Dictionary* defines 'secret' as "kept or meant to be kept private, unknown or hidden from all but a few", and the practical requirements of political strategy have meant that a full understanding of the ambitious breadth of his way forward has been confined to a few within his inner circle. (The same was true of the "neoconservative" program during Bush's presidency.)

My title also alludes to, and turns around, the title of *The Secret*

Founding of America. In that work 'secrecy' had a negative connotation: the secrecy of Freemasonry's hidden role in the founding of the federal Union and of *élites* with Masonic links pressing to hijack America's destiny for their own ends. In this work 'secrecy' has a positive connotation: a hitherto-much-hinted-at but less-than-fully-disclosed role that when fully disclosed (as we shall see in Part Four) will receive the admiration and applause of the entire world. Between them the titles of the two books convey how a secret agenda in its negative sense is being transmuted into an ambitious ideal for all humankind that is still understandably undeclared, veiled in secrecy in a positive sense.

To many observers America's current stance is bewildering. While writing my previous works I saw that their bewilderment had much to do with the contradictions of the seven past paths in relation to America's coming destination.

My cumulative consideration of America's role in these works placed me in the centre of the 'Star crossroads', and I researched the way forward Obama is planning for America. I was fascinated that Obama has said, "No one nation can or should try to dominate another nation."[11] And yet Obama sent 30,000 additional troops to fight in Afghanistan.

North-American civilisation's seven-banded rainbow and world unity
In the work I presented to President Bush, *The Fire and the Stones*, I see each civilisation in terms of a rainbow which appears to have seven bands. These bands are only differentiated through the refraction of light in raindrops, and in the human eye, as they are part of a unified spectrum. In that work, I saw these seven bands as the essential ingredients of every civilisation: the vision of Reality that inspires the genesis of each civilisation; alternative inspirations; a civilisation's religion, which eventually degenerates into coteries; the stones (temples, cathedrals, mosques) which are inspired by the vision of Reality and are later destroyed; the peoples who join the civilisation and contribute to its cultural unity, and the seceders who later cause cultural disintegration; a foreign military threat which brings foreign cults; and the secularising State which expands into empire.

When I was writing this passage in *The Fire and the Stones*, which identified 25 civilisations, I had a crystal hanging in my window and in the morning sun it cast 25 rainbows on my desk and carpet, which represented my 25 civilisations and their sevenfold bands. In the North-American civilisation it is possible to perceive these bands as also representing the seven bouts of expansion since the planting of the first settlements. The eighth band is the entire unified spectrum which embraces all seven differentiated components: the unified rainbow that thrusts upward toward the arch, as does the North-American civilisation now.

I see the Statue of Liberty, the Colossus that is America, standing beside the upward curve of a rainbow which represents the apparently differentiated seven directions the North-American civilisation has tried. Liberty's empire spans the globe, but has been notoriously difficult to describe. In fact many authors describe just one of the bands of the unified rainbow. I resolved to see Liberty's rainbow as a whole and to follow its rise.

To define America's new direction we must first distinguish it from America's past directions. To see America's way forward we must go back to when Liberty's empire apparently began, somewhere near the base of the curve of the thrusting North-American civilisation; distinguish its expansion; identify America's mission; and chart its stunning and continuing rise.

Notes:
1. The traditional seven seas are the Mediterranean Sea (including the Tyrrhenian and Aegean), the Adriatic Sea, the Black Sea, the Red Sea, the Arabian Sea, the Persian Gulf, and the Caspian Sea. The seven continents are Asia, Africa, North America, South America, Antarctica, Europe, and Australia. (To arrive at seven rather than five, North and South America have to be separated and Antarctica included.)
2. See https://edition.cnn.com/2013/07/03/us/statue-of-liberty-fast-facts/index.html.
3. See http://en.wikipedia.org/wiki/Colossus_of_rhodes.
4. See http://en.wikipedia.org/wiki/Colossus_of_rhodes.
5. *Anthologia Graeca*, 4, p.171, ed. Hermann Beckby, Munich, 1957.
6. Some thought has been given as to whether the omission of the comma was a bronze-worker's error or a deliberate mistake. Emma Lazarus was addressing the ancient lands of Europe, saying in effect, "You can keep your pomp but give America your poor." The omission of the comma creates an imperative that may address the people of Europe, saying in effect, "You can keep your ancient lands and pomp, but give America your poor." It has been suggested that Liberty is addressing the American people and is urging an imperialistic destiny: "Keep (i.e. hang on to) the ancient lands that you have occupied." This is unconvincing as America had very few colonial possessions before 1883, about which there was little "storied pomp". The missing comma is likely to be an error rather than a deliberate change of meaning.
7. James Truslow Adams, *The Epic of America*, p.404.

8. Donald Rumsfeld, interview with *Al-Jazeera* TV, February 25, 2003, press release, Department of Defense, http://www.defense.gov/transcripts/transcript.aspx?transcriptid=1946.
9. See www.empirenotes.org.
10. President George W. Bush speaking at a press conference held at the White House on April 13, 2004, http://www.nytimes.com/2004/04/13/politics/13CND-BTEX.html.
11. Remarks by President Obama to the UN General Assembly in New York on September 23, 2009, https://obamawhitehouse.archives.gov/the-press-office/remarks-president-united-nations-general-assembly.

34

A New Philosophy of Literature

The Fundamental Theme and Unity of World Literature
The Vision of the Infinite and the Universalist Literary Tradition

Prologue
The Fundamental Theme of World Literature

This book presents the fundamental theme of world literature. It argues that its main thrust is the revelation that the universe is ordered and permeated by an infinite Reality which human beings can know. It shows that this traditional material has been restated in the literature of every culture and age, and that the quest for an ordering Reality that is behind and within everyday life was originally stronger than secular writing.

However, in many literary works, this level of Reality is missing. Especially today, writing is secular and there is only a personal and social reality. Consequently, many contemporary works are secular and materialist in presenting life in an accidental universe of purely physical processes that are devoid of purpose or meaning. This book argues that there needs to be a revolution in thought and culture to perpetuate the traditional material in a new literary movement so that once again it co-exists with secular writing. In other words, this book calls for a revolution in Western literature.

This call to revolution is in fact a call back to tradition, and I seek to carry forward the thinking in T.S. Eliot's essay, 'Tradition and the Individual Talent' (1919), in which Eliot urged poets to cultivate a historical sense and a feeling for "the whole of the literature of Europe from Homer", and to be aware of "the mind of Europe" as "no poet... has his complete meaning alone". In this work I evoke the literary tradition since Homer.

An investigation of the fundamental theme in world literature transports the reader into different cultures and civilisations, and focuses on all humankind. It therefore necessarily enters the uncharted territory of literary Universalism.

Universalism
Universalism's global perspective can be found in various disciplines

outside literature. Historical Universalism sees the history of all humankind as a unity, as did Toynbee in his *Study of History*. Political Universalism sees all humankind as one political entity, to be governed under a World State and a benevolent world government. Religious Universalism sees all religions as unified on the basis of a common experience known to all mystics in all ages and cultures: the experience of the Light, known to Christians as "the Divine Light" and to Catholics as "the Light of Glory" (*lumen gloriae*). Philosophical Universalism focuses on the universe, as did the great philosophers of the past. Following a philosophically lean century dominated by logic and language, it sees a unified, orderly universe operating within "the infinite" as did the early Greek philosophers, and it too focuses on the unity of all humankind.

I have written extensive studies of historical Universalism (*The Fire and the Stones, The Rise and Fall of Civilizations*), religious Universalism (*The Fire and the Stones, The Light of Civilization*), political Universalism (*The World Government, The Secret American Dream*) and philosophical Universalism (*The Universe and the Light, The One and the Many, The New Philosophy of Universalism*).

In *The New Philosophy of Universalism* I set out a philosophy that focuses on the universe – indeed, an ordered cosmos – and challenged modern philosophy's focus on language and logic. I looked back to the Greek Presocratic philosophers who offered empirical explanations for the workings of the universe at the source of Western philosophy. I considered their metaphysical view of the universe. 'Metaphysics', "*ta meta ta phusika*", were originally "the [works of Aristotle] *after* the Physics", but their study of first principles came to be misinterpreted as meaning "the science of things transcending what is physical or natural" (*Shorter Oxford English Dictionary*). 'Metaphysics' therefore came to mean what is *beyond* physics, and as "*meta*" can be translated as "behind" as well as "after", 'metaphysics' has also come to mean "what is *behind* physics": "the science of things behind, and therefore transcending, what is physical or natural". Metaphysics asks what had infinite being before the Big Bang that could account for how the finite, physical, natural universe came to emerge from its fiery birth, and what has continued to be behind, and order, the physical, natural universe ever since the Big Bang. Metaphysics has not been impressed by Materialist assertions that nothing pre-existed the Big Bang and that the universe is an accident ruled by random chance and without order.

In *The New Philosophy of Universalism* I blended a scientific, evidential view of the universe with a scheme for its metaphysical structure: out of the One (or Nothingness) manifested Non-Being, from which emerged Being and eventually Existence. I saw unified Being as behind and within the diversity of Existence, the world of appearance. Within a new centre of the self, the universal being, humans can look beyond Existence into Being, which they can receive as the metaphysical Light, and can grasp that the universe is layered, tiered, with the invisible energy of Being operating behind the surface Existence. (See diagram of Universalism's view of the structure of the universe, p.353.)

The faculty that perceives unity is what Coleridge called "the esemplastic power of the imagination",[1] 'esemplastic' coming from Greek words *"eis en plattein"*, meaning "moulding or shaping into one". (Coleridge in *Biographia Literaria*, ch.X, wrote, "I constructed it myself from the Greek words *eis en plattein*, to shape into one", whereas the *Shorter Oxford English Dictionary* derives the word from *eis en plassein*, "moulding into unity, unifying".) All my studies of Universalism have been written from this faculty, which perceives similarities. It is very different from rational analysis, which perceives differences and makes distinctions.

Besides focusing on the universe and the universal order principle, Universalism focuses on humankind's place in the universe, and therefore on the oneness of humankind. Universalism also probes the natural world, the universal cosmic energies which stimulate the growth of organisms and plants, and the universal being within the self where these energies or rays are received by human beings.

The unity of humankind is a theme suited to times when there are attempts to govern the whole known world: the times of the Athenian Empire, Augustus's Roman Empire, the Crusades, the post-Renaissance European empires, and in our time the British Empire, the American Empire and globalisation.

Literary Universalism
Literary Universalism reflects the Universalist approach in philosophy, history, religion and politics. In *The New Philosophy of Universalism* I devoted a few pages to the applications of Universalism, and spoke of literary Universalism, which received a scanty two pages. I pointed out that literary Universalism sees all literature – the literature of all countries – "as one, an interconnected unity, one supranational Literature". This book extends Universalism to world literature. I use 'literature' in its primary meaning: "literary productions as a whole, the writings of a country or period or of the world in general" (*Shorter Oxford English Dictionary*). This definition is descriptive. It describes the process of literary production, publication and circulation, and includes any works written in the ancient cultures that have survived. To this definition has

accrued a further definition first used during the Romantic Age, in 1812: "writings esteemed for beauty of form or emotional effect". This is a more evaluative definition, and suggests that some works are to be evaluated as literature while others do not qualify in terms of the Romantic criteria of beauty of form and emotional effect. Different movements and ages have different criteria by which to evaluate what is and what is not literature, and a coming Universalist movement, and eventually Universalist Age, will have its own distinctive criteria.

Literary Universalism is concerned with the literary productions of the world as a whole, and focuses on works of art rather than printed matter which has no literary merit. Its criteria include whether a work of art reflects specific Universalist characteristics.

Twelve Universalist Characteristics
What are these characteristics? Within literature (and philosophy) the term 'Universalism' incorporates 'universe', 'universal' and 'universality'. It focuses on the universe, on a universal principle of order and on humankind as a whole. It focuses on inner transformation to the universal being, the deeper self below the rational, social ego which is open to universal cosmic energies, the manifesting metaphysical Light. It focuses on universal human virtues, the standard from which writers have ridiculed the follies and vices of humankind.

In all times and ages, Universalist literature seeks confirmation that the universe is ordered by a Reality that surrounds it, which Greek Presocratic philosophers such as Anaximander of Miletus (who flourished c.570BC) described as the infinite, "boundless" (*to apeiron*).

It holds that this Reality is perceived in many cultures as Light or Fire; that all humankind is one; and that there are consequently similarities between cultures and civilisations. It holds that the universal being (or spirit) can know the Reality as the Light and (according to all cultures) achieve immortality; and that there is a universal virtue which measures human behaviour.

This book is a work of literary Universalism. It sets out the long tradition of Universalist literature that reflects this view and adheres to these criteria. In fact, in all ages each particular work of Universalist literature reflects the idea of Reality found in their culture and civilisation, the metaphysical aspect of the fundamental theme; and until relatively recently the outlook of the traditional material could be located within the society and rituals that nourished it. In the interests of clarity it is worth setting out the twelve characteristics by which Universalism can be recognised. Universalism, and the metaphysical aspect of the fundamental theme, focuses on:

- the infinite (*to apeiron*) that surrounds the universe;
- the metaphysical Reality perceived in all cultures as Light (or Fire, which is a universal cosmic energy);
- the universal principle of order in the universe (universal in the sense that its effects are found in all aspects of Nature and its organisms);
- the oneness of known humankind behind its apparent diversity;
- the similarities in cultures and civilisations;
- the universal being (or self) that opens to the Light behind the rational, social ego;
- universal virtue, a standard by which to measure human follies, vices, blindness, corruption, hypocrisy, self-love and egotism, and [focuses] on vices in relation to an implied universal virtue (when human interaction is considered from a secular perspective, as separated from its context of Reality);
- the promise of immortality of the universal being or spirit;
- an inner transformation or centre-shift from ego to universal being;
- the quest of the purified soul to confront death, in the ancient cultures by journeying to the Underworld, and to receive the secret Light of infinite Reality;
- a sensibility that approaches Reality through more than one discipline, the sensibility of a polymath; and
- a new perspective of unity in key disciplines: seeing world history as a whole; seeing the common essence (the inner experience of the Light) of all world religions; seeing the One that can be revealed by philosophy and science; seeing the World State that can unify international politics; and seeing the unity of world literature.

In the ancient world, in which religion was strong, these characteristics dominated society's rituals and were reflected in literature. Despite weakenings of this cultural activity which gave rise to periods of secularisation in literature, this fundamental Universalist and literary perception of the universe can be found in all places and times. It is the archetypal literary theme that has been repeated in each generation. Each generation restates the traditional Universalist theme.

Outline of the Fundamental Theme
There are in fact two sides to the fundamental theme: the traditional metaphysical quest for Reality and, in periods of greater secularisation, a more secular view of social reality that focuses on vices in relation to an implied virtue. In Part One of this book I trace the two aspects of

the fundamental theme from their origins in the ancient world (ch.1) through the classical world (ch.2) to the medieval world (ch.3), the Renaissance (ch.4) and the Baroque (ch.5). I trace the conflict between the two aspects in the Neoclassical and Romantic traditions (chs.6 and 7) and their short-lived reunification in the Victorians (ch.8) and Modernists (ch.9). I examine the position in the later 20th century (ch.10) and conclude that the two aspects are still a force, despite widespread secularisation.

In Part Two, drawing on the literary summaries at the end of each of the ten chapters in Part One, I outline how Universalism can reconcile and perpetuate the two aspects of the fundamental theme today (ch.1), and dwell on the reconciliation in poetry (ch.2). In the Epilogue I chart a new direction for world literature and consider the role of the Universalist tradition in the health of each civilisation in which it flourishes.

The fundamental theme is the unifying principle of world literature, and through its lens world literature can be seen as a unity. I will inevitably be restricted in the number of poems, plays and novels I will be able to cite as complying with one or other of the two aspects of the fundamental theme, but the same principle (quest or vices) can be applied to texts that will not be mentioned in this work, with similar results. In this work I am concerned to establish the principle of the fundamental theme from a sample of highly respected texts rather than to analyse every existing text in world literature (an impossibly gargantuan task) to demonstrate the principle.

The title of this book, *A New Philosophy of Literature*, of course echoes *The New Philosophy of Universalism*, but it also states that this work introduces a philosophy of literature and falls under the category of philosophy of literature.

Philosophy of Literature
The philosophy of literature has been approached by analytic philosophers, who have related literary problems to aesthetics. The analytic perspective defines literature, distinguishing between oral and written literature, and discusses the identity of literary works. It addresses the nature of fiction and our emotional involvement with fictional characters. It discusses the concept of imagination and its role in the apprehension of literary works. It looks at theories of metaphor and postmodernist theory regarding the significance of authors' intentions and the interpretation of their work. And it examines the relevance of truth and morality to literary appreciation. These questions are raised in Christopher New's analytic *Philosophy of Literature*, and in

an analytic anthology by Eileen John and Dominic McIver Lopes, also entitled *Philosophy of Literature*.

An analytic approach to the philosophy of literature sees a poem, a play, a novel, a short story as also being a work of literature, and the same applies to a work of oratory, an essay, philosophy or scripture. All these *genres* may also be literature. However, there is also popular or light literature, mass-market fiction written for escapist entertainment, which some would say is not good enough to warrant being called 'literature'. The analytic approach defines literature as "linguistic composition that has a certain property or properties of literariness". "Literariness" involves "figures of language such as rhyme, metre (whether 'strict or free'), onomatopoeia, alliteration and eye rhyme".[2] It also deals with value theory, metaphysics (the definition of literature, theories of fiction and the ontology of literature) and the philosophies of language and mind (theories of fiction, emotional engagement, interpretation and metaphor).[3]

There is, however, an alternative approach to the philosophy of literature: the historical, traditional, Universalist approach. This is more pragmatic. Based on principles rather than theory, and perceiving through the creative "esemplastic" faculty that sees unity, it sees literature (to echo the definition on p.4 [of *A New Philosophy of Literature*]) as all literary writings or works of art of the world as a whole that have ever been produced. Starting with the literature or written works produced in the ancient world, it considers the direction the fundamental tradition has taken, whether it has stuck to its course and the extent to which it has been challenged and superseded by a rival view of what literature is. This book pursues this tradition of the philosophy of literature.

Direction of the Fundamental Theme
The philosophy of history explores the direction of historical events and its interpretations of the rise and fall of civilisations, and seeks the pattern in and behind human events. Similarly, the philosophy of literature explores the direction of literary events and its interpretations of movements and literary traditions, and seeks the pattern in and behind the themes of the works of the most significant authors of each age. It examines the fundamental theme of world literature in each age, and explores the direction it takes in the course of more than 4,600 years of recorded history. Literary events or works of course reflect, and often comment on, the historical events of their age.

This work falls under the category of "philosophy of literature" in the sense that it identifies the core literary theme of the last 4,600 years and explores the direction it has taken (while continuing to reflect the order within the universe and experience of the hidden Reality that traditionally bestows immortality). It traces the direction this fundamental literary theme has taken in recent years and draws conclusions regarding its weakening in the present time. We shall see that the quest for Reality in metaphysical periods encompasses and incorporates the second aspect of the fundamental theme: the outlook in secular periods that human vices should be exposed. The fundamental theme consists of two opposites which alternate in their periods of dominance and which are reconciled from time to time.

Until now no attempt has been made to trace the direction of the universal fundamental literary theme. This book therefore breaks new ground. It attempts something that has not happened before. However, although the tracing of the traditional theme is "new" as a statement, the outlook of Universalism is as old as civilisation. The Universalist tradition of literature has ancient roots and has always been with us. Detailing it may be new, but there have been many Universalist writers who have reflected the twelve characteristics and criteria of Universalism. Literature has always recorded intimations of Being and humankind's instinctive longings for order in the universe.

The quest for Reality as Light and its opposite motif within the fundamental theme, the exposure of vices, can be seen in terms of light and shadow. Light and shadow can best be approached through an image or symbol. At Copped Hall in Essex in the UK, an eighteenth-century ruin that is being restored, there is a remarkable 1890s sundial in the marble pediment above four Ionic columns. (See front cover and p.x [of *A New Philosophy of Literature*].) Two male reapers recline on either side of the gnomon, back to back, holding scythes above reaped ears of corn. The one on the right is tousled-haired and bare-chested, and very much awake, having turned his head to look at us, gripping his scythe. The one on the left, also bare-chested, has wound his half-discarded cloak into a cowl-like hood round his head to shade him from the fierce sun and is at rest, with his eyes closed. He appears to be asleep as his hands limply rest on his scythe, which is propped on one knee. Above them is an hourglass. The two figures could represent Work and Sleep, Day and Night. Underneath there is a Latin motto: *Me umbra regit vos lumen*. The sundial says, "Shadow rules me [i.e. the sundial], light rules you [i.e. all mortals who look at the sundial]".

I see the pediment as a symbol for the fundamental theme. One figure (*lumen*) represents the quest for a metaphysical Reality as Light. The other figure (*umbra*) represents the world, the shadows cast by the Light, the shadowy world of human vices which are measured in terms of its counterpart, virtue granted by the influx of the Light. From the secular perspective, light (in the sense of sunlight) rules us mortals as we depend on ripened grain.

We shall encounter the symbol again in Part Two. But it is now time to see how the two motifs of the fundamental theme, the metaphysical and the secular, are contrasted and conjoined within the literature of the last 4,600 years.

Notes:
1. Kathleen Raine, *Defending Ancient Springs*, pp.121–122.
2. Christopher New, *Philosophy of Literature*, pp.18, 36.
3. *Philosophy of Literature*, ed. by Eileen John and Dominic McIver Lopes, p.xii.

35

A View of Epping Forest

Prologue
History Shaping Places

I have known Epping Forest since 1943. It was the cradle of my growth, and it has hardly changed since my childhood. This book tells the story of Epping Forest's history, places and institutions. It is not a guidebook, detailing every region of the Forest, but more a reflection of the Forest's variegated history which still confronts us wherever we look.

Objective narrative

As I draw on decades of personal experience this book has the flavour of a personal memoir. However, I see it as an objective narrative as it tells the story of Epping Forest's history and the evolution of its places and permanent buildings. Even the most objective narrative must inevitably be coloured by the personal observations of the narrator, and in my objective narrative the personal and the objective are intertwined. The personal element is in the "view" of the book's title, the objective in its focus on the Forest.

View

This book presents a view of Epping Forest, of 6,000 acres of ancient woodland. It is *a* view, just one of a number of possible views, *my* view, for the Epping Forest I describe is the one I have known.

According to the *Shorter Oxford Dictionary* a 'view' has two main components in its meaning. The first, referring to the view that can be seen from a window, is "a sight or prospect of some landscape or extended scene; and extent or area covered by the eye from one point". The second, referring to a reflective opinion, is "mental contemplation, a single act of contemplation or attention to a subject; a particular manner or way of considering or regarding the matter or question; a conception, opinion or theory formed by reflection or study".

My 'view' presents both a description of the landscape of Epping Forest from the single point of my eye and a reflection (or contemplation) on the Forest that leads to a "conception, opinion or theory". The description and reflection are inextricably entwined in my view of the Forest.

Perspectives: four periods of history

The theme of this book is that the places of the Forest cannot be fully appreciated without a firm grasp of four periods of history which have shaped them. These four periods are conveyed in Part One as pairs of contraries or opposites: Celts and Romans; Anglo-Saxons and Normans; Medievals and Tudors; and enclosers and loppers. In Part Two I attempt to show how history has shaped the main Forest places in my Loughton, Chigwell, Woodford, Buckhurst Hill, Waltham Abbey, High Beach, Upshire, Epping, the Theydons and Chingford Plain. The Appendix [of *A View of Epping Forest*] reproduces some of my poems about these places.

I am partly known as a local educator, and I have taken the opportunity to include my three* Oak-Tree schools, which form a triangle largely within Epping Forest, and to put little-known facts on public record as although thousands of local people have been through these schools over the years published information on the schools is relatively scanty and often factually incorrect.

The book thus presents different perspectives of the Forest: the four very different periods of history; the continuity of the flow of historical tradition; the effect of the cumulative tradition on individual places; and my reflective contemplation on the places in my Epping Forest in poetry. I blend history, recollection and poetic reflection in a quest for a rounded view of the Forest.

Whole sweep

As a Universalist, in my works I present the whole sweep of history and its context. I use what Coleridge called the "esemplastic power of the imagination". (The Greek *eis en plattein* means "to shape into one".) Such a historical mind shapes conflicting events into one and understands the progression that leads to the present. I have used this approach in writing of the rise and fall of civilisations;[1] of a period of history;[2] of an episode in history and its consequences;[3] and of the evolution of local history.[4]

The historian who knows that all history is ultimately a unity wants to find out what really happened by close reference to historical texts and sources, and presents local history in terms of a whole. I am not a local historian in the mould of W.C. Waller and the producers of booklets for the Loughton & District Historical Society who publish records, documents and diary entries – in themselves useful sources – without much attempt to relate them to a narrative that reflects a whole view. Writers on Epping Forest must be able "to see the wood for the trees". A view of Epping Forest has to be "wholist" rather than partialist while necessarily being eclectic.

My approach is closer to Sir William Addison's. He wrote of Epping Forest's literary and historical associations, focusing on well-known individuals or "Essex worthies". His topic-based *Portrait of Epping Forest* is supplemented by its companion volume, *Figures in a Landscape*, which dwells on the Forest's landscape, people and history and retells anecdotes. He recorded the social whims of his figures but was alert to the movement in the age behind the sweep of local events and fortunes of local notables. As a Universalist I look for the underlying movement of each age and relate it to the actions of its significant individuals.

Sources

Unfortunately, Addison did not provide his sources. In this day and age sources are crucial, and writing must be evidential. I endeavour to be accurate and meticulous in locating sources.

I have found that many of the books on Epping Forest get facts wrong and repeat and perpetuate mistakes made in other books on blind trust, without scrutinising or supplying sources. For this reason I have made a fresh start. I have resolved not to trust anything for which there is no source. Wherever possible I have gone back to original sources and looked at them with an open mind. I have ignored the consensus of books that do not give sources. When books say, for example, that there is no connection between Ambresbury Banks, Loughton Camp and Celtic or Roman occupation I have re-examined the sources and have sometimes come to surprising conclusions. I hope that there will be a broad welcome for a fresh approach that explores the history of Epping Forest as if coming to it anew.

I present evidence, probe behind the surface and revise any judgement that is not soundly based. I challenge orthodoxy when necessary and iron out inconsistencies to arrive at the truth. This is the method I have used in my historical works.

What the Forest means

Epping Forest has meant different things in different ages. To the Neolithics it was a dark, forbidding place, and primitive humans were happy to settle along the Roding. To the Romans it was wild and dangerous, and hid hostile Celts. To the Normans the Forest of Waltham was at first a place from which Saxons could launch attacks and then became the hunting-ground of kings. The 14th-century forest of *Sir Gawayne and the Grene Knight* was wild and inhospitable, removed from the fire on the lord's hearth. The Norman and Tudor forests, including Waltham (later Epping) Forest, were dangerous places:

hunting zones, entry to which was illegal and might result in fines or death. In the Elizabethan Age, like Shakespeare's forests Waltham (or Epping) Forest was a place of natural beauty in whose solitude transformation could take place and individuals could discover inner truths. To the German and English Romantics forests were holy and uncorrupted by the taints of civilisation. In reality, during both these times Epping Forest was haunted by footpads and highwaymen, and locals had to venture in to lop branches for firewood to keep warm. Nevertheless, to Tennyson and Clare Epping Forest was a place of natural beauty and purity.

Epping Forest has meant something different, again, to me. It is a place of inspiration. It teems with life and reveals Nature's system and the universal order. It offers still ponds that reflect the universe. It flows with the seasons, from winter bareness to smiling spring's tender green, to summer profusion and autumnal tints in myriad reddening and yellowing leaves.

Like an oak
The places of Epping Forest have been shaped by the history and tradition of the Forest just as the branches of a tree are shaped by its trunk. Epping Forest is like one of its ancient oaks: its roots are in prehistory, its trunk is the tradition of the last 2,500 years and its branches are the Forest settlements and communities that have grown out of its evolving history.

I, too, am like one of its oaks. And I am happy that one of my acorns has grown into these leaves that are prints of its parent and of the long tradition and history of Epping Forest.

*The Oak-Tree Group now comprises four schools.

Notes:
1. *The Fire and the Stones; The Light of Civilization; The Rise and Fall of Civilizations.*
2. *The Secret History of the West; The Syndicate.*
3. *The Secret Founding of America; The Secret American Dream.*
4. *The Last Tourist in Iran; The Libyan Revolution.*

36

My Double Life 1: This Dark Wood

A Journey into Light
Episodes and Pattern in a Writer's Life

Prologue
The Path and Pattern

Without Contraries is no progression. Attraction and Repulsion, Reason and Energy, Love and Hate, are necessary to Human existence.
(Blake, 'The Marriage of Heaven and Hell', c.1793)

My Double Life presents my life in two volumes: 'a life in two slices'. I led a double life in several senses. From early on I developed an everyday social life that found employment as a lecturer and kept a family; and an adventurous life that approached the One in literary works and quested in the Middle and Far East. From my mid-twenties I was living at social and metaphysical levels and experienced a First Mystic Life. Then I took on my secret work and lived the double life of an undercover intelligence agent, during which I experienced illumination and a Second Mystic Life. Later still I was a teacher, and then a Principal of schools and employer, while writing books. Like many Geminis I had twins within my mind.

Each of the two volumes of *My Double Life* tells of a dual life. I sometimes think I was ladled a double helping for I crammed so much experience into my life that I seem to have lived two lives within the span of one lifetime. This impression has been redoubled by the diversity of my work life – looking back, I seem to have had several professions – and by the variety of the literary *genres* and forms in which I have written. Yet I was always aware that I had an underlying single life that lived in harmony with the oneness of the universe.

The path through a dark wood
My Double Life *belongs to a genre of transformation*
My Double Life 1: This Dark Wood narrates a personal journey along a perilous path through a "dark wood": the influences, belief systems, ideological conflicts and political causes of the 20th century. As I progressed along the Mystic Way I came to understand that I could not reach the goal of my quest – Reality, the One – until I had undergone

a transformation, a metamorphosis: a centre-shift after purgation from sensual attachments, followed by illumination, which I had sought in Zen temples in Japan and which burst upon me inconveniently in 1971 when I was grappling with secret work. This profound experience changed my way of seeing [see Appendix 1, pp.437–447], and I found that I now instinctively saw the universe as a unity behind all the differences. *My Double Life 1: This Dark Wood* describes the changes in my circumstances that led to this experience, which I came to see as universal – Universalist. Its sequel *My Double Life 2: A Rainbow over the Hills* completes the story of the transformation and development in my life and thinking during a remarkable odyssey that led me from Oxford materialism to the metaphysical outlook of my literary, philosophical and historical works.

During my journey I had four Mystic Lives in all. The first two of these can be dated from the chronological list of experiences of the Light (see Appendix 1, p.489 [of *My Double Life 1: This Dark Wood*]). There are 16 experiences of the Light in *My Double Life 1: This Dark Wood* and 77 in *My Double Life 2: A Rainbow over the Hills*, a total of 93 experiences of the Light, each of which is documented from *Diaries* written at the time. Between the First and Second Mystic Lives I endured a Dark Night of the Soul, and between my Second and Third Mystic Lives I experienced the first part of my Dark Night of the Spirit, in which I was fed new powers. *My Double Life 1: This Dark Wood* ends near the beginning of this Dark Night. In *My Double Life 2: A Rainbow over the Hills* the story continues, and between my Third and Fourth Mystic Lives I experienced the second part of my Dark Night of the Spirit in which I was confronted with ordeals. My Unitive Life began after my Fourth Mystic Life.

My Double Life belongs to a literature of transformation, a tradition of 'process works' that began with Ovid's *Metamorphoses*, continued with St Augustine's *Confessions*, Bunyan's *Pilgrim's Progress* and the Continental *Bildungsromans* (novels about early life and development) – Crebillon fils' *The Wayward Head and Heart*, Goethe's *Wilhelm Meisters Lehrjahre*, Constant's *Adolphe* and Hesse's *Demian* and *Siddhartha*; and reached new heights in Wordsworth's *Prelude* and T.E. Lawrence's account of his life as a British intelligence agent, *Seven Pillars of Wisdom*.

In *A New Philosophy of Literature* I identified the metaphysical and secular aspects of the fundamental theme of world literature that can be found in the literature of every culture since the *Epic of Gilgamesh*, c.2,600BC: the quest for metaphysical Reality, the One; and condemnation of social follies and vices. *This Dark Wood* is a quest for the One, and I encounter many follies and vices on the way.

Pattern: life as a succession of episodes
Pairs of opposites; concept of time
I covered some of the ground of *My Double Life 1* and *2* from a different angle in *A Mystic Way* (1994), which showed how my life influenced my poems.

My Double Life 1 and *2* incorporate, revise and update *A Mystic Way* while retaining its concern to catch the cumulative process of my thinking and avoid imposing a present construct on past experience. In the two new volumes I have deliberately followed the wording of passages in *A Mystic Way* that have not been updated or presented from a new angle, preferring to retain the original account and (as they incorporate the earlier work) I have generally not referred to pages of *A Mystic Way* in the Notes and References.

In *A Mystic Way* I brought a philosophical principle to my treatment of time. Time cannot be seen; only its effects can be detected as a succession of events. In *A Mystic Way* I stated that "time is a succession of events" and that "the present is added cumulatively to the past so that new layers are endlessly added to previous layers".[1]

I have since developed that concept of time. In *My Double Life 1* and *2* I focus on a life, and time, in terms of successive episodes. I see that I lived my life in a succession of episodes. Time is now an episodic succession of events: a succession of events within an episode – and, indeed, a succession of episodes. And as time progresses, memories of successive episodes are continuously stored in layers within the memory.

An 'episode', according to the *Concise Oxford Dictionary*, is "one event or a group of events as part of a sequence", "an incident or set of incidents in a narrative". I have come to see that in each episode of my experience, on each stage of my path, the "group of events" or "set of incidents" consisted of pairs of 'contraries'. In each episode within my narrative there was a pair of conflicting sequences of events or opposites. That meant that in each episode I was living a kind of 'double life'.

The episodes inspired my memories. As I journeyed from episode to episode, memories of successive pairs of conflicting sequences of events – pairs of opposites – formed round my self. In my earliest episode the two conflicting sequences of events were imposed on my self and stored in my memory. As I grew older I found myself living through a new episode in which a second pair of conflicting sequences of events superimposed itself as a new layer on my self and my memory. And as I grew older still I lived through a new episode in which a third pair of opposites superimposed itself as a new layer on my self and my memory. And so on. Most episodes do not begin and end abruptly. Their opposites grow out of the previous episode and fade during the next episode.

I have come to see that the pattern of my life – its "repeated decorative design" (*Concise Oxford Dictionary*) – can be found in my progression through these episodes, these pairs of opposites and memories which formed – accreted – round my self, each of which controlled my life for a period of time. Tracing my progress through these episodes – these successive pairs of opposites, these sequences of events within episodes – reveals how I found my particular path and journeyed up it to this particular sloping hill.

This view of a life as a succession of episodes of conflicting sequences of events (and the layered memories of successive pairs of opposites that formed on my self) is in harmony with the view of the universe I expressed in my books. These see the universe as a unity that reconciles pairs of opposites or contradictions: day and night, spring and autumn, life and death. In a *saké* (rice-wine) bar in Tokyo in 1965 I asked the Japanese poet Junzaburo Nishiwaki (a contemporary of Eliot's) for a distillation of the wisdom of the East. He wrote on a business reply card now framed on my study wall, "+A + –A = 0, great nothing". (See p.186 [of *My Double Life 1: This Dark Wood*].) He explained to me that the universe is a unity that reconciles all contradictions, that the One combines day and night, life and death. I brought this Eastern idea back from Japan. Each pair of opposites – of conflicting sequences of events that form memories on my self – in different periods of my life is a "+A + –A" that reflects Eastern thinking.

The cone-like self: a pine cone's scales, pairs of opposites
I have come to see the layered memories of successive episodes that formed round my self, and the origin of my literary, historical and philosophical works, in terms of the image of a cone borne by an evergreen conifer: a pine, spruce, yew, cedar, cypress, larch or redwood tree.

I first made this association in August 2011. I was reflecting on how at every stage of my growth my life has been an accumulation of successive pairs of contradictions when I travelled from Cornwall to stay on Dartmoor, at Gidleigh Park. I was shown to my room and sat in the window looking down at the river that gushed through boulders beyond the lawn and rushed headlong like the course of a life. I noticed dark humps of woods beyond it. On the window-sill between me and the open window was a bowl of pine cones.

I picked one out and examined its open arms or 'scales'. I realised it was a female seed-bearing cone that shed seeds when the scales opened, and opened and closed in response to the weather. I realised the cone would one day be significant. A bowl of pine cones was an image for something, but I had not yet fathomed what. I wondered if it was an image for clusters or sequences of events. I brought the cone back with me and placed it on my desk.

Several months passed. Then, sitting in this window and looking out over this dark wood from this hill, I ruminated again on the pattern of a life, of episodes and memories, and on the structure of the self; and found myself again holding the pine cone. I examined it and realised that each scale or arm was one of a pair. A cone is formed of pairs of scales. They are in layers that are arranged in two spirals. I was holding a double-spiral structure consisting of layers of pairs of opposites, whorls around an axis. It was a perfect image for the concept of a life that I had been forming: successive episodes with pairs of contradictions, memories of which formed round the self.

A spruce cone has at least 42 pairs of scales or opposites
I have a conifer in my Essex front garden. It is a Norway spruce (*picea abies*), the species of Christmas tree donated each winter by the people of Norway and erected in Trafalgar Square. I wandered outside and picked up a five-inch-long spruce cone that was lying on the ground. (Once I might have called it a 'fir-cone' but that generic description is scientifically inaccurate as spruces and firs are different species of conifer.) Its scales were closed but as I examined it I found the same principle applied: the scales were in pairs of opposites, layer upon layer from bottom to top. I counted in zigzag up each of the two spirals and reckoned there were about 42 layers of scales. I brought it in and laid it on my desk. I knew the hard scales protected seeds that grew beneath them. During the next two days the scales opened and deposited small winged seeds. I put the spruce cone and the seeds in a small box, and within a few days it had shed more than 130 seeds.

I now intuitively grasped that the structure of the self is similar to the structure of a conifer's female cone. From childhood onwards we progress along a path through episodes, and as our cone-like self experiences and remembers our path in our memory we grow layers of scale-like pairs of opposites: memories of conflicting pairs of sequences of events, contraries, each of which is an expression of the Eastern $+A + -A = 0$. Beneath each scale of a conifer cone are two ovules that develop into seeds. The scales at the base and top of the cone are sterile, without seeds. I grasped that as we grow a new layered episode of a pair of opposites we at the same time grow the seeds of our own creativity.

I knew that the analogy of the conifer cone should not be taken too literally. Conifer cones have two seeds per scale, i.e. four seeds per layered pair of opposites. It does not follow that a fully-grown self living to about 105 with 42 layers and pairs of opposites, and therefore 84 'scales', has exactly 168 seeds or projects. But I intuitively felt that the principle of seeds being produced from beneath layers and pairs of scales does apply to the self, that the germs of potential creative works and projects are produced from beneath layers of memories of pairs of opposites based on episodes with conflicting pairs of sequences of events, even though the number of creative works and projects achieved differs from the number of seeds in a cone.

Fibonacci spirals, 13 counter-clockwise and 8 clockwise
My thinking was carried forward in January 2012. My wife had a locally well-known naturalist and environmentalist[2] to lunch. I produced the small box containing the two cones and the deposit of seeds. I remarked on the pairs of opposite scales. As she handled the cones the environmentalist said, "Of course, they're spirals. It's the Fibonacci sequence. It determines their form." Her remark dropped into my mind like a stone. I did some research.

As in many growing things, from the base of a cone spirals whirl upwards in two opposite directions. There is a double set of spirals, one going in a clockwise direction and one in a counter-clockwise direction. In a fully-grown pine cone there are 13 counter-clockwise spirals and 8 clockwise spirals, a total of 21 spirals. In all cones these conflicting spirals go in the same differing directions. In a fully-grown spruce cone the same applies. The number of these spirals is determined by the sequence of numbers named after Leonardo of Pisa, who was known as Fibonacci and who in 1202, in his *Liber Abaci*, introduced the sequence (which was already known in Indian mathematics) to the West: 0, 1, 1, 2, 3, 5, 8, 13, 21, 34, 55, 89, 144, 233, 377 and so on. The first two numbers are 0 and 1, and each subsequent number is the sum of the previous two.

If we divide each number (e.g. 13) by the number that precedes it in the sequence (e.g. 8), it gives a value of approximately 1.6180339, the golden ratio or mean which is represented by the Greek letter *phi*. To successors of the early-13th-century Fibonacci such as Leonardo da Vinci this was the ratio of beauty. Thus the perfect face contains this figure of design proportion – the width of the mouth is 1.618 times the width of the nose, for example – whereas in a lopsided, unbeautiful face this is not the case. The same is true of the proportion of the limbs of the body. Each finger bone is 1.618 times the length of the preceding finger bone, and the distance from elbow to wrist is 1.618 times the distance from wrist to fingertip. The distance from belly button (or navel) to the soles of the feet is 1.618 times the distance from the top of the head to the belly button, and ideal height is 1.618 times the distance from shoulder to fingertip. Fibonacci saw a mechanism in Nature that implements proportion. He did not say how or why the drive or thrust within Nature spurs the DNA to reproduce this ratio.

Sunflowers by and large obey the Fibonacci sequence of numbers. Different types of sunflower have 55 spirals (34 clockwise, 21 counter-clockwise), 89 (55 clockwise, 34 counter-clockwise) or in the case of very large sunflowers even 233 (144 clockwise, 89 counter-clockwise). The counter-clockwise spirals appear to limit their growth to accord with the golden ratio. The arrangement of the Fibonacci numbers maximises the number of seeds that can be packed into a seed head. Spiralling growth is found in the leaf arrangements, stems and branches of other plants, in their petals and seed heads and in the whorl of a nautilus shell. It is found in the growth of many flowers and fruits, the uncurling of fern fronds, and the positioning of branches on tree-trunks as well as in the growth of mollusc shells. Plant cells turn at 0.618 of a revolution (222.5 degrees) to maximise space, forming spirals. Not all plants obey the Fibonacci sequence. For example, corn grows in straight lines.

I was startled to discover that Alan Turing, the father of computer science who helped break the Enigma code at Bletchley Park, spent two years working on the Fibonacci numbers in sunflowers to understand how plants grow. He wrote a paper on form in biology in 1951 and devised a theory to explain why Fibonacci sequences appear in sunflowers and plants, but before the theory could be tested he died after biting an apple injected with cyanide in 1954. A Turing's Sunflowers project led by the Museum of Science and Industry in Manchester in 2012 analysed sunflower specimens sent by 12,000 people in seven countries and found that of 557 heads analysed, 458 (82%) had their rows arranged in Fibonacci spiral patterns, and that of the rest 33 had patterns based on the Lucas series, a modified Fibonacci sequence that begins with 2 and 1 and proceeds on the same basis (3, 4, 7, 11, 18, 29 and so on).[3]

Looking at my spruce cone again, I realised that the cones are imbricate – arranged so as to overlap each other like fish scales (or roof tiles) to protect seeds. I saw that the scales are different sizes and that their ends are curled up to different extents so that when the scales are closed the ends fully protect the seeds above from predators and rain. (A cone closes if soaked in water.) Sequoia cones, including those of redwood trees, the tallest trees on earth, feel heat from fires. They wait until fire threatens the seeds before scattering them, probably because in primeval times, long before the advent of man, lightning strikes started forest fires. Such intricate organisation and ordering was truly wonderful, and I marvelled that the DNA instructs each spruce scale to grow to a precise specification that differs from that of all the other scales.

I was again struck by the 8 clockwise and 13 counter-clockwise spirals. They twist in opposite directions, the spirals are also opposites, their own +A (i.e. 8) + −A (i.e. 13) = 0. I dwelt on the image and concept of a self as spirals of memories of experiences. I saw mind as clockwise and counter-clockwise spirals of sequences of memories of experiences.[4]

I sensed that the whole intricate structure of the self consists of pairs of opposite memories of experience. That is to say, I sensed that each episode passes into our memory as a pair of opposite sequences of events, and that within each opposite are subsets of further sequences of events. And that each memory may be within a pair of 'scales' that is simultaneously stored within two opposite spirals and has an essential part in the whole.

I grasped that each episode in a life could be shown as a pair of opposite experiences, and that a self could be shown as spirals of sequences of memories of experiences. In each of my pairs of opposites, one half of the pair would be part of a spiral on one side of the cone of the self, and the other half of the pair would be part of an opposite spiral on the other side of the cone of the self. Just as one can look at a cone as pairs of scales, as clockwise spirals and as counter-clockwise spirals, so one can look at a self as pairs of opposites, as clockwise spirals and as counter-clockwise spirals of memories, all winding up to the cone-shaped self's present outlook at its top. For our earliest memories are at the cone-shaped self's base, and our most recent are in our present episode, towards the top.

The double helix, two entwined spirals
It is worth pointing out that if my memories of the pairs of opposites within the episodes of my double life are held within two entwined spirals that formed round my self, then they resemble the pairs of opposites within the double helix, or two entwined spirals, of DNA. (See below.) If this is so, then human memory and inheritance can be seen to follow the same process, pattern and law: another confirmation of the unity between human consciousness and biological Nature.

8 clockwise (left) and 13 counter-clockwise (middle) spirals of a pine cone; and (right) diagram of the double helix of DNA showing two ribbon-like (phosphate-sugar) chains with horizontal rods connecting pairs of bases or opposites that hold the chains together.

The structure of My Double Life: *successive episodes –* My Double Life 1 *as the first 15 of 42 episodes and pairs of opposites*
Through such musings I arrived at the form of *My Double Life*. I realised that I had been confirmed in my thinking about its structure. I could see 30 episodes along the path of my life so far, of which the first 15 are covered in *My Double Life 1: This Dark Wood*, ending with the end of my career in intelligence. I have structured *This Dark Wood* round the first 15 of the 30 layered episodes I have lived through. They begin on p.22 [of *My Double Life 1: This Dark Wood*]. In each of the numbered episodes in my life there was a pair of conflicting sequences of events that are reflected in the title of the section devoted to each episode. Each episode, or rather each conflicting sequence of events within the pair, is also a layer of memories stored within my self. I shall consider the pattern of these 15 episodes in the Epilogue. The remaining 15, and a review of all 30, can be found in *My Double Life 2: A Rainbow over the Hills*.

These 30 episodes – so far, and the 42 episodes of my fully-grown self if I live to be 105 and the average length of an episode is 2.5 years – can be seen as having a linear chronological progression from episode 1 to episode 30 and eventually to episode 42, and we shall see that the pairs of opposites have their own progression within their double helix. (See p.474 [of *My Double Life 1: This Dark Wood*].)

I sensed that as my finished life – if it achieves its full span – will have 42 layers and pairs of opposites, I have just completed the 30th layer, and the 31st–42nd layers are still in the future.

Inclusion of my intelligence work – Sir John Masterman, Asa Briggs

> I said, "I will watch how I behave, and not let my tongue lead me into
> sin; I will keep a muzzle on my mouth as long as the wicked man is near
> me." I stayed dumb, silent, speechless.
> (*Psalm 39, Jerusalem Bible*)

When I discussed my experiences in Libya with the historian (Lord)
Asa Briggs, Provost of Worcester College, Oxford in October 1978
and told him what I had been doing immediately before and during
Gaddafi's *coup* as an intelligence agent, he told me very strongly,
"You must write a book about your experiences. You have told me
something I have often wondered about and did not know, you must
write it down. You have just explained how the West came to accept the
Gaddafi Revolution. I have not seen this written anywhere else. You
must write the *full* story. It is of historical importance." He followed
this up with a letter: "I feel that you ought to write up your experience,
and I am sure that it would be of very wide interest."[5]

I did not know that he had worked in Bletchley Park for two years
from early summer 1943 to May 1945 and that he would write his own
account, *Secret Days* (which would be published in 2011 when he was
90). Nor did I know that my Provost when I was at Worcester College,
Sir John Masterman, had been Chairman of the Twenty Committee
('XX Committee') during the Second World War and in charge of the
'double-cross system' that turned German agents round and duped
German intelligence into believing that D-Day would take place in the
Pas de Calais rather than Normandy. I did not know that the account
he wrote immediately after the war in 1945 was walled round with
silence in the UK until it was finally published as *The Double-Cross
System in the War of 1939 to 1945* in the US in 1972. (See p.119 [of *My
Double Life 1: This Dark Wood*].) Without realising it until later on, I
came through a college that has a strong tradition – as Masterman and
Briggs demonstrated – of publishing accounts of individual dealings
with intelligence. In response to Asa Briggs' 1978 urgings I brought
out *The Libyan Revolution* in 2009, which told only half the story: the
events I lived through in Libya in 1968–1970. I have now fully acceded
to Briggs' 1978 urgings and (35 years late) here include the whole story
of my four years of intelligence work from May 1969 to the summer
of 1973.

As to the merit of such secret work, Masterman and Briggs had
the advantage of working against the murderous Nazis. All agree that
it was splendid to decode Enigma, make D-Day a success and stand

up to the Nazis during the war against Hitler. Collecting information on the expansionist Soviet Union and China in Africa, a continent in which Nelson Mandela struggled against *apartheid* in South Africa in the 1950s and Smith's UDI (Unilateral Declaration of Independence) in Rhodesia alienated the world in the 1960s, seems on the face of it a less clear-cut case, especially as liberal opinion supported the struggle of the Africans. Nevertheless there was still a real strategic prospect that the Soviet Union would invade Western Europe, and standing up to post-Stalinist Soviet expansion in Europe and Africa during the Cold War and to Maoist Chinese expansion in troubled African states such as Tanzania was as vital to British interests in the 1970s as standing up to Nazi expansion was in the late 1930s and 1940s.

Standing up to Gaddafi's Libya is a more clear-cut case as at a very early stage after his 1969 *coup* Gaddafi began to fund and arm international terrorist groups, including the IRA, and opposing Gaddafi meant opposing terrorism. Those who endangered themselves to defend the West against terrorism in the early days of Gaddafi's tyranny have been dismayed by claims in the press that after 2004 the British intelligence services allied with Gaddafi; systematically targeted Libyan dissidents and opponents of Gaddafi living in Britain and worked to send them back to Gaddafi for detention and torture,[6] betraying the risky work carried out a generation earlier by anti-Gaddafi intelligence agents.

My book *The Libyan Revolution*, which presented Gaddafi in a less than flattering light as a despot, may have been caught up in an operation to implement this policy that included walling books round with silence. The generation of Masterman and Briggs would have been astounded if the British intelligence services had suddenly taken Hitler's side towards the end of the war, delivered his opponents to him for detention and torture and impeded books that were unenthusiastic about him, yet the operation to assist Gaddafi after 2004 is just as astonishing. Something went badly wrong with the West's response to Gaddafi's attempt to acquire weapons of mass destruction in the first decade of the 21st century. Now Gaddafi has fallen, the Libyan part of this record speaks for a generation that stood up to Gaddafi immediately after his *coup* and is a contribution to undoing the betrayal of 2004.

On his opening page Asa Briggs gives three reasons for writing *Secret Days*: his duty to contribute a personal memoir to the collective Bletchley-Park inheritance while he has time to record it; his duty as a historian to recall his own experiences in perspective, which he considers to be of importance; and his wish to answer the question as to why a historian should work in Bletchley Park. Similar considerations apply to my reasons for including my four years with the SIS in this account. I feel I have a duty to contribute a personal memoir to the SIS inheritance; I have a duty to recall my own experiences in perspective, which I consider to be of importance; and I want to answer the question as to how I came to work for the SIS. I have weighed my contribution in a measured way and have taken other considerations into account. I believe it is in the public interest that I should leave behind an appropriate record of my experiences during that long-ago time.

Although it is more than 40 years since I discontinued my intelligence work and we are now in a different era, I have adhered to the principles of disclosure and have not named members of the Secret Intelligence Service I had dealings with, who are referred to by Christian names and surnames other than their own to protect their anonymity. I have not revealed full details of the operations that involved me. I have borne in mind that in much of my intelligence work I was sharing what I was already doing – after the event. I have waited until Gaddafi's death before saying what I was really doing in Libya, and I have waited for a clear 40 years to elapse before writing about aspects of the Cold War, during which time the world has changed, the Cold War has ended and most of the participants have died, including the leaders Edward Heath, Leonid Brezhnev and Mao Zedong. The pre-internet methods that applied in my day may now look antiquated, but there is historical merit in telling what happened, as Asa Briggs was quick to see in 1978. Members of the armed forces are able to refer to their 'war record'. I have judged that the time is now right for me to refer to my 'secret-war record'.

I have another reason for writing this work: to make clear key events in my life which members of my family have found baffling. Some of these events have been reflected without explanation in my literary work. Some of my poems, including a few in *The Gates of Hell* sequence, cannot be fully understood without an understanding of the pressures of coping with the dangers of an agent's life and their role in triggering the break-up of my first marriage. Furthermore, my progress from nationalism to Universalism in my literary, historical and philosophical works cannot be fully understood without a grasp of the significance of my four years of being instructed to think nationalistically and of my disturbing discovery that I was working not just for my country but within a latent, self-interested New World Order (see pp.414–415 [of *My Double Life 1: This Dark Wood*]). For 40 years I have kept silent about these events. In the words of the version of *Psalm* 39 quoted above, I kept a muzzle on my mouth and stayed dumb. Now that I am in the year of my 75th birthday it is time to set the record straight about events that began 45 years ago.

I believe that my inclusion of my intelligence work for the first time in *My Double Life 1: This Dark Wood* enables me to present the full extent of the darkness within my Dantean wood, which at times was as impenetrable as Conrad's "heart of darkness". It is important to me to bring out that my illumination burst upon me and left me reeling during a month when in the London streets outside I was being tailed by surveillance squads: a combination of two extremes that could not be more opposite. I believe that the contrast between my intelligence work and my early mystical life makes my narrative unique and that the inclusion of my intelligence work makes *My Double Life 1: This Dark Wood* a unique contribution to the *genre* of transformation. There is not another work like it in this *genre*: T.E. Lawrence left his intelligence links out of *Seven Pillars of Wisdom*. Although opening to the mystic Light and operating as a latter-day James Bond are extreme experiences, and at opposite extremes, I believe this account of my perilous path through a dark wood has a universal resonance.

Personal pattern: the story of my quest for Reality, the One
My Double Life tells the story of my quest and its pattern. It is not a conventional autobiography that describes the progress of a social ego but rather an objective narrative that focuses on my personal quest, an epic journey available to all wayfarers. In the later parts of my story I have frequently quoted from my *Diaries* as they were written immediately after the events described and give 'at-the-time' authenticity to my recollection. 'At-the-time' wording bypasses fallible memory and inadvertent embellishing-in-hindsight. It adds vividness by recapturing with precision long-forgotten details relating to the day on which events happened, and reproduces how events struck me at the time. My aim has been to get as close to the original experience in the moment as is possible at such a distance, and my method has enabled me to achieve a fidelity to the moment which many memoirs that look back over decades fail to achieve. The moments all belong to a process, and my double life is a 'process life'. My *Diaries* add immediacy and bring the past alive in the dynamic, baroque, process-led Universalist manner. I have sourced the quotations from my *Diaries* so that my memoir has the flavour of being evidential and objective as well as vividly detailed and 'at the time'.

My personal quest led me into a transformation (or metamorphosis) that began on the other [eastern] side of the world. The episodes (or successive conflicting sequences of events) along my path were reflected in layered memories which contain my projects and indicate the structure of my self and the pattern of my life. Just as a cone sheds its seeds, so our layered memories contain seed-like projects we shed while we are alive. My layered memories contain my seed-like projects, my works, most of which I have already shed (or spread before humankind).

To what extent was the path of my life subject to chance, choice or destiny?
My narrative in the two volumes of *My Double Life* is objective because its main focus is not on me but on objective aspects of my quest: my path, the pattern of my life and the development of Universalism. It subordinates my personal, individual experiences to the objective presentation of a universal quest. My narrative describes events that seem to be chosen by free will; or seem to happen by chance; or seem to fulfil a destiny. All my experiences (+A + –A) were useful and essential to the shape of my life when viewed as a whole, and they too fulfilled a destiny. 'Destiny' is what is predetermined and fated to happen to a particular person. There is no place for the concept of destiny in a materialist world that is governed solely by chance, accident and coincidence. The concept of destiny is only meaningful if Providence presides over our path. An objective narrative of my quest will bring out the interconnection between free will, chance and destiny.

Universal pattern: the pattern of the path of my life reflects a universal pattern
In *My Double Life 1: This Dark Wood* I have tried to identify the pattern behind my experiences and how I remember them. The content of my personal, individual experience is unique as is everyone else's, but I regard the structure of my experience, of episodes that are remembered in layers within the self, as being universal. This work suggests that the principles that underlie my individual experience and everybody's experience are universal principles.

Besides describing a personal, individual journey *This Dark Wood* is a universal work that reflects the experiences and development of many young people. The objective pattern of the path I set out is a universal one, and there *is* a universal pattern of experience. The pattern of the path of my life reflects a universal pattern.

So *My Double Life 1: This Dark Wood* focuses on the relationship between the personal, individual and local on the one hand and the universal on the other hand; on personal and universal pattern; on the episodic structure of all experience; and on my developing awareness that the universe is a unity. It is therefore a Universalist work. As with all my works, it came with an urgency and effortlessness that sometimes seemed inspired: I completed the research and writing in seven months (from 14 January to 14 August 2012). I have to thank my PA Ingrid Kirk for her role in enabling me to complete this work so quickly.

So much for the principles behind the pattern and structure of *My Double Life*. I can now proceed to the origins of my double life.

Notes:

1. Nicholas Hagger, *A Mystic Way*, pp.159, 776–777, Note [see Preface 5, p.85, of *Collected Prefaces*].
2. Tricia Moxey.
3. Michael Hanlon, 'Turing's flower theory blossoms', *The Sunday Times*, 28 October 2012.
4. It may be of interest to record that I had already outlined 21 pairs of opposites for an early draft of these two volumes, subsequently discarded, which I viewed as two spirals: 13 + 8. The first 13 would take me to the point of illumination, the 8 would cover the next 8 episodes and take me to the beginning of my writing career. Between them they would cover the birth of my outlook. I saw that the next 21 pairs of opposites would continue the first 21 within the two spirals, and cover the next 21 episodes and take me to the development of my outlook. The first 13 episodes of these would complete my development of the world, and the next 8 episodes would complete my new view of the world and take me to the end of my life, with a capacity to store memories to the end of my life. The last 12 are still ahead of me.
5. Letter from Asa Briggs to Nicholas Hagger, 20 October 1978; in the Hagger archive.
6. Two Libyan dissidents brought civil actions against an MI6 official and the ex-Foreign Secretary relating to rendition and torture allegations. See, for example, *The Independent on Sunday*, 21 October 2012, p.34.

37

My Double Life 2: A Rainbow over the Hills

The Vision of Unity
Episodes and Pattern in a Writer's Life

Author's Note

Episodes and pattern in My Double Life 1: This Dark Wood
My Double Life 1: This Dark Wood presented the first 15 episodes of
my life. This book, its companion volume and sequel, continues the
story and presents the next 15 episodes. They are numbered 1–15 to
give this work the feel of a self-contained volume but they could have
been numbered 16–30. *My Double Life 1: This Dark Wood* dealt with
my travels in the Middle and Far East, including China, my work for
British Intelligence in Europe and Africa, my emergence from darkness
into Light and the birth of my vision of unity. This work deals with my
emergence to Universalism (whose different activities, disciplines and
*genre*s are symbolised in the bands of a rainbow) and the gestation and
production of my first 40 books. It deals with how the books came to
be written, the pressures behind them, the processes that brought their
Universalism to birth and their attempt to convey my vision of the
universe as a unity.

My Double Life 1: This Dark Wood contains a very full Prologue, which
deals with all the main issues, including the presentation of my life as
a chain-like succession of episodes, in each of which there is a pair of
conflicting sequences of events that resemble the pairs of opposites
in the double helix of DNA and in the two spirals [of the scales] on
a spruce cone. This book therefore does not have a Prologue, which
is replaced by this Author's Note. *My Double Life 1: This Dark Wood*
contains an Epilogue that looks back over the first 15 episodes. This
work's Epilogue looks back over the next 15 episodes, and assesses all
30 episodes. Through their episodic structure the two books together
convey the pattern in my life, and it is my contention that a similar
episodic approach will reveal the pattern in all lives. I see both works
as therefore being Universalist works.

In the Prologue of *My Double Life 1: This Dark Wood* I said that I have
had four Mystic Lives. I wrote:

During my journey I had four Mystic Lives. These can be dated from the chronological list of experiences of the Light (see Appendix 1, p.903 [of *My Double Life 2: A Rainbow over the Hills*]). There are 16 experiences of the Light in *My Double Life 1: This Dark Wood* and 77 in *My Double Life 2: A Rainbow over the Hills*, a total of 93 experiences of the Light, each of which is documented from *Diaries* written at the time. Between the First and Second Mystic Lives was my Dark Night of the Soul, and between my Second and Third Mystic Lives was the first part of my Dark Night of the Spirit, in which I was fed new powers. *My Double Life 1: This Dark Wood* ends near the beginning of this Dark Night. In *My Double Life 2: A Rainbow over the Hills* the story continues, and between my Third and Fourth Mystic Lives was the second part of My Dark Night of the Spirit in which I was confronted with ordeals. My Unitive Life began after my Fourth Mystic Life.

My unitive life within seven disciplines: method, and opposites within episodes
In *My Double Life 2: A Rainbow over the Hills* I narrate my progress into unitive life within seven disciplines.

Taken together, these two works recount how during my quest my glimpses of the metaphysical Reality known as the One inspired me to write Universalist works in seven disciplines: transpersonal psychology and mysticism, literature, science and philosophy (including cosmology), world history, international politics and statecraft, comparative religion, and world culture. They therefore narrate the development of my world view, Universalism, which focuses on the unity of the universe and the universality of humankind and seeks to bring in a harmonious world in the near-future; and which I have expressed in my 40 books.

In the Prologue of *My Double Life 1: This Dark Wood* I wrote the following regarding my method:

I have frequently quoted from my *Diaries* as they were written immediately after the events described and give 'at-the-time' authenticity to my recollection. 'At-the-time' wording bypasses fallible memory and inadvertent embellishing-in-hindsight. It adds vividness by recapturing long-forgotten details relating to the day on which events happened with precision, and reproduces how events struck me at the time. My aim has been to get as close to the original experience in the moment as is possible at such a distance, and my method has enabled me to achieve a fidelity to the moment which many memoirs that look back over decades fail to achieve. The moments all belong to a process, and my double life is a process life. My *Diaries* add immediacy and bring the past alive in the dynamic, baroque, process-led Universalist manner. I have sourced the quotations from my *Diaries* so that my memoir has the flavour of being evidential and objective as well as vividly detailed and 'at the time'.

As will be seen, the bands of the rainbow represent the disciplines in which I have worked (see pp.260, 873 [of *My Double Life 2: A Rainbow over the Hills*]). It will become apparent that within each episode many of the italicised subheadings begin with one of the two 'opposites' of that episode, and as the episodes of Part Two reflect these disciplines many of the subheadings reflect one or more of these disciplines. The subheadings therefore connect the reader to the seven bands of the rainbow.

Time taken
Finally I should add that, having finished *My Double Life 1: This Dark Wood* in seven months, I took longer on this work, which spans 40 years and 40 books. I completed the research and writing in eleven months (from 19 August 2012 to 7 September 2013), and amended both books for another seven-and-a-half months (until 25 April 2014, see pp.844–845 [of *My Double Life 2: A Rainbow over the Hills*] for further details). I would like to pay tribute to my PA Ingrid Kirk who helped me complete both books so quickly.

38

Selected Stories

Follies and Vices of the Modern Elizabethan Age

Preface to Selected Stories

The 86 stories of Parts One and Two were written during a period of 40 years between 1966 and 2006. They describe the fortunes of an Englishman, Philip Rawley, in the UK and other countries from late youth to early old age during five decades of the second Elizabethan Age. Most of these stories originally appeared within four separate volumes between 1995 and 1998: *A Spade Fresh with Mud*; *A Smell of Leaves and Summer*; *Wheeling Bats and a Harvest Moon*; and *The Warm Glow of the Monastery Courtyard*. Others appeared in a fifth volume, *In the Brilliant Autumn Sunshine*, which was in *Collected Stories* (2007). *Collected Stories* presented 1,001 stories, a tally that echoes *A Thousand and One Nights* (also known as *Arabian Nights' Entertainments*).

The fundamental theme of world literature
In *A New Philosophy of Literature* I identified the metaphysical and secular aspects of the fundamental theme of world literature: the quest for metaphysical Reality, and condemnation of social follies and vices in relation to an implied virtue. This selection reflects the fundamental theme. It presents stories exposing the follies and vices of our time (Part One), and stories on Philip Rawley's quest and his growing awareness of the unity of the universe (Part Two).

The quest for Reality
The quest for Reality and the promise of immortality go back 4,600 years to the Mesopotamian *Epic of Gilgamesh* and follow the Mystic Way which can be found in the literature of every culture and generation. Confronted with the seeming finality of death, the soul turns away from bodily attachment, is purged and illumined, and undergoes a transformation that enables it to perceive the unity of the universe and sense the possibility of its own survival. The stories in Part Two are in the 4,600-year-old tradition of the metaphysical aspect of the fundamental theme. See pp.238–241 [of *Selected Stories: Follies and Vices of the Modern Elizabethan Age*] for quest themes in Part Two, all of which involve intense experiences of the oneness of the universe, Nature and history and awareness of the One.

Follies and vices

In every decade from the 16th century to today literary works have also looked back to the classical world and reflected its condemnation of social follies and vices.

What is the difference between 'follies' and 'vices'? Folly is associated with foolish acts; vices are associated with immoral, depraved or evil behaviour. Folly exposes people to vice. Some foolish acts are due to poor decisions. Sometimes people are too trusting and are taken advantage of by unscrupulous people whose behaviour is immoral or evil. An example of such gullibility can be found in the painting by Hieronymus Bosch, *The Stone Operation*, which is also known as *The Cure of Folly* (c.1488 or later). The painting shows a man being treated for a mental disorder by having a stone removed from his brain. The 'surgeon' (shown wearing a funnel hat which at the time indicated a charlatan) drills into the man's skull to remove a stone. Both he and a woman who is probably his wife (who has a book on her head, suggesting folly) are being conned. They will pay the 'surgeon' an extortionate fee for the pointless operation. The folly of the couple has made them victims of the immoral, evil 'surgeon' whose unscrupulous money-seeking is a vice. Follies are different from, but inextricably linked to, vices. Many vices could not be indulged without compliant foolishness.

A comprehensive list of the follies and vices in world literature can be found in the index of *A New Philosophy of Literature*. The list includes (F indicating folly):

abandonment; acquisitiveness; alcoholism; ambition; arrogance; asperity; betrayal; bigotry; blindness; boastfulness; bravado; brutality; bullying; capriciousness; concealment; confidence tricks; corruptibility; corrupting worldly power; corruption; credulousness (F); cruelty; cynicism; debauchery; deceit; defiance; denial of principles; destructiveness; dictatorial behaviour; discontent; dishonesty; being domineering; drunkenness; duplicity; eagerness to marry (F); egotism; egotistical sensuality; enmity; envy; excessive mourning; exploitation; fantasies; fortune-hunting; frivolity; greed; hatred; hedonism; hubristic contentment; hypocrisy; idleness; illusions (F); impudence; inconstancy; infatuation; infidelity; inhumanity; insincerity; interference; jealousy; lack of truthfulness; lust; lust for power; massacres; meanness; mercenary motives; miserliness; misjudgement; mistreatment; money-seeking; moral blindness; murder; naïve beliefs (F); neglect; nihilism; obstinacy; overreaching (F); patricide; pedantry; persecution; petulance; pretension; pride; prodigality; rebelliousness;

revenge; ruthlessness; seduction; self-centredness; self-conceit; self-deceit (F); self-interestedness; self-love; shadiness; shrewishness; snobbishness; social climbing; strictness; swindling; thieving/stealing; threatening behaviour; treachery; trickery; troublemaking; tyrannical ruthlessness; tyranny; unscrupulousness; usurpation; vanity; villainy; voluptuousness; war; warmongering; and pursuit of wealth.

These same follies and vices can all be found in the 1,001 stories in my *Collected Stories*. They can all be found in this selection (with the exception of 'patricide'). The list below replicates the one above, and each bracketed number indicates a numbered story in Part One of this selection in which each folly or vice can be found (Q before a number indicating a story in Part Two, 'Quest for the One'):

abandonment (39, 42); acquisitiveness (10, 24, 25); alcoholism (23, 42); ambition (18, Q29); arrogance (6, 29); asperity (38, Q28); betrayal (2); bigotry (Q1); blindness (22, Q32, Q34); boastfulness (12, 34); bravado (12, 15); brutality (16); bullying (17, 24); capriciousness (15); concealment (Q15); confidence tricks (3, 12, 23, Q19); corruptibility (13); corrupting worldly power (10, 16, 28); corruption (10); credulousness (F, 12, Q19); cruelty (16, 27); cynicism (20); debauchery (14); deceit (12); defiance (Q14); denial of principles (32); destructiveness (42); dictatorial behaviour (24, 36); discontent (14); dishonesty (12); being domineering (17); drunkenness (1); duplicity (10); eagerness to marry (32); egotism (3, 23); egotistical sensuality (12); enmity (4); envy (8); excessive mourning (14); exploitation (13, 23, 26, Q29); fantasies (23, 35); fortune-hunting (11); frivolity (Q32); greed (10, 24, 41); hatred (33); hedonism (11); hubristic contentment (4, 6, 11); hypocrisy (1, 36); idleness (Q20); illusions (F, 34, 35); impudence (43); inconstancy (1); infatuation (12, 14); infidelity (1, 13, 28); inhumanity (33, 36); insincerity (11, 12); interference (7, Q26); jealousy (8); lack of truthfulness (39, 41); lust (12, 14); lust for power (28); massacres (33, 36); meanness (4); mercenary motives (41); miserliness (24); misjudgement (32); mistreatment (37); money-seeking (24, 41); moral blindness (33); murder (9, 20, 24); naïve beliefs (F, 5, 15, 25); neglect (42); nihilism (14, Q2); obstinacy (3, 32); overreaching (F, 37); pedantry (4); persecution (27); petulance (38); pretension (4); pride (6, Q5); prodigality (1); rebelliousness (10, 22, Q3); revenge (10, 27); ruthlessness (9, 36, 41); seduction (12, 14); self-centredness (12, 19, 43); self-conceit (6); self-deceit (F, 5, 35); self-interestedness (12, 19); self-love (18, 32); shadiness (24); shrewishness (4, 8, 19); snobbishness (8, 40); social climbing (8); strictness (17); swindling (23, 24); thieving/stealing (24); threatening behaviour (24); treachery (2); trickery

(23); troublemaking (24); tyrannical ruthlessness (9); tyranny (36); unscrupulousness (11, 12); usurpation (8, Q3); vanity (3, 23, 32); villainy (24, 31); voluptuousness (32); war (9, 16, 27); warmongering (33); and pursuit of wealth (3, 41).

Additional follies and vices which are also exposed and condemned in the numbered stories in Part One of this selection are in the list below, which is also in alphabetical order (Q again indicating stories in Part Two):

absent-mindedness (F, 22, 30); aggressiveness (4); anger (20, Q14); bitterness (24, Q40); boredom (14); bribery (31); burglary (10, 24); childishness (25); covetousness (8); deception (12); desertion (12); egocentricity (25); egoism (19); extortion (11); false jokiness (21); falsely claiming knowledge (Q15); gluttony (excessive drinking and drugs) (39); gullibility (F, 31, 32); hero-worship (23); idealisation (2); imperiousness (19, 38); trying to impress (21); injury (9); intolerance (36); know-all superiority (8); lack of good sense (F, 2, 3, 14); long-windedness (30); manipulativeness (7); mendacity (12, 36); nuns' worldliness (22); overbearingness (37); peremptoriness (26, 29); phoniness (23, 40); pomposity (18); posing (15); not facing reality (Q25); rivalry (35); robbery (24); roguery (3); self-deception (F, 5, 12, 35); self-importance (18, 29, 40); self-righteousness (4); servitude (17); sloth (14); stinginess (23); suicide (42, Q2); terrorism (33); theft (10); and yobbishness (43).

These two lists correspond to the list of follies and vices in each story in Part One of this selection, which can be found on pp.235–237 [of *Selected Stories: Follies and Vices of the Modern Elizabethan Age*]. They total 151 vices and 10 follies. In fact, follies can be found in most of the stories in Part One, particularly in 2, 4, 5, 7, 8, 11, 12, 13, 14, 15, 21, 26, 30, 32, 34, 35, 37, 38, 40, and in some stories in Part Two, for example 1.

All these follies and vices can also be found in *Selected Poems: Quest for the One*, a companion volume to this work. Its Preface sets out numbered groups of poems and excerpts in which each of these follies and vices can be found. Readers may like to compare the treatment of follies and vices in *Selected Stories* and *Selected Poems*.

These lists in fact cover the vices identified by Chaucer and Shakespeare in their works (as shown in *A New Philosophy of Literature*), and the stories in Part One of this selection are in the tradition of Chaucer's and Shakespeare's treatments of follies and vices as well as in the tradition of the secular aspect of the fundamental theme.

Universalist balance of fundamental theme's two aspects
At different times one of the two aspects of the fundamental theme
of world literature dominates the other in contemporary works,
depending on the metaphysical or secular outlook of the particular
Age, civilisation and time within which the works have been written.
Universalism seeks to reconcile contradictions, and the Universalist
ideal seeks a balance between the two aspects, between social virtue
and the soul's perception of the One. This selection is deliberately
balanced: both Part One and Part Two contain 43 stories. In the
Epilogue I have included two hitherto unpublished 'communications
from Giza' c.2600BC, which encapsulate and balance the secular and
metaphysical aspects of the fundamental theme from a time that
predates its appearance in world literature.

This selection introduces Philip Rawley's reflections, his growth
and development, the wide range of characters he encounters from
all backgrounds, their follies and flaws, and his glimpses of the One
in fleeting 'epiphanies' (revelations). Death lurks behind the social
situations, and though social life is presented as a Dance of Death there
is a growing sense that the universe has a higher order that reconciles
the contradictions of life, death and eternity and offers the hope of
immortality. These stories reflect the Age and the One Reality behind
the many phenomena, and suggest an ordered universe in which
glimpses of meaning and purpose can transcend nihilism and despair.

Inspiration from the 17th century
These mini-stories present a new literary form. They are prose-
poems whose titles (such as 'An Important Star and a Fossil-Lady' or
'The Bride and a Forgotten Joint') effect, in the words of Johnson's
description of the wit of Metaphysical poets in his 'Life of Cowley', "a
combination of dissimilar images" in which "the most heterogeneous
ideas are yoked by violence together". In so far as their connections
adhere to (and carry forward) Johnson's description of Metaphysical
wit they can be regarded as Metaphysical stories, stories in the 17th-
century Metaphysical tradition. Besides conveying an image with a
poet's eye for significant detail, concreteness and realism they make a
statement and therefore represent a Universalist synthesising blend of
image and statement. They are verbal paintings that present an image
in action, as if on a canvas, and can startle the soul into a new mode of
perception and enlightenment.

This said, I must emphasise that this selection and my *Selected
Poems: Quest for the One* (also 2015) anthologise my treatment in my
stories and poems of the fundamental theme of world literature set out

in *A New Philosophy of Literature*. Many of the situations that inspired these stories – and the poems in my *Selected Poems* – can be found in my two-part autobiography, *My Double Life 1: This Dark Wood* and *My Double Life 2: A Rainbow over the Hills* (2015).

14–15, 21, 25 April 2011; 19 September,
9 October, 1 November 2012; 30 April 2014

39

Selected Poems

Quest for the One

Preface to Selected Poems

This selection of my poetic works spans 52 years. It includes poems and extracts from poems taken from my *Collected Poems 1958–2005* (which incorporates my *Selected Poems: A Metaphysical's Way of Fire*, 1991 and *Collected Poems: A White Radiance*, 1994); a few of my odes from *Classical Odes* (2006); and a few extracts from my two poetic epics, *Overlord* (1994–1996, one-volume edition 2006) and *Armageddon* (2010), and from my five verse plays.

The fundamental theme of world literature

In *A New Philosophy of Literature* I identified the fundamental theme of world literature as having metaphysical and secular aspects: the quest for metaphysical Reality (the One), and condemnation of social follies and vices in relation to an implied virtue. This selection presents poems on my quest and growing awareness of the unity of the universe (Part One), and poems exposing the follies and vices of our time (Part Two). The two Parts, 'Quest for the One' and 'Follies and Vices', reverse the titles of the two Parts of my *Selected Stories: Follies and Vices of the Modern Elizabethan Age* (a companion volume to this work), in which 'Follies and Vices' precedes 'Quest for the One'.

The quest for Reality

The quest for Reality (or quest for the One) in literature goes back 4,600 years. It originates in the Mesopotamian *Epic of Gilgamesh*, c.2600BC, and it follows the Mystic Way, which has been found in the literature of every culture and generation since then and is the universal path trodden by Dante, who was lost in a Dark Wood, and more recently by T.S. Eliot. Faced with the seeming finality of death like Gilgamesh, the soul awakens from the social consciousness of the ego; undergoes purgation in a Way of Loss in which things go wrong in the outer world; and turns away from its attachment to the body and the senses. It has its first experience of illumination by the universal Light which is Reality, and basks in visions; and, transformed in the course of a centre-shift from the ego's control, begins to live through a new centre of consciousness that has a growing awareness of the Oneness of the universe. It experiences further illumination and visions, perceives the unity of the universe instinctively and senses the possibility of its own survival.

In my case the centre-shift and first glimpse of illumination happened in 1965 [see Appendix 1, pp.437–439], and the experience can be found in extracts from *The Early Education and Making of a Mystic* and 'The Silence'. After a Dark Night my second illumination took place in 1971 [see Appendix 1, pp.439–447], and the experience features in poems in *The Gates of Hell* such as 'Visions: Golden Flower, Celestial Curtain', 'More Visions: The Judge' and 'Visions: The Pit and the Moon'. (A few of the poems in *The Gates of Hell* refer to being "seized" or "snatched" by "God", a term used by mystics suggesting the Hound of Heaven. I do not want to undermine the words I used at the time as I struggled to understand the experience, but I would now describe the experience as being opened to the One and the poetic imagination.)

The sensing of unity involves what Coleridge called "the esemplastic power of the imagination" (*Biographia Literaria*, ch.X), "*eis en plattein*" meaning "shape into one". The soul shapes the fragments of the universe it perceives "into one" like an archaeologist piecing together the fragments of an unearthed urn. In contrast, the social ego's reason analyses and dissects, sees distinctions rather than similarities, breaks the One into bits and is separated from the unitive vision. An image can often catch the One more deftly than a statement, and some of my quest poems present images of the One. Others touch on the poets of the literary tradition I draw on to help reflect it, which includes some Roman poets.

In my Preface to my *Collected Poems* I wrote:

> It is characteristic of the journey along the Mystic Way that those lost in its "Dark Wood" and experiencing its Dark Night are unaware of the explanation for what is happening to them and what lies ahead; this is only grasped later when, from the serene calm of unitary consciousness, the self can look back and understand the detaching that suffering brought as a gift.

My prose work, *My Double Life 1: This Dark Wood*, throws light on one aspect of what happened to me during this part of my journey. It unveils that – in the footsteps of Marlowe, Defoe, Maugham, Greene and T.E. Lawrence, and probably of Wordsworth (whose name is in the Duke of Portland's secret book of payments next to the chief British intelligence agent in Hamburg as receiving £92.12s on 13 June

1799) and possibly of Byron (who spent a lot of money that may not have been his own when refitting the Greek fleet and paying the anti-Ottoman freedom-fighting Souliotes as commander-in-chief of the Greek army in Western Greece in 1824) – for four years, from May 1969 to the summer of 1973, I was a British intelligence agent, a role that plunged my personal life into turmoil. For part of this time I was Edward Heath's Top-Secret 'unofficial Ambassador' to the African liberation movements, monitoring the Soviet and Chinese expansion in Europe and Africa during the Cold War. The earlier 'Archangel', which is on Soviet and Chinese Communism, takes on a new significance in view of this secret work. I have included a few poems, such as 'On the Waterfront', 'Mephistopheles' and 'The Code', that have not been fully understood until now because what I was doing at the time was not in the public domain.

Quest themes
Notes at the end of poems and extracts in Part One of *Selected Poems* state their quest themes. They include, in the order in which they appear, the following themes: early yearning for truth; awakening to higher consciousness; the power of Nature; experience of the One; encounter with a future self; transformational centre-shift; the vision of the unity of the universe; the Way of Loss; purgation; illumination; visions of the One; unification of contemplation and action; hindrances of intelligence work; intense moments; glimpses of the One; images of the One; and reconciliation of contradictions within the harmony of the One. All the poems in Part One state different aspects of my Reality.

As a poet, I have found that the myth of Orpheus has spoken powerfully to me: his descent into the Underworld, his loss of Eurydice and of his ego, his discovery of his soul, his charming of all creation with his lyre, his vision of unity, his dismemberment by Maenads and his head continuing to sing after his death.

Condemnation of follies and vices
The secular aspect of the fundamental theme, condemnation of follies and vices, has co-existed with the quest for Reality since early times. It can be found in the classical world and was particularly strong in the 16th-century Renaissance. It can be widely found in the social satire of the Augustan poets: the mock-heroic couplets of Dryden's 'Absalom and Achitophel' and of Pope's 'The Rape of the Lock' and 'The Dunciad' expose vice.

My satire on society can be found in 'The Expatriate', 'The Silence',

'Old Man in a Circle', 'Zeus's Ass', 'Pastoral Ode', 'At Beckingham Palace'; in the two visits to Hell in my poetic epics *Overlord* and *Armageddon*; and in the extracts of dramatic verse from my verse plays. In poems such as 'Attack on America' and 'Shock and Awe', in my two poetic epics and in my verse plays I evoke some of the major events of our Age: D-Day, 9/11 and the invasions of Afghanistan and Iraq. Part Two includes evocations – in the case of 'Attack on America' and 'Shock and Awe', questionings – of these events and therefore reflects the Age. As readers of my books on contemporary history will know, my version of contemporary events does not always accord with the official version. I am confident that one day my version will come to be seen as being more right than the current official version.

The following follies and vices are exposed and condemned in Part Two of this selection, and are mentioned in the notes that summarise themes at the end of the poems or extracts of Part Two. They are listed below in the order in which they appear in Part Two (numbers in brackets indicating numbers in Part Two where they can be found, F indicating folly, * indicating already mentioned):

self-love (1); genteelness (2); dictatorship (3, 15); brainwashing (3); disharmony (4); discontent (4); destruction (4, 15); escapism (5); lust (5, 7); systemic killing (6, 7, 14, 15); power (6); deviousness (6, 10); ruthlessness (6, 10, 11, 12, 14, 15); cunning (6); ingratitude (6); unscrupulousness (6); ambition (6); pride (7); gluttony (7); greed (7); anger (7); violence (7); sloth (7); executions (7); cruelty (7); tyranny (8); self-importance (8); spin (9, 12); population reduction (9); popularism (9); usurpation (7, 9, 15); vacuousness (9, 12); eccentricity (9); impersonation (9); faking images of institutions (9); delusion (9); frivolity (9); heedlessness (9); rashness (9); naivety (F, 10); manipulation (10); vindictiveness (10); tyrannical censorship (10); showing-off (10); hypocrisy (10, 11); wrongful banishment (10); shallowness (10, 14); *usurpation (11); *delusion (11); bribery (11); regicide (11); murder (11); slyness (11); deception (12); mendacity (12); ostentation (13); chaviness (13); blinginess (13); flaunting (13); gullibility (F, 14); credulousness (F, 14); fancifulness (14); mass destruction (14); deceit (14); bombings (15); opulence (15); *murder (15); and blackmail (15).

A comprehensive list of the follies and vices in world literature can be found in the index of *A New Philosophy of Literature*:

abandonment; acquisitiveness; alcoholism; ambition; arrogance; asperity; betrayal; bigotry; blindness; boastfulness; bravado;

brutality; bullying; capriciousness; concealment; confidence tricks; corruptibility; corrupting worldly power; corruption; credulousness; cruelty; cynicism; debauchery; deceit; defiance; denial of principles; destructiveness; dictatorial behaviour; discontent; dishonesty; being domineering; drunkenness; duplicity; eagerness to marry; egotism; egotistical sensuality; enmity; envy; excessive mourning; exploitation; fantasies; fortune-hunting; frivolity; greed; hatred; hedonism; hubristic contentment; hypocrisy; idleness; illusions; impudence; inconstancy; infatuation; infidelity; inhumanity; insincerity; interference; jealousy; lack of truthfulness; lust; lust for power; massacres; meanness; mercenary motives; miserliness; misjudgement; mistreatment; money-seeking; moral blindness; murder; naive beliefs; neglect; nihilism; obstinacy; overreaching; patricide; pedantry; persecution; petulance; pretension; pride; prodigality; rebelliousness; revenge; ruthlessness; seduction; self-centredness; self-conceit; self-deceit; self-interestedness; self-love; shadiness; shrewishness; snobbishness; social climbing; strictness; swindling; thieving/stealing; threatening behaviour; treachery; trickery; troublemaking; tyrannical ruthlessness; tyranny; unscrupulousness; usurpation; vanity; villainy; voluptuousness; war; warmongering; and pursuit of wealth.

All these follies and vices (with the sole exception of 'patricide') can be found in my *Selected Stories: Follies and Vices of the Modern Elizabethan Age*, the companion volume to this work. Its Preface details numbered stories in which each of these follies and vices can be found, and a section at the back lists stories' follies and vices. Readers may like to compare the treatment of follies and vices in the two works.

These same follies and vices can be found in *Selected Poems*. The list below replicates the one above – there is some overlapping with the previous list of follies and vices mentioned in the end-of-poem notes – and each bracketed number indicates the numbered group of poems or extracts in Part Two where each folly or vice can be found (F again indicating folly, * indicating already mentioned):

abandonment (7, 15); acquisitiveness (2, 7, 15); alcoholism (7); *ambition (7, 15); arrogance (7); asperity (7, 15); betrayal (7, 15); bigotry (15); blindness (15) boastfulness (15); bravado (15); brutality (7); bullying (15); capriciousness (7. 15); concealment (7, 12, 15); confidence tricks (7, 15); corruptibility (15); corrupting worldly power (7, 15); corruption (7, 15); credulousness (F, 12); *cruelty (7); cynicism (7, 15); debauchery (7, 15); *deceit (7, 14, 15); defiance (8); denial of principles (7, 15); destructiveness (4, 7, 15); dictatorial behaviour (7, 15); *discontent

(7); dishonesty (12); being domineering (7, 15); drunkenness (7, 15); duplicity (7, 15); eagerness to marry (7, 15); egotism (15); egotistical sensuality (7); enmity (7, 15); envy (7); excessive mourning (7, 15); exploitation (7, 15); fantasies (12); fortune-hunting (7, 15); *frivolity (12); *greed (7); hatred (7, 15); hedonism (2); hubristic contentment (12); *hypocrisy (10); idleness (7, 15); illusions (F, 7); impudence (4, 12); inconstancy (15); infatuation (7, 15); infidelity (7, 15); inhumanity (3); insincerity (2); interference (7, 15); jealousy (7, 15); lack of truthfulness (12); *lust (14); lust for power (15); massacres (7); meanness (7, 15); mercenary motives (7, 10, 15); miserliness (7, 15); misjudgement (12); mistreatment (7, 15); money-seeking (7, 15); moral blindness (7, 15); *murder (7); naive beliefs (F, 13); neglect (14); nihilism (7); obstinacy (7); overreaching (7); pedantry (7, 15); persecution (7); petulance (6); pretension (12); *pride (11, 14); prodigality (7); rebelliousness (7, 15); revenge (15); *ruthlessness (6, 10, 11, 12, 14, 15); seduction (2); self-centredness (7, 15); self-conceit (15); self-deceit (15); self-interestedness (7, 15); *self-love (2); shadiness (7, 15); shrewishness (15); snobbishness (7, 15); social climbing (7, 15); strictness (7, 15); swindling (7, 15); thieving/stealing (7, 15); threatening behaviour (7, 15); treachery (7, 15); trickery (7, 15); troublemaking (7, 15); tyrannical ruthlessness (7, 15); *tyranny (6, 8); *unscrupulousness (7, 15); *usurpation (7, 9, 15); vanity (15); villainy (7, 15); voluptuousness (15); war (6, 7); warmongering (6, 7); and pursuit of wealth (7, 15).

Additional vices referred to or implied in the poems or extracts of Part Two and not in the previous two lists are, in alphabetical order:

abusiveness (7, 15); adultery (7, 15); attention-seeking (7, 15); avarice (7, 15); cheating (7, 15); excessive materialism (7, 15); false language (9); falsehood (12); fickleness (6); flattery (12); fraud (7, 15); grumpiness (7, 15); impertinence (7, 15); implausibility (10); incontinence (7, 15); lechery (2, 15); misanthropy (7, 15); phoniness (12); preening (12, 15); pretentiousness (7, 15); provocativeness (2); self-harm (7); selfishness (7, 15); sneering (15); superficiality (12); triviality (12); vacuity (12); vandalism (1, 3); *violence (7, 14); and wrath (7, 15).

The following follies and vices (listed in alphabetical order, * indicating already mentioned) are condemned in my *Selected Stories*. They are touched on in *Selected Poems*, if only in the descriptions of Hell:

absent-mindedness (F, 10); aggressiveness (7, 15); *anger (3, 14); bitterness (7); boredom (3); *bribery (7, 11, 15); burglary (7, 15);

childishness (7, 15); covetousness (7); *deception (7, 14, 15); desertion (7, 15); egocentricity (7); egoism (7); extortion (7, 15); false jokiness (12); falsely claiming knowledge (12); *gluttony (excessive drinking and drugs) (7, 15); gullibility (F, 12); hero-worship (12); idealisation (12); imperiousness (7); trying to impress (12); injury (7, 15); intolerance (7, 15); know-all superiority (12); lack of good sense (F, 12); long-windedness (15); manipulativeness (6, 12); *mendacity (7, 12, 15); nuns' worldliness (15); overbearingness (6); peremptoriness (6); *phoniness (12); pomposity (12); posing (12); not facing reality (7, 15); rivalry (7, 15); robbery (7, 15); roguery (7, 15); self-deception (F, 12); *self-importance (8); self-righteousness (12); servitude (7, 15); *sloth (14); stinginess (7, 15); suicide (7); terrorism (15); theft (7, 15); and yobbishness (2, 4).

If we do not count the asterisked vices, which are duplicated within the lists, the four lists present 62, 93, 29 and 37 vices; and 10 follies. The total number of vices referred to in all the lists is 221.

Universalist balance of fundamental theme's two aspects
One of the two aspects of the fundamental theme dominates in every age. Now one, now the other has the upper hand. In the English Augustan Age, exposing follies and vices dominated. In the Romantic Age the quest for the One – Reality – was uppermost. The Universalist ideal, which seeks to reconcile opposites and contradictions, seeks to balance the two aspects: the soul's perception of the One and criticism of social vices. Universalist poetry attempts to balance inner quest and outer social harmony. In our present time, the secular social outlook dominates and my allocation of Part One to the quest for the One in these poems goes some way to restoring the balance and preparing for a new metaphysical poetry. This selection deliberately balances the two aspects, a broadly equal number of pages being devoted to each aspect in each Part. The balance is Universalist. The poems within each Part are dated and arranged in chronological order to make the quest and condemnation of social vices truly sequential and easier to follow.

The poet of the One who senses the unity of the universe and captures it in poems is also aware of society and should also be an exposer of social follies and vices. To the poet of quest, the reason for writing poetry is to capture the truth about the universe. Glimpses of the One are 'epiphanies' or revelations. The poet puts himself in readiness to approach and receive the One by restructuring the universe in poems. His poems are models of the One, orderly simplifications of chaotic complexity that bring out the order in the cosmos. In this state of readiness the poet receives a passing glimpse or vision of the One that confirms that the universe is an ordered Whole with meaning and purpose, and not a chaotic mess. Within the Whole, social virtue has a place – hence the necessity of exposing social follies and vices. Man belongs to the universe as much as he participates in society and the two Parts of this selection also balance these differing perspectives of man, which have in the past given rise to differing traditions of poetry.

Basis of selection
Selection has not been easy. There are nearly 1,500 poems in the 30 volumes of *Collected Poems*, and in addition I have written more than 300 classical odes, two poetic epics of 41,000 and 25,000 lines of blank verse respectively, and five verse plays; so there is an enormous amount to choose from. There are poems in every kind of form: lyrics, sonnets, elegies, odes, a quartet, a quintet and longer poems in sonata, fugal and symphonic form. There are poems in every rhyme scheme and metre, including stress metre and blank verse. Because this selection highlights the fundamental theme's two aspects in my work I have necessarily had to omit a number of poems that are jostling for inclusion, including many poems on Nature's *flora* and *fauna*. It would be possible to compile a selection of my Nature poems as long as the present volume. To conform to my two aspects I have distributed excerpts from my pivotal poem 'The Silence' and from other poems between the two Parts, and have reluctantly decided there is no room for excerpts from my longer sonata, fugal and symphonic poems 'The Four Seasons', 'Lighthouse', 'The Weed-Garden' and 'The Labyrinth'.

The two Parts include poems capturing the unity of the universe that could be grouped under five headings: Philosophical, Nature, Spiritual, Historical and Topical. Poems for all these five genres can be found in both Parts of this selection:

- Philosophical poems showing the universe as One include 'A Metaphysical in Marvell's Garden', 'Night Visions in Charlestown', 'Ode: Spider's Web: Our Local Universe in an Infinite Whole', 'The Laughing Philosopher' and 'The One and the Many'.
- Poems seeing the universe as a Oneness that shapes Nature as an energetic force include 'Sea Force', while poems seeing Nature as a vital rather than a mechanistic force imbued with the One include 'A Crocus in the Churchyard', 'Pear-Ripening House' and 'Clouded-Ground Pond'.
- Poems showing the rational, social ego giving way to the mystical life of the soul and spirit as it progresses from awakening to illumination

and the unitive vision include 'An Awakening in London', 'Flow: Moon and Sea', 'Visions: Golden Flower, Celestial Curtain', 'More Visions: The Judge', 'Visions: The Pit and the Moon', 'February Budding, Half Term', 'Visions: Raid on the Goldmine', 'Visions: Snatched by God, a Blue Light' and passages towards the end of 'The Silence'. After the experience of illumination the soul can bask in the mystic Light as can be seen in poems such as 'Contemplations by a Sundial', 'Iona: Silence' and 'Sunbathing'.

- Poems seeing history as a unity, and drawing on the cultural tradition of Europe, the West and the world, and of the cultural legacy of Western civilisation, include my two poetic epics (represented in extracts) and poems from my *Classical Odes*, which revisit the past at specific geographical places and give history a contemporary relevance. This selection includes 'At Otley: Timber-Framed Tradition' and 'At Catullus's Sirmione'. Many of the classical odes are about visits to the historical and cultural sites of Europe. In a sense, each is a localist poem but the combined effect of the classical odes presents the culture of Europe, to which England belongs, and the classical odes must therefore be regarded as Universalist poems. (In a sense, all my work is about the relationship between localist and Universalist poetry.)
- Poems on contemporary, topical issues and current affairs include 'Pastoral Ode: Landslide, The End of Great Britain'; my poems about America, Afghanistan and Iraq: 'Attack on America' and 'Shock and Awe'; and mock-heroic poems after the manner of Dryden and Pope that include 'Zeus's Ass', 'Groans of the Muses' and 'Authorship Question in a Dumbed-Down Time'.

It should be emphasised that poems are cross-disciplinary and can deal with the philosophy of the universe, metaphysical Nature, the mystical, history and the topical in one work as Oneness pervades all levels and layers. This can be seen in such poems as 'Connaught House' and the second 'Epitaph'.

Ted Hughes latched on to my work in 1993. An early letter from him to me can be found in *Letters of Ted Hughes*, selected and edited by Christopher Reid (2007), and he corresponded with me until his death in 1999. He wrote to me about *Overlord*, which originally came out in four parts, and my handling of the history of the Second World War in verse: "I started reading it with fascination – I rose to it, the omnivorous masterful way you grasp the materials" (20 March 1995); and "I'm admiring the way you bit off and chew up these great chunks of history in your epic. It's good for verse – to become the workhorse for sheer mass of material. Pressure of the actual – the resources to deal with it drawn from elsewhere" (28 January 1996). Later he wrote: "One of the mysteries about you is – when do you get it all done? How many of you are there? Do you never blot a line?" (4 March 1998). [See Appendix 2, p.517.]

My transformation

The poems present my transformation in the course of five decades in both subject matter and technique. In subject matter they reveal my growing sense of the unity in the universe. There is a progression from my early discontent within Great Britain (as I then thought of the UK) to my metamorphosis in Japan; to my reflection of the Cold War; to the anguished suffering and chaos of my Dark Night; and to a serene consciousness that is outward-looking, unitary, at one with the universe. They also show the transformation of my technique during my exploration of, and experimentation with, technical innovations in the 1960s and 1970s – compressed or abbreviated narrative in a sequence of images, stress metre and sonata, fugal and symphonic form – and in the 1980s and 1990s: the quartet and quintet. I then settle back into more traditional stanzaic forms and metres.

Inspiration from the 17th century

As can be seen from 'A Metaphysical in Marvell's Garden' I derive my inspiration from the Metaphysical poets of the 17th century, in whose works thought and feeling were fused. I make use of the 17th-century love of learning, drawing in a cross-disciplinary way on several disciplines – such as history, philosophy, archaeology, physics, geology and astronomy – within one poem as Donne did. In some of these poems "a combination of dissimilar images" can be found, in which "the most heterogeneous ideas are yoked by violence together". In so far as these yokings carry forward Johnson's description of Metaphysical wit in his 'Life of Cowley', my poems can be seen as carrying forward the 17th-century Metaphysical tradition in which they are rooted. But while the Metaphysical poets were universalists, Universalist poetry is independent of the 17th century and reconciles the Romantic and Classical perspectives, blending image with statement, organic with structural form and seeing the artist as both apart from society – indeed, isolated from society – and as participating in society by exposing its follies and vices.

Universalist poems

The poems in this selection are Universalist poems: poems about the universe and the shift to the "universal being" which replaces the rational, social ego and perceives the Oneness of the universe. They blend image and statement and reconcile sense and spirit in a neo-Baroque style. They synthesise Romantic and Classical approaches, and implement Universalism's reconciliation of opposites. They present the transformation of the soul on the Mystic Way, its perception of the One and its reflection – and criticisms – of the vices of the Age. They carry forward literary Universalism and continue in our time the 4,600-year-old tradition of the two aspects of world literature's fundamental theme.

I must emphasise that this selection and my *Selected Stories: Follies and Vices of the Modern Elizabethan Age* (also 2015) anthologise my treatment in my poems and stories of the fundamental theme of world literature set out in *A New Philosophy of Literature*. The situations that inspired many of these poems – and many of the stories in my *Selected Stories* – can be found in my two-part autobiography, *My Double Life 1: This Dark Wood* and *My Double Life 2: A Rainbow over the Hills* (2015).

June 2011; 28 August, 11–12, 16 September 2012; 30 April 2014

40

The Dream of Europa

The Triumph of Peace
A Masque

Preface
Masques and Europe

Masques in the 16th and 17th centuries
The masque was a courtly entertainment performed in 16th and early-17th century Europe, including England. A masque was only played once, and celebrated an event at court. It often flattered the monarch, who often had a masked non-speaking part as did Henry VIII, James I and Charles I. It included music, dancing and singing, and the professional actors hired to speak and sing varied between eight and sixteen in number and wore elaborate costumes. On special occasions a band of masked players unexpectedly appeared at a nobleman's gates, performed at a social gathering in his Great Hall and danced with the guests. At the end of the entertainment they took off their masks and mingled with the audience, which in London comprised courtiers.

In England Ben Jonson's masques were performed in the Banqueting Hall of the Whitehall Palace during the Christmas holiday, often on Twelfth Night. (The Banqueting Hall preceded the Banqueting House, which was built between 1619 and 1622.) *The Masque of Blackness* was performed before the Stuart court in the Banqueting Hall on 6 January 1605. It was written at the request of Anne of Denmark, queen consort of James I. The masquers were disguised as Africans and their blackness was supposed to be cured by James I. This was impossible to show, and after Jonson's *Hymenaei*, or *The Masque of Hymen*, which was written for the Earl of Essex's wedding before a Roman altar on 15 January 1606, there was a sequel, *The Masque of Beauty*, which was also performed in the Banqueting Hall, on 10 January 1608. *The Masque of Queens* was performed on 2 February 1609 and contained an antimasque, unlike the previous masques.

Jonson's *Oberon, The Fairy Prince* was performed in the Banqueting Hall on 1 January 1611. The front curtains displayed a map of the British Isles, and the fairy prince Oberon (based on James I) arrived to bestow order and rule benevolently. Nymphs and satyrs danced joyfully. *Christmas, His Masque* was performed at the court during

Christmas 1616, when Christmas entered with his attendants. *The Masque of Augurs* was performed on 6 January 1622. It praised the arranged marriage between Prince Charles (the future Charles I) and the Spanish Infanta, and Prince Charles himself led the dance of the masquers. The masque included some thoroughly-researched Roman augury.

Shakespeare's masque scenes in *The Tempest* were influenced by Jonson, and there had also been masque scenes in *Romeo and Juliet* and *Henry VIII*. Spenser's *Faerie Queene* (book 1, canto 4) contains a processional masque of The Seven Deadly Sins. John Milton wrote *A Masque Presented at Ludlow Castle, 1634 (Comus)*. Such dramatic masques ended in 1640 with *Salmacida Spolia*. Masques were dependent on the court, and the fall of the monarchy and consequent collapse of the court brought them to an end. The Puritans closed the theatres in 1642, and in the 1660s when they reopened the masque turned into opera. The poet John Dryden and the composer Henry Purcell collaborated on productions that were part-masque and part-opera. Thomas Arne wrote a masque, *Alfred* (1740), which included the first performance of 'Rule Britannia'. Shelley wrote *The Masque of Anarchy* about the Peterloo Massacre of 1819. Several musicians wrote masques, including Ralph Vaughan Williams, who wrote *Job: A Masque for Dancing*. Also, in the 20th century William Empson wrote a masque, *The Birth of Steel*, in honour of the Queen's visit to Sheffield on 27 October 1954. Its relatively undramatic verse only took 15 minutes to perform. In the course of the masque Queen Elizabeth II was addressed as a "goddess" in keeping with the masque's tradition of flattering the patron. (The Queen returned the compliment by bestowing a knighthood on Empson in 1979.)

Origins of the masque
The origins of the masque are in doubt. In England Richard II took part in "mumming" (masked mime) as early as 1377. In Italy the masquerade was a carnival entertainment akin to "mumming". In France the performance became more of a spectacle. Throughout Europe there were "guisings" or "disguisings" in which a masked allegorical figure addressed a courtly audience. In England the masque's immediate forerunner was the dumb show of the kind found in Thomas Kyd's *The Spanish Tragedy* (first performed 1587) and in Shakespeare's *A Midsummer Night's Dream* (1595–1596, the wedding of Pyramus and Thisbe), *Hamlet* (1600–1602) and *Pericles, Prince of Tyre* (1607–1608). Masques performed for Elizabeth I emphasised the unity of her kingdom and the peace and concord that flourished in her realm.

Masques' five parts
Formally, the masque had five parts: the prologue or poetic induction; the antimasque (a spectacle of disorder and chaos) which preceded the masque; the masque (which transformed the disorder into order and harmony, and provided a resolution); the revels (which rejoiced at the resolution and broke down the barrier between stage and spectator); and the epilogue.

The dream of Europa: the birth of a unified Europe
This masque, *The Dream of Europa*, is about the birth of a unified Europe. The representatives of 50 European states are on stage throughout the playing time. In the prologue, Zeus entrusts Europa (the goddess of Europe) with the task of bringing peace to a Europe ravaged by the Second World War. In the antimasque, Europeans chant their misery and wretchedness at the disorder and chaos in Europe, aided by film on a large screen. In the masque, Europa turns the disorder into order and brings the resolution of a unified state that begins with the implementation of the Treaty of Lisbon. In the revels, Europeans rejoice at the new unified Europe and celebrate. And in the epilogue, Europa hands the European Union back to Zeus on course to become a United States of Europe and to have 50 states like the United States of America. His problem solved, Zeus looks ahead to a World State.

Disorder contrasted with order
The Dream of Europa, which is subtitled *The Triumph of Peace*, contrasts the disorder of Europe in 1945 with the order in Europe 70 years later in 2015, and by rooting the Treaty of Lisbon in the ruins of Berlin I am reminding the audience of why a unified Europe has been created and of the peace that has been achieved.

Discordant voices and the UK's dissent
However, despite the order that has been established there are still discordant voices – from Greece, Italy, Spain and the UK – and the revels are interrupted by disputes within Europe that still have to be resolved. Not all Europeans were pleased that the European Community passed into a more unitary European Union as a result of the Maastricht Treaty of 1993, and Eurosceptics now regard the European Union and its eurozone as a failed experiment.

There is evidence that Russia wants to recover the Baltic states, which it still regards as being within the Russian sphere of influence, and keeping Europe together will prevent Russian expansion whereas fragmenting Europe with exits (by Greece and the UK) would open the way for Russian expansion. *The Dream of Europa* calls for European unity at a time when the unity of Europe is threatened.

Towards the end of the revels, Churchill (my MP during the war) lambasts the UK representative for having forgotten the war and for putting domestic concerns such as immigration and the abuse of the benefit system above its vision of unity. He reminds her of the chaos in 1945 and the triumph of peace in 2014. It is my hope that the UK will come to share Churchill's perspective.

The dream of 50 European states
Europe has done extremely well during the last 70 years. It is a Union of 28 states, and as can be seen from the diagram on p.xviii [of *The Dream of Europa*] the remaining 22 of the 50 European states are members of one or more of the 17 supranational bodies that form groupings of European nation-states. The dream of Europa is that one day the EU will consist of 50 European states, a step towards a Universalist World State. My work, *My Double Life 2: A Rainbow over the Hills*, was subtitled *The Vision of Unity*, and the vision of unity is what is now needed to create a United States of Europe that can lead all the continents of the earth into a coming World State. Such a State can abolish war, famine, disease and poverty by international law and greatly benefit humankind.

Genesis of this masque
I had the idea for *The Dream of Europa* in April 2010, and I was in touch with the European Agency for Fundamental Rights. The project was shelved in May 2010 due to the euro crisis involving Greece (a problem still with us in 2015), and the idea was pushed to one side until late 2014, when the European debate intensified in the UK. As a man of letters I am pleased to be able to add this masque to the other *genres* in which I have worked, which include lyric poems, classical odes, epic poems, verse plays and short stories. The masque has always been a court entertainment, and it is my hope that there will be a production of this work in Brussels to mark an anniversary attended by European leaders.

19–20 January 2015

41

Life Cycle and Other New Poems
2006–2016

Preface

My *Collected Poems 1958–2005* contained 30 volumes of my poems, 1,478 poems spanning 47 years. *Life Cycle and Other New Poems 2006–2016* contains volumes 31–34, a further 210 poems (if the 11 poems in 'India: Revisiting the British Raj' are counted separately). None of these new poems appeared in my most recent selection, *Selected Poems: Quest for the One* (2015). These new poems include four of the 318 poems in *Classical Odes* (see below), and if these are discounted they bring my total tally of poems (excluding my two poetic epics *Overlord* and *Armageddon* and my five verse plays) to just over 2,000: to be exact, 2,002 (1,478 + 318 + 206).

In event order
By and large these new poems are in event order within each volume (the order in which events happened). They are therefore not always in chronological order (the order in which poems were written), as can be seen from the index on pp.351–359 [of *Life Cycle and Other New Poems*] (poems within each volume). The dates on which all the poems in all four volumes were written are listed in the index on pp.361–370 [of *Life Cycle and Other New Poems*]. Each poem in the text ends with the date (or dates) on which it was written and notes (if any).

Uniting Augustan and Romantic traditions
Readers of my works will know that I derive my poetic inspiration from the 17th-century Metaphysical poets and have sought to unite the later Augustan and Romantic traditions. They will also know that in the 1960s some of my poems (such as 'The Silence') were in the Modernist tradition, and that following my visit to Ezra Pound in Rapallo on 16 July 1970 [see Appendix 2, pp.498–501] I returned to Wordsworthian and Tennysonian principles and narrative. I asked Pound if compression – which he had used in *The Cantos* – was really a good method for a long poetic epic, and unconvinced by his answer moved away from compression to the narrative blank verse of Tennyson's *Idylls of the King* in my two poetic epics, *Overlord* and *Armageddon*. In many of my poems that focus on Nature, including those in volume 32, *In Harmony with*

the Universe, I am aware of following Wordsworth's principles. I have consciously sought to continue the poetic tradition of Wordsworth and Tennyson, but also the classical tradition of ancient Greece and Rome: many of my poems (for example those in *The Gates of Hell*) were rooted in the works of Catullus, Ovid and Virgil. In my poetic works I have sought to reconcile the Classical and Romantic traditions.

Poems reflecting the fundamental theme of world literature
As readers of my works will know, my poems reflect the fundamental theme of world literature, which I identified in *A New Philosophy of Literature* as having metaphysical and secular aspects that are in conflict: a quest for metaphysical Reality (the One); and condemnation of social follies and vices in relation to an implied virtue. My Universalist approach reconciles and unites these two very different aspects.

The four volumes
Volume 31, *Life Cycle*, presents a poem with a title I first glimpsed in 1962 when, sitting with my eyes closed in the air above Ur, Iraq, I received the words 'life cycle', which seemed to come from the beyond. It is a reflection on the pattern in our lives. Volume 32, *In Harmony with the Universe*, conveys the vision of oneness with Nature to which the quest leads. (It includes some poems omitted from *Collected Poems*.) Volume 33, *An Unsung Laureate*, focuses on public events within the British nation-state and on international political themes that include the contemporary history of the UK and the EU and their dealings with Russia and the Middle East. The first four poems appeared in *Classical Odes* (2006) and are reproduced here as they anchor the volume's political theme: development from a nationalist to a supranationalist outlook. I condemn follies and vices in 'Zeus's Emperor', which is a sequel to 'Zeus's Ass' (a poem in volume 29 in my *Collected Poems*). Volume 34, *Adventures in Paradise*, reflects the questing of my travels to remote places thought of as Paradise and ends with the greatest adventure that awaits us all: death.

The European thread: decline of European nation-states and the resurgence of Europe as a supranationalist superpower
I would like to say a little more about the European thread in volume 33. My poetic works have mirrored the state of European civilisation: the horror of ruined Europe at the end of the Second World War (*Overlord*), the declining Europe of the 1960s ('Old Man in a Circle', 1967) and the resurgent European Union after the Lisbon Treaty of 2009 (*The Dream of Europa*). In my study of civilisations I saw the European nation-

states passing into a resurgent conglomerate, the European Union, that subsumes them just as the Soviet Union subsumed the regions of the Russian Federation. I attempted to catch the dismay at the passing of an era of nation-states and hopes for the new regional union in the odes in *Classical Odes*, which are represented by the first four poems of volume 33. Over the years I have tried to catch the feelings of nation-staters opposed to a European superpower – feelings that can be found in supporters of Brexit, of a British departure from the EU – and the feelings of pro-Europeans who support the EU and in many cases a coming World State (*The Dream of Europa*). Having worked as a British intelligence agent for my nation-state and having then journeyed through to an international, supranationalist perspective, I have been well-placed to hold a mirror up to both sides and harmonise them within volume 33.

The universe as opposites reconciled within the whole
In my poems and my prose works I have often used "algebraic thinking" which reconciles opposites. I have seen the universe as a dialectic of opposites reconciled within a synthesis: $+A + -A = 0$. Volume 33 presents both sides of the dialectic – $+A$ (supporters of nation-states and Brexit) $+ -A$ (supporters of regional and international conglomerates, of the EU and a World State) – and attempts to reconcile them within the whole that includes them.

My experience of Iraq
Volume 33 contains two poems on Iraq. I am still amazed that at 22 I intuitively knew I should find my way to Iraq and lecture at the University of Baghdad, and that Iraq would somehow be central to the world's problems in the late 20th and early 21st centuries. Since I was in Iraq Saddam used mustard gas to kill 5,000 Kurds at Halabja, and his Sunni successor in Iraq, IS (or Daesh), has used mustard gas in Marea, north of Aleppo, on at least four occasions after April 2015 – Saddam's unaccounted-for stock which our weapons inspectors could not find? My second poetic epic *Armageddon* told how (according to the ex-1st Executive Chairman of the UN Monitoring, Verification and Inspection Commission, Hans Blix, in 2004) bin Laden acquired 20 nuclear suitcase bombs the size of laptops and targeted 10 American cities, and there is concern that these were not retrieved when bin Laden was killed and may have found their way into the hands of IS. I sometimes feel I was shown the Middle East early as I would have to write about it in later years. Sometimes there seems to be something Providential about the Way I chose, or which chose me.

Awakening, purgation, illumination and unitive vision
Volumes 1–30 traced this Way, along which the soul is awakened, undergoes purgation and illumination, is transformed and progresses to a unitive vision in which it instinctively perceives the universe as a unity, all contradictions reconciled. Volumes 31–34 contemplate the pattern in our lives, the soul's harmony with the universe, the conflicts within Western society, and truths and echoes of Paradise that can be gleaned from the inspiring cultures of remote civilisations reached by adventurous journeys.

Progression of 34 volumes of my poetic works
Volumes 31–34 are a natural progression from volumes 1–30. One day a new *Collected Poems* including all 34 completed volumes may confirm this progression and end with a 35th volume of poems in the narrative tradition of Shakespeare's *Sonnets* and Wordsworth's *Prelude*, to which I intend to devote my last years.*

12–13, 26–27 January, 11, 13 February, 23 March, 1, 4, 14 April 2016

*The 35th volume will be *The Oak Tree and the Branch,* poems on Brexit, and there may be a 36th volume, *The Tapestry,* poems in the narrative tradition of Shakespeare's *Sonnets* and Wordsworth's *Prelude.*

42

The First Dazzling Chill of Winter

Collected Stories

Preface

My *Collected Stories* contained 1,001 short stories covering five volumes and spanning 50 years, 1966–2006. *The First Dazzling Chill of Winter* is a sixth volume containing a further 201 stories written between 2009 and 2016 and takes my total tally of stories to 1,202. These new stories did not appear in my recent *Selected Stories: Follies and Vices of the Modern Elizabethan Age* (2015).

Stories that reflect the fundamental theme of world literature
Readers of my stories will know that they reflect the fundamental theme of world literature, which I identified in *A New Philosophy of Literature* as having metaphysical and secular aspects that are in conflict: a quest for Reality (the One) and the heightened consciousness it brings which perceives the universe as a unity; and condemnation of social follies and vices in relation to an implied virtue.

Universalist reconciliation of contradictions
My Universalist approach seeks to reconcile these contradictions. It blends image and statement and seeks a balance between social virtue and the soul's perception of the One; between the outlooks of the Augustan and Romantic periods in English literature.

Mini-stories of early old age
My mini-stories follow Philip Rawley from his late twenties to his seventies and impending old age. Rawley's growth and development is presented in terms of the many people he encounters, who reflect the ways of the modern Age. During his quest his soul undergoes a transformation that changes his outlook. In this sixth volume Rawley instinctively perceives the unity of the universe in his "early evening sunshine", and is dazzled by what he sees. He feels at peace despite his advancing winter, and grasps that wisdom is a way of looking. Despite his serenity he is increasingly preoccupied by death, which is ever-present behind the social situations.

A new literary form: dissimilar images yoked together
These miniature stories present a new literary form. They offer a complete literary experience in a few minutes. Their vivid titles reflect Dr Johnson's description of the wit of the 17th-century Metaphysical poets in his 'Life of Cowley' as "a combination of dissimilar images" in which "the most heterogeneous ideas are yoked by violence together". Many of these stories reflect the One and have a metaphysical ambience.

Verbal paintings
My stories are vivid verbal paintings that present an image in action. Some of the stories are like portraits in the National Portrait Gallery and concentrate on conveying a particular character. I have tried to bring a poet's eye for significant detail, and some stories seek to startle the soul into a new mode of perception.

12–13, 26–27 January, 8 April 2016

43

The Secret American Destiny

The Hidden Order of the Universe and the Seven Disciplines of World Culture Universalism and the Road to World Unity

Prologue
The Universalist Vision

This book is the third of my American trilogy. It follows *The Secret Founding of America*, which dwelt on the founding of the North-American civilisation in 1607 and the consequences of the advent of Freemasonry in the next decade; and *The Secret American Dream*, which dealt with America's ambition to export the American Dream of prosperity to all humankind in the form of a democratic World State.

In those two books I looked at America's materialistic achievement: Liberty's awesome technology, which in my lifetime has enabled man to reach the moon, send spacecraft to explore our solar system and produce images of our galaxy. American satellites send instant pictures to our television screens and American computers send messages round the globe. American drones operated from the Nevada desert take out targets in the Middle East thousands of miles away, and precision bombing and use of co-ordinates have taken warfare to a new level of accuracy, minimalising civilian casualties. In commerce American multi-national corporations and globalisation have transformed the world.

In *The Secret American Dream* I set out the seven paths America has taken during the last 400 years, and covered the growth and expansion of America up to Barack Obama's first two years. I set out an eighth path the North-American civilisation has begun to take under Obama "as the benevolent bringer of political and spiritual unity to all the peoples of the world".[1] Liberty, who welcomed the "poor" and "homeless", has the ambition to protect the "huddled masses yearning to breathe free"[2] throughout the world and raise their material standard of living.

America's Universalist destiny and world culture
The Secret American Destiny carries the story forward. It takes up the Epilogue of *The Secret American Dream*, 'Liberty's Universalist Destiny', and focuses on the spiritual worldview behind the American global

achievement. A World State will seek to unite the religious and non-religious world citizens. According to a Pew Research Center survey in 2010 there were 5.8 billion religiously affiliated (Christians, Muslims, Hindus, Buddhists and followers of other faiths): 84 per cent out of a total world population then of 6.9 billion.[3] (See p.3 [of *The Secret American Destiny*] for more recent surveys.) America's spiritual vision must accommodate all world citizens regardless of their religious or secular outlook.

Film from space has made us aware of the oneness of the tiny Earth and of the potential unity of its nation-states and world culture. From space it seems only natural that America should attempt to create a political structure that reflects the unity of humankind. The Earth is widely perceived as a disunited complexity racked by local wars. Through American technology Liberty perceives its underlying unity and Universalist destiny – and the unity of the universe which has been mapped by American science.

A new philosophy of Universalism lurks behind America's globalisation. The new outlook has several layers. In its narrow theological meaning a 'universalist' "holds that all mankind will eventually be saved" (*Concise Oxford Dictionary*). A Christian universalist sees all mankind as potentially being saved, including non-Christians. From this narrow meaning 'Universalism' has come to have a wider sense: a focus on the role of all humankind on Earth and in the universe.

'Universalism' incorporates the words 'universe', 'universal' and 'universality'. It focuses on the universe, universal science and the universal principle of order whose effects are found in every aspect of Nature and its organisms. It examines humankind as a whole in its seven disciplines, and the place of humans on Earth and in the universe. It draws attention to the universal being, the deeper self below the rational, social ego which is open to universal cosmic energies that convey the principle of order and structure the growth of plants and organisms.

Universalism is the study of the whole of humankind's activities: the whole of history, international relations, philosophy and the sciences, religion and culture. It incorporates seven disciplines: mysticism, literature, philosophy, history, politics, religion and culture. And so we can speak of seven separate Universalisms – mystical Universalism, literary Universalism, philosophical Universalism, historical Universalism, political Universalism, religious Universalism and cultural Universalism. But ultimately they all belong to one Universalism. I have presented these seven disciplines as seven bands within a rainbow.[4] The bands are separate but they all belong to one rainbow.

Universalism unifies the seven disciplines of world culture
Universalism's perspective unifies the seven disciplines of world culture and focuses on the rainbow rather than on its separate bands. It presents a fundamental understanding of the universe by unveiling a whole view that includes all disciplines, which at present appear to be divided. Individual disciplines are separated in university syllabuses, and their approaches are to fragments of a greater whole. Universalism seeks to restore the view of the whole by combining and reconciling divisions in seven partial disciplines of world culture, and in the fragmented disciplines themselves.

In this study I am not concerned with everyday popular culture – what people do in their leisure time: going to shopping malls and restaurants and bars, taking vacations, watching sporting fixtures and talent shows on television, listening to music, news of the Presidential or Royal families, and the like. I am sifting the way 7 billion live by (for example) probing a more fundamental culture that includes how many take part in religious worship and how many do not, and what they understand by the universe. I approach world culture from the seven disciplines and therefore the seven Universalisms. To me, the fundamental world culture is a rainbow with seven bands that overarches the globe and affects everybody.

In 1959 C.P. Snow delivered a Rede lecture, 'The Two Cultures',[5] in which he drew attention to the gulf between the literary and scientific cultures, which, he argued, should be bridged. Universalism provides that bridge, and the literary and scientific are different bands of the same cultural rainbow.

Metaphysical and secular approaches within seven disciplines of world culture reconciled within Universalism
This book argues that in each of the seven disciplines of world culture there is a conflict between a traditional metaphysical approach and a more modern secular, social approach. These conflicting approaches make for a disunited world culture and a climate of opinion not conducive to a united World State. I argue that they can be reconciled within Universalism and that the reconciled conflicts make a contribution towards reunifying world culture and thereby preparing the ground for a coming World State. In this book I approach each of these seven disciplines from four different perspectives: the metaphysical (ch.1); the social (ch.4); the Universalist reconciliation (ch.5); and the contribution of the metaphysical and social perspectives to a one-world movement within world culture and therefore to the climate of order a coming World State would need (ch.6).

America's destiny is to restore a sense of order and reunify world culture
A study of the whole reveals the order in the universe. 'Order' is "the condition in which every part or unit is in its right place, tidiness" (*Concise Oxford Dictionary*). This definition of order suggests that insects, fish, birds, mammals and humans have a "right" place within Nature's system, that the behaviour of each creature reflects the underlying order of Nature and the universe. This order is hidden when the universe is seen partially, but is revealed when the universe is perceived as a whole. 'Order' is also "a state of peaceful harmony under a constitutional authority" (*Concise Oxford Dictionary*). This definition of 'order' draws attention to the fundamental organisation within Nature and the universe, which is behind this harmony. Again, Nature has to be seen as a whole through Universalism's perspective for this apparently hidden order to be revealed. All things are then seen to have their place within the organised and orderly system of the universe.

America's destiny is to restore this sense of order and reunify world culture, and so make possible a new conception of civilisation: a World State that can abolish war, famine, disease and poverty. An image for this destiny is: the statue of Liberty beneath a rainbow showing all seven cultural bands.

American destiny and World State
This book examines the Universalist perspective on world culture that makes possible this American destiny to bring the world together into a World State. It carries forward a section in the Epilogue of *The Secret American Dream* regarding America's political and religious Universalism. My study of 25 civilisations shows that Universalism is already a feature of the North-American civilisation's present stage,[6] and will feature in a coming – indeed, imminent – stage. The North-American civilisation is at present in the same stage of its development as the Roman Empire was in its early days, after the two Punic Wars, and the Roman Empire's Universalism brought unity to the culture of the known world during Roman times.

Civilisations' rise-and-fall pattern
In my study *The Fire and the Stones*, updated as *The Light of Civilization* and *The Rise and Fall of Civilizations*, which I began in Japan, I see 25 civilisations passing through 61 stages. Each civilisation is shaped in a parabola like a rainbow: it rises through a metaphysical vision which passes into its religion, and declines when it turns secular and loses some of the *élan* which carried it upward in its early stages. (See

Appendix 2 [in *The Secret American Destiny*].) The North-American civilisation is the youngest of my 25 civilisations, having been founded in 1607, and has reached stage 15, the stage the Roman Empire was in at the beginning of its expansionist phase. This North-American stage began c.1913. The vision through which the civilisation rose was then expressed in American ecumenical Protestantism. Europe's comparable expansion was between c.951 and 1244 and included the Crusades (as can be seen in the table on pp.227–228 [of *The Secret American Destiny*]).

Stage 15 is soon followed by the creation of a Light-based heretical sect, after which a "new people" graft the heresy onto the civilisation's main religion and central idea. In Europe's case, the new "heresy" was the early Protestantism of the Reformation and the "new people" were the Renaissance Humanists. The equivalent North-American heresy is a coming Universalism[7] which will draw on the Freemasonic Deistic Illuminatists I wrote about in chapters 4 and 5 of *The Secret Founding of America*, and on the more recent New Age. The "new people" in the North-American civilisation will be new Universalists who affirm a universal God drawn from all religions and perceived or experienced as Light.

If my vision of coming history is right, America's expansionist phase (which began in its stage 15) will create a democratic World State with a Universalist outlook that will include a universal God perceived as Light or Fire. This will be grafted on to Christian ecumenical Protestantism and will absorb it and offer a global religion. Just as Renaissance Humanists grafted Protestantism on to the Catholic Light, so new Universalists will graft Universalism on to the American Protestant Light.

The Universalist Light
I have written about my encounter with the ordering Light in *My Double Life 1: This Dark Wood*. [See Appendix 1, pp.437–447.] It was this experience that took me into the seven disciplines of world culture. I had had external, pantheistic experiences of the oneness of the universe in 1946, 1954, 1959 and 1963. While working in Japan – I was Visiting Professor at three universities from 1963 to 1967 and taught Emperor Hirohito's younger son world history – I visited Zen meditation centres and temples in 1964 and began writing poetry seriously. In 1965 I visited the Zen Ryoanji stone garden in Kyoto twice, and recognised its message: stones raked by the monks into different swirling patterns with large rocks among them presented an image of the universe. This could be seen as stones and rocks, or sea and rocks, or earth and hills, or clouds and mountains, but however it was seen, existence was

composed of only one substance – in the stone garden represented as stone – and was a unity. The swirls made the unity appear diverse, but all existence was one. In September 1965 I underwent a centre-shift from the rational, social ego to universal being.

My understanding of oneness deepened soon afterwards when in October 1965 I drank *saké* with Junzaburo Nishiwaki, a poet who was attached to one of my universities, Japan's T.S. Eliot, and asked him his view of the wisdom of the East. He wrote out on a business reply card he took from my copy of *Encounter* which I happened to have on the table: "+A + –A = 0". Above the 0 he wrote "great nothing". I immediately saw what the algebraic formula meant. Life was pairs of opposites or contradictions: day and night, life and death, time and eternity – and they were all reconciled in the unity of zero, the great nothing. Nishiwaki told me: "The Absolute is where there is no difference."

Soon after this, one morning my mind was filled with an inner sun, a 'light' I could "see" within, and I knew this was significant. My opening to oneness found its way into my long poem 'The Silence'.

My first full encounter with the metaphysical Light took place in London on 10 September 1971.[8] [See Appendix 1, pp.439–447.] For an hour and a half I saw behind my closed eyes "white light" flowing up, and then many visions, and a centre of Light shining down from a great height, a white flower. (In the current book 'Light' is spiritual, 'light' physical.) This was my equivalent of what Pascal experienced in 1654. After his death in 1662 the following lines were found sewn into the lining of his doublet:

The year of grace 1654,
Monday, 23 November....
From about half past ten in the evening until about half
past twelve
FIRE.[9]

The experience was so important to him that he *wore* a reminder of what had happened for the last eight years of his life, which he spent in a Jansenist convent. I was at first inclined to think that I had had the fundamental poetic experience – and I still believe that this is what many of the great poets have written about, particularly the 17th-century Metaphysical poets – but I quickly grasped that my experience was metaphysical, and to date I have had a total of 93 experiences of the Light, all of which are covered and listed in appendices in *My Double Life 1* and 2.

I was recently asked, "Do you visualise behind closed eyes?" I replied, "No, I'm like a puddle reflecting the sun. The puddle doesn't visualise, it just reflects the reality of the sun." I now see this Light as the One, as Reality. It is the zero or great nothing of "+A + −A = 0". In the East, Nothingness, the Void, is also a plenitude, a fullness.

So having found myself as a poet in Japan, I had now found myself as a mystic who trod the traditional Mystic Way from awakening to purgation, illumination and eventually the unitive life. The centre-shift from the rational social ego which perceives differences and makes distinctions to the universal being which perceives unity – a shift all mystics experience – opens the way to Universalism's unitive perspective.

Increasingly I wanted to understand the experience that had happened to me, and while still writing my poems I collected all the recorded experiences of the Light or Fire from all the world's countries – from world culture – during the last 5,000 years in my first full-length work, *The Fire and the Stones*. I then realised that the experience was crucial to many religions: Christ the Light of the World, the first words of the *Koran* seen as written in Fire, the Buddha's enlightenment, Hindu *samadhi* and the Chinese *Tao* all attempted to describe this experience. I saw that civilisations grow after an experience of the Light or Fire has found its way into their religion. Energy is transmitted back to the civilisation and pushes it to grow.

I passed from comparative religion to history and unveiled my Grand Unified Theory of world history and religion which presents 61 parallel stages of 25 civilisations. (See Appendix 2 [in *The Secret American Destiny*].) I showed all the world history of the last 5,000 years as being parallel patterns of Light-inspired civilisations.

I then turned to philosophy and realised that there was a tradition of the Light which some philosophers followed, but not others. I wrote *The Universe and the Light, The One and the Many* and eventually *The New Philosophy of Universalism* about the order in the universe ignored by linguistic and analytical philosophy.

I was led to world culture. I gave a lecture in Aldeburgh, Suffolk, 'Revolution in Thought and Culture', which found its way into *The One and the Many*. I had been involved in international relations and statecraft (see *My Double Life 1* and 2), and I dealt with the political implications of Universalism in *The World Government*.

The metaphysical tradition and the secular, social outlook within unifying Universalism
In the course of my previous 43 books I have come to see that the

fundamental experience of the Light needs to be restored to world culture so that there can be a balance between the metaphysical tradition (which has inspired the world's higher religions) and the secular, social outlook. While continuing my literary work I was able to cover mystical, literary, philosophical, historical, political, religious and cultural Universalism and develop the idea of Universalism as unifying seven disciplines. I have trodden the way of the Renaissance polymaths who were at home in many disciplines, and I have been able to do this because all the disciplines are interconnected and united within one Universalism.

I was inspired to write this book at a gaudy (college reunion) at Worcester College, Oxford, on 6 September 2014. I had talked again with the new Provost, the Shakespearean scholar and author Jonathan Bate, and dined in hall at a long table among those of my contemporaries who were still alive. An academic at Bristol University, a physicist, leaned across the table and asked, "What are you saying in your books?" I tried to explain what I had to say regarding the fundamental unity of the universe, and described my way of looking at all the disciplines of Western civilisation – the North-American and European civilisations – in terms of pairs of opposites (+A + –A = 0). I mentioned physics and metaphysics, the finite and the infinite, in relation to the Greek philosophers. He was a secular sceptic. "The Greeks' beliefs were wrong," he said, "so they're irrelevant. We don't need to hear them." His line was that only contemporary Materialism is true, because it looks at scientific evidence. "I won't accept any theory such as multiverses being down a black hole," he said. I agreed with him about multiverses – I stick with the universe I know, and mathematics that posit parallel universes offer unproven theories – but I countered and put the other side, the side he wanted to ignore, in each of seven disciplines.

I said, "There are two ways the mind works. Analysis drops this glass of water and smashes it into pieces. Synthesis discovers broken potsherds and pieces them together. You're advocating the first but not admitting the second. You're saying everything must be analysed and tested. I'm saying synthesis is a valuable way of arriving at truth: piecing fragments together and returning to the whole." He said, "I am not competent to pronounce beyond the evidence. Seeing the whole is very ambitious." I said, "But necessary. It has to be done. The whole has to be seen. All the opposites have to be reconciled within the origin and evolution of the universe and man's place in it."

The conversation continued after dinner in the Buttery and a group gathered round us, listening. I wished I had a book that summarised my thinking over the past few decades which I could send him. This book about the secret American destiny to bring a Universalist vision and outlook to all humankind in the seven disciplines of world culture *is* that book.

Notes:

1. Nicholas Hagger, *The Secret American Dream*, p.229.
2. Emma Lazarus, 'The New Colossus', a sonnet written in 1883 and engraved on a bronze plaque and mounted on the inside of the pedestal of the Statue of Liberty in 1903.
3. See Pew Research Center's 2012 survey, https://www.washingtontimes.com/blog/watercooler/2012/dec/23/84-percent-world-population-has-faith-third-are-ch/.
4. Hagger, *My Double Life 2: A Rainbow over the Hills*, p.873.
5. C.P. Snow, *The Two Cultures: and A Second Look*.
6. Hagger, *The Rise and Fall of Civilizations*, pp.112, 116–117.
7. *Ibid.*, pp.131–132.
8. Hagger, *My Double Life 1: This Dark Wood*, pp.372–375.
9. Pascal's 'Fire' parchment: facsimile in Abbe Bremond's *Sentiment Religieux en France*, iv, 368; quoted in Dom Cuthbert Butler, *Western Mysticism*, p.74.

44

Peace for our Time

A Reflection on War and Peace and a Third World War

Prologue

Now after a writing career of nearly sixty years that has included two poetic epics on war, one on the Second World War and one on the War on Terror, I sit above a calm sea and reflect on war and peace in my lifetime and how best to bequeath peace to my grandchildren. I have lived an active as well as a contemplative life and through extraordinary circumstances found myself involved in humanity's best hope of establishing world peace. To my amazement I found myself a participator in the West's efforts to prevent a Third World War. I cannot but recount the strange events that led to this pass. But I am also drawn back to my own wartime childhood, and, seeking to understand it, my mind goes back to Munich in July 1994.

Munich and war
My wife and I had taken our two nearly-adult boys on a coach tour through seven countries in Europe, and the coach party were served beer in Munich's Hofbräuhaus, a beer 'cellar' that could seat 3,000 on the ground floor where Adolf Hitler made an impassioned speech on 8 November 1923.

"We will be here at least half an hour," our guide said.

I said to my wife, "Come on, we're going for a drive in Munich." We slipped out, leaving our two boys with enormous glasses of German dark beer under our guide's watchful eye, and found a nearby taxi rank.

The driver of the first car spoke English and I said, "All the Hitler places in half an hour." He talked in German to his controller and plotted a route and set off.

We found Hitler's nine-room second-floor apartment in Prinzregentenplatz which Neville Chamberlain visited during the morning of 30 September 1938 following the 2am signing of the four-power Munich Agreement (backdated to 29 September). Chamberlain took from his pocket a typed sheet of paper, the Anglo-German Declaration, and read three paragraphs, one of which stated that the British and German nations considered the 1938 Munich Agreement and the 1935 Anglo-German Naval Agreement "symbolic of the desire of our two peoples never to go to war with one another again".

According to Chamberlain, Hitler exclaimed *"Ja, ja"* ("Yes, yes").

Later that day, the German Foreign Minister Joachim von Ribbentrop remonstrated with Hitler for signing the Declaration.

The Führer replied, "Don't take it so seriously. That piece of paper is of no further significance whatever."

Hitler renounced the Anglo-German Naval Agreement on 28 April 1939. The apartment now houses the headquarters of Munich's regional police.

We saw the Odeonsplatz, where Hitler was caught on film at a rally to celebrate the declaration of war in 1914. We saw the arches of the Feldherrnhalle where Hitler's 1923 *Putsch* was stopped by Bavarian police. We went on to the public building near the Gate of Victory in which Heinrich Hoffman had a photographic shop, where Hitler met Eva Braun. We passed three buildings in Königsplatz that housed the Nazi Party and were associated with Hitler. Hitler spoke from the Greek-looking columns of the Propylaea (German Propyläen). We went on to the site of the Bürgerbräu beer hall from which Hitler launched his 1923 putsch. I was doing local research for my epic poem on the Second World War, *Overlord*.

We re-entered the Hofbräuhaus half an hour after leaving it. Our party were still sitting over their beer, but I had seen the apartment where Neville Chamberlain produced his Anglo-German Declaration that Hitler signed at the end of his visit to Munich on 30 September 1938, the day German troops entered the Sudetenland.

Peace for our time

After his meetings with Hitler in Munich and the surrender of the Sudetenland Chamberlain flew back to Heston aerodrome and waved the Anglo-German Declaration "which bears his name upon it as well as mine". This paper Chamberlain and Hitler had signed on 30 September 1938, that said that the 1938 Munich Agreement and the 1935 Anglo-German Naval Agreement were "symbolic of the desire of our two peoples never to go to war with one another again", was in fact a declaration of appeasement. It handed Hitler the Sudetenland despite Czech opposition.

Later in the day Chamberlain stood outside 10 Downing Street and announced: "For the second time in our history a British Prime Minister has returned from Germany bringing peace with honour. I believe it is peace for our time."[1]

The first Prime Minister in British history to return from Germany with a promise of peace was Benjamin Disraeli. Back from the Congress of Berlin in 1878 Disraeli stated, "I have returned from Germany with peace for our time." The British had just balanced their interests with Russia's and Austria-Hungary's, and the Congress had been a success. Chamberlain was echoing Disraeli's phrase.

There is a line in the *Book of Common Prayer*, "Give peace in our time, O Lord", which I often heard in Chigwell School's chapel in my boyhood and which may have been based on a 7th-century hymn: *"Da pacem, Domine, in diebus nostris."* In a popular reinterpretation (probably influenced by the *Book of Common Prayer*) Chamberlain's "peace *for* our time" became 'peace *in* our time', a misquotation that passed into Noel Coward's 1947 play, *Peace in our Time*.

Looking at the rippling waves I now reflect that Chamberlain's "peace for our time" proved illusory, for the reality turned out to be impending war with Germany. I am haunted by the possibly illusory 'peace for our time' I have sought, for perhaps that will turn out to be impending war with Russia, and perhaps a proxy Third World War has already begun. I have wanted to work for a universal peace my grandchildren will know so they do not have to live through war from the air as I did as a small boy.

V-1s and V-2s

I was conceived around 29 August 1938. As far back as in 1934 Hitler told his military leaders that 1942 was the target date for going to war in the east.[2] As Goebbels' *Diaries* make clear, Hitler was already planning the Second World War – war against Britain and eastward expansion following an invasion of Czechoslovakia on 1 October – from early 1938.

In March 1938 Hitler had successfully invaded Austria and turned his attention to the Sudetenland. On 20 May he presented his Generals with a draft plan to attack Czechoslovakia codenamed Operation Green. On 28 May he ordered an acceleration in the construction of U-boats and in the building of two new battleships. Ten days later he signed a directive for war against Czechoslovakia to begin not later than 1 October 1938.[3]

Hitler was already planning the Second World War in May, and certainly in early August 1938, well before the signing of the Munich Agreement on 30 September 1938. Hitler invaded Poland on 1 September 1939 and Chamberlain's declaration of war in his radio broadcast followed on 3 September 1939.

I was born into war. We lived in Norbury and Caterham, suburbs of south-west London, and after Caterham was bombed on a Sunday in May 1940 we moved to East Grinstead in Sussex to live with my maternal grandmother out of harm's way. In November 1942 my father began a new job in Loughton, Essex as chief accountant in the treasurer's department of the Chigwell Urban District Council. He lived in digs until March 1943, when my mother, my infant younger brother and I, not yet four, moved to a rented semi-detached house near his work.

We were in Churchill's constituency and therefore had to endure nightly air attacks. In March 1944, when I was four, a string of German bombs blew out our windows. I was leaving our house with my father one late afternoon when it was nearly dark to walk to the Post Office, and had reached the end of our garden path. I can still see the early night sky light up in a flash as bright as day.

In June 1944 a first V-1 (Vengeance-1) pilotless doodle-bug rocket landed in our part of the UK. I was just five. Between June and the following March over 9,500 V-1 rockets were fired at south-east Britain and from September to the following March these were supplemented by over 1,400 silent V-2 (Vengeance-2) rockets which also targeted south-east Britain.

For nine months I lay in bed each night and listened to the doodle-bugs cut out. When the drone of their engines stopped they fell to earth and exploded ten seconds later. Lying in bed I would count to ten and when I heard a distant bang I sighed with relief, for we were still safe, the rocket had fallen elsewhere. We had no warning of the silent V-2s. There was a sudden bang. Lying in bed I was aware that any second there could be a sudden deafening bang that would wipe us all out. During those nine months, lying in bed at night I longed for peace.

Having lived with the imminent prospect of attacks from the air in 1944–1945 we faced sudden extinction from Soviet missiles all through the Cold War. I recall the imminent prospect of sudden extinction from the Soviet Union during the Cuban missile crisis of 16–28 October 1962. And a hostile Russia has again pointed nuclear missiles at European capitals from its exclave in Kaliningrad. We now face admittedly less-imminent sudden extinction from jihadist terrorism. I have lived with the prospect of sudden extinction in varying degrees of imminence all my life, and long for a true 'peace for our time' that will remove this dread from the lives of future generations.

World State and peace
For more than seventy years after the end of the war European peace has been safeguarded by the EEC, EC and EU, which have locked

France and Germany into the same institutions so both sides settle their differences by talking rather than by going to war; and by NATO, which watches over the former Soviet states of Eastern Europe that have broken away from Russia and preserve a fragile democratic independence.

Now we live in a time when Islamic terrorists are targeting France, Belgium, Germany and the UK. I lectured at the University of Baghdad from October 1961 to June 1962, and a pupil there three decades later founded the IS (Islamic State), who are reported to have seized enough radioactive material from government facilities to have the capacity to build a large and devastating 'dirty bomb', according to Australian intelligence reports.[4] IS are reported to be developing a radioactive dirty bomb they can let off in a Western capital, perhaps borne by a drone.[5]

I observe the intensifying war in the Middle East, centred round a war in Syria that has lasted more than five years, longer than the First and Second World Wars. It has the feel of a Third World War. And I observe the fragility of peace in Asia and see nation-state at loggerheads with nation-state. Since the war the UN has failed to stop 162 local wars.[6] The UN is 'inter-national', 'between nation-states'. It has no supranational authority over nation-states, and conflicts between nation-states are still settled by war. During the last seventy years I have seen collisions between nation-states lead to 162 wars, and I have seen terrorist war seek to undermine nation-states.

Over the decades I have developed the new philosophy of Universalism, which sees the universe as one and studies the activities of the whole of humankind. My Universalism, as set out in *The New Philosophy of Universalism*, includes political Universalism: a plan for the government of the whole of humankind that sees the 7.33 billion of the world's population as a potentially unified electorate.

Over the decades I have come to the view that the best guarantee of world peace in future generations is a World State: a democratic world government that reins in all oligarchs and *élites* who have sought to enrich their families by seizing the world's gas and oil.

I believe that a World State should be created as soon as possible. Partly federal, it will have enough authority to control all radioactive material, end terrorism and abolish war. In my view this is the most effective way of achieving 'peace for our time'. In the 20th century such a World State was advocated by Winston Churchill, President Truman, Albert Einstein, President Eisenhower, Bertrand Russell, Mahatma Gandhi, President John F. Kennedy and President Mikhail Gorbachev. I believe that following my book *The World Government* I am the only Western literary author continuing this tradition.

Over the decades amid the desolated landscapes of what looks like a Third World War I have seen beyond nation-statehood a partly-supranational World State that can bring in a universal peace. I see a contrast between nation-statehood that leads to war and a partly-supranational World State that brings peace. This is the essence of my reflection on war and peace.

I gaze at the sea. It is so calm and peaceful now, yet how quickly it is whipped up by stormy wind so waves boil through rocks and crash onto the beach. The same is true of the international landscape. It has both calm and turmoil at different times and in different places at the same time. I see the conflicting tides and currents of world history in this serene sea. And though I know the universe enfolds opposites – day and night, life and death, time and eternity – it is this serenity I would like to prevail.

In the East I was told by the then elderly distinguished Japanese poet, Junzaburo Nishiwaki, "+A + –A = 0", that all opposites are reconciled in a unity. I did not know that I would come to found a World State and be asked to lead an international peace initiative. Now I have a deep conviction that I would like to see war and peace, the shattered streets of Syrian towns and the tranquillity of the English countryside, reconciled in an enduring World State in which violent passions and gentleness are unified as exquisitely as the wind-rustled calm of the sea beneath my window now.

Notes:
1. See http://ww2today.com/chamberlain-announces-peace-for-our-time.
2. Richard J. Evans, *The Third Reich in Power*, pp.338–339.
3. See http://www.bbc.co.uk/bitesize/higher/history/roadwar/munich/rev isio n/1/.
4. See http://www.independent.co.uk/news/world/middle-east/isiss-dirty -bomb-jihadists-have-seized-enough-radioactive-material-to-build- their-first-wmd-10309220.html.
5. See http://www.telegraph.co.uk/news/2016/04/01/isil-plotting-to-use- drones-for-nuclear-attack-on-west/.
6. See http://www.war-memorial.net/wars_all.asp.

45

World State

Introduction to the United Federation of the World
How a Democratically-Elected World Government Can Replace the UN and Bring Peace

Prologue
The Need for a World State

A 'World State' is "a state comprising the whole world; a state possessing world-power" (*Shorter Oxford English Dictionary*). There has never been such a state, and although there have been attempts to create one we are used to nation-states and so a state comprising the whole world seems difficult to imagine. Yet our television cameras take us to the United Nations and show us the representatives of all nations in the UN General Assembly.

A democratic World State and its early supporters
A democratic World State's lower house will resemble the UN General Assembly. It will be a Parliamentary Assembly representing all nations like the UN General Assembly, and indeed will possibly initially meet in the great hall of the UN General Assembly.

However, unlike the UN General Assembly it will have a partly-federal, partly-supranational structure that will allow nation-states to be internally independent. Through its federal power it will impose disarmament; abolish war, famine, disease and poverty; and govern the world in accordance with internationalist thinking and principles. It will run the world for the benefit of humankind and will bring peace and prosperity to all.

This book is about a State that will cover the whole world and exercise world-power. The two atomic bombs dropped on Hiroshima and Nagasaki in Japan in 1945 shocked and appalled the world, and many of the world's leaders and prominent men called for such a democratic World-State.

President Harry S. Truman was among the first, in 1945:

> It will be just as easy for nations to get along in a republic of the world as it is for you to get along in the republic of the United States. When Kansas and Colorado have a quarrel over the water in the Arkansas

River, they don't call out the National Guard in each state and declare war over it. They bring a suit in the Supreme Court of the United States and abide by the decision. There isn't a reason in the world why we can't do that internationally.

(Dedication of war memorial in
Omaha, Nebraska on 5 June 1948)

Winston Churchill, Prime Minister of the UK, called for a democratic World State in 1945:

Unless we establish some form of world government, it will not be possible for us to avert a World War III in the future.

Also:

Unless some effective world supergovernment for the purpose of preventing war can be set up... the prospects for peace and human progress are dark.... If... it is found possible to build a world organisation of irresistible force and inviolable authority for the purpose of securing peace, there are no limits to the blessings which all men may enjoy and share.

Albert Einstein, whose scientific papers contributed to the splitting of the atom and therefore the explosion of the atomic bomb, added his voice in 1945:

There is no salvation for civilisation, or even the human race, other than the creation of a world government.

Also:

A world government with powers adequate to guarantee security is not a remote ideal for the distant future. It is an urgent necessity if our civilisation is to survive.

And in 1946:

A world government must be created which is able to solve conflicts between nations by judicial decision. This government must be based on a clear-cut constitution which is approved by the governments and nations and which gives it the sole disposition of offensive weapons.[1]

The philosopher Bertrand Russell spoke in 1946:

It is entirely clear that there is only one way in which great wars can be permanently prevented, and that is the establishment of an international government with a monopoly of serious armed force.[2]

And:

A scientific world society cannot be stable unless there is a world government.[3]

Also:

Our goal should be the creation of a world government.

The Indian leader Mahatma Gandhi was of the same view in 1947:

I would not like to live in this world if it is not to be one world.[4]

Atomic scientists through a 1948 UN Resolution supported their view:

The emergency committee of atomic scientists, having explored for two years all means other than world government for making responsible the control of atomic energy [meaning nuclear weapons, really, and by implication, all weapons of mass destruction], has become convinced that no other method than world government can be expected to prove effective, and that the attainment of world government is therefore the most urgent problem now facing mankind.

In 1955 Russell and Einstein made common cause in their call for world peace in the Russell-Einstein Manifesto:

We invite this Congress, and through it the scientists of the world and the general public, to subscribe to the following resolution: 'In view of the fact that in any future world war nuclear weapons will certainly be employed, and that such weapons threaten the continued existence of mankind, we urge the governments of the world to realise, and to acknowledge publicly, that their purpose cannot be furthered by a world war, and we urge them, consequently, to find peaceful means for the settlement of all matters of dispute between them.'[5]

Subsequently other prominent people called for a democratic World State.

President Dwight D. Eisenhower added his voice:

The world no longer has a choice between force and law; if civilisation is to survive, it must choose the rule of law.

And:

We have been warned by the power of modern weapons that peace may be the only climate possible for human life itself.... There must be law, steadily invoked and respected, for without law, the world promises only such meagre justice as the pity of the strong upon the weak.

Jawaharlal Nehru, the first Prime Minister of India, called for the world to unite:

Either the world will unite or it will perish.

John F. Kennedy called for a world-wide law:

We must create... world-wide law and law enforcement as we outlaw world-wide war and weapons.

Ronald Reagan echoed Kennedy in his address to the UN General Assembly on 26 September 1983:

Our goals are the same as those of the UN's founders, who sought to replace a world at war with one where the rule of the law would prevail, where human rights were honoured, where development would blossom, where conflict would give way to freedom from violence.

And more recently Mikhail Gorbachev expressed the same sentiment:

There is an increasing awareness of the need for some form of global government.

Pope John Paul II also envisaged a World State:

The international community should support a system of laws to regularise international relations and maintain the peace in the same manner that law governs national order.

In 1946 Einstein saw the need for new thinking to take humankind beyond nationalism to supranationalism:

> A new type of thinking is essential if mankind is to survive and move toward higher levels. The fundamental problems we face cannot be solved at the same level of thinking with which we created them.[6]

New thinking in Europe and America: 50 European states and New World Order
Europe implemented this new thinking regarding a democratic World State immediately after the war. Churchill called for a United States of Europe at Zurich University on 19 September 1946:

> We must build a kind of United States of Europe.... We must recreate the European family in a regional structure called, it may be, the United States of Europe, and the first practical step will be to form a Council of Europe.

And from 1946 to 2016 Europe enjoyed 70 years of peace after being riven by wars between nation-states every 30 years or so for two thousand years – through conflicts between the Romans and the Gauls and the Germanic tribes, the Anglo-Saxons, the Normans and the wars of the Middle Ages – and most recently in 1870, 1914 and 1939. Devised by Jean Monnet in conjunction with the Council on Foreign Relations in the early 1920s, first the European Economic Community and the Common Market, then the European Community and most recently the European Union and the Single Market implemented and progressively constructed a European system of governance that brought peace and prosperity to the EU's 510 million out of Europe's 739 million citizens and absorbed 28 member states with another 22 waiting to join, making 50 in all:

> 28 members of the EU: Austria, Belgium, Bulgaria, Croatia, Cyprus, Czech Republic, Denmark, Estonia, Finland, France, Germany, Greece, Hungary, Ireland, Italy, Latvia, Lithuania, Luxembourg, Malta, Netherlands, Poland, Portugal, Romania, Slovakia, Slovenia, Spain, Sweden, the UK (which in March 2017 triggered Article 50 to leave the EU).

> 22 states not yet members of the EU: Albania, Andorra, Armenia, Azerbaijan, Belarus, Bosnia and Herzegovina, Georgia, Iceland, Kazakhstan (Kazakhstan's bilateral agreement with the EU secures

Kazakhstan's common foreign policy and trade relations with the EU), Kosovo, Liechtenstein, Macedonia, Moldova, Monaco, Montenegro, Norway, Russia, San Marino, Serbia, Switzerland, Turkey, Ukraine.[7]

America also implemented this new thinking in the 1960s. An American-led New World Order called for a world government of free liberal democracies. It was advanced by Nelson Rockefeller, who had called for world federalism in his *The Future of Federalism* (1962), claiming that current events demand a "New World Order", "a federal structure of the free world", and echoed by Richard Nixon in 1967 and by George Bush Sr on 11 September 1990 after the pulling-down of the Berlin Wall and the end of the Cold War ("a New World Order can emerge"), and used secrecy and deception. The New World Order favoured liberal interventionism to overthrow the dictatorships of the Middle East and Asia. It worked to create a worldwide liberal democracy and sought to cover the earth with oil and natural-gas pipelines. These pipelines benefited élitist families who were more interested in making fortunes for themselves than in benefiting humankind, and who were responsible for many local wars. My view of a World State has no truck with these élitist families.[8]

Populism and nationalism
The rise of populism in Europe and America in 2016 challenged the European and American élitist Establishment, which was entrenched on both sides of the Atlantic. In Europe, populism took the form of a revolt against the EU and the flow of refugees from wars in East Asia, the Middle East and North Africa which threatened livelihoods. Populists called for anti-immigrant nationalistic policies and challenged supranationalism. There was a similar revolt against the US Establishment that saw Trump come to power. 'UK First' policies in the UK and 'America First' policies in the US (whose Statue of Liberty symbolised America's welcoming of immigrants) sought to strengthen nation-states' borders with walls and block the free movement of peoples.

European populism spread to the 'France First' policies of the neo-Fascist Front National of Marine Le Pen, the 'Netherlands First' policies of the Party for Freedom of Geert Wilders (who did not win the Dutch election), the 'Italy First' policies of Five Star, the 'Germany First' policies of the Alternative for Germany (AfG) party and the 'Hungary First' policies of the Fidesz party. Populism's roots in Fascism, itself a 'national socialism' (a combination of ultra-nationalism and improving the people's working and social conditions), were pointed out by the

Archbishop of Canterbury. The eurozone was divided between rich northern states like Germany and indebted southern states such as Greece, Italy, Portugal and Spain.

Although all the anti-Establishment parties had relatively minor support and it was statistically unlikely that they would take power like Trump, it seemed the EU might collapse before the UK had completed its exit, that there would be no EU from which the UK could exit. A European Golden Age looked as if it might disintegrate into a new Dark Age, and the feeling among supranationalist defenders of the European Union seemed elegiac. As at the end of Camelot, a noble Arthurian world seemed as if it was coming to an end.

Revival of calls for a democratic World State
As a result of this populist and nationalistic revolt against supranationalism, the 20th-century calls for a democratic World State are no longer heard. Today I believe I am the only Western literary author and thinker to continue the tradition of those 20th-century calls. I called for a democratic World State in my acceptance speech when I received the Gusi Peace Prize for Literature in Manila in November 2016.[9] In that speech I pointed out that since 1945 the United Nations has failed to prevent 162 wars[10] and the manufacture of (at the time, autumn 2016) 15,375 nuclear weapons, a total that had fallen to 14,900 in spring 2017 (see Appendix C9 [in *World State*]):[11]

> In my lifetime I've seen the world go through a miserable period and we could be heading for a *Third* World War. Since 1945 the UN has failed to prevent 162 wars – *162 wars* – and the world has accumulated 15,375 nuclear weapons: *15,375 nuclear weapons*. There were none when I was born. In my books I've tried to analyse what's gone wrong, and find solutions. I've concluded that ideally we need a *democratic* World State with the nation-states staying as they are and a partly-federal government that's *strong* enough to prevent wars and control nuclear weapons. The present United Nations lacks overall authority, and nation-states go to war too readily.
>
> The first two atomic bombs left many international figures in shock and calling for such a democratic peace-bringing World State. These included Churchill, Truman, Einstein and Eisenhower. I have the same vision, and so I'm carrying on this call in *my* works.
>
> As I see it, the UN General Assembly could eventually be turned into a lower house of democratically-elected Representatives in a partly-federal government that includes a World Senate, as set out in my work *The World Government*. I see the UN eventually becoming a UF,

a United Federation. A *UF*.

Such new thinking could create a world government with enough authority to abolish war, enforce disarmament and alleviate famine, disease and poverty.

However, there were signs of a reawakening regarding the need for some sort of world government. There was now an increasing feeling among many that, with Europe under threat, the noble supranational European idea should be applied to the world, and a revival of calls for a strong central authority could be detected in the international reactions to IS (Islamic State), or Daesh. It was asserted that IS had captured 40 tonnes of nuclear material from Mosul University and was trying to convert it into a 'dirty' bomb that could be delivered by drone and contaminate a Western capital with radioactive material, creating Western refugees.[12] President Obama was so worried about this prospect that he summoned 50 Western leaders to a conference in Washington from 31 March to 1 April 2016, and asked them what they would do if a drone-borne dirty-bomb spread nuclear material on their territory.[13] IS was defeated in Mosul in July 2017.

Threat of a Third World War
There was talk of the world's being on the verge of a Third World War. It looked as if a proxy Third World War had already broken out in the Middle East, with the superpowers on opposite sides and fighting each other through intermediaries. If a new front opened with a Russian invasion of the Baltic states of Estonia, Latvia and Lithuania then there would be a World War on two fronts – a Baltic front as well as a Middle-Eastern front – and technically the Third World War, a world war on more than one front, would have broken out. The retreat of European states into the nation-statehood of the past brought no solutions to the world's problems, and a democratic World State, a State covering the whole world and exercising world-power, is much needed today.

In each region of the world humankind lives under the threat of war and annihilation, and the lives of many are blighted by famine, disease and poverty, especially in parts of Africa, Asia and South America.

Dream of a strong supranational authority
There seems to be a recognition that there should be a stronger central authority than the UN so that wars can be stopped, including the interventionist wars involving pipelines in Afghanistan (the Trans-Afghan Pipeline from the Turkmen Dauletabad fields through Afghanistan to Multan in Pakistan and then India); in Iraq (the Kirkuk–

Haifa pipeline); and in Syria (the Qatar–Jordan–Syria–Turkey pipeline and the Iran–Syria pipeline).

Under a stronger central authority full nuclear disarmament can happen, and there can be global drives on famine, disease, poverty and global warming to benefit the lives of all humankind. To achieve this there must be supranational planning, and so the UN General Assembly needs to be turned into the lower house of a World State with democratically-elected representatives. Supranationalist supporters of Europe who are bruised by the populist movement's successes may now look beyond Europe to the world itself and throw their weight behind a movement that can bring all 193 nation-states under one global governance with democratically-elected representatives.

An objective study of history's civilisations shows that 'sovereign' nation-states are competitive and self-interested, and that their obsession with borders and walls inevitably leads to war as wars begin out of fear. Einstein understood this:

As long as there are sovereign nations possessing great power, war is inevitable.

And:

With all my heart I believe that the world's present system of sovereign nations can only lead to barbarism, war and inhumanity, and that only World law can assure progress towards a civilised peaceful community.

Dr Sarvepalli Radhakrishnan, the second President of India, grasped that some sovereignty must be surrendered to achieve a World State:

There will be one central authority to which the instruments of coercion will be surrendered and a fraction of the sovereignty of independent nation-states will have to be given up for the security of the whole world.

Jan Tinbergen, Nobel Laureate in Economic Sciences, saw the need for a World State:

Mankind's problems can no longer be solved by national governments. What is needed is a world government.

The next few years may see the beginning of a general disillusionment with nation-states as Trump's ban on immigrants is seen to be unconstitutional, reactionary and not conducive to economic growth while Brexit nation-statism is seen to lead to a lowering of living standards. It may become very evident that the solutions to the world's problems of wars, disarmament, famine, disease, poverty and global warming can be found through a co-operative democratic World State rather than economic self-interest, protectionism and isolationism.

Political Universalism
My championing of a World State came out of my philosophy. In *The New Philosophy of Universalism* I set out Universalism, which sees the universe and humankind as a unity in terms of several disciplines. I maintain that history should be about the history of humankind as a whole and all civilisations; that philosophy should be about humankind's place in the universe; that literature should be about the fundamental theme of world literature, which I stated in *A New Philosophy of Literature*; and that international politics and statecraft should be about humankind as a political unity – in other words, a democratic World State. It was appropriate that, to show that a World State can be created, when chairing the World Philosophical Forum's Constitutional Convention in 2015 I brought in a World State, the Universal State of the Earth.[14]

Political Universalism holds that all humankind can be organised under a World State and that this is the best structure for solving the world's problems, which have not been solved by nation-states and the UN. The UN is 'inter-national', and hosts meetings of nation-states, some of which have vetoes, and it has no supranational power to impose an abolition of war and an enforcement of disarmament. Political Universalism sees a stronger authority running the world. The League of Nations was seen to have failed when the Second World War broke out, and its replacement the United Nations may now be seen to have failed as the war in Syria has lasted longer than the First and Second World Wars and seems to have no end in sight; and as according to many a Third World War has already begun. Political Universalism sees the UN as being replaced by a 'UF', a United Federation of the World.

Despite populist nationalism, political Universalism has our worldwide lifestyle on its side. Air travel, satellite television and instant communications via the internet have all brought humankind together. Globalisation – the expansion of global linkages, the organisation of social life and trade on a global scale and the growth of a global consciousness – has spread and integrated different countries' ideas, values, norms, behaviour and ways of life. The way the world is linked is Universalist, and our globalised way of life, with goods coming from China and all parts of the world, lends itself to a Universalist political structure.

In short, the time of the World State is approaching and the concept and model of the World State can be expected to receive increasingly serious attention in the next two decades. Hence this objective study.

Surprisingly there has been no accessible study of the concept of a World State until my pioneering (and therefore necessarily tentative) book *The World Government* (2010). This current book describes the evolution of the World State, the longings for it and attempts to impose it by force, and the nation-states' failures that have made it possible. It sets out the World State's supranationalist identity; the new structure it requires which goes beyond the structures of the UN and regional unions; and its ideal form, supranationalist structure and agenda. It seeks to be sufficiently comprehensive and authoritative to last for several decades while a coming World State can be formed. This book is therefore a manifesto for a World State, and implementing its principles can unite humankind and bring in a Golden Age of peace and prosperity.

Notes:

1. Albert Einstein, 'Towards a World Government' (1946), in *Out of My Later Years: The Scientist, Philosopher and Man Portrayed Through His Own Words*, New York: Wings Books, 1956.
2. Bertrand Russell, 'The Atomic Bomb and Prevention of War', in the *Bulletin of the Atomic Scientists*, 1 October 1946.
3. In Dennis Laurence Cuddy, *Secret Records Revealed: The Men, the Money & The Methods Behind the New World Order*, p.89.
4. Gandhi, speech, March 1947. In Gandhi, *All Men are Brothers: Autobiographical Reflections*, p.112.
5. The Russell-Einstein Manifesto (1955), issued in London on 9 July 1955 by Bertrand Russell.
6. From 'Atomic Education Urged by Einstein', *New York Times*, 25 May 1946.
7. For Europe's eventual 50 member states, see http://geography. about.com/od/lists/a/officiallist.htm?p=1 for 48 member states, with Azerbaijan and Kazakhstan also in line to become member states. The UK, one of the 48 member states, was preparing to leave the EU at the time of writing. See also Nicholas Hagger, *The Dream of Europa*, p.83.
8. For detailed coverage of the New World Order, see Nicholas Hagger, *The Syndicate*; and *The Secret American Dream*, chs.7 and 8.
9. Nicholas Hagger, *Peace for our Time*, pp.181–183.

10. See Hagger, *Peace for our Time,* p.xvi and source, http://www.war-memorial.net/wars_all.asp.

11. See Hagger, *Peace for our Time,* p.98 and source, https://fas.org/issues/nuclear-weapons/status-world-nuclear-forces/. In autumn 2016 there were 15,375 nuclear weapons, in early 2017 14,900.

12. See https://www.rt.com/news/338086-isis-chemical-lab-mosul/; http://www.independent.co.uk/news/world/middle-east/isiss-dirty-bomb-jihadists-have-seized-enough-radioactive-material-to-build-their-first-wmd-10309220.html; and http://www.telegraph.co.uk/news/2016/04/01/isil-plotting-to-use-drones-for-nuclear-attack-on-west/.

13. See https://www.theguardian.com/uk-news/2016/apr/01/a-terrorist-dirty-bomb-us-summit-asks-world-leaders-to-plot-response.

14. See *Peace for our Time,* pp.48–49 and elsewhere; and *The Secret American Destiny,* pp.250–253.

46

World Constitution

Constitution for the United Federation of the World

Preface on Constitutions

Definition of 'constitution'
A 'constitution' is "the mode in which a state is constituted or organised", "the system or body of fundamental principles according to which a nation, state or body politic is constituted and governed" (*Shorter Oxford English Dictionary*). It is "the body of fundamental principles or established precedents according to which a State or other organisation is acknowledged to be governed" (*Concise Oxford Dictionary*). A good constitution has clarity, sense and succinctness, and inspires and resonates.

Written constitutions dictate the rules that are to govern societies. The American constitution was agreed after a Constitutional Convention in Philadelphia involving 55 delegates and lasting 116 days (25 May–17 September) that brought in the Federal Constitution in 1787.

Number of past constitutions and precedents
A total of 158 sovereign nation-states now have written constitutions, as do 9 partially-recognised countries and 13 dependent territories, and there are 6 uncodified constitutions and 18 constitutions of former countries, making a total of 204 constitutions (see Appendix 1 [of *World Constitution*]). The UN has a Charter and the Universal Declaration of Human Rights, NATO has a Treaty and the EU has a succession of Treaties that include the Paris, Rome, Maastricht, Amsterdam, Nice and Lisbon Treaties. It also has the European Convention on Human Rights and the Charter of Fundamental Rights of the European Union. There are 26 constitutional precedents (see Appendix 1A [of *World Constitution*]). The UK does not have a written constitution, and this may be one of the reasons for Brexit: the British do not like to be tied down to the written rules of the EU.

Since the establishing of the UN there have been two flawed attempts at writing constitutions with the intention of founding a new World State. Neither seeks to replace the UN. The Constitution for the Federation of Earth (1968, 1991) is very short on rights and presents an approach so moderate that its supporters seek to amalgamate with the UN. The Constitution for the Universal State of the Earth (USE), whose Constitutional Convention I chaired at the World Philosophical Forum in Athens and brought into being on 7 October 2015 (see *Peace for our Time*, 2018, pp.46–50), has a democratic deficit. It is aimed at its paid-up members, not all world citizens through the UN, and it will take decades for paid-up members to be in sufficient quantity to form a world majority, or even the 100,000 members the USE has to reach for it to be formally recognised, according to its constitution.

The World State my works and this Constitution introduce
My work within political science/international politics and statecraft draws on my early study of Roman Law and of Justinian I's 6th-century *Codex Justinianus* (Code of Justinian), the Roman Empire's codification of World Law (the law of the known world) that is the Roman World State's equivalent to this Constitution. My pioneering of Universalism has led me in the direction of this Constitution for a new World State arguably since *The Fire and the Stones* (my study of the rise and fall of civilisations) appeared in 1991 with an 'Introduction to the New Universalism'; and certainly since work I was doing in 2006, which culminated in my section on political Universalism in *The New Philosophy of Universalism* (2009). My books *The World Government* (2010) and *World State* (2018), which includes an updating of the evidence and data on which a World State should be based, are introductions to the new World State, which I have named the United Federation of the World (UF).

When it comes into existence the UF will be a partly-federal, democratically-elected world government with an inter-national World Parliamentary Assembly (an elected lower house that will initially be based in the UN General Assembly) and a supranational, federal World Commission and World Senate (an elected upper house). The hyphen in 'inter-national' suggests a secondary meaning that distinguishes it from 'supranational': "between [Latin *inter*] nation-states", as distinct from "above [Latin *supra*] nation-states". As I see it, the World Parliamentary Assembly will eventually replace the UN General Assembly, and under the new federal arrangement the United Nations, UN, will be replaced by the United Federation of the World, UF.

Three reasons for naming the World State the 'United Federation of the World'
The name 'United Federation of the World' is the most appropriate name for a new World State for the following three reasons, which take

possible alternative names into account:

1. *Name to reflect partial, not total, federation*. The word 'federation' comes from the Latin *'foedus'*, meaning "league, covenant". So a 'federation' is "the action of uniting in a league or covenant", "a union of several states under a federal government, each retaining control of its own internal affairs" (*Shorter Oxford English Dictionary*). In other words, a federation is a union of partially-self-governing states or regions under a central (federal) government. Under the United Federation of the World, all the existing nation-states will remain internally independent but will be subject to central federal control in seven areas. In Appendix A2 in *World State* I list 27 federations that involve unions of several states. These include the United States of America. As the Federation this Constitution will bring in includes all nation-states it may seem to resemble a 'United States of the World'. However, in a 'United States of the World' the federal control would be total, over everything outside the internal administration of the nation-states, whereas the federal element of the United Federation of the World is partial, limited, restricted to the seven federal goals listed in Article 1 of this Constitution (which were first stated in my books *The World Government* and *The Secret American Dream*).

2. *Name to reflect Tennyson's vision and anthem*. In the name 'United Federation of the World', 'United' echoes the 'United' in 'the United Nations'; 'Federation' suggests a union of all nation-states under a federal government limited to the seven federal goals; and 'the World' emphasises that the federation is of all the nation-states and extant civilisations in the whole world. It is the "Federation of the world" the English poet Tennyson foresaw in 'Locksley Hall' (1842), which is in the anthem (see Article 133 [of *World Constitution*]): 'United' (as in 'United Nations') + Tennyson's "Federation of the world".

3. *Name to reflect solution to, not causes of, world's problems*. My introduction to the United Federation of the World, *World State* (in which Part One is titled 'Beyond the Nation-State'), makes clear that sovereign nation-states are the cause of the world's problems, notably the problems of wars, nuclear weapons, refugees and migrants, and that the solution to these problems requires a federal, supranational level of government that is strong enough to achieve the seven federal goals: to abolish war, impose disarmament, share energy, tackle disease, famine and poverty, and sort out global warming and financial crises. As competing nation-states have caused the world's problems and the solution to the world's problems is the seven federal goals and

a limited federalism of all the world's nation-states, it is better that the new World State should be named the 'United Federation of the World' (which focuses on the solution) than the 'Federation of Nation-States' (which focuses on the problems and would be a confusing name as it suggests a total rather than a partial federation and as there have been 27 federations of nation-states). (I referred descriptively to a "Federation of nation-states" in *Peace for our Time*, 2018, p.99, quoting my paper 'Urgent Global Problems, Inactive Nation-States and Decisive Supranationalism' which can be found in Appendix 6 in that work and has been online since soon after it was written on 22–23 September 2016. However, my descriptive reference was not intended to be a name for the new World State.)

Failure of the inter-national UN to prevent wars
The United Federation of the World (or UF) will need to be much stronger than the existing inter-national United Nations, which has no supranational power and is really just a debating chamber for nation-states and a club where world leaders can meet. The UN has failed to prevent 162 wars since 1945, of which a shocking number of 72 wars are still continuing at present (for the evidence, see Appendix C6 in *World State*) and has failed to control the 2017 tally of 14,900 nuclear weapons.

On the subject of nation-states causing wars, President Trump's strong and statesman-like, internationalist address to the UN General Assembly on 18 September 2017 was about the need for secure and prosperous sovereign nation-states, national self-interest. In a place valuing peace he attacked North Korea, Venezuela, Iran, and the Islamic jihadist organisations, and threatened to destroy North Korea. There was no word on the need for a federal supranationalism that could bring lasting peace, and unsurprisingly the horrified delegates of the UN General Assembly did not persistently interrupt his speech with applause as they did when President Obama addressed them. As could be seen from their response, the world is crying out for a vision of unity that goes beyond self-interested nation-states and wars. Only a body with some supranational authority can achieve the seven goals.

Precedents legally sound
In assembling this Constitution I have consulted the precedents listed in Appendix 1 [in *World Constitution*], which contain wording that has been tried and tested over many years and found to be legally sound. I have amalgamated the thinking in these precedents, and where possible I have echoed the legally tried and tested phrases. This

Constitution and its Articles can therefore be seen to have evolved from the precedents and their legally sound Articles. For full coverage of the thinking behind this Constitution's presentation of the United Federation of the World, see my companion volume *World State: An Introduction to the United Federation of the World*.

Need for a Constitutional Convention in the UN General Assembly
No constitution has force until it is ratified. As this Constitution for the United Federation of the World will have to be ratified, there will need to be a Constitutional Convention in the UN General Assembly to approve and no doubt amend its Articles, and at that stage a committee of lawyers will comb through this Constitution. It is my hope that the UN Secretary-General's office will look at this Constitution in conjunction with *World State*, and allow me to give a presentation to the UN General Assembly to initiate this process.

26, 30 August, 1, 28–29 September, 2, 7, 9–11 October 2017

47

King Charles the Wise

The Triumph of Universal Peace
A Masque

Preface
A Court Masque and Universal Peace

Early English court masques
The 16th- and early-17th-century masques in Europe and England were court entertainments. They celebrated an event at court, sometimes a royal marriage, and flattered the monarch.

In the early English masques Henry VIII, James I and Charles I all had masked non-speaking parts. In England Ben Jonson's early-17th-century masques were performed in the Banqueting Hall of the Whitehall Palace during Christmas, often on Twelfth Night. The Banqueting Hall was replaced by the Banqueting House, which was built between 1619 and 1622. Masques can be found in the works of Shakespeare (*A Midsummer Night's Dream, Henry VIII, The Tempest*), Milton (*Comus*), Shelley (*The Masque of Anarchy*) and most recently William Empson (*The Birth of Steel*). Empson's masque was in honour of the Queen's visit to Sheffield in 1954 and addressed Queen Elizabeth II as a "goddess". (The Queen returned the compliment by knighting Empson in 1979.)

Origins of the masque
The masque seems to have originated in "mumming", a masked mime which Richard II took part in as early as 1377. The Italian masquerade was a carnival entertainment, and in France there were masked performances. Throughout Europe there were "guisings" or "disguisings" in which an allegorical figure addressed a courtly audience. Dumb shows can be found in Kyd's *The Spanish Tragedy* (first performed 1587) and Shakespeare's *A Midsummer Night's Dream* (1595–1596, the wedding of Pyramus and Thisbe), *Hamlet* (1500–1602) and *Pericles, Prince of Tyre* (1607–1608). Masques performed before Elizabeth I (including an anti-Catholic masque performed before her at the Whitehall Palace on Twelfth Night, 6 January 1559) emphasised the unity of her kingdom and the peace and concord that flourished in her realm.

Masque's five sections
The masque had five sections: the prologue; the antimasque (a spectacle of disorder and chaos); the masque (which transformed the disorder into order and harmony, and provided a resolution); the revels (which rejoiced at the resolution); and the epilogue.

The Dream of Europa: The Triumph of Peace
My first masque, *The Dream of Europa* (2015), celebrated the 70 years of European peace that followed the Second World War. It was in five sections and was subtitled *The Triumph of Peace*.

King Charles the Wise: The Triumph of Universal Peace
This masque, *King Charles the Wise*, is about the UK's global role after the disorder of Brexit and the birth of a united and unified world. In the prologue Zeus asks Minerva (the goddess of Wisdom) to work for world peace by promoting a democratic, federal World State strong enough to abolish war. He sees the founding of such a World State as the UK's new global role and asks her to establish whether the UK's Prince of Wales can be persuaded to support the concept when talking to world leaders. In the antimasque world citizens chant their misery and wretchedness at the disorder and chaos in the world, and the goddesses Britannia, Europa and Columbia (speaking for the UK, the EU and the US respectively) give their own discordant perspectives on the UK's future role. In the masque Minerva turns the disorder into order and provides a resolution: a coming World State that will unify humankind and bring the prospect of universal peace. Prince Charles approves the humanitarian principles and concerns on which this new age of peace will be based, and she crowns him with her Wisdom. In the revels, historical figures and contemporary world citizens rejoice at the prospect of a unified world. In the Epilogue Minerva reports back to Zeus, who will now send her to the Secretary-General of the UN.

This masque contrasts the contemporary disorder with the order of a coming democratic World State which will be strong enough to abolish war. It calls for a unified world with a limited supranational World Government that can solve humankind's problems. Its call comes at a time when in every continent there are divided nation-states and problems – such as wars, terrorist attacks, refugees and the threat of nuclear extermination – that seem insoluble within the present world structures.

Although the coming coronation of the Prince of Wales is referred to, the court event this masque celebrates is the UK's role in delivering a new structure that can bring universal peace. It presents humankind's need to bring the world together beyond the separateness of populism and isolationism. Political Universalism, a form of global governance in which all humankind can have a say, is on the world's coming political agenda and aims to establish universal peace. And so *King Charles the Wise* is subtitled *The Triumph of Universal Peace*.

Dialectic between opposites
In all my works there is a dialectic in which two opposites are reconciled in a unity in accordance with the algebraic formula I found in the East, +A + –A = 0. My two masques conform to a dialectic involving disorder and order. *The Dream of Europa* celebrated the peace-bringing EU, and this masque, *King Charles the Wise*, celebrates the UK's new global role that can bring in universal peace. These two masques are themselves opposites that suggest +A and –A, the first being on Europe and the second on the UK's Brexit, both of which are reconciled within the World State. Similarly, this masque about the UK's post-Brexit future, *King Charles the Wise*, will be contradicted by its opposite, a mock-heroic long poem in progress about the circumstances surrounding the UK's departure from the European Union, *Fools' Paradise*, and both are similarly reconciled within the World State.

Performance and production
A word on performance. A production could be performed by a cast of six (Zeus, Minerva, Prince Charles and the three royal household staff) with all the other characters – the five goddesses, the nine Kings and leaders and various choruses – shown on screen. Indeed, the Prologue and Epilogue could be shown on screen to indicate the remoteness of the gods' Olympus, and so Zeus could be pre-recorded on screen, leaving a cast of five on stage. However, if all the other characters are pre-recorded on screen the interaction between Prince Charles and the goddesses on stage would be lost, as would the on-stage audience for Minerva's crowning. The principle is that the left screen is the link between Buckingham Palace and Olympus (Zeus and the goddesses)/ the future, and the right screen is the link between Buckingham Palace and choruses (from the past, present and future, alive or dead, including the nine Kings and leaders and the shades of the dead). Such an approach would cut performance costs.

Genesis of this masque
I have had this masque in mind for some time. In a letter to the Prince of Wales on 1 August 2016 I wrote:

I see your coming reign as being distinctive, as I predicted in 'Night Visions in Charlestown' in 1983 (p.499 in *Collected Poems* with notes on pp.554–556). It can bring new hope for humankind by pioneering a new solution to the world's problems: a new spiritual vision of the unity of all humankind that can advance the lives of all people everywhere. As King you can be perceived as standing for universal values – Defender of the Faiths and more – and can come to be seen as King Charles the Wise. I do seriously intend to put this vision into a masque when I get clear of my immediate duties.

I had been thinking deeply about the UK's future global role after Brexit and the UK's possible hand in a coming World State, but first I had to write *Peace for our Time* and then *World State* and *World Constitution* (all 2018).

Although it may seem that my Muse put my poetic inspiration in touch with Zeus and Minerva as I sipped at the Pierian spring in the shadow of Mount Olympus, this masque presents the UK's innovative shaping of a new world structure that can bring in an era of universal peace and prosperity and benefit the whole of humankind.

21 August, 22 September, 16, 18 October, 16 November 2017

48

Visions of England

Poems Selected by the Earl of Burford

Preface
The Visionary Tradition

Meaning of 'Visions' and 'Visionary'
A 'vision' is "something which is apparently seen otherwise than by
ordinary sight; especially an appearance of a prophetic or mystical
character, or having the nature of a revelation, supernaturally presented
to the mind in sleep or in an abnormal state"; or "a mental concept of a
distinct or vivid kind; a highly imaginative scheme or anticipation"; or
"the action or fact of seeing or contemplating something not actually
present to the eye; mystical or supernatural insight or foresight"
(*Shorter Oxford English Dictionary*). ('A revelation' is, according to the
same dictionary, "the disclosure of knowledge to man by a divine or
supernatural agency".)

'Visions of England' therefore means "views of places in England
which are also seen otherwise than by ordinary sight, with prophetic,
mystical, revelatory and imaginative insight, not by the bodily eye".
Or more simply "seeing England with prophetic, mystical, revelatory
and imaginative insight".

'Visionary' means "able or accustomed to see visions; capable
of receiving impressions by means of visions"; or "presented or
apprehended in a vision"; or "existing in imagination only" (*Shorter
Oxford English Dictionary*). The 'visionary tradition' in poetry is
therefore "the tradition of seeing visions and reflecting them, and
imaginative vision, in poems".

These poems, all written before 1999, are views of England filled
with prophecy and mysticism and looking back to the work of the
Metaphysical poets and the visionary tradition of Blake.

Provenance of this selection: places in England
On 20 February 1979 I visited the English Neoclassical literary critic
Christopher Ricks, then Professor of English Literature at Cambridge
University, in Christ's College, Cambridge to discuss my early
Metaphysical poems, which he had been reading. He gave me a tutorial
and rattled through sixteen points on the poems for two hours and

then said, "There are too many poems. Get a friend to make a selection of 30 and bring them out, and make your *entrée*." Having edited his definitive *The Poems of Tennyson* (1969), he advised me to follow Tennyson's practice of amending lines, advice I took to heart and have implemented ever since. He then took me for lunch in Christ's Senior Common Room. I sat next to him at a long table among a dozen dons.

I was in a creative time and more poems kept coming, and I was still working full-time and coping with my new poems in the evenings and at weekends. My lengthy *Selected Poems: A Metaphysical's Way of Fire* (146 poems or excerpts) came out in 1991, followed by my *Collected Poems: A White Radiance*, 1958–1993 in 1994 (1,272 poems), and – following a further visit to Christopher Ricks on 27 January 1993 and a day walking round Oxford with him on 21 June 1993 – my first epic poem *Overlord* about the Second World War from D-Day to the Fall of Berlin (41,000 lines of blank verse in four separate volumes, 1995–1997). And I wrote two verse plays. There were now even more poems along with works of epic and dramatic verse, and I had still done nothing about getting a friend to select 30. I thought John Ezard of *The Guardian* might assume that role, but he was busy writing articles and meeting deadlines and we met increasingly infrequently.

In March 1998 the Earl of Burford, the heir to the Dukedom of St Albans, became my Literary Secretary following an interview at my then home in Albion Hill, Loughton which doubled up as Head Office of the Oak-Tree Group of Schools. He worked five days a week at Otley Hall in Suffolk, a historic Tudor house I had acquired and opened to the public, and I drove down twice a week to oversee the restoration and running of the stately home and work with him. His ancestor the 3rd Earl of Southampton, Shakespeare's patron, had been closely involved with the Earl of Essex, whose secretary Robert Gosnold III had owned it and lived there, and with his Cambridge friend Bartholomew Gosnold, Robert Gosnold III's nephew. Both Southampton and Bartholomew Gosnold had joined Essex's Cádiz and Azores expeditions in 1596 and 1597 – Southampton had captained Essex's ship on the second of these – and Southampton had funded Bartholomew Gosnold's expedition to America in 1602, which had been planned at Otley Hall and during which Bartholomew named Martha's Vineyard (after his daughter Martha) and Cape Cod. So Otley Hall had strong family associations for the Earl of Burford. A full account of Otley Hall's historical and literary associations can be found in my illustrated guidebook *Otley Hall* (2001), which can still be obtained at the property.

At one of our early meetings in my study, which had been an Elizabethan tiring-room (or attiring-room, dressing-room) for travelling players, the Earl of Burford remarked, "Your work is like a cathedral amid modern buildings." I told him about the need for a new selection and the idea emerged in our discussions that he would select 100 poems, not 30, focusing on places in England featured in my poems and on my metaphysical perspective. As my Literary Secretary he read all my poetic works.

Principles, thought processes and categories behind selection
On 30 April 1999 the Earl of Burford messaged me that he had selected 152 poems, mostly from *Collected Poems: A White Radiance* and a few from what would become *Classical Odes*. Under the heading 'Poems: British Selection' he set out the principles and thought processes behind his selection:

> I have selected 152 poems, some long, some short, some very short, from which I shall make a final selection of about 100 next week. I shall also put them in order, according to what scheme I'm not yet sure. I am tempted, however, to begin with 'Elemental Sea' because it contains the image of the hermit, which I think should be the defining symbol of the selection.
>
> You, the poet, are the hermit. You give your readers a tour of Britain, guiding them by the light of your metaphysical lamp. Like a hermit of old, you tramp the length and breadth of the country, teaching the mystic tradition. Suddenly you light on an ancient stone and holding your lamp over it cry, "Look here! See, see!"
>
> Thus you cast yourself in the role of psychopomp [in Greek mythology, "a conductor of souls to the place of the dead" (*Shorter Oxford English Dictionary*) and so a spiritual guide for the souls of the living]; or of the shaman, willing – by a huge effort of mind – his country's renewal.
>
> One of the advantages of using the image of the hermit at the very beginning is that it lets the reader know that there is a vital exchange between mind and landscape. The mind's ecstatic charges not only apprehend the landscape, they vivify it. For this reason, I've also been keen to include poems that open a window on the landscape of the poet's mind, as for example 'Bumble-Bee: Correspondence'.
>
> Included also are poems whose central images are symbols of Britain and British life: the sea, the oak tree, bluebells in spring, the snail etc. All these help to give insights into the peculiar spiritual life of the country. In addition, it makes sense that certain images that are both powerful and intrinsic to the poet's metaphoric world (e.g. a tree as the universe) should recur in the selection. Ultimately, then, a metaphysical

vision of the country emerges.

The overall impression should be of a poet with a strong sense of Britain's special destiny – the country, after all, that has fostered his own special insights into the universe.

In the event he did not begin with 'Elemental Sea' or include 'Bumble-Bee: Correspondence'. Among the papers is his handwritten list of the 152 poems with strike-throughs to bring the tally down to 101 (in fact 102 as one of his numbers merges two poems).

He also identified 26 poetic categories in the poems in *Collected Poems: A White Radiance* and what would become *Classical Odes*, which he considered for the selection:

England; Britain; English Heritage/History; British Heritage/History; Essex; Cornwall; East Anglia; The Celtic World; Europe; The Sea; The Far East; The Middle East; Decline of the West; Christian Culture; Greece/Rome/Classical Culture; History; The Modern Age; World Politics; Gardens; Love; Death; Nature; The Spiritual Quest; Mysticism; The Artist and his Art (The Imagination); The Fire/Light.

It is for the reader to judge how many of these categories can be found in the poems he chose, but his focus on England excluded many of the categories beyond England's shores.

There is a later note in my handwriting among these papers: "Call it *Visions of England*?"

Visions of England was the outcome: 102 poems celebrating places in England and my metaphysical outlook. These were in fact universal – indeed Universalist – poems with a significance that went far beyond England's borders.

Visions of England, then, covers what was in 1999 about one-thirteenth and is now about one-twentieth of my poetic works (excluding my two epics and five verse plays), and sees me as a hermit. I should point out that a later selection, *Selected Poems: Quest for the One* (211 poems or excerpts, 2015), sees me as a quester for Reality and observer of social follies and vices in all my poetic works, and that it would be possible to see me in a different light in a different one-twentieth of my poetic works: for example, as a journeyer along the Mystic Way (as in *Selected Poems: A Metaphysical's Way of Fire*); as a developing Universalist; as a poet within the perspective and tradition of seven disciplines; as a social, satirical poet; as a reflector of Western culture; as a Nature poet; as a war poet of the Second World War, Iraq and Afghanistan; and as a poet carrying forward the tradition of the Metaphysical poet in

Baroque work that unites sense and spirit, the Augustan and Romantic perspectives. *Visions of England* may include aspects of all of these eight alternative approaches, but the point I am making is that it would be possible for a selection of a similar length to offer a completely different view of my poetic works.

Overtaken by events
Visions of England was overtaken by events. In 1998 I had written a verse play, *The Tragedy of Prince Tudor*, about a Prince who protests against the impending break-up of the United Kingdom by hostile international forces, and the prospect of the loss of its sovereignty. Dismayed at the Blair Government's Reform Bill to abolish the hereditary peers' voting rights in the House of Lords and end a 700-year-old tradition, the Earl of Burford told me he detected Brussels' hand at work and was going to protest.

As a descendant of Shakespeare's patron the 3rd Earl of Southampton (and also of the 17th Earl of Oxford who Oxfordians regard as Shakespeare, and of Charles II and Nell Gwyn) and mindful of Southampton's involvement in the Earl of Essex's march through London and abortive *coup* of 1601 that led to Southampton's imprisonment in the Tower and Essex's execution (and Robert Gosnold III's being fined £40), he felt he had to rise to his family's tradition of making a stand in critical times and make a similar protest in what would be a "beautiful act" that would also be remembered for 400 years. He told me he was planning to climb onto the throne in the House of Lords, stand on its seat and address the assembled peers. I talked him out of violating the seat of the throne.

On 26 October 1999 he went ahead and made a principled protest in a packed House of Lords by leaping onto the Woolsack, the Lord Chancellor's wool-stuffed seat, and denouncing the Third Reading of the Reform Bill, which he branded treasonous. His speech would today be regarded as anti-EU: "This Bill, drafted in Brussels, is treason. What we are witnessing is the abolition of Britain.... No Queen, no culture, no sovereignty, no freedom." His spirited "act" led to 92 hereditary peers remaining in the Lords to this day, of whom 90 are now elected.

In a further protest the Earl of Burford stood for Parliament in a by-election. He left my employ in April 2000 and then changed his name to Charles Beauclerk. In August 2000 my publisher went into receivership and the manuscript was put away. It was soon buried under other papers.

Nearly twenty years later, in January 2018, I was assembling papers for my next deposit in my literary Archive at the Albert Sloman

Library, University of Essex and came across *Visions of England*. As a celebration of places in England it looked perfect for the UK's post-Brexit time. I immediately saw that my poetic treatment of the places reflected aspects of England's history and culture. I contacted Charles Beauclerk and he gave his blessing to the selection remaining under the byline of 'the Earl of Burford' as he had still been known as the Earl of Burford when he made the selection. I am delighted that *Visions of England* can at last see the light of day.

Shakespeare asked the 3rd Earl of Southampton to support his poems 'Venus and Adonis' and 'The Rape of Lucrece' in two letters/dedications written in 1593 and 1594 (the only letters by Shakespeare that have survived, both written to the 3rd Earl of Southampton), and just over 400 years later the 3rd Earl of Southampton's descendant made a selection of my poems in Tudor Otley Hall, which Southampton is thought to have visited. Of the many remarkable events that have happened in my life, this is one of the more extraordinary.

In the visionary tradition of the Metaphysical poets; Blake; and Shelley
My "visions" are rooted in the 17th-century Metaphysical poets, especially Marvell – as can be seen in 'A Metaphysical in Marvell's Garden'.

The title *Visions of England* echoes volume 12 of my poetic works, *Visions Near the Gates of Paradise*, and looks back to Blake's "fourfold vision" (for example, in my 'Beauty and Angelhood'); to his critique of the materialist outlook in his letter to Butts in 1802, "May God us keep/From Single vision & Newton's sleep"; and to his 'Visions of the Daughters of Albion' ('Albion' being another word for 'England' and the name of the road in which I then lived). I must point out that Blake's daughters' visions were troubled whereas my visions were in harmony with Nature and the universe.

My 'visions' also looked back to the 1845 painting by Joseph Severn of Shelley composing *Prometheus Unbound* in the Baths of Caracalla in Rome in early 1819, in which he is sitting in a historical setting with his mind elsewhere, seeing something "otherwise than by ordinary sight", setting down an imaginative vision.

In *Visions of England* I show an England that is a green and pleasant land as in Blake's 'Jerusalem' but has its own culture within European culture. And the last two poems of this selection, written in December 1998 and May 1999, anticipate feelings that the UK faced being fragmented and might need an English Liberation Front, the discontented outlook that led to the vote for Brexit in 2016. In 1991, in *The Fire and the Stones*, I had prophesied that the European Community would become an integrated United States of Europe, which the EU's European Commission now want to create, and several of the poems in this selection can now be seen to have been prophetic in anticipating Brexit and to accord with the current English mood of independence.

Since 1999 I have had all 34 of my poetic volumes published – *Collected Poems 1958–2005* (1,478 poems, 2006) contained the first 30 volumes, and volumes 31–34 appeared in *Life Cycle and Other New Poems 2006–2016* (206 new poems, 2016) – along with *Classical Odes* (318 poems, 2006), a total of 2,002 poems in all; and I have written a second epic poem *Armageddon* (2010) about the War on Terror (9/11, Iraq and Afghanistan, 25,000 lines of blank verse). I have also had three more verse plays published. Now, looking back on the poems in *Visions of England* I am struck by their vividness and vitality.

When they appeared in *Collected Poems: A White Radiance*, in *Collected Poems 1958–2005* and in *Classical Odes* – the last four poems in this selection are classical odes – they were accompanied by sometimes extensive notes, and readers who want to know more about poems such as 'Beauty and Angelhood' can consult these. Withholding the notes emphasises the involvement of the spirit and its visions, intensifies the poems' spiritual focus and brings out their vividness and the vitality of their rhythms. In a few instances – following Ricks' advice in 1979 that I should amend like Tennyson – I have made minor amendments to the original versions of poems.

When I was discovering myself as a poet in Japan while writing 'The Silence', I was accompanied during my afternoon walks in the hot sun by my shadow, a constant companion that became an image for the future wise self I hoped I was heading towards and (in my mind then) would become in my old age. Now, at 78, looking back from the wisdom of my Shadow which I believe I have become, I marvel that Providence, in its wisdom, left me sufficiently clear of public duties to have time to write my works. I cannot help feeling that I did well to spend long hours writing at my desk with (wherever I was living) an inspiring view of my garden, a corner of the universe whose seasonal growth and decay nourished my soul with its vitality just as rustic surroundings nourished the souls of Nature hermits – and Marvell – in bygone times.

The picture of me on the front cover, taken without my knowledge on 14 April 1986, shows me sitting near the cottage believed to have been the "dwelling" of Wordsworth's Solitary, Blea Tarn House between Little Langdale and Great Langdale in England's Lake District, and opening to an imaginative vision that would become 'At Blea Tarn House' (15–16 April 1986, not in this selection) and 'At Cartmel Priory:

Taming the Unicorn' (written on 18 April 1986, in this selection). It is a modern equivalent of Severn's picture of Shelley writing in the Baths of Caracalla in Rome (see p.xix [of *Visions of England*]), and my eyes, too, are in imaginative vision within an inspiring landscape.

15–16, 21, 24, 26, 31 January, 1–3, 5 February 2018

49

Fools' Paradise

The Voyage of a Ship of Fools from Europe
A Mock-Heroic Poem on Brexit

Preface
The Mock-Heroic Tradition

Social satire
The first tutorial I had with Christopher Ricks in the early summer of 1959, 60 years ago, he took me out to a seat in the Worcester College gardens on a warm summer morning and asked me what poems I liked. I said, "Mystical poems about the universe as in Wordsworth, Blake and Shelley." He said, "I shall teach you to like social satire." From the very outset we had different casts of mind but I was open to his guidance and embraced Swift, Dryden and Pope.

The tradition of mock-heroic verse
The tradition of mock-heroic verse is a long one. It looks back to the elevated heroic style of the classical epic poems of Homer (*The Iliad* and *The Odyssey*) and Virgil (*The Aeneid*) and more recently Milton's *Paradise Lost*, all of which were unrhymed, and adapts it to a trivial subject to suggest the unheroic character of the modern age. It satirises epic poetry, and it arguably began with an anonymous burlesque of Homer's *The Iliad* in the ancient world, *Batrachomyomachia* (*Battle of the Frogs and the Mice*), which was perhaps written in the 4th century BC but may not have been written until the 2nd century AD. In the battle between the frogs and the mice Zeus proposes that the gods take sides and tries to persuade Athena to help the mice.

In English Literature social satire looks back to the narrative poems of Chaucer. The naïve narrators in *The Book of the Duchess* (1368–1369) and *The House of Fame* (1378–1381) satirise the narrator-guide relationship of Dante and Virgil in Dante's *Divine Comedy* (1308–1320). *The Parliament of Birds* (*Parlement of Foules*, 1378–1381) satirises the social classes, which are represented by different birds. Chaucer lived on the fringe of political intrigue and was very alert to the politics of his day, having in 1366 married the sister (Philippa Roet) of Katharine Swynford, the love of the Lancastrian John of Gaunt's life and last wife, and having held public office during the power struggle between the Houses of Lancaster and York for the succession after Edward III's death in 1377, which led to the Wars of the Roses. (Gaunt's son eventually became Henry IV.)

The tradition of mock-heroic being applied to English politicians in English literature looks back to Dryden's 'Absalom and Achitophel' (1681), which is in rhymed heroic couplets. It deals in allegorical form (scriptural disguises) with Lord Shaftesbury's party's attempt to exclude the Duke of York from the succession and replace him with the Duke of Monmouth. Dryden wrote the poem to influence the outcome (then in the balance) by revealing the true characters of the politicians he described, most notably Shaftesbury (the false tempter Achitophel) and Monmouth (Absalom).

The mock-heroic approach was adopted by 'modern' writers seeking to ridicule contemporary classicists, the 'ancients', as in Nicolas Boileau's mock-heroic poem '*Le Lutrin*' ('The Lectern', 1674–1683) in which a quarrel between two ecclesiastics about where to place a lectern in a chapel ends in a battle in a bookstore, with books by 'ancient' and 'modern' authors being flung about by the two ecclesiastics. Jonathan Swift varied this theme in 'The Battle of the Books', part of the *prolegomena* to *A Tale of a Tub* (1704), which is in mock-heroic prose.

Alexander Pope's 'The Rape of the Lock' (1712–1714) is in heroic couplets. It was first published in two cantos and then enlarged to five cantos. It describes a society beau's trivial cutting of a lock of hair from the head of a society belle as if it were comparable to the abduction of Helen which began the Trojan War. Lord Petre cuts a lock of Miss Arabella Fermor's hair, causing a quarrel between the two families, and Pope seeks to allay this quarrel on the model of Boileau's '*Le Lutrin*'. He shows Belinda (Arabella Fermor) at her dressing-table, at a game of *ombre*, and drinking coffee, when her lock is snipped. He shows her wrath and describes how the lock becomes a new star in the sky.

The first two versions of Pope's mock-heroic poem *The Dunciad* ('book of dunces'), bks I–III, were published anonymously in 1728 and 1729, and Pope acknowledged authorship in 1735. Bk IV was added in 1742 and a revised version of all four books was published in 1743. *The Dunciad* celebrates the goddess Dulness and the progress of her chosen dunces (including many of his contemporary poets), who filled Great Britain with chaotic ignorance and tasteless drivel.

My interpretation of the mock-heroic tradition

I came to mock-heroic after writing my epic poem *Overlord* (1994–1996), which is about the Second World War from D-Day to the Fall of Berlin, with Eisenhower as its hero (41,000 lines of blank verse); and again after the publication of my second epic poem, *Armageddon* (2008–2009), which is about the War on Terror after 9/11, especially the wars in Afghanistan and Iraq, with George W. Bush as its hero (25,000 lines of blank verse). Having adopted an elevated tone in these two epics I was able to use epic devices such as invocations to the Muse and supernatural interventions in my mock-heroic.

In my interpretation of mock-heroic I have followed Dryden's focus on politics but have drawn on Pope's social satire. In 2000 I wrote 'Zeus's Ass' in seven cantos about UK Prime Minister Blair's vacuity and spin. It focuses on Blair's being barracked by an audience of women, all members of the Women's Institute. In 'Zeus's Emperor' (2009/2015, three cantos) I focused on Blair's attempt to be appointed the next President of the European Council ('EU President') in 2009, a post that went to Herman Van Rompuy. Both these poems have political overtones, and they are modern attempts to write in the tradition of Dryden's 'Absalom and Achitophel' and Pope's 'The Rape of the Lock' and *The Dunciad* in rhymed heroic couplets.

In *Fools' Paradise* I have followed the mock-heroic tradition by writing in heroic couplets (rhyming couplets) in iambic pentameters, as in 'Zeus's Ass' and 'Zeus's Emperor'. My basic foot is of course the iamb (◡ –), but I have been alert to stress and when the sense has required I have resorted to trochees (– ◡), anapaests (◡ ◡ –) and dactyls (– ◡ ◡), and occasionally to amphibrachs (◡ – ◡). My poetic notation has been adapted to the demands of conveying international negotiations and the conflicts surrounding them.

In his preface to *Paradise Lost* under a heading *The Verse* Milton champions "English heroic verse without rime, as that of Homer in Greek, and of Virgil in Latin" and laments "the troublesome and modern bondage of riming" which is "the invention of a barbarous age, to set off wretched matter and lame metre". In my two epic poems, *Overlord* and *Armageddon*, I have agreed with Milton's analysis and used unrhymed blank verse, but in 'Zeus's Ass', 'Zeus's Emperor' and now *Fools' Paradise* I have followed the mock-heroic convention established by Dryden and Pope and have submitted myself to the "troublesome... bondage" of rhyme. I have sought to avoid lame metre by varying my iambic feet with trochees, anapaests, dactyls and amphibrachs. I would not disagree that the matter, which has presented itself in the news of the last two-and-a-half years, is "wretched".

Fools' Paradise

In *Fools' Paradise* I focus on Brexit, the most important decision the UK has taken since the declaration of the Second World War, and in particular on the promises of the Brexiteers which led to the referendum's being won by Leave and the non-delivery of their promises and the chaos they caused. Following my presentation of leaders in my other works – Eisenhower and Hitler, George W. Bush and bin Laden, Blair and Van Rompuy – I present the Chequers gathering at which the Chequers proposal was first introduced, the subsequent resignation of two leading Brexiteers, and the slide towards 'no deal' with a hostile European Union being unsympathetic to the British proposal, and the delays to leaving and long-term prospect of staying-in. I show the divisions within the Conservative party and in the country, and the chaotic May leadership which could not enforce collective Cabinet responsibility.

The Conservative leadership and, indeed, the politicians of all parties in Westminster seemed to be unable to agree on what course to take, in what direction the UK public should be led, and lurking behind the poem is the 1494 poem *Ship of Fools* by Sebastian Brant (published in Basel, Switzerland), which describes a voyage of fools who possess all the follies and vices of their time to Narragonia, the Fools' Paradise, which does not exist except in the minds of the captain and the crew. The caption under a later English version of the woodcut of *Ship of Fools* (see p.xxvii [of *Fools' Paradise*]) states that they were bidding "farewell to Europe".

The idea of a ship making a daft voyage is based on Plato's comparison of a philosopher being ignored by society to a ship's captain being ignored by his dysfunctional crew in *The Republic* book 6 (c.380BC), which I had to read in Greek at school. As Plato's description originated the allegory of a Ship of Fools with a dysfunctional crew and also the metaphor of the Ship of State – which was anticipated in the poetry of Alcaeus of Mytilene (621–560), Aeschylus's *Seven Against Thebes* (c.467BC) and Sophocles' *Antigone* (c.441BC) – it is worth quoting:

Suppose the following to be the state of affairs on board a ship or ships. The captain is larger and stronger than any of the crew, but a bit deaf and short-sighted, and doesn't know much about navigation. The crew are all quarrelling with each other about how to navigate the ship, each thinking he ought to be at the helm; they know no navigation and cannot say that anyone ever taught it them, or that they spent any time studying it; indeed they say it can't be taught and are ready to murder anyone who says it can. They spend all their time milling round the captain and trying to get him to give them the wheel. If one faction is more successful than another, their rivals may kill them and throw them overboard, lay out the honest captain with drugs or drink, take control of the ship, help themselves to what's on board, and behave as if they were on a drunken pleasure-cruise. Finally, they reserve their admiration for the man who knows how to lend a hand in controlling the captain by force or fraud; they praise his seamanship and navigation and knowledge of the sea and condemn everyone else as useless. They have no idea that the true navigator must study the seasons of the year, the sky, the stars, the winds and other professional subjects, if he is to be really fit to control a ship; and they think that it's quite impossible to acquire professional skill in navigation (quite apart from whether they want it exercised) and that there's no such thing as an art of navigation. In these circumstances aren't the sailors on any such ship bound to regard the true navigator as a gossip and a star-gazer, of no use to them at all?

In the woodcut of *Ship of Fools* the captain, crew and passengers all wear jester's hats and the captain is on the prow pointing forward and calling to the other fools. They are not looking at him or listening to him, they are too busy pushing a fool overboard or drinking wine, and those at the helm at the rear of the ship have their back to him and are steering in a different direction. The fools are already fighting among themselves, and mutiny is not far off. It is a truly chaotic voyage.

The metaphor of the Ship of State was carried forward by Horace (*Odes* 1.14) and in more modern poetry, for example Longfellow's "Sail on, O Ship of State" in 'The Building of the Ship' (quoted by Churchill in a speech on 13 April 1941).

Brexit
The British attempt to exit the European Union has dominated the newspapers since the 2016 UK referendum. In 2017 44% of the UK's trade (worth £274 billion) was with the EU, the most significant trading bloc in the world. The UK electorate voted to walk away from half the UK's income to make better trading arrangements with the US, India, China and the Commonwealth countries. Continuing alignment with the EU would make these new trading arrangements impossible. However, continuing alignment with the EU seemed inevitable as the only way to preserve a frictionless border between Northern Ireland and the EU without turning the Irish Sea into a border, separating Northern Ireland from the rest of the UK and breaking the UK up and without preventing Scotland from declaring independence was to remain in the EU. Consequently the UK could not agree on how to implement the new trading arrangements. The European Commission was disinclined to reach a deal with the UK

as it did not want any of the other 27 member-states following the UK's example and breaking away.

The momentum in the EU was now for more integration and for allowing more European nation-states to join. With Russia threatening the Baltic states a United States of Europe was looming with its own army and defence, and it seemed that the UK had turned towards isolationism at a time when most European nation-states were preparing to resist a menacing Russia. The UK seemed to be sailing against the tide of history. The negotiations led to an impasse and parallels were drawn with the miscalculation that led to the Suez crisis, which lasted for several weeks.

Today the world order seems to be breaking down – hence the momentum for integration within the EU. The US, leader of the West for most of the 20th century, has turned inwards and unpredictable and stands for 'America First'. Putin menaces unpredictably on Europe's eastern front. China is showing signs of expansionism in the South China Sea and in Africa, and is engaging in a trade war with the US. To believe that the UK can have a greater influence on world events on its own than it could as part of the integrationist EU when the world order is breaking down is seen by many to be a fantasy.

Essentially Brexit has been a battleground between conflicting ideologies: between supranationalism and nationalism. Neither Brexit nor Trump's nationalistic isolationism will deflect the rise of a coming World State.

Dialectic between opposites

As I wrote in the Preface to my masque *King Charles the Wise*, in all my works there is a dialectic in which two opposites are reconciled in a unity in accordance with the algebraic formula I found when living in the East, $+A + -A = 0$. My two masques conform to a dialectic involving disorder and order. *The Dream of Europa* celebrated 70 years of peace achieved by the EU; and *King Charles the Wise* celebrated the UK's new global role that could lead to universal peace. Both contradictory masques would be reconciled within a coming World State.

I pointed out that *King Charles the Wise*'s view of the UK's post-Brexit future would be contradicted by *Fools' Paradise*, which would be about the UK's departure from the European Union. I said that both would be reconciled within a coming World State. It is worth quoting my exact words to make my message clear:

Similarly, this masque about the UK's post-Brexit future, *King Charles the Wise*, will be contradicted by its opposite, a mock-heroic long poem in progress about the circumstances surrounding the UK's departure from the European Union, *Fools' Paradise*, and both are similarly reconciled within the World State.

I did not start writing the "long poem in progress" until 7 August 2018. I wrote the first five cantos and the first two sections of canto VI in Charlestown, Cornwall between 7 and 17 August 2018. The poem was only supposed to be seven cantos like 'Zeus's Ass'. I was clear that I should start with the Chequers plan but Prime Minister May's delaying kept prolonging the negotiations and therefore my poem, and I needed to wait for the outcome. I wrote the last six cantos and the Epilogue between August and December 2018 and rhymed from some way into canto IX to the third section of canto XII between 19 December 2018 and 1 January 2019. I added cantos XIII and XIV and redistributed the text of cantos XI–XIV to even out the length of the sections on 30 January 2019, added more in February and March and completed the poem on 12 April. I redistributed the text of cantos XIII and XIV to even the length in the evening of 12 April. I completed the amendments on 16 April 2019.

In *Fools' Paradise* I present the Brexiteers – and all the politicians – as being on a Ship of Fools. Both *King Charles the Wise* and *Fools' Paradise* would have their contradictions reconciled within a coming World State. In my ongoing dialectic of opposites I am following a method Blake used: his *Songs of Innocence* and *Songs of Experience* contained opposite views (symbolised by the innocent gentle lamb and the experienced savage tiger) which were fundamentally reconciled in the underlying unity that contains both.

So am I for or against Brexit? I am neither. I present both sides in *King Charles the Wise* and *Fools' Paradise*. I am like the reporter who is sent to the Emirates Stadium to report on Arsenal's latest home match and reflects what happens with a degree of objectivity. I may be an Arsenal supporter, but in my report I am balanced and present an objective view of the performance of both sides in the game. Although Brexiteers may be aggrieved by the mock-heroic tone of this work and by my dwelling on the Ship of Fools, they will find their case presented in my work as a whole, for example in the words of Britannia in *King Charles the Wise*. I look beyond the pros and cons of Brexit for both are ultimately reconciled within a World State.

The UK belongs to the European civilisation
In *The Fire and the Stones* and later in *The Rise and Fall of Civilizations* I have shown that the UK belongs to the European civilisation. The UK

and the European nation-states share a common heritage in belonging to the Roman Empire and in medieval Catholicism and the Reformation. I show that 25 civilisations, including the European civilisation, all pass through 61 similar stages and share a unified pattern. They rise and fall in a rainbow-like parabola. I show that they rise round their 'central idea', a metaphysical vision of the Fire or Light that is embodied in religion and reflected in European literature by poets such as Dante, Milton, the Metaphysical poets and T.S. Eliot, and they fall through secularisation.

During this fall they pass into my stage 43, a Union (in the case of the European civilisation currently the European Union), and stage 44, in which there is syncretism as religious sects draw together in the shadow of a new conglomerate (the EU) and espouse Universalism, which in one of its tenets sees the Fire or Light as the common source of all religions.

In stage 45 there is a rejection of the present, a reassertion of the national perspective, a yearning for the nation's lost past and a revival of cultural purity as has happened in the Arab world with IS's longing to return to the 7th century AD – and, in a less violent way, in the UK with Brexiteers' longing to opt out of the European civilisation and return to the conditions of the British Empire. In stage 46 civilisations pass into a federation. In our time the Soviet Union passed into the Russian Federation, and eventually the European Union will pass into the European Federation, as the United Kingdom can be expected to do. (I wrote in *The Fire and the Stones*, 1991, of the "dismemberment of the United Kingdom when Ireland is reunited with the European conglomerate", and it remains to be seen whether in view of the backstop this was prophetic.)

The role of the true poet
The true poet timelessly reflects the central idea of his civilisation even when the civilisation is in decline and heading for its end (when it will be absorbed into another civilisation as the ancient Mesopotamian and Egyptian civilisations were absorbed into the Islamic Arab civilisation). The true poet stands apart from society even more than the Church and channels the mystic Fire or Light into his civilisation in his poems. The true poet – such as Dante, Milton, the Metaphysical poets, the Augustan and Romantic poets, and T.S. Eliot – beams metaphysical Reality into his society, and does not shrink from criticising the aims and goals of the Government of the day as I did in *The Dream of Europa* and *King Charles the Wise*, and do now in *Fools' Paradise*.

The role of the true European poet is to be a truth-bearer in a mendacious Age, to make a principled stand for true values and to reflect the driving force and central idea of European society to its regional readers. In the past poets have been exiled by their civilisation's rulers for telling the truth as in the Roman civilisation Ovid was exiled by Augustus, which I covered in my verse play *Ovid Banished*. The role of the true poet is not to flatter those in authority but to hold them to account for their misdeeds, using the time-honoured, tried-and-tested form of social satire. Both Byron (in the 'Dedication' to *Don Juan*) and Shelley attacked Castlereagh, the British Foreign Secretary and Leader of the House of Commons from 1812 to 1822.

The true European poet uses language in a truthful and unmendacious way, which conflicts with politicians' bland and deceptive use of language. I knew Sir John Biggs-Davison for many years. He succeeded Winston Churchill as my MP and sent me a ticket to hear Prime Minister Eden speak in the main Suez debate in the Commons on 12 September 1956. He invited me to the Commons on many occasions and said I had had experience in Libya and elsewhere that would be valuable in the House, and on several occasions hinted that one day I might become his successor. When he announced his impending retirement due to ill health in 1988 he asked me via an intermediary if I wanted my name to go forward to succeed him. I said no. I had more than fifty books to write and I had chosen to be an author and for me that was the right decision. I knew that Andrew Marvell was an MP at various times between 1659 and 1678 as well as a Metaphysical poet, but I would not have been happy to use language to obfuscate as politicians often do, as a smokescreen. The true poet uses language to reflect experience with clarity, and although ambiguity and verbal play have a place in poetry, conveys experience of the universe with integrity and is wary of politicians' dissembling language.

I wrote about the role of the poet in my letter to Ted Hughes of 28 March 1994, which is in my *Selected Letters*. It was a reply to a long letter Ted Hughes wrote me on 19 March 1994 which appeared in *Letters of Ted Hughes* (selected and edited by Christopher Reid, Faber & Faber, 2007). Hughes was Poet Laureate at the time, and I discussed the Poet Laureate's role with him:

Traditionally the Archbishop of Canterbury provided the context of the Fire or Light for the monarch which makes possible the divine right of kings. The present incumbent at Canterbury, I am reliably informed by a friend of the woman who designed it, did not understand why his enthronement robe showed flames of Fire. (The designer knew of *The Fire and the Stones*.)

Where is the true poet in relation to the procession? The Church no longer fulfils its traditional function and so needs to be prompted by the true poet, who like Dante is actually positioned higher than the Archbishop in relation to Reality, for in his high dream (which he receives in obscurity and isolation) he has the vision and passes it on, as did Dante (the sempiternal rose, the Light of Glory). When a civilisation is still growing, the poet and Church co-exist in harmony, the one reinforcing the other as did Dante. When the parabola turns down and the civilisation declines into secularisation and materialism, the Church goes with it, *but the true poet's vision remains constant, the poet stands firm*; apart, calling the monarch and the people to adhere to the vision of the civilisation's central idea, as Yeats and Eliot did to some extent. The Church has become materialistic and secularised, and being apart, the poet becomes Universalist (see stage 44 in *The Fire and the Stones*, which today reflects our new identity in the European Union, the advent of which I first predicted in 1967).

Most poets are not true poets; they are not inspired '*rsis*', and the high vision is not to be found in their work. In each generation the true poets need to find their way to the front so that they can endeavour to offer to the people the direction the Church traditionally provided. They're fighting a losing battle because the civilisation is in progressive decline and is therefore continually moving further away from its central idea which it is less and less interested in, but in each generation if a few can get the message across they hold the line and temporarily arrest further decline.

The true poet is therefore a fairly unwelcome presence at the coronation, as he offers his Holy Water and points to the light in the basket from which the Archbishop derives his authority and [which he] prefers to ignore. I would say your role as Poet Laureate is to ignore the Archbishop and represent the civilisation's central idea to the monarch, and to embody Reality. To interpret the role in purely social-rational terms would be a dereliction of duty in relation to your sacred office; just as, for all his wit, polish and good humour, being a great entertainer like Betjeman and striking a poetic echo with the masses was, for all its entertaining popularisation, a dereliction of duty in relation to the sacred office. I can see the role you can perform very clearly.

I said something similar in an earlier letter to Christopher Ricks of 4 May 1991, which is also in my *Selected Letters*:

I thought you might be interested in the change in the role of the poet which the Metaphysical Revolution seeks to bring about. The poet is no longer a marginal or peripheral entertainer. As the metaphysical poet renews the vision of the Fire which is crucial to our civilisation's renewal and survival (see *The Fire and the Stones*), he is once again a central figure. The Metaphysical Revolution brings a new importance to the writing of poetry so long as it keeps society in touch with its central vision.

So in such a crisis for the European civilisation as the departure of the UK from the coming United States of Europe the role of the true poet is to keep the European civilisation in touch with its central vision of the Fire or Light and to tell the truth to imperfect politicians without being locked up in the Tower of London like the first Metaphysical poet, Sir Walter Raleigh, who wrote his *History of the World* during his thirteen years of incarceration in three rooms in the Bloody Tower, and without being banished beyond the civilised world like Ovid.

In *The Dream of Europa* (2015) I showed a united Europe celebrating 70 years of peace within the European civilisation and a fractious UK representative being told off by *Churchill,* who called for a United States of Europe in Zurich in 1946. What this UK representative said anticipated Brexit. In *King Charles the Wise* I wrote about the UK's post-Brexit global role outside an increasingly integrated European Union. (The UK is still, and will always continue to be, within the European civilisation.) And now in *Fools' Paradise* I write about the UK's departure from Europe (while remaining within the European civilisation), and look forward to the unification of all extant civilisations in a democratic World State that will reconcile all the world's conflicts, including the conflict between Leave and Remain. In doing this I revert to the traditional role of the true poet who is a central, not a marginal or peripheral, figure who keeps society in touch with its central vision and points the way – calls on the UK to go forward from its reasserting of national independence to participating in a global democracy.

In all times the true European poet reflects the central idea of the European civilisation as did Dante, Goethe, Milton and Eliot, but in the present time secularised readers who do not know the Fire or Light may not recognise or understand the truth of his vision. It is a fact of life that the true Metaphysical poet is today scarcely recognised within a civilisation that has lost contact with and ceased to recognise its own metaphysical central idea, and therefore may not be welcome at State events.

My Universalism
But I am above all a Universalist poet. Universalism focuses on humankind's position in the whole universe and sees all disciplines

as interconnected wholes. I reflect the unity of the universe that is expressed in its literary, philosophical, historical, mystical, religious, political (in the sense of 'international politics and statecraft') and cultural disciplines – and reconcile the conflicting sides of all dialectical arguments. In this respect I understand the mind-set of Zeus, the reconciler of all who as I show in *King Charles the Wise* wants a World State – see my *World State* and *World Constitution* (both 2018) – and who appears again in this work. As an artist I identify with all conflict, but like a good Universalist I am aware of the bigger picture beyond conflicts, the reconciling context of a coming World State.

I have a bust of Apollo at the foot of the spiral staircase to my study here at Connaught House – Apollo is the god of the Light who inspires holistic poems in structured form and metre as opposed to the raw energy and free verse inspired by Dionysus – and I am now seeking a complementary bust or statue of Zeus to place on the balcony outside my window to remind me that my overriding concern in my contemplation of the universe and the role of Brexit is to reconcile all conflicting points of view and opposites in an underlying unity, in the true Universalist manner.

27 August, 9–14 September, 3 October 2018;
3–4, 17 January, 1, 5, 15–16 April, 3, 9 May 2019

50

Selected Letters

Nicholas Hagger's Letters on his 55 Literary and Universalist Works

Preface
The Epistolary Tradition and Universal Truth

The tradition of letter-writing
The letter has always been a universal literary form. Roman letters were often addressed to historical people, and Horace's epistles (published in two books in 20BC and 14BC), Ovid's letters from exile, Seneca's epistolary guide to Stoic initiates and Pliny the Younger's letters that included a letter to the historian Tacitus on the eruption of Vesuvius in AD79 all seem to have been written for publication rather than for posting. Cicero's letters to Atticus show that political discussion was natural in a friendly letter. The self-revelation and self-representation of the letter-writer were appreciated. Seneca wrote to Lucilius, "I thank you for... revealing your real self to me in the only way you can. I never receive a letter from you without being in your company forthwith." *Moral Letters* (*Ad Lucilium Epistulae Morales*), 40.1.

The great age of letter-writing was the 18th century when postal services expanded and the epistolary novel emerged. Letter-writers described the self and explored everyday experience. Alexander Pope's letters to Jonathan Swift, William Fortescue and Lady Mary Wortley Montague (just three of many correspondents) were modelled on Horace's gently-satirical epistles and conveyed informality and spontaneity. Pope published from his own correspondence in his lifetime, and we know he revised and edited his letters as his translation of *The Iliad* was written on the backs of his edited personal letters. Samuel Richardson's *Pamela* and *Clarissa* and Fanny Burney's *Evelina* promoted letter-writing as a cultural activity. Both 18th-century letters and the Roman letters on which many were modelled sought to convey the ideal of universal virtue by which society was expected to live.

More recently, letter-writing has had to compete with the writing of literary works. Writers as different as Wordsworth, Keats, Iris Murdoch and Hemingway wrote letters when they were not writing literary works, and the arrival of emails has led to abridged, functional letters written against time. Some writers believed in replying to every letter they received, as did Darwin. I have always regarded readers as having a right to write to writers about their works and to receive a reply. I have always said that it's like asking a question at the end of a lecture. Everyone should have the right to ask one question, and the writer should reply courteously.

The best letters have something to say and express it clearly and directly, and writers' letters are often about aspects of their works. Keats' letters throw light on his works, as does his letter on "negative capability" to his brothers George and Tom Keats of 22 December 1818. Ted Hughes' letters – I was the recipient of several between 1993 and 1999 – focused on things he wanted to know that related to his writing in some (sometimes obscure) way.

Selected Letters *and Universalism*

These letters by a man of letters are all literary letters in so far as they refer to, and throw light on, my 50 books and on the development of my Universalism, which imbues them. I write within seven disciplines: literature, mysticism, philosophy and the sciences, history, comparative religion, international politics and statecraft, and world culture. My Universalism focuses on the oneness of the universe and the fundamental unity of all apparently diverse disciplines, each of which must be seen as a whole that is itself within a greater whole. So I see the fundamental unity of all literature, the common essence of all religions in the mystic Light, the whole of recorded history as the rise and fall of 25 civilisations and the whole of international politics in a coming Universalist World State. I have symbolised this unity behind diversity as a rainbow, which has seven bands of apparently diverse colours that together form one rainbow.

I have also symbolised the unity behind diversity as the seven-branched antlers of a stag. One of the antlers symbolises the seven disciplines, the other symbolises the seven branches of literature in which I have written: poems and poetic epics; verse plays and masques; short stories and novellas; diaries; autobiographies; letters; and my statement of the fundamental theme of world literature in *A New Philosophy of Literature*.

My Universalist approach to literature is innovatory. My published literary works include: 2,000 poems, two epic poems, five verse plays, two masques and 1,200 short stories. In the course of my long quest for the One as a latter-day Metaphysical poet, I have departed from literature to make more detailed studies of the philosophical, historical and political aspects of the universe and have produced innovative works of philosophy, history and international politics and statecraft. I have explored the place of metaphysics within philosophy; the rise-and-fall pattern of European civilisation within the world's civilisations; and the progress of European nation-states towards a World State. All these more detailed views have supplemented my poetic quest.

I have sought to be a Metaphysical poet, man of letters, philosopher, cultural historian, and writer on contemporary international politics. In my works I have tried to reflect the Age.

Recipients of these letters
These letters were written over a period of nearly 60 years and many of the recipients are now dead. They include some prominent national and international figures: well-known writers and critics such as Frank Tuohy, Christopher Ricks, Kathleen Raine and Ted Hughes; the historian Asa Briggs; the Continental philosopher Chris Macann; and several well-known politicians. A glance down the list of letters in the Contents reveals a number of well-known names in all walks of life.

Asa Briggs remarked on reading my two autobiographies *My Double Life 1: This Dark Wood* and *My Double Life 2: A Rainbow over the Hills* that I seem to know the top people in many fields. My correspondents include: a Professor of Poetry at Oxford, two Poet Laureates, a colleague of Einstein's, a collaborator with Hawking, Montgomery and his aide, a Bletchley Park code-breaker, the rediscoverer of Jamestown, the Head Master of Eton, England's cricket captain, an Oscar-winning actor, an earl descended from the Earl of Southampton (Shakespeare's patron), and the Queen's representatives in East Anglia.

There are letters to: academics, actors and actresses, archaeologists, aristocrats, artists, courtiers, diplomats, educationalists, farmers, film-makers, historians, philosophers, poets, politicians, Royals, scientists, Shakespearean scholars, soldiers and writers.

A list of the recipients' brief biographical details can be found on p.929 [of *Selected Letters*].

Principles behind this selection
These letters all refer to one or more of my works. I have written many letters that do not mention my works, for example to members of my family at different times of my life, including weekly letters from Oxford, Iraq, Japan and Libya. These are not included as they do not refer to my works.

These letters track my literary development and the development of my thinking about Universalism; and of my metaphysical thinking. They contain many insights, for example into my thinking about classical epic poems. All were written without any thought of publication.

These letters cover six decades. They are arranged chronologically, not under individual books or disciplines, and it is important to stress that they surfaced out of my life. They therefore reflect situations and issues that were current in my life at a particular time, some of which gave rise to my works.

Looking through my letters I am amazed at how many throw light on my books. Each of the letters in this volume contributes something to understanding.

Selected Letters *and my works*
These letters have been selected because they touch on aspects of my works and add to the reader's knowledge about them. The development of my poetic method can be tracked, as can the development of my thinking about Universalism in seven disciplines and the unification of knowledge. Situations in different parts of my life are backdrops in some of the letters. As I have already said, these letters were not written for publication. They were interactive engagements with the recipients. Following in the tradition of Alexander Pope, who also edited his own letters as we have seen, I have added asterisked editorial notes to illumine what may otherwise be obscure.

I should point out that *Selected Letters* is to have a companion volume, *Collected Prefaces*. In 1991 I revived the Preface, as I wrote to Tony Little on 3 May 1991, and most of my books contain a Preface like this one. My two *Collected Poems* and three *Selected Poems*, two epic poems and my *Collected Verse Plays* all have Prefaces in the tradition of Wordsworth's *Preface to the Lyrical Ballads* (1801/1802) and Shelley's Preface-like 'A Defence of Poetry' (1840). Another *entrée* into my works and the development of my Universalism can be gained by reading all my Prefaces in conjunction with each other.

Universalism and universal truth
In all my Universalist writings I have pursued universal truth. In other words, I have seen poems, short stories and other works as statements – descriptions – of aspects of a Reality that is always true. At a mundane physical level, it is always true that flowers and trees grow from seeds and that the sun rises every day. At a metaphysical level it is always true that the universe is a unity, and that the soul can relate to the Reality that is always One and reveals itself as the Light. Our lives are surrounded by opposites – day and night, life and death, time and eternity – but it is a universal truth that all contradictions are reconciled within the underlying unity of the universe. Universal truth takes us to the order within the universe, and the similes and linkings,

contrasts and contradictions within the titles of my poems and short stories are glimpses and revelations of its fundamental unity.

There are many instances in these letters where my interpretation and elucidation of my writings reveals the fundamental unity of the universe, and therefore of all apparently different disciplines. In the course of writing about my books to correspondents from different disciplines I am never far from touching on the metaphysical oneness of the universe and the Reality which is the Light. And so, whether a letter is about my literature, mysticism, philosophy and the sciences, history, religion, international politics and statecraft or world culture, there is often an underlying interaction with universal truth. Collectively, these letters make a statement about how to approach life and about its meaning; and about how a poet reflects the Age.

The epistolary tradition's early emphasis on virtue was an approach to universal truth in a time of formalised religion when society was expected to follow standards of virtue. Since the 18th century, advances in science and metaphysical thinking about Reality have widened the approach to universal truth, which now includes a way of perception, a way of looking, a perspective that is a consequence of direct mystical experience.

Approach to my works
Looking back at the early letters I am struck by how definite I was in my early years, in the sense of direction my work needed to follow. This sense of direction is present in the first (fateful) letter. I have gone on my own solitary way, always focusing on the next work. I am also struck by the clarity with which I saw my own destiny nearly 60 years ago: to quest for and find the metaphysical Light overseas and reflect it in my works, to find a way of doing this and to contribute to arresting the decline of Western civilisation, which in *The Fire and the Stones* I hold to thrive when the Light is widely seen and to decline when it is not. I have always regarded the true poet as the saviour of his civilisation by keeping the tradition of the Light going, and I say this to Ted Hughes in my letter of 28 March 1994. I am for the most part very sure of my views, and in this letter I am not averse to telling the Poet Laureate of the day what his role should be. This sureness may be a consequence of metaphysical living.

In individual letters again and again I get to the heart of one of my books by explaining (or describing) to a correspondent what it is about in a couple of lines. These explanations (or descriptions) must form part of my collected *oeuvre*, which is like 50 pieces of an interlocking jigsaw that convey a picture. The picture these letters convey via my books is of a unified, metaphysically-interactive universe. These letters describe our civilisation and universe in different terms from those used in the media, and present and hold up a vision of the universe whose Reality and Truth are points of reference that we must never lose.

The vision of Reality I found in seven disciplines can be found here along with the true meaning of Universalism. My final *oeuvre* would not be complete without my approach to my works in these letters and the illuminations they provide.

2, 9–13 December 2018; 14 January; 20 April; 9 May 2019

51

The Coronation of King Charles

The Triumph of Universal Harmony
A Masque

Preface
A Coronation Masque, the Carolingian Age and
Universal Harmony

Masques

The early European masques were court entertainments and often celebrated royal marriages. The English masques of the 16th- and early 17th-centuries were performed in the Banqueting Hall of the Whitehall Palace, often over Christmas or on Twelfth Night, and later in the Banqueting House, which was built between 1619 and 1622 and replaced the Banqueting Hall.

Between 1605 and 1631 Ben Jonson wrote 28 masques (starting with *The Masque of Blackness* and finishing with *Chloridia*), and this long run is closely associated with the site of the Banqueting House, the last surviving room of the Whitehall Palace through which Charles I walked to his execution. It has a fine ceiling painted by Rubens showing his father James I being taken to Heaven by angels, and he stopped and looked up at it before leaving the Palace through a first-floor sash-window to be beheaded on a high scaffold erected in the street outside.

Coronation processions and pageant entertainments

In the early days coronations were celebrated with pageant entertainments rather than masques. These took place in streets during coronation processions. During her coronation procession Elizabeth I was carried through the streets of London from the Tower to Westminster on a golden litter from which she viewed five pageant entertainments in Gracechurch Street; Cornhill; Soper's Lane; Little Conduit in Cheapside; and the Conduit along Fleet Street. This happened on Saturday 14 January 1559, the day before her coronation.

James I's coronation procession passed under seven triumphal archways in the city of London on its way to the Palace at Whitehall and he viewed pageant entertainments under all seven arches: under a Londinium arch at the east end of Fenchurch Street (which focused on the monarchy); an Italian arch in Gracechurch Street (which focused on succession, continuity and unity); a Dutch arch at the Royal Exchange, Cornhill (which focused on foreign policy); an arch above Great Conduit in Cheapside (which showed *Arabia Britannica*); an arch close to Little Conduit, Cheapside (which portrayed peace and bounty); an arch above the Conduit along Fleet Street (which addressed the new world), where the dramatist Thomas Middleton made a speech; and an arch at Temple Bar, a representation of the Temple of Janus (which portrayed power, peace and wealth). See Michelle Castelletti, *A Picture of Pageantry and the Arches of Triumph*, and its lengthy bibliography of primary and secondary sources.

It is reported that Thomas Dekker wrote pageant entertainments for five of these archways (half the total performance) and that Ben Jonson wrote two (for Fenchurch Street and Temple Bar, the other half of the total performance) – and that as he devised four of the seven archways Ben Jonson preferred to ignore Dekker's contribution in a subsequent book of his two pageant entertainments titled *Part of the King's Entertainment in Passing to his Coronation*.

James I's coronation took place on 25 July 1603, but because of an outbreak of the plague his ceremonial procession through the city of London was postponed until 15 March 1604. (As the new calendar year began on 25 March in England at that time, the procession was originally recorded as happening in 1603.)

The Coronation of King Charles: *a masque with three pageant entertainments*
In this masque on the coronation of King Charles III I have revived the tradition of pageant entertainments, which was last in use in 1661.

This tradition was in operation in 1377 when the 10-year-old Richard II was crowned, and it was in use in the coronations of Elizabeth I and James I as we have just seen, and of Charles I and Charles II (1661). Their pageant entertainments took place on street corners when their coronation processions stopped. James II abandoned the tradition of pageant entertainments to pay for jewels for his Queen, Mary of Modena. A sketch of William III's coronation procession shows the Banqueting House in the background, but by then there were no pageant entertainments. Since then there have been processions at every coronation, but no pageant entertainments. There are three pageant entertainments in *The Coronation of King Charles*.

In *The Coronation of King Charles* I have combined the masque and pageant entertainments. The three pageant entertainments are within a masque form that is traditionally in five sections: prologue; antimasque (a spectacle of disorder and chaos); masque (which transforms the disorder into order and harmony and provides a resolution); revels (which rejoice at the resolution) and epilogue. The three pageant entertainments are in the prologue, antimasque and masque.

The Coronation of King Charles is set in the Banqueting House, and Ben Jonson would recognise the approach of his masques and his pageant entertainments in this work. In *The Coronation of King Charles* I have moved the pageant entertainments from street corners into the Banqueting House, which was built for James I within the Whitehall Palace to put on masques.

The first pageant entertainment is on King Charles's lineage and refers to the tradition of the Royal Family's descent from the House of David. This descent is traditionally thought to go back to Abraham's grandson Jacob, who dreamed of a ladder that reached to Heaven – while sleeping with his head on a stone pillow believed by many to be the Stone of Scone, the British coronation stone – and of God's covenant and promise that his descendants would rule Israel (*Genesis* 28.11–13, 18). This prophecy was fulfilled by Jacob's descendant David, to whom the covenant was renewed. (In *2 Samuel* 7.12–17, God spoke to Nathan the prophet promising to establish David's dynasty for ever.)

To some this descent is controversial as there is no historical evidence for early Biblical legend. But the tradition is a strong one, and it featured in several publications during Queen Victoria's reign (see p.72 [of *The Coronation of King Charles*]). It is an important tradition as the genealogical link (which is set out in full in Appendix 2 on pp.61–72 [of *The Coronation of King Charles*]) establishes that the Royal Family are heirs to the Biblical covenant between God and King David's descendants and enjoy the divine right of kings through the Royal Family's successive coronations.

Trilogy and dialectic
With this work I have completed a trilogy of masques.

The first masque, *The Dream of Europa: The Triumph of Peace* (2015), celebrated 70 years of peace in Europe following the disorder of the Second World War.

The second masque, *King Charles the Wise: The Triumph of Universal Peace* (2018), was about the UK's global role after the disorder of Brexit. Minerva, goddess of Wisdom, arranges for the goddesses Britannia, Europa and Columbia (speaking for the UK, Europe and the US respectively) to visit Prince Charles in Buckingham Palace and give their discordant perspectives on the UK's role. The UK's opposition to the EU is presented and a way forward is suggested, through the humanitarian vision of benefiting all humankind by setting up a democratic World State.

The third masque, *The Coronation of King Charles: The Triumph of Universal Harmony*, synthesises the conflicting supranationalistic-European and nationalistic-British themes of the first and second masques in the coming Carolingian Age, in which groundwork will begin for a democratic World State that will bring in an Age of Universal Harmony. This masque contrasts the disorder and chaos of the modern Elizabethan Age with the order and harmony that will be sought in the coming Age when political Universalism will be prevalent and the prospect of a World State will bring humankind together.

There is a tradition in English literature in which the protagonist wrestles with his soul, as does Dr Faustus when he is visited by Mephistophilis. King Charles also wrestles with his soul in coming to terms with what God and the Prolocutor want his Carolingian Age to achieve.

I said in my Preface to *King Charles the Wise* that in all my works there is a dialectic based on the algebraic formula I found in the East, +A + −A = 0. In the first two masques of the trilogy there is a dialectic between supranationalism (+A, the EU in *The Dream of Europa*) and nationalism (−A, the UK/Brexit in *King Charles the Wise*), which is reconciled in the synthesis of a World State (0, *The Coronation of King Charles*). This masque therefore completes the dialectic between opposites of the other two masques. In each of the three masques there is also a dialectic between disorder and order that is resolved in harmony.

Verse: the tradition of the iambic pentameter with variations as the English heroic line
A word about the verse. For 600 years (1380–1980) from Chaucer to after Tennyson metre was traditional and the iambic pentameter was prominent. It was widespread in Latin as the second line of the elegiac couplet (the first line being a dactylic hexameter), and it has been estimated that three-quarters of English verse written since Chaucer has been in iambic pentameters. Varying the iambic pentameter by including trochees (– ◡), anapaests (◡ ◡ –) and dactyls (– ◡ ◡), and other less-well-known feet, allows individual words to be stressed within the regularity of the metre.

When thinking of this tradition in 1779 Dr Johnson wrote of "the music of the English heroic line". In his 'Life of Milton' in *Lives of the Poets* he wrote: "The music of the English heroic line strikes the ear so faintly that it is easily lost, unless all the syllables of every line co-operate together."

Some poets in the 20th century appeared to sweep traditional metre aside in favour of free verse and stress metre, and yet the musical iambic pentameter with variations lurks at the back of apparent irregularity. The opening of Eliot's 'The Waste Land', for example, can be re-lined. The first four lines are in fact three lines of pentameters.

I have stuck with the tradition of the iambic pentameter with variations – indeed, I am one of the few poets, if not the only poet, writing in the 21st century who has continued the tradition in a large body of verse, which puts me treading in the footsteps of the pentameters of Chaucer, Spenser, Shakespeare, Milton, Marvell, Dryden, Pope, Byron, Keats, Shelley, Wordsworth and Tennyson. The Royal Family spans – and precedes and succeeds – these 600 years, and it is appropriate that a masque celebrating a modern coronation should be in iambic pentameters with variations, an approach that has been in existence in the UK at least since Richard II, who had pageant entertainments at his coronation in 1377. Iambic pentameters with variations have been prominent throughout the British Royal Family's rule since then, and throughout the time of British heraldry since the battle of Agincourt (1415) and the collation by the College of Arms of coats of arms worn on knights' surcoats and shields.

Performance and production

There may seem to be a large cast in the Dramatis Personae, but this masque could be performed by a cast of three (King Charles, Prolocutor/Minerva, God of the One) and the Chorus of the pageant, who sing all the coronation music. All the live choruses in A within the Dramatis Personae can be drawn from this Chorus, which is present for the whole masque. Some of these live choruses marked † in A within the Dramatis Personae could be filmed prior to the production and be shown on screen so they do not need to be present in the Banqueting House. This would reduce the size of the cast. All the choruses in B within the Dramatis Personae are only on screen and will not be present in the Banqueting House. The size of the cast will depend on how many of the choruses are being put on screen, which will be the Director's decision depending on how lavish the performance of the coronation masque should be.

There are Notes to the Director and the Director of Music on pp.xxi–xxii [of *The Coronation of King Charles*]. I would like the role of Director to be offered in the first instance to Sir Jonathan Bate, who can be contacted via Worcester College, Oxford; and the role of Director of Music to be offered in the first instance to Ian Skelly, who can be contacted via BBC3 where he has presented a music programme, *Essential Classics*, for 20 years. I have spoken with both of them.

Genesis and protocol

I already had the idea for a masque to celebrate the coronation in the autumn of 2015. In a letter to the Prince of Wales on 6 November 2015 (in which I sent him two of my books he had requested, *Selected Poems: Quest for the One* and *Selected Stories: Follies and Vices of the Modern Elizabethan Age*) I wrote:

> Having celebrated 70 years of peace in Europe with a masque in the tradition of Ben Jonson's early 17th-century masques, I would like to write a masque on your accession and coronation when the time comes, expressing hopes that a new Carolingian Age will see the solution of many of the world's problems. I glimpsed such a Universal Age in 1983 in 'Night Visions in Charlestown' (Charlestown, the Cornish harbour where I can be found six times a year in what used to be the Harbour-master's house). I have flagged part two of this poem on p.87 [of *Selected Poems: Quest for the One*], and "Charles's town" indicates that more than 30 years ago I associated this new age with your coming reign.

In the same letter I spoke of "the coming Carolingian Age as an era that brings hope to all humankind", an idea that had surfaced as "an Age of Hope", a "Universal Age of Light", in my poem 'Night Visions in Charlestown' (section II of which is titled 'Flight of the Soul to the Coming Age') on 6 August 1983. In a sense in this masque I am delivering (36 years later) a vision I had in August 1983, within a year of writing the first version of my Preface to *Selected Poems: A Metaphysical's Way of Fire* (which was written in September–October 1982).

In a letter of 1 August 2016 to the Prince of Wales I wrote that as King he could "come to be seen as King Charles the Wise", and that "I do seriously intend to put this vision into a masque when I get clear of my immediate duties." *King Charles the Wise* dealt with this and was not linked to his coming coronation. In a letter of 31 July 2017 I wrote that I was preparing to begin this masque (*King Charles the Wise*).

On 30 October 2018 I encountered the Prince of Wales's Assistant Private Secretary, Dr Grahame Davies, at a meeting at the Oxford and Cambridge Club and talked with him privately for 20 minutes. I told him (before giving him a signed copy of my masque *King Charles the Wise*) that I wanted to write a masque that could be performed in the Banqueting House at the time of the coronation. He agreed that as I could see how to do this coronation masque now and would be 80 in May 2019 I should complete the work while I am still *compos mentis* and lodge it with him until the time for a performance is due.

The next day, 31 October 2018, I put this in a letter to him:

> I said I would like to write a masque for the coming coronation. I see this as being in the tradition of Ben Jonson's early 17th-century masques, which were performed in the Banqueting House, the successor of the Banqueting Hall in Whitehall, where my masque could be performed. I said that Garter has suggested I should write on this subject to the Lord Chamberlain. You said yesterday a masque was unlikely to be formally commissioned until HRH ascends the throne, and that I could write it now and lodge it with you until that time comes. I propose to do this.

He wrote back that in view of "the sensitivities" protocol would not allow any commissioning. I would have to write this masque on my own initiative and it could be "lodged" until the time came.

In a letter dated 21 November 2018 to Thomas Woodcock, Garter Principal King of Arms, I confirmed the arrangement:

> Last week he wrote to me and said that a masque for the coronation cannot be commissioned at present in view of the sensitivities (of commissioning anything for the coronation before the Queen's demise), but that I can send a masque to him as we had previously arranged. I propose to start this in March, but officially it must be on my own initiative.

In fact, I was delayed by an unexpected invitation to Russia and by the completion of *Fools' Paradise* and *Selected Letters*. I could not make a start until late June 2019, by which time I had mulled over the idea for at least three-and-a-half years.

Russia: 'Vision for Future'

I was invited to Moscow to speak in the semi-governmental Civic Chamber on 22 April 2019, the first day of the new Year of the Phoenix in the Mayan calendar. This only comes round every 2,000 years and is associated with world states, as the audience all knew. The last time it came was shortly after Augustus's reign during the Roman Empire, and with a new World State ahead I was asked to speak for 20 minutes about my *World State* and to launch a new era of universal peace and harmony, which I did. (See my website, Sources, for this speech.) I began by bringing greetings from the UK, "Russia's wartime ally", and I called for better relations between Russia and the West.

I had been asked to bring greetings from Prince Charles, but the Foreign and Commonwealth Office had strict guidelines regarding royal involvement in Russia following the Novichoking in Salisbury, and I was sent a long letter by Sir Alan Duncan, who was in charge of Russia for the FCO, setting out the guidelines I should operate within. I nevertheless received letters from the Office of the Prince of Wales wishing me well on the eve of my departure to Moscow, and sending best wishes shortly after I returned.

At the end of my speech I was awarded a Golden Phoenix by the Russian Ecological Foundation. It was presented by a Russian cosmonaut. I was also given a silver medal by the BRICS countries (Brazil, Russia, India, China and South Africa) for 'Vision for Future' (the wording on the medal). There were members of the Russian military present, and I was joined on stage by an Admiral and Vice-Admiral, both in full uniform with several rows of ribbon bars, who stood either side of me. Each grasped one of my hands and held it aloft in a victory salute.

My 'vision for future' (to quote my silver medal) was for seeing a united world in my *World State* and *World Constitution*, and for my Universalism (outlined in *The New Philosophy of Universalism*), and the content of my vision must still have been in my mind when I began *The Coronation of King Charles* two months later, on 20 June 2019.

I wrote to the end of the masque section at Connaught House in Essex between then and 24 July, and finished the coronation masque in Charlestown, Cornwall, between 26 July and 3 August 2019.

Banqueting House and Universalist God of the One
On the subject of things still being in my mind, I first visited the Banqueting House in 1966. From 1963 to 1967 I had been living in Japan, where I was a Professor in English Literature at three universities and tutor to Emperor Hirohito's second son, Prince Hitachi, whose State visit to the UK in October 1965 I helped plan. I returned to the UK for a 10-week vacation in 1966 and did extensive literary and historical research while visiting many literary and historical places.

On 8 July I went to the Banqueting House, the only surviving room of the old Whitehall Palace, to walk in Charles I's footsteps and see what he saw on his way to being beheaded on the scaffold outside. I did not then know that I would be able to use this research in my verse play *The Rise of Oliver Cromwell* (2000). The inside of the Banqueting House has been in a deep place in my mind for 53 years, and it is extraordinary – one of the many extraordinary things that have happened in my life – that I should have drawn on those mental images while writing this coronation masque. I would have been amazed to be told then that I would write a masque and pageant entertainments to be performed in the Banqueting House at the time of King Charles III's coronation.

During my time in Japan I became familiar with Buddhism and Taoism, and when I left in 1967 I travelled back through eleven countries and had experience of Hindu India. In 1961–1962 I had lectured in English Literature at the University of Baghdad, Iraq, when Iraq was a backwater that Churchill had created 40 years previously, and I had experience of Islam, which I intensified during my time lecturing at the University of Libya in Tripoli from 1968 to 1970. Throughout that decade I steeped myself in religions other than Christianity and discovered that they all had a common essence in the experience of the mystic Light. I later wrote this up in *The Light of Civilization*. My own experiences of the Light in 1965 and 1971 and subsequently – 93 experiences in all – can be found in my two autobiographical works *My Double Life 1: This Dark Wood* and *My Double Life 2: A Rainbow over the Hills*.

In the 1960s and 1970s I had naturally acquired a Universalist approach to 'God of the One', and saw mystics' experiences in many religions as relating to one God. As I look back again on my visit to the Banqueting House in 1966, it seems perfectly natural to locate God of the One above a balcony in the Banqueting House for the duration of a masque and pageant entertainments.

30 July, 10, 23, 27 August, 5 October 2019

52

A Baroque Vision

100 Verse Selections from 50 Volumes

Preface
The Baroque Vision behind Universalism, and the Tradition of Wordsworth and Tennyson

Ricks urges me to select 30 poems in 1979 and 1982, and my poetic identity
As can be read in my *Selected Letters* p.58, when I met him on 20 February 1979 the eminent English literary critic Christopher Ricks asked me to select 30 poems that represented my range and the best of my work.

At the time I was struggling to see what sort of poet I was. I had had some remarkable, indeed extraordinary, inner experiences while writing my poem 'The Silence' from 1965 to 1966 when I was a 26-year-old Professor in Japan, and I was still trying to understand them. I had grappled with them on my own, trying to evaluate vivid images that flooded in seemingly from the beyond but perhaps from my imagination (or Muse), and an experience of the mysterious Light ("a round white light"), and I wrote of my future self, which I called my "Shadow" (my shadow being ever beside me as I walked to and fro under the hot Japanese sun): "My Shadow sees/With a metaphysical eye." (Now that, in my 81st year, I have become my Shadow, to reach which required a subjugation of my "Reflection" or social ego, looking back I can say this was remarkably prescient.)

I sent some of my poems to Christopher Ricks, and wrote him three letters between 1979 and 1982, attempting to pinpoint my poetic identity and the tradition in which these new experiences placed me. These three letters are in *Selected Letters*.

The first letter (dated 18 February 1979) saw me as a Metaphysical poet. On 20 February I visited Ricks at Christ's College, Cambridge. He gave me a brilliant tutorial in the Buttery and, following notes he had made, dwelt on the technical differences between my ruminative approach and the approach of the Metaphysical poets. He said I should make a selection of 30 poems. We then lunched together in the Senior Common Room.

The second letter (dated 1 May 1982) saw me as a Romantic poet. Ricks more or less went along with this. The Romantic poets

Wordsworth and Shelley had dwelt on the One – Wordsworth's "A motion and a spirit, that impels/All thinking things, all objects of all thought" and Shelley's "The One remains, the many change and pass" – and my ruminative approach was akin to Wordsworth's "emotion recollected in tranquillity". On this view I could be seen as continuing the tradition of Wordsworth and Shelley.

The third letter (dated 17 October 1982) took account of a development since late 1979 and early 1980 when I reconciled my vision with social and historical events. This letter saw me as a Classical poet, as blending the Classical and Romantic in what I called the Baroque after writing in my poem 'The Silence' "A new Baroque age is born" (see two early typed drafts at the end of *A Baroque Vision*). Ricks went along with this.

I visited Ricks at Christ's College, Cambridge (room B6), on 29 October 1982, after my third letter, and he said I had sharpened my ideas. He said: "I believe in the Baroque, but though everything that is Baroque is Classical and Romantic, not everything that is Classical and Romantic is Baroque." I replied that the mysterious Light is central to the new Baroque. He said: "I think your work is Baroque. You got there, even though your itinerary surprised you. You must anthologise 30 poems, each no longer than a page. Make your entry and then expand."

On 31 October 1982 I wrote to Ricks, "To be Baroque a work must have the Light, a sense of transformation, an awareness of the dynamic nature of the material world, and a mixture of sense and spirit, so yes, although Baroque is Classicism and Romanticism, Classicism-and-Romanticism is only Baroque if it has these elements." See 'The Genesis and Shaping of the New Baroque Vision' in the Appendix of *Collected Poems* ('Vision and Technique in the Collected Poems'), section 3; which is also in Appendix 1 of *Collected Prefaces*.

My non-delivery
By then I had written *The Fire-Flower* (1980), a volume of my most Metaphysical poems that included 'A Metaphysical in Marvell's Garden'. Even then my poetic output was bulky, and it was hard to come up with 30 pre-1979 poems that caught my poetic identity clearly. I was also a busy Head of English with 'A'-level marking to keep abreast of, and new poems kept coming.

Immersed in my ever-increasing output during the 1980s and 1990s I found it impossible to whittle either my pre-1979 or my life's work down to 30 poems, the challenge Ricks had set me in 1979 and 1982. Every time I wrote down a poem that might be included in a draft selection of 30 poems a dozen other poems clamoured to replace it like unruly children, and I could not be sure that in relation to my true poetic identity they did not have a better claim. I was also aware that I had works ahead of me, including the work I discussed with Ezra Pound in 1970 (*Overlord*), and I felt that if I delayed I would be able to include passages from what was still to come. So I bided my time.

Ever since then my poetic output has increased each year. My *Collected Poems 1958–2005* contains 1,478 poems in 30 volumes, and *Life Cycle* (2006–2016) contains a further 210 poems in four more volumes. *Classical Odes* (1994–2005) contains 318 classical odes in four books, and I have also written two poetic epics: *Overlord* about the Second World War from D-Day to the Fall of Berlin (1994–1996 in four volumes, collected edition in 2006, 41,000 lines of blank verse) and *Armageddon* about the War on Terror from 9/11, which includes the American invasions of Iraq and Afghanistan (2008–2009, 25,000 lines of blank verse). I have also written five verse plays, having revived the verse play in 1994 with *The Warlords*, and these are in *Collected Verse Plays* (2007); and I have written three masques and *Fools' Paradise*, a poem on Brexit, and am working on a sequel, *Fools' Gold*, and on a volume of new poems.

My three Selected Poems had different perspectives. My first selection, *Selected Poems: A Metaphysical's Way of Fire*, was a selection of key poems written before 1991 that reflected my Mystic Way, which transformed my consciousness into an instinctive unitive vision. (On 21 August 1984 I had written in my diary that my "Ricks collection", then titled *A Way of Fire*, should reflect my Mystic Way.) My *Selected Poems: Quest for the One* (2015, 423 pages) demonstrated that my poetic work reflects the fundamental theme of world literature: a perennial dialectic and tussle between a quest for the One and satirical condemnation of follies and vices, one of which has always predominated for over 4,000 years during any generation or time. *Visions of England*, poems selected by the Earl of Burford (2019), presented 100 poems about places in England written before 1999. None of these presented the 30 poems (and by implication, the poetic identity) Ricks had requested in 1979 and again in 1982.

A new perspective and this selection
In 2019, after my 80th birthday, I completed *Selected Letters*, letters I had written about all my works including my poetic works, and then *Collected Prefaces*. In 1991 I had revived the Preface, a form Wordsworth used so effectively in his Preface to the second edition of *Lyrical Ballads* in 1801 and, greatly expanded, in the third edition in 1802, and in

Collected Prefaces I present my 56 Prefaces (including this Preface).

Rereading my letters relating to Ricks' urging of 30 poems (see pp.58 and 71 of *Selected Letters*), and all my Prefaces, gave me a new perspective, and I suddenly saw how I could choose 30 poems written before 1979 (the year Ricks first mentioned 30 poems) as Part One of a two-part selection that would end in 2019. I jotted down titles, and later drew up a spreadsheet with decades across the top, from the 1960s to 2010s, and all the key subjects, genres, forms, techniques and verse lines I had used down on the left. I posted the titles of key poems into the spreadsheet so I could check that my selection covered every decade, key subject, genre, form, technique and verse line that I had used in 61 years of writing poetry.

My initial task was to choose 30 poems written before 1979, so I have devoted Part One to delivering 30 Baroque poems from the 17 volumes written before then, an average of 15 poems per decade. Part Two presents another 70 Baroque – Classical and Romantic – poems (an average of 17.5 poems per decade for another even more prolific four decades) from another 33 volumes written between 1979 and 2019. My life's poetic output at present is in 50 volumes – 34 volumes of poems written over the years that can be found in *Collected Poems* and *Life Cycle and Other New Poems*, two epic poems, four books of classical odes, five verse plays, three masques and two poetic volumes to be published in 2020/2021, *Fools' Paradise* and *The Oak Tree and the Branch* – and I have drawn on all 50 of these 50 volumes in this selection, which now reflects my life's poetic work.

I arrived at 100 numbered poems by counting each titled poem as one poem. My two epic poems therefore count as two of the 100 numbered poems (even though *Overlord* was published in four separate volumes before being published in one volume). Each is represented by excerpts which are all under one title and together count as one poem. I have regarded these two epic poems as special cases as (at 41,000 and 25,000 lines of blank verse) together they comprise over 66,000 lines, and my excerpts total around 3,440 lines, around 5% – the minimum amount needed to give a feel for their narratives, root them in the epic tradition (via invocations to Homer, Virgil, Dante, Milton, Tennyson and other forerunners) and bring out their Baroque features (including visits to Heaven and Hell and focus on the Light).

The Baroque vision
This selection tells an underlying story within my 61 years of writing poetry, a kind of subliminal narrative that invites connections between poems. The selected poems show why I saw myself in my three letters

to Ricks in 1979 and 1982 as a Metaphysical poet writing of the Mystic Way and came to see myself as being in the Romantic, and later the Classical tradition, and as blending the Classical and Romantic in what I called the Baroque vision after two lines in 'The Silence' (1965–1966): "While naked on the petalled lawn,/A new Baroque age is born." The second line came straight from the beyond, and for some years I did not fully understand it.

I see from consulting my archive, which is held in the Albert Sloman Library at the University of Essex, that it did not find its way into the poem until April 1973, when it was handwritten in the margin of a version of the poem corrected in blue ink, and that it later appeared in a typed version in April/May 1973. (See two early typed drafts at the end of *A Baroque Vision*.) (Looking at the many papers connected with 'The Silence' in my archive in the University of Essex, I was stunned by how many vivid lines I cut out of the final version. There must be a hundred or two which would grace any of my poems.)

I also described 'The Silence' in the poem's dedication as "This string of baroque pearls". This was written in Japan some time after the writer Frank Tuohy took my wife and me to the office of a pearl dealer called Meiras, so he could buy two necklaces of irregular baroque pearls in Tokyo on 20 October 1965. I returned to Meiras with my wife on 16 December 1965 and bought her a necklace of baroque pearls. The dedication "To Mr F.T." was to Frank Tuohy, who, having read the poem and suggested I should add marginal glosses in the manner of Coleridge's 'The Ancient Mariner' to present a clear narrative, would understand how my irregular chunks of verse in 'The Silence' could be described as misshapen baroque pearls. (See my diary entries for these two days in *Awakening to the Light*, pp.202 and 222.)

The full dedication at the beginning of 'The Silence' was: "To Mr F.T./This string of baroque pearls,/To be told like a rosary." The last line of this dedication brings out the poem's religious associations – each irregular chunk of my verse was like a bead in a rosary to be meditated over as if in prayer – and evokes the religious associations of the historical Baroque.

I believe it was in 1967 that I found in a bookshop in Tokyo's Kanda district Germain Bazin's description of the Baroque in *A Concise History of Art*. (It is first mentioned in my diary entry in *Awakening to the Light* for 7 February 1967.) Bazin sets out a life cycle of artistic styles first suggested by Déonna in Geneva in 1913 and developed by Faure (in 1927) and Focillon (in 1934): a primitive, archaic pre-classical stage or Age; a classical stage or Age; an academic or post-classical stage or Age (Neoclassicism); and then a pre-baroque Mannerist stage or Age.

The end of Mannerism – its cure – is the baroque stage or Age in which "the spirit is again in contact with the world, the imagination drinks deeply of its forms, and at the very source, with an eagerness born of long deprivation. The cosmos itself seems to be throbbing in the soul, filling it with inspiring emotion" (Bazin, p.528). I now began to understand how my work might be regarded as Baroque.

The historical Baroque period which produced the artistic baroque style began around 1600 and ended around 1750. It influenced all the arts, and in literature it inspired the Metaphysical poets, Milton's *Paradise Lost*, and the Augustans. The Baroque consciousness is open to, and combines, both the spiritual and the sensual: the Romantic infinite and the Classical social outlooks, the soaring grandeur of Heaven and the sensuous, emotional exuberance and movement in the everyday. Bach, Handel, Bernini and Rubens – in all the arts the Baroque soars to Heaven, as in Rubens' painting *The Apotheosis of James I* (see front cover [of *A Baroque Vision*]), which was installed in the Banqueting House, London in 1636. James I was the father of Charles I, who commissioned the painting, and in his 'apotheosis' (elevation to divine status, deification) he is shown being drawn upwards to Heaven on the Banqueting-House ceiling, which I first saw when I visited the Banqueting House on 8 July 1966. (See my Preface to *The Coronation of King Charles*.)

In literature the Baroque includes the profound poems of Donne (including 'Aire and Angels'), the Metaphysical poets and Milton that confront death, and the social satire of Dryden and Pope. And, because they blend the spiritual and the sensual, the poems of Tennyson which succeeded the poems of the Romantic Wordsworth can be seen as blending the Classical and Romantic as neo-Baroque. I have sought to achieve a similar blend between the Classical and Romantic in my neo-Baroque poems.

Baroque poetic inspiration can be seen as images bursting into the poet's mind from the beyond like windfalls bursting through the leaves of a tree, like my image of a new Baroque age being born on a petalled lawn. In 'The Tree of Imagination', first written on 31 December 1979 and ruminating on my visit to Ricks on 20 February 1979 (not included in this selection), I wrote: "So images burst round a poet's head,/ Windfalls from a leafy beyond that heal/A sick society...."

My inspiration derives from the 17th century, the time of the Metaphysical poets, masques and Milton's epic poem (as I had realised by 1963, when I wrote 'The 17th-Century Pilgrim'); but also from the 18th century, the time of social satire, and the 19th century, the time of the Romantic poets, of Wordsworth's 'Preface to *Lyrical Ballads*' and of

Tennyson's blend of Romanticism and Classicism in his *'In Memoriam'*, his "Nor winks the gold fin in the porphyry font", his long narrative works and his poems on national events such as 'The Charge of the Light Brigade' about an event in the Crimean War.

My poem 'The Silence' (1965–1966) derives from Modernism, but after an evening with Ezra Pound in 1970 I decided that abbreviated narrative in an emotionally-linked sequence of images was not for the epic and narrative poems I wanted to write, and I consciously headed back into the 19th century and the 17th-century Baroque for my inspiration, where it already was subconsciously.

My range

My questing poems led me to look into disciplines outside poetry, and these were reflected in my poetry and extended its range. I now regard my poetic works as drawing on seven disciplines: literature, of course; mysticism; philosophy; history; religion; international politics and statecraft; and world culture.

In this selection can be found poems on aspects of my literature ('Authorship Question in a Dumbed-Down Time', 'On the Death of Mr Nicholas Hagger'); on my mysticism ('The Power by the Lake', 'The Silence', 'Visions: Golden Flower, Celestial Curtain', poems from *The Fire-Flower*); on my philosophy of the universe ('Night Visions in Charlestown'); on history (an excerpt from 'Old Man in a Circle', 'At Otley: Timber-Framed Tradition'); on religion (excerpts from *Beauty and Angelhood*); on international politics and statecraft (excerpts from 'Archangel', *Ovid Banished* and *The Tragedy of Prince Tudor*); and world culture (my classical ode 'At Virgil's Tomb', *Overlord*, *Classical Odes*).

A stag with seven-branched antlers

I see myself as an Epping-Forest stag with seven-branched antlers. One antler's seven branches symbolise the above seven disciplines. The other antler's seven branches symbolise the branches within literature I have pursued as a man of letters: poems and poetic epics; verse plays and masques; short stories and novellas; diaries; autobiographies; letters (*Selected Letters*); and my statement of the fundamental theme of world literature (*A New Philosophy of Literature*).

My Universalism

As can be tracked in my *Selected Letters* and *Collected Prefaces*, my writings show a developing Universalism in the above seven disciplines and in all branches of literature. At both finite and infinite levels, Universalism deals with every known idea and so can focus on: transformation by the Light; seeing from the perspective of the Whole and therefore seeing things as a whole; the blend of sense and spirit in (for example) Rubens' *The Apotheosis of James I* (which shows a king becoming a god and reinforces the Divine Right of Kings, but also shows a man with a divine soul); the transcending of death; the possibility of Angelhood (which can be found in 'Archangel' and *Beauty and Angelhood*); and the prospect of Heaven.

At both finite and infinite levels (Classical and Romantic) Universalism sees the universe as a unity and sees humankind and all disciplines as a whole. So philosophical Universalism studies the whole universe in its finite and infinite aspects (hence *The New Philosophy of Universalism*); historical Universalism studies all history, including the rise and fall of civilisations (hence *The Rise and Fall of Civilizations*); political Universalism sees one political union of all humankind (hence *World State* and *World Constitution*); and literary Universalism sees the whole of literature, the fundamental theme of world literature: hence *A New Philosophy of Literature*, which sets out the fundamental theme as a generational dialectic between a quest for the One and satirical condemnation of follies and vices, between the Metaphysical-Romantic and the Classical – Universalism synthesising or reconciling both. See *The Essentials of Universalism* (coming shortly) for the key passages about Universalism in my prose.

Looking back on my works and on my experiences of the Light and the way I received crucial ideas and understanding in my sleep (recorded in *My Double Life 2: A Rainbow over the Hills*), I sometimes wonder if I was sent down to the earth and took human form in the year the Second World War began to confront the world's problems, reconcile all the disciplines and promote peace. I resonate with the feeling in Donne's 'Aire and Angels' that "Angells affect us oft" and are sent down to earth to complete a mission and tasks, and that at the very least we have divine souls, as Rubens showed in his painting of James I.

My Baroque development, forms, genres and verse
The poems and verse excerpts in this selection catch my development over the decades, my Universalism, my early mysticism, my Metaphysical approach ('The Silence', *The Gates of Hell*, 'A Metaphysical in Marvell's Garden' and other poems in *The Fire-Flower*), my Romantic outlook (*The Gates of Hell*, 'The Four Seasons'), my later Classicism (*Classical Odes*), my war poetry (*Overlord, Armageddon*, 'Shock and Awe'), and my awareness of the One ('The Silence', *The Gates of Hell, The Fire-Flower*, God of the One in *The Coronation of King Charles*). Elements

of Classicism and Romanticism can be found in all my works, which I therefore regard as neo-Baroque.

In this selection can be found examples of the forms and genres I have written within: my sonnets; my lyrics; my odes; my social satire; my verse plays; and my masques.

My verse has become more Classical as the decades progressed. I began by exploring stress metre (four or five stresses in a line) but soon opted for iambic pentameters and blank verse, and on occasion heroic couplets. The turning-point was the evening I spent with Ezra Pound in Rapallo on 16 July 1970. I discussed the best line for writing an epic and became convinced that his Modernist approach in *The Cantos* of abbreviated narrative in emotionally-linked sequences of images (which I had defended in an essay in a book to mark Eliot's death, *T.S. Eliot: A Tribute from Japan*) was not the way I should pursue narrative verse, and when we walked round Oxford on 21 June 1993 Ricks confirmed my feeling that I should write an epic poem in blank verse. My classical odes on the culture of Europe are in rhymed or alternately-rhymed lines, and I use rhyme in most of my lyrics, odes and of course my many sonnets.

In this selection can also be found narrative, lyrical, reflective and dramatic verse; my early stress metre; lines of 2, 3, 4, 5, 6, 7 and 8 feet either rhymed or alternately rhymed; my standard iambic pentameters, blank verse and heroic couplets; and stanzas of 4, 8, 9 and 10 lines.

Alternative views of my poetry

In poems in this selection can be found the alternative views and perspectives of my poetry I identified in my Preface to *Visions of England*: my journeying along the Mystic Way (*The Gates of Hell*, 'Journey's End', 'Pear-Ripening House', *The Fire-Flower*); my developing Universalism ('Crab-Fishing on a Boundless Deep'); my social, satirical poetry ('Zeus's Ass'); my reflecting of Western culture ('On the Waterfront', 'Question Mark over the West'); my Nature poetry ('The Flight', *The Four Seasons, The Weed-Garden*, 'Sea Force'); my war poetry (*Overlord, Armageddon*, 'Shock and Awe'); my carrying forward of the tradition of the Metaphysical poets ('A Metaphysical in Marvell's Garden', *The Fire-Flower*); and my Classical and Romantic neo-Baroque poetry.

Also can be found poems on my local Epping Forest ('An Inner Home'); on my home town and childhood memories ('Among Loughton's Sacred Houses'); on my old school, which I later acquired ('Oaklands: Oak Tree'); on my Cornish sea ('Sea Force', 'Crab-Fishing on a Boundless Deep'); and on life and death ('A Crocus in the Churchyard').

In the tradition of Wordsworth and Tennyson
I have pictures of both Wordsworth and Tennyson within the vicinity of my study desk.

I see myself as being within Wordsworth's tradition of *The Prelude* and his 'Preface to *Lyrical Ballads*' (1801/1802), and the picture on the cover of *Visions of England* shows me sitting with the Wanderer's cottage in the background.

Ricks, arguably the leading world authority on Tennyson after his standard *Tennyson*, urged me to model myself on Tennyson, who had a vast range that included lyrical and narrative verse and events of international history such as 'The Charge of the Light Brigade' (set in the Crimean War, 1854), and who lived at Beech Hill House, High Beach, from 1837 to 1840 (very near where I live in Epping Forest), and heard the "wild bells" ring out from Waltham Abbey.

He urged me to correct my past poems as Tennyson did to improve lines, and I have always done this, as in my reworking of 'Strawberry Hill' (1974) into 'Clouded-Ground Pond' (1980, not included), and 'In Marvell's Garden, at Nun Appleton' (1973, not included) into 'A Metaphysical in Marvell's Garden' (1980). He said to me as we walked round Oxford on 21 June 1993 and I settled on blank verse for *Overlord* (the subject behind my discussion with Ezra Pound in 1970): "Nothing's changed since Tennyson technically. Go back to him."

I describe in a letter to Ricks in *Selected Letters* (dated 29 July 2008) how I was aware of Tennyson's presence when I spent several days staying at Farringford House, his home on the Isle of Wight from 1853 until his death in 1892, both while I wrote in his study and slept in the bedroom he used.

Since then I have sensed that Tennyson has often been with me as a Muse, and frequently acts as an editor and draws my attention to where I could improve a word (see *Fools' Paradise*, p.145). Tennyson wrote after the Romantic Age and blended Romanticism and Classicism in his own way that was neo-Baroque. It may be significant that I took the world anthem for *World Constitution* from six lines in Tennyson's 'Locksley Hall', and in *World State* named my World State 'The United Federation of the World' after Tennyson's lines in that poem. I also quoted at length from Tennyson's 'Ulysses' in my speech in Moscow's Civic Chamber on 22 April 2019 (see my website for video). Besides deriving from Wordsworth I also derive from Tennyson, as I hope this selection will demonstrate.

Having had an early interest in Modernism and having taught the poems of T.S. Eliot in great detail to Japanese students between 1963 and 1967 when I was a Professor of English Literature in Tokyo (part of the time in a room where William Empson taught between 1931 and 1934), and having turned back to the 19th century after my evening with Ezra Pound, I returned to the 600-year-old tradition of the iambic pentameter that dominated English verse from 1380 to 1980 and was followed by both Wordsworth and Tennyson. My essay 'A Defence of Traditional Poetic Method or: Poking the Hornets' Nest' (1999, revised in 2005) can be found at the end of my *Collected Poems* and of *A New Philosophy of Literature*.

My "mission" and project: to develop my Baroque vision into Universalism
Ricks, with whom I have corresponded for 40 years as *Selected Letters* shows, spoke with me at Worcester College, Oxford, on 1 July 2019, before giving a lecture about the iambic pentameter as "the music of the English heroic line" (Dr Johnson, 'Life of Milton' in *Lives of the Poets*, 1779). Over drinks before his lecture we discussed my recent visit to Russia and my call there for better relations with the West, and he said to me (two octogenarians together who had known each other a long time), "You have been on a mission since you left University." And I wondered if I had indeed worked on one lifelong project ever since I left Oxford in 1961, 58 years previously, even longer than the 57 years that Pound had been writing *The Cantos* when I visited him in 1970. (See my letter to Ricks in *Selected Letters* dated 3 July 2019, which also mentions that he told me I had used the heroic line in *Overlord*.)

I thought he meant that during all my travelling of the world and my writing I had been on a mission to arrive at Universalism and to set out my Universalist vision in literature and extend it to six other disciplines. (He had once said to me that art comes out of a quarrel with oneself, not with the world, and he knew that I had sought to understand the universe so I could elevate my poetry – while preserving the approach of Keats' "negative capability", responding to life fully in the moment.) But, having completed the selection of the poems in Part One of *A Baroque Vision*, I awoke on Christmas Day 2019 with the realisation (which had come to me in my sleep) that he had remembered my three letters to him in 1979 and 1982 and meant that my Universalism was rooted in and grew out of my Baroque vision in my poems, that my "mission" and project was to develop my Baroque vision into Universalism. Whether he meant this I do not know – and it may already be obvious to diligent readers of my *Collected Prefaces*; but I had woken with what was for me a new perspective, and I was stunned.

Evidence for the connection between my Baroque vision and my Universalism

I got up and looked in my Prefaces for evidence of the connection between my Baroque vision of 1982 and my Universalism of 1991.

I saw I first stated my Baroque vision in my Preface to my *Selected Poems: A Metaphysical's Way of Fire*, 'On the New Baroque Consciousness and the Redefinition of Poetry', which, though published in 1991, was first written in September–October 1982 (and revised in August and October 1989 with the addition of "as Classical Baroque" at the end of the title). I saw I first stated my Universalism in a Preface written in April 1989 and also published in 1991 (Preface to *The Fire and the Stones* titled 'Introduction to the New Universalism').

I looked in my *Collected Poems*, and I now saw that the turning-point which shows my Baroque vision giving birth to my Universalism was in my poem 'Night Visions in Charlestown', first written in 1983 and revised in 1990 ("So hail the Universal Age of Light!.../New rising of Baroque in its own right...").

I looked in my diaries. I saw that on 21 August 1984 I wrote that a selection of my poems for Ricks should be called *A Way of Fire* (which became *Selected Poems: A Metaphysical's Way of Fire*, published in 1991, on my Mystic Way). I saw that in early April 1985 I had a number of intense experiences inspired by Charlestown in Cornwall, and in my diary entries for 7 April (which are in *My Double Life 2: A Rainbow over the Hills*, pp.185–187) I wrote:

> Soul and body together – the very essence of Baroque.... Artists create the next age, which will be a Baroque one, uniting Classicism and Romanticism. A new word for it?... A new flowering of the Romantic age amalgamated to Classicism.... So what is the Age?... Think. It is a new -ism, after Romanticism and Classicism, in artistic terms Baroque.... I still need a word for the next age.

On 9 April, inspired by the night view of the stars over the sea from Charlestown, in my diary I pondered the next age, a Universal Age, and came to the brink of declaring a Universalist Age:

> I see so clearly from a Cornish cliff, and that is why I must buy a cliff-top house in Cornwall, e.g. Charlestown.... My 'trade mark' is man in the universe, against the stars, not the social man.... I see a man against the stars, a frightening vision that permeates my '[The] Silence' and which should still permeate my work.... I am a Universalist – a word that has the idea of Holism, the whole, i.e. all universes, and all that

is universal; while going for the Light which permeates the universe. Universalism.... That is the new philosophy, which has characteristics of the Baroque. Especially if Universalism includes soul and spirit, 4 levels of man's being.... A Universal Age. After Realism and Nominalism came Humanism, the human scale (mind and body, not soul). Now Universalism, the scale of the universe, which includes the soul, for entry into the soul takes us out into the universe. The Universal Age.... There are as many stars as sparkles, and they fade and form like the jumping lights on a sunlit sea – one perception I have had which takes me to the truth about the universe – "bunches of grapes of 5,000 galaxies each". An age that raised its eyes from the street and social concerns to its place in the universe.

I saw that in April 1985 I had described Universalism as "the" new philosophy with "characteristics of the Baroque". I added in *My Double Life 2: A Rainbow over the Hills* (p.188):

After a few days of intense thought I now regarded myself as a Universalist announcing and heralding in a Universal Age, in which Universalism would succeed Humanism. I wrote [in a later diary entry on 9 April 1985] that any selection of my poems "must go with the Universal Age" and that I should write "an essay on our Universal Age which has Baroque features: on communications, the global view, but also on man's role in relation to the universe, which the new Renaissance is making possible.... The new science has opened up the stars and enlarged the soul, and my work must respond to this."

This passage written in my diary on 9 April 1985 caught the turning-point from "a new Baroque age" to a coming Universal or Universalist Age "which has Baroque features", and I was now clear that my Baroque vision had given rise to my Universalism, which opened to the universe and the perspective of Heaven as in Rubens' *The Apotheosis of James I* and took Heaven's view of the whole universe, all civilisations and a united humankind in a World State – God of the One's view in *The Coronation of King Charles*. I had dealt with this in *My Double Life 2: A Rainbow over the Hills* and had somehow forgotten, and Ricks had reminded me in his throw-away mention of my "mission".

I saw in my 1987 diary that on 10 October 1987 I was at the Frankfurt Book Fair and spoke with a German representative of the publishers Fischers, Reiner Stach. I told him about my coming work *The Fire and the Stones* and explained that just as Einstein had a hunch about varying speeds of travel, which led to his Relativity theory, lying in a meadow and mentally travelling back up a sun-ray, so I had a hunch about the cause of civilisations, which grow out of a mystic vision similar to the Baroque vision into a religion. He said, "You have developed a universalist theory of world civilisations," and his use of the word 'universalist' chimed with my own earlier use of the word on 9 April 1985 ("I am a Universalist").

A new Baroque Age behind a new Age of Universalism

I saw that I recorded in my diary on 29 April 1989 that I "woke with the beginning of my 'Introduction to the New Universalism' [the Preface to *The Fire and the Stones*] in mind and wrote it in vest and pants". I had received it in sleep, just as I received the meaning of what Ricks meant by my "mission" in sleep, and I was in such haste to write it down before the words I had seen evaporated that I did not wait until I had finished dressing. In the Preface I wrote, "A new baroque Age, an Age of Universalism, is ahead." In my diary entry for 29 April 1989 I added, "I believe I have devised a new discipline.... I have devised Universalism."

The Baroque vision behind Universalism has unified all my literary and Universalist works

I was now sure that my Baroque vision was behind my Universalism, that I had developed my Baroque vision into Universalism, that Ricks had known this on 1 July 2019, and that I had been on a "mission" and had followed one project throughout my life.

I could now see that all my books came out of the third part of 'The Silence', and that it was the origin of both my Baroque vision ("A new Baroque age is born") and of my early Universalism. In Part III of 'The Silence' (excerpts included) can be found all the features of the Baroque – the Mystic Way, a centre-shift and transformation, the Light, the sensual and the spiritual, the unitive vision, the One, the Romantic infinite and Classical order – and, in the cross-disciplinary context of Freeman's experience, all the disciplines Universalism (which sees the universe as a unity, embodies the unitive vision) unites: mysticism and religion (the irregular chunks of verse as beads on a rosary, "In the meditation hall", the "round white light"); philosophy (the universe seen from a beach in lines 896–913, and lines 1438–1442); history (vision of the ruin of European civilisation in lines 1414–1426); international politics ("all men are a part of One", at one with all humankind); and world culture (the meeting of East and West in the poem).

Also written in 1966, the year I finished 'The Silence', were other poems with Baroque/Universalist features: 'Archangel' (history, international politics and closing vision of a World State); 'Old Man in a Circle' (history and international politics, the decline of the British Empire and the rise of Europe); and 'Two Moral Letters after Horace' (not included), the first being 'An Epistle to an Admirer of Oliver Cromwell' (history), and the second, addressed to His Imperial Highness Prince Hitachi, Emperor Hirohito's second son whose tutor I then was ("Imperial Highness on your birthday,/Spare a thought for the poor of the world./Use your influence like your father...").

All this came as a staggering revelation that Christmas morning for it thrillingly unified my literary and Universalist works. I now saw the jigsaw pieces of my 52 interlocking books as one picture, a whole. Once again my mentor Ricks had been breathtakingly discerning, and, in a seemingly-casual remark, with a true mentor's skill had guided me into seeing that my Baroque vision grew into and was behind my Universalism.* I had put a new gloss on my Baroque vision: Universalism. I saw that my Baroque vision passed seamlessly into Universalism, which is fundamentally Baroque.

I now saw that the poems I wrote between the mid-1960s and early 1980s embodied a truth that I had not fully understood at first and had not fully grasped rationally until then. I was reminded of Yeats writing in the year I was born, "A man can embody truth but cannot know it" (letter to Lady Elizabeth Pelham, 4 January 1939). With age sometimes comes wisdom. Now I am 80 I would amend what Yeats wrote to: "A man can embody a vision of Truth and he can come to understand it."

Having waited 40 years to present a selection of 30 poems I wrote between 1961 and 1979, I am very pleased to be presenting this selection of 30 poems (40 years late) in Part One of A Baroque Vision. And, having now understood that the Baroque poems I wrote between 1982 and 1991 were the seed-bed of my Universalism, I am very pleased to be presenting a selection of 70 poems I wrote between 1979 and 2019 in Part Two. These Baroque poems in this selection represent my life's poetic work over six decades, and the realisation that their Baroque vision is behind and has grown into my Universalism and the coming Universalist Age has satisfyingly unified all my Prefaces and all my 52 literary and Universalist works within one lifelong "mission" and purposeful project which, if political Universalism is fully implemented in a World State, can only be to the eventual benefit of all humankind.

17–21, 23–25, 27–28, 30–31 December 2019;
2, 8–13, 21–22 January, 15 February 2020

*See Appendix 3 for five letters written by Nicholas Hagger to Christopher Ricks on *A Baroque Vision*, the last two in reply to an image he received from Ricks on 2 March 2021 (see his letter of 2 March 2021 in Appendix 3).

53

The Essentials of Universalism

A Philosophy of the Unity of the Universe and
Humankind, of Interconnected Disciplines and a
World State
75 Prose Selections from 25 Works

Preface
The Unitive Vision and Seven Disciplines

The thread of Universalism in my books
Looking back on my 53 books at the age of 80, I can see that a thread
runs through all my prose works: bringing Universalism to birth and
parenting it towards adulthood. Universalism sees the universe, all
humankind and all branches of knowledge as wholes that form an
interconnected unity. The 'essentials' of Universalism are its 'basic
elements' or principles, which this anthology conveys through key
passages from my works.

How I arrived at Universalism: first, the Mystic Way and the unitive vision
I arrived at Universalism first through my early mystic life. At Oxford I
knew I had to get myself to Japan, and when I was 24 I became a Professor
of English Literature at three universities in Tokyo. Surrounded by
images of the Buddha's enlightenment and taken to meditate in Zen
temples, without at first realising it I found myself on a 'Mystic Way'.
The Mystic Way begins with an awakening and is followed by a centre-
shift from one's social, rational ego to a deeper part of oneself, the soul
which is in contact with the enduring spirit. There is an early glimpse
of the Light, the Reality behind the universe, and a long involuntary
process of purgation while there is a shift from sense to spirit, which
heightens sense perception. This is followed by a Dark Night of the
Soul when much is harrowingly taken away, and then illumination,
and then a long Dark Night of the Spirit and the emergence (like a
butterfly emerging from a chrysalis) of a new self that instinctively sees
the unity behind apparent contradictions and rational differences. My
early works show me trying to make sense of what was happening to
me: my diaries 1958–1967 were titled *Awakening to the Light*, and my
first autobiographical work was titled *A Mystic Way*.

Absorbing the wisdom of the East
In 1965 I asked Junzaburo Nishiwaki, my colleague at Keio University and Professor Emeritus, often called Japan's T.S. Eliot, to sum up the wisdom of the East as we drank together in a *saké* bar with sawdust on the floor near Keio University, and he took a business reply card from a copy of *Encounter* I had with me and wrote on it: "+A + −A = 0", and over the '0', "great nothing".

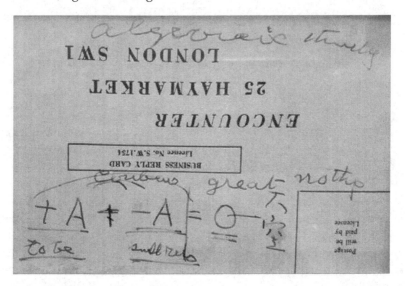

Card on which Junzaburo Nishiwaki wrote +A + −A = 0 on 5 October 1965

I immediately understood: all pairs of opposites – good and evil, day and night, peace and war, life and death, time and eternity – are reconciled in an underlying unity, the 'great nothing' which in the East is called the *Tao*.

I was on a quest and in Japan, in my twenties, I found and absorbed the wisdom of the East. I have written about my mystic life and (drawing on my diary entries) my 93 experiences of the Light in my two autobiographical works *My Double Life 1: This Dark Wood* and *My Double Life 2: A Rainbow over the Hills*.

How I arrived at Universalism: secondly, the unitive vision in my Baroque poems
The instinctive unitive vision that comes from progressing along the Mystic Way underlies my Universalism, but I would not have developed it without the grappling and discoveries of my early poems, in particular 'The Silence' (1965–1966), which is subtitled 'A

402

Meditation on a Quest for Meaning and Self-discovery', during the writing of which I underwent my centre-shift, found I was on the Mystic Way and experienced my first glimpse of the Light and of the unitive life that has been so important to my work. As the Preface to *A Baroque Vision* shows, in a dedication I called 'The Silence' "a string of baroque pearls" for it was written in the Modernist style of abbreviated narrative in emotionally-linked sequences of images and there were uneven chunks of verse like misshapen and rough-hewn baroque pearls. While revising the poem in 1973 I received two mysterious lines from the beyond:

> While, naked on the petalled lawn,
> A new Baroque age is born.

The Baroque vision of a Universal Age gives birth to Universalism
At the time I did not really understand what these two lines meant, just as I was still struggling to understand the mystical developments that had been happening within me, but I came to understand that my poetic work was Baroque. It was rooted in the historical Baroque Age which flourished c.1600–1750, and therefore in the Metaphysical poets, Milton, Dryden and Pope, and like the Baroque it blended sense and spirit, and the Classical and the Romantic, as did Tennyson, and was increasingly interested in the perspective of the universe and the view from space of the earth's globe as a seemingly unified ball. My Preface to *A Baroque Vision* makes it clear that I regard my verse as neo-Baroque.

An important landmark in my turning away from Modernism to a blend of Classicism and Romanticism in neo-Baroque poems was my visit to the 85-year-old Ezra Pound in the late afternoon and whole evening of 16 July 1970 (see pp.498–501). He urged me to write the epic poem I had ahead of me, which I eventually did as *Overlord*, but talking with him convinced me that I should turn back from Modernism's abbreviated narrative to the traditional approach of Milton and Tennyson, and write in blank verse, not Modernism's stressed lines. Just over a year later I had my profound experience of illumination on 10 September 1971 while working as a British Intelligence agent in extreme situations in London, and coped with it in rhymed sonnets and structured poems. This experience led me to my chrysalis-like Dark Night of the Spirit and my emergence to unitive vision, as I describe in *My Double Life 1: This Dark Wood* and *My Double Life 2: A Rainbow over the Hills*.

As my Preface to *A Baroque Vision* shows, an important work in taking my Baroque vision to Universalism was 'Night Visions in Charlestown' (1983), in which I presented the Baroque vision in terms of the universe and wrote of a "Universal Age". By the time I wrote my 'Introduction to the New Universalism' for *The Fire and the Stones* in 1989, my Baroque vision – which was essentially the expression and implementation of my instinctive unitive vision – had given birth to my Universalist vision of the unity of the universe.

As I proceeded on my quest I had become aware that I needed to go into other disciplines very deeply to link them to what my poems were discovering, and I had begun with history.

The genesis of this work
This work has its roots in a visit I made to Colin Wilson, author of *The Outsider*. I first visited him in Cornwall in 1960, and I stayed with him at Gorran Haven from 6 January 1961. I woke early on the morning of Sunday 8 January alone in his garden chalet, and after an hour or two's thought I walked down to Gorran Haven's harbour and stood on its wall and, feeling an exile like the Wanderer and Seafarer in Old English poems, I made an existential decision to go abroad and quest for Reality, and in particular try and get to Japan.

Colin took me for lunch that day in The Rising Sun at Portmellon, and I told him, "I shall become a wanderer, an exile, for ten years, an itinerant lecturer, and search among foreign cultures and religions" (see *My Double Life 1: This Dark Wood*, p.125). This is exactly what happened, and The Rising Sun prophetically suggested Japan's flag.

I visited Wilson three times in August 1991, and during the last visit he gave me, and signed to me ("For Nick, warm regards, Colin, Aug 22, '91") a copy of *The Essential Colin Wilson*, which had appeared in 1986 when he was 54 or 55 and then (according to his 'Introduction') the author of "over fifty-odd books".

I thought he should have delayed it as it seemed an end-of-life rather than a mid-life book, but from that day I always had it in mind that when I had finished my innovatory writings I would do something similar that might be called *The Essential Hagger*. But anthologies like *The Essential Einstein* are generally compiled by others after the subject of the work is dead. It made better sense to focus in this work on the thread of Universalism with a degree of objectivity, and I am grateful to my publisher John Hunt for advising me that this book should be called *The Essentials of Universalism*.

Companion volumes: A Baroque Vision *and* The Essentials of Universalism
It can be said, however, that *The Essential Hagger* can in effect be found in companion volumes, one covering my verse and the other my prose:

A Baroque Vision: 100 Verse Selections from 50 Volumes, which presents the Baroque thread in my poems, verse plays and masques through key poems and excerpts; and its companion volume *The Essentials of Universalism*, which presents the Universalist thread in all my prose works through key excerpts.

My Preface to *A Baroque Vision* sets out the evidence for how the Baroque brought Universalism to birth during the 1980s, and both volumes, in which the Baroque and Universalism are inextricably linked, are rooted in my experience of the Mystic Way and of the 17th-century Metaphysical poets. The cover of *A Baroque Vision* shows James I being taken up to Heaven, and in a sense in these two works I have 'Heavenised' the universe: presented Heaven's unitive view of the whole universe, all civilisations, a united humankind and a coming democratic World State.

Principles behind this selection
My aim in this work has been to set out in Part One some early passages which shape the emergence of my Universalism; then in Part Two to show Universalism's approach in seven disciplines (mysticism, literature, comparative religion, history, philosophy and the sciences, world culture, and international politics and statecraft), proceeding discipline by discipline; and then in Part Three to draw together some conclusions from these passages and all the strands of Universalism, and offer a forward vision. This book traces the thread of Universalism in my main works.

Quite simply, I have selected key passages from those of my books I have primarily focused on: *My Double Life 1: This Dark Wood* and *My Double Life 2: A Rainbow over the Hills*, *The Universe and the Light*, *The Syndicate*, *The Secret History of the West*, *A New Philosophy of Literature*, *The Light of Civilization*, *The Rise and Fall of Civilizations*, *The New Philosophy of Universalism*, *The Secret American Destiny*, and *World State* and its companion volume *World Constitution*, just 12 of my 53 volumes. Also key passages from some of my other works: *Selected Poems: A Metaphysical's Way of Fire*, *The Fire and the Stones*, *Collected Poems 1958–2005*, *The One and the Many*, *Classical Odes*, *Armageddon*, *Selected Poems: Quest for the One*, *Selected Stories: Follies and Vices of the Modern Elizabethan Age*, *Peace for our Time* and *A View of Epping Forest*.

Universalism in seven disciplines
To absorb the knowledge within seven disciplines took me many years. I was motivated from within – driven – to see each discipline as a whole and to take the Universalist vision and perspective in each

405

discipline as far as it would go.

I discovered from the tradition of the most prominent mystics that mystical Universalism involves opening to the Light in illumination and experiencing the One behind and within all natural phenomena – in an intuitional, concrete, existential mystical experience rather than as an abstract idea of a purely rational philosopher. (In this sense, Universalism continues Existentialism.)

Religious Universalism involves seeing the Light as the common essence of all religions, the fundamental religious experience that is common to all the traditional faiths.

Historical Universalism involves going to the traditional study of all civilisations and seeing all civilisations as part of a pattern of history. I found that each of 25 civilisations goes through the same 61 stages – I have them on a 7-foot-long chart that accompanied *The Fire and the Stones* – and this shows that all the civilisations have sprung from religions. First there is a mystical vision, like Mohammed's in his cave, which passes into a religion, as Mohammed's did into the *Koran*, and a civilisation forms as people flock to know more and congregate, and champion it in relation to other peoples and religions; and then a civilisation grows round it, as the Arab civilisation grew round Mohammed's vision.

Nicholas Hagger shows Iain McNay the 7-foot chart of 25 civilisations each going through 61 stages while being interviewed by him on Conscious TV.

Philosophical Universalism involves seeing the unity of the finite universe and the infinite which surrounds and permeates it. In the course of establishing this I summarised the up-to-date findings of all the sciences and assembled their positions (see *The New Philosophy of Universalism*).

Literary Universalism involves seeing the literature of all countries as an interconnected unity. It can then be seen that there is one fundamental theme in all world literature, which I set out: a quest for the One, and condemnation of social follies and vices. These two contradictions alternate for over 4,000 years, from Gilgamesh's Romantic quest for the One in *The Epic of Gilgamesh*, which appeared in the Mesopotamian civilisation c.2600BC and featured in successive versions over several centuries; down to the Roman Augustan times of Horace's Classical focus on follies and vices; to the 18th-century Augustan focus on follies and vices in Dryden and Pope; to the Romantic quest for the One in Wordsworth and Shelley. Periodically Universalists, such as Dante, Milton and Tennyson, have combined both (as I do in my literary work, my poems and short stories).

Cultural Universalism involves seeing all cultures as an interconnecting unity, and seeing that there can be one world culture which combines the metaphysical approach to the One and Truth and the social approach which ends in atheism – and sees the +A of the metaphysical and the –A of the social and atheistic as being reconciled in the = 0 of an underlying unity.

Political Universalism involves seeing the whole world as one interconnecting unity and therefore political entity, and when taken to its logical conclusion champions a democratic World State for all humankind, bringing an end to war and nuclear weapons and solving the world's problems, including its division of climate change.

My Universalism as distinct from Christian Universalism

In 1989, as I have said, I wrote 'Introduction to the New Universalism', and I must stress that my Universalism is a neo-Universalism. It is not the Christian Universalism which holds that all Christians (and no other religious participants or non-communicants) will be saved. My Universalism extends to all humankind, all 7.79 billion at the time of writing who are born and will die, and to giving all humankind a right to live under a democratic World State, free from tyranny.

The Universalist tradition within seven disciplines

In each of the seven disciplines there is often a tradition of visionaries and thinkers who have grappled with seeing unity, my forerunners. I say 'often' because the idea of Universalism is novel and in some cases original, and in some disciplines there does not seem to be much of a tradition. The traditions behind each of the seven disciplines are as follows:

- In mystical Universalism, my forerunners who have opened to the Light include: Zoroaster, the Buddha, Plotinus, St Augustine, Pope Gregory the Great, Hildegarde of Bingen, Dante, Julian of Norwich, St John of the Cross, Marvell, Milton, Blake and T.S. Eliot.

- In religious Universalism, account is taken of all the gods of 21 distinctive civilisations with differing religions, and it can be argued that the Light is common to all. Blake wrote in 'The Marriage of Heaven and Hell' "All Religions are One" and came close to seeing the Light as the common essence of all religions. Augustine was close to this vision when he wrote of "the City of God".
- In historical Universalism, my forerunners in the linear tradition include Bossuet's *Discours sur l'histoire universelle* (Discourse on Universal History), Gibbon's *Decline and Fall of the Roman Empire*, Spengler's *Decline of the West* and Toynbee's *A Study of History*. Toynbee's study of civilisations is the closest to my historical Universalism, but he chopped and changed as to what was an admissible civilisation and he admitted he never found the genesis of civilisations – because he was looking within historical events and not with the eye of a mystical Universalist.
- In philosophical Universalism, the tradition of seeing the universe as a unity can be found in Plato rather than the scientific, analytical Aristotle. The philosophers in the Vienna Circle have been analytical rationalists who have ruled out asking questions like "What is the meaning of life?" as they are considered to have no meaning, and similar analytical objections can be raised to 'the unity' of the universe. 'Unity' is perceived intuitively and existentially, not through the reason which seeks differences and distinctions. Such a tradition as there is can be found in the Vitalists at the beginning of the 20th century: Whitehead, Bergson, T.E. Hulme, Husserl and William James. Of these Whitehead is the most important.
- In literary Universalism my forerunners include many writers who have combined the quest for the One and condemnation of follies and vices, and Classicism and Romanticism, including Homer, Virgil, Dante, Shakespeare, Marlowe, Marvell, Wordsworth, Coleridge, Shelley, Tennyson and Eliot. There are experts on Classicism such as Gilbert Highet and on Romanticism such as Frank Kermode, but as yet no single authoritative work for the new literary Universalism. (I believe my work *A New Philosophy of Literature* breaks new ground.)
- In cultural Universalism, the cultural historians who focused on world cultures and civilisations were thinkers such as Edward Burnett Tylor. The metaphysical sap of European civilisation began to fail with the Renaissance and since then 50 'isms' or doctrinal movements have risen, that demonstrate fragmentation, loss of contact with the One and disunity within European civilisation.
- In political Universalism, those who have seen all humankind as

a political entity include Dante and Kant, but in recent times the tradition of those who have called for a World State includes my immediate forerunners: Truman, Einstein, Churchill, Eisenhower, Gandhi, Russell, J.F. Kennedy and Gorbachev.

Universalism therefore includes the seven strands of these traditions which collectively form a new Universalist tradition.

What Universalism can do in all seven disciplines
As can be found in *The Secret American Destiny*, all the seven disciplines, and indeed all the sciences, are divided in a conflict between a traditional approach preferred by some and a modern approach preferred by others:

- Mysticism is divided between the traditional approach to the Light, and a modern approach that emphasises social communities.
- Religion is divided between the traditional approach to prayer, and the Church's (or in other religions, Establishment's) modern support for social causes such as loneliness.
- History is divided between traditional linear historians who (since Thucydides) see forces and patterns, and modern pragmatic, fact-based historians who see a succession of patternless events and social movements.
- Philosophy is divided between the traditional Greek philosophy of the universe, and modern linguistic and logical philosophy which is largely semantic and excludes much of Nature.
- Literature is divided between traditionalist poets who write in metre, and modern poets who write in stressed rhythms; and between traditional writers who convey inner Truth, and modern writers who show purely social settings and characters.
- World culture is divided between traditional thinkers who see life as having order and a purpose, and modern atheists who (citing Darwin) see life as being chaotic and meaningless.
- Politics are divided between traditional religious control of governments and peace-loving regional groupings that favour open borders, and modern nationalist populists who want borders to be guarded and emphasise secular and social relationships of sovereign nation-states.

Universalism, the philosophy of all humankind and a World State, can heal these conflicts and divisions. All of them involve a +A and −A, and Universalism can provide an extra context that can include both contradictions and defuse and reconcile both sides. It is possible to write about both the quest for the One *and* condemnation of follies and vices, as I have done.

A new subject at universities

Universalism should one day be a new subject at universities. The young should be taught the conflicts in disciplines and how they can be reconciled into an underlying unity. Such a course would have breadth and depth.

Until such a breakthrough takes place, Universalism will be resisted by those who do not fully understand what it involves. Earlier I said that the Baroque – and therefore to a degree Universalism – 'Heavenises' the universe: presents Heaven's unitive view of the universe. Such a 'Heavenised' view will not be popular with atheists, who dominate the universities and literary journals in the West.

Interestingly, recent global surveys downgrade the influence of atheists and agnostics. According to a Pew Research Centre Survey in 2010 there were 5.8 billion (84 per cent) religiously affiliated out of a total world population (then) of 6.9 billion. By the time of the WIN (World Independent Network) Gallup International global survey in April 2015 only 11 per cent regarded themselves as atheists or agnostics out of a world population of (then) 7.33 billion (at the time of writing 7.79 billion), and adherents to the traditional metaphysical approach outnumbered adherents to the secular, social approach by nearly 6 to 1.

The influence in the West of the one in six is out of all global proportion. As the rational, social intellect is analytical and looks for differences and distinctions as if breaking a jar into pieces, not having undergone a centre-shift, it has little understanding of the soul which synthesises as if piecing a smashed jar together to restore it to the unity it originally was. Such analytical and atheistic thinking will wish to ban unity-based thinking.

In the West we like to pigeon-hole what people do and are identified with. Universalism by its all-encompassing nature is unpigeon-holeable, and to the extent that it is original it flummoxes those who are uncomfortable with a completely new way of looking and thinking. For all these reasons Universalism will have a struggle to establish itself in the universities, but I am confident that one day this will happen.

Coming Universalism in the European and North-American civilisations

History seems to be on Universalism's side. In my history I have shown that the European civilisation has reached stage 43 of the 61 stages in each civilisation, a union (the EU) that takes sovereignty from its constituent nation-states; that stage 44 is syncretistic and brings in Universalism; and that in stage 45 a constituent nation-state wants to revert to being by itself with its own cultural purity (as in the case of the UK's Brexit). Ahead is stage 46, federation, like the Russian Federation into which the Byzantine-Russian civilisation's union of the USSR (stage 43) has passed.

I have also shown that the young North-American civilisation is in stage 15, the same stage that the Roman Empire was in when it ruled the world, and that it can be expected to exert global leadership again after Trump; that in stage 16 heroic epic literature is created – both my two epics have American heroes, *Overlord* having Eisenhower and *Armageddon* Bush Jr; that in stage 17 a heretical sect, which can be expected to be Universalist, comes to the fore – there are signs that this is happening in the spreading US New Age movement; and that in the later stage 27 this heresy is grafted onto the civilisation's central idea just as Protestantism was grafted onto European Catholicism. This suggests that one day Universalism will be grafted onto American Puritanical Protestantism.

Universalist history states a pattern that can be found in all civilisations and so can make predictions, that coming stages will be similar to the same stages in civilisations that have already passed through those stages.

My role in bringing Universalism to birth
In my early days, then, I was a poet and mystic, and was groping towards my world view through mystical poems and eventually history and philosophy. After my first published works and my Prefaces on the Baroque (in *Selected Poems: A Metaphysical's Way of Fire*) and the Universalist vision (in *The Fire and the Stones*), both published in 1991, I explored Universalism in a long epic poem (*Overlord*, 1994–1996) and widened into more comparative religion, history, philosophy and literature, and eventually into international politics and world culture, in a huge operation which would take the best part of 30 years. By then I was acting as a poet, man of letters, cultural historian and philosopher.

Renaissance man: one energy from mystic life, and Baroque and Universalist outlooks
By the time I reached 80 I had led a literary life in Nature and had written 2,000 poems including over 300 classical odes in four books, 1,200 short stories, two epic poems, five verse plays, and three masques and was refining my vision in seven disciplines as something

of a Renaissance man at home in many disciplines. I looked back to Michelangelo, a painter and sculptor but also an engineer and writer of letters, architect and poet who wrote over 300 sonnets and madrigals; and Leonardo da Vinci, primarily a painter but also an inventor who made contributions in drawing, sculpture, architecture, science, music, mathematics, engineering, literature, anatomy, geology, astronomy, botany, palaeontology and cartography.

By now I was expressing my Universalism as a poet and man of letters in epic poems, classical odes, verse dramas, masques, short stories, letters, diaries, autobiographies and the philosophy of literature; and making contributions in books on mysticism, comparative religion, history and the philosophy of history, philosophy, world culture and international politics and statecraft – with an American trilogy, a focus on world government and a contribution on the structure of a coming World State and its constitution. All these were outcomes from the one energy that came from my mystic life and illumination, my Baroque outlook in my poems and my Universalist outlook in my prose.

Symbolism for Universalism in seven disciplines: stag and rainbow
I have written elsewhere that my trade mark as a writer is an Epping-Forest stag with two seven-branched antlers. I put what the two antlers stood for in *Peace for our Time*:

> Privately I saw one of my antlers as my works in seven disciplines: mysticism; literature; philosophy and the sciences; history; comparative religion; international politics and statecraft; and world culture. I saw the other antler as my literary works within seven branches of literature: poems and poetic epics; verse plays and masques; short stories and novellas; diaries; autobiographies; letters; and my statement of the fundamental theme of world literature.

I have also written elsewhere that my Universalism in seven disciplines is like the seven bands of a rainbow: each discipline, like each band, is separate; but together the seven disciplines, like the seven bands, form one rainbow, which is Universalism. The rainbow is on the cover of *My Double Life 2: A Rainbow over the Hills*, and is in the last passage in *The Essentials of Universalism*.

In 2019 I was awarded my own coat of arms and crest by Garter Principal King of Arms at the College of Arms. It is the kind of coat of arms and crest that identified the knights in armour on the battlefield at Agincourt in 1415.

**Nicholas Hagger's coat of arms and
crest showing stag and rainbow**

On the crest can be found both the stag and the rainbow, and the oak-tree and endless-knot motifs on the coat of arms represent the finite and infinite in my works, the +A world of time and the –A Baroque eternity. At the bottom on either side of my motto – containing four Latin words I urge my descendants to emulate – are the earth and the sun, suggesting my Universalism, a perspective that goes beyond the concerns of the earth and takes account of the sun and the whole universe.

I am fortunate to have been blessed with such an image which contains many cryptic details of my life. It is a reminder that in my life I rode into battle with a coat of arms and crest that embodied the principles of Universalism which I believe will be taken up in the future, as the stages 17 and 43–45 in the pattern of my Law of History suggest, and will come into their own when a democratic World State is set up with a World Constitution and brings in an era of peace and prosperity for all humankind: a true Golden Age.

54

The Promised Land

Universalism and a Coming World State

Preface
The Promised Land of Moses, and Universalism's Coming Democratic World State

The Biblical Promised Land
'The Promised Land' goes back to God's promise of the land of Canaan to Abraham (*Genesis* 12.7, 15.18–21): "Unto thy seed will I give this land." Abraham had left Haran and travelled south to Shechem, midway between and towards the coast from Lake Galilee and the Dead Sea when God spoke to him.

God renewed his promise to Isaac (*Genesis* 26.3) and Jacob (*Genesis* 28.13), and finally to Moses (*Deuteronomy* 34.1–4), who

> went up from the plains of Moab unto the mountain of Nebo, to the top of Pisgah, that is over against Jericho. And the LORD shewed him all the land of Gilead, unto Dan, and all Naphtali, and the land of Ephraim, and Manasseh, and all the land of Judah, unto the utmost sea, and the south, and the plain of Jericho, the city of palm trees, unto Zoar. And the LORD said unto him, This is the land which I sware unto Abraham, unto Isaac, and unto Jacob, saying, I will give it unto thy seed: I have caused thee to see it with thine eyes, but thou shalt not go over thither.

Moses saw the Promised Land from the top of Mt Nebo and died soon afterwards, before he could enter it, and was buried somewhere on Mt Nebo, the highest peak in the mountain range of Pisgah. And it was left to his "minister" Joshua to conquer Canaan and take the Hebrews into the Promised Land, which was described as including the territory from the Nile ("the river of Egypt") to the Euphrates (*Genesis* 15.18), from the Red Sea to the Mediterranean, "the sea of the Philistines" (*Exodus* 23.31).

My view from Mt Nebo and a coming World State
During a visit to Jordan in early March 2020 I stood on Mt Nebo where Moses stood, and looked down from 2,650 feet across the Dead Sea and

the Sea of Galilee towards the coast, the western half of this Promised Land. I saw what Moses saw, allowing for the fact that Jerusalem and Jericho were larger clusters of buildings than when Moses saw them. I saw Palestine (the land of the Philistines) in the distance and Israel, which had been in conflict with the Philistines since before the single combat between David the Israelite and Goliath the Philistine, and I saw across the Holy Land. But I was interested in more than the historical lands promised by God to Abraham and his descendants. What I saw was a symbol of the coming World State, which would one day be created by political Universalism.

It hit me while I was on Mt Nebo. There was quite a wind 2,650 feet above the Promised Land. The symbolism came to me as a revelation and I stood scribbling the places I could see in my notebook and was struck by their resemblance to the nations of the earth. I stood for a long time completely lost to my surroundings, and when I came to I was alone, my fellow travellers had gone and the wind was blowing my hair.

There on Mt Nebo I was haunted by the parallels between my life and Moses' life. I was haunted by his 40 years in the wilderness, his receiving of the Ten Commandments on Mt Sinai, below which I had stood in 2005 before visiting St Catherine's monastery and looking at the place where according to tradition Moses saw the burning bush, now protected by a wall overhung by the bush's green leaves. I had developed Ten Principles of Universalism. I was haunted by the thought that he had been allowed to look at the Promised Land "but thou shalt not go over thither". According to the *Bible* Moses died at the age of 120, but if generations and dates were calculated on a more realistic basis he would have died around 80, my own age. I saw through his eyes and his advancing years, and I had the same feeling he must have had, that he could see the Promised Land but would not live long enough to enter it.

My Promised Land is all the kingdoms of the earth unified under a democratic World State with a limited federal supranationalism that would give it sufficient authority to abolish war, enforce disarmament, impound nuclear weapons, combat famine, disease and poverty, solve the world's financial and environmental problems including climate change – and solve the world's medical and health problems such as the menacing coronavirus that threatened to end my travels.

My travels and developing Universalism
I completed my tour of Jordan, got on our ship at Aqaba – and was told that our ship had been barred from docking in Israel because it was

closing its borders due to coronavirus. I would not be allowed to enter Canaan just as Moses had not been allowed to enter it.

We visited Luxor and Cairo. The 95 on our ship were told we would be going to Alexandria, but a huge storm came up from the south of Egypt and the harbour of Alexandria was closed for two days. We steamed through the Suez Canal and headed for south Turkey and saw Roman ruins. We were then barred from landing in Cyprus to catch our flight home. We eventually flew to Istanbul, and after a night there flew back to the UK.

During my travels in Jordan, Egypt and Turkey I saw links between my earlier visits to these countries and my developing Universalism. Before I left the UK I had completed *A Baroque Vision*, which presents 100 selections from my poems, verse plays and masques taken from 50 poetic volumes to show how my early Baroque verse became Universalist; and had started *The Essentials of Universalism*, which showed the developing Universalism in my works and the essential principles of Universalism. My tour of key places in Asia Minor and Egypt awakened memories from previous visits in 1961, 1970 and 2005 and brought them to the fore, and in Cairo I again stood before the unwrapped mummy – the dead body – of Ramesses II, which I last saw in 2005. There are good grounds for seeing him as the Pharaoh who opposed Moses. This hook-nosed brown man I stood before had met Moses.

My tour now seemed to reveal how my Universalism emerged in a way that would not have been so clear had I been allowed to land in Israel and Cyprus. It was as though these had been pruned to leave me a clear insight into how my works led to the formation and revelation of all aspects of Universalism, and of the political Universalism which pointed to the new Promised Land. The Lord did not stand beside me and show me my Promised Land as He showed Moses, but a pattern was fed to me through the order in which I wrote my works, and it was as if my Muse had guided me to write my works in the order in which they were written and had presided over the reception of my poems and ideas from the beyond.

Coronavirus

The disruption caused by COVID-19 (the Corona Virus Disease 2019) in itself cried out for a coming World State. Every day brought news of more and more deaths as fatalities in Italy overtook fatalities in China. We had hand gel on the ship and in our coaches, we had our temperatures checked with a hand-held 'gun' pointed at our temples or foreheads, and every Turkish port had a 'movie camera' on a tripod that detected high temperatures. Anyone with a temperature spike as they walked past such a camera would be detained and barred from entering. A Roman theatre in south Turkey had a team of spacesuited men spraying the stone seats and columns after our visit. Turkey was keeping its ruins open but spraying them after tourists' visits.

There were unconfirmed rumours about the coronavirus COVID-19. We were asked to believe that it had surfaced in Wuhan, China but had no connection with the Institute of Virology there, where research into viruses takes place as at the UK's Porton Down. There were suggestions coronavirus had been extracted from horseshoe bats or pangolins (scaly anteaters). There were suggestions that researchers were seeking a bio-weapon in Wuhan, and also that coronavirus had leaked when a virologist had not scrubbed down thoroughly enough after working in the Institute of Virology. There were rumours that bats and pangolins used in research were legally required to be incinerated, but that some had been sold illegally on the black market to nearby restaurants for soup. A couple of dozen non-Chinese scientists have said that the virus was not genetically engineered and had simply transferred from wildlife to humans. Any mention of the Institute of Virology resulted in accusations of spreading a "conspiracy theory", but the coincidence of the virus's having surfaced near the Institute of Virology in Wuhan seemed too coincidental for there to be no connection.

I was reminded of Spanish flu, which was said to originate in Kansas, USA (although that may have been a weaker and different strain of flu) or in north China before reaching Spain, and which killed 50 to 100 million between January 1918 and December 1920 after infecting 500 million people, about a quarter of the world's population. It was called Spanish flu because King Alfonso XIII was gravely ill with it, creating a false impression that Spain was especially hard hit. It was an H1N1 influenza virus like the swine flu epidemic of 2009. Again there were suggestions that the Spanish flu virus was linked to research into germ warfare in an American laboratory to bring the First World War to an end, but nothing conclusive was ever proved. To this day it is a mystery as to how the pandemic of Spanish flu killed a huge number of 50 to 100 million people at the end of the First World War, many millions more than died in battle during the whole war.

A World State will solve all problems
The Promised Land that I envisage will control and regulate virology more rigidly than at present and will make such pandemics a thing of the past. The coming World State has been longed for from Dante's medieval treatise on the need for a universal monarch in *Monarchia*

(1309–1313) and Kant's arguing in *Perpetual Peace* (1795) that an international state (*civitas gentium*) would "continue to grow until it embraced all the peoples of the earth"; and in my lifetime by Truman (who oversaw the founding of the UN after the Second World War and kept in his wallet the six lines from Tennyson's 'Locksley Hall' I quoted in Article 133 of *World Constitution* as the anthem of the United Federation of the World, see p.341), Einstein, Churchill, Eisenhower, Gandhi, Russell, J.F. Kennedy and Gorbachev.

For some reason I seem to be the only Western writer who is calling for a World State within this tradition, and it is entirely appropriate that at 80 I should find myself standing where Moses stood and seeing the Promised Land as all the unified countries of the world as promised by a long line of thinkers since Dante and founded on the principles of Universalism that I have set out in the Prefaces to *World State* and *The Essentials of Universalism*, in my Ten Principles of Universalism set out in this book, and in at least 22 of my 55 works (see p.405).

21–22 March 2020

55

Fools' Gold

The Voyage of a Ship of Fools Seeking Gold
A Mock-Heroic Poem on Brexit and English Exceptionalism

Preface
The Man of Letters and the Cultural Consequences of Politicians, Reconciling Eliot and Tennyson

A sequel to Fools' Paradise

Fools' Gold follows on from *Fools' Paradise* (2020) in telling the story of Brexit, Britain's exit from the European Union.

Fools' Paradise focused on Theresa May's premiership and her inability to get her Withdrawal Agreement through Parliament, which resulted in a paralysis widely derided in Europe. The poem describes the UK's attempt to leave the EU in terms of the voyage of a Ship of Fools to Narragonia, the Fools' Paradise, in Sebastian Brant's German poem, *Das Narrenschiff* (*The Ship of Fools*), first published in Basel, Switzerland in 1494.

The Brexiteers had been promised a paradise funded by savings from annual budget payments to the EU, which would provide an extra £350 million a week for the NHS, and new trade deals would replace the European single market that took 43 per cent of UK exports. Zeus was exasperated by Brexit as his plan to create a United States of Europe as a staging post to a World State that will solve all the world's problems has received a setback.

Fools' Gold

Fools' Gold continues the story by focusing on Boris Johnson's premiership. Johnson won support at the hustings to select May's successor by announcing there would be no deal with the EU. He succeeded May and announced that the UK would be leaving the EU on 31 October 2019. However he was unable to get the Withdrawal Agreement through Parliament, which was the most unpleasant Parliament in living memory, completely deadlocked and full of personal abuse. After winning a general election with a stunning majority of 80, during which many promises were made of coming 'gold', Johnson tweaked May's Withdrawal Agreement – of the 599 pages less than 5 per cent of the divorce deal was changed – and got it through Parliament. The UK exited the EU on 31 January 2020. There was then a transitional period in which a trade deal was supposed to be agreed.

There was now alarm that the Withdrawal Agreement with the EU had created a border down the Irish Sea, and that Northern Ireland had in effect been lost to the United Kingdom. With Scotland and Wales having voted Remain and wanting independence in varying degrees, there were fears that the United Kingdom would break up and would pass into a Federation of the British Isles.

The costs of leaving the EU were estimated by Bloomberg Economics at £203 billion by the end of 2020: £39 billion for the divorce settlement; £125 billion in loss of growth amounting to 6 per cent of gross domestic product (GDP) worth £2.2 trillion over two years; and a proportion of £160 billion to repay loans. These costs were soon swamped by further costs as a result of the Covid-19 pandemic that spread from China, and lockdown: borrowing estimated at £391 billion by the end of 2020; at least £174.6 billion in loss of growth amounting to 9 per cent (possibly 14 per cent) of GDP; and unemployment rising to 2.5 (possibly 4) million.

All the promises of 'gold' turned out to be worthless fools' gold, and ahead was the worst recession for 100 years (since the outbreak of Spanish flu from 1918 to 1920), and possibly for 300 years (since the bursting of the South Sea Bubble in 1720). And with the world order breaking down and the breakdown now compounded by Covid-19, the simultaneous rise of China (where Covid-19 originated) and the paralysis of the Western economies, there were fears that the West would be in decline for a long while and that power was shifting from the West to the East.

At a time when there was such economic devastation in the West and little prospect of the promised trade deals as other trading nations had their own problems relating to Covid-19, it was questioned whether this was the right time to be leaving a single market that took 43 per cent of British exports and precipitate a 'double whammy' to the British economy: paying for four months' of lockdown and lack of economic activity *and* for the departure from the EU.

The Foul Parliament
UK parliaments are often known by nicknames: The Mad Parliament (1258–1264), The Addled Parliament (1614–1621), The Happy Parliament (1624–1625), The Useless Parliament (1625–1626), The Short Parliament (April – November 1640), and Barebone's Parliament (1653–1654).

The 54th UK Parliament (2005–2010) was known as "The Rotten

Parliament" because of the expenses scandal: so many MPs were found to have overclaimed their expenses and to be "rotten". The 57th Parliament from the general election in June 2017 to December 2019 was a fetid swamp in which both parties were stuck. May's three Meaningful Votes were lost, and though Johnson won a vote on his tweaked version of May's deal it was felt to be worse. Johnson made the keynote speech at Northern Ireland's DUP's 2018 conference and promised there would be no economic border down the Irish Sea, and then broke his promise and cancelled May's red line on having no economic border down the Irish Sea.

This Parliament was one of broken promises, intemperate language and shouted abuse. In 1381–1382 Chaucer entitled a satirical 700-line poem 'Parlement of Foules' (in the sense of 'birds'), and, writing in his tradition, I echo Chaucer in calling this Parliament 'The Foul Parliament': a Parliament of foul deeds and behaviour.

Covid-19

The coronavirus Covid-19 (SARS-CoV-2) had been worked on in a laboratory in the Institute of Virology, Wuhan in China.

There had been a US-funded program to work on a benign bat coronavirus for five years from 2014 with a view to discovering the aetiology of diseases, and US and Chinese research scientists had worked together without a problem, funded by the US NIH (National Institutes of Health, $3.7m for the program). This was renewed for a further six years in 2019 (funded by the US NIH and NIAID, the National Institute of Allergy and Infectious Diseases, another $3.7m for the program). This time the experiments modified a benign bat coronavirus with gain-of-function add-ons to make benign bat coronaviruses more airborne, attach themselves to the ACE-2 receptors in lungs and enter human cells, and with an envelope protein from HIV (GP141) impair immune systems. Whether it was wise to be creating a pathogen, an organism that causes a disease and is therefore a quasi-bio-weapon, to research into diseases is a moot point. But out of the first program seems to have come Remdesivir, which was sponsored by NIAID, an antiviral drug used against Ebola and later promoted as a treatment for Covid-19.

Covid-19 is thought to have escaped from Wuhan City's Biosafety Level (BSL) 4 laboratory between 6 and 11 October 2019, presumably by accident but at the time of writing deliberate intent cannot be ruled out. There were Wuhan phone records mentioning roadblocks and satellite images of full hospital car parks from 14 to 19 October. This second joint US-Chinese research programme was terminated on 24 April 2020.

The Americans knew of the escape in November 2019, and alerted Israel that same month. Covid-19 seems to have reached the UK by early December 2019 as Professor Stefansson, who was then in charge of Iceland's track-and-trace, has said that Covid-19 arrived in Iceland that month via skiers returning from the Alps and travellers from the UK. It was probably active in the UK during the general election of 12 December 2019. Yet Prime Minister Johnson did not attend five consecutive Cobra meetings on the coronavirus on 24 and 29 January and 5, 12 and 18 February 2020 when arrangements for a pandemic could have been put in place. Hancock, chairing the meetings in his place, described the risk from the virus as "low". Johnson spent two of these weeks in Chequers with his pregnant fiancée formalising his divorce, and did not attend a Cobra meeting on the virus until 28 February 2020.

There was talk of a second 'spike' or outbreak, but in fact the virus was permanently present as was the plague of 1347–1351, the Black Death which killed half England's – and Europe's – population via rat-fleas. The 1347 plague had forty 'spikes' during the next 318 years, the last one being the Great Plague of London of 1665, when blind Milton left for Chalfont St Giles with his family and dictated *Paradise Lost* to his daughter while isolating or 'shielding' with the plague outside. It was not impossible that there would be further outbreaks of Covid-19 for years to come if no vaccine could be developed that worked.

The plague turned all necks, armpits and inner thighs black, and death followed within 12 hours. Covid-19 was dangerous for the elderly and those with underlying health conditions, but it was not as severe. Nevertheless, the UK suffered the highest death rate in Europe and also the highest number of excess deaths, despite Prime Minister Johnson describing the Government's arrangements to contain the virus as "world-beating", a claim so at variance with the facts that it turned many against his Government.

Poetry as quarrelling with oneself: the cultural health of Europe
The poet Yeats wrote: "We make out of the quarrel with others, rhetoric, but of the quarrel with ourselves, poetry" (*'Anima Hominis'* in *Per Amica Silentia Lunae*, 1918). The critic, and world authority on Tennyson and Eliot, Christopher Ricks quoted this during his walk round Oxford with me on 21 June 1993, when he advised me to use blank verse in my epic poem *Overlord*. He said that great poetry comes from a poet quarrelling with himself. So Keats wrote in the 'Ode on Indolence':

O, for an age so shelter'd from annoy,
That I may never know how change the moons,
Or hear the voice of busy common-sense!

He was arguing that he should live in "honey'd indolence" with negative capability, just receiving impressions and working on them with his imagination, not understanding them scientifically. It can be argued that a poet *should* know how the moons change, but the point is, Keats wanted a life of ease he had not got, he was arguing with himself. Ricks said to me, "Yeats was right. Great poetry is produced from a quarrel with oneself. I hate Yeats, but he said something that is true. You must quarrel with yourself."

A poet should not present a political point of view in his work as it then becomes one-dimensional propaganda and probably invective, certainly rhetoric: "the art of effective or persuasive speaking or writing; language designed to persuade or impress (often with an implication of insincerity or exaggeration)", *Concise Oxford Dictionary*. A poet should present both sides in a balanced way, reconciling opposites, in accordance with the wisdom of the East which the Japanese poet Junzaburo Nishiwaki wrote out for me in Japan on 5 October 1965: +A + −A = 0. Just as all opposites – day and night, life and death, time and eternity – can be reconciled within "great zero", so all political opposites can similarly be reconciled within an underlying harmony.

Christopher Ricks sent me a 1944 first edition of *Horizon* containing T.S. Eliot's essay 'The Man of Letters and the Future of Europe' in July 2004, when I was putting the finishing touches to my *Classical Odes*. Many of my odes were on the culture of Europe, and a handwritten message from Ricks tucked inside the magazine said: "Apt to your thinking, no?" In this essay Eliot wrote:

The man of letters as such, is not concerned with the political or economic map of Europe; but he should be very much concerned with its cultural map.... The man of letters... should be able to take a longer view than either the politician or the local patriot.... The cultural health of Europe, including the cultural health of its component parts, is incompatible with extreme forms of both nationalism and internationalism.... The responsibility of the man of letters at the present time... should be vigilantly watching the conduct of politicians and economists, for the purpose of criticizing and warning, when the decisions and actions of the politicians and economists are likely to have cultural consequences. Of these consequences the man of letters should qualify himself to judge. Of the possible cultural consequences of their activities, politicians and economists are usually oblivious; the man of letters is better qualified to foresee them, and to perceive their seriousness.

In this important extract (the first epigraph in both *Fools' Paradise* and *Fools' Gold*) Eliot is saying that the man of letters has to be very concerned with the cultural health of Europe as it is incompatible with extreme forms of nationalism and internationalism. (Writing in 1944, he was thinking of Fascism and Communism.) He argues that the man of letters should vigilantly watch the conduct of politicians and economists as their decisions and actions are likely to have cultural consequences – of which the politicians and economists are usually oblivious. He argues that the man of letters is better qualified to foresee these consequences and to perceive their seriousness than the politicians and economists.

The Europeanness of the British
In both *Fools' Paradise* and *Fools' Gold* I have foreseen the cultural consequences of Brexit, and have quarrelled with myself on the Europeanness of the British while at the same time putting forward the case for a global Britain that is scarcely credible in view of the UK's woeful lack of resources.

In *Fools' Gold* the Europeanness of the British is a historic fact. Practically all the UK's population has arrived from Europe – the Celts, Romans, Anglo-Saxons, Vikings, Normans and many other such ethnic groups – and it seems that my own ancestor Carolus Haggar arrived from Bruges in 1366. The UK has always been a part of the European civilisation, especially since the Dark Ages, and has shared Christianity, the Church and the Pope with the rest of Europe. The UK's history has been intricately connected with European history from the time when England ruled part of northern France through to fighting two world wars in Europe, and helping the Eastern-European nations break free from the Soviet Empire and join the European Union.

Nationalism versus regionalism
I have also quarrelled with myself over nationalism and regionalism (the European Union). The UK is a Union of four nations in current danger of breaking up, and it acts as one nation-state and is represented at the UN as such. Having been a British intelligence agent for four years and risked my life many times for my nation-state, I am arguing with myself regarding the merits and demerits of nationalism as opposed to regionalism (the European Union), and, I have foreseen a coming World State not in my lifetime but perhaps in my grandchildren's lifetimes.

For this to happen the US, a coming United States of Europe including Russia (an integrationist EU with fiscal union) and a Pacific Union including China need to form a united federation of the world that will preserve internal independence but combine externally to abolish war and nuclear weapons, solve the world's problems relating to poverty, famine and disease, and have a united policy towards climate change and on viruses to prevent future pandemics. The Eastern wisdom of seeing that all opposites – *yang* and *yin* – are reconciled in the *Tao*, +A + –A = 0, applies to nationalism + regionalism (Europe), which are reconciled in the political Universalism of a World State: +nationalism + –nationalism (regionalism) = the Universalism of a World State.

As a quarreller-with-myself in *Fools' Paradise* and *Fools' Gold* I am seeking to preserve the cultural health of the European civilisation, to which the UK has always belonged and always will belong, by arguing with myself about both the Europeanness of the British and the nationalism of nation-states which always leads to wars and trade wars, as the experience of the two 20th-century world wars and colonial competition, and Trump's 'America first', fully bear out. Brexit is a move away from Europeanness to a new nationalism, and, I would argue, from a Union to a new Federation of the British Isles. This move has profound cultural consequences the politicians and economists may not have foreseen, but which are apparent to a discerning man of letters.

Mock-heroic verse
In *Fools' Paradise* I wrote in the mock-heroic tradition – heroic couplets with an epic tone – of Dryden's political perspective in 'Absalom and Achitophel' (1681) and of Pope's social satire in 'The Rape of the Lock'(1712–1714) and *The Dunciad* (1728–1729, 1742, published as a whole in 1743). Like these works by Dryden and Pope, my *Fools' Paradise* is in rhymed heroic couplets, which I used in my 'Zeus's Ass' and 'Zeus's Emperor', poems about Blair.

It is appropriate for the man of letters to hold politicians to account for the need to maintain the standards of the cultural health of Europe, as Eliot urged, and one way of doing this is via the heroic couplet, which affirms standards while ridiculing and satirising follies and vices. A prose model for such an approach would have to be the incomparable Swift. In *Fools' Paradise* I continued the tradition of the rhymed heroic couplet, which is admirably suited to mock-heroic and ridicule.

Heroic verse
In *Fools' Gold* I have, on reflection, gone back to heroic verse, blank verse, which I used in my two epic poems *Overlord* and *Armageddon*,

to hold politicians to account and uphold the standards required to maintain the cultural health of Europe as advocated by T.S. Eliot in 'The Man of Letters and the Future of Europe' (1944). The catastrophic turn of events that saw Brexit overtaken by Covid-19 has shifted the public tone, and the nature of responding to politicians, beyond mock-heroic into the territory of epic, my two poetic epics and my three masques (*The Dream of Europa, King Charles the Wise* and *The Coronation of King Charles*), all of which have serious implications and are also in heroic verse.

In this I am reminded of Milton's preface to *Paradise Lost* in which, under a heading *The Verse*, he champions "English heroic verse without rimes as that of Homer in Greek and of Virgil in Latin" and laments "the troublesome and modern bondage of riming" which is "the invention of a barbarous age, to set off wretched matter and lame metre".

Quite simply, in *Fools' Gold* the coronavirus pandemic compounds Brexit in bringing disaster to lives and livelihoods, and to the UK's economy. At the time of writing there have been 141 million cases of Covid-19 worldwide and 3.01 million deaths, and Covid has killed more than 567,000 Americans and more than 127,000 British citizens. For comparison, more than 291,000 Americans were killed in combat in the Second World War, and 40,000 British citizens were killed in the Blitz.

To put it another way, the tone of *Fools' Paradise* is of the follies and vices of the politicians which have led to a colossal mistake, the biggest mistake in British history since the Second World War (and perhaps since the loss of America). The tone of *Fools' Gold* is of the consequences of this mistake, which are compounded by Covid-19, and the heroic verse of my epic poems and masques is more suitable and appropriate to the rawness and mortality of these consequences.

Fools' Gold, then, is in heroic verse. What the heroic line loses in rhyme it gains in music. Dr Johnson wrote in his 'Life of Milton' in *Lives of the Poets*: "The music of the English heroic line strikes the ear so faintly that it is easily lost, unless all the syllables of every line co-operate together." In my heroic line I use the iambic pentameter, which has been central to English verse over 600 years from Chaucer to Tennyson, and I have sought to avoid "lame metre" (Milton) by varying my iambic feet with trochees (– ◡), anapaests (◡ ◡ –) and dactyls (– ◡ ◡) that add a lively skip. I recall a rhyme that conveys what these metres do:

The iamb saunters through my book,
Trochees rush and tumble;
While the anapaest runs like a hurrying brook,
Dactyls are stately and classical.

I also use and other less-well-known feet such as tribrachs (◡ ◡ ◡), bacchiuses (◡ ◡ –), cretics (– ◡ –) and amphibrachs (◡ – ◡), that allow individual words and syllables to be stressed within the musicality of the regular metre.

In this I am conscious of being the son of two musicians: my mother was a violinist who gave recitals in the 1930s and my father was a singer, a tenor with a very rich voice, and they performed together at many musical evenings in the 1950s. Such musicality as can be found in my verse can be attributed to the classical music that was constantly played and performed in the family home when I was a child.

When I was nearing the end of *Fools' Gold*, on 10 November 2020 (the morning after a new Pfizer vaccine against Covid had been announced) I was woken early from sleep by a series of seemingly pre-prepared revelations from the beyond that reminded me of how I encountered the heroic line and its varying skips at school. I was shown chunks of verse I had learned while reading the heroic couplets of Chaucer's *Prologue* and the heroic verse of Shakespeare's *Macbeth* for 'O' level English Literature at the age of 14, and the skips in Chaucer's "As wel in cristendom as in hethenesse" and in Shakespeare's "Tomorrow, and tomorrow, and tomorrow" and "To the last syllable of recorded time". I was shown chunks of verse I had learned during 'O' level Greek and Latin from Euripides' *Alcestis* and the dactylic hexameters of Homer, Virgil and Ovid, and dwelt on a particular skipping line from book 12 of Homer's *Odyssey*:

ἀλλ᾽ ὅτε δὴ τὴν νῆσον ἐλείπομεν, οὐδέ τις ἄλλη
φαίνετο γαιάων, ἀλλ᾽ οὐρανὸς ἠδὲ θάλασσα....

I was shown myself sitting reading Milton's *Paradise Lost* by the Seine in Paris in April 1959 when I was 19 and a skipping line from the opening passage: "And chiefly Thou, O Spirit, that dost prefer" I was also shown that my use of cantos in 'Zeus's Ass', 'Zeus's Emperor', *Fools' Paradise* and *Fools' Gold* came from my reading of Dante in the summer of 1957, just after I turned 18, and from my visit to Ezra Pound in Rapallo. And I was shown that my use of Zeus in my poems and masques came out of my Greek studies at school.

In short, I was alert to varying the heroic iambic pentameter at school while I was getting 89 per cent for 'O' level English Literature and three As for my 'A' level Latin, Greek and Ancient History (which won me an Essex County Major Scholarship and enabled me to go to Oxford, hence my lifelong loyalty to Essex). In giving me a good grounding in traditional syllabic verse, which is beneath the stress-based system of modern European poetry, my early education worked. There are many instances of varying skips in my heroic lines – my epic poem *Overlord* has over 41,000 heroic lines and my epic poem *Armageddon* 25,000 – and there are many instances in *Fools' Gold*, for example in the last two lines of canto XXIV: "And where is British pragmatic common sense,/ The realistic eye that detects fools' gold?"

This extraordinary pouring-in of revelations ended in a sequence of at least a dozen expanding circles of Light each radiating outwards into my mind one after the other like rapid ripples from a stone thrown into a pool but with the force of the expanding shock wave of an exploding nuclear bomb, as if the Muses and angelic orders were priming my earthbound consciousness for my coming work on *Fools' Gold*, indicating that they were working with my heroic verse to chart the end of the pandemic in *Fools' Gold*.

The good thing about English Literature is that it is a tradition and one can link oneself to previous models within the tradition – in the case of *Fools' Gold*, Milton and Tennyson – while avoiding slavish imitation, varying what the masters of the past did to achieve effects more appropriate to our time when today's readers follow "24-hour news" and the phrases of news reports form part of their everyday language. I have used the heroic line to hold politicians to account and uphold the standards required to maintain the cultural health of Europe in a more serious way, as the cultural future of the UK and wider Europe during the rest of the 21st century will be affected by the blunders associated with Brexit and Covid-19.

Poet of decline and world unity

I became a poet in Japan in 1965–1966. My Modernist poem 'The Silence', written during 18 months while I was a Professor there, reflects Western decline and Eastern wisdom, and in 1966 I visited China, and then Russia twice (on my way back on leave from, and again during my return to, Japan). In those days I was thinking deeply about Western decline – the Japanese asked me to teach me a year's course to my postgraduate students called 'The Decline of the West' from 1966 to 1967 – and while on leave in England in the summer of 1966 I wrote in 'Archangel', my poem on Communism:

How but by containing both sides, can we heal
This split down the mind of Europe and the world?

In Moscow I had visited the Cathedral of the Archangel within the Kremlin compound on 9 June 1966, and staring at the icon of the

Archangel Michael I glimpsed a united Europe and a united world, and I wrote of a "World-Lord" who presided over a World State, and its leaders:

Decades of contemplation
Show in their white-haired peace
As, trusting to perfect feelings,
They value each equal they greet;
Until, whispering on silence,
They glide to the Leaders' Hall,
Their hearts, with a World-Lord's wholeness,
At the centre of life, of all,
Their hearts where all past and future meet.

On 22 April 2019 I told an audience in Moscow that I had first glimpsed a united world inside the Kremlin, and was roundly applauded. The audience included a number of Russian servicemen in military uniform.

In 'Old Man in a Circle', which I also wrote on leave in 1966, I saw the West in deep decline. I wrote of the strength of the UK's military at the time of the First World War, and its weakness in 1966:

And all down Piccadilly, the indomitable Grand Fleet steamed,
71 battleships and battlecruisers, 118 cruisers,
147 destroyers and 76 submarines;
And on the dreadnoughts our guardian angels sang
"Rule Britannia, Britannia rules the seas."...

Aegospotami and Midway. Ah the maritime:
One blink and a whole armada is knocked to bits
Or sold abroad, or stored, as "obsolete",
And shipless Admirals' voices float from aerials
To 4 aircraft carriers, 2 commando ships,
2 cruisers and a few destroyers and frigates –
O Senior Service.
As I left Downing Street during the Seamen's Strike,
Big Ben peered over the trees and pulled a face
And Nelson raised an arm.

Today's ship count would show an even steeper decline.

I have seen the European civilisation rising into a United States of Europe and the UK declining towards the break-up of its Union and the establishing of a Federation, further on towards decline, similar to Russia's decline from the Soviet Union to the Russian Federation. In a sense, *Fools' Paradise* and *Fools' Gold* are within the tradition of my 'Old Man in a Circle' and similarly hold a mirror up to Nature to reflect the UK's decline. I have written what I have seen, the dwindling and diminishing of my nation-state from ruling a quarter of the world when I was born before the Second World War to Little England, at odds with Scotland, Wales and Northern Ireland, and the European Union.

In the Victorian time the British Poets Laureate were expected to reflect national events in their works. Hence Tennyson's 'Ode on the Death of the Duke of Wellington' (1852) and 'The Charge of the Light Brigade' (1854). Their works were expected to lift the morale of the serving forces throughout the British Empire. The last thing a Poet Laureate should be doing is dwelling on national decline. I am grateful to have been left free to be a court poet (in the sense that my subject matter is drawn from the court) who reflects what I have seen even though it dismays me, and has dismayed me for 54 years.

The poet is a truth-teller who holds his mirror up to Nature, the universe, the Age, and the court. Like Hans Holbein the Younger he reflects the main royal and political figures of his day. Holbein truthfully painted Sir Thomas More, Henry VIII, Jane Seymour, Anne of Cleves, Thomas Cromwell, Erasmus and (on the day they heard that England was finally leaving the Catholic Church of Rome) The Ambassadors. I have truthfully painted Eisenhower, Churchill, Montgomery, George W. Bush, Hitler, bin Laden, Tony Blair, Van Rompuy, Theresa May, Boris Johnson and Prince Charles. In the course of painting the universe the poet will truthfully paint what is going on in the court. The poet should aim to put his easel up in the seat of government and power and paint the court from an independent point of view.

The true poet reflects the Truth and is not a propagandist for his administration or regime. Queen Elizabeth I in 'The Rainbow Portrait' is shown clutching a rainbow – a symbol of the State's control of the dramatists' inspiration in the 16th century – and there may still be an expectation that a State appointee today will be a flattering propagandist and not be truthful.

As I wrote in the Preface to *Fools' Paradise*, the true poet stands apart from society and reflects the true state of his civilisation's cultural health. The true poet has to be a truth-bearer in a mendacious Age to reflect the central idea of his civilisation and culture, in my case the European civilisation and culture. I believe I caught its positive vision in *The Dream of Europa*, the first of my three masques. This has to be read alongside my second masque, *King Charles the Wise*, in which the case for Brexit is put to Prince Charles by Britannia. All my works have to be read in conjunction with another of my works as there is a dialectic, +A + −A = 0, at work between pairs of my works, behind the scenes.

All my works are aspects of winning through to world unity: my vision of a coming World State, as forecast in my third masque, *The Coronation of King Charles*. And a vision of a united world lies behind both *Fools' Paradise* and *Fools' Gold*. My quarrelling with myself enables me to tell the truth to imperfect politicians without being locked up in the Tower of London like the first Metaphysical poet, Sir Walter Raleigh, but in such a way that the positive side of the politicians' message is also shown, and there is a tension between the two. For in +A + −A = 0, the +A and the −A are tethered together and are inseparable, even though they are reconciled within a larger underlying vision.

A Universalist poet: reconciling Eliot and Tennyson

Fundamentally I am a Universalist poet. In *Fools' Paradise* and *Fools' Gold* I endeavour to show all conflicting points of view and opposites within an underlying unity. Universalism affirms the fundamental unity of the universe and of all humankind, and the Universalist poet shows where the misjudgments and self-interested decisions and actions of nationalist and internationalist (regionalist, European) politicians make things worse for their civilisation and culture with cultural consequences, as T.S. Eliot urged men of letters (including himself) to do in 1944 when the British Empire was at its height.

Fools' Paradise and *Fools' Gold*, two national poems by a man of letters, attempt to foresee, take a longer view, criticise and warn of the cultural consequences and seriousness of the decisions and actions of the UK's nationalist and the EU's internationalist politicians, of which the politicians and economists – and SAGE scientists – may be oblivious and need to understand. As Sebastian Brant wrote in the introduction to *Das Narrenschiff* (*The Ship of Fools*) in 1494:

Wer sich für ein Narren macht
Der ist bald zû eym wisen gemacht.

This can be translated: "He who recognises himself as a fool will soon become wise."

In following Eliot's concern for European civilisation and culture and in warning of the cultural consequences of politicians, and in following Tennyson's focus on national events and a "Federation of the world" in 'Locksley Hall' in Tennysonian narrative rather than in the abbreviated, concentrated narrative of the Modernist sequence of images, both within the Classical heroic couplet of Dryden and Pope and the Classical heroic line of blank verse of Milton and Tennyson, I believe I have brought about a Universalist reconciliation of the approaches of Eliot and Tennyson in *Fools' Paradise* and *Fools' Gold* – and, indeed, in all my poetic works that use the heroic couplet ('Zeus's Ass' and 'Zeus's Emperor' as well as *Fools' Paradise*), the heroic line of blank verse (my two epic poems *Overlord* and *Armageddon* and my five verse plays as well as *Fools' Gold*) and rhymed stanzas (my *Classical Odes* and the majority of my poems in *Collected Poems* and my more recent poems).

8–10, 18, 21, 25 August; 10–11 November 2020; 5 March, 20 April 2021

APPENDICES

Collected Poems and the one-volume *Overlord* each has an Appendix. These Appendices are referred to in the Prefaces, and as they supplement the Prefaces to these two and other books they are reproduced here.

Appendix 1

Vision and Technique in the Collected Poems
(See Collected Poems, pp.853–888)

1. The Experience of Illumination

Extracts from Nicholas Hagger's Autobiography [A Mystic Way]

(1) Zen, Japan 1964–1965
I went to Kogenji temple with the graduate student Mr Munekata. We passed tombs and a statue of the Buddha, and the Master was bald and bespectacled and in a *yukata*. I meditated in a great heat among rows of silent cross-legged Japanese and then slept, and meditated again just before dawn with the rice-paper doors open to the night and the whirring cicadas. The meditation lasted an hour and a half, and through my half-closed eyes, sitting like a Buddha, I now and again glimpsed the progress of the dawn in the polished floor. I went very deep and got below the level of time and differences and becoming to a timeless being in myself that could have existed forever, and I did not want the meditation to end and afterwards felt very peaceful and inwardly whole. I saw how the Buddha might have reached a state in which his bodily aura was enlightened from within....

A further development began on 11 September 1965. I had worked on my essay all day and could not sleep. I closed my eyes and a succession of images rose: scrivenings in a foreign language – Arabic or Hebrew – in yellow and blue; a puddle and an orb of fire within it; corn stalks with many ears of corn; a whirlpool. Then it seemed I was going down a well, and saw the orb of the sky getting smaller as I descended. Two days later, on 13 September, I had more images behind closed eyes, also late at night. A series of gold heads went slowly by as if on a conveyor belt: some Egyptian, some Negroid, some Babylonian. Then there were exquisite diamonds in green and mauve which lasted 30 seconds. When I got off to sleep I dreamt I was on the second floor of a Turkish Byzantine café and there was an earthquake and I rushed down the stairs and out into the courtyard through falling masonry to find everything in ruins, all foundations crumbled. Then I was in a morgue among many corpses, which suddenly sat up and came to life, jingling their bones.

I did not finish my essay until the end of September, and had then written almost no poetry for six weeks. The essay [see 2 in this Appendix, pp.447–457] was a vindication of the method I was groping for in 'The Silence', abbreviated narrative in an emotionally linked sequence of images, and although I was tired from the heat and the effort of the reading and research, I felt I had justified my poetic method. Now I had time to walk to the Cathedral and gaze at symbols which trap the eternal. I was still sleeping very badly, and on 6 October, still awake at dawn, I thought I understood the Absolute in terms of the Stone Garden: at the underlying level of unity there is no difference between the particular forms of existence, and the Absolute manifests itself through unity.

My development reached a climax in mid-October. On 8 October I went to a Tutankhamen exhibition, and saw the gold mask which had arrived in Japan from Egypt. It corresponded to one of the Egyptian gold heads I had seen in mid-September. The next day we went to Nobe. The trees were full of autumnal tints, the sky was blue, the rice had been harvested from the paddy fields, which were full of stumps, and dry rice hung like straw from poles. The sea had a typhoon swell. On 10 October, back in Tokyo, I wrote the passage about the Stone Garden in 'The Silence'. Later that same evening I went for a drink with Tuohy, who invited me to go to China with him the following spring, and write some articles.... In the late evening of 11 October I went to the bathroom from our dark bedroom and, turning on the light, was flooded with golden light behind my closed eyes. The pattern was of rings, each linked into a golden net.

The next few days I worked very intensely on sections of 'The Silence', in the course of which I fulfilled my teaching commitments and attended a farewell reception at the palace of Prince and Princess Hitachi.... I spent much of 16 October searching for an image for my centre, which became the image of a child between a husband and wife (Nadia's role in my marriage) and writing the 'poet of the self' passage and on Sunday 17 October I was so tired in the afternoon that I slept.

I seemed to sink down within myself, and when I awoke at 4.30pm and went to my study and looked out of the bungalow window I seemed to be a floor below my thoughts. I sat down and thought about the centre of myself in relation to the cosmos, and as my *Diaries* record: "... I understood *Tao*, that just as my self-centre unites me, so *Tao* could unite life and death and all cosmic opposites and pluralities, so that all men are brothers." The next morning, 18 October, a Monday, I stayed at home, and as my *Diaries* record: "All morning I have been filled with a round white light: I cannot see it, except occasionally when I glimpse it and am dazzled, but I know it is there. It is like a white sun. This is, I suppose, what Christians refer to as the soul – the centre of the self. And the mystical experience is given meaning by the relation between the centre and the sun, so that everything is one." I observed that it was not the universe that had changed, but my self and my perception of it "so that it now seems more harmonious". I observed that it "would be easy to follow a path of sainthood".

Looking back I can see that these brief gleams in 1965 represented my first illuminative life, a first glimpse of *satori* or enlightenment following a shift from my rational, social ego to a new centre within my self, my soul. I had no doubt that the development was a consequence of my long process of self-discovery as I wrote 'The Silence' and that I had glimpsed a Light within my soul. On 31 October I connected the experience with a passage I found on "luminous phenomena, photisms" in William James's *The Varieties of Religious Experience* in which James quotes Charles Finney's *Memoirs* (1876): "A light perfectly ineffable shone in my soul.... This light seemed like the brightness of the sun in every direction. It was too intense for the eyes.... I think I knew something then, by actual experience, of that light that prostrated Paul on the way to Damascus." This quotation is in a chapter on "conversion", and James shows that conversion cures and unifies the sick soul and divided self and takes it to potential sainthood.

(2) London, September 1971
On the Saturday morning I read Evelyn Underhill's *Mysticism* (which I had happily packed) in my Worthing room and read of the Dark Night as "this last and drastic purgation of the spirit"... I wrote in my *Diaries*, there in my Worthing room: "I am on the journey and I am not sure how far I have gone, how far I have got to go.... Something is happening to my perception: the glow that unites the moon and the corn.... The white that unites sky and sea – yet it is hardly there.... Something is happening to my way of seeing, and I do not understand." Later I wrote of "this mystic glow around beautiful everything, this strange white light round the sea, the sky". The experience found its way into my poem 'Flow: Moon and Sea'.

On the Sunday morning I woke and lay with my eyes closed and was surprised by two visions: one of a cross with a white light behind it, and one of a small figure of the Virgin Mary. I thought nothing more of these....

I was on the verge of the two most intense months of my life. I was whole, alive, fresh, and had had a glimpse of what was to come. A spring in my clear consciousness was about to wobble visions up, like the bubbles in the spring of Ain el Faras at Ghadames.

I now come to the momentous day, Friday 10 September 1971, the equivalent for me of what Monday 23 November 1654 meant to Pascal, who wrote down his experience and sewed the parchment into his doublet and *wore* it until he died, so important was his illumination to him.

The day began unpromisingly as an ordinary school day, the last day of the first week of the autumn term. I returned home and wrote a letter.... Margaret came into my room.... I picked up Underhill's *Mysticism* and opened the book at random.... I read aloud a passage about the philosopher's stone, how it turns metal into gold.... (I) carried on reading to Margaret. I read passages on different mystics: St Teresa, Mme Guyon. There was more on the philosopher's stone and mention of the Light.

I felt a quickening within me. Margaret said, "It's a Flowing Light, it flows upwards. Just sit and feel the peace." We sat side by side and looked at the plane tree for about half an hour. Then she said quietly, "Lie down." I lay down. She said, "Shut your eyes." I shut out the world, and waited, watching within. At her direction I gave my breathing to the twilight until I fell into a trance. And from behind my closed eyes, looking into my closed eyes I saw white light, flowing upwards: a tree, white against the black inside me, a bare winter tree of white fire, flowing, rippling as if in water. I put my hands over my eyes, I wanted nothing outside to spoil the brightness of what I saw within, and then, as it were, a spring opened within me like the spring in the Sahara, and for a good hour and a half the visions wobbled up inside me like the wobbling bubbles in Ain el Faras. I remembered the first two most clearly: a centre of light shining down from a great height, and then a white flower, like a dahlia or a chrysanthemum, with very detailed, breathtakingly beautiful cells. This was my first glimpse of the celebrated Golden Flower, the centre and source of my being.

There were too many visions for me to remember one quarter of what I saw. But almost immediately a sun broke through my inner dark and hung in the "sky" with a dazzling whiteness. Then I saw a fountain of light and then all was dark and I saw stars, then strange patterns, old paintings I had never seen before, old gods and saints. When I came out of it, I was refreshed. I felt turned inside out and wobbly at the knees, as if I had made passionate love.

Having been born a Catholic, Margaret went off to pray. Alone, I fell on my knees in the dark. I screwed up my eyes to shut out the outer world, and there was a white point, a small circle of light that went deep up into the heavens. I said aloud, "I surrender", and the light moved and changed until it became a celestial curtain blown in the wind, like the *aurora borealis*.

Then I felt limp, exhausted. I had to stop. Blissfully happy I went and drank in the Bunch of Grapes. I just wanted to forget. I was filled with an afterglow, and my fingers were moist.

In the interests of faithfulness as to what I experienced, I now quote from my *Diaries* entry, which was written at 8.20pm:

It came in me: a tree, white against black inside me, a bare winter tree of white fire, flowing, rippling as if in water…. And more. A centre of light shining down as if from a great height, rays coming down like rocket blasts or fireworks. Then a white flower like a chrysanthemum (detailed cells). And so much more…. A sun breaking through cloud (a moon?). Stars. And a fountain of white light. Patterns like my *mandala*. And I was behind my chest – in my *heart* – lying down, breathing slowly and deeply with half closed eyes, near sleep as at Worthing when I had two visions… but this was what I tried to find in the temple. When I sat up I felt as if I'd made love, I felt refreshed, turned inside out, and wobbly at the knees. I asked to be alone. Margaret had seen a bishop with a crozier ("God" she said) and a painting with "God sitting on a throne". She went to pray. I wanted to write this…. It was dark, my window was open. The clock ticked, distant traffic roared. I fell on my knees in the dark, hands clasped and there was a white point, then a circle of light that went deep deep up into the heavens. I said "I surrender" and the light moved and changed till I felt exhausted – but again, as after love. I want to push it away now, forget about it and have a drink in the Bunch of Grapes. I feel relaxed. After all my seeking, I have found my heart, my centre, my soul, I have found my white light. I feel exhausted but blissfully happy. Full of love. It is as if I had made love in my chest, my knees. And now, I do not feel alone. There is an aura around me.

"Prayer".… I now have something to commune with. A round blob, sometimes like a jellyfish, sometimes like a celestial curtain blown in a wind – the *aurora borealis* in the *Marvels of the Universe*. That is what I now have found. Feel too limp and exhausted to write any more. Or to communicate my weary jubilation.

Almost immediately afterwards I began to interpret:

Me and my Flowing Light. Nothing else. Everyone has it. The saints are ordinary people who have well-kept gardens – there is nothing 'heroic' about them. They are no more forward than me. I was like a child that does not know it can walk until it has been told it can… until it has been taught. I am like a little boy – worn out by such little effort. Though as I grow…. I am quite drunk with it. So wobbly on my knees. Drunk with love. Can't take any more now. Too tired. At great peace. At such peace that if I were pastor Bonhoeffer, I could die with tranquillity.

The next day I closed my eyes, buried my eyes in the crook of my arm, and it happened again. I saw a beautiful dome made of light, like a spider's web, and then a sumptuous yellow and purple tomb. Then, like an old gold death mask, on a primitive shield, the magnificent face of God. When I finished I felt shaky again, like a child taking its first tottering steps.

Almost immediately I made another attempt to define what had happened in my *Diaries*:

At peace. Feel turned inside out still, infinitely relaxed, totally un-nervous.... I have been loved by a great light. I still feel as if I have made love. This is enlightenment. *Satori. Illumination.*

And again:

Fingers wet after vision: inside a cave, which became a beautiful dome seen from inside in spider's web like, filigree light. Also, earlier, a sumptuous tomb (yellow and purple here). An old primitive OE (Old English) shield with a face, looming up – the face of God, like an old gold death mask.... All this after Margaret returned from confession at the Brompton Oratory and we talked about the Way and read the three temptations (don't ask for proof, don't want) and discussed the poor in spirit. Margaret: "If people throw stones at me – revile me – I give them bread.... I have fallen from the pinnacle of the temple, I shouldn't be up there.... The Catholic Church is the only one for me." Now feel shaky again, like a child that has taken tottering steps.

I had enough strength to walk to the Brompton Oratory. Its Italianate baroque splendour always uplifted me, and I later found it appalling that the KGB would use St Patrick's Chapel as a dead-letter box. For some time I stood in the aisle. At length, for the first time for years I went into the pews and knelt and gave myself to the silence. I concentrated on the point of white light between my closed eyes, and observed the eternal light in the basket, the light which is never put out and from which all candles are lit. And I felt an immense peace.

That night I lay again for an hour and a half. I saw a silver egg which I thought was the philosopher's stone; a round mirror; a shadowy Christ on a cross; a flaming devil in white light; a saint with a halo round his head. The visions poured up: a yellow rose; black thorns against squirming, moving white lines; a child that looked foetal; a high death-mask, like an Eastern god, with a high crown. And then, with breathtaking clarity, Christ: a man with dark brown hair, a crown of thorns, and a reddy-brown robe worn round his shoulders and gathered by a pin under his chin. It was a direct frontal view, the vision gazed straight at me.

Then there were more patterns, like frost on glass. And all the time there were hints of a white flower and suns and shafts of light. My arm was across my eyes to black out the dusk, and every so often I had to stop and rest. Then I saw a starless night, with an outline of something at the top, as though I were looking up at the universe from the bottom of a round pit. Through this a point of white light always broke, and as it got larger, everything started again. In the end I saw a long white-hot line like the trunk of a tree, down the centre of my being, and I again knelt and said "I surrender." And, as if in answer, the point of light swelled into a vivid moon.

And again I need to record what I wrote in my *Diaries*:

Shaky moist fingers, cold feeling on forehead after spending 6.30pm–8pm lying on my bed with Margaret having visions. An egg, in silver, empty inside – I thought it was the Philosopher's Stone: a round mirror: Christ on the cross – shadowy, and a flaming devil or demon in paisley blotches of white light: a saint with a halo round his head in full length facing to the right: and then – how can I remember out of the abundance of them – a yellow rose; black thorns against squirming, moving white lines; a child – a foetus; a death-mask, like the Buddha, with a high crown, probably in gold though it looked white of course; and, with breathtaking clarity, Christ – I think in effigy: with a crown of thorns, brown – dark – brown hair and a Roman robe gathered at a pin under the chin (he looked straight at me) and worn round the shoulders; then... what? Patterns? Like frost on glass. And a primitive shield. All the time there were hints of a white flower and suns, and shafts of light fell towards me. Sometimes after a rest (for my arm was across my eyes to black out the dusk outside and it ached every so often and I had to rest) I saw a starless night, I was looking up into an empty universe... very aware of distance and space. Then it would all begin again, starting from a point of white light which got larger, then broke, like a moon through clouds, scattering spider's webs of shapes. The long white-hot line like the trunk of a tree in the centre. After Margaret went to her room I fell on my knees and covered my eyes with my palms and said again, "I surrender", and the still point came up and broke through the night into a vivid moon, as if in answer. Then worn out and wobbly on my knees, I knew it was time to stop. I have found my heart, the centre of myself. *Practice*, knowledge is not enough, there must be practice.

After that I had several evenings of visions. I saw the Flower a number of times. I saw the philosopher's stone – an egg in the heavens above a tree. I saw prison gates, and, gathering in a majestic splendour among the stars and floating down, nearer and nearer and nearer, looking slightly to the right, full of experience-frowns and bearded like a Greek sculpture or a Rodin, the magnificent aged face of God. I saw the sky as van Gogh painted it, and a recurring vision was of a river of Flowing Light. This made me say: "Time is the cutting up of eternity, which can be known through the Silence." Yet when it came to evaluating what had happened to me, I was reluctant to give it any metaphysical significance. I preferred to think, 'I've made direct contact with my imagination.' I regarded my visions as being no more metaphysical than the opium vision Coleridge had of Xanadu.

I fell asleep on the Saturday night exhausted. Once again in the interest of faithfulness to the visions I experienced when I awoke the next morning, I quote from my *Diaries* for 12 September: 'This morning more visions: a red flower and, after streaks of white, then red light across the centre of my being – the great cable of my soul: prison gates with arrows, in black; an egg in the heavens above a tree, an egg which turned into the Philosopher's Stone; and again, gathering in majestic splendour among stars and then floating down nearer and nearer, the magnificent aged face of God, looking slightly to the right, all experience-frowns and bushy-moustached and bearded, like a great Rodin or Greek sculpture. And so much more, I have temporarily forgotten. Now do not feel so weak on my knees. I am learning to walk. How long will this period of illumination last?' On that Sunday, "both my clocks stopped within a quarter of an hour of each other." Looking back, I am sure the intensity of the energy that flooded in stopped the clocks.

And again, still from 12 September:

Before lunch. Lay on my bed, hands over my eyes. More visions. In colour against stars, paintings in blues and yellows and reds and browns. The face of God again, as an old master. Again, as a Russian icon. Earlier, a white wheel. I emerge from these contacts with my imagination and soul fresh and whole in my centre.... Still the images come. A tree, wide trunk, a white light behind it.... Earlier red lights – red for my throbbing passion.... And more: the night sky and star seen through a crown of black thorns. A yellow mountain range sloping down and a blob of a moon. And hundreds of van Gogh rings round the stars – all in white. Perhaps I should become a painter of these visions. Also, life spreading like roots or nerves round blobs – in thin and white map contours.

And again at 3.30:

Vision: a golden star (two triangles?) on a blue wall, golden rays pouring out of it. Then a silver star in the heavens, white round it, turning into an amoeba? A jellyfish? An iced-cake ceiling melting into a sky and whirling stars.

At Dino's, a waitress had caught my eye and smiled. She was from Columbia. I spent the next two hours out with her and then: "Back to visions: Tudor suns, bamboo leaves, wrought iron gateways." The next day was a Monday, and I spent most of it at school. My *Diaries* record of the evening: "Vision: Tudor rose." And the following day: "Visions abating."

I now understood that in my soul I had an inner television, and I understood how man lived life before the 1880s, before electricity when there were dark nights and no external television and merely inner prayer to keep one feeling at peace. And I did feel at peace. I had the Mystic Peace. I was not in Hell now. I sat, utterly still, and gazing at the plane tree outside my window brought an ecstatic serenity. I felt at one with my surroundings, I was a stranger to nothing. I had found that joy and love of everything which is the highest meaning and the justification of suffering. "Stop looking and you will find," Margaret had told me, meaning I would find my heart. I had found.

It was now apparent that something had happened on 10 September. At the very same moment that I made the breakthrough into a life of imaginary [imaginative] vision, Margaret felt a call back to the Church – at the very same time. Now she spoke more and more of the Church, telling me it was the centre which stopped one from "pulling people to pieces", and she urged me to speak to a priest. But I knew I wouldn't. I was not interested in relating my experience to any doctrinal belief. Margaret told me: "Your task is to teach the younger generation, be a prophet to the younger generation. They will take it from you. Then you can say: 'I did it the hard way – at my school.'" I knew that I had a role in relation to the younger generation, but I felt it would be as an artist now, not as a priest. "No more mountains for you," Margaret said. "You've climbed the last one."

There was a lull for a few days… and then on 24 September I brought

Margaret some dahlias and thrilled at how like my golden flower they were. Later that day I had more visions: "The flowers in my soul. Streaks of white light inside me. The picture book of my imagination – leafing through it like an old scrapbook of strange patterns."

I still thought of having located my imagination rather than an external metaphysical Reality, and I wrote in my *Diaries* on 25 September: "After the suffering, the gain that justifies the suffering, the meaning…. I have found the source of my being, the fountain of my imagination, the spiked dahlia of the golden (white) flower." And again: "The meaning of life – the highest meaning – is to be found in joy, to get which you have to suffer. A stern message to the young…. To find the joy, and live, you must suffer." I meant that you must suffer at a deep level, at the deep level of losing everything, for it gives you meaning; not at the level of shallowness when there is no accompanying meaning, only futility.

But I was groping towards God. I saw we are on the threshold of a new epoch, that a European rebirth was in the air, one that restored the soul after a time of doubt, that a new view of man and of the universe was ahead and consequently a new philosophy [Universalism]. It would be based on the mystic six: self-stripping, not-wanting (or detachment), discarding (or purifying), growing, flowing and peace. Perceptivism was the word I used, for man must change his perception so that he perceives the unity of the universe. The philosophy would recover the inner life our age has lost. I now knew deep down that I had found the source of my being, the fountain of my imagination, the 'God in myself'.

Margaret put a completely Christian interpretation on what had happened to me. "Visions such as yours only happen to someone with a calling," she said at the beginning of October. "The spirit needs solitude to grow in the heart." And she announced that she was preparing to leave 13 Egerton Gardens, so that I would have the best conditions of solitude in which to grow.

The Illuminative Way is tidal. The beyond approaches and for a while covers the sand and shingle of the social ego like a tide, but after the tide has receded the sand and shingle are there again, and the ego is apt to explain the encroachment in terms that do not threaten it. So it was that my rational, social ego, when faced with interpreting my visions and the Light in my *Diaries*, immediately saw it in terms that were familiar to itself: the imagination. That explanation enabled me to assimilate what had happened, adjust to it, but looking back now I believe my interpretation was only partially correct. For although, yes, the visions were from my imagination, my imagination itself was part of the tidal flow of the Light from the beyond, which was always behind the white crests and surf of the visions. Beyond all the visions was the Light. Or to change the image and see it in terms of the Ghadames spring, the visions were the bubbles but the Light was the underground spring from which they wobbled to the surface of my gazing mind.

It was only as time went by that I realised that I had been through a conversion, a "turning around". Eventually I would see that the events of 10 September appeared to 'turn me around' from a materialistic outlook to a metaphysical outlook, but in fact those events were themselves part of a process, much of which was subterranean, unconscious....

2. The Method and Form of 'The Silence'

Extracts from 'In Defence of the Sequence of Images', essay by Nicholas Hagger
(This was first published in *T.S. Eliot: A Tribute from Japan, 1966*.)

Everyone agrees that T.S. Eliot was a really great innovator and liberator, yet it is the *Four Quartets*, the "proper modern colloquial idiom" and some of the early poems that are generally praised, not the experiments. There is doubt as to what the influence of the experiments should be. This doubt applies to the entire Modernist movement, and is one of the main critical questions today. Consider the following two judgements:

> The theory and influence of Eliot... seem to me the most dangerous and nearly the least defensible of our time. They have grown upon our time with all the benumbing energy of a bad habit....
> (Yvor Winters, The Anatomy of Nonsense, 1943,
> reprinted in *In Defense of Reason*)

> It is hard to believe that poetry in the future can make any further progress in the Imagist-Symbolist direction.... If we are to use metaphors, mine would not be a cul-de-sac but a detour, a diversion from the main road. Traffic along the main road has been proceeding all the time.... The most brilliant poetic innovations of the most original poetic talents of our day are probably inimitable and unrepeatable. They cannot be developed any further, and they have been of a kind from which it is very difficult to learn.
> (Hough, *Image and Experience*, 1960)

These two judgements, in their varying degrees of dissent, constitute what Frank Kermode called a Counter-Revolution, and judgements similar in spirit have been passed by such 1950s poets as D.J. Enright (*Poets of the 1950s*, 1955) and Robert Conquest (*New Lines 2*, 1963). The Counter-Revolution, however, has not established itself and Philip Toynbee echoed the feelings of many when he concluded his obituary notice on Eliot by writing:

> It is 43 years since 'The Waste Land' was published, and very little has happened in English poetry since then to suggest that its true potentialities have been grasped.

Only the poet can really show what these potentialities are.... In spite of such judgements as the ones quoted above, Eliot's device of the sequence of images has potentially much to recommend it to poets....

There are two rival and mutually hostile theories of poetry in the twentieth century.... The first, the Imagist-Symbolist theory, conceives of a poem as an image – "an image composed... of images" to quote C. Day Lewis (*The Poetic Image*, 1947). An image presents an object, and it can vary in its complexity. At its simplest it is "a picture made out of words" (*The Poetic Image*); at its more complex it is an object or picture which suggests something more than external reality and which is significant through having some emotion, experience, memory or comparison invested in it, so that object, emotion and idea are unified. Whatever its degree of complexity, it works quite differently from discourse: it reveals, often in a thrilling flash, whereas plodding discourse states, and what it reveals the reason could not express half as well twice as cumbrously – think of all the cumbrous rational attempts to express the idea behind 'The Waste Land'. Exactly what a poem is an image of – exactly what an image-poem reveals – will of course depend on what the individual images add up to, and, without getting involved in the traditional, symbolist 'epiphany' of some sort of 'another world', I think it can be said that a good image-poem "is able to express a general truth; retaining all the particularity of... experience, to make of it a general symbol" (T.S. Eliot, 'The Poetry of W.B. Yeats', 1940). C. Day Lewis has seen this "general truth" in terms of a journey: "Every poem is created by a journey through darkness and a return to light... and the finished poem is the image of that journey." And this might certainly be true of 'The Waste Land' and of Pound's quest through civilisation in the ideogram which is *The Cantos*. This pictorial conception of poetry largely derives from the Imagist-Symbolist process of creation. Whether the images or central image are visions from the imagination or memories fished up from places deeper than the reason, involving "depths of feeling into which we cannot peer" (T.S. Eliot, *The Use of Poetry and the Use of Criticism*, 1933) and succeeding a development of experience which is "largely unconscious, subterranean" (T.S. Eliot, 'Introduction to Pound', 1928), or whether they grow more directly and consciously from observations of the external world, the process begins pictorially, and rational order and interpretation come later. Indeed, for the more subterranean Imagist-Symbolist, the interpretation of images is one of the main aims of writing. The second theory, the Counter-Revolutionary theory, conceives of a poem as an unpictorial, rational statement. As Winters has written in *In Defense of Reason*:

> The poem is a statement in words about a human experience. Words are primarily conceptual, but through use and because human experience is not purely conceptual, they have acquired connotations of feeling. The poet makes his statement in such a way as to employ both concept and connotation as efficiently as possible. The poem is good in so far as it makes a defensible rational statement about a given human experience... and at the same time communicates the emotion which ought to be motivated by that rational understanding of that experience.

And Hough in *Image and Experience*:

> A poem... ought to make the same kind of sense as any other discourse.

In Winters' case this conception is founded on a moralistic view of the aim of poetry. According to Winters the statement should be a moral judgement on a situation, in terms of a moral absolute, and this aim is quite different from the Imagist-Symbolist aim of revealing through the image.

This Counter-Revolutionary theory differs from the Imagist-Symbolist theory in its aims, its assumptions and its process of creation, and it is important to see judgements that are unfavourable to the Imagist-Symbolists in this context.... Although the Counter-Revolution may be perfectly valid as a theory of poetry it has no business to pass judgements as if it were *the only* theory.... To question the validity of the image-poem is like questioning the validity of Yeats' words, "Man can embody truth but he cannot know it." The assumptions of both theories are equally valid, and in the last analysis many of the unfavourable judgements on the sequence of images – how bad an influence it is and so on – have the force of personal preference rather than of objective evaluation.

*

What are the potentialities of the image and of the sequence of images? Let us look into the potentialities of the image by comparing the following:

(1) The apparition of these faces in the crowd;
     Petals on a wet black bough.

                                        (Pound)

(2) Streets that follow like a tedious argument
    Of insidious intent
    To lead you to an overwhelming question.

    I should have been a pair of ragged claws.

                                        (Eliot)

There are two completely different conceptions of the image here, and as Donald Davie has shown in *Ezra Pound: Poet as Sculptor* (1965) they both derive from Rémy de Gourmont. In number (1) – a juxtaposition and sequence of two images – Pound's view of the image is realistic. It may not contain the view of the image as a scientific and detailed observation that came from de Gourmont and therefore less directly from the scientist J.H. Fabre, and which is to be found in the later ideographic method of *The Cantos*, but it begins in the external world with line one and then interiorises the faces by recording a subjective impression in line two. In number (2), however, the movement is the other way round, from interior to exterior, so that a subjective state of mind or emotion is projected out, as from a magic lantern, and Prufrock's indecision finds its correlative in the maze of streets and his social diffidence in the crab. This is the "objective correlative":

  The only way of expressing emotion in the form of art is by finding an "objective correlative"; in other words, a set of objects, a situation, a chain of events which shall be the formula of that *particular* emotion; such that when the external facts, which must terminate in sensory experience, are given, the emotion is immediately evoked.

                                        (Eliot, '*Hamlet*', 1919)

Eliot was of course claiming too much with the "only". The "objective

correlative" is founded on de Gourmont's theory of impersonality,
which Eliot restated in 'Tradition and the Individual Talent' as the
"anti-Romantic" division between the man who suffers and the artist
who creates, emotion having its life "in the poem and not in the history
of the poet". This view of the image is very subjective, for the streets
do not exist as solidly as Pound's faces, and it can be regarded as
symbolist in the second of the two meanings of 'symbolism'. In its first
meaning a symbol is a concrete particular which embodies a general
truth. There is, strictly, no meaning outside the symbol: Yeats' beast
embodies a new scientific age, and Yeats' chestnut tree embodies his
view of the wholeness of man. In its second meaning, a symbol is a
concrete particular which refers to another particular by a one-to-one
correspondence – Mallarmé's swan = the poet – and it is chiefly in this
sense that the objective correlative is symbolist, the one-to-one idea
being contained in an equation, emotion = object....

I am inclined to think that the potentialities of the image are on the
realistic side. Consider this realistic image of Eliot's:

> Yet when we came back, late, from the Hyacinth garden,
> Your arms full, and your hair wet, I could not
> Speak, and my eyes failed, I was neither
> Living nor dead, and I knew nothing,
> Looking into the heart of light, the silence.

The lines record a near-mystical memory of a woman against the sun.
It could be argued that the hyacinth girl is a correlative for an intense
state of mind, but she clearly belongs to a real experience Eliot has
had.... What makes the experience an image is the abbreviation, the
fact that it is made into a picture by being cut out of its context like the
snapshot images in 'Gerontion':

> In depraved May, dogwood and chestnut, flowering Judas,
> To be eaten, to be divided, to be drunk
> Among whispers; by Mr Silvero
> With caressing hands, at Limoges
> Who walked all night in the next room;
> By Hakagawa, bowing among the Titians;
> By Madame de Tornquist, in the dark room
> Shifting the candles; Fräulein von Kulp
> Who turned in the hall, one hand on the door.

Neither the hyacinth girl nor Fräulein von Kulp are any more symbolic than a scientific image in Pound.

The significance of this is startling. A common objection to the image is that it excludes actual experience, the experience of thinking, feeling and acting human beings. Hough's title, for example, suggests that image and experience are antithetical and mutually exclusive. In the case of the less realistic images, they often are, in the sense that an image takes experience and transforms it. As Yeats wrote:

> Those masterful images because complete
> Grew in pure mind, but out of what began?...
> Old kettles....

And we remember the image for old age in *The Tower*:

> A sort of battered kettle at the heel.

But in this realistic image Eliot has combined image and experience. The lines about the hyacinth girl record an experience, yet, being part of a sequence and being abbreviated, the experience itself is an image. This 'imaged experience', as I would call it, is clearly a cinematographic device: a 'moving image' with more movement than any vortex. The possibilities it suggests are vast: sequences of abbreviated experiences.

It will immediately be objected that abbreviation and compression have one weakness: they obscure. 'We don't know who the hyacinth girl is' is a frequent cry. Or 'Fräulein von Kulp is name-dropping', a charge which Winters terms "reference to a non-existent plot". The answer to this is: 'If Eliot does not tell you then there is no real need for you to know.' The hyacinth girl produced a near-mystical experience, and Fräulein von Kulp's name is given to internationalise the theme of the decay of the communion service; we do not need to know more. To the objection 'But we don't know what they are doing', however, there is a much more positive answer, an answer which is a positive argument for compression: compression generalises by taking people out of their particular context. It would narrow the application of each illustration if we knew why Mr Silvero walked all night or whether Madame de Tornquist is shifting the candles for a séance or a black mass or whether Fräulein von Kulp really feels guilty. As they stand, the lines include all possible meanings, which is why they are so evocative, and Winters is not justified in requiring a particular motive on the grounds that to get a poetic emotion you must understand an experience rationally, and to understand an experience rationally you must "know and correctly judge its motive".

We can now consider how such realistic abbreviated experiences should be linked together, how one such image should be connected with the next. This raises the problem of linking in a sequence of images and its potentialities. There are two different kinds of sequence, and the distinction can be extracted from Eliot's introduction to St-John Perse's *Anabasis* (1930):

> Any obscurity of the poem, on first readings, is due to the suppression of "links in the chain," of explanatory and connecting matter, and not to incoherence, or to the love of cryptogram. The justification of such abbreviation of method is that the sequence of images coincides and concentrates into one intense impression of barbaric civilisation. The reader has to allow the images to fall into his memory successively without questioning the reasonableness of each at the moment; so that, at the end, a total effect is produced. Such selection of a sequence of images and ideas has nothing chaotic about it. There is a logic of the imagination as well as a logic of concepts.

The first kind can be called 'abbreviated narrative', that is, narrative without the connecting links. The advantage it has over conventional logical narrative is that it can do away with all the "wadge" in poetry, all the prosaic connecting passages which serve only to link the intense moments the poet is really interested in. Take the diffuseness of these lines from *The Prelude*, for example:

> Well I call to mind
> ('Twas at an early age, ere I had seen
> Nine summers) when....

It may be argued that Wordsworth is trying to relate the "low breathings" to his everyday life, and that the lines are therefore a necessary part of his intention, but one sees the point of Eliot's reference (in *The Use of Poetry and the Use of Criticism*, 1933) to poets who "become impatient of this 'meaning' which seems superfluous, and perceive possibilities of intensity through its elimination". These intense moments, Eliot is saying, can be linked without the "wadge" through an emotional "logic of the imagination", a logic which the Counter-Revolution has savaged, for to the rationalist logic can only be conceptual. So in the first eighteen lines of 'The Waste Land' this logic emotionally connects the intense moments of a narrative which might run: 'In April we went into the Hofgarten and in the course of conversation I remembered an experience from my childhood when we were staying at the archduke's.'

The second kind is linking without the narrative. Here the "logic of imagination" works solely by a progression through feelings and moods, so that intense moments are linked by their internal similarities. Consider the following sequence:

I will show you fear in a handful of dust.
> *Frisch weht der Wind*
> *Der Heimat zu.*
> *Mein Irisch Kind,*
> *Wo weilest du ?*
'You gave me hyacinths first a year ago;
They called me the hyacinth girl.'
– Yet when we came back, late, from the Hyacinth garden....
Oed' und leer das Meer.

In these lines the "logic of the imagination" develops an emotional theme, the need for rebirth to a real state of mind. Line one, which images death, is first linked to four lines of symbolist objective correlative, Tristan's impatience for Isolde representing the poet's impatience for some sign of spiritual regeneration. The force of the connection is to suggest the need for a rebirth that will take account of death. Then, without any "wadge" we pass straight into the realistic memory of the woman against the sun. There is clearly a connection between *"Mein Irisch Kind"* and the hyacinth girl, and the significance of the connection is to suggest that the experience connected with the hyacinth girl is an example of a real state of mind, that it is a possible answer to the poet's impatient question in line five. The last line, 'Waste and empty is the sea', represents the true answer to the poet's question, and the force of its connection with the passage about the hyacinth girl is to suggest that people have ignored what is possible.

I think that this second kind of sequence can be defended so long as the images relate to an emotional theme. Hough has written "the collocation of images is not a method at all, but the negation of method", but he is only right to reject collocation if (as in some 'pure' poetry like Dylan Thomas's 'A Grief Ago') the images go on breeding until what emotional theme there was originally is lost. I think also that there are some false objections to it – the unfounded gibe that Pound was responsible for it, much to Eliot's consternation, for example, and Winters' judgement in terms of the quite different assumptions of rational discourse that it is "the progression either of random conversation or of reverie" – and I think that besides music, modern art can be invoked in its favour: for example, a Braque collage which "concentrates into one intense impression". Nonetheless, I think that the potentialities lie in the largely untried first kind of sequence. The first kind is a more suitable medium for the cinematographic abbreviated experience: as we see from Fellini and Godard, a film without a narrative does not really work, and the result can be very arbitrary. Before advocating such an "abbreviated narrative in imaged experiences", however, I want to examine Eliot's substitute for narrative in 'The Waste Land' and this raises the problem of form and its relation to society....

*

I have just argued that there is a structure in 'The Waste Land' but I must now say that I think it just that, for all the mythological interest in the 1940s, it has not been followed. There is something very artificial about mythological structure and parallel, even when the myth is treated from the point of view of psychology, ethnology and anthropology. And there is something very ready-made about symbolism spawned from and dependent on a myth. 'The Waste Land' will always be an image for states of mind we must know in order to mature, like Ivan's story 'The Grand Inquisitor', but an *experience* invested in an object will make a better image. "Mr Joyce is pursuing a method which others must pursue after him. They will not be imitators, any more than the scientist who uses the discoveries of an Einstein in pursuing his own, independent, further investigations...." Despite their originality, neither Eliot nor Joyce split the structural atom. Although mythological situations will continue to lurk behind real situations in art – and what powerful responses they are capable of evoking – poets must find another way of giving "a shape and a significance to the immense panorama of futility and anarchy which is contemporary history". And because poets have so far failed to find another way it does not mean that there is no other way; which brings us back to abbreviated narrative in emotionally linked realistic images, the narrative linking each image to the total Image.

To this we can add a dimension. The social view of the sequence of images should have indicated that abbreviated narrative need not be purely technical, that it can accommodate a social use of the device of juxtaposition and contrast and gain from it. Although Eliot employed the device to get into poetry the "variety and complexity" of a breaking culture, I think we should avoid seeing it solely as a dated attempt to come to terms with social conditions that were peculiar to the second and third decades of the twentieth century – I think we should see it as a device which, through its ability to relate similars and opposites like a camera, is admirably suited to the immense variety and complexity, confusion and fragmentation of our knowledge and living today.

We are now confronted with the main objection to abbreviated narrative in images, an objection we have already touched upon in connection with the abbreviated experience: inevitably it will cause poetry to become more difficult and more obscure than it is at present. I think it is impossible to separate the problem of obscurity from the aims of the poet; which is another way of saying that obscurity is to some extent justified if ambitious, untrivial things are being attempted – aims connected with the complexity of living in our age, for example – and if the obscurity is in some way necessary to their achievement so that the achievement would be less without the obscurity. And, more negatively, I wonder whether, taking into consideration the achievements of the best Movement poems, we can really be satisfied that ready comprehension and lucidity are such poetic virtues. There is no need to be difficult in a complex age, goes the chant for the usual defence; Arnold's answer to "this strange disease of modern life" was the simple and traditional form of 'The Scholar Gipsy'. Yes, but look at 'The Scholar Gipsy'. There is no need to write about a complex age, goes the refrain. The neo-Georgian subjects of the past decade testify to the truth of that.

And this brings us to what is perhaps the most important point about abbreviated narrative in images. I have already argued that abbreviation can enlarge and generalise. I now want to propose that one of the secrets of the best poetry is that it generalises the particular, and that basically the act of communication proceeds along these lines: the poet translates a particular into a general, and the reader translates that general back into his own particular, which is of course by that time very different from the poet's particular. The particular hollow men I see in the subway are not the particular hollow men Eliot saw. I am sure that generalisation is often bound up with the generic image and the symbol, and I am also sure that the trouble with many of the carefully motivated Movement poems is that for all the generalising moral they are too particular for too much of the time, or at any rate, insufficiently generalised. A poem is not just a story with a moral in verse. "Don't imagine that a thing will 'go' in verse just because it's too dull to go in prose" – Pound's warning is pertinent today. To me, at any rate, the total effect of the particularised tour round the church is not half as haunting as Fräulein von Kulp's moment by the door, and this is because Fräulein von Kulp's emotion is generalised by being presented as an image of a general action. I would further suggest that when Winters insisted on the connecting links and the particular motivation, he particularised away the one quality which really haunts, and which no theory of syntax can restore. "The poem is good in so far as it makes a defensible rational statement about a given human experience...." There is nothing about the general. A theory of poetry can only be judged finally by the greatness of the poems it has produced – one test of greatness being contained in a stanza of Yeats' 'Vacillation' – and I think it is true to say (with all due respect to Elizabeth Daryush) that no great poems can emerge from a theory which stresses the particularly motivated experience and the moral judgement.

I think it is true to say that the aim of great poetry is... the eternal aim of recreating order from chaos, of seeking pattern and purpose in self and contemporary history and the universe, and therefore of seeing old things in new ways. In short, it is the record of a spiritual or existential quest, and the poet's technical task is to find a form that can give expression to this quest.

3. The Genesis and Shaping of the New Baroque Vision

Extracts from letter written by Nicholas Hagger to Frank Tuohy on 11 December 1977:

Dear Frank,

I went to Kathleen Raine's poetry reading in the end. I only made the decision to go at 7.30pm on the evening, so there wasn't time to contact you. I have now got her in perspective.

I had forgotten that she wrote to the *TLS* [*Times Literary Supplement*] in 1956, attacking the *New Lines* Movement poets for writing out of personal memory rather than "inspiration", and for apparently not knowing that they have a *"daimon"* or Muse who puts the words into their heads. I reminded her of this in the interval – she was very friendly – and she followed it up during question time, the second half of the evening, when she distinguished "poetry of the soul, which comes from the imagination", and "poetry of the temporal self in the external world", which is inferior, according to her, being mixed with journalism, politics and prose. Thus Auden is "an enemy of the imagination". One obviously objects: but what about Wordsworth's *Prelude*, which approaches the soul through personal memory?

She approves of Wordsworth because he gets back to the soul. The tradition she follows is Blake, Coleridge and Yeats (on whom she has written books), Eliot (who is merely "great", having introduced quite a bit of personal memory in the *Four Quartets*), Edwin Muir (for his dream poems), David Jones, Robert Graves, Vernon Watkins, Dylan Thomas and, of course, David Gascoyne, who has "a prophetic voice" that speaks what deaf ears cannot hear and what blind eyes cannot see. She is totally uninterested in ironic or satiric works – never reads them....

Kathleen Raine ought, therefore, to be one of my heroines, as an anti-Movement embodiment of a mystical tradition. The trouble is: her rejection of personal memory, which (like Gascoyne's rejection of personal memory) gives her work a chillingly abstract quality behind the superficial imagery. Inspiration pure and simple, without being fused with human situations, is rather remote, and Blake, Coleridge and Yeats were all good at bringing out human situations, even when inspired from their "*daimons*". Kathleen Raine's work is too much between her and her "*daimon*", and too little between her and us.

Nevertheless, she did sound rather splendid when she spoke of having to rebel against a materialistic age, and of being aristocratic – in Plato's sense, admiring the *best* – and of loathing democracy and the masses and a "wider public", all of which are the concern of politicians and journalists and inferior enemies of the imagination like Auden. She was very good on the standard all should aim for – that of "Homer, Dante, Shakespeare, Wordsworth and Yeats" – and it was good to hear her say that Menuhin is *better* than the Beatles....

I think she is probably shackled by her Neoplatonism. I feel that her poems express the Platonic *idea* in imagistic *forms*, and in seeking to catch the *idea* she leaves out personal experience and human situations. Like Gascoyne, she catches the *idea* of mysticism; she does not record her own direct experience of the One. And so her work appears enfeebled – and she finds the *idea* of mysticism in Yeats and Gascoyne and pronounces them mystics, whereas the truth is, neither Yeats nor Gascoyne, like Kathleen Raine herself, appears to have had one remotely mystical experience....

Yours ever, Nicholas

Extracts from letter written by Nicholas Hagger to Kathleen Raine on 18 December 1977:

Dear Dr Raine,
... The mystical tradition I have followed so far is different from

your inspirational-imaginative tradition. The word 'mystic' can be derived from the Greek *muein*, meaning "to see", just as a 'seer' can be regarded as a "see-er", and the tradition I have been continuing includes St Augustine, Pope Gregory the Great, St Bernard and St John of the Cross, who were *see-ers* of the Light. I actually *see* the Light on my inner eye, along with the various images I record in *The Gates of Hell*, and can therefore describe the Light and the images in terms of sense-experience, although they are of course beyond sense-experience. My Elizabethan rational intelligence has recorded what it received from deeper places, the Uncreated Light and archetypal images. So far, I agree, my voice has been a thoughtful one, while my subject matter has come from the beyond; in the tradition of the developing mystical awareness of Donne, Wordsworth and Eliot. I have been concerned to record the experience of the Golden Flower and its consequences for both the soul and "the temporal self in the external world", i.e. the whole man. I have aimed for a certain amount of plain speech, as Herbert did, and to reveal the whole man I have drawn on a line that runs from Wyatt, through Shakespeare's *Sonnets* and Tennyson's *In Memoriam*, to Hardy.

I believe that my mystical tradition and your inspirational-imaginative tradition converge. Coleridge was very close to the *visible* Uncreated Light in 'Dejection: an Ode', lines 43–75, where the light that issues from the soul, the "luminous cloud", is the true source of poetic inspiration and the "shaping spirit of Imagination" by which things of higher worth are seen; and in chapter 12 of *Biographia Literaria*. Coleridge was not really a mystic – an illumined soul who saw the Uncreated Light – any more than Yeats was, but he shared the mystic's source. Shelley was similarly close in 'Alastor' ("obedient to the light/ That shone within his soul") and 'Adonais' to cite just two poems. The images of the imagination and the Light of the mystic both come from the same source, the eternal world....

Yours sincerely, Nicholas Hagger

Extract from postcard written by Frank Tuohy to Nicholas Hagger on 3 January 1978:

Thank you for your letter about K. Raine.... Vaughan, Blake, Traherne are perhaps visionary, meaning that they actually experienced the vision, and communicated it, whereas K.R. (i.e. Kathleen Raine), Æ, Gascoyne etc. are among the would-bes – if the vision was there, they have not given any signs of being able to communicate it....

Best to you all, Frank

Extracts from letter written by Nicholas Hagger to Frank Tuohy on 5 January 1978:

Dear Frank,

Many thanks for the beautiful Egyptian fish, and for your comments on visionaries, with which I entirely agree.

Since I wrote to you, I have sharpened the distinction between the Raine tradition and my tradition. I put it in a letter to her and received a long letter back. Her tradition, the imaginative-inspirational tradition, is different from my mystic-contemplative tradition, but both have the same source: Coleridge writes of the imagination in terms of the Light. Her imaginative-inspirational poets see images (visions), whereas the mystic-contemplatives, like later Donne and Eliot, see the Light which is behind the images-visions. The imaginative-inspirational poets write from the point of view of the images-visions, and omit the rational intelligence and the social setting of the Neoclassical Movement poets. The mystic-contemplative poets, on the other hand, write from the higher mind of contemplation, which unites thought and feeling (cf. Eliot's admiration for Donne, and the time before the dissociation of sensibility) and which is different from the rational intelligence of the Movement poets, for contemplation is a different exercise from rational thought. The mystic-contemplative sees life as a whole and includes society, but is essentially a see-er, for 'mystic' can be defined from the Greek *'muein'*, meaning "to see".

A 'visionary' poet, then, sees pictorial images, while a 'mystical' poet sees the Light, like St John of the Cross. Kathleen Raine is quite wrong to call either Yeats or Gascoyne 'mystics', for they are 'visionaries', one true and one *manqué* (fishy) as you say. Kathleen Raine writes that she dislikes the word 'mystical'. I don't think she knows very much about the experience of the mystic, which is harder to have than, and of superior quality to, the images which precede the breaking of the Light.

I dare say the distinction will seem an occult quibble, but it is important enough to register a parting of the ways for the Raine tradition (see her *Defending Ancient Springs*) and me. This is not to say that I am not going to express any visions. A mystic contemplative can also be a visionary, but a visionary cannot also be a mystic-contemplative unless he (she) has made the great breakthrough into Light....

Yours ever, Nicholas

Extracts from letter written by Nicholas Hagger to Christopher Ricks on 3 February 1979:

Dear Christopher,
  ... You will find numerous instances of verbal play which are doubtless 'Ricksite' in origin, in the sense that your tutorials alerted me to the various layers of ambiguity....
  In the case of my long poems, the sample of course shows few of the cross-references and balancing echoes: 'The Four Seasons', for instance, is constructed on a host of parallels. There are so many short poems that I could have made half a dozen different selections, and I have had to choose between basing this selection on the theme of my mystical development alone, and reflecting the whole spectrum of my work, in which my mysticism is but a part. This problem of where to place emphasis is no doubt one that faces any anthologiser of anyone's work (e.g. Tennyson's), but it is particularly acute when one is anthologising one's own work, and I have inevitably fallen between two stools; and hence now incline to the view that if I should indeed start with a selection, then someone other than me should make it. The mystic theme surfaces properly towards the end of 'The Silence', and it is developed in *The Gates of Hell*, and particularly in the poems that follow 'Flow: Moon and Sea'. For the enlightenment theme in English poetry, see pp.21–22 of the synopsis, which I can support with numerous quotations. At the end of the poems I include some work in progress, a few sonnets from a mystical sequence that already numbers 20 and which will be called *Lady of the Lamp*, in which the Mystic Marriage is seen in terms of a frank, modern sexual relationship. These seem to be moving towards what is for me a new form of Symbolism, and it is perhaps significant that Aleksander Blok's statement of the Mystic Marriage, 'Verses about the Lady Beautiful' (which I have not read) made him the founder of Russian Symbolism....
  This package states the problem, defines my dilemma.... I need advice on the basis of a selection.
Yours, Nicholas

Extracts from letter written by Nicholas Hagger to Christopher Ricks on 18 February 1979:

Dear Christopher,
  I feel I may have resolved some of the difficulties I expressed in my last letter.... As a slight change of focus is involved, I would like to set it down on paper before we meet.

I now feel that I am, perhaps, above all a *Metaphysical* poet. My strengths may be metaphor, verbal play, and possibly (in some of my work) wit, and these are blended with a Metaphysical subject matter, a search for Reality, i.e. enlightenment. A Metaphysical poet must have a metaphysic to be metaphysical about, and the background to mine is in the synopsis I sent you. Being a Metaphysical, I: start naturally with personal situations; am interested in the theme of love; am fairly learned and certainly interested in "the new philosophy"; am fascinated by the relation between the spirit and the senses (e.g. in *The Gates of Hell*); tend to compress and fuse thought and image; and am interested in the way symbols reflect my metaphysic. My present tendency towards Symbolism, which I referred to in my last letter, can, perhaps, be partly seen in terms of layers of ambiguity, a Metaphysical fascination with poems that move at two or more different levels at the same time.

If all this is so, then the relationship between my mysticism and verbal play becomes understandable. The mysticism is but one part of my Metaphysical sensibility and outlook, the other part being the verbal play and ambiguity (the part that Kathleen Raine would be against). This part surely originates with the Metaphysicals, but more recently it goes back to Empson (your ancestor, some say) and *Seven Types of Ambiguity*. Empson absorbed the East when he was a predecessor of mine at my University in Tokyo – I was told by a contemporary that he was sacked in 1934, I believe, for sitting nude in a taxi after some nude bathing spree – and he was an admirer of Marvell's 'Garden' ('There is something very Far-Eastern about this'). He surely goes back to the Metaphysicals, whereas so many of his Movement followers only go back to the 18th century. In so far as you have carried forward the Empson tradition, my verbal play is very definitely Ricksite. A selection or anthology of my poems should therefore aim to reveal its Metaphysical qualities, which include both the mysticism and the verbal play.

I have said that the background of my metaphysic is in the synopsis for... *Oceans of Light*. This partly deals with how the new science (subatomic physics and biology) has debunked the old philosophies and made a metaphysics of enlightenment possible again.... Such a book about our new age could resemble a book by Donne or Marvell about the new ideas of the Age of the Metaphysicals.... I regard such a book as a background to the Metaphysical outlook of these poems, and I am all the more convinced that there should be a selection or anthology of my poems.

This letter is really an attempt at self-definition. You may disagree and have another definition, change the focus. It will be interesting to hear. Understanding (as opposed to knowing) oneself is a terrible problem when one has written so many different things, and I am reminded of Eliot's remark about Tennyson: "He was incapable of illumination which he was capable of understanding." I am not sure that this definition would have taken place had we not arranged to meet, so I am already grateful to you for sharpening the focus.

I hope to appear soon after midday on Tuesday.

Yours, Nicholas

Extracts from Nicholas Hagger's autobiography:

On 20 February I visited Christopher Ricks at Christ's College, Cambridge on a snowy day. I passed the mulberry tree Milton knew when he was a pupil there. Ricks was waiting for me in his large room, dressed in blue denim shirt and trousers. I had sent him some of my poems and we walked to the Buttery and there, dome-headed with round spectacles and wispy grey hair, he gave me a tutorial whose brilliance took my breath away. He made sixteen technical points about my poems one after the other with great rapidness, declaring that they were not Metaphysical in the sense that the Metaphysical poets' poems are Metaphysical. He was not thinking of the metaphysical content at all (for me, the central issue), but purely of beginnings and endings, syntax, imagery and such matters. He launched into a long monologue while I listened, saying Marvell had done this and Hagger that; Milton and Tennyson had treated a particular theme one way, Hagger another; Keats and Eliot had done such-and-such, while Hagger had done so-and-so. For a good hour he related my work to the highest standards, and I felt as though I were listening to a tutorial in which my work had already joined the canon.

We had lunch in the Senior Common Room at Christ's. I sat next to Ricks and in between making general conversation with the other dons I said to him at one point that Coleridge distinguished imagination and fancy, to which Ricks replied: "I've never found that distinction particularly helpful." We had coffee in a snoozy room aglare with snow, and Ricks suddenly said "You're very learned," which I took as a compliment rather than as a criticism....

After my meeting with Ricks I resolved to write a more impersonal poetry, to focus attention on the object "like an artist rubbing himself out of the scene he has painted". I wrote: "Wittgenstein and Empson are two in whose tradition I am, but also Lowell (mystic and confessional and a reviser). Transmute and generalise the autobiographical, and in particular catalogue the strategies for saying 'I sit....', e.g. 'Let us' or 'We sit' or 'All who sit', etc., i.e. ways of generalising the particular.... I am verbal and write in ambiguities, but that does not mean I am a rationalist, à la Winters; rather I am an imagist/symbolist. So go back to Empson – and Ricks – on images and symbols, and forget the rational side for the contemplative."

Extracts from letter written by Nicholas Hagger to Christopher Ricks on 1 May 1982:

Dear Christopher,

First, many congratulations on becoming King Edward VII Professor of English. I always knew you would sooner or later succeed Leavis as the major literary influence at Cambridge, so I am not surprised. I have long thought of you as *the* curator of the tradition; hence my use of the term 'Ricksite'.

Secondly... I would be very interested in your reaction to a new *perspective*, if you could find the time to give it.

I have spent over three years pondering the anthology of thirty poems, which you suggested. The trouble was, if I discounted the longer works and merely chose 30 of the smaller ones, I did not even touch on the main theme of my work. As I pondered, it slowly dawned on me that the "Metaphysical" model I proposed three years ago is incomplete, and that I have in fact all along been continuing *the Romantic tradition* of Blake, Wordsworth, Coleridge and Shelley, albeit as a pretty Metaphysical Romantic. I have now written a Preface to this effect. It appears at the beginning of the accompanying selection, and I would be very interested in your opinion, if you could spare the time to read it.

It seems to me that seeing my poems in a Romantic perspective accounts for many of the things that made you uneasy when we last met, and solves a number of the problems. You found my poems: (1) ruminative instead of immediate – ruminative like Wordsworth instead of Metaphysical; (2) personal rather than individual – a Romantic trait; (3) explicit in places – again a Romantic feature; (4) sometimes arbitrary as to what appears in the next line – explained by Romantic organic form dressed as musical form, and by post-Romantic emotional linking or juxtaposition of images. You disliked (5) some of the 19th-century diction – an extension of the Romantic tone; and (6) the ending of some poems with a question – which is allowed in Romantic poems, e.g. 'Ode to the West Wind', 'Ode to a Nightingale', 'Grantchester'. Romantic and post-Romantic criticism are very different from Neoclassical criticism, and allow many things (e.g. organic form, and a freer line as in 'Christabel') that Neoclassical 'statement' criticism cannot allow, and I would like to know if you agree that relating my poems to their correct genre clears up some of the difficulties.

I have been reticent about *The Gates of Hell* till now, allowing it to gather dust on a shelf for ten years, as many of the poems in it were written in the sort of pain Shelley must have felt when he wrote 'To the Lord Chancellor'; but they certainly fit in with a Romantic view of my work, as outlined in the Preface, and may even be among my best works in terms of Romantic (as opposed to Neoclassical) principles. The emotional Romantic approach explains some of the relationships between things; for example, "child's balloon" in 'Flow: Moon and Sea', which you commented on, is now appropriate as it suggests a fear of making the girl pregnant and creating a child who will have a balloon.

In this selection I have included whole works rather than excerpts you have so far seen, so that the organic form can show itself to best advantage. (Imagine an anthology of any Romantic without some of the longer works.) I have concentrated on the longer works which illustrate the theme of the Preface, rather than on the hundreds of short poems. *The Fire-Flower* you have not seen at all as these poems were all written since we last met (although some are rewrites), and you will see that 'The Tree of Imagination' is partly about you and our last meeting. I don't know how it reads, but it is meant to be complimentary in making you the number-one critic and guardian of the Tree of Tradition.

I am aware that you are on the Neoclassical rather than the Romantic side – you were very interested in social satire in the early 1960s and have approached Keats from the viewpoint of social embarrassment, and have championed Mary Douglas – but on the other hand the subjects of your books are all on the Romantic side, and I know from our tutorials that you like Wordsworth. I know you will take a fair and balanced view, and will judge Romantic poetry by Romantic standards and not by the hostile Neoclassical standards Yvor Winters used in *In Defense of Reason*....

Your ever-devoted, Nicholas

Extracts from letter written by the Neo-Romantic Sir George Trevelyan to Nicholas Hagger on 27 May 1982:

Dear Nicholas,

... Now I have read the preface with delight and excitement. It is a splendid statement and it is fine to have it made by one who has the authority of the scholar and poet. I gained a lot by reading it. I am sure we are approaching the new Renaissance which should be a wonderful period since mankind is lifting consciousness to enter the realm of the archetypal Ideas. The experience must express itself through the arts.

I really enjoyed reading the preface.... Kathleen Raine is the sort of critic who could really advise and assess.

I look forward to meeting and talking more. You are a lecturer on this theme? If you can really put over the 'living idea' then we ought to do something together!

Yours ever, George Trevelyan

Extracts from letter written by Christopher Ricks to Nicholas Hagger on 31 July 1982:

Dear Nicholas,

... I reminded myself of some of the poems, and brought down with me to the country the latest (3rd?) draft of your preface. I believe that you're right to divine that this is the right context for your own work.... The price paid (a) for your sense of what Romanticism is (as against W. Jackson Bate's sense of the essential continuities of Augustan into Romantic; and (b) for your own such Romanticism; does seem to me very considerable. (But then you cd. reasonably retort that huge prices are paid for, say, Spenser's or Pound's decisions – and then I'd agree.)...

Best wishes, Christopher

Extracts from letter written by Nicholas Hagger to Christopher Ricks on 17 October 1982:

Dear Christopher,

As promised, I enclose version 4, the last version, of my Preface. It is well over double the length of version 3. You will see that there is a considerable shift of ground from a Romantic position to what I call a 'Baroque' position (i.e. Classicism plus Romanticism, sense plus spirit). The word appears in the dedication to 'The Silence' (1965–1966), and in line 1332 of that work. Version 3 was but another stepping-stone to the finished idea, which was there as long ago as 1965 if I could but have grasped it.

I have tried to define myself – retrospectively – in terms of first the Metaphysicals and then the Romantics, but each time I have been unable to explain the distinct *Classical* elements in my work, e.g. the 'Ricksite' verbal play and the fact that much of what I have written is actually from the 'social ego' (although admittedly it generally opens to 'the beyond'). In what must be seen as a significant development, I have now faced the fact that though my work obviously draws on the Metaphysicals and the Romantics – I was clearly right in seeing my roots as immediately being in Romantic Idealism – it also has a Classical element, to which your remark about W. Jackson Bate indirectly drew my attention, and that in art a combination of Classicism and Romanticism is 'baroque'. (See pp.23–29 [of the Preface, pp.41–47 of *Collected Prefaces*] for a deepened view of this term and recurring cycles in art.) I have – seriously – in all modesty and humility – of the kind I learned from you – tried to relate myself to the past, to place myself somewhere within the great tradition. The attempt has not worked. No matter how hard I tried, I could not 'fit my work in' with what is already there. I was telling half the truth about my work but I was not doing justice to the whole of it. Therefore I have (almost reluctantly) been forced to consider that I am doing something *new*, that I have been somewhat original and innovative all along in creating a new 'baroque' poetry which shares some of the assumptions of the Metaphysicals and the Romantics and blends with the New Age consciousness of Sir George Trevelyan and others. I am sure I have now come to rest and have finally achieved my 'public stance', and that there will be no more developments, only modifications. I am sure you will not receive a letter next year putting forward another view.

Of course, it will now be even harder for me to get the poems across to the public. Like a third political party, I would be attacked from both sides: by the Neoclassicals like Larkin for being too romantic and mystical in my subject matter, and by Neo-Romantics like Kathleen Raine for being too concerned with the classical social ego as opposed to the Platonist "other mind". Nevertheless, my primary concern is not getting the work across, but correctly identifying what it is (as if I were writing an essay for you), and the getting it across is secondary. Wordsworth wrote that "every great and original writer, in proportion as he is great or original, must create the taste by which he is to be relished; he must teach the art by which he is to be seen". In so far as I *have* been original in writing 'baroque' poetry, the onus has been on me to create a taste for it, and now that I know the taste, I can set about creating it. The Preface is a start, and I now have an 'ideological' basis for an anthology, if I can get round to the agonising business of making a very small selection.

I think this definition of my work allows me more latitude in the future. The "price" you spoke of in your letter was presumably a price in human terms, and Baroque poetry, which allows the social ego in in a way that Neo-Romantic poetry does not, affords more human scope, and accounts for the considerable human interest in my many short poems; and therefore reduces "the price". I am also now set to embark on the 12-book epic which I have had in mind for 20 years, and which I consulted Ezra Pound about in Rapallo in 1970. (Pound gave me his blessing, saying "T.E. Hulme said to me in 1914, 'Everything a writer has to say can be put on half a side of a postcard, and all the rest is application and elaboration.' Have you got that? If you have, then two ends of the twentieth century are now meeting.") This epic will draw heavily on the external world and the human Classical side, and it is itself a Baroque conception. (Milton, after all, lived in the original Baroque Age.)

My life has undergone a dramatic change within the last year, as if in preparation for this enterprise. In July I exchanged contracts on the private Essex day preparatory school (3–11) which I attended from 1944–1947, and have installed my wife as Headmistress. We are sole owners.... I will soon be able to retire from teaching in Marxist ILEA..., and I will be able to spend the mornings writing my epic in the midst of Nature. The time, in the sense of leisure, and the freedom for which I have long yearned are now within my grasp. I will be able to reread many of the books I read for you at Oxford. Meanwhile the local community will come to my door. Yes, the Baroque is a very appropriate reconciliation between the social and contemplative forces I will meet during the next two or three decades.

As a result of this latest and *last* development, I do not now need to see Kermode or any of the Romantic specialists at Cambridge. I have thought my way out of my quandary on my own, despite all the hectic Essex activity and commuting. I think you will welcome my development as it includes rather than excludes the Classical. I think you will regard it as a step in the right direction, even though, while I acknowledge the continuity of Augustan into Romantic (largely thanks to your last letter, your tutor's knack of opening up new vistas with a phrase), there is still some tension as the Romantic part of the Baroque synthesis pulls against the Augustan; and you will probably still withhold appreciation....

With very many thanks for bearing with me and helping me in labour, and of course looking forward to hearing your reaction to version 4 of the Preface,

Your ever-devoted, Nicholas

Extracts from Nicholas Hagger's autobiography:

I had finished my Preface on 17 October and sent it to Christopher

Ricks. I noted: "The imagination is seeing the Idea within the form – it is a Platonist idea. Romanticism and Platonism. (The breakthrough I had in writing to Tuohy..., when I grasped that Plato transcended sense experience, and really felt the Romantic Idealism to be a true reflection of my state of mind then.)"

On 29 October I visited Ricks at Christ's, Cambridge. I went up to B6 and saw him through the open door wearing jeans, and immediately warmed to his endearing smile beneath his bald head and small round spectacles. He said I had sharpened my ideas: "I believe in the Baroque, but though everything that is Baroque is Classical and Romantic, not everything that is Classical and Romantic is Baroque" – to which I replied that the Light is central to the new Baroque. He said: "The proof of the pudding is in the eating. I think your work is Baroque. You got there, even though your itinerary surprised you. You must anthologise 30 poems, each no longer than a page. Make your entry and then expand. I know selection is painful, it's painful for me to leave out bits from my lectures." I told him that I had temporarily disowned *The Gates of Hell* because they were not metaphysical, and more recently, the Neo-Christian poems because they did not fit in with Romanticism. "Both fell within the Baroque." He nodded. Ricks had skilfully diagnosed the position ahead of mine and was leading me forward.... Of Oaklands, he said "It's Providential", an adjective I did not expect to hear from him.

Extracts from letter written by Nicholas Hagger to Christopher Ricks on 31 October 1982:

Dear Christopher,

As I promised in your room on Friday – for which *very many* thanks – I enclose the annotated *Fire-Flower* and *Beauty and Angelhood*.... You should be able to see that in *Beauty and Angelhood*, like the Baroque artists of old, I stand fairly and squarely on the tradition of Christian mysticism. Your question "Where from here?" may be answered to some extent in 'Against Materialism' and in the 30 or 40 linked poems I wrote after watching the death of my mother during the night of Hallowe'en and All Saints Day last year – a year ago today – but I feel it may not be fully answered until I have tackled the epic and faced, and answered, the question of the Light's responsibility for the evil of Auschwitz. A Baroque work if ever there was one.

To be Baroque, a work must have the Light, a sense of transformation, an awareness of the dynamic nature of the material world, and a mixture of sense and spirit, so yes, although Baroque is Classicism and

Romanticism, Classicism and Romanticism is only Baroque if it has these elements.

The "fourfold vision" is a very ancient one that goes back to the Kabbalah, long before Blake (who got it from the Kabbalah). I have adapted it to redefine what a human being is and to demonstrate that the view Humanism has is incomplete. I would be very interested in your reaction if you could spare time to give it....

Your ever-devoted, Nicholas

Extract from letter written by Christopher Ricks to Nicholas Hagger on 20 December 1982:

Dear Nicholas,

... It's good of you to have sent me *The Fire-Flower* and *Beauty and Angelhood*; I read them with interest, and with some awe at your energy of mind and synthesising (*not* synthetic) aspirations. The notes are I think a genuine help, and done (both proffered and enacted) with tact and modesty. Touches of the best of Empson in them – and in some things in the poems (that despair/rare rhyme, for instance)....

With best wishes, Christopher

Extract from Nicholas Hagger's Diaries, *5 August 1984:*

Classical and Romantic – the difference (I decided as I peed into the bracken at the back of Greenfield,... looking across at the distant mountains in early twilight) is between town and country: in the towns, man is the measure of all things, and there is society; in the country man is absorbed into nature and natural rhythms, which dominate. Town *and* country – the Baroque. The world is Baroque and doesn't realise it. The Space Age – whirling clouds past a space rocket – and Tippett's *Mask of Time* are Baroque works. When the world realises we are living in a Baroque time, there will be a great change in the arts, which I have anticipated, and man will be redefined to include more than the mere mind and body accorded him by the Renaissance.

4. Extracts from 'Revolution in Thought and Culture', an essay by Nicholas Hagger

(This was a public address given at the Jubilee Hall, Aldeburgh on 3 October 1997 and published in *The One and the Many*.)

There was a time in the Middle Ages when European culture was unified and all the disciplines interconnected round a central idea, like branches round a central trunk, the Christian religion, and the whole was fed by a metaphysical sap. 'Metaphysical' suggests a "Reality beyond the world of physics and of Nature", "beyond the senses", "energy manifesting into the universe from beyond it". In the time of the Crusades European art, literature and music all received the nourishing sap of the metaphysical via the Christian trunk, and there was unity of culture and "unity of being" (Yeats' phrase). Before the Renaissance the great cultural works of the European civilisation's art, sculpture, music, literature and philosophy all expressed a vision (as leaves express sap) of the illumined soul (or halo), which they associated with the examined life, progress to sainthood, serene and ordered Gregorian chantings, stone angels and thought about the divine. It was a vision which made the human condition less grim and bleak, and during the Renaissance Plato-inspired Ficino and Botticelli shared Dante's vision. Despite the Reformation, unity of culture continued during the Elizabethan time and the time of the Metaphysical poets. Since the 18th century, the metaphysical idea expressed through Christianity has dwindled, and our culture has turned secular.

These days we have cultural diversity and multi-culturalism. This is another way of saying that our culture is fractured and fragmented and supplemented by new grafts from ex-colonial territories (Caribbean and Indian). Many would say there is richness in diversity, that the branches of humanistic diversity are preferable to the tree-trunk dictatorship of religion, but the trouble is, diversity of branches with too little metaphysical sap means that the branching out in all directions is brittle and may fall apart. Hardly any of the branches of our culture these days draws on metaphysical vigour. A study could demonstrate in devastating detail the secular nature of the main contemporary works and how little they reflect the metaphysical. Secularisation of culture is a consequence of a civilisation's decline. And, conversely, a civilisation's decline is a consequence of the secularisation of culture. A civilisation grows through a metaphysical sap that expresses itself in green-leaf-like culture, and declines when the sap stops and culture turns secular and sere. A metaphysical idea gives every civilisation its sap, and civilisations last so long as the sap lasts, so long as it flows and they are renewed, and when the sap fails the civilisation declines and its leaf-like culture turns dry and brittle and its branches look bare.

If we think of European culture (our cultural diversity) as our integrated knowledge, beliefs and behaviour – our language, ideas, customs, codes, institutions, rituals, ceremonies, works of art and other intellectual achievements – and if we distinguish 'popular' culture (light entertainment, war films, sport, pop concerts, music, television and the lottery) from 'higher' culture (art exhibitions, concerts, literary events, museums, libraries, bookshops, book reviews, lectures), most of the products of our higher culture in recent times (our art, sculpture, music, literature and philosophy) share attitudes of humanism, secularism, philosophical materialism and scepticism. In other words, the products of our culture share a concern with the human and the mundane, hold that matter is the only reality and that no other vision of Reality is possible; which means there is no God or soul or spirit and life is a purposeless accident; death is the end, and culture offers perceptions of character in terms of human values – hence Beckett's half-buried figures, Bacon's screaming Popes and shock art at the Royal Academy. Such works express horror at the horror of the humanistic version of the human condition, human interest and warmth, and a diversity of disbelief.

I speak up for the metaphysical idea in our culture, the vision of energy or power which is at the root of our civilisation. I do not do so as a committed Christian or as an evangelist or as a hater of humanistic, secular writings; I have the interest in *all* culture of any man of letters, and I am an admirer of the best humanistic works and a devotee of English Literature: Chaucer's *Prologue*, Pope's 'Epistle to Boyle' and Keats' Odes. I accept that for many secularisation and diversity are irreversible, that the world has moved on (which is another way of saying that our civilisation has declined from its metaphysical beginnings and middle). On the other hand, I am worried at how *little* the metaphysical idea is found in our culture. It has become virtually non-existent, the sap is just not reaching the branches at all. I believe there is still room for the metaphysical and that many people derive sustenance from it, that our culture needs a strong metaphysical presence, that the young need to encounter metaphysical works on their largely humanistic, secular courses (works such as "honey-tongued" Shakespeare's Platonic Sonnets, Milton's *Paradise Lost* and Eliot's *Four Quartets*). And it is in this spirit, to correct an imbalance, that I want to start a 'Revolution in thought and culture'. My Revolution is to get some sap moving round the almost dried-up tree to arrest decay.

Besides being a man of letters I am a cultural historian and observer who shares many of Matthew Arnold's views on our culture, which has become further secularised since *Culture and Anarchy* first appeared in 1869, and I am cross-disciplinary, and still see our culture as a sap-energised whole even though today it is fragmented, its sapless parts separate. Today there are many specialists, but few cultural historians who are in contact with the vision that reconciles all disciplines, restores the unity of culture and makes a Theory of Everything possible. The poet is allowed to move between disciplines – there are precedents in Matthew Arnold's *Culture and Anarchy*, T.E. Hulme's *Speculations*, T.S. Eliot's *Notes Towards the Definition of Culture* and Graves's *White Goddess* – and, claiming such cross-disciplinary licence and looking back to the example of Coleridge, I seek to unify; I look for what is in common between disciplines and different cultures. Specialists analyse and seek differences and make distinctions with rational analysis, I, on the other hand, follow the "esemplastic power of the imagination" as Coleridge called it (*eis en plattein* – "shape into one") and unify, help parts that have fallen apart grow back together again, get the sap flowing through the broken branches of our culture so they put out leaves again, and seek to restore the whole view.

That is why I raise the standard of revolt in the name of Tradition. I believe it is the first time in the 20th century that anyone has attempted such a Revolution (or reversal of decay) in so many branches of thought and culture....

Our higher culture is today separated from a long Tradition which used to be central to it, that the highest experience we know is the sublime vision of Reality or vision of God, the vision of Paradise. This Reality has traditionally been regarded as being of a higher order than secular, humanistic social life and is independent of the soul or mind that has the vision. It is known in all cultures and civilisations. European painters have tried to capture it: Jan van Eyck's *Adoration of the Lamb*; Fra Angelico's angels in *Christ Glorified in the Court of Heaven* (much-used on Christmas cards); and Michelangelo's Sistine Chapel vision. European composers have tried to capture celestial music: in medieval and Renaissance vocal music (notably Gregorian chants); in the sacred choral music of Palestrina, Tallis, Byrd and Monteverdi; and in the Hallelujah chorus in Handel's Messiah. European poets have offered it as the goal of man's quest: Dante's sempiternal rose in his *Paradiso*; Milton's "God is light,... celestial light" in *Paradise Lost* (bk. 3); Eliot's "crowned knot of fire/And the fire and the rose are one" in 'Little Gidding'. Philosophers have seen the brightness in this vision as the source of creation and Nature: Heracleitus's "ever-living" Fire ('Fragment 30'), Plato's Fire or "universal Light" which causes the shadows to flicker on the walls of the cave, and Plotinus's "authentic Light" which "comes from the One and is the One". The Fire or Light is what creation manifested from.

This Paradisal vision of Fire or Light can be traced through many cultures where it has surfaced at many times during the last

5,000 years, from the Indo-European civilisation to ancient Egypt to Mesopotamia, Iran and India, down to the European, and most recently, the North-American civilisation. The religious teachers refer to it and are identified by it. The Buddha was the Enlightened One, Jesus the Light of the World, Mohammed saw the first page of the Koran written in Fire. The experience is behind Patanjali, the Fire cult of Zoroaster, Mahavira, Lao-Tze, Mani and George Fox (who founded the Quaker Inner Light). The great European mystics have known it in all cultures: Saint Augustine, Pope Gregory the Great, Bayazid, Al-Hallaj, Omar Khayyam, Suhrawardi, Hafiz, Symeon the New Theologian, St Hildegard of Bingen, Meister Eckhart, Suso, Ruysbroeck, Kempis, Rolle, Hilton, Julian of Norwich, St Catherine of Siena, St Catherine of Genoa, St Teresa of Avila, St Gregory Palamas, Padmasambhava, Sankara, Guru Nanak, Hui-neng, Eisai, Dogen and many others. The vision is to be found as the central idea of many poets: St John of the Cross, Herbert, Vaughan, Crashaw, Traherne, Norris, Law, Marvell, Milton, Blake, Wordsworth, Coleridge, Shelley and, in our century, Yeats and Eliot. My own work contains a number of visions of the Fire or Light.

All these people saw the Fire or Light within their soul. They closed their eyes and moved behind their rational, social ego into their universal being and sat and waited, the mystics in contemplation, the poets waiting for images like anglers waiting for fish to bite, and the Fire or Light opened to them like sunlight breaking in water as it did for St Augustine in AD400 and St Hildegard of Bingen in c.1140. Baroque art symbolised these experiences of illumination in the sunburst, and sunbursts can be seen in Catholic and Protestant churches throughout Europe. The vision of Fire or Light is sometimes described as the vision of God or of Being....

The vision of the Fire or Light, which I have described as the highest experience during the growth of the culture (philosophy, music, art, literature and religion) of a civilisation, and which is its central idea, round which it grew, must be revived in every generation if the civilisation is to be revitalised and stay alive. The vital, revitalising sap is released by mystics into the trunk of religion and by philosophers, artists and writers into the civilisation's various branches.

Traditionally, the philosophers have contributed to this renewal by interpreting their civilisation's central idea of the Fire or Light. In the west, the Church was behind the philosophy of the Middle Ages – Aquinas and the Scholiasts – and at the back of traditional philosophy has been metaphysics. A branch of philosophy. Having started as the "philosophy *after* physics" (Aristotle's *ta meta ta phusika*) and having become "the study of the first principles of things, including such concepts as being, substance, essence, time, space, cause, identity" or "the ultimate science of Being and Knowing" (*Shorter Oxford English Dictionary*), metaphysics came to focus on what is *beyond* physics, or what is *behind* or *hidden within*, physics; what E.W.F. Tomlin called "the concealed Absolute". Metaphysics became the science of a universal Whole, concerned with "the endeavour to frame a coherent, logical, necessary scheme of general ideas in terms of which every element of our experience can be interpreted" (Whitehead, *Process and Reality*, 1929), and in the course of offering a metaphysical scheme, philosophers touched on and renewed their civilisation's central idea for their generation...

The dead-end philosophy reached after 1910 has had an effect on European literature, which after Pound, Eliot and Yeats has been concerned with the phenomenal world and the social ego. The scepticism and materialistic cosmology of modern philosophy has resulted in sceptical, reductionist scientists such as Hawking filling the void left by philosophy and influencing literature. Hawking says we have no special place in the universe, as first the earth, then the sun has been dethroned from being its centre. (As Hubble has discovered there is no centre to the universe, which is expanding and inflating like a balloon, while the chemistry of our bodies is the same as the chemistry of the stars, suggesting we are just stardust.) I, on the other hand, hold that as everything began in one point and the metaphysical source of that point, the moving Fire, radiates into us, we have a very special place in the universe. Neo-Darwinists claim that we live in a purposeless universe – indeed, that as a result of the Second Law of Thermodynamics, everything is running down and we are living on a "dunghill of purposeless interconnected corruption" – which is the view of Beckett's characters. In Sartre, Camus, Kafka, Beckett, Hemingway and Orwell, the phenomenal world is all and man is a defeated, purposeless, "useless passion" (Sartre) who lives under the "benign indifference of the Universe" (Camus) or the political reality of a regional branch of world government (Orwell's Big Brother), unable to attain the Castle which he seeks (Kafka) and which, despite its hint of metaphor, is set in an uneasy phenomenal world. Some writers like Greene and Waugh are concerned with social Christian dogma, and many novelists convey a social view of characters without suggesting the new perception of man and its possibilities.

Very few writers have reflected the new view of Reality in literature. Eliot attempted to absorb it in his *Four Quartets*, Durrell reflected it in the structure of his *Alexandrian Quartet* (in which the four books are supposed to represent three dimensions of space and one of time) and C.P. Snow called for writers to acquire more knowledge of science, something that has manifestly failed to happen in a way that is fundamental to their work and their view of Reality (as opposed to influencing a technique or gimmick). For the world of most contemporary writers is still granular and materialistic and blind to a new model of Reality. It is simply not good enough that the great majority of novelists, dramatists and poets are setting their works in the phenomenal world alone, writing about social egos and relationships, and making partial statements that ignore the Whole and amount to endorsements of mind-body humanism (which discounts soul, spirit, and an afterlife), Rationalism, Empiricism, reductionism, materialism, mechanism, scepticism, positivism (giving primacy to the reason, sense data, parts, matter, mechanical explanations, doubt and observable facts) – in sum, the false views that have dogged the 20th century and have contributed to the huge wastage of human life in wars and similar disasters.

The new Universalist view of man restores all his traditional powers which the false views have eroded. In the Middle Ages, man was body, mind, soul and spirit, operating within a dualistic Christianity that frowned on and subjugated the body. The revolution that we know as the Renaissance shifted the focus to the body and mind from the soul and spirit, which were marginalised along with the halo, the illumined vision of the spirit, and then largely eliminated from art. Representing the phenomenal world alone was the business of the artist, even though he still drew on Christian stories, parables and themes. The Romantic revolution, among other things, focused on feelings at the expense of the reason and restored the metaphysical perspective of contact with the "Wisdom and Spirit of the Universe" (Wordsworth), with an "unseen power" (Shelley). The Modernist revolution turned against post-Romantic, Georgian feeling for the countryside and dwelt on the agony of fragmentation following the wreckage of Europe in the First World War, in which nothing made sense. Man became an alienated, shocked, purposeless, futile creature who could connect "nothing with nothing" (Eliot). Since then there have been minor movements (such as the Movement in English Poetry in 1956, which was anti-Romantic and Neoclassical and insisted on poems being rational statements set in social situations). Now the new Universalist view of man and the universe restores human immortality. Man is an invisible body within a visible body, infinite within his finite envelope, and this spiritual body can survive death – that is what reports on the near-death experience tell us. Man is again a body, mind, soul and spirit, and it is the soul-spirit which channels the universal energy of the Fire or Light, and knows the Reality of philosophy in the post-Existentialist Universalist *gnosis* (or knowing).

A Universalist Revolution is essential in literature. A fundamental, sudden and abrupt change needs to take place, and must be called for. The phenomenal world is not the only Reality. Man is not merely body and mind, he has immortality. Novels need to include a dimension of the universal, metaphysical Whole, the One, behind their focus on narrative relationships and character in parts of the Whole (reductionist parts). So do plays (as Shakespeare's did, for example the reference to "the lark at heaven's gate" in *Cymbeline*) and so do poems. So do painting and music. I am not calling for an end to exclusively secular literature – some of the outstanding English literature from Chaucer to Pope and Jane Austen has contained sharp social observation, focusing on character defects and espousing the human virtues of kindness, tolerance, mercy, decency and consideration and care for one's fellow human beings, all of which are in harmony with the infinite Whole and are much admired by metaphysical philosophers. Some of the different *genres* in literature (e.g. the dramatic monologue, narrative verse) usually require exclusively secular treatment. Nonetheless the spectrum of differing *genres* reserves a central place for Truth-bearing contemplative-reflective odes in secular settings, and for the sublime vision. Like the greatest philosophy and art, the greatest literature reflects the writer's highest perceptions of Reality and of the Age, and leads readers forward to Truth. The greatest literature is Truth-bearing.

The Universalist Revolution bears the metaphysical Fire or Light within social settings in literature and combines sense and spirit – the phenomenal world of the senses and the spiritual beyond – as they were in Baroque art, which showed both dynamic movement in the world (often symbolised by wind) and the world of spirit (often symbolised by clouds). (I think of Bernini's sensuously sculpted, swooning, mystic St Teresa.) The new Universalist literature is taking its place alongside existing humanistic secular literature and the Universalist Revolution in literature follows the Baroque and is neo-Baroque in mixing the metaphysical and the secular. Just as the Baroque threw up epic (Milton's *Paradise Lost*), a mixture of metaphysical and secular, so has neo-Baroque. My *Overlord*, a poetic epic on the struggle between Eisenhower and Hitler at the end of the last war at the secular level, and on the struggle between Heaven and Hell for differing New World Orders on earth at the metaphysical level, is an attempt at a Universalist epic: a latter-day Sistine chapel vision of the metaphysical world's involvement in secular manoeuvres for war and peace. Epic requires a common metaphysical-secular culture in which all can find common ground, and I have produced my epic because I have been to the past and revisited the common ground of metaphysical belief which allows a panoramic sweep of the Whole. I am not impressed when secular critics who are self-confessedly anti-metaphysical say that epic is impossible today because there is no common ground of belief or common culture. (Of course there isn't, if the metaphysical is rejected in favour of total secularism. Of course there isn't, if the past and the Whole are ignored.)

A Revolution is happening in subject matter and technique (i.e. there is a new concern with metaphysical Reality) as the neo-Baroque style mixes Classicism and Romanticism and combines traditional and organic form, statement and image: Classical statement in social situations in traditional form, and fresh Romantic image and mystic vision in organic form. Universalist poems are about the Quest, illumination, glimpses of Reality, and their soaring vision is grounded in a return from rhymeless rhythm or free verse to rhyme and metre. Universalist verse plays show man's aspirations in relation to the One Reality behind the universe. Universalist stories contain revelations of Being. Kingsley Amis wrote in the first Movement anthology *New Lines* (1956), "Nobody wants any more poems on the grander themes for a few years." In a lean time of sharp and ironic ordinariness in literature, the Universalist Revolution is bringing back the sap that produces grander, loftier themes (which Wordsworth knew) along with the new view of man and of the universe that amounts to a new or Second Renaissance.

Traditionally philosophy, history and literature were branches on one unified tree-trunk, religion, and were permeated by the sap of a metaphysical vision which was central to religion and arts alike. In a unified, rather than a fragmented culture – in a growing rather than a declining civilisation, or in a reviving phase of a declining civilisation – this is the case: philosophy, history and literature are all sap-fed branches from one trunk, religion, as they were in the Europe of the Middle Ages. Today, following vandalistic shakings since Newton, the sap has dried up and the brittle branches are almost severed from their trunk.

Today the whole of our European culture is fractured at both the popular and higher levels and in deep malaise. Practitioners in the arts today are separated from the metaphysical energy which thrust their civilisation into being, and so they are impoverished, rootless. In *Culture and Anarchy* Matthew Arnold defines culture as the "study of perfection", of the works of the "best self", which he says are of "like spirit with poetry", what Swift in his *Battle of the Books* called "sweetness and light" – that which is achieved by *"euphuia"*, the finely tempered nature that looks beyond bodily activities and seeks to nourish the soul. Culture involves the pursuit of perfection (an "inward condition of the mind and spirit") by getting to know "the best which has been thought and said in the world". I would say culture is the best aspirations of the human spirit within a civilisation, as expressed in the arts and architecture, and that it has transmitted knowledge from past generations to our generation and will pass knowledge on from our generation to future generations.

The "most perfect" works of our time have nothing in common save humanism and scepticism (i.e. their focus on human life and doubt). Our higher culture is not bearing the fruit it should be bearing. It has secular leaves and shrivelled metaphysical fruit because its sap has ceased to flow from its roots in the One, the metaphysical vigour which in the Middle Ages found expression in the illumined vision of the Church. Landscapes (like Constable's) which show the serenity, unity, composure and tranquillity of Nature, have been replaced by disjointed abstract art. Spatial art, atonal music and doodle poems represent a huge decline in quality in relation to Michelangelo, Beethoven and Dante. The secular works being produced often invite the question: "So what?" A memory – so what, unless it points us to Truth? The pervasiveness of popular culture has meant that many higher culture novels and poems have the same humanistic, secular outlook on the world as *Mrs. Dale's Diary* or *The Archers*, at a more sophisticated and subtle level of character and language, no doubt, but still in their part of the spectrum. At the secular level, such works may be entertaining – in poetry they may lead to phrases of praise such as "cool syntactical windings", "concision", "tactile sonorities", "clever glooms and charmed lightenings" or "self-deprecatingly funny", "salvaging beauty from squalor" or "wonderfully sardonic and ironic" and in novels "full of linguistic inventiveness", "creates an authentic narrative voice", "well-observed", "keeps one's attention" – but in relation to the principles of the highest or profoundest art they are simply below the standard of the best, a shallow "dumbing down" from the high vision of the tradition.

We now live in a fractured culture in which anything goes: performance takes the place of substance, PR gimmicks and sensationalist "shock art" crowd out classical painting, music and literature. Standards have collapsed and no one is sure of what is good any more. Conveying Truth is now less important than capturing attention. To improve their own ratings newspapers and the media pitch their articles and programmes at the greatest number of potential 'consumers', who are sometimes deemed to be more interested in a review of a book on Elvis than in one on Reality. (Eliot wrote, "Humankind cannot bear very much reality.") Our fractured culture is one in which bemused, sceptical people who are unsure of their own beliefs or believe nothing occupy key positions within the Establishment and, unsure of what to do, find it safe to stick with the secular and ignore those whose work challenges the received 'wisdom' of scepticism, and so keep the secular sceptics in business and advance our culture's terminal decay. Presiding over the British scene is a Ministry for Culture, Media and Sport, the linkage of which evidently regards our higher culture as being on a par with secular, popular media and sport.

The Universalist Revolution in modern thought – in philosophy, history and literature and other disciplines such as the sciences and art – can heal the malaise in our culture for it is actually a counter-Revolution which restores the Tradition that we have forgotten, which is the central idea of European civilisation; and if enough practitioners join the Revolution and convey its sap, their revival of the European vision will revitalise and reunify our now desiccated and brittle European culture. A group of Universalist thinkers, writers, artists, painters, sculptors and composers can act as a kind of latter-day Pre-Raphaelite Group and recreate philosophy, history, literature, art and music round European civilisation's traditional central metaphysical energy, and so reunify Europe's culture at a higher level. Each renewal of a declining civilisation's central idea revives that civilisation as sap revitalises dry and brittle branches, and so it is desirable that Europe's current secularisation should be arrested by such a metaphysical movement for cultural renewal.

There would be one central idea in the work of such a Group: the metaphysical vision of the Fire or Light, which all would reflect in their work. This idea would draw sustenance from the deepest roots of European culture by renewing the European metaphysical vision as it was when it was strong and there was growth in the European civilisation. Just as the 19th-century Pre-Raphaelite artists themselves (Holman Hunt, Millais and Dante Gabriel Rossetti) sought to emulate the work of Italian artists before the time of Raphael, so the Group I envisage would be a pre-Rationalist Group to emulate the unified art of the Middle Ages, Renaissance and Baroque before the Age of Reason split European culture into reason and (later) feeling, and developed scientific materialism from Newton's discoveries. It would anyway be a pre-Vienna Circle Group that would be a pro-Einstein-and-Vitalist Group.

In calling for the metaphysical to exist alongside the secular through such a Group, I am not siding with Christianity against the art of the Renaissance or of Greek Hellenism before it (which Arnold distinguished from Christian "Hebraism"); I seek to renew the metaphysical idea within Greek Hellenism and the Renaissance. The Greek art of Pheidias perfectly captured the Greek metaphysical central idea, the serene divinity of Zeus, in his statue at Olympia which was one of the seven wonders of the ancient world, and the artists of the Renaissance – Giotto, Leonardo, Michelangelo – are all imbued with the metaphysical idea. In both Greek and Renaissance artists beauty, harmony and inner and outer human perfection have been expressed with the highest and most perfect skill. Far from calling for metaphysical Hebraism to be admitted to a secular Hellenistic dictatorship, I am lamenting the fact that modern Hellenism has lost contact with its own metaphysical roots which Pheidias exemplified, and I am seeking to help it make a reconnection by paving the way.

A latter-day pre-Raphaelite Group can rediscover a common cultural vitality by returning to the past. As all civilisations grow from the same metaphysical vision, in a healthy civilisation and culture (in Europe's case until 1660) there is a core of belief around that vision which is vital, and cultural vitality is reflected in creative vitality – the relationship between cultural vitality and creative vitality is very close – and poets and philosophers, artists and scientists all have common ground and creative vitality in the culture of the civilisation's vital central idea. As I have said, Dante, Ficino and Botticelli all share a vision. In an unhealthy civilisation and culture (in Europe's case after 1660, but especially after 1910) there is no central essence of belief associated with the vision that inspired its growth, and consequently there is no cultural vitality in relation to a metaphysical idea, only humanistic diversity. Without cultural vitality to nourish him, the artist-Seeker must go back to the past and rediscover his roots in the cultural vitality of the past, which is then reflected in his own newly discovered creative vitality.

The artist needs to derive his creative vitality by rediscovering his roots in the civilisation's and culture's metaphysical idea, and he draws fragments of this idea into his work, as did the poets of 1910–1920. Pound in his *Cantos* turns away from his Age's "grimace" and searches through the past (through scenes from Homer, Virgil and Chinese history) to renew contact with what is nourishing, the mysteries of Eleusis for example. Eliot in 'The Waste Land' turns away from the "stony rubbish" of contemporary secular culture and finds fragments from Indian and later early European thought with which to "shore up" (as with beams) his "ruin". And Yeats sees "things fall apart, the centre cannot hold" and finds his values in images of metaphysical Byzantium. My own foray into the past took place in Roman Italy and Presocratic Greece, and in Japan where in my youth I discovered the practice of enlightenment in Zen meditation, and the unitive Zen view of the universe in the imagery of the Ryoanji stone garden in Kyoto, as can be read in my poem, 'The Silence'. These fragments took me on to the essential European vision. The only way for the artist in an unhealthy culture to recover contact with his culture's roots is to go back to the past and rediscover the vitality his culture once had in its early years (perhaps via another culture) and to reflect its early vitality in images which have creative force; and in so doing he renews his own creative vitality and transforms his own contemporary culture by putting it in touch with its common ground of belief during past growth.

In philosophy, history and literature, there is salvation today in going back to the past. In philosophy metaphysical Reality was abandoned around 1910; the vision of the metaphysical Whole was abandoned like a disused Cornish tin mine, and some philosophers need to return to 1910 and Einstein's discoveries and continue going forward from there, connecting themselves to the long mining tradition of empirical metaphysical inquiry. Despite Toynbee, history has failed to see all differing civilisations and cultures as parts of a Whole, as one interconnecting flow (Heracleitus would have said "flux") of events, and is not revealing the full pattern of human life but merely reductionist slices of a particular nation's history in a particular decade. Historians need to return to Toynbee's example and go forward from there, seeking patterns in the metaphysical Whole as I have tried to do in *The Fire and the Stones*. After Pound, Eliot and Yeats (who stood firm to the end of their lives, as can be seen from Pound's later *Cantos*, Eliot's *Four Quartets* and Yeats' 'Byzantium' poems), literature failed to present a vision of the metaphysical Whole, and Kingsley Amis saying "Nobody wants any more poems on the grander themes" in 1956 is a consequence of its academicist Augustanism or neo-Rationalism (in which statement was preferred to image). Literature has abandoned the metaphysical vision of Yeats and Eliot (who followed the occult and Christian traditions) and is heading for a secular wilderness of increasingly techniquey self-consciousness. Writers need to return to the metaphysical Whole that was still known in Tennyson's day and during the Modernist concern with civilisation.

By in the first instance reviving the essence of European culture, such a latter-day pre-Raphaelite Group may seem to run counter to multi-culturalism. It is fair enough that as the European nations had empires, ex-colonials should be writing in English (Rushdie about India, Walcott about the Caribbean, Soyinka about Africa), but secular treatments of the Moslem religion, however interesting in their own right, do not do much to reconnect us to the European civilisation's metaphysical idea, and to that extent multi-culturalism (another term for cultural diversity found in declining civilisations) has not helped European writers rediscover their cultural vitality and purity within the essential European vision and its common ground. On the spectrum of European literature, which rightly includes multi-cultural, ex-colonial diversity, literature that revives the European civilisation's essential vision must have a prominent, if not central, place. The very fact that I should have to say this is a measure of how much the metaphysical has been marginalised by the secular in our time (which is another way of saying that in our time secularised literature has lost contact with the metaphysical Search).

A European and world common culture can come from reviving the essence of European culture, the vision that began our culture's metaphysical growth, for this is at one with the essence of all other cultures. As I have shown in *The Fire and the Stones* on the Universalist principle that all the metaphysical ideas of all 25 civilisations are the same, each essential vision has a universal aspect and is universal to all cultures. If each living civilisation revives the essence of its early culture, which on the Universalist principle has the same vision behind it as every other living civilisation, then internationally and globally there will be different, diverse revivals of metaphysical ideas which are essentially the same. A worldwide movement in which each civilisation returns to its metaphysical idea would create the common ground from which every civilisation could opt to join a world association that can bring an era of peace. A return to the unity of European culture could therefore mark the beginning of a Universalist movement to unite all cultures round a revival of their initial unity, and therefore of a worldwide movement for world peace. Certainly, such a worldwide movement to create a common culture based on the Fire or Light of every civilisation can only be good for world peace. The contemplative practice of Universalist metaphysics is conducive to world harmony, not discord. Universalism is a metaphysical movement but it also has the potentiality to take regional blocs towards world peace....

The Revolution is a restoration of the metaphysical, mystical Tradition in opposition to humanism, Rationalism, Empiricism, materialism, mechanism, scepticism, positivism and reductionism.... It renews the Vitalism of early 20th-century philosophy (the view that life originates in a vital principle, not chemical and other physical forces) and can reunify and renew our fragmented culture round our civilisation's central idea, so that Western artists and composers reflect the One.

5. The Approach of the Later Poems

Extracts from 'Questioning Modern Secular Poetry: A Defence of Traditional Poetic Method or: Poking the Hornets' Nest' by Nicholas Hagger

> "Yet let me flap this bug with gilded wings,
> This painted child of dirt, that stinks and stings."
> (Pope, 'Epistle to Dr Arbuthnot', lines 309–310)

For 600 years (1380–1980) the different branches of English culture all grew out of one healthy Christian trunk like the branches of a tree, and all the disciplines were fed by the same metaphysical sap from the Christian religion. In the Middle Ages, religion pervaded philosophy, painting, music and poetry, the earliest form of literature. Over the years secularisation weakened English culture and by the 20th century the English cultural tree was pretty dry.

For 600 years English poets have had something to say, and the intensity, pressure and urgency of their message elevated their verse into poetry. (Verse is metrical patterns with rhyme heightening their effectiveness, whereas poetry has an additional quality that is hard to define but which has much to do with the poet's vision.) The sap of European culture imbued their lines, leading to reflections on time and eternity and on the metaphysical nature of the universe. Shakespeare wrote of the lark at Heaven's gate in *Cymbeline*. Marvell saw the soul gliding like a bird into a tree in General Fairfax's Garden in Nun Appleton, Yorkshire. Milton justified "the ways of God to man" in *Paradise Lost*. Pope vindicated "the ways of God to man" in his 'Essay on Man'. Wordsworth wrote of the "Wisdom and Spirit of the Universe" in his *Prelude*, and of "a motion and a spirit, that impels/All thinking things, all objects of all thought/And rolls through all things" in 'Tintern Abbey'. Shelley wrote in 'Adonais', "The One remains, the many change and pass." Similar sentiments can be found in the poets of the European tradition, such as Dante and Goethe. What the poet had to say was often lofty and elevated, sometimes sublime. Shelley wrote in his 'A Defence of Poetry' that "a poem is the very image of life expressed in its eternal truth".

For 600 years the mainstream of poetry has involved metre and rhyme or blank verse, which act like banks beside a river, as borders that order, without which there would be an anarchic flood. Within the restrictions of these banks poets paddle with the flowing currents of spiritual energy. The Greek and Latin iambic measures entered English Literature with the Normans and the Renaissance, pushing out the Old English alliterative line of stresses. St Godric (who died c.1170) was the first to reject Anglo-Saxon forms. From Chaucer to Tennyson readers knew clearly where they were technically, whether a line scanned well or badly and rhymed well or badly. Shakespeare had his irregularities but these were exceptions rather the rule. The Metaphysicals, Milton, the Augustans and the Romantics all used the stanza, blank verse, the heroic couplet and the formal Ode. The Victorians continued the metrical tradition with the dramatic monologues of Browning and lyrics of Tennyson, though Matthew Arnold loosened his verse and Hopkins introduced feet of one stress with sprung rhythm.

As poets used forms that enabled readers to know precisely where they were their verse could take on reflective philosophical weight as they communicated what they had to say. This weight can be found in Shakespeare's soliloquies and Platonist sonnets, Donne's probing of metaphysical truth, Milton's speeches about God, Pope's 'Essay on Man', Wordsworth's autobiographical *Prelude* and Keats' great Odes about the ephemerality of life. There was a general awareness that humans have a spiritual and divine spark as well as a social mind and body. After the freeing rhythms of Whitman and Pound, Eliot and Lawrence, Yeats maintained the metrical tradition in the 20th century with reflective poems about life and death, and Eliot himself returned to profound philosophical considerations in his formal *Four Quartets*. The word-drunk Dylan Thomas sang about the mysteries of time and death, Betjeman surveyed life in his strictly formal poems. Larkin and the Movement poets (for all their rationalism and concern with statement rather than image) used their formal concerns to reflect on society. For 600 years it has been possible to understand the content and method of Chaucer, Shakespeare, Milton, Pope, Coleridge, Shelley or Tennyson without requiring any fundamental change in the nation's poetic taste. Just as the domes of Islamic mosques express the beauty of God in art over a thousand years, so the poets of the British tradition created their own testaments to divine beauty in their life's work.

The collapse of religious belief in the late 20th century, and of belief in immortality, has had consequences for 'the traditional' poetic method. For poetry then becomes a record of the world of the self, which is dark and lacking in the beauty of the cosmos. Since 1980 many practitioners of English verse have had nothing to say and they have moved away from the readily comprehensible forms, preferring that words should be put down on paper as they happen to come out instinctively, without the shaping constraints of stanzas or metrical form. A climate of "anything goes" has arisen. Metre and rhyme were largely abandoned and with them a 600-year-old tradition of poetic method. Rooting himself in Lawrence's free verse, Eliot's early stress poetry and American free verse practised by William Carlos Williams, Roethke and of course Sylvia Plath, Ted Hughes (with whom I corresponded from 1993 until his death in 1998) encouraged this tendency and some of his poems seem to be written in chopped-up 'prose' (though pentameters, five-feet lines, *can* be found by piecing short lines together). In 1982, the introduction to the *Penguin Book of Contemporary British Poetry*, co-written by Andrew Motion, the new Poet Laureate, and Blake Morrison, stated: "A body of work has been created which demands, for its appreciation, a reformation of poetic taste." Verse without metre and rhyme, with irregular lengths of lines, sometimes (but not always) using rhythm, requires a different kind of understanding. (Of Motion, Michael Schmidt wrote approvingly in *Lives of the Poets*, "He has a subtle ear for speech so that the poems seldom settle into metre." The implication is that any poet who is alert to speech does not need to use metre, and that metre is a crutch for bad poets. This is a wrong view of poetry, and is a necessary consequence of the reformation of taste.)

The effect has been to make it harder for readers to know what is going on and for practitioners of this alternative method to approach reflective, philosophical themes, for the new-way verse forms are slight and sometimes have only one or two words per line. Practitioners have in effect demanded that the old way of responding to poetry for 600 years should be unlearned – poetry like Chaucer's, Shakespeare's, Milton's and Wordsworth's which is rooted in English culture and appeals to the soul – and that appreciation of the new way should focus on word-choice, sounds and image and applaud its slight subject matter and lack of depth. It is as if painters were to have a revolution against the traditional art of portrait-painting and declare that doodle-cartoons are now the norm, that there needs to be a "reformation of taste" so that the public can appreciate the new art and that the advantages of the cartoon should be stressed so that portraits can be ignored in future. Pope understood the thinness behind such thinking and lampooned banality in his *Dunciad*.

I could now invite you to consider half a dozen fairly typical examples of the new-way poetry, which new-way critics have praised for their power; lyric beauty; intense emotion; biting satire; punning eloquence that makes the language sing; intense imagery, inventiveness and jewelled language.

I decline to offer selections from these new-way versifiers (whose permission I would have to seek) as I am defending the old way; but informed readers will readily be able to supply their own examples from the best-known new-way poets. "Old-way" sensibilities see such metreless, rhymeless offerings differently as evidence of the bankruptcy of the new-way secular-humanist vision.

In the majority of new-way poems, language is decorative rather than descriptive – meaning is sacrificed to decorative effects – and its source is the rational ego and many, the world of the self which has lost contact with the soul. It is therefore shallow. In the great majority, meaning, grace and beauty are not obviously apparent. A comparison to, or rather contrast with, the two Poets Laureate of the 19th century, Wordsworth and Tennyson, shows what a huge decline in communication of meaning through language there has been in the last hundred years, and that the beauty of the best verse of Wordsworth and Tennyson is missing. Many of the new-way works deliberately do dirt on the sacred; all amount to a kind of anti-poetry that is now held up as the norm and defended by the poetic Establishment for the above versifiers – my examples would include two Poet Laureates, a Chairman of the Literature Panel of the Arts Council and the Oxford Professor of Poetry.

The new way of writing is user-friendly to poets. Whereas Yeats on at least one occasion spent all morning hunting for a rhyme and Betjeman spoke of the surprising simile that can be thrown up during the search for a word within the constraint of rhyme, a two-or-three-words-per-line poem without metre or rhyme (which is spurned as "predictable") and precious few other rules can be dashed off in a minute or two at a bus-stop or while waiting for tea in a *café*. Ease, brevity and convenience have brought followers to this disposable, sketchy kind of art. A reader may be forgiven for feeling unable to judge the result as the criteria by which its worth can be deemed are not obviously apparent.

I have come to hold grave reservations about free verse. Eliot wrote that there should be a ghost of a pentameter behind the arras of free verse, and he had strong opinions on the matter: "There is no freedom in art"; "No verse is free for the man who wants to do a good job.... Only a bad poet could welcome free verse as a liberation from form." Lawrence's free-verse poems seem unsatisfactory, dashed off in varying lengths of lines that do not really lodge in the memory.

The great drawback of the new metreless, rhymeless way is that it produces poems that cannot be remembered, and are therefore unmemorable. Memory, the ability to remember, is fundamental to a shared rooted culture. Consider the following passages which, by contrast, *can* be remembered and *are* memorable:

> When icicles hang by the wall,
> And Dick, the shepherd, blows his nail,
> And Tom bears logs into the hall,
> And milk comes frozen home in pail.
> When blood is nipp'd and ways be foul,
> Then nightly sings the staring owl,
>   Tu-who;
> Tu-whit, tu-who – a merry note,
> While greasy Joan doth keel the pot.
>   (Shakespeare, *Love's Labour's Lost*, v.ii)

> About, about, in reel and rout
> The death-fires danced at night;
> The water, like a witch's oils,
> Burnt green, and blue and white.
>   (Coleridge, 'The Rime of the Ancient Mariner')

> The One remains, the many change and pass;
> Heaven's light forever shines, Earth's shadows fly;
> Life like a dome of many-coloured glass,
> Stains the white radiance of Eternity....
>   (Shelley, 'Adonais')

Rhyming lines from Shakespeare, Coleridge and Shelley drop into the memory like a stone into a well, and are retained without effort. But none of the new-way verse lends itself to memory and retention. After several readings a poem by Hughes or by other new-way versifiers fails to lodge in the memory. Sir Philip Sidney pointed out in his 'An Apologie for Poetrie' (1580/1581) that "verse far exceedeth prose in the knitting up of the memory..., one word... begetting another as, be it a rhyme or measured verse, by the former a man shall have a near guess to the follower". In Sidney's terms the unguessable new-way verse is closer to prose.

Another drawback of the new-way verse is that it diminishes the standing of both the poem and of the poet. For 600 years the poet was a cross-disciplinary reflector who held the mirror up to human nature and the universe and, as one who often embodied the central idea of his culture, reflected on the state of his civilisation as a leading figure in it and often the embodiment of its central idea and its culture. Now the poet has become an ordinary bloke who produces small disposable and unmemorable offerings that may secure throw-away laughs at a poetry reading. The new-way verse is invariably humanist (i.e. concerned with human rather than divine matters) and is unaware of the One behind the many. I am reminded of the Ship of Fools. It is as if the new-way versifiers have no sails on their ship because they do not believe in the breath of God. Chaucer's *Prologue*, Shakespeare's Platonist sonnets, Dryden's 'Absalom and Achitophel', Shelley's 'Adonais' and Eliot's *Four Quartets* have set an exalted standard for the poem and the role of the poet in his culture which the new-way verses and versifiers ignore or reject.

*

My work continues the traditional poetic method; sometimes I think I am the only poet continuing it in contemporary Britain. I have retained metre/rhyme and blank verse for ready communication and I have made the quest for Reality my subject matter. Many of my poems are rooted in the English countryside, and are reflective approaches to the One behind the many (to put it in the terms of the Presocratic philosophers Parmenides and Heracleitus and of my own philosophical work, *The One and the Many*). They are Universalist poems. Universalism is a restatement of the metaphysical vision which sees the universe as a Whole and assimilates every known experience and all possible concepts, including infinity. Universalist philosophers see the universe as fundamentally One, a whole; Universalist historians see history as a whole; and Universalist poets and men of letters look at the whole of life, in both its physical and metaphysical layers, rather than from a purely humanist, social perspective. Many of my poems therefore interlock. They are about connections between the world of Nature and the metaphysical Reality hidden within it and behind it; between tradition and the individual.

This idea is expressed in my re-creation of an Elizabethan knot-garden at Otley Hall in Suffolk (later reproduced in my garden in Essex), where a single white point in the centre of the garden can be seen as sending energy that becomes the events of physics and history. The 25 beds of herbs represent the civilisations of history, the forms of physics and the isms of philosophy. My poetic output is a kind of knot-garden in verse that also makes a statement about the events of physics, history and philosophy.

My subject matter aims to be both universal and local. I have poems about the universe, about Europe, about English places that evoke the tradition of English culture and Englishness (for example, Warwick Castle); and I have written many pastoral poems set in Essex, Suffolk and Cornwall in which the One is never far away. Epic poetry has been regarded in all countries and at all times as the highest form of poetic achievement because it narrates heroic events on a grand scale. My epic poem *Overlord*, written in 42,000 lines of blank verse, is about Eisenhower's conflict with Hitler in the last year of the Second World War but at another level it is also about the rival New World Orders of Christ and Satan.

I have tried to ensure that the range of my verse is wide. I have written sonnets; lyrics in trimeters and tetrameters that are rhymed or alternately rhymed; elegies; odes in 8, 10 or 12 stanzas, each of 8, 10 or 12 lines that are rhymed or alternately rhymed; blank verse; stress metre (my own exploration and eventual abandonment of 4-stress lines); narrative poems; epic; and dramatic verse (i.e. my four verse plays, *The Warlords*, *The Tragedy of Prince Tudor*, *Ovid Banished* and *The Rise of Oliver Cromwell*).

In traditional poetry there are perennial tensions between Romantic image and neo-Augustan Movement statement; between solitary-mystic-spiritual Romantic and rational-social Augustan outlooks. I have tried to combine the Romantic and Classical approaches in a style I have called the Neo-Baroque, which unites sense and spirit, the social and the individual, feeling and thinking. It is important for a traditional poet to reflect a sense of what has traditionally been thought of as the divine in creation. No great poetry can be written by atheists who have an exclusively social view of the world because it fails to reflect the beauty of the cosmos. An image of the true poet can be found in the Middle English poem, 'Pearl'. In a late 14th-century illustration, the 'Pearl' poet stands on one side of a river and sees his dead daughter (the pearl without price) on the far bank clothed in light. He communicates with her across the barrier between the mundane and spiritual realms. The swirling water that separates him from the beyond is full of fish, the images of his poems. The true poet is in constant touch with the "eternal truth" (Shelley) behind everyday life.

Traditional poetry is the product of Imagination. In his *Biographia Literaria* (1814–1817) Coleridge refers to the "esemplastic power of the imagination", "esemplastic" meaning "shaping into One". Imagination – Coleridge's "esemplastic" power – is the intuitive, unitive faculty that sees the Whole behind the parts, One behind the many. Where reason analyses and reduces into parts, Imagination puts the parts back together into a Whole and takes us to the hidden metaphysical unity behind multiplicity. Fancy, by contrast, is rational and decorative. A simile within a secular humanist poem in which one "part" of the Whole is compared to another "part" of the Whole is an example of such decorative fancy. Imagination is the capacity to image in a creative, Whole-seeking way, and in doing so to perceive the Oneness of the universe. Shelley, in his 'A Defence of Poetry' (1821), defines poetry as "the expression of the imagination" in vitally metaphorical language whose harmony excites. Poetry therefore "lifts the hidden beauty of the world".

Modern irregular new-way verse has lost the intuitive, unitive vision that can soar to the Whole and has settled for existing in confusion among the parts in the world of the self. The new way is lost among the many phenomena of multiplicity and ugliness and is unable to relate them to the One. And the loss of this esemplastic faculty is accompanied by a loss of feeling in poetry. The highest feeling is where the One is glimpsed, the "unknown modes of being" of Wordsworth's *Prelude*. Feeling of a high order can be found in Keats' Odes, Shelley's 'Adonais' about the death of Keats and Tennyson's *In Memoriam* but not in the impersonality of Modernist work, except very obliquely – when emotion is invested exclusively in images as in Eliot's hyacinth girl – and not in the cool, rational statements that are Movement poems. Modernism and the Movement both hold emotions and feelings at a distance. The new-way verse is even more pallid in its emotion. I have tried to restore emotions and feelings in my poetry (for example in *The Gates of Hell*, 1969–1972).

Since Tennyson poets have sought for a modern colloquial idiom. My fusion of Romanticism and Classicism through esemplastic imagination and its focus on history and tradition has attempted to blend image and statement, feeling and reason within the same poem. Poetic diction and dead form do not make for vibrant language, but Wordsworth's concern to find a language of the common man, of "a man speaking to men" ('Poetry and Poetic Diction', 1800), and Eliot's concern to "purify the language of the tribe" (*Four Quartets*) can be fused in a voice speaking through metre and rhyme and moving in and out of images to create a new approach to the Oneness behind the many phenomena in the universe, to approach (as Wordsworth did) the "Wisdom and Spirit of the Universe". The colloquialness of the new-way verse does not justify the banality of much of its language, which is not purified by the constraints of metre and rhyme.

I am a poet who seeks to reflect Truth in all its layers in my poetry. I am open to insights into the metaphysical Whole as well as social truths; and to a mystical awareness of the way the universe has been created and of the way human beings relate to it. Human beings' consciousness has always been held to be superior to that of the animals – the animalistic, shamanic Hughes reversed this when he gave equivalence to a thrush, Mozart and a shark in one of his poems – and Nature poems should be about the place man occupies in the divine universe. Artists are of two kinds: Apollonians, who are makers of art and follow Apollo, god of art and the divine Light; and Dionysians, who are possessed by a dark raw energy, like van Gogh; Lawrence; and Hughes, who wrote Dionysian, neo-Blakeian works about tiger-like jaguars and lambs. I am an Apollonian in my poetic approach, and see the consciousness of man aspiring to visionary heights and the mystical perception of the One. The tradition of the Whole, which metaphysics passed on in philosophy and which poets absorbed when our civilisation was healthier and its branches were filled with metaphysical sap, is an important subject in the poetry of any Universalist. As Eliot pointed out in 'Tradition and the Individual Talent', tradition cannot be inherited, it has to be obtained "by great labour" and it involves the historical sense, a perception not only of "the pastness of the past, but of its presence" and "a feeling for the whole of the literature of Europe from Homer".

I am a poet who writes in verse partly to reflect on life, to make statements (which draw on all disciplines) of images of the One, of Truth, in specific places and situations and therefore to instruct – there is a semi-didactic purpose in Universalism; and partly to delight and please. (Horace in his *Ars Poetica* wrote that a poet should instruct or please or both: "Poets aim at giving profit or delight, or at combining the giving of pleasure with some useful precepts for life.") I am a poet who uses the esemplastic power of the Imagination to reach – and teach – my perception of the One and of its embodiment in historical and traditional scenes, and I use traditional versification – metre, rhyme and blank verse – to make this vision readily accessible.

Contrary to the disparaging views of new-way critics, it is the vision of the One that needs to be defended in our secular-humanist, declining time in which most poems are like brittle leaves which are not nourished by the metaphysical sap of the One that once unified our culture. The defence of traditional poetic method has to be fought partly at the philosophical, mystical level. The One still presses into some poets, and I certainly aim to keep it alive in my writing – and I sometimes think that I am doing so on my own. The new-way versifiers of sapless, rhymeless, metreless doodle-cartoons want a reformation of the public taste so that their sapless works will be better appreciated. In other words saplessness, metrelessness and rhymelessness are to become the norm along with multiplicity, ugliness and Onelessness. I say there has already been a huge decline in taste – and in our culture – which has allowed the debased forms of the new-way verse to be elevated to a position of superiority over traditional poetry and to enter newspapers, poetry magazines and journals as the superior successor to traditional versification. What a con! The tree has dried up, the branches of our culture are desiccated, the leaves are sere and lifeless – and are now being promoted as superior to green, tender leaves. To say it is to poke a hornets' nest (or puff smoke into it) but new-way verse is accelerating the decay in our culture.

The secularisation of the 600-year-old metaphysical poetic tradition by critics, universities, Arts Council bureaucrats and recent poets has resulted in Shakespeare, Donne, Milton, Wordsworth, Keats and other poets of the tradition losing their metaphysical meaning and becoming literary tourist sites or a literary theme-park – a counterpart in literature to the recent secularisation of sacred stones (pyramids, cathedrals, temples and mosques) that once embodied and housed the metaphysical Fire but which are now tourist attractions as I described in *The Fire and the Stones*. Traditional poets have been forced off school and university curricula – and replaced by new-way poets. By writing secular humanist poems the new-way poets have played a part in the further desecration of this tradition. English poetry already looks like being in terminal decline.

Traditional poetry must be defended against this decline. What is needed is not a reformation of taste but a relearning of the traditional taste by which for 600 years poets from Chaucer to Eliot were appreciated, to arrest the decline and the advance of debased work whose apologists would like to see off works with residual signs of health. In a time when a blank canvas with a hole in it is perceived as being better than a Constable or a Gainsborough and a cacophonous symphony is felt to be better than Mozart or Beethoven, it is vital that the techniques and attitudes behind the unhistorical doodle-verse should not be allowed to dismiss epics, lyrics, sonnets and verse plays rooted in the tradition of the last 600 years as "old-way" and not worthy of consideration by the public.

I have drawn a distinction between verse and poetry. Not all verse (i.e. metrical patterns of sound and language with rhyme heightening their effectiveness) is poetry. Poetry has an indefinable something that transcends verse – a pressure of intensity, a soaring into the One, a glint of Truth. The new-way is struggling to be verse. It seeks a vision of the universe, a sense of the divine, and to redefine verse as patterns of loose cadences of free verse. It lacks the vision of the One. It is not poetry. The continuation of poetry in the 21st century requires a rejection of debased taste and a return to the traditional poetic method defended by Sir Philip Sidney, Wordsworth and Shelley and to the taste by which it is relished.

3–4 June 1999; revised 27 October 2005

Appendix 2

The 25-year Gestation and Birth of *Overlord*
[See *Overlord*, pp.933–947]

1. Extracts from Nicholas Hagger's *Diaries*/Autobiography [*A Mystic Way*]

5 May 1968, Loughton, England
On the Vikings, it is the ON (Old Norse) tradition I really belong to, and which I must explore, see Bronsted. (NB, '*sted*' in Stansted, near here, is ON.).... My poetry is ON in origin, I now feel. It is pre-Snorri Sturluson, it is battle and conflict and heroism within, the traditional epic interiorised.... I must go into the ON epic, its long swinging lines and pagan religion.

30 July 1968, Loughton
What am I aiming at? To create giant, monumental images of eternal things in contemporary garbs.... I must think more about interiorising the traditional epic. *Life Cycle*, that elusive cycle of Baudelairean-type poems that has haunted me since I flew from Baghdad to Basra and got the idea among the clouds, that is my epic. How can I give a relationship an epic quality? By concentrating on the eternal, the heroic, by plumbing the depths of suffering, by shrinking from nothing in my pot-holing down the mind.... If I am allowed only five books in Libya, they must be a book on epic, ON poetry, Baudelaire, Michelangelo and Rodin.... Epic: "a poem that celebrates in the form of a continuous narrative the achievements of one or more heroic personages of history and tradition", e.g. Homer, Virgil, Milton, [*Chanson de*] *Roland, Ramayana* etc. How to give form to a contemporary epic without doing a Joyce?... What is the story? What Paradise lost?... Aristotle: an epic poem should deal with a single action. So Homer avoids the chronological method or telling the life-history of his hero or proceeding episodically... – he gives his poem organic unity by selecting one theme, the wrath of Achilles, and weaves it into the background of the war, and he thus begins near the end and narrates retrospectively and avoids a biography of his hero. An organic whole in treatment of a subject – the working out of theme. Through the theme Homer traces the pattern of the war – the Trojan story is present to his mind and to that of his listeners. The *Iliad* and *Odyssey* were composed in and for a society that no longer exists; consequently the

conditions for reproducing such poetry no longer exist.... This work I have just glimpsed is my *magnum opus*: my *Paradise Lost*, my *Ulysses*... I will get onto this epic – as soon as I can *afford* the time. Meanwhile I must be ready. I must wait on the theme and when she pays me a little attention I must remember every line on her face.

13 September 1969, Tripoli, Libya
A Biblical work on modern times, a modern *Ecclesiastes?*... A visionary poem on London.... Theme in full: After World War 2 a settled way of life broke up: the Empire, class system, rural life became urbanised, Christianity.

20 October 1969, Tripoli
An active mood; can't sleep. Dogs barking, night silence.... I feel I am and always have been a poet, whose mission should be the image.... Think about epic.

11 June 1970, Tripoli
The Arab world is in a barbarian heroic stage, so epic is possible – the battle poetry of the Arabs against the Israelis. Homer, Virgil, the *Beowulf* poet, Milton – the epic poets are on the side of their fighters. Only the mock-heroic poets and novelists (Fielding, Pope) show detachment. Epic is impossible today, with an anti-war spirit.

17 June 1970, Tripoli
Woke up at 8.30, though I had an exam to invigilate at 9.... Made it at 8.59. Corrected my exam from 12.30 to 3.... Returned, was followed by two secret police in a VW; they parked round the corner, so did my washing, then washing-up, then went on the roof to see if they were still there. They weren't. Read the papers in the boiling sun on the roof.... Got the idea of visiting Ezra Pound in Rapallo.... Pound is the only writer of epic today in poetry.... So visit him at all costs. Who am I? A writer of epic.

20 June 1970, Tripoli
More on the epic. It is basically about a group of people in a hostile world: they band together and have allegiances for mutual self-survival. That is why it is produced by national migrations. The Greeks going to Troy. The [Trojans in Italy] under Aeneas. The Danes invading England and bringing with them a story of the Geats and the Danes being harassed (pushed out) by Grendel. Lucifer leaving Paradise. Migrations produce epic,* hence the sense of loss and exile in heroic

poetry; for the heroic scale it has to be about the centre of the world. So Tolstoy writes of the Russians resisting the Napoleonic invasion (Napoleon being the centre of the world) and the epic I saw in Peking about Yuan Wen Tsé is of the VC (i.e. Viet Cong) resisting American invasion (America being the centre of the world). The shouting over loudspeakers in the streets today [in Tripoli] is the same thing: America, the centre of the world, has been 'shoved' out of Wheelus (Air Base). (Today [in Tripoli] is a fantasy-epic.) The Arabs resisting Israel, however, is too off-centre to be heroic (but what about the *Edda*? Iceland?). Nonetheless, this is a barbarian, heroic *Völkerwanderungen*, this Tripoli war-council. Epics are written from the point of view of the invaders (Greek, Roman, *Beowulf*) or invaded (Tolstoy). There is Israeli epic or Palestinian epic. Maoist epic (*The East is Red*) or Chiang epic (full of exile, loss of home). The *Beowulf* poet must have been a Dane who crossed to England… and who, though in the invading situation, told a story about home, why he was driven out. (Grendel is the tribe that drove him out and his fellows.) For the invaded, the elegiac tone: gone is that former happiness…. The Seafarer and the Ancient Mariner – *having* to tell a story. Later the group became individual. Why?… What must you do to have a modern, peacetime epic? Distance to the timeless, have an adversary…. Have a great event, great people, great feelings. Don't use myth…. Think about the modern conflict in epic. We are in the time of *Satyricon*, in a late Silver Age, an age of comedy, or Plautus and Terence and debased coinage and language, in the time of *koiné*, the melting-pot, the mixing-up of styles. The Universal State is about to begin…. But N.B. Virgil's *Aeneid* was written at the beginning of a Universal State, the feeling of a new Renaissance can give birth to national epic ('Great Augustus' etc.). Reread *The Aeneid*…. Who is Faust's enemy? The Devil. And Lucifer's? God…. My enemy has nothing to do with national enemies, or wars, or the centre of the world. It is internal….

Externally since 1957 a line has become clear, a '*limes*' (frontier), and "the geographical transition from civilisation to barbarism is now no longer gradual but is abrupt" (Toynbee). External proletariats react to civilisations they come into contact with by producing epic poetry (written in later Dark Ages) that reflects their gods (Greek Homer against Crete; Teutonic epic poetry – *Beowulf* – and Scandinavian saga of Iceland; cf. French *Chanson de Roland* against Andalusian Umayyad Caliphate, 11th century). "No poetry from civilisation… can equal… Homer." (A reference to *Paradise Lost*.)…. Epic has no relation to periods of history…? No. It has. Cromwell was a barbarian leader of a heroic time. (But "Drama develops in the home country, epic among migrating peoples.") A time of war? A law: epics are written by wandering tribes (the oral tradition); after revolutions – through myth; or before/on the foundations of Universal States, e.g. Virgil, when they celebrate.

*D-Day was a migration (Nicholas Hagger's *Overlord*), as were the US invasions of Afghanistan and Iraq (Nicholas Hagger's *Armageddon*).

7 July 1970, near Oran, Algeria
1 July. Left Tripoli in haste, pursued by police. (They had tried to arrest me under the pretext of stealing my own grapes.) Uneventful drive to the border, where I got two nails stuck in my back tyre; the Libyan farewell.

16 July 1970, Rapallo, Italy
A visit to Ezra Pound in Rapallo, Sant'Ambrogio. Found his red house (*"casa rossa"*) on top of a mountain about 7, knocked on the back door. He appeared and fled, living in total silence as he does, like Hess. I waited and knocked again and his companion came up the garden. She had got my letter ("E. Pound, Rapallo"), said it would be more convenient for me to see him then. I went in. He sat apart, bearded, 85, in great silence. For fifteen minutes he did not speak a word, it was like the Delphic Oracle. You put the question to it and listened for the answer you wanted to hear, and the silence confirmed it. I outlined my poetic epic method and asked, "Why can't you compress at length?"... I persisted, and he said, "It's worth trying" and "Have you had twelve experiences that sum up the culture of the last thirty years?" I insisted that I had. His (companion [Olga Rudge]) then interrupted with coffee and was a little rude.... I: "I want to hear from the author of *The Cantos* if the method is worth following for forty years." Then in came an Italian writer, "Pescatore – like a fish", with his mistress and an Italian boy, and they talked a lot, and Pound sat in silence in the open window, under a full moon, very sad and apart, blinking constantly, and I was able to take in the room: the sculptures, the books (Gaudier-Brzeska, Yeats' *Mythologies*), the handwritten notes: "A place of skulls".... When (they) left Pound grabbed me by the arm and pointed to the chair in front of him and said, "Here, sit down, sit down," and "You've been around a lot, I think you can do what you want to do: put the culture and the Age into twelve poems."... I said... I could *see* this poem. He: "If you can see it, then you've already done it." I told him... that two eras in English Literature were spanning each other, and he shook me warmly by the hand and then lapsed into oracular silence, as silent as the future, and I left.

Extract from Nicholas Hagger's autobiography, A Mystic Way; *a fuller account of this meeting (the above abbreviated account having been written in a hotel room at 1am when he was extremely tired and facing a very early start later that morning, conditions favouring haste rather than full recollection):*

On 16 July I found a hotel and then drove to Sant'Ambrogio and asked directions from passers-by and was told to go to a *"casa rossa"* (red house) on the top of a mountain. I arrived about seven and knocked at the back door and Pound appeared, bearded, in his slippers. He turned away and went back in, and his companion Olga Rudge came up the garden. Yes, she said, she had got my letter (which was simply addressed Ezra Pound, Rapallo) and it would be convenient to see him immediately. I followed her in and was shown into a large room with many books, some sculptures, a circular table with papers on it, and a sofa. Pound sat apart beside a window in great silence. He had a serene face and troubled eyes. I spoke about my knowledge of Japan and China, including the Cultural Revolution – he had got Yeats to look at Japanese Nō plays, hence Yeats's own plays, and he had got the idea for his own *Cantos* from China through Fenollosa in 1913 – and I spoke about my interest in developing his innovations and my plans to write a poetic epic, and said: "You've been writing the *Cantos* for fifty-seven years, so you're the best person to ask about a method which is going to involve me in many years of work. You compressed twenty-six lines into two: 'The apparition of these faces in the crowd;/Petals on a wet black bough.' Is it possible to compress at length over twelve books?" He listened to me for fifteen minutes in complete silence – he was like the Delphic Oracle, you asked a question and listened to the silence which revealed your own heart – and then he merely said, "Wait until Antonio comes, he'll answer these questions better than I can. Or ask Desmond O'Grady or Graves," and later, as I persisted: "It's worth trying." I continued to persist, saying the epic can sum up the culture of the last thirty years in twelve books, and Pound asked suddenly: "Have you had twelve experiences that sum up the culture of the last thirty years?" I said, "Yes. For example, my experience of China."

At that point Olga Rudge, a violinist brought up in Italy, his mistress and mother of his child, returned with coffee. She was younger than he was, in her seventies I judged, and she was rather rude: "If you put everything on a postcard, then he'll take you seriously." To which Pound said: "T.E. Hulme said to me, in 1915, 'Everything a writer has to say can be put on half a side of a postcard, and all the rest is application and elaboration.' Have you got the application and elaboration?" Then in came an Italian neighbour and writer, who introduced himself as "Pescatore, like a fish" with his mistress and an Italian boy, and suddenly the room was filled with talk. Pound did not say a word. He sat in silence in the open window, a full moon over his shoulder, very sad and apart, blinking constantly, and I noticed a sculpted head carved by Gaudier-Brzeska and saw a copy of Yeats's *Mythologies*. I spoke about my visits to China and Russia and talked about my travels, and about 9 Pescatore turned to me and said, "You know, I've been visiting Mr Pound for ten years, but I've never heard his voice." He stood up to go, and I stood up to go with him, thinking I wouldn't get much more out of Pound.

But as the neighbours trooped out with Olga Rudge and I lingered to say goodbye to the Oracle, unexpectedly Pound stood up and grabbed my arm and pointed to the chair in front of him and said: "Here sit down, sit down, you don't have to go yet do you? I've been thinking and listening to you. You've been around a lot, I think you can do what you want to do: put the culture and the Age into twelve poems." Inspired, I sat down on the chair at the circular table and told him I knew I could. He said "Your long preamble about myself wasn't necessary" – he did not seem to want to acknowledge his technical innovations – and when I said that I could *see* the pattern ahead, "I can *see* the poem," he said: "If you can see it, then you've already done it. Seeing it's half the battle." We talked on. On the circular table, upside down as I looked, was his handwritten text of his latest canto – I could read "A place of skulls" – and as we discussed the technical side of writing an epic he said: "It doesn't matter where you begin. It's like making a table, it doesn't matter which leg you put on first so long as the table stands up at the end." Olga Rudge kept intruding, saying "Ezra, it's time for your orange juice", which she put in front of him and later, "Ezra it's time you went to bed." To which he said flatly, "Leave us alone, woman." (I'm sure I heard the "woman" at the end of his muttered sentence.) I asked him about many details in his study, including the statue by Gaudier-Brzeska. When eventually, just before midnight, I stood up to take my leave, he stood up too, and we stood together. I was surprised he was so tall. I told him, "When I am seventy… I will think of this evening. I believe two eras in English Literature are spanning each other, although this will not be apparent until the next century." He extended a hand and shook me warmly by the hand – there was nothing feeble about his handshake and he held onto my hand and looked intently into my eyes like a healer transmitting an energy and brightening my aura, like a poet passing on a seed from a tradition he has grown, and in what I took to be an endorsement of what I had just said he repeated: "If you can see it you've already done it." Then he lapsed into oracular silence and returned to his chair and sat as silent as the future, the full moon over his shoulder, and I left while Olga Rudge scolded him (and by implication me) for staying up so late. I thought it sad that Modernism and all his questionings should have ended in a silence.

17 July 1970, Geneva
With J. Conversation in the mountains. Man is proud, his intelligence is guided by his pride not his reason. In the 19th century, the mountain was the measure of man; in the 20th century, it is his drives that measure him – for we drive on the road and in the spirit. (The road has killed everything. It has made 19th-century villages attract cars for business. Hence neon, big notices, petrol stations, garages, motels and competing hotels, street lights, traffic lights, pedestrian crossings, bend-signs, speed-signs, motorways, flyovers, bridges.) In the 20th century we drive towards our ideal: to realise everything we want.... Man has got to the moon, and he thinks he has conquered nature.... Man defined or measured in terms of the mountain (19th century) is replaced by man dwarfed and baffled in the city – the motorcar has done that. I explained my task to her, above Lake Leman, under Mont Blanc, which looked very permanent. It was to search through everything, I said, through literature, art, philosophy, every culture, every country, different people, until in the end I have a total knowledge about what man is, i.e. in terms of himself. Then I shall hope to know what he is in terms of nature and his society and context. This distinction is very very important. Man between his birth and his death – vertically, waiting in the desert; and man measured horizontally in relation to nature and his society and other people. My huge 40-year task must do both of these.

20 July 1970, Loughton
On my art. My destiny... is my huge work, my series of poems that will take 40 years to finish and that will be as long as *Paradise Lost*. It will be Tchaikovsky and Brahms in poetry, a great symphony of suffering and joy.

24 July 1970, Loughton
On epic. Unity should be organic, through the theme, not chronological or based on the life history of a particular hero or episodic. The poet's question: how to organise his material? He must look for the artistic centre of the material, the unifying principle; i.e. select his theme and weave it into the broad fabric of... the 20th-century world. In

the *Iliad* it is the Will of Zeus (he sides with Achilles' wrath against Agamemnon); in the *Odyssey* it is the wrath of Poseidon (his son the Cyclops is blinded); in the *Aeneid* it is Juno versus Aeneas; in Milton it is the cause of the Fall. The poet can by-pass the chronological: he can use retrospective narrative and begin near the end (the shipwrecks in the *Odyssey* and *Aeneid*). The first book should propose the whole subject and then "the Poem hasts into the midst of things" (Milton, [*Paradise Lost*, bk1, 'The Argument']).... Consider structure and style.

6 December 1975, Kensington
Decided to call my epic *Overlord*.... I travelled [in Europe, the Middle and Far East] to prepare for *Overlord*.

22 December 1975, Kensington
Milton's question in 'Lycidas' – why be a poet, why not give up the hard work of rhyming the Muse and have the pleasure of Amaryllis and the other nymphs?

28 December 1975, Kensington
It is my destiny to write a 12-book epic about the Second World War.... I have planned the twelve books and must now fit in the Christ-Devil theme and get the form right.

15 April 1976, Rouen
Observations on the French trip, 13–15 April. From Cherbourg to Valognes and Sainte-Mère-Église.... On to Utah beaches... the Omaha beaches. The cliffs.... The American Military Cemetery. Nearly 10,000 crosses. On to Bayeux – William the Conqueror's Cathedral, the tapestry and the war, an epic in pictures; mine to be in words. Arromanches and the Mulberry. Juno and Sword beaches, then on to Pegasus Bridge.... On to Cabourg – Le Home;... then Deauville, Trouville. Back to Caen. Then Ouistreham.... On to.... Hill 112. Also Falaise.... On to Versailles. Trianons. On to Paris. This morning Rouen.

22 July 1979, Wandsworth
I, too, like Milton, am worried about the present state of the world. Just as his *Paradise Lost* was about the Puritan cause, so my *Overlord* is about the Second Coming of Christ and a united Europe, i.e. the European cause. The equivalent cause of our time, our battle, is between the pro- and anti-Europeans. I must remind people of the horrors of war, the need for change.... I write about a vision of Paradise: a universal peace, harmony and concord which Christ will bring about through Europe,

a relief from all the terrorists and violence.

12 January 1993, Wandsworth
My epic will be like *Paradise Lost*, with a reference to the New World Order. This is a struggle between Christ, who wants it to be within the framework of civilisations, simultaneously bringing in a new stage (43) in the European civilisation and developing a new stage (15) in the American civilisation; and the Devil, who wants it to be a worldwide Baalite order which has never happened.... The New World Order has two meanings. It is both Christian and diabolical in conception. There is in fact a struggle between *two* New World Orders. I have got there! The Christian view will include Universalism, a Light-based common ground for all cultures. The Diabolical view will attack all religion.

27 January 1993, Oxford
Drove to Oxford, put my car in the pay-and-display area and waited outside Blackwells for Ricks, who came out open-necked, grey-haired, round glasses, warm and smiling but very exact.... We walked to the Turf.... I bought him a cider and myself an orange juice and we sat on the right of the bar on wooden seats, I leaning on the table, and we talked. I talked about Ezra Pound and the Rothschilds and Mullins and Pound in Italy, and my desire to write an epic post-Virgil, -Dante, -Milton (all of whom were in Italy). He asked what I am about. I said I had seen something which is everywhere in the Metaphysical poets and realised it was the centre of religion and history's civilisations and also the Reality behind physics and philosophy. This is new and I am doing an interlocking jigsaw, I said. He mentioned holism. I: "In the sense that everything is a whole. My close reading of the universe and what is hidden – perhaps in the tradition of the Ricksite way of looking. You taught me to read closely, and now I am reading the universe closely, for what is hidden behind Nature and Western civilisation." But, I said, my base is Literature and like a *Times* reporter or barrister mastering his brief I go out into disciplines. I: "A poem is a wonderful medium for a cross-disciplinary approach. In Donne for example." He: "It can be small in subject and huge in range. Tennyson's library – there's a precedent for it. Tennyson was very interested in science." I: "Darwinism in *In Memoriam*." He: "Yes."...

3 May 1993, Pisa, Italy
I... took a bus to the Arno and walked to where Shelley lived. The plaque on the wall, near Ponte alla Fortezza. The house may have been pulled down and the plaque may be on next door. Here he wrote

Adonais. An emotional walk along the end of Lungarno Galileo (via San Sepolcro, a Templar church) across the river to Lungarno Mediceo where, after looking at a Roman wall, I pondered my future, knowing I could live on the Pisan waterfront. I had written poems, and after being opened up by (Fra) Angelico and at the Carmine yesterday, I was filled with higher feeling as I sensed my future and destiny, to write an epic as great as Homer's, Virgil's, Dante's, Milton's, Pound's. I had done my basic work *à la* Ficino – my history and cosmology – and only had the political and religious Universalism to do. Like Virgil I had shelved the huge task for twenty years, having been caught up in worldly things, and now was the time to get on and do it. I could hide here in Pisa.... This was the Arno of Dante (in Florence) and of Shelley and Pound (who was detained here) – the medieval, Romantic and Modernist union, the tradition.... I had all the qualifications needed to write an epic: the Fire, history, cosmology, science. All, achievements in themselves, were but preludes to the epic, clearing my head for what is to come, a work that would plumb the height of goodness and the depth of evil, the struggle between the universal Christ and Lucifer whose Seven Deadly Sins are winning (Hitler, Stalin, Cold War, Conspiracy).... The elemental, high, *pure* feeling overflowed in me, and my eyes were wet, I trembled inside at the intensity of what I must do: to embody all the culture of Western civilisation in a twelve-book poem. The exalted vision of perfection brought with it a sense of the inadequacy of my realisation of the vision (or so I thought). My vision was one of meaning and awe, of optimism, not despair. I was in a bar on the Lungarno Mediceo, drinking a cup of tea and my eyes were filled with tears on and off for about ten minutes. I could not speak, blinking back the tears. I had found my next stage in my work.... I had had the equivalent of Dante's vision of 1301.... I knew what I had to do.... I would choose art and incorporate the Italian (and Greek) tradition into my epic.... In Pisa I discovered a spring of creative feeling and imagination.

Extract from Nicholas Hagger's autobiography, based on Diaries, *21 June 1993*
Christopher Ricks rang, inviting me to Oxford, where he was finishing his Sabbatical, to discuss my coming epic. "I like what you said" (i.e. that I am now aiming to be a man of letters) "and I want to see you but I've got to pack up a house by the end of June.... I don't think I can get away, but you can come here and have tea...." And so on 21 June I met Ricks outside Blackwell's at 3.30.... He was open-necked and in jeans material and carrying nothing; wrinkled bald pate and round glasses

and grey hair and kind smile.... We walked to Worcester College.... We went to Worcester Gardens past staircase 8 (his room) and sat on a seat looking at the lake before the arch; the situation of our first tutorial and looking at the spot where I chose to be a poet – a neat twist on his part. I told him about my epic... explained the higher world and the lower one. Explained the New World Order. He on the difficulties. First, my predecessors Homer, Virgil, Dante, Milton and Pound: "Don't be in competition with them, don't be hubristic, people will snipe, it is very ambitious of you. Second, are you Manichaean, i.e. dualistic? Is it good versus evil or are both reconciled in one? Thirdly, it is easier to do evil than good. Blake said Milton is of the Devil's party. Regicide, deicide, Heaven and Hell. There is something wrong with God that makes the poem *Paradise Lost* go wrong, as Dryden, Addison and Pope pointed out, and which defeated Tennyson. The mightiest of your predecessors have failed in getting the art right; Milton's Heaven was not a 'glory'. 'Justifying the ways of God to men' (Milton) is not the primary poetic theme; 'making friends with the necessity of dying' (Freud) is, to me. Empson, when he returned from Japan, once he had got his book on complexity done, could say *'Nunc dimittis'* (i.e. 'now I can die'). Fourth, there is a problem regarding the future, which is left unrealised. A lump of futurity. Look at the end of Marvell's 'Horatian Ode'. What happens in the future?" I: "I can show the future without predestination, and still believing in free will." He: "Prediction and prophecy or prescience, Eliot's distinction: be prophetic, don't predict. Fifth, there is a moral position."... He on the difference between a religious position and a technical position or artistic problem. "And so, sixth, long poems tend not to be as good as shorter ones, e.g. *Paradise Lost* books 11 and 12 are not poetically achieved, and Milton writes 'Egypt divided by the river Nile' (a flat line). The lesson of the failures of the geniuses of the past in respect of points five and six, for example *Idylls of the King* and the problems of the historical novel. Seventh, there needs to be a common belief or body of agreement or consensus, which (I assert) is not achievable as it's Christianity or nothing, and our multi-ethnic society and atheism deny consensus." I identified this problem and said it was solvable by Universalism and by Michelangelo's unitive vision in which everything is a hierarchy. He: "Without a universal figure, and it can't be Christ, you're like Blake with a private mythology, for example Los. Eliot's objection to Blake: lack of orthodoxy. Dante was the beneficiary of sustained and coherent thinking such as Aquinas – but Dante was Christian and not Universalist (although in his time Christianity covered the known world and so was Universalist). Look at Tennyson's 'The Ancient Sage' and *In Memoriam* and consider what failed Tennyson, the inequalities of accomplishment. Tennyson's late poems are not as good, for example 'St Telemachus' is not as good as 'St Symeon'. Eighth, religion still means Christianity and Christ cannot stand for holism, and homogeneity of culture is an assumption. Christ as messiah and avatar? ('In Vishnu-land what Avatar', Browning.) Have a Hellish Council and a Heavenly Council. Use Tillyard but be more alive." I reflected on the [definition of] avatar: "Descent of deity to earth in incarnate form or manifestation; the Second Coming of Christ as Messiah and Avatar." He: "Homer, Virgil, Dante, Milton and Pound were geniuses who made mistakes and failed in their efforts. You must learn from their mistakes."

We then walked back to Worcester and peed in the "lavatory", a "sump" (Ricks), very primitive – the Fellows' loo for guests near the chapel by staircase 2. He insisted I went first: "Guests first." We walked to Longwall Street, and I said to him as we walked round Oxford: "Tuohy went for walks with Wittgenstein. I have the feeling of what it was like when I walk with you." He is the Leavis of our time. Ricks said: "Yeats says we make poems out of the quarrel with ourselves and rhetoric out of the quarrel with others. Quarrel with yourself – art, quarrel with others – rhetoric. Keats quarrelled with himself when he wrote: 'O for a life of ease'. He wanted a life he had not got. I hate Yeats but he said something that is true…. Religions are bad things and there should be a government health warning about holism and unity…." We passed his bike, propped against the wall outside Balliol, much battered, with a crossbar, and I raised the line (most appropriate for an epic). He: "Blank verse is better than stress metre, but 'Maud' is an alternative as it contains every known line except blank verse; but lacks dignity. Look at *Dynasts* again, Hardy's long poem." I settled for blank verse…. He: "Don't have a stanza for an epic like (Byron's) *Don Juan*." I raised similes and said I was looking forward to using Miltonic similes from everyday life. He: "Slightly demotic." He quoted Wordsworth's "How oft, amid those overflowing streets,/Have I gone forward with the crowd…" (*Prelude* VII, 626–627) and the smell of sewers and city fumes in the air….

We found a tea-room opposite Eastgate… and he ordered coffee and I ordered tea from a mini-skirted waitress and I showed him some of my poems…. Regarding my epic, he said: "The danger is that you will feel too strongly about (world events) and will quarrel with others and not make art out of the quarrel with yourself." I replied: "I can paint my Sistine chapel. My art is not propaganda." I reflected: 'I need to withdraw from quarrelling with others to quarrel with myself.' And I observed his sneezing with hay fever and violent and loud blowing of his nose. I showed him the title of a volume of my poems: *A Sneeze in the Universe*. He smiled. He spoke of my 'gigantism'. I: "The New World Order is gigantic – there has never been a world government – and so I have a gigantic theme, like Milton's *Paradise Lost*."... He: "Nothing's changed since Tennyson technically. Go back to him." He remarked:... "You've done your thinking and thought it all out and so you can use it in an epic." Suddenly at 5.45 he leapt up, said "I've got to be back by six", darted over to the counter and paid, and as I followed him out into the street, said "I shall shake you by the hand and say goodbye because I'm going that way", and with a brief shake of the hand he had gone before I could properly thank him.

8 April 1994, Loughton
The Devil's plan is to flatten cities for urban renewal and put Stalin in control so there can be killing of some of the 2 billion people. He believes 'I won'. But God is using him to bring about a benevolent world government.... A benevolent not a malevolent world government.... An epic does not have a hero. It is Churchill v. Hitler, Eisenhower v. Churchill, Stalin v. Eisenhower and Churchill. Christ has to support Churchill who is under the will of the Illuminati. Churchill and Monty have to be goodies, Hitler and Stalin baddies, but the Devil is beating Christ, setting the agenda, defending.... *Overlord* deals with a struggle for power.

28 May 1994, Southampton
War. The *Iliad* was based on Troy; the *Aeneid* began with the departure from Troy. D-Day was the largest seaborne invasion ever; *and* a phoney invasion that never happened. It was larger than the Spanish Armada, Trafalgar or Waterloo, or even the Somme, where Haig killed 1 million. Or Agincourt. It was the most momentous day of the 20th century.... D-Day, the hugest battle ever.

29 May 1994, Loughton
Do I go for the American or British version? Eisenhower or Montgomery version? Probably the Eisenhower one, that Monty's plan went wrong; Caen was to have been taken the first day along with Bayeux, and the Americans got him off the hook. But Eisenhower was under the Illuminati, and that is the point. Eisenhower is the hero, is he not; not Montgomery (who was over Churchill). Think. Was it Monty v Hitler? Until 1 September 1944, yes; then it was Eisenhower.

31 May 1994, Lisieux, France
After supper and a jug of red wine, pressed the guide to go to Villers-Bocage.... On the way back was tackled by Willie, who told me he was at D-Day. He invited me to his room to meet Jo (82, loud-voiced and drunk) and Robert (now an Aussie), who was in a vehicle at H plus 2 hours on D-Day, Gold beach.... Talked about their memories, drinking three whiskies with them, matching them drink for drink until Jo became inarticulate and Robert spilt his drink on his knee.

1 June 1994, Lisieux
Dinner with the veterans.... Talk about the storm on the mulberries, how they worked through the storm and knew it worked. They ate the night before, Robert ate nothing until that evening, Willie had breakfast on 6 June and was given two tots of rum in the evening. "You slept in your clothes and carried a pack of about 20 lbs with your greatcoat, clean shirt. You had a gas mask and cape to put on when it rained. You got wet and when the sun came out you dried." Willie said they didn't get ill as the pills the army gave them filled them with vitamins, but Robert had two boils from not eating greens. "When the mortars began you got into an earth hole you'd dug and kept your head down.".... Thoughts on my epic.... Split the first book into sections and do it. Get the landings out of the way. And Hitler: make him a towering figure of evil, committed to a policy of population reduction to please his masters. Begin with a flashback of the horrors of war. "Say Muse how."

2 June 1994, Lisieux
Felt good..., and on the way out in the coach, started writing the epic, on my knee: the theme, *Overlord*, and some other bits I could see. Little by little the technical problems seemed to solve themselves and I am resolved to finish bk 1 of the epic while I have it in mind.

1 May 1996, Charlestown, Cornwall
Rang Svetlana Stalin, i.e. Svetlana Peters.... Told her Stalin ("your father") was a Martinist Rosicrucian. She: "I didn't know." "He lived with Gurdjieff for a year." "When was that?" She said, "You are obsessed by my father." Mentioned her mother, what a remarkable lady she looked.... Told her I had been to Russia in October, to St Petersburg, Moscow and Yalta. "Oh, you *are* obsessed by my father. Cornwall reminds me of the Crimea." Stalin was "like the Tsar", he told his mother.

4 May 1996, Charlestown
I… returned to Mullion, where Svetlana was standing outside the gate waiting for me. She was small with blue eyes (her father's) and browny hair which used to be red. We shook hands and I apologised for being late (1.45), she led me round the back to her bedsit…. She started talking about herself…. She carried on talking while I asked all my questions. Her mother… opposed Stalin and wrote him a suicide letter and shot herself. She hurt him very much and he moved out of the Kremlin apartment in 1932… and built himself a *dacha* at Kuntsevo fifteen miles outside Moscow. He and her brother Jacob by his first wife were then looked after by a housekeeper found by Beria, and Stalin came back for dinners. She had moved apartments and was now in the Senate building on the first floor; the flag visible from Red Square was not in his block. He ran the war in the building opposite, on the second floor where the Soviet People's Commissars were. He had the whole floor and ran the war from a large room; a table with a green cloth and a main desk; runner carpets typical of the Kremlin, secretaries in the next room…. I: "As a Tsar, your father extended the Russian Empire to its farthest extent since Ivan the Terrible." She nodded and mentioned Peter the Great…. The frankness of my questions has reached a new high, even for me; in putting to Svetlana some of the things her father did.

2. Visits by Nicholas Hagger to Countries/Places Relevant to *Overlord*

1953	September	France: Paris, Normandy – Cabourg, Caen, Ouistreham and the D-Day beaches
1957	March/April	Italy – Rome, Licenza (Horace's villa), Naples, Pompeii, Herculaneum, Mt Vesuvius, Sorrento, Capri, Paestum, Syracuse, Catania, Mt Etna
1958	August/ September	Greece – Athens, Thermopylae, Delphi, Thebes, Sounion, Marathon, Mt Parnassus, Eleusis, Dafni (Daphnae), Megara, Corinth, Patras, Olympia, Pylos, Sphacteria, Kalamai, Tripolis, Argos, Nauplion, Epidavros (Epidaurus), Tiryns, Mycenae, Crete (Knossos, Phaestos, Gourna), Rhodes, Mykonos, Delos; return via Belgrade

1959	April	France – Paris
	June/July	Spain – Barcelona, Valencia, Malaga, Coin, Torremolinos, San Sebastian
1960	July/August	Greece, via Belgium, Amsterdam, Yugoslavia – Athens, Spetsai, Spetsopoula, Porto Cheli, Calchis, Sciathos; return via Skopje, Dubrovnik, Split, Rijeka
1961–1962	September–June	Iraq – Baghdad, Ctesiphon, Rutba, Babylon, Gourna, Basra, Shatt al-Arab; visit to Jerusalem, Mount of Olives/Gethsemane/Calvary/Garden Tomb, Jericho, Qumran, Bethany, Damascus, Beirut
1963–1967	November–November	Japan – Tokyo, Hiroshima, Kyoto, Nara, Nikko, Gora, Kurihama/Nobe, Kamakura/Kitakamakura, Karuizawa
1966	March	China via Hong Kong, Kowloon – Canton, Shanghai, Hangchow, Nanking, Peking
	June/August	USSR – Nakhodka, Khabarovsk, Moscow, through Brest, Warsaw, Berlin, Flanders
1967	November	Hong Kong, Macao, Vietnam – Saigon/Cholon/Bien Hoa; Cambodia – Pnom Penh/Siem Reap (Angkor Wat); Bangkok; India – Calcutta, New Delhi; Nepal – Katmandu; Istanbul; Budapest; Vienna; Paris
1968–1970	November–June	Libya via Avignon/Marseilles, Tunis/Carthage – Tripoli, Sabratha, Leptis Magna, Gorna (or Souk El Juma'h), Ghadames
1969	July	Tunisia – Djerba
1970	February	Egypt – Cairo/Pyramids, Memphis, Saqqara, Luxor, Alexandria, El Alamein

	April	Malta – Valetta, St Paul's Bay, Sliema
	July	Tunisia – Medenine, Gabes, Hammamet; Algeria – Souk Ahras, Algiers, Oran; Morocco – Tangier; Spain – Marbella, Barcelona; Italy – Rapallo; Geneva – Annemasse, Mont Blanc/Lake Leman
1972	March	Germany – Frankfurt, Arnoldsheim
	May	Belgium/Brussels
	September	Tanzania – Dar es Salaam, Tanzam railway, Zanzibar; return via Nairobi
1976	April	France – D-Day beaches; Cherbourg, Valognes, Sainte-Mère-Église, Utah/Omaha beaches, Bayeux, Arromanches, Juno/ Sword beaches, Pegasus Bridge, Cabourg, Deauville, Trouville, Caen, Ouistreham; Hill 112, Falaise; Chartres; Versailles, Paris, Rouen
1985	February	France – Paris, Versailles
	May	France – Paris
	June	France – Rouen via Normandy
	July	France – Dordogne: Orleans, Blois, Périgueux, Les Eyzies, Sarlat, St Cyprian, Buynac, La Roque, Domme, Gourdon, Rocamadour, Padirac, Souillac, La Madeleine, Les Combarelles, Cap Blanc, St Emilion, Bordeaux, La Rochelle, Nantes, Mont St Michel, Rouen, Boulogne
	October	Germany – Frankfurt

1986	August	Belgium – Dunkirk, Bruges, Ghent, Antwerp, Waterloo, Brussels; Holland – Amsterdam; Germany – Bonn; Luxembourg – Echternach, Luxembourg City, Bourscheid (Ardennes); France – Lille
1987	August	Denmark – Esbjerg, Rynkeby, Ladby, Kertminde, Svendborg, Trelleborg, Fyrkat, Nodebo, Gilleleje, Helsingor (Elsinor), Kobenhavn (Copenhagen), Odense, Jelling
	October	Germany – Frankfurt
1990	April	Hungary – Budapest, Szentendre, Visegrad, Esztergon, Tura, Kocskemet
	December	Czechoslovakia – Prague
1991	October	Germany – Frankfurt
1993	April/May	Italy – Florence, Pisa
	July	USA – New York, Boston, Niagara Falls, Washington, Philadelphia, Florida (Orlando, St Petersburg, Daytona)
1994	May/June	France – D-Day beaches via Southwick House, Broomfield House, Fort Southwick, Fort Nelson: Caen, Villers-Bocage, Banville, Pegasus Bridge, Ouistreham, Sword and Juno beaches, Arromanches (Gold), Mulberries, Bayeux, American beaches (Omaha, Pointe du Hoc), Colleville, Lisieux, Falaise, Chambois, Montormel (Falaise Gap), Sainte-Foy-de-Montgommery, Rouen, Atlantic Wall, Calais
	July	Southwick

Appendix 2

	July	Europe – Brussels, Hanover, Berlin, Poznan, Warsaw, Auschwitz, Cracow, Budapest via Slovakia, Vienna, Salzburg, Munich, Cologne via Rothenburg, Rhine, Moselle, Meuse
	October	Germany – Munich, Berchtesgaden, Dachau, Ingoldstadt, Nuremberg
1995	March/April	Germany – Obersalzburg/Berghof, Dresden, Goslar via Colditz, Brocken, Gottingen, Flossenberg, Weimar, Buchenwald, Wewelsburg, Externsteine, Hermannsdenkel, Padeborn, Verden, Sachsenhain, Belsen, Luneburg, Deutsche Evern
	April/May	Holland, Germany, France – Hoek van Holland, Arnhem, Oosterbach, Nijmegen, Rhineburg, Buderich, Wesel, Straelen, Venlo, Maastricht, Bastogne, Reims, Clervaux, Saar, Forbach, Trier, Ardennes, Echternech, Our, St Vith, Losheim, Elsenborn, Malmédy, Stavelot, Calais
	July	Turkey, Greece – Istanbul, Troy, Guzelyali, Kusadasi, Ephesus, Seljuk, Didyma, Samos, Patmos, Athens, Kefalonia, Ithaca, Athens, Eleusis
	October	Italy – Sorrento, Mt Vesuvius, Solfatara, Cumae, Avernus, Pompeii, Herculaneum, Oplontis, Amalfi, Paestum, Capri, Naples
	October	Russia – St Petersburg, Moscow, Yalta
1996	July	Greece – Athens, Sounion, Thebes, Delphi, Naupactus, Patras, Olympia, Pylos, Sphacteria, Mistras, Sparta, Mycenae, Epidavros (Epidaurus), Peiraeus, Aigina (Aegina), Mykonos, Ephesus, Patmos, Rhodes, Crete (Knossos), Santorini (Akrotiri), Dafni (Daphnae), Athens
	September	Italy – Rome, Licenza (Horace's villa), Tivoli, Vatican

3. Inside Front Covers of First Edition of *Overlord*

Books 1–2
Written in blank verse with a panoramic visionary sweep that embraces higher and lower worlds within his Universalist scheme, *Overlord* is a contemporary epic poem in the tradition of Homer's *Iliad*, Virgil's *Aeneid* and Milton's *Paradise Lost*. Continuing the mystical vision of Dante's *Divine Comedy* and the concern for civilisation of Pound's *Cantos*, the poem focuses on the last year of the Second World War viewed from the higher world by its conflicting leaders, the Universalist Cosmic Christ and Cosmic Satan.

Hagger's cosmos is one of two conflicting forces, an expanding Fire which is behind the creation and expansion of the universe, and a contradicting force of darkness, destruction and gravity, of dark matter and black holes. These opposites, which recall *yang* and *yin*, are held in balance by a transcendent and immanent God, universal energy of Fire or Light, and it is under these divine powers that General Eisenhower, Supreme Commander of the Allied Expeditionary Force, Hagger's Aeneas-like hero and *homme moyen sensual*, defeats Hitler and dreams of a new world order of universal peace and world government.

This epic poem will comprise 12 books. In this volume, books 1 and 2 take the story from D-Day to the 20-July plot against Hitler's life and reveal the essential laws of the universe.

Books 3–6
Following on from books 1 and 2 which present D-Day and the plot against Hitler's life, books 3–6 cover the last year of World War II and feature Falaise, Arnhem, the Holocaust and the Ardennes campaign (or Battle of the Bulge). They record the struggle between Eisenhower's forces to defeat Hitler and, at another level, the Cosmic Christ's struggle with Lucifer.

Written in the tradition of Homer's *Iliad*, Virgil's *Aeneid* and Milton's *Paradise Lost*, Nicholas Hagger's Universalist 12-book epic poem about the most significant event of the 20th century reflects the conflict between the forces of Light and order which seek to restore peace, and the forces of darkness and devastation which lay behind the evil of Auschwitz. In the course of treating this hugely important, Tolstoyan metaphysical theme in a work that recalls Michelangelo's Sistine Chapel ceiling, Nicholas Hagger reveals the laws that govern history and the ordering of the universe.

Books 7–9
Following on from books 1–2 and 3–6, which tell the story of Eisenhower's advance towards Hitler through D-Day, the plot against Hitler's life, Falaise, Arnhem, the Holocaust and the Ardennes campaign, books 7–9 feature the Yalta conference, the crossing of the Rhine and the squabbling during Hitler's defence of Berlin. At another level Eisenhower visits Hell, and the forces of heaven under the Cosmic Christ repulse an invasion by Hell's forces led by the Cosmic Satan, and counter-invade. In both the lower and higher worlds, the forces of Light have begun to triumph over the forces of Darkness during the long battle of Armageddon.

Written in the tradition of Homer's *Iliad*, Virgil's *Aeneid* and Milton's *Paradise Lost*, Nicholas Hagger's Universalist epic draws on the hidden history of the 20th century to tell the truth about World War II. The conflicts between Stalin, Roosevelt and Churchill, Eisenhower and Montgomery, and Hitler and his generals are handled with a Homeric mastery that moves easily between formal diplomacy and bitter antagonism. As the powerful forces who influenced the outcome of Yalta are still operating in our own time and seek to mark the millennium by creating a world government, *Overlord* makes sense of the 20th century and gives a new understanding of the present. Nicholas Hagger's writing unifies many poetic traditions: in Elizabethan style he finds his theme in historical events, and takes his structure from classical epic and Milton. While reconciling classical balance with the Modernists' concern with civilisation he reveals a divine universe in which Light and Darkness are in perpetual conflict (but underlying harmony) and the forces of Light have to retain their upper hand on earth.

Books 10–12
Contained within three volumes, the first nine books of *Overlord* tell the story of Eisenhower's advance towards Hitler through D-Day, the plot against Hitler's life, Falaise, Arnhem, the Holocaust, the Ardennes campaign, the Yalta conference, the crossing of the Rhine and Hitler's defence of Berlin. Books 10–12 present the fall of Berlin (a contemporary Troy) and death of Hitler, the Nazi surrender and the birth of the atomic age at Hiroshima. At another level, Hell falls to Heaven's invasion, and Satan, the power behind Hitler, now cut down to size, goes into exile and foments the Cold War with his new ally Stalin. With the defeat of Hitler, the Antichrist, Armageddon is over, and Eisenhower is given a vision of Paradise and the coming Millennium, the Cosmic Christ's Thousand-Year Reign on earth and benevolent world government which triumphs over Satan's plans for

a new world order.

Conceived in 1969, discussed with Ezra Pound in 1970 and begun in 1994, *Overlord* is the first 12-book poetic epic in the English language since Milton's *Paradise Lost*, and as in the case of Milton's classic it had a 25-year gestation. Like Virgil's *Aeneid*, which celebrated Augustus' new order, its underlying theme is the yearning for universal peace which can be found in contemporary attempts to create a world government to coincide with the new millennium. Nicholas Hagger's Universalist epic reaches a triumphant conclusion with Eisenhower's defeat of Hitler and the Cosmic Christ's victory over the Cosmic Satan, and a vision of the divine order behind the universe reconciles the Tolstoyan conflict between war and peace and Michelangelesque contrast between Heaven and Hell. In Hagger's classical unitive vision, harmony and balance are restored between the eternally conflicting forces of Light and Darkness, with Light just predominating.

Combining imagination, spiritual vision, a penetrating understanding of history and a metaphysical eye that draws on the new science and philosophy, Nicholas Hagger has created an impressive work that towers above the contemporary European literary scene like a mountain half-hidden in cloud over a flat landscape.

4. Letters from Ted Hughes, then Poet Laureate, to Nicholas Hagger about *Overlord*

8 July 1994
Dear Nicholas,

... I look forward to seeing your epic – but are you sure about publishing books 1 and 2 before 5, 6 and 7 are written? Or is it all written? My experience is: publishing a book annihilates the factory that produced it. Rather like – first prototypes of a new weapon, in a war, bring the enemy to demolish the source. Robert Frost never published a book until he'd completed the next. He called it "keeping an egg in the nest". I know I've two or three times regretted publishing the first specimens in a new line of production. Obviously, those serial novelists didn't feel that way. On the other hand, the response finally stopped Hardy – in his series of novels. Not quite the same thing....

All the best, Ted H.

20 March 1995
Dear Nicholas –

Thank you for the copy of the big work. I started reading it with fascination – I rose to it, the omnivorous masterful way you grasp the materials. But same day was swept out of the country on hectic business and got back only last night. Look forward now to reading the rest. I'll try to get something by tomorrow. But will it help? Do comments help? Doesn't the whisper go further than the shout?

Yours – Ted

28 January 1996
Dear Nicholas –

You certainly are industrious. I'm admiring the way you bite off and chew up these great chunks of history in your epic. It's good for verse – to become the workhorse for sheer mass of material. Pressure of the actual – the resources to deal with it drawn from elsewhere. I want to see the whole thing finished, though, before I make any comment....

Keep up the good work – Yours ever, Ted

3 December 1996
Dear Nicholas –

Thank you for the epic. What a prodigious amount of work!

You hit a pace, a tilt, that really carries your reader along – through what could be impassable masses of detail. Weirdly readable – considering the blizzard of data. Everything comes as a subordinate clause to your dramatic momentum – a hand waving out of the express train window.

I have only dipped in here and there so far. You're obviously serious about the Rothschilds and the Illuminati – can any human endeavour be so successfully organised?

I liked your riff on de Vere.

But I have to get the whole sweep.

Well – what now?

Yours ever, Ted H.

4 March 1998
Dear Nicholas –

I didn't get to see the programme but your coin trove sounds pretty interesting.

One of the mysteries about you is – when do you get it all done? How many of you are there? Do you never blot a line?

You know on that Sir Thomas More manuscript in the British Museum – which contains a wonderful passage, top quality circa *All's Well That Ends Well* vintage – Shakespeare makes several quite radical corrections. (But the whole thing written at top speed obviously. Only about 5 punctuation marks in thirty or more lines.) So it is permitted.

Yes, debased coinage.* In a sense, that has happened to poetry –
we're all guilty. Main thing is – keep the metal pure, at least, if you can.
Keep well, Ted

*Extract from Nicholas Hagger's earlier letter: "It's all wrong. The purity of
the word on the page has a tiny audience, and the debasing of it conveys it to
millions. It's like the debasing of Roman coinage between Augustus and the
Fall of Rome: the coins of Augustus had a relatively limited audience whereas
the later ones included all the barbarians. Or so I like to think."

Appendix 3

Letters from Nicholas Hagger to Christopher Ricks on *A Baroque Vision*

To Christopher Ricks
Buckhurst Hill, 13 January 2020, Em
Subject: *A Baroque Vision*: revelation, homework 40 years late

Dear Christopher,

A Happy New Year to you and Judith (and your son David, who I sat next to during your lecture on 1 July).

I have been thinking of you a lot over Christmas. I had completed my current round of books: *Fools' Paradise* (seeing Brexit in terms of Sebastian Brant's 1494 Ship of Fools voyaging to non-existent Narragonia – there will be a sequel which I have already drafted, *Fools' Gold*); *The Coronation of King Charles* (a masque, reviving the pageant entertainment from 1661, perhaps to be performed at the next Coronation – early copy to be handed to Prince Charles's Assistant Private Secretary for safe-keeping); *Selected Letters* (letters by me that refer to all my books); and *Collected Prefaces* (54 Prefaces showing the development of my literary thinking and my Universalism). While I was assembling *Selected Letters* I saw that you asked me select 30 poems in 1979 and again in 1982, when we corresponded about my blend of Romanticism and Classicism, my Baroque style.

I should have made the selection then, 40 years ago, but I was still feeling my way on my poetic identity and was exceptionally busy at work, as a Head of English keeping abreast of A-level marking and acquiring my old school (Oaklands). Before Christmas I saw what this selection should look like, and I have now chosen the 30 poems. These will appear in Part One, poems written between 1961 and 1979, of a new selection I am doing of 100 poems from 50 poetic volumes, *A Baroque Vision*. Part Two will continue the thread of showing my Baroque roots, and will present 70 poems written between 1979 and 2019. I know it won't be the thin volume of 30 poems by themselves that you envisaged, but 40 years on it makes sense to continue the Baroque thread and this is the most feasible way of getting the selection out today.

A Baroque Vision will show that the Baroque vision we corresponded about grew into Universalism, and I must tell you how I arrived at this perception. While making my selection I had recalled your throw-away remark before your lecture at Worcester College, Oxford on 1 July, "You have been on a mission ever since you left University." I thought at the time you meant that I had done my travelling and writing in the 1960s to arrive at what would become Universalism and state it in seven disciplines, and write *World State*, which I spoke about during my visit to Russia. I woke on Christmas morning with the revelation (received in sleep) that my Baroque vision of the early 1980s had grown into my Universalism by the late 1980s, that you may have meant that my "mission" was to develop my Baroque vision of 1982 into Universalism.

I was stunned. I saw that my Baroque vision probably *had* grown into Universalism but that I had not consciously realised this. I got up and looked at my Prefaces, poems and diary entries written in the 1980s, and the evidence is very clear. It's as my revelation showed. I am so pleased to have had this revelation. It unifies all my literary and Universalist works.

As soon as I could I wrote this revelation into a Preface I had finished in draft, now titled 'The Baroque Vision behind Universalism, and the Tradition of Wordsworth and Tennyson'. I made it clear that all my works have been jigsaw pieces with one picture: a project which, chameleon-like, changed its appearance (or at any rate, nomenclature) between 1982 and 1991, from Baroque to Universalism. My Preface has drawn everything together and unified my work, and it will appear as the last of my 54 Prefaces at the end of *Collected Prefaces*, a strong ending that binds all the Prefaces together.

I have been looking to see when 'Baroque' first appeared in my work. On Friday 3 January I went to the University of Essex and looked in my archive at versions of 'The Silence' and found handwritten lines "And naked on the petalled lawn/A new Baroque Age is born" written into 'The Silence' in April 1973. The dedication mentioning "This string of baroque pearls" was earlier, written in Japan some time after December 1965, when I bought a necklace of baroque pearls for my (then) wife. This was on 16 December 1965, according to my diary entry in *Awakening to the Light*, p.222 – she still wears that necklace, and it will eventually pass to my daughter. So events that seem everyday at the time can assume a deeply-symbolic importance over 50 years later.

Perhaps when we get to 80 we do become wise. Certainly your (then) 85-year-old-and-very-wise throw-away line on my "mission" on 1 July set off reverberations – shock waves, Eliot's "My words echo/ Thus, in your mind" – in my subconscious that finally erupted and set off a tsunami on 25 December nearly six months later. Thank you, my excellent mentor, for such an unexpected and welcome Christmas present that brought everything together for me, with insight and understanding, in my 81st year.

So I can report that I'm doing my homework and will finish it in early February. Sorry to be 40 years late in handing it in, but Ezra Pound told me (regarding my epic *Overlord* on 16 July 1970), "If you can see it, then you've already done it. Seeing it's half the battle." And I hadn't properly *seen* it until Christmas morning. It should be out in early 2021, and I will make sure you have an early copy. The front cover will show Rubens' Baroque painting *The Apotheosis of James I*, which is on the ceiling of the Banqueting House. It shows James I as a divine soul being drawn up to Heaven on an eagle with the help of supporting Angels, and Charles I stopped and looked up at it as he walked to be beheaded on a scaffold outside. (The Banqueting House, James I's room in the Whitehall Palace for masques, is on the cover of *The Coronation of King Charles*.)

In July 2008 I told you about my visit to Tennyson at Farringford House [see letter of 29 July 2008]. I said at the time that my contact with him there did not persist on my return to Essex, but he followed me back to Essex soon afterwards. For the record, for the last ten years, I have felt, and I still feel, in an active daily relationship with Tennyson, who acts as a Muse and an editor. I hear his words (or at any rate, words) when I wake from sleep, what to amend in the previous days' work. 'He' will tell me to look at, for example, the middle of page 43, often a specific line, and I'll look and find something that needs improving or amending. The subconscious is amazing, I'm filled with awe that all this seems to be happening at one remove from me, during my sleep and on waking. I haven't forgotten that when we walked in Oxford on 21 June 1993 you advised me to go back to Tennyson, and it was that advice that took me to Farringford House when it was still possible to stay there, from 20 to 25 July 2008.

With thanks for your mentoring over the years, in 1979 and 1982 and subsequently, which I greatly appreciate in my 81st year, and long may you continue to be the inspiration you have been and make throwaway remarks that unify a life's works, Your ever-devoted, Nicholas

NH's works referred to: *Fools' Paradise*; *The Coronation of King Charles*; *Selected Letters*; *Collected Prefaces*; *A Baroque Vision*; *Fools' Gold*; 'The Silence' in *Collected Poems*; *Overlord*

To Christopher Ricks
Buckhurst Hill, 26 July 2020, Em
Subject: Onwards despite the virus/'The Silence'/reconciling Eliot and
Tennyson/the heroic couplet

Dear Christopher,

It's more than a year since I heard you on the heroic line and more
than six months since I last wrote, and since then the world's changed.
I hope you and Judith have stayed well amid the ravages of the virus.
We are all fine.

I have been isolating – shielding – and working full writing days,
then feeding the carp and walking every afternoon in our meadow,
watching how the clover and bird's-foot trefoil are growing amid the
meadow browns, looking for small tortoiseshell butterflies among
the blackberries on the brambles and singing to my new friends,
"Swallows" – and their hearing is so good that four swallows dart from
behind trees, recognising my song, and swoop round me. On Thursday
I walked with my son Tony and a swallow swooped and described a
perfect circle round us, skimming at knee level, clearly saying "Hello".
In short I've been reconnecting with Nature as Wordsworth and
Tennyson were able to do in unpolluted air and vivid colours and have
had a glorious four months of nineteenth-century living, back in 1881.
I am frequently reminded of blind Milton shielding from the plague
in 1665 in Chalfont St Giles and dictating *Paradise Lost* to his daughter
with a virus menacing beyond his curtilage.

We visited Jordan and Egypt from a ship in February and March
and were banned from Israel and Cyprus because of the virus and came
back via Turkey, landed just before lockdown. With my PA working
remotely I have kept going. *Fools' Paradise*, on Brexit during May's
premiership in heroic couplets, is completely finished; it's not out until
December but early copies have arrived. I will be posting to you in due
course. Its sequel *Fools' Gold*, on Brexit during Johnson's premiership
and the virus, is nearly finished in draft but I now have to work on the
couplets. I have finished *A Baroque Vision*, 100 selections from 50 poetic
volumes, and also *The Essentials of Universalism*, 75 selections from 25
prose volumes. No proofs yet. *Collected Prefaces* has been copyedited,
no proofs yet. *Selected Letters* is at the proofs stage. *The Coronation of
King Charles* is done but not at the proofs stage yet. I am about to start
The Promised Land. In Jordan I stood on the top of Mount Nebo where
Moses stood and saw the Promised Land stretched out beneath him
(the Dead Sea, Jerusalem, Jericho, Galilee), and I realised that I too
have seen a Promised Land which, like Moses (who died on Mount

Nebo and was buried there), I will not live to enter.

The Indian-created World Intellectual Forum wrote to me during lockdown, mentioning my early work on a coming World State *The World Government*, and asked if I would join their Executive Board. I agreed on the basis that I'm not travelling anywhere for them or taking part in distracting Zoom meetings. So now I'm in touch with more than 20 intellectuals from different countries, including a Nobel prize-winner from Tunisia. One of them, Thomas Daffern, who has lectured at Oxford and is based in France, told them that he'd followed and admired my books for years and that my masterpiece is *The Fire and the Stones*, which they should all read if they haven't read it already. But having reviewed all my poetic and prose works recently I now think that if a writer has to regard one of his works as his masterpiece irrespective of its reception – which would be yours? – then I would have to regard my masterpiece as 'The Silence', which I wrote in Japan during 18 months between 1965 and 1966 when I was struggling to understand the bewildering sequences of images and glimmerings of Light that were happening to me, as it's about the wrestling and inner transformation that turned me into a poet and made my Universalism, my perspective of all humankind and my 55 books possible – as you've been aware, as your throw-away remark on 1 July last year made clear.

I think it's true to say there's nothing remotely like 'The Silence' in English poetry, which is why I had such difficulty in connecting myself to the tradition to do your selection of 30 poems in the three letters I wrote you in 1979 and 1982. Perhaps its nearest equivalent in prose is Joyce's *A Portrait of the Artist as a Young Man*. Like Joyce's *Portrait* it's a Modernist work, full of sequences of images and juxtapositions, and, having transformed myself through Modernism and thinking about writing a poetic epic, I turned my back on Modernism's concentrated narrative after my evening with Ezra Pound in 1970 and went back to the 17th, 18th and 19th centuries, which was right as it opened the way to Tennyson, a path you later endorsed. My boss in Japan (as Representative of the British Council there), the metaphysical philosopher E.W.F. Tomlin, who knew Eliot and arranged for me to lecture on Eliot for a year at Tokyo University and wrote *T.S. Eliot, A Friendship* about the hundred letters Eliot wrote him, told me in the late 1980s just before he died that he had arranged for me to visit Eliot when I returned to the UK on leave in mid-1966. Eliot of course died in 1965, and I contributed 'In Defence of the Sequence of Images' to a book Tomlin got out in Japan, *T.S. Eliot, A Tribute from Japan*, while I was teaching Eliot and writing 'The Silence', and I sometimes wonder what would have happened had I met Eliot in 1966 – would I have remained a Modernist? Anyway, that didn't happen, and I didn't. Now you are the leading authority on both Eliot and Tennyson and may appreciate the struggle I had in choosing between their conflicting approaches. But they're both in the tradition and I've reconciled them (+A + -A = 0): Eliot's, Pound's, Yeats' and Tennyson's concerns for our civilisation and culture within classical blank verse (or heroic line), rhymed stanzas, heroic couplets and musical language – and no concentrated and obscure narrative.

When the system is unjammed there will be a flurry of books and I will put them in the post as they come through in dribs and drabs. Meanwhile if you are giving another lecture in the UK do let me know. It was such a pleasant surprise that your billed lecture on Mailer's rhythms turned out to be on the heroic line, which is close to my heart as you know, and I found what you said riveting. Several of your throw-away reflections have lingered in my mind. In particular, do please let me know if you are lecturing anywhere on the heroic couplet – or if you are going to be in the UK soon and somewhere within driving distance where we can meet and talk about the heroic couplet in Dryden and Pope and modern times, perhaps looking at *Fools' Paradise* and seeing how I can improve my couplets in *Fools' Gold*; if so I'll send you a copy now....

With very best wishes for continued good health, ongoing energy and more abundant wisdom, percipience, perspicacity and perspicuity (the three mentorial – a neologism? – Ps featuring perception, discernment and clarity), and many more throw-away lines that enable self-understanding, to my mentor from your ever-devoted, Nicholas

NH's works referred to: *Fools' Paradise*; *Fools' Gold*; *A Baroque Vision*; *The Essentials of Universalism*; *Collected Prefaces*; *Selected Letters*; *The Coronation of King Charles*; *The Promised Land*; *The Fire and the Stones*; 'The Silence' in *Collected Poems 1958–2005*; 'In Defence of the Sequence of Images' in *T.S .Eliot, A Tribute from Japan* (1966, by NH), edited by Masao Hirai and E.W.F. Tomlin

To Christopher Ricks
Buckhurst Hill, 28 October 2020, Em
Subject: Heroic couplet/heroic line

Dear Christopher,

I hope you have been keeping well amid the ravages of Covid. We are all well.

As promised, I am putting in the post (to the College of Arts and

Sciences) a copy of *Fools' Paradise*, which deals with Brexit in the May years in heroic couplets. It's mock-heroic, in the tradition of Dryden and Pope (more Dryden than Pope).

I am up-to-date on its sequel, *Fools' Gold*, which deals with Brexit and Covid in the Johnson year. After days of intense thought (when I could have done with chatting to my mentor) I have decided to do this in the heroic line, blank verse. The tone is different in view of the many deaths caused by Covid: 226,000 Americans dead, approaching the 291,000 killed in combat in the Second World War, and 60,000 British dead, more than the 40,000 British killed during the Blitz. It's in the tradition of the heroic verse of Milton and Tennyson.

Both books hold politicians to account to uphold the cultural health of Europe in accordance with T.S. Eliot's 'The Man of Letters and the Future of Europe', the first with ridicule, the second in a more serious way as becomes the death toll, the implications of a national event and the heroic line. The heroic couplet is good at exposing follies and vices, the heroic line is better suited to a catastrophe that includes mass deaths and widespread economic devastation, which has to be taken more seriously. And it escapes "the bondage" of rhyme (Milton's preface to *Paradise Lost*).

Had we been able to meet this is what I would have said. Without realising it you helped me greatly by talking at Oxford on 1 July 2019 on the musical heroic line. Your talk helped me make this choice, with hindsight it almost seems to be a call, before we had heard of Covid, to return to the heroic line of 600 years of English verse from Chaucer to Tennyson. I hope this approach will have your blessing when you eventually see *Fools' Gold*.

I'll be thinking of you on 4 November and of America's future direction. Stay well, and with best wishes to my mentor from your ever-devoted, Nicholas

NH's works referred to: *Fools' Paradise*; *Fools' Gold*

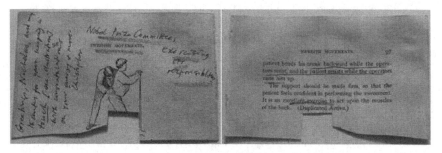

A half-page front and back entitled Swedish Movements, which Nicholas Hagger received from Christopher Ricks on 2 March 2021

To Christopher Ricks

Buckhurst Hill, 2 March 2021, Em

Subject: Swedish Movements

Dear Christopher,

Your half-page arrived this afternoon, and after feeling relieved that you are clearly well in this plaguey time I knew immediately and with delight that it is one of your Vorticist images with many associations, an at-first baffling conundrum which little by little becomes more clear. What an excellent image, and what a rush of ideas it set in motion. Let me react step by step:

1. The background is my having thanked you for having been an excellent mentor for over 40 years and for introducing me to the heroic couplet, which I used in *Fools' Paradise*. And my saying what a tussle I had between my early Modernism on 'The Silence', out of which all my work has come, and the Tennysonian narrative of my epics and other poems, and that you are the leading authority in both Eliot and Tennyson.

2. The half-page comes from George Taylor's American *An Exposition of the Swedish Movement-Cure: Embracing the History and Philosophy of this System of Medical Treatment, with Examples of Single Movements and Directions for their Use in Various Forms of Chronic Disease, Forming a Complete Manual of Exercises,* 1860 – the date perhaps suggesting the time of Tennyson, the text drawing on the Swedish Movement of Ling in the 1830s, and the subtitle perhaps touching on my bringing history and philosophy to bear on the chronic disease of British Brexit in *Fools' Paradise*.

3. Your "keeping in touch [see illustration]" refers to you, my operator/ mentor, straightening the stance and posture of me, your patient, as I resist Modernism and am raised up by Tennysonian narrative in heroic verse and heroic couplets. When I bent backward you resisted, and now I am resisting Modernism I am raised.

4. "Excellent exercise", underlined in mentor's red, is perhaps encouraging support to give me confidence in performing the next movement (perhaps *Fools' Gold* in heroic verse, to which I am adding finishing touches).

5. Swedish Movements, the running header on the back of p.97 above the illustration, is underlined in red as is "Nobel Prize Committee, exercising its responsibilities", i.e. the stooping mentor has now become the examining Nobel Prize Committee. This could have a number of meanings. I mentioned that *Fools' Paradise* has been put

in for the Ondaatje Prize, and the Swedish Nobel Prize Committee may be a rush, an association in the same idiom, developing the idea of Swedish Movements; or it could mean that it should be entered for a Nobel Prize as "an excellent exercise"; or it could announce a movement in Sweden, veiled news that the Nobel Prize Committee is examining something – if so, I hope this applies to you as you deserve a Nobel Prize. The Japanese poet Junzaburo Nishiwaki told me that his intuition was seldom wrong and forecast that I would get a Nobel Prize (see *My Double Life 1: This Dark Wood*, p.167), but although Michael Nobel saw me receive the Gusi Prize for Literature in 2016 and told me that he had read a several-page publisher's leaflet about my works and was very interested, he has little influence within the Nobel family now, and though I was nominated for the Templeton Prize for 5 years (three years to go) I don't think I'm well enough known to be on the Nobel watchlist. I have written my books in the wilderness.

6. I should add that the World Intellectual Forum (WIF) I told you about have latched onto my works. The Indian founder, Dr Swaminadhan of Hyderabad, has written a short book calling for a democratic, Presidential, federal world government, which is based on my books *The World Government*, *World State* and *World Constitution* (which he's got), and he has described our work as "a meeting of minds" and said that he and I will be expressing our view to the UN General Assembly. He has now founded the Global Network for Peace, Disarmament and Development (GNET-PEDAD) to bring in a World State like the one I have called for (the United Federation of the World, the last four words taken from Tennyson's 'Locksley Hall'). I have no idea whether this will become a Swedish Movement.

So all these ideas are rushing about in your half-page, which I will treasure. I hope my understanding is on the right lines. It's an inspiring half-page, especially the brilliant illustration of you, my mentor, correcting my literary posture, for which I am very grateful and deeply appreciative.

Swedish Movements, it's such a powerful idea with so many ambiguities and associations, and I am full of admiration for your symbol, which is like a communication from the Delphic Oracle, capable of more than one interpretation. As the Japanese say, "*Sensei, dormor*" – "Professor, thank you." Now may be a time to follow a Japanese proverb: "*Shiranai ohotoke*" – "Be wise and know nothing, like a Buddha."

The books are slowly making progress despite lockdowns, and I'll send them as they trickle out.

Stay well, and with best wishes from your ever-devoted, Nicholas

NH's works referred to: *Fools' Paradise*; 'The Silence' in *Collected Poems*; *Fools' Gold*; *My Double Life 1: This Dark Wood*; *The World Government*; *World State*; *World Constitution*

To Christopher Ricks

Buckhurst Hill, 13 March 2021, Em

Subject: Swedish Movements, further thoughts

Dear Christopher,

I had my second Pfizer jab yesterday and half-expected to wake with a temperature this morning. In fact, I woke with a normal temperature but with more sleep inspiration. I was told (Tennyson told me) that the background to Swedish Movements was *A Baroque Vision* and letters I wrote you in 2020 as well as my movement from Modernism to Tennysonian narrative.

The Swedish Movements of your oracular image in fact refer to my acceptance that my pre-1979 Baroque vision developed into Universalism during the 1980s, which unifies my literary and Universalist works, and that I have been on a "mission" since leaving Oxford as you told me on 1 July 2019, which unifies my life. I received confirmation of this in sleep on Christmas morning 2019 (as I described in my letter to you of 13 January 2020 about *A Baroque Vision*). They also refer to my movement from Modernism to the Tennysonian heroic line (as I described in my letters to you of 26 July and 28 October 2020). A third movement may be my call to replace the United Nations with a United Federation of the World (the last four words taken from Tennyson's 'Locksley Hall'). Your image is saying that when I pushed back on these developments, including the selection of 30 poems, I had to be resisted, but now I have reconciled Eliot and Tennyson and am pushing forward and am going with them as in *Fools' Paradise* I can be raised up and there is nothing to stop my being considered by anyone for a Prize, even by the Nobel Prize Committee. Or something of the sort.

I think I have now got there. Like the Delphic Oracle you make an ambiguous pronouncement and I, the supplicant, try to make sense of it without following a wrong interpretation like Croesus, King of Lydia (modern Turkey), who asked if he should go to war with the Persian Empire and was told, "If Croesus goes to war he will destroy a great empire." He went to war and destroyed his own empire in 546BC.

Once again your baffling image teased me out of thought as doth eternity, and it needed a Pfizer jab and a sleep amid antibodies to bring full understanding.

I look back on your memorable symbols in recent times: the *Victoria* and the *Triton*, circumnavigation of the globe by wind-dependent Magellan in 1519 and by nuclear submarine in 1960 (the metaphysical and Neoclassical routes), sent in 2012; the Barnes 1903 cloister (the Edwardian tutor room at Worcester College, Oxford of my Provost Masterman, which he blew up c.1910, 50 years before asking me if I would be interested in a career in intelligence), sent in 2014; Barrie's picture postcard of a watcher on the 18th-century way over the Boldre bridge and a toiler loading a two-horse cart with reeds in 14th-century muddy river conditions (my two-part autobiography being spied on with Neoclassical and metaphysical associations), sent in 2015; the founding members of *Mosaic, A Journal for the Interdisciplinary Study of Literature*, one of them you with the prospect of being the last survivor and getting the whole tontine annuity (my literature-based mosaic-like interdisciplinary works presenting one picture and perhaps my being the last survivor in this mosaic tradition and like you getting the whole tontine annuity), sent in 2017; and your page from *Notes and Queries*, 1881, showing that literary men are listed and general readers buy (without the interfering State gripping their rainbow as Elizabeth I did and controlling their publicity and confining them to the wilderness if, like Marlowe, they worked in intelligence), sent in 2019. (Long live 1881.) And now Swedish Movements, 1860. Not to forget the first edition of the *Horizon* (December 1944) that contained Eliot's 'The Man of Letters and the Future of Europe', which is relevant to my *Classical Odes* and is at the heart of my holding politicians to account for the consequences of the effects of their actions on the culture of Europe in *Fools' Paradise* and *Fools' Gold*, sent in 2004. Seeing all this, Zeus can't wait for you to be his mentor on Olympus. What a mentor, there's never been one like it!

With gratitude from your appreciative and ever-devoted, Nicholas

NH's works referred to: *A Baroque Vision*; *Fools' Paradise*; *Classical Odes*; *Fools' Gold*

INDEXES

1.

Index of Works

Nicholas Hagger's published works that have Prefaces in chronological order. Dates in brackets refer to publication dates.

The Fire and the Stones (1991) xi, xiv, 3–8, 10, 31, 45, 46, 49, 53, 65, 66, 79, 80, 81, 84, 88, 97, 117, 158, 191, 234, 244, 245, 250, 262, 314, 317, 340, 354, 363, 364, 365, 366, 367, 373, 396, 397, 398, 403, 405, 406, 411, 482, 483, 493, 523, 524, 543

Selected Poems: A Metaphysical's Way of Fire (1991) xi, 9–77, 289, 350, 352, 380, 387, 396, 405, 411, 548

The Universe and the Light (1993) 66, 78–81, 80, 84, 117, 250, 317, 405

Collected Poems 1958–1993: A White Radiance (1994) 9, 60, 77, 83–84, 289, 350, 351, 352, 355

A Mystic Way (1994) 83, 85, 87, 88, 98, 105, 117, 265, 401

Awakening to the Light (1994) 83, 87–89, 389, 401, 520

A Spade Fresh with Mud, Collected Stories, Vol 1 (1995) 91–92, 105, 127, 129, 187, 283

Overlord, bks 1 and 2 (1995) 93–98

The Warlords (1995) 99–103, 115, 119, 120, 157, 165, 166, 167, 168, 172, 178, 182, 387, 490

A Smell of Leaves and Summer, Collected Stories, Vol 2 (1995) 105–106, 127, 129, 187, 283

Overlord, bks 3–6 (1996) 107–109

Overlord, bks 7–9 (1997) 111–114

Overlord, bks 10–12 (1997) 115–118

2.

Subject Index

The main subjects in *Collected Prefaces* are presented within a whole structure in A – the same structure that is in *Selected Letters* – to provide a context for the individual entries in B. Most of the entries in A can be found in alphabetical order in B. The Subject Index contains key Prefaces on these main subjects.

"If you can see it, then you've already done it. Seeing it's half the battle."
Ezra Pound in conversation with Nicholas Hagger on 16 July 1970

A. Structure of Subjects

(1) Literature – man of letters in seven branches of literature:
poems and poetic epics
poems: classical odes, lyric poems, social satire
epic poems: blank verse for *Overlord* and *Armageddon*, visit to Pound,
epic on American Civil War
verse plays and masques
short stories and novellas
diaries
autobiographies
letters
the fundamental theme of world literature

Literary development and technique (progress to self-understanding as poet):
poetic criticism; poetic identity – Metaphysical, Romantic, Baroque (blend
of Classical and Romantic) approaches to poetry; thirty poems; poetic
method; poetic subject matter; poetic technique; true poet; development of
literary Universalism

(2) Universalism (inner transformation, instinctively seeing the oneness of
humankind within the oneness of the universe): manifesto; Universalism
and Existentialism; universe

Universalism in seven disciplines (seeing the oneness of all disciplines
internally and in relation to each other with cross-disciplinary thinking)
Mysticism (seeing the Light as the universal mystical experience, perceiving
the unity of the universe): transformation, illumination; Light; mystic-
contemplative tradition; imaginative-inspirational tradition; psychic stream

Literature (the fundamental theme of world literature as quest for the One and condemnation of follies and vices): blend of Metaphysical, Romantic and Classical approaches reflecting the unity of the universe. See (1).

Philosophy and the Sciences (seeing all humankind in relation to the One, the unity of the universe): Becoming and Being; metaphysical thinking; Nothingness and plenitude; Providence; sciences; surfer

History (seeing the underlying patterns of world history with 25 civilisations following the same stages, seeing all history as one and where it is leading): European history; Grand Unified Theory of world history; Law of History; philosophy of history; rise and fall of civilisations; Kurgans; universal/world history

Comparative religion (seeing the Light as the common essence of all religions, which are therefore one)

International politics and statecraft (seeing the dangers of an élitist new world order with the sources owned by a few families, and seeing the benefits of a new democratic World State; and the art of crafting a new State)

international politics: view of revolutions; intelligence works; Heroes of the West; Libya; New World Order; world order

statecraft: World State; World Constitution

World culture (seeing the underlying unity of world culture)

(3) Symbolism (symbolising the seven branches of literature, the seven disciplines and European civilisation): stag; rainbow; tree (tree of tradition); crest and arms; symbols in Ricks' cards

language 2, 7
mature work 4
Metaphysical poet 2
neo-Baroque 2, 4, 6, 13, 39, 'The Genesis and Shaping of the New Baroque
    Vision', Appendix 1
Neo-Baroque Age 2, 6
Neoclassical 2
Neo-Romantic 2
poet of decline and world unity 55
poet receives vision of the One 15, 21, 23, 39, Appendix 1
reconciling Eliot and Tennyson 55
Romantic Infinity 2
Romantic poet 2
self in process of development 23
symbols of Reality 2
'The Approach of the Later Poems', Appendix 1
thirty poems, Appendix 1
true poet, role of 2, 49, 50, Appendix 1
turning-point 4
Universalist poet 4, 21, 31, 39, 49, 55, Appendix 1

Prefaces 2, 21, 38, 39, 49, 50, 51, 52, Appendix 1

Seven branches of literature 50, 52

Seven disciplines 33, 37, 43, 48, 50, 52

Short stories 7, 10, 16, 17, 25, 38, 42
    a painter in words 7, 16, 25, 42
    and Death 25
    and retirement 25
    and the One 25
    A Smell of Leaves and Summer 10
    A Spade Fresh with Mud 7
    associative order 7
    Being 7, 10, 16, 17, 25
    belief, harmony, acceptance 16
    Collected Stories 25
    condemnation of follies and vices 38, 52
    dissimilar images yoked together 42
    follies and vices 38
    fundamental theme 38

BOOKS

O-BOOKS

O is a symbol of the world, of oneness and unity; this eye represents knowledge and insight.